Further Pra

THE G

Longlisted for the Andrew Carn̄ͤ——————————————

A *Kirkus Reviews* Best Book of 2017

"A sensitive and sturdy work of environmental history. . . . [Davis] has a well stocked mind, and frequently views the history of the Gulf through the prism of artists and writers including Winslow Homer, Wallace Stevens, Ernest Hemingway and John D. MacDonald. His prose is supple and clear." —Dwight Garner, *New York Times*

"In the tradition of Jared Diamond's bestseller *Collapse* and Simon Winchester's *Atlantic* comes Jack E. Davis' nonfiction epic, *The Gulf: The Making of an American Sea*, which strives both to celebrate and defend its subject—the Gulf of Mexico. . . . Detailed and exhaustive, written in lucid, impeccable prose, *The Gulf* is a fine work of information and insight, destined to be admired and cited." —William J. Cobb, *Dallas Morning News*

"Splendid. . . . Davis is a historian, and this book is packed with research, but *The Gulf* does not read like a textbook. He is a graceful, clear, often lyrical writer who makes sometimes surprising, always illuminating connections—it's not a stretch to compare him to John McPhee. And he is telling an important story, especially for those of us who live around what he calls the American Sea. What happens to it happens to us, and the more we know, the better equipped we'll be to deal with a future on its shores." —Colette Bancroft, *Tampa Bay Times*

"An incisive, comprehensive and entertaining portrait of the world's most diverse and productive marine ecosystem—from its lusty birth in the chaos of shifting continental plates to its slow and agonizing death of a million cuts inflicted by oil and gas extractors, dredge-and-fill operators, 'condo-canyon' developers, industrial-scale fishers, fertilizer-dependent farmers, chemical plant entrepreneurs, love-it-to-death snowbirds and so many more. . . . Amid all of the pollution and exploitation, this could easily have been a grim history of 'Paradise Lost.' But in Davis' skilled hands it is as much love story as tragedy."

—Ron Cunningham, *Gainesville Sun*

"This vast and well-told story shows how we made the Gulf of Mexico, in particular, into what local activists have begun to call a 'national sacrifice zone,' at enormous cost to its residents of all species. It's a sobering tale, and one hopes that reading it will help us hit bottom and acknowledge the need to change."

—Bill McKibben, author of *Eaarth: Making a Life on a Tough New Planet*

"A tremendous book. Davis is not only one of our preeminent environmental historians, but also a first-rate storyteller and prose stylist. Lay readers and scholars alike will be delighted by *The Gulf*, a lovely evocation of the natural world and the problematic ways our nation has profited from it."

—Blake Bailey, author of *Cheever*

"*The Gulf* takes on troubling environmental issues with a lyrical voice and a steady appreciation of history."

—Mark Kurlansky, author of *Paper: Paging Through History*

"With the narrative force of the Gulf Stream, Jack E. Davis takes readers to an unforgettable geography of wonders, oddities, and characters famous and unknown. Davis's writing shimmers with salt haze, delights like a flock of pelicans, and threatens like oil on a white sand beach. If you thought you knew the Gulf, guess again. If this is your introduction to it, lucky you."

—Jordan Fisher Smith, author of *Engineering Eden* and *Nature Noir*

"*The Gulf* starts with the geology of plate tectonics, proceeds through Indian settlements before the arrivals of Europeans, advances to hurricanes, the Dead Zone, and oil pollution, then analyzes the future. And it does all this very, very well. Books that attempt such comprehensive treatments of a subject are too often, as the saying goes, a mile wide and an inch deep. This book is 1,000 miles wide and 10,000 feet deep. It's an extraordinary achievement."

—John M. Barry, author of *Rising Tide* and *The Great Influenza*

"Like its subject, *The Gulf* is big, beautiful, and beguiling. Meticulously researched and sparklingly written, it is also a cautionary tale about a paradise ill-served by humankind."   —William Souder, author of *On a Farther Shore*

"An astonishing work of environmental history, sweeping in its narrative scope while also being wonderfully intimate in its richness of detail. The march of history and the vibrancy of place live on its every page, and the environmental story it tells could not make for more urgent reading in these perilous times."

—Darcy Frey, Harvard University

"[A] magnificent chronicle of the Gulf of Mexico. . . . A work of astonishing breadth: richly peopled, finely structured, beautifully written. It should appeal equally to Gulf coast residents and snowbirds, students of environmental history, and general readers."

—Robert Eagan, *Library Journal*, starred review

"A perceptive historical survey of America's Gulf Coast, this fascinating work accents the region's nexus between nature and civilization. . . . Marked by thorough knowledge and fluid writing, this work will enhance any collection of American and environmental history."

—Gilbert Taylor, *Booklist*, starred review

"Comprehensive and thoroughly researched. . . . Davis makes the convincing argument that wiser, far-sighted practices—including those aimed at combating climate change—could help the Gulf region to remain a bastion of resources for the foreseeable future."

—Publishers Weekly, starred review

ALSO BY JACK E. DAVIS

An Everglades Providence: Marjory Stoneman Douglas
and the American Environmental Century

Paradise Lost? The Environmental History of Florida
(editor, with Raymond Arsenault)

Making Waves: Female Activists in Twentieth-Century Florida
(editor, with Kari Frederickson)

The Wide Brim: Early Poems and Ponderings of
Marjory Stoneman Douglas (editor)

Race Against Time: Culture and Separation in Natchez Since 1930

The Civil Rights Movement (editor)

Only in Mississippi: A Backroads Guide for the Adventurous Traveler
(with Lorraine Redd)

THE GULF

The Making of an American Sea

JACK E. DAVIS

LIVERIGHT
PUBLISHING CORPORATION

A DIVISION OF W. W. NORTON & COMPANY

Independent Publishers Since 1923

NEW YORK   LONDON

For information about permission to reproduce selections from this book,
write to Permissions, Liveright Publishing Corporation, a division of
W. W. Norton & Company, Inc., 500 Fifth Avenue, New York, NY 10110

For information about special discounts for bulk purchases, please contact
W. W. Norton Special Sales at specialsales@wwnorton.com or 800-233-4830

Manufacturing by LSC Harrisonburg
Book design by Lovedog Studio
Production manager: Anna Oler

Library of Congress Cataloging-in-Publication Data

Names: Davis, Jack E., 1956– author.
Title: The Gulf : the making of an American sea / Jack E. Davis.
Description: First edition. | New York, NY : Liveright Publishing Corporation,
2017. | Includes bibliographical references and index.
Identifiers: LCCN 2016051692 | ISBN 9780871408662 (hardcover)
Subjects: LCSH: Mexico, Gulf of—History. | Mexico, Gulf of—Environmental
conditions. | Human ecology—Mexico, Gulf of. | Environmental degradation—
Mexico, Gulf of. | Nature—Effect of human beings on—Mexico, Gulf of.
Classification: LCC F296 .D38 2017 | DDC 909/.096364—dc23
LC record available at https://lccn.loc.gov/2016051692

ISBN 978-1-63149-402-4 pbk.

Liveright Publishing Corporation
500 Fifth Avenue, New York, N.Y. 10110
www.wwnorton.com

W. W. Norton & Company Ltd.
15 Carlisle Street, London W1D 3BS

5 6 7 8 9 0

For Willa, and to the memory of Jimmy (1956–1970),
taken by the sea that captivated us

Contents

Chronology   1

Prologue: History, Nature, and a Forgotten Sea   3

Introduction: Birth   12

Part One

ESTUARIES, AND THE LIE OF THE LAND AND SEA:
ABORIGINES AND COLONIZING EUROPEANS

One   Mounds   23

Two   El Golfo de México   41

Three   Unnecessary Death   51

Four   A Most Important River, and a "Magnificent" Bay   75

Part Two

SEA AND SKY:
AMERICAN DEBUTS IN THE NINETEENTH CENTURY

Five   Manifest Destiny   97

Six   A Fishy Sea   114

Seven   The Wild Fish That Tamed the Coast   150

Eight   Birds of a Feather, Shot Together   184

Part Three

PRELUDES TO THE FUTURE

Nine	From Bayside to Beachside	*223*
Ten	Oil and the Texas Toe Dip	*261*
Eleven	Oil and the Louisiana Plunge	*280*
Twelve	Islands, Shifting Sands of Time	*304*
Thirteen	Wind and Water	*335*

Part Four

SATURATION AND LOSS: POST-1945

Fourteen	The Growth Coast	*375*
Fifteen	Florida Worry, Texas Slurry	*411*
Sixteen	Rivers of Stuff	*440*
Seventeen	Runoff, and Runaway	*465*
Eighteen	Sand in the Hourglass	*476*
Nineteen	Losing the Edge	*490*

Epilogue: A Success Story amid So Much Else	*509*

Acknowledgments	*531*
Notes	*533*
Additional Selected Sources	*559*
Illustration Credits	*565*
Index	*567*

THE GULF

Chronology

DATE	EVENTS
10,000 BP–1513	First people settle and live on Gulf shores.
	Sea rises to current-day levels.
	Ecology and geography evolve to modern-day characteristics.
1513–1821	Spanish, French, and English explore and settle parts of the Gulf coast.
	Europeans discover major geographic features and physical contours of the Gulf.
	European diseases devastate indigenous populations.
1821–1900	Americanization of the Gulf begins.
	The five U.S. Gulf states are formed.
	Commercial fishing begins.
	Significant exploitation begins to show toll on some natural endowments, including fish and birds.
	Conservation on the Gulf is born.
	Tourism begins with sportfishing before expanding to include beachside vacations.
	Diking of the Mississippi River begins.
1900–1945	Oil is discovered.

The internal combustion engine advances tourism and commercialization of natural endowments.

Population growth is steady along most parts of the coast.

Devastating hurricanes raise questions about that growth.

Some sea life populations exhibit a major decline.

Gulf bird flyways are discovered, and birding becomes popular.

1945–2000   The population explodes across the Gulf and on the waterfront.

Hurricanes continue to expose dangers of waterfront living.

Offshore oil exploration and the petrochemical industry move into modern times.

Chemical and wastewater pollution peaks.

The Gulf dead zone is discovered.

Engineering projects significantly change the contour of the coast.

Coastal erosion is discovered as a major problem.

Animal and plant populations suffer significant losses.

Ecological science broadens the understanding of Gulf nature.

Organized efforts to protect the coast and natural endowments of the Gulf increase.

Some water bodies undergo major cleanup.

2000–present   The worst oil spill in history occurs in the Gulf.

Pollution is abated in some areas and continues unabated in others.

Organized efforts to protect natural endowments continue.

Sea-level rise presents new challenges.

Coastal erosion becomes more rapid and widespread.

Aquaculture offers sustainable use of the Gulf's natural assets.

Prologue

HISTORY, NATURE, AND
A FORGOTTEN SEA

Man is to be studied as a part of the physical Universe.
He belongs to the realm of Nature.

—HANS FERDINAND HELMOLT (1901)[1]

History without the wildlands is no history at all.

—EDWARD O. WILSON (2016)[2]

❖ ────────────────────────────

IN 1904, WINSLOW HOMER SPENT THE MONTH OF JANUARY fishing midway up Florida's west coast, where the Homosassa River quietly slips into the Gulf of Mexico. The painter laureate of the Atlantic had never been on the Gulf, and it delighted him with its natural palette of sea and shore—its color, movement, and history.

Behind reedy coastal marshes rose a dense woodland—a jungle of green, as Homer portrayed it—where splaying air plants and ferns hung in mottled sunlight, and the scent of aromatic cypress and red bay trees vied with traces of rotting organic muck. Homer likely listened for the double knock of ivory-billed woodpeckers sounding from interior corners, and studied the stealth pose of herons and egrets quietly fishing in the water. Its sweeping, calm surface was the perfect vision of contentment, though a deceptive veneer over the restless energy below. Wherever Homer drifted with bait and tackle, the water beneath his rowing skiff was clear several feet to a grassy bottom, flush with crabs, mollusks, and a thousand living things unseen. Among the most scintillating of sights were fish in schools as long as freight trains, running with the invisible Gulf tide. Their imposing numbers invited eagles and ospreys that circled overhead, and the wading birds tending to the shallows. They invited Homer, too, on return trips for years after.

He was sixty-eight years old, trim as ever, mustached as always, and at the height of his fame as a painter, acclaimed for his Atlantic seascapes. He was also an immensely passionate angler, as practiced at reeling in a fish as rendering one on canvas or paper. Come winter, he'd shutter his studio on Prouts Neck, Maine, and steal away to southern latitudes for a season of restorative recreation, usually on breezy sea islands.

Surprisingly, he had not seen the Gulf of Mexico beyond its fringe waters of Cuba and the Florida Keys. For years, sporting journals had been extolling the sea in America's backyard as an angler's paradise, a last unspoiled frontier where wildlife still outnumbered people. Among all the outstanding fishing holes around the long, arcing coast from south Florida to south Texas, Homosassa was a perennial favorite. *Forest and Stream* called it "truly an enchanting spot," where the "knight of the rod can land fish of large size as rapidly as he can bait and secure his hook." Conquests came with such ease that Homer wrote home to his brother declaring the fishing to be the "best in America as far as I can find."[3]

What also caught the attention of sporting journals was the distinct imprint of a historical place, one wholly excluded from the central narrative of the American experience. You could travel the coast all day without seeing another person, yet everywhere encounter signs of a vibrant human past in the countless aboriginal mounds that rose out of the flat wildlands. Compositions of earth and shells, typically overgrown with vegetation, they seemed as much a part of the natural burnish as fish and trees. They were built-environment remnants of people who had occupied Gulf shores for thousands of years, though long since departed. There were tall ceremonial mounds, and more modest burial mounds, some predating the birth of Christ by 250 or more years. Most were refuse heaps, called kitchen middens, that contained the shell-and-bone evidence of indigenous seafood diets and abundance, connective threads to the modern anglers' bounty, and to a history still unfolding.

Together, Gulf nature and the patina of the past aroused Homer's artistic sensibility. He was prepared for such moments. Wherever he traveled with rod and reel, he carried paints and brushes. As he matured as an artist, the native scenery migrated on his canvas and paper from backdrop to focal point. In many of his Atlantic seascapes, human subjects appear in detail front and center, and often in contest with spirited, sometimes raging, seas that speak to nature's paramount authority.

Retaining this forthrightness in a composition of the Gulf, where the water was often as unruffled as a millpond, required adjusting the scale of complementary elements. Among several watercolors that Homer completed at Homosassa, human subjects recede into a dab of color against a slate of restful water and a wall of green, over which palm trees ascend toward buff clouds and into the center of each work. In one such painting, *Shell Heap*, sabal palms shade an aboriginal mound spilling discarded oyster shells down to the water's edge where two anglers float in a skiff, suggesting a continuity between the ancient and the recent. Like all of Homer's Homosassa paintings, *Shell Heap* conveys an intimate and vital connection linking humankind, nature, and history. I call this triad Homer's truth, and it lies at the heart of this book.

In Homer's day, most people, including historians, were not accustomed to thinking of the sea, or nature generally, as asserting itself in human activities and progress. Oceans cover seventy-one percent of the globe, yet historians chose to write about major events, figures, and wars, and great cities and nation-states. As is still true today, seas were typically looked upon as merely corridors for exchange and exploration, and, most often, as passive backdrop. In a little-known essay on the Pacific Ocean from 1901, the historian Count Edward Wilczek suggested the unconventional when he acknowledged that the ocean "has played a noticeable part in the course of human history." Yet even Count Wilczek, a member of the Austrian nobility, reverted to the norm and treated the sea in his writing as essentially an inert pool of geography that connected or divided distant places and cultures.[4]

Not until the mid-twentieth century did a new generation of historians adopt a more expansive attitude, beginning with the French scholar Fernand Braudel. Braudel was a leader of the innovative Annales School, which examined the past through the experiences of ordinary people, turning bottom side up the traditional top-down approach of interpreting the actions of a few leading individuals as the drivers of events. Braudel went one farther to engage the "sea itself, the one we see and love," as a powerful agent in human affairs. Giving a nod to Wilczek's observation, and unwittingly to Homer's truth, he published a groundbreaking two-volume "biography," as he called it, of the Mediterranean Sea. Released in 1949, with new editions issued in 1966 and 1972, *The Mediterranean* inspired a wave of ocean studies. Historians dispersed across the globe to write histories of the Atlantic, Pacific, and Indian Oceans. Over the years, more and more studies appeared, several of the Mediterranean. Yet the endeavoring sea scholars always paused at the Gulf of Mexico, and never immersed themselves in its important past.

Even today, the Gulf is lost in the pages of American history.[5] This book, then, covering the period from the Pleistocene to the present, is the discovery of a sea of many ages and many civilizations. The Gulf was not only a panorama of flourishing aboriginal cultures; it was a dynamic enabler in European imperial wealth, and a critical component in the geographic expansion and economic rise of the United States. The architects who pieced together the country one treaty, conquest, and real-estate parcel at a time believed the Gulf was rightfully American. Years before the Louisiana Purchase of 1803 and the subsequent opening of the Great West, Thomas Jefferson saw what was then a Spanish-controlled sea as fundamental to the future of his young republic. Yet it is the rare history that looks at the Gulf through Jefferson's eyes, as an object of national desire and embodiment of the

American spirit. Even a quick investigation of the Gulf's past illuminates the values and ambitions of the American people no less than does the history of the Great West, recounted in a mountain of books, with most seeking to define what it means to be American.

The Gulf's history, as we shall see, is America's history; the energies of one are shared with the other. Our school books taught us that there were thirteen British colonies caught up in the war for American independence, yet in truth there were fifteen: the forgotten two were the Gulf colonies of East Florida and West Florida. The Gulf was on the frontier line that advanced from the original US states, delivered opportunities to Americans and immigrants searching for a better life, and nourished the nation's coming-of-age—doing so not in just western woodland, mountain, and river valley, but on the southern sea itself. At the beginning of the nineteenth century, the New England fishing fleet introduced its trade to the Gulf, and at the end, leisure seekers from the Northeast and Midwest booked excursions south, à la Homer, for warmth and outdoor attractions. Around this time, a fellow angler trying his luck on a little back bay in Texas discovered oil beneath his boat. Wildcatters eventually converged offshore searching for a foul gummy substance below the water deep in the earth, ultimately turning the Gulf into the country's most important oil and gas repository.

With every new train line that reached the coast, every new hotel that opened, and every new craving for a marketable resource, the region drew closer to the furious pace of change and consumption that possessed the rest of the nation—and then surpassed it. The Gulf had become America's sea.

None of this happened apart from nature's influence. Embracing Homer's truth that we cannot divorce ourselves from the physical context, this book diverges from the traditional historical narrative that leaves humans gamboling across unacknowledged landscapes, nature erased and dismissed. Even the many ocean biographies that followed in the wake of *The Mediterranean* render the historical agency of the environment as "almost imperceptible," to use Braudel's words from nearly seventy years ago. Nature was always present, as the French scholar argued, and far more than ambiguous backdrop.[6]

It was participant, impetus, and catalyst. It was the riches that made nations wealthy and powerful, and over which their armies fought; it was the wildness our ancestors insisted on taming, the scourge that left them despairing, and the blessing that kept them alive. How and where and by what design people built their homes and businesses depended on natural conditions and endowments. Inspirations for what people wrote and painted, what they wore and said to each other, how they planned their day and spent their leisure time, and what they chose as a livelihood all flowed from an organic setting. Nature shaped strategies in war and gave form to economies, and its wealth or privation determined that of the people and their enterprises.

Revealing the sensibilities of his predecessor Winslow Homer, the Mississippi artist Walter Anderson once asked, "Why does man live?" Writing in one of the logs he kept of Gulf island sojourns in the mid-twentieth century, he answered, "To be the servant and slave of all the elements." Anderson wasn't propagating an ideal but speaking to the Gulf's intrinsic place in the lives of fellow humans. Its rich fishery is more accurately the legacy not of enterprising New Englanders but of the Gulf's phenomenal estuaries. Its first leisure seekers were lured by a native fish—a fighter among fighters, coveted by sporting anglers— and then later by spectacular beaches and sunsets. Rivers connected the American Sea to the rest of the country, including its agricultural and industrial heartlands, and stimulated the Gulf-side rise of the nation's busiest cargo ports. Chance geological conditions, related to rivers, mountains, changing seas, fossilized marine life, and the aging Earth, enriched the Gulf with petroleum resources that transformed modern society in inconceivable ways.[7]

Western tradition holds up history as the record of civilization's progress and the genius of great leaders. But progress in the traditional sense—growth, accumulated wealth, technological advances—has, alas, historically come with an ecological downside. Birds of the Gulf once fell from the sky in bewildering numbers to support commercial and recreational endeavors. The region became a favorite sandbox of the earth-sculpting US Army Corps of Engineers, and a sump for the nation's agricultural and industrial waste. Its magnificent estuaries have been so depleted that only a fraction of the schools of fish that swam waters in Homer's day remain—and waters not nearly as clean and clear.

The sea has not been a lone casualty either, for growth-induced erosion has long been eating away at mainland and islands. The Gulf is the country's hurricane alley, yet Americans have been aggressively committed to building in the middle of it. Many of the Gulf's beaches, where migrating hordes have amassed, are not altogether natural, but the product of a continuing taxpayer-funded struggle against the sea. All these inauspicious particulars are symptom and symbol of prevailing cultural values, which have weakened the natural struts of our existence and wrought an uncertain future.

Looking back can help in finding a smarter way forward. "Consider the future / And the past with an equal mind," T. S. Eliot wrote in his famous poem about the sea, "Dry Salvages." We live with priorities that differ from those of Homer's contemporaries, engaged in daily conversations about our relationship with the environment and with a deeper grasp of it. Nevertheless, in many ways our relationship with nature remains the same. We still insist on harnessing it to our will, as we perpetuate waste and blight in the natural world.[8]

Arguably, humanity's most pressing challenge in the current age is confronting climate change and sea-level rise, and no region in the US is more vulnerable than the Gulf. As we search for fixes, we have an available past that is full of edifying precedents: in the way other cultures connected with their surroundings, how our own once lived more sustainably than now, how nature acted differently and perhaps more disagreeably after we tried to change it, or how, when left alone, it bestowed a surfeit of offerings that has since been lost. History can expose counterproductive behavior at the same time it can reclaim positive symbols that informed past understandings. It can reveal the effects of ecological conditions on the human condition, and restore the idea of nature as a human place.

I have therefore organized the book's chapters around natural characteristics of the Gulf—from fish and birds to estuaries and beaches—to explore how they intervened in human affairs, and how, in turn, humans intervened in the natural world, and thus affected their own. For a number of related reasons, the pages ahead focus on the United States. Unlike the Atlantic, which has some forty-three countries sharing its shores, or the Pacific, nearly a hemisphere in itself, the Gulf is not an international sea of the same extent. Only three countries flank its shores, with the US occupying half its coastline miles. Yet waterfront views are not the whole of the story. The narrative reveals geopolitical, geographic, economic, and, especially, ecological circumstances that make the Gulf largely American.

The book's focus also derives from the imperative I see in knowing the more complete story of a place that is important to our lives and history. Since the *Deepwater Horizon* tragedy of 2010, oil has hijacked the Gulf's identity. It frames how we—from journalists to policy makers, even scientists and tourists—perceive the American Sea. That eighty-seven-day nightmare, including the loss of eleven lives and the ominous sinking of the ruptured platform on Earth Day, represents the worst accidental spill in history, and perhaps the most poorly conceived cleanup response. The Gulf, as a result, will be living with fatal and unknown consequences far into the future—consequences that writer Rowan Jacobsen has incisively observed in *Shadows on the Gulf.*[9]

The book in hand was not written as a prelude to *Deepwater Horizon's* 200-million-gallon torrent. For one, as Jacobsen and a few others who appear in these pages have recognized, that milestone spill is not the greatest assault to befall Gulf nature—not even close. Every day in the Gulf is an environmental disaster, originating from sources near and far, that eclipses the spill. For another, no person or place is the sum of a single tragedy or continuing ones.

The Gulf and its history—its biography, Braudel might say—should be celebrated, not mourned. The American Sea has long been and will continue to be a gift to humankind. It brings beauty into our lives and invigorates the human spirit. It gives us food, moderates our climate, removes carbon dioxide from the atmosphere, and puts oxygen we breathe into the same. There is a kind of nourishing energy out in the Gulf that doesn't pump from a well. It is the wholeness of living things, the dynamic energy moving from sun to plant to animal, a ceaseless flow that in the long scheme of things is far more important than mineral deposits to our future existence.

Introduction

BIRTH

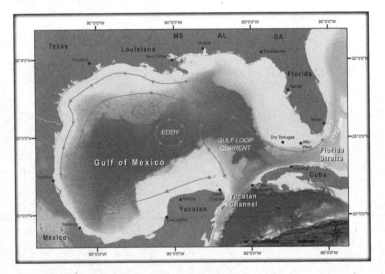

The Gulf of Mexico's loop currents feed the Gulf Stream, which
changed European navigation from the New World.

*The environmental story of the Gulf. . . . This is where it all
ends up.*

—WILLIAM WHITSON,
GULF OF MEXICO PROGRAM (1993)[1]

ONE HUNDRED AND FIFTY MILLION YEARS AGO, A THIRD
of the distance from the equator to the North Pole, the Gulf of Mexico
began taking shape. Its development was unhurried but spectacular,

midwifed by the breakup of what was then Earth's sole landmass, Pangaea, surrounded by a single global ocean, Panthalassa. Arising in episodic disturbances across eons, earthquakes preyed on the supercontinent, splitting open the land and spewing methane gas. Volcanoes erupted as a thousand rings of fire that spilled over with radiant mountain-building lava. They layered the sky with ash and sulfur dioxide, both of which contributed to the "Great Dying," the most severe extinction event in Earth's history, eliminating nearly all marine life and most vertebrate land species. Beneath the tearing and convulsing, massive plates of the upper mantle and crust shuddered, shifted, collided, and folded one over another, heaving up into more mountains while prying apart the sacrificial supercontinent into megacontinents, Laurasia (North America and Eurasia) and Gondwana (South America and Africa). The cleaving forced a massive chunk of land, the Yucatán Peninsula, to separate from Florida, and a basin opened in between.

Slowly, yet inexorably, the basin assumed the aspects of a gulf. Water poured in from the southwest and Panthalassa, before the Yucatán, still creeping counterclockwise, joined with Mexico into an earthen dam. To the east, a rift channel severed lower Georgia and invited additional water in from the vicinity that would later become the Atlantic Ocean. In time, the channel closed, leaving the Caribbean the basin's only source of seawater, entering through a strait east of Yucatán. Before permanent ice sheets materialized at the Earth's poles, the gulf filled to the point that its northernmost bay lay where Cairo, Illinois, is today.

Many millions of years passed as rifting, subsidence, and erosion polished the basin into the familiar shape and dimension of the Gulf of Mexico. Dinosaurs appeared and disappeared. Some evolved into birds, survived the geological mayhem, and made homes on ever-changing Gulf shores. The sea rose and fell two, three, four, maybe a dozen times. During the Pleistocene, the basin cradled water in a much-shrunken pool, more or less 250 feet lower and considerably colder than temperatures today. Glaciers impounded a quarter of the Gulf's future water

hundreds of miles to the north before ice melts gorged the basin with a
rush down through the Mississippi River valley.

How the Gulf came to be remained a mystery in earth science for
a long time. Geologists can sometimes glance at one of the planet's
features, as with the Gulf of Suez, and determine its origins. From
above, this narrow water body looks like a split seam in the Incredible
Hulk's shirt, indicating its birth as a rift formation. But in the case of
the Gulf, its shape brings to mind the profile of a camel's head turned
passively to the west, bearing no resemblance to a violent laceration
in Earth's skin. Origin theories advanced in the nineteenth century
were little more than unproven hunches. Some scientists speculated
that a giant asteroid-born meteor punched through the atmosphere,
slammed into Earth, and forged the Gulf basin. It was the wrong
guess, something you might find in science fiction, yet not altogether
far-fetched.

Late in the next century, oil geophysicists identified a 110-mile-
wide meteor-made depression at the northwestern edge of the Yucatán
Peninsula, and named it the Chicxulub crater. This was the meteor
that many believe touched off the legendary Cretaceous-Paleogene
extinction, when the particulate plume from impact blocked out the
sun, disrupted photosynthesis, and deprived plants and plankton of
energy-fixing sunlight, and animals, including dinosaurs, of food.

Definitive evidence revealing the Gulf's beginning stayed buried in
the earth until early in the twentieth century, when help unexpectedly
arrived from oil hunters. Typically, the scholarly work of geologists
aids mineral exploration, but in this case petroleum companies sinking test wells across the region provided scientists with core samples
unavailable before, and a physical record that pointed to rifting and
the connection to Pangaea's breakup. The industry's own successful
discoveries reinforced this conclusion. Where rifting has occurred, oil
has usually been found.

Confusion over the Gulf's birth no doubt contributed to an ambiguous identity that has long plagued it. While visiting the island city
of Galveston, Texas, in 1895, the writer Stephen Crane expressed a

common notion when he observed that the "Gulf of Mexico could be mistaken for the Atlantic Ocean" without "its name . . . printed upon it in tall red letters." Decades later, the International Hydrographic Organization, charged by maritime nations with charting the world's waters, designated the Gulf as a part of the Atlantic. This downgrade to appendage obscures the Gulf's separate birth, physical attributes, demeanor, and individuality, and it provides part of the *raison d'être* for this book.[2]

Here again Winslow Homer can be instructive, this time as artistic interpreter of the Atlantic. When placed against his portraits of the larger sea, his Homosassa watercolors affirm the Gulf's distinctive qualities. Homer's Atlantic is a roaring, agitated giant, gray and intense, stirring with water spouts, thrashing seas, and sharks. Its coastline is a display of crashing waves on jagged rocks, as dark and turbulent as the sky above. Human subjects often struggle against the crosscurrents of cold remoteness, for the Atlantic is less "place" than entity, bearishly expansive and disengaged. By contrast, Homer's Gulf is a sea of another color, with a cordial disposition. The water lies flat and serene in his paintings, except when a fish jumps to throw a hook. But this is thrill, not threat; the angler's boat continues to drift at ease, his fishing line drawn back in a flourish. In the white-cloud sky, birds peaceably ride invisible updrafts on open wings.

A very essential difference Homer captured lies in the special sense of place the Gulf fosters. It draws you in, though not into some watery vortex, a looming danger in his Atlantic portraits. The Gulf calls you to partake in its essential self, to dangle bare feet off the edge of a weather-grayed dock. When Edward O. Wilson was seven, he spent a summer on such a dock on the Gulf in the 1930s, a summer he called a "season of fantasy," endlessly discovering living "treasures," and embarking on an undeviating course in his intellectual and spiritual development. After growing tall and lanky and into one of the nation's preeminent evolution biologists, he wrote, experiences like his "must have been repeated countless times over thousands of generations."[3]

None of this is to say the Gulf promises only inviting conditions. It will turn brutal shades when foul weather rolls in from the Atlantic or when it brews its own. To be sure, as British travel writer Henry Major Tomlinson said long ago, it can "kick up a nasty sea."[4]

If those contemplating the Gulf were not folding its identity into the Atlantic's, they were often trying to equate it with the Mediterranean (another Atlantic appendage, according to the International Hydrographic Organization). In 1934, when the American poet Wallace Stevens was at Key West taking in watery sights of the Gulf of Mexico, he imagined at times he was looking out at another sea. The Gulf, he wrote to his wife, Elsie, back home in Connecticut, "has what must be a Mediterranean beauty." Comparisons of this sort date back to early European contact, when observers were trying to recreate a familiar place in spite of obvious physical differences. The Mediterranean is younger, larger, deeper, and bluer than the generally shallow and greenish-blue Gulf of Mexico. Whereas the younger sea has barely detectable tides rising and falling on cliff-faced shores, the older has vivid ebbs and flows, and hardly a single rock, no vertical projections taller than sand dunes and the rare red-clay bluff. The Mediterranean is also technically a *sea*, and the Gulf, indeed, a *gulf.*[5]

Stevens's comparison consequently raises a couple of questions: what makes a body of water a gulf, and where do such bodies fall in the taxonomy of oceans, seas, bays, coves, and the rest? Size is the principal distinction, with oceans taking the top spot. They are Earth's vast deeps and bounding mains, the collective of all interconnected saltwater. Seas come next in size, and then gulfs, although the division lacks a fixed standard, a little like inconsistent size charts across the clothing industry: one brand's medium is another's large. The 600,000-square-mile surface area of the Gulf of Mexico is one-fifth more expansive than the Sea of Okhotsk off east Russia, and even more so the Sea of Japan.

One hard-and-fast rule is that while it's fine in casual conversation to call a gulf a *sea*, you should never call a sea a *gulf.* Another, and one that prompted comparisons between the Gulf of Mexico and

Mediterranean, is that gulfs and seas are both connected to an ocean and partially enclosed by land. Save for the nine-mile-wide narrows of the Strait of Gibraltar, the Mediterranean is wholly bounded by land, while Cuba, Mexico, and the US shelter ninety-four percent of the Gulf of Mexico. Gulfs are, by rule, larger than bays, coves, and the like, and usually encompass these features. Still, geography, like everything else, has its rule breakers. The dimensions of North America's Hudson Bay* are greater than every gulf in the world, except one: the Gulf of Mexico.

The planet's largest gulf is tenth in size among the Earth's bodies of water. The surface area of a hundred Gulfs of Mexico would fit in the Pacific; fifty, in the Atlantic. The sailing distance between Philadelphia and London is roughly equal to the Gulf's perimeter, along which are five US states and six Mexican. Some 1,500 miles of coastline run from Tamaulipas to northern Quintana Roo, and 1,631, from Florida to Texas. Ten times that distance in US tidal shoreline wraps around Gulf islands, bays, and other knotty features. Cuba's 236-mile Gulf front seems comparatively insignificant, except this elongated and elegant island lies in the middle of the Gulf's only portals to other seas. From Cuba's westernmost point, Mexico's Yucatán Peninsula is 125 miles across Caribbean water entering the Gulf through the Straits of Yucatán. Around to the northeast at Havana, Key West lies 99 nautical miles (115 statute) away. The water between is the Florida Straits and part of the Gulf Stream, rushing out toward the Bahama Channel and the Atlantic.

The Gulf Stream is a warm and massively powerful current that travels up the Florida east coast to North Carolina before swinging out across the Atlantic toward Europe. Essentially a river within the sea, the Stream pushes nearly four billion cubic feet of water per second, more than all the world's rivers combined, up to 5.6 miles per hour. The identity of its source stoked the curiosity of scientists soon

---

* Hudson Bay has the characteristics of a gulf and, if not for its historical name, might properly be called one.

after Europeans began sailing it to expedite return trips back home, often starting out from the Gulf in ships carrying New World gold and silver. In 1575, André Thévet, a French priest and cosmographer, asserted incorrectly that the Mississippi River was the Stream's headwater. He wasn't far off.

The Stream builds from a vigorous loop current in the Gulf, formed from the heat and energy of the Yucatán and Caribbean currents and the sun. Prominent enough to appear on satellite images, the Gulf's loop current looks something like an inchworm in motion. Its back end rises up from the Straits of Yucatán toward the Louisiana coast. The torso loops over along the Florida panhandle and drops in line with the peninsula, turning nearly parallel to the equator as it winnows through the Florida Straits, between Cuba and Key West, as the worm's head might push along the ground. The loop current repeatedly moves up and down, slowly, about one up and down a year.

Rachel Carson, who wrote classic works about life in the sea, called the Gulf Stream an "indigo flood." It is a shade or two darker than the surrounding water, visually discernible in part because it is full of drifting life, from microscopic plankton to macrosized sea turtles. Ernest Hemingway loved to fish the Stream between his homes in Key West and Havana for a chance battle with a big marlin or tuna. Combined with Hemingway's tenaciousness and superior angling skills, the Stream delivered him world records and tournament championships, and a reputation as a saltwater sportsman extraordinaire.[6]

Wallace Stevens, who never fished with Hemingway but once brawled with him outside a Key West bar, quipped that he first got to the Gulf when a hurricane "pushed" him out of the Florida Keys. This wasn't altogether a bad outcome (not nearly as bad as the broken hand he suffered from a punch to Hemingway's jaw). Stevens learned that the Gulf could inspire with a distinct non-Mediterranean beauty, much like a poem drawing on its own rhythm and tonality. The American Sea became a siren to him—his own Lorelei—during many visits on which he explored Cuba and the five Gulf states.

Imagine him, for a moment, on packet boats hopscotching the

Gulf. If the first steamed out of Havana Harbor, leaving behind the old Spanish fortress of Morro Castle and bearing north to Alabama's Port of Mobile, on the uppermost shore—where the scenery moved him to write a winsome poem about a fish-catching eagle, "Some Friends from Pascagoula"—he would travel nearly seven hundred miles. If, next, a second packet set out from the west coast of Florida at Tampa, famous for its Cuban-leaf hand-rolled cigars ("good fat" ones best suited his taste), stood down the bay's long ship channel, and entered the Gulf toward the setting sun, the boat would ply five miles shy of a thousand upon making port in Mexico.[7]

Between the two journeys, he would crisscross a basin that holds 643 quadrillion gallons of water, which is not really a lot for the dimensions cited. That's because the Gulf's mean depth is but a single mile. Satellite images show what looks like underwater snow drifts packing around the entire coast, with the heaviest accumulations fronting Yucatán, Louisiana, and Florida. This is the continental shelf and its slope, and why the Gulf contains more shallow water (about thirty-eight percent) than deep water (about twenty percent).

The continental shelf was once dry land surrounding that much-shrunken pool of blue many thousands of years ago. Stand beside the Gulf today and the Earth's curvature will prevent you from seeing all the way to where the waves broke at the foot of the old Pleistocene beach. Back then, conditions were cold, dry, and blustery, very different from the warm-weather place of today. Mastodons, saber-toothed cats, giant bears, camels, and ground sloths the size of oxen stalked steppe-like savannas of golden-tawny grasses, and boreal forests of tree species that today are limited to the continent's northern tiers. People lived out there too, on that windswept land with those animals that no longer exist. The doomed megafauna struggled for survival against a common implacable predator—humans with spears and shell clubs—and against a changing climate. Lost causes both, as it turned out.

270 · · · 275 · · · 280 · · · 2

FLOR

FLOR

R. de Spirito Santo

R. de Matanzas

Aminoia

Chicagua

30

Terlichichimechi

R. de la Madalena

Gaços

Culias

C. de Mando
B. del Spiritu Santo
C. de Cruz

C. de Arbolida

25

Vachus

R. de las Palmas

R. Montalto
Chila

PANUCO

Tancacana

Ta meco

St. Ester

Tancuie Puerto

Panuco

S. Iago de

los Valles

Nachapalan

Tuzeluco

Tanquinitl

Pachca

Chuchica

Quastlavaca
Mexico

Chalco

Cuerna buca

los Angeles

las Casas

Yxionyan

MEXICO

Chiaytla

Pucla

Antequera

R. Panuco

C. Roxo
I. Lobos

R. de Tuspa

R. S. Pedro
S. Paulo

Chalechicoca

Almeria ó
Villarica

Tlascala

R. de Zempoal

Aquigaustiam
la Vera Cruz

Medellin

R. Ant Sardo

R. Alvarado

S. Iuan d'Ulua

S. Ilefonso

Spiritu Santo

Negrillo

la Bermeja

las Bivoras

Baixo de Sisal

I. das Arenas

Triangulo

os Arcas

P. de Terminos

Tabasco ó N.S.
de la Vitoria

TABASCO

20

GOLFO

DE

MEXICO

Iuc

Va

S. Fran
Camp

La
Bac

Chetum

I.
Chetumi

270 · · · 275 · · · 280 · · · 2

Uytgevoerd te LEYDEN door PIETER VANDER AA met Privilegie.

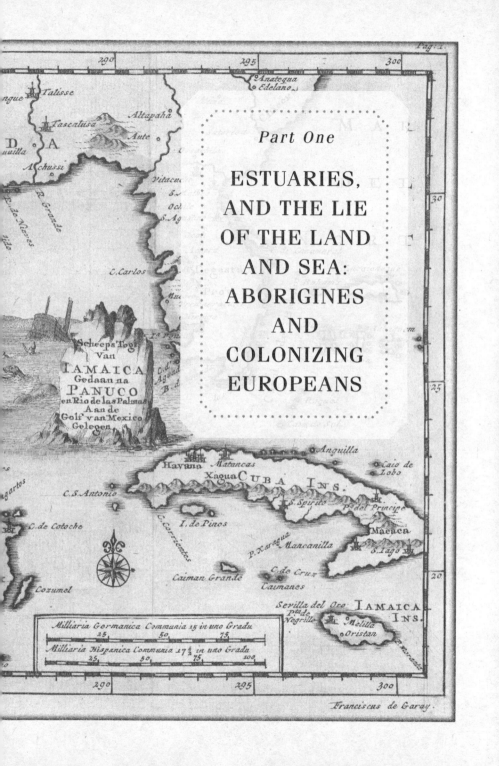

Part One

ESTUARIES, AND THE LIE OF THE LAND AND SEA: ABORIGINES AND COLONIZING EUROPEANS

Scheeps Tog
Van
JAMAICA
Gedaan na
PANUCO
en Rio de las Palmas
Aan de
Golf van Mexico
Gelegen.

Franciscus de Garay.

One

MOUNDS

Shell mounds circled the Gulf in huge numbers, symbolizing
the wealth of the estuarine environment and flourishing
precontact aboriginal life.

*The romance of it all, the old old mounds from the top of which
way off in the distance the green gulf sends its iridescent color
up to the deep sky.*

—WELLS MOSES SAWYER (1896)[1]

ONE OF THE MOST EXCITING DIGS IN THE HISTORY OF
American archaeology began with a deceptive thud. It came early in
1895 when the shovel of a wage worker struck hand-carved wooden

artifacts buried in a muck swamp on Marco Island, lying in the Gulf off southern Florida. The worker was excavating peat for his boss, William D. Collier, who used it to nourish the soil of his vegetable garden. Captain Collier, as people addressed him, grew citrus and coconuts, harvested clams, built and captained charter boats, and operated the island's grocery and small inn. He was also the postmaster of Marco, which had fewer residents than its five hundred acres. One vocation he couldn't claim was archaeologist.

Nevertheless, when his man's shovel plunged into hidden treasure, Collier wasn't clueless. You didn't live on the Gulf all your life without knowing about the aboriginal shell mounds that circled its shores, practically shoulder to shoulder, all the way around into Mexico. People were constantly digging in them hoping to find Indian gold and silver. Sometimes they'd discover a trinket from the Spanish colonial period, likely acquired in trade, but the more common finds were spear points and seemingly worthless shell objects. Collier's artifacts and their interment in a swamp rather than a mound were uncommon, as was his lack of greed. He was acting in the interest of historical research when he sought the counsel of an amateur archaeologist, Charles D. Durnford, a retired British military officer visiting from Edinburgh.

Durnford had a distant connection to the Gulf. His great-grandfather, as surveyor general with the Corps of Royal Engineers, had laid out the city of Pensacola in the 1760s, when the territory west to the Mississippi River was part of the British colonial empire. The great-grandson came to the Gulf on occasion to fish for tarpon and explore the ancient mounds—something of a mystery to everyone who had investigated them. People debated over whether they were built by long-vanished Gulf natives or migrants from elsewhere. Writing in *Forest and Stream* twenty years earlier, Charles Kenworthy, a New York sportsman who regularly fished on the Gulf, dignified racial myth when he maintained, "It is a well-known fact that the Indians were too indolent to engage in such an undertaking." He called upon "our scientific men" to investigate. But the Gulf stirred little scholarly interest at the time, and a proper response had to wait until Collier let Durnford recover a few samples.[2]

The amateur archaeologist knew to get them in front of experts, and that Philadelphia was the logical place to do this. Durnford's home, Edinburgh, had been the center of the Enlightenment in Scotland, as had Philadelphia in the US. Among men of science, the cities maintained strong ties that dated to Benjamin Franklin. Durnford personally delivered the artifacts to the University of Pennsylvania's Museum of Archaeology and Anthropology, to be evaluated by William Pepper, the museum's founder and a respected physician, known in professional and social circles as Dr. Pepper. On hand at the museum was a frail-looking ethnologist named Frank Hamilton Cushing, who was on sick leave from the Smithsonian Institution and under Pepper's care. A quick inspection was enough to satisfy Cushing that the pierced shells and strands of fish netting laid before him originated in the depths of native antiquity. Ignoring his poor health, he insisted on leaving straightaway to investigate the Marco site.

Talented, meticulous, possessing a strong sense of self, Cushing was the right man for the job. Virtually everyone in anthropology and ethnology knew him as a leading authority on aboriginal cultures. When he was a boy, an arrowhead tossed up by the plow on the family farm in north-central New York—literary province of James Fenimore Cooper's Indian tales, including *The Last of the Mohicans*—predetermined the "calling" of his "whole life." At seventeen, Cushing published his first scientific paper, reporting on a native fort he had begun excavating three years earlier. At nineteen, he landed a curator position at the Smithsonian.[3]

The public got to know him too. Big-city newspapers documented the six years he lived with Zuni Indians in New Mexico, where he established himself as American social science's first practitioner of participant observation (credit that erroneously went to others in the years after his death). A *Washington Post* headline said he was "one of the most famous western experts," and his boss at the Smithsonian, John Wesley Powell, himself a brilliant scientist and intrepid explorer of the West, called Cushing a "man of genius." Thirty-seven years old at the time he met Durnford, Cushing was all mustache, slight of build but stouthearted, and always restless for fieldwork, even though exposure to the elements beset him with any number of physical ailments. He was like a seasick-prone sailor who wouldn't stay off the water.[4]

Despite the outstanding contributions he made to aboriginal studies, and the sensation his discoveries created at the time, history barely remembers Cushing or the lost indigenous civilization he would disinter on Marco. Yet the people he named the "Key dwellers" and the estuaries that sustained them were no less an important part of American history than better-known native peoples of woodland environments, the fabled birthplace of America.

THE GULF OF MEXICO is one of the largest estuarine regions in the world, with more than two hundred estuaries (more than one-quarter of all North American estuaries) occupying nearly eight million acres around its shores. Densest around the five US states, these cradles of life give the American Sea its distinct ecological quality. To exist, they demand a few conditions. One is land—island or peninsula, wet or dry—partially enclosing a body of shallow water, which might take the form of a bay, bayou, cove, lagoon, inlet, sound, delta, or marsh. The Gulf has no shortage of these.

Another condition is suggested by the estuary's Latin antecedent, *aestuarium*, which means "tidal place." Central to these marine ecosystems is a dynamic exchange between seawater and freshwater, the latter pouring in from a stream, river, or overland runoff. The sixty-five rivers that trundle out of the US into the Gulf collaborate in the cultivation of a nearly solid band of estuaries that runs its shores. Bearing nutrient-provisioned sediment, the flowing freshwater stirs its charge into the salty sea tide. This brackish broth stimulates spectacular vegetable and animal growth, setting a table for hungry wildlife. Cosmopolitan, industrious, and purposeful, estuaries are bustling communities of the sea and shore, and among the world's most productive habitats. They were responsible for the Key dwellers' existence and, indirectly, Cushing's trip to the Gulf.

Getting to southwest Florida from Philadelphia in those days required patience, not to mention endurance. Shortly after meeting with Durnford, Cushing boarded a New York–bound train to take passage on the Clyde Steamship line to Jacksonville, high on the Florida east coast. From there, he proceeded down and halfway across the fecund peninsula on a stern-wheeler to the top of the north-flowing St. Johns River at Sanford, a citrus community scarred and blackened by back-to-back freezes that winter. A second train followed. Then he went "in the saddle" the last thirty miles, finally arriving at Punta Gorda at the head of Charlotte Harbor on Florida's southwest coast. He likely spent a night at the Hotel Punta Gorda, recently built for sporting enthusiasts who followed a similar route from the Northeast each spring to fish for tarpon. There he hired John Smith, a fishing guide who captained a "little sloop," the *Florida*, to take him down the coast to Marco.[5]

Outside the fuss of the inn's seasonal guests, southwest Florida was home to only a few hundred homesteaders, ranchers, fishers, and wildlife poachers scattered over a thousand square miles of scrubland, swamps, and windblown barrier islands. Cushing was back on the frontier, although it looked different from the western one he came to know when he lived among the Zuni—the one that colored the American imagination. The immense sky and profusion of light were similar, but where his eyes might have fallen on red and brown desert sands and still rock, he saw white beach, green islands, and great expanses of water. The scene, he later wrote, cast him back to "boyhood fancies . . . of Buccaneers and Spanish romance and adventure."[6]

For recording his real adventure, Cushing carried a journal in his pocket. The first Florida entry is dated May 28 (1895), the day Captain Smith and his mate set sail with Cushing on a "glorious evening" across the "bright waters" of Charlotte Harbor, a dogleg-shaped bay that reached toward the Gulf. By civilization's definition, those waters were a harbor; by nature's, they were an estuary, absorbing the sea tide and sweetened by the Peace and Myakka Rivers, a slew of creeks, and a mantle of encircling wetland. Charlotte Harbor was Cushing's introduction to an environment that increasingly beguiled him.[7]

The *Florida* had been under way an hour when "a low blue band on the horizon" appeared; it was the Gulf of Mexico, and Cushing was seeing it for the first time, "opalescent" and "magnificent." If the *Florida* had been bound for Texas or the upper Gulf coast, Captain Smith would have sailed into its languid swells. To make Marco, he followed the more commonly traveled route toward Key West and Cuba, navigating south into the wide swath of Pine Island Sound—another prosperous estuary, this one "sand-locked" by "palm-clothed" barrier islands.[8]

From Punta Gorda to Marco, a trip that would take a day on a good wind without stops, ended up taking eight. Cushing requested that the *Florida* call at every island revealing a shell mound, which turned out to be most. There were more than seventy-five mounds between Charlotte Harbor and Marco, by his estimate, and forty were "gigantic" ones he described as "truncated pyramids." "Ancient" canals, which he believed had been canoe passes, "threaded" the land, and dotting it were what appeared to be artificial lakes. He also came upon conch-shell seawalls several feet high that encircled lagoon-like areas he called "water courts," which he determined had been settlement areas. He was beginning to realize that the indigenous population was much larger than he had imagined, and likely not one of sojourners from another land, but of permanent residents.[9]

Initially, Cushing seems to have regarded the natural landscape as did most other visitors—as part of a colorful tropical setting. Then he began noticing a profusion of wildlife activity around the mounds and water courts, and he started making connections. From his gunwale-side seat on the *Florida*, he saw everywhere on mainland and island shores "clustering deep-green mangroves." These are shoreline trees common to estuaries in warmer climes. Of the more than fifty mangrove species worldwide, three lived on the US Gulf, primarily in expansive coastal forests Cushing called "sunless jungles of the waters." The most prolific, colonizing only in Florida, were red mangroves, named for their dangling russet-colored seedpods, pencil thin and long. The trees put out leggy prop roots that made them look ready to strut. Black mangroves, more geographically widespread, were known for their dark trunks and iron-hard heartwood. They bore thousands of specialized roots called pneumatophores, "bended like the legs of centipedes" up from the wet sand, Cushing wrote, enabling them to breathe in varying tides. Preferring dry feet, less dramatic white mangroves grew behind their amphibious counterparts.[10]

Red and black mangroves are both shelter and market for estuarine communities. When the tide runs high, the trees' webwork of roots become a catchall for the flotsam of the sea—decaying vegetation, shells, broken corals, uprooted sponges—food store for many. Mangrove oysters clinging to roots sift free-floating plankton that comes in with the tide; in turn, fish that ride the same feed on the oysters. Mangrove tree crabs similarly consume floating and falling detritus and pass energy up the food chain when eaten by fish and birds. In the tidal mud, solitary hermit crabs and scrums of fiddler crabs do much the same. Coffee-bean snails press up the trees to avoid fish predation, only to become avian edibles. Mosquitoes, too, which settle in a fog on mangroves, are an important part of the system. Their larvae at the base of the food chain are sustenance for small fish.

Life beneath the surface was less visible to Cushing, yet crowded like no city on the Gulf, with blue crabs, oysters, shrimp, turtles, and a range of young and mature fish. "No waters in the world so teem with food-producing animals," Cushing concluded, "as do these waters of the lower Florida Gulf-coast." On shoal and shore, mangroves accumulated peat around their roots and stimulated sea grass, full of nutrients and life. In Cushing's day, easily more than a million acres of sea grass meadows spanned Gulf estuaries, with Florida waters hoarding most. By some estimates, an acre of sea grass makes enough food in a year to support tens of millions of invertebrates and tens of thousands of fish, from small fry to lunkers. "Enormous" schools crossed Cush-

ing's path, often "wildly leaping . . . fleeing noisily before several puff-
ing porpoises and monster sharks."[11]

The throngs of fish hailed birds, too, the showiest wildlife. Cushing saw thousands at a time. The long-legged ones—herons, egrets,
ibises, spoonbills, and wood storks—tended to nests and nestlings in
the "thicket-bound" mangroves, and waded in shallows for food, from
sunrise to sunset, and sometimes beyond. Eagles and ospreys grabbed
nourishment on the wing at the water's surface. Brown pelicans
plunged for it headlong from the sky and "made short work of securing their evening meals." The fish and birds, the animated scenes of
the estuaries, and the mounds and water courts always next to them,
became a revelation. They "suggested to me in a vivid and impressive manner" why people centuries earlier "had begun their citadel of
the sea," Cushing wrote. "What more natural, then, that these people
should have followed the example of the pelican and cormorant, and
located their stations for food-winning, and finally their dwelling
places themselves, out in the midst of the navigable, but still not too
deep, shoreland seas?"[12]

AT NIGHT, THE *FLORIDA* put up at remote commercial fish camps.
Their overseers were people partial to their isolation and accustomed
to the bugs and sticky heat that kept Cushing awake at night. Never
hard to come by, dinner was often the day's catch. One evening's meal
was a heron Smith had shot—"fine eating," wrote Cushing; another
evening's, a sea turtle Cushing had turned on its back while strolling-
ing the beach collecting shells—"better than steak." When the sloop
finally reached Key Marco, their host, Captain Collier, put out a plate
of venison. Apparently finding it comparatively unremarkable, Cushing recorded nothing of its taste.[13]

He put down his impressions of Collier, though—a "civil" man yet
"bursting with irreligion," which was to say he livened his speech with
foul language. Slender, bearded, middle-aged, Collier was more or
less the potentate of Marco, a realm bedecked with native saw palmet-

tos and sabal palms, both common throughout the Gulf.* At low tide, a mangrove swamp joined his island to another key, Caxambas, many times the size of Marco.† Amid the insular green lived a handful of fishers, hunters, and guides in whitewashed plank-board houses and fishing shacks.

The island had been Collier's home since he was a boy. Uprooted by the Civil War, he, his parents, and eight siblings traveled the Gulf coast on a schooner his father, a millwright from Tennessee, had built and named the *Robert E. Lee.* When the family happened upon Marco in 1870, following a misadventure with a storm, they settled—the same as countless fresh-starters were doing on 160-acre government-granted homesteads in the western territories.

Collier's wife, Maggie Eliza McIllvaine, was also raised island-hardy, up the coast at Cedar Keys, where he did a lot of his trading. She ran their twenty-room inn and helped oversee the workers they hired to tend their spread of vegetables. Produce not shipped to markets they served to their guests, mostly northern men and women of the leisure class fond of the sporting life. The main appeal was recreational fishing, though some hunted on the mainland in the Big Cypress, a thousand-year-old wetland forest still untouched by loggers, hoping to bag a panther or bear, while rarely failing to take an alligator.[14]

Cushing went straight to work at the dig site and "struck relics almost immediately." "Splendid success," he reported in his journal on June 5 (1895). A single day's toil in the muck revealed he was onto something big. It was an aboriginal settlement of people, he was certain, who had not come with effects from elsewhere, but had

---

* William D. Collier was not related to the advertising millionaire Barron Collier, who later became the largest landowner in the area and state, and namesake of Collier County, Florida.

† The Key Marco of Cushing's day is now called Old Marco Village. In the 1980s, a developer renamed Horr's Island, south of Marco Island, Key Marco. The two were joined by a dredge-and-fill project in the 1960s.

adapted to their local surroundings. He returned to Philadelphia in fairly quick order. His samples, a wooden mask and conch-shell ladle among them, persuaded Dr. Pepper and Phoebe A. Hearst, mother of William Randolph* and a dedicated patron of anthropological research, to fund a full expedition. By December, Cushing was back in Florida.[15]

THIS TIME, HE SAILED out of Tarpon Springs, Florida, a Gulf-side village of Greek-immigrant sponge divers. He obtained papers to command the *Silver Spray*, a fifty-two-foot sponging schooner that carried "lots of sail," six in all. The truth is he was happiest at the helm. According to Wells Sawyer, the expedition's artist, Cushing possessed a "limitless and all-pervading . . . ardor and enthusiasm" that made an inspiring temperament for his handpicked crew of eleven. Leaving Tarpon Springs, Cushing, necktied and wearing a wing-collar shirt and suit vest and coat, in pitiable health as always, joined by his spouse of thirteen years, Emily Tennison, piloted the *Silver Spray* down the Anclote River to the Gulf. They put out to sea on Sunday and gained Marco Pass on Wednesday. It was a "pretty sight to see coming down before the wind," Sawyer said of the *Silver Spray* in a letter to a friend. Off the port side, mangroves fronted the estuarine coast for the entire two-hundred-mile run.[16]

Collier put Marco at Cushing's full disposal, asking only that the crew set aside salt-free peat for his crops. On the surface, the dig site was a "muck hole." The "whole place was like a thick sponge," Cushing wrote, "saturated with water holding a great quantity of salt and a large variety of smells"—yet he wasn't discouraged. The rank muck, an anaerobic mire and effective quarantine against oxygen, preserved the objects within. But he was unprepared for the terrible thing that happened when wooden artifacts came into contact with air. They began

* Virtually every source on the expedition identifies her incorrectly as Hearst's wife.

rapidly decomposing. Sawyer worked frantically with pen, paint, and sketch pad before a ceremonial mask or amulet lost its original color and shape. For some objects, his illustrations turned out to be their only form of preservation.[17]

Another frustration was constantly thrumming mosquitoes, hardly daunted by the crew's burning smudge pots, and potentially dangerous. Sawyer contracted a mild case of malaria. Cushing's health, amazingly, held up. Six weeks of digging, he appearing daily in white shirt and vest but eager to get dirty, turned out to be one of the most fruitful excavations in the history of US archaeology. "When they find anything nice," Maggie Collier wrote in her diary, "they all give a yell and Mr. Cushing shakes hands with the one who made the find." There was a lot of yelling and handshaking. Cushing's crew recovered about a thousand artifacts: ceremonial masks, tools, and weapons hundreds of years old. Powell, his boss, came down from Washington to see, and Frank W. Putnam, the curator of archaeology at Harvard University's Peabody Museum, said it was "almost beyond belief that so much of importance could have been found." The masks, Putnam maintained, were the "most marvelous archaeological evidence that has ever been brought out."[18]

More important to Putnam and other anthropologists, Cushing established that the people of southwest Florida had developed an organic society. They may have come originally from Central or South America, or even the North, but they were culturally reborn in the marine environment of the Gulf, and it sustained them for thousands of years. This became clearer when Cushing later began linking the physical artifacts of the tangible past with firsthand accounts in colonial Spanish documents. The Spanish were the first Europeans to arrive on the Gulf, and by the time they did, in the sixteenth century, the native population of southwest Florida had reached perhaps twenty thousand, ranging across fifty villages. These people were the descendants of Cushing's Key dwellers, part of a highly structured chiefdom secured with strategic marriages and military might. They maintained feudal control over all the native groups of the lower third of the Florida peninsula, who, collectively, were members of what researchers coming after Cushing would identify as the Glades culture.

Spanish conquistadors and missionaries referred to the aborigines they met in southwest Florida by the name of their cacique (supreme leader), "Carlos," which evolved into "Calusa." According to Spanish records, subordinate native groups translated the Calusa name to mean "fierce ones." That image quickly crossed the Atlantic. An early historian of the New World described the Calusa disposition as "very surly and very savage and bellicose and ferocious and uncontrollable and not accustomed to tranquility."* That was, undeniably, the disposition they took toward European invaders, and the first place they exhibited it was on the water.

The Calusa carved cypress-log canoes—using fire to break down wood at the log's center, and shell scrapers to hollow it out—that, when lashed two together, held forty warriors. Trimmed with sails, the worthy crafts took them to Cuba, perhaps as far as Yucatán, and the Lucayos (the Bahama Islands).†

When Juan Ponce de León made his maiden voyage to Florida, reaching Charlotte Harbor or thereabouts in 1513, he encountered those canoes. His three ships entering controlled waters and putting to shore armed and armored soldiers affected an aggressive posture, which led to two skirmishes, eight Indian captives, and deaths on both sides. After the sun rose one day too many over the anchored intruders, warriors in eighty canoes positioned themselves on the water, quietly at first. Sharp cries then went up, and a storm of arrows and darts arced overhead, falling short of the ships. It was a warning. The Spaniards retreated and eventually returned to Puerto Rico.

---

* The historian was Gonzalo Fernández de Oviedo y Valdés, quoted in Robert H. Fuson, *Juan Ponce de León and the Spanish Discovery of Puerto Rico and Florida* (MacDonald and Woodward, 2000), 165.

† The sixteenth-century historian Francisco López de Gómara claimed that women of the Lucayos possessed a beauty that lured men across broad waters. Francisco López de Gómara, *Historia General de las Indias y Vida de Hernan Cortes* (Biblioteca Ayacucho, n.d.), 23.

Nearly four centuries later, material evidence of indigenous power emerged from Cushing's dig site. It revealed itself in remnants of military instruments and domestic tools. As native peoples to the north used stone, the Calusa used available materials in their environment, which produced scarcely a pebble or rock outside of limestone. Bone and shell were the hard stock of south-Florida cultures. "Their art," Cushing wrote, "is an art of shells and teeth, an art for which the sea supplied nearly all the working parts of tools, the land only some of the materials worked upon." Warriors armed themselves with spears made of alligator and fish bones, and stingray spines, which also made good cutting edges and gaffs for domestic use. Fish harpoons doubled as war spears. Shells were used as dippers, spoons, bowls, hammers, awls, and digging and hacking tools. Big spiky conch shells were strapped to the heads of war clubs.[19]

Eight years after his reconnaissance voyage, an incorrigible Ponce de León faced these instruments of defense again. He returned in two ships, this time intending to colonize the centuries-occupied land, and once again the Calusa turned back the Europeans. Spanish chroniclers subsequently described the Calusa as raven-haired giants. They weren't giants, but the hyperbole is forgivable. With the men standing between five feet eight and five feet ten, they were inches taller than the average Spanish soldier—taller than Cushing. The twice repulsion of a formidable conquistador and the dispossession of his dreams made the Calusa larger-than-life figures in European New World mythology.

What accounts for the Calusa's notable political and physical stature? The simple answer is Gulf ecology. The more complex one, provided by Cushing's expedition, is that other hunter-gatherer societies faced food shortages, even starvation, in winter months when dry stores and wild game ran short. It was a time of uncertain survival for the weak and elderly, though not for the Calusa. Their people were firmly fettered to the coastal estuaries, wellsprings of protein—self-generating and perennial—that spared the Calusa of wintertime fasting. They had no need for agriculture, yet they stayed in one place and devoted themselves to developing a stable society and strengthening defenses.

For a people to be permanently settled without the requirement of food crops was rare in North America and across the globe—a luxury, in a way. There was no imperative, either, for the Calusa to migrate from hunting ground to hunting ground stalking food, because it came to them. Big fish, little fish, shrimp, sea turtles, crabs, lobsters, manatees, and even sharks, whales, and West Indian seals—it was all easy gathering with spear, net, or quick hand. Waterfowl, deer, and plants contributed only slightly to the local diet; all told, marine life supplied more than ninety percent. The Calusa were tall in stature because they were rich in food.

Their daily sustenance was easily deciphered from the shell-and-bone mounds that Cushing and later researchers troweled into. The concentration and type of shell in the mounds corresponded with local ecology. Oyster shells dominated those near the mouth of a river, and conch shells, those beside saltier water. Cushing was one of the first to recognize that what people called aboriginal trash heaps, or kitchen middens, were often something more. Since natural rises are rare on the Gulf coast, natives used shell refuse to create high ground that their cultures typically accorded places of worship and political honor. Coastal dwellers were wise to natural conditions too, and elevated their houses above tidal and expected storm surges, and up where breezes might knock back biting insects.

Cushing was quite certain that the Gulf natives heeded the wind and the sea when they sited their houses and towns. When enough shell wasn't available, or if one's social standing didn't ensure solid undergirding, they pounded log piles in the muck and built high and dry on those. Marco's aboriginal residents sheltered themselves at the north and mainland side of the island, semiprotected against storms and hurricanes. A good blow, nevertheless, could rip away a native dwelling. The architecture was a standard one-room round hut of pine poles, palm- and grass-thatch roof, and lattice walls. Woven floor mats were made of the same material.

The chiefdom's council house, where in more peaceful times the cacique would host Spanish emissaries with a feast of fish and oysters (no vegetables or land food), could hold two thousand people. The council house resided on Mound Key, one giant earthwork of shell substrate elevating the structure sixty or more feet, and other lesser dwellings twenty to thirty.

Cushing's subjects were not exactly children of a snakeless Eden. They spooked no bison off the edges of cliffs, as did other North American hunter-gatherers, burned no forests to draw out game, and worked no growing fields to exhaustion. But they drained wetlands and cleared dry land for their townships, which were individual and meticulously planned developments. As was the case with all New World aborigines, the Western Hemisphere gave them no horses or donkeys to pull carts, but the Calusa had their canoes. Around their mounds, they dug scores of miles of watercourses on the order of Venetian canals; one allowed them to punt their craft two and a half miles across Pine Island between the sound and Matlacha Pass, saving themselves from a ten-mile paddle around either end of the island. Following their disappearance in the mid-1700s, and before white settlement the next century, clearings returned to woodland, and wetlands reformed—just as the Collier/Cushing dig site had evolved from vacated settlement to swamp.

There was nothing inorganic about the Calusa's way of life, though; they lived and worked in and with their environment. Cushing observed this dynamic when he recovered their fishing nets. Busy hands had spun and twisted Spanish moss and palm fiber (sabal palm or saw palmetto) into tight cordage that, with equal care, they wove into nets, and along the lower course they threaded pierced mollusk shells for bottom weights. To stand nets in the water vertically, they attached buoyant gourds—domesticated papaya or *Cucurbita pepo* (squash)—to the upper cording (today known as the cork line). And they caught fish, lots of fish. The sea grass–carpeted, tropics-clear estuaries kept incubating them. The enduring abundance was reaffirmed year after year through generations, as was the native understanding of the interconnectedness of sea and avian life. The Calusa also saw links between the effects of lunar cycles and seasons: moon tides drew mollusks closer to shore; the deep, ebbing tides of winter exposed oyster beds; and spring lured sea turtles to beaches to lay eggs, and big fish to inland waters to feed.

Even as the Spaniards marveled at the robust physical stature and healthful existence of their native adversaries, they failed to make an association with the productive estuaries. In the sum of their Gulf endeavors, they retained a strident disregard for how aboriginal culture organized itself around the physical world. They might comment on it in their reports and journals, but they did not attempt to duplicate it. Cushing's dig into the past is the record of a lost culture and lost legacy. European conquest, as the pages ahead tell, introduced a future of imprudent relationships with nature in place of successful ones.

A HALF CENTURY AFTER Ponce de León's first run-in with the Calusa, the Spanish settled the east coast of Florida but had yet to affix themselves permanently on the Gulf outside Mexico and Cuba. They wasted no time, however, in establishing missions in Indian villages. It was their Christian obligation, reinforced by papal mandate, to spread the word of God and bring the uninitiated to Christ. Jesuit Juan Rogel settled in with the Calusa, who by then tolerated the Spanish, though barely. His mission lasted all of three years. During that time, Rogel went from village to village, in canoes navigated by natives along hand-dug canals. No matter the season, he dressed in a black cincture-tied woolen cassock and a tuftless biretta, a Bible often pressed to his side. The Good Book told him that God was the master of man, and man the master of all on earth, where he should reign as sovereign over the fish of the sea, the birds of the sky, and everything else. Different from the "beasts" God had made, humans were a race apart, of intelligence and reason, a divinely blessed counterpoint to nature, separate from and above it.

The contrasting spiritual enlightenment of Calusa religious leaders came not from a book, but from the earth and sea. They wore no robes, but masks, of the like Cushing unearthed, carved in the image of animals for use in ceremonies, some of which paid tribute to the bounty of the sea. Statuettes, carved from stock of local buttonwood trees, combined human and animal physical characteristics. The Calusa believed that when they died, their spirit passed to a land animal or fish, and when they took either for sustenance, its spirit departed to yet another. Life in all forms was a world of common spirits, of humans and animals.

Rogel could neither comprehend the meaning of the masks and statuettes, nor make them go away. He wanted to prevent the Calusa religious leaders, whom he called "witch doctors," from partaking in their rituals, but couldn't. After a year, he expressed his frustration in a letter to the governor in St. Augustine: The Calusa "said to me that their forbears had lived under [their own] law from the beginning of time and that they also wanted to live under it, that I should let them be, that they did not want to listen to me." Religious conversion meant more than saving souls. Rogel tried to prohibit the Calusa from painting their bodies, and he gave them cloth to cover their nakedness, shears to cut men's long hair, and tools to plant food crops. The Calusa rejected the tools. Food crops would have fed Rogel and the small garrison attached to him. The Calusa preferred ordering their lives around the nature of estuaries, not the cultivation of fields.[20]

Three hundred and twenty-six years later, Frank Hamilton Cushing explored the ground once brushed by Rogel's priestly robe. The ethnologist would not live to see the scholarly dividends of his discoveries. He had five more years before an untimely death, not from illnesses born in the field—the poetic way to go—but, according to some accounts, by choking on a fish bone while organizing his Gulf notes at a retreat in Maine called Haven.

Cushing had journeyed to southwest Florida to learn about an ancient civilization, whose members he came to regard as "amongst the brainiest of the prehistoric peoples." He had learned something about the Gulf of Mexico too. Embodied in the muck-concealed relics was the answer to his Key dwellers' prosperity. Wells Sawyer summed it up with a lyrical salute: "With nature face to face / In all about them thought they saw / In bird and stream and flower / The working of Nature law / Enduring all with power." The Gulf provided. That was the central lesson of Cushing's exceptional finds, although it was one the Spanish never quite grasped after they discovered the Gulf and claimed it as theirs.[21]

Two

EL GOLFO DE MÉXICO

Hundreds of thousands of aborigines lived on the Gulf coast before
European contact and thrived beside the sea's rich estuaries.

*Water is friendly to man. The ocean, a part of nature farthest
removed in the unchangeableness and majesty of its might from
the spirit of mankind, has ever been a friend to the enterprising
nations of the earth.*

—Joseph Conrad (1906)[1]

In June 1519, Alonso Álvarez de Pineda, a Spanish
explorer of little notoriety, then and now, sailed into the Gulf of
Mexico and around the coast, and made a map. The Spanish had

been to Florida and were colonizing Mexico, but before Álvarez de Pineda's map, they were uncertain whether the water between was an ocean, large bay, or gulf. In this age of exploration, a vast world had already begun opening to imperial European powers, which Joseph Conrad called "enterprising nations of the earth." Their mariners had discovered Mexico, Central America, South America, Greenland, Newfoundland, Bermuda, Madagascar, Zimbabwe, and the Amazon River. They had sailed the rugged waters around Africa's Cape of Good Hope to India, Thailand, Vietnam, and China. Vasco Núñez de Balboa had anchored in the Caribbean and marched across a sliver of jungle and mountain, the Isthmus of Panama, and looked out to the Pacific Ocean. *Mar del Sur*, the "South Sea," he named it. That was six years before Álvarez de Pineda's Gulf reconnaissance.

After Christopher Columbus arrived in the New World, expanding across the Caribbean and subduing the islands and natives took precedence over determining what kind of body of water lay to the north. There was also the matter of sorting out the regional geography. Between the Gulf and the Spaniards' Caribbean domains lay a long, slender tropical land of sloping green mountains they would one day name Cuba. It blocked their view beyond it, and it, too, initially remained unexplored. For all they knew, Cuba was the outer edge of a new continent. Even as they lingered off it for some years, there was the ever-present pull toward new land and water, and the prospect of wealth and glory in discovery.

The first to sail up to Cuba was Columbus, searching for that illusory portal to the delights and riches of the Far East. In October 1492, he briefly passed along Cuba's northeastern edge and drew close to the Gulf, before a stiff sea current turned him back. He had sailed into the Gulf Stream but didn't know it. What he did know, or insisted he knew, was that Cuba was a peninsula and the eastern tip of continental Asia.

Juan de la Cosa, the owner of the *Santa Maria*, Columbus's flagship, and himself a pilot and master, was left with a different impression. He had sailed with the admiral when he skirted Cuba, and despite signing a pledge demanded by Columbus attesting that they had reconnoitered a peninsula—lest he have his tongue cut out—he subsequently produced a map showing the terra firma in question as an island. Drawn in 1500, De la Cosa's map is as much art as cartography, depicting in vivid color cultural artifacts as well as geography. Little wonder, after being lost in a Paris archive for centuries, that it caught the eye of Alexander Humboldt, among the nineteenth century's greatest scientific minds and one of the first to propose that South America and Africa were two pieces of a broken continent. Humboldt argued for De la Cosa's genius. The Spaniard had captured Cuba in remarkable light, with a large bay or gulf to its north opening into the hollow of a landmass. Perhaps he had learned of the island and the water above from Spanish slavers, who routinely traveled uncharted seas, or from the seafaring native Taíno people, who lived throughout the Caribbean. Two other maps appeared later with similar cartographic speculations. Finally, the governor of the Indies, Nicolás de Ovando, sought the help of Sebastián de Ocampo to end the uncertainty.

In some ways, Ocampo was an unlikely candidate. Although he commanded a fleet of trading ships, he wasn't supposed to. A royal decree confined him for life to Hispaniola (today the island of Haiti and the Dominican Republic) for trouble—unrecorded—he had gotten into in Spain. Governor Ovando had always looked the other way, although he paid close attention in 1508 after dispatching Ocampo to determine Cuba's geographic truth. Ocampo's two ships proceeded to Cuba's north shore and then west against the current as Columbus had done. Ocampo pushed ahead, discovering a harbor he named Puerto de Carenas (later to be renamed Havana), where he careened his vessels for routine maintenance. Ships readied, he continued on and rounded Cuba's westernmost point, Cabo San Antón, with the great Mexican peninsula of Yucatán off his right shoulder, probably beyond sight. He returned to Hispaniola knowing that Cuba was an island, and that a broad sea of some type reached beyond the northwest horizon.

Governor Ovando could not exploit this discovery without bringing trouble to the truant Ocampo and himself. Still, word about insular Cuba got out. Two years later, one of Ovando's lieutenants in the conquest of Hispaniola, Diego Velázquez de Cuéllar, launched a successful invasion of the island. As its first governor, Velázquez devoted his attention to colonizing Cuba, securing a sound economy and enslaving the Taíno, scores of whom tended to his personal drove of swine, which grew from a handful to a remarkable thirty thousand. He had no time to give to the northern sea that bordered his island—not at the moment. His preoccupation consequently opened the way for Juan Ponce de León to become the first European of record to enter the Gulf beyond its outer edge.

NEXT TO COLUMBUS'S VOYAGES, few expeditions of the period have become as famous as Ponce de León's 1513 discovery of *La Florida*. His quest lacked the "dazzling doings" of others, said the late historian Charles Arnade, and among his contemporaries his accomplishments were notable but not the stuff of greatness. Ponce de León's posthumous celebrity is the product of the Fountain of Youth legend, first advanced by early chroniclers and given immortality by the likes of Nathaniel Hawthorne, Orson Welles, and the Florida tourism industry. Foremost on the agenda of any self-funded conquistador, as was Ponce de León, was finding land that would net a profit. His royal charter prioritized the search for gold and silver and the enslavement of Indians. It made no mention of a fountain.[2]

The mission of the man that myth would make famous was relatively routine. With no maps to guide him, he set out in early March to discover unknown waters and land north of the Bahamas. When his three ships made the east coast of Florida, he thought he had happened upon an island. Following the coast northward, he named the terra firma off his port side *La Florida* in recognition of the Easter season, known in Spain as *Pascua Florida*, "feast of flowers." Present-day Floridians prefer to think of the Spaniard as coming upon a land that spoke to him with the colors, fragrance, and, indeed, flowers of subtropical exuberance. It's a quaint notion that says less about a conquistador's inclinations than about a contemporary people who use the orderly landscaping around their homes and in their parks to picture early Florida, and know little of the harsh wildness that the Spanish often engaged in North America.

Ponce de León's view of the shore would have taken in dune grass, vine-tangled forests, and long stretches of scrubland of virtually impassable saw palmettos. There would have been few flowers. As devout Roman Catholics, the Spanish often named a place for the religious day on which they discovered it. If the expedition had made landfall farther north, then Delaware or New Jersey, still waiting for spring flowers, might be known today as Florida. The little convoy instead came about somewhere off Cape Canaveral and steered south, rounded the curving end of the peninsula, and followed the west coast to the present-day Charlotte Harbor area. Ponce de León had entered the Gulf but gave it little thought. After a fortnight of conflict with the Calusa, the Spaniards left. On return to Puerto Rico, they stopped at a string of eleven islets and ransacked the wildlife, killing thousands of birds and several manatees. Their commander named the islands *Los Tortugas*, this time after neither a saint nor religious commemoration, but after the 160 sea turtles his men slaughtered or took away.

Ponce de León had slipped around peninsular Florida's mangrove-trimmed point without realizing that the sea lying to the west was a gulf. Nor did he know that Florida clung to a continent. He assumed it was another New World island. His 1513 entrada would have amounted to little, if not for one extraordinary discovery on the east side of the peninsula. After turning south near Cape Canaveral, the ships beat against a powerful current that sometimes stopped them dead. The Spaniards were unaware that they were full sheets into the Gulf Stream. Later, they figured out that this ocean torrent could drive a ship east across the Atlantic to Europe. One Gulf Stream scientist puts it this way: "Christopher Columbus found the way to the New World, but Ponce de León found the way back."[3]

The discovery of the Stream's potential actually belongs to Ponce de León's observant chief pilot, Antón de Alaminos. A native of Palos, Spain, the staging point of Columbus's historic voyage and producer of countless ocean navigators, Alaminos as a boy joined Columbus on his fourth New World trip. Ponce de León was fortunate to land his services years later; Alaminos was coming into his own as a top-notch navigator—one of the most knowledgeable of the Indies. The strength of empires lay not only in the initiatives—if also arrogance and sanguinity—of leaders like Velázquez and Ponce de León, but equally in the fine navigational skills of pilots like Alaminos.

Those pilots labored closer to yet a deeper truth. The age of exploration had an indelible ally in nature: the ocean currents and wind that propelled and the stars and sun that guided their sailing vessels, the natural resources from which those vessels were constructed, and the discovered resources—hoped-for gold and silver—that paid dividends upon the risk taking of exploration. As a pilot, Alaminos relied on human inventions—navigational instruments—but his astrolabe and quadrant brought him closer to the celestial bodies that were his beacons, and his compass let him see the Earth's magnetic force that gave him direction. A mere glance to stars in the clear night sky and a quick calculation told him his latitude and distance traveled, and positioned him in relation to places he knew—Spain or Hispaniola. He might curse nature when a storm threw him off course or when impertinent clouds obscured his view of the guiding heavens. Still, to traverse the Atlantic or to guide Ponce de León into the still-uncharted Gulf, Alaminos had to put his faith in nature.

That's how he approached the alien current that slowed his headway. In it he saw advantage rather than hindrance. Six years later, in 1519, the same year Álvarez de Pineda circled the new sea, Alaminos used the yet-to-be-named Gulf Stream for the first time to push heavily laden vessels of the Spanish treasure fleet back home from Mexico. Approaching Europe, the Stream forks, with one tine reaching up toward the British Isles and Norwegian Sea, and another toward Spain. Sailing the Stream could shave a week off a crossing. Less time on the water reduced shipping costs and the risks of encountering dangerous storms and pirates. For the Spanish, the Gulf Stream would transport not just precious metal, but timber, naval stores, sugar, and rum. It became an ocean highway of global trade and, wrote the late geographer Carl Ortwin Sauer, a "lifeline" of "empire."[4]

In the American version of the past, Benjamin Franklin is credited with producing the first map of the Gulf Stream. The great flow of dark blue intrigued him, but he wasn't its original cartographer. A century earlier, in 1665, the German Jesuit scholar Athanasius Kircher charted the Stream on a map he made of the world's oceans. Other pre-Franklin maps also featured the expediting waters. These were privately commissioned by trading and settlement companies exclusively for private use, kept under lock and key and out of the hands of competitors. Franklin did create a map, based on earlier ones and the testimony of sea captains. Colonial postmaster at the time, he was trying to speed up mail delivery from Britain by directing packets around the current's pushback. Sea captains tended to be a stubborn lot, however. They ignored Franklin's cartographic advice, and the mail moved across the Atlantic as slowly as before. Nearly a century elapsed before the first modern and precise survey of the Stream was made. The person directing it was US Coast Survey chief Alexander Bache, Franklin's great-grandson.

IF CURIOSITY WAS THE FACILITATOR of exploring and charting the New World, profit seeking was the motivator. When Bartolomeu Dias of Portugal first rounded the Cape of Good Hope in 1488, he did so to open a trade route to Asia. After cobbling together watery pathways of global commerce, merchant mariners swelled the treasuries of Europe's enterprising nations and gilded its cathedrals with gold. New ship designs—from the agile sixty-foot caravels to much larger carracks—accommodated longer voyages at higher speeds. Pilots connected more dots on world maps, and explorers grew bolder—if that's possible. One of the most impressive feats was the circumnavigation of the globe, launched by Ferdinand Magellan, a native of Portugal flying the flag of Spain and representing the premier sailing powers of the time. He took his departure around the time Álvarez de Pineda was completing his map of the Gulf.

After Ponce de León, three expeditions intersected with the Gulf. West from Cuba, each passed along Mexico's Yucatán Peninsula and the pyramid-peaked towns of the Maya, and reached points along a broad, elliptical bay at the bottom of the Gulf. The pilot on one of those voyages, Alaminos, named the bay Campeche. The first expedition had been organized as a slaving quest of cavaliers without captive labor, considered essential to establishing oneself on a profitable plantation in the Caribbean. The last, yielding Mexican gold and silver, was led by the maverick conquistador Hernán Cortés. One month later, Álvarez de Pineda took leave from Jamaica for the Gulf.

Little is known about Álvarez de Pineda—next to nothing of his nationality, experiences, and the figure he cut. Was he, like Ocampo, an exile sent out on a mission, in this instance initiated by the governor of Jamaica? Not only did the governor covet precious metals; he needed slaves to replace those on his island lost to punishing labor and Old World diseases, and the northern Gulf offered fresh territory.

Álvarez de Pineda left Jamaica with four ships in spring, and likely accessed the Gulf through the Straits of Yucatán. From there, his exact course is uncertain. But it is clear he followed the perimeter of the entire Gulf coast in one direction or the other, or perhaps both. The evidence is in his map. Crude and spare, without tracking lines, compass rose, or cardinal directions, it is little more than a ghostly outline of the coast. It does not seem the kind of map bound to change a pilot's life, but it did. That ghostly outline is a decent representation of the Gulf's physical shape, and it solved two mysteries. It revealed that Ponce de León's Florida island was actually a peninsula, and that land encircled that curious body of water north of Cuba; it was a gulf.

Álvarez de Pineda became the first European on record to sail the Gulf's upper rim and the Texas coast. En route, he identified a few rivers, including what seems to be the Mississippi (a river he named

Espiritu Santo, after "Holy Spirit"), which to European nations would become the most important river in North America. The Gulf's first cartographer also met Hernán Cortés at Villa Rica in the midst of his Mexican conquest. North of there, Álvarez de Pineda scooted up Mexico's Río Pánuco and laid out a settlement. It was short-lived. Historians are ninety-nine percent sure he died there when native Huastec massacred the colonists.

His map survived him, and subsequent maps reveal his carto-graphic influence. The once-hidden sea eventually got a name too. The unknown maker of a 1541 map called it *Seno de Mejicano*, the "Mexi-can Gulf." Sebastian Cabot, son of Newfoundland discoverer John, issued a map in 1544 with the designation *Golpho de la Nueva España*. A Portuguese cartographer chose a geopolitically neutral Latin vari-ant, *Sinus Magnus Antiliarum*, which means "large, round bay." As with the others, the name was doomed, perhaps by its clunkiness (unlike the mapmaker's own, Lopo Homem, Latin for "wolf man"). The words that finally stuck were *Golfo de México*.

If Álvarez de Pineda gave the Gulf a name, we don't know it. He did not imprint one on his map, and unfortunately, no written records survive his expedition. As a result, history may have been denied some poetic summation of the sea and shore he mapped so skillfully. As did every expedition leader, Álvarez de Pineda surely kept a log. In it would have been the only first-person observations of native cul-tures of the upper Gulf at the time of contact. According to second-hand accounts, he came across as many as forty native groups, which would have exhibited the fullness of aboriginal life, thousands of years old, before the sweeping carnage of European pathogens, biological imports transported on every ship crossing the Atlantic. Archaeologi-cal evidence suggests he would have seen well-kept villages of round huts of pole construction, covered in animal skins, grass thatch, or palm thatch, many atop shell mounds, as with the Calusa, and some older than Egypt's pyramids. Traveling in June, he perhaps saw par-tially vacated villages. Outside the Calusa, hunter-gatherers of the Gulf coast headed inland during the warmer months to collect nuts and fruits and pursue wildlife, eventually returning to the perennial fare of the estuaries.

Álvarez de Pineda's log most certainly would have described the lie of the land too, which, in a word, was flat. Unlike the upshooting volcanic islands of the Caribbean familiar to him, the Gulf commands no impressive heights. There were no mountains or rocky promontories to record, no valleys or plunging ravines. Making up for the horizontal monotony was diversity of another sort: coastal prairies, salt marshes, broad beaches, mangrove bulkheads, sounds, lagoons, barrier islands, and river deltas. They were the natural settings of estuaries—the environment that enabled Gulf natives to live healthy and strong, and vigorously defend themselves against European invaders, of which so many died.

Three

UNNECESSARY DEATH

NARVAEZ IN TAMPA BAY.

To aborigines, Spanish ships reaching the coast in the sixteenth century were symbols of hostility. In turn, three celebrated conquistadors lost their lives on the Gulf's alien coast.

> *Our pity is much lessened upon finding a reasonable man so debilitated by fright and despair that he cannot make use of a plenty provided by providence.*
>
> —BERNARD ROMANS (1776)[1]

THE MANCHINEEL TREE GROWS ACROSS THE TROPICS, often sharing space with mangroves. About the same size as the mangrove, with wriggling exposed roots, the manchineel probably got to Gulf shores from Central America after its seeded fruit bobbed along the loop current. The tree has flawless green leaves, a sweet-scented blossom, and a cute, palm-sized apple-like fruit—an appearance that belies its lethality. The Spanish named it *manzanilla de la muerte*, "little apple of death."

When Ponce de León returned with colonists on a second voyage to south Florida in 1521, a Calusa defender using a hand-carved projectile thrower, called an atlatl, hit him in the thigh with a dart. The thwarted settlers fled, carrying away their semilucid leader. The tip of the dart was almost certainly laced with the manchineel's poison. Ponce de León was dead within days of retreating to Cuba. Centuries later, the American poet William Carlos Williams wryly observed that the Calusa had "let out his fountain."[2]

Thousands of natives lived on the Gulf coast at the time, with strong defenses and effective communication networks that reached great distances across land and water. Seafaring people, they did not live in primitive isolation, as the Spanish assumed. Their world reached beyond horizons. Indeed, they knew of the Spanish before the Spanish knew of them. They were aware of the enslaving and killing of Indians in the Bahamas, Hispaniola, and Cuba. Shipwrecks, too, so common in the age, gave away the presence of others. Flotsam had been washing onto Indian shores around the Gulf since the early days of European exploration, and the "gear of foreign dead men," to quote T. S. Eliot, sometimes included dead men themselves, their faces oddly covered with hair and their bodies weighted with clothing. On occasion, a live one crawled onto the beach, revealing even more about the foreigners. The first time Ponce de León met the Calusa, whom he knew nothing about, a native greeted his expedition with Spanish words.[3]

That the conquistador returned eight years later, when he succumbed to the apple of his would-be Eden, would not have surprised Gulf Indians. Nor would they have been surprised when, seven years after, there came another, Pánfilo de Narváez. The conquistadors were known to be relentless, as well as ruthless, and Narváez was as cold-blooded as any. Historians have described him as an Olympian brute—a "hollow-voiced bully," as one put it—burdened by a vindictive streak to settle a score with Hernán Cortés, no sweet lamb himself. A Castilian by birth, wreathed in a red beard, Narváez was a major player in the conquests of Jamaica and Cuba. Cortés had been part of the Cuba campaign too. He and Narváez served under Diego Velázquez de Cuéllar, who prosecuted the conquest before becoming governor and the husbander of thirty thousand swine.[4]

In addition to fostering his massive drove, Velázquez's island was fertile ground for profitable cash crops—such as cassava (called yucca in Cuba)—but worthless without a healthy labor source. Much of the indigenous supply had been lost to either foreign pathogens or the brutality of enslavers. Following two mostly unsuccessful slaving raids to Yucatán, Velázquez dispatched Cortés on a third in late 1518. It turned out to be a mistake. Once Cortés gained Aztec gold and silver, he showed no inclination to return and share the bounty with Velázquez, who had funded the expedition. After a year, the governor appointed Narváez to bring Cortés back. One of Cortés's swordsmen, Bernal Diaz, later remembered Narváez as a "mad dog [out] to destroy us all." But Cortés proved the shrewder of the two. As he did with the Aztecs, he did with his Castilian rival: he defeated Narváez's larger force with a smaller one. Narváez lost an eye but was spared his life. He spent nearly four years imprisoned on the Veracruz Gulf coast—the first permanent European settlement in North America—before his wife secured his release.[5]

Freedom was merely an opportunity to deal with unfinished business. Narváez sailed to Spain to petition for a royal charter to compete with Cortés. Charles V was generous. He granted Ponce de León's old territory and more: the Florida peninsula up to the modern northern border, west twenty-five hundred miles to the Pacific, and down into Mexico, abutting the contested domain where Narváez had wasted in chains. Two-thirds of the Gulf shoreline fell under his authority, a coast barely touched by white men. Aside from monarchs, no individual had ever possessed so much waterfront. Narváez walked away with a satchel full of titles too: governor, captain-general, chief law enforcer, superintendent of fortresses, and *adelantado* (civilian authority). His return to the Gulf was to be self-funded. But, presumably, there would be payoffs (gold, silver, and slaves) and the opportunity to settle accounts with Cortés—the kinds of motives that might impair a leader's judgment. There was the investment in lives too. Some six hundred soldiers, sailors, and colonists wagered on his venture. It was a bad bet.

Historians have long said that Narváez was not only the most ruthless, but the "most unfortunate of the conquistadors." Risk sailed with every transoceanic trek; a safe passage was epic, so dangerous was each. Narváez's fleet of five ships made its Atlantic crossing in the summer of 1527 without mishap. But misfortune could be epic too, and once he was in the New World, bad luck latched onto his expedition like a leech and slowly sucked the life out of it. A rare November hurricane took two ships, sixty men, and twenty horses. Narváez replaced the vessels while in Cuba, where he also hired a pilot, Diego Muerlo, who claimed the expertise required to navigate the unfamiliar Gulf. Four days on the job, he ran the fleet up onto hidden shoals on Cuba's southern coast, where the boats rocked on grounded keels for a fortnight. Then a storm, typically the mariner's worst enemy, blew up from the south, fattened the water, and set them free. Proceeding to refreshment and supplies in Havana, they yawed and pitched through another storm, then a second, and a third.[6]

After regrouping in Havana, the hexed Spaniards were finally ready to depart for Mexico. Finding one's way around the New World still depended on instruments of ancient-Greek vintage: the magnetic compass to determine direction, and the astrolabe to measure latitude, although imprecisely before the development of the sextant two centuries later. Charts of the day were unreliable, often misplacing landmarks and giving incorrect distances between them. Mariners had to wait until later in the century for the chip log, which calculated sailing speed, and until the eighteenth century for the chronometer, which determined longitude, east–west positioning. No less important than the limited technology a pilot had at his disposal was an ability at dead reckoning, which is to say, guesswork based on the speed of the ship— gauged by bubbles passing on the water's surface—and the direction of prevailing currents, still a mystery in the Gulf.

When the fleet left Cuba, something went terribly wrong. The pilot Muerlo would have set his compass for a westerly course toward his destination at Rio de las Palmas, 125 miles south of the Rio Grande, and then watched the bubbles on the water to track his whereabouts and progress. After an unknown number of days at sea, however, the crew sighted land, not at Rio de las Palmas, but nine-hundred-plus miles on the other side of the Gulf near Tampa Bay—not due west of Havana, but due north.

Muerlo and the other pilots insisted they had gotten the fleet to Mexico—even though the sun set behind the sea rather than the land—and that Rio de las Palmas lay ten to fifteen leagues up the coast. How the little flotilla ended up so far off course remains a mystery. Some historians believe yet another storm cursed Narváez; others say the ships got caught in the Gulf Stream and loop currents. Either theory is plausible.

What is certain is that critical questions demanded Narváez's immediate attention. Should the lost Spaniards try to find the Rio de las Palmas? If so, by foot or by boat? How would the natives respond to them? Did the natives have gold or know where it could be found? Did they have food?

Replenishments were the first priority of the passenger-colonists. They were a fair picture of Spanish society—artisans, merchants, lawyers, physicians, hidalgos, and friars. All were Christians, save for some of the slaves, duty bound to follow their lord and Narváez, soldier of Christ, and among them were surely the qualities of discipline, endurance, faith, and charity. But increasingly, doubt, if also fear and regret, characterized their mood, and ominously, none among the hungry lot was familiar with estuarine abundance.

It would be to their peril that they never took full measure of the life below the water's surface, beginning with Tampa Bay. Estuaries are the bustling urban centers of oceans—cities that never sleep—and Tampa Bay is the Big Apple of the Gulf's east coast. Fish are like the hordes at a market or souk. Nothing on the land above an insect resembles their density. Throughout Gulf sea grass beds, up to two hundred fish species engage in an unending contest of hide-and-seek with shrimp, crabs, and smaller fish, and they freely take at the beds of oysters, clams, and scallops. Sharks, rays, bottlenose dolphins, otters, and more than two dozen species of birds lengthen the food chain to the uppermost links below humans.

The best guess of scientists is that many millennia back, Tampa Bay was a freshwater drainage basin that took shape when sections of the region's limestone substructure collapsed. Swelling Gulf water began sluicing into the basin perhaps six thousand years ago, encouraging the tenancy of marine flora and fauna that exists today. Four rivers draining twenty-two hundred square miles infused the estuary with bracing freshwater, changing its biology ever so slightly between cycles of drought and seasonal upwellings. Some areas stayed more turbid or clear, and more salty or fresh, than others, and the shoreline supported mostly mangroves and salt marshes.

The Spanish early on called Tampa Bay *Bahia Honda*, "deep bay." Although its twelve-foot average depth was fine for the Narváez fleet, the bay was later unsuitable for large-draft vessels without dredged channels. Perhaps a more fitting name would have been *Bahia Muchos*. Sprawling across four hundred square miles, Tampa Bay is a bay of bays (Terra Ceia, Boca Ciega, Hillsborough, Old Tampa, Little Cockroach, Miguel, Mobbly, Double Branch, East, McKay, and Joe) and of bayous (Coffee Pot, Cabbagehead, Boat, Mullet Key, Clam, Cooper, Little, Big, Emerson, Cambar, Champlain, Critical, Custer, Tillette, and Williams). Although estuaries are constantly changing, today's Tampa Bay is a fair outline of the one Narváez mistook for Mexican waters.

MOST OF THE HISTORICAL DETAILS about his expedition come from Álvar Núñez Cabeza de Vaca, a survivor who set down events in a report to the Crown. Historians regard Cabeza de Vaca as a reliable eyewitness, short of his overlooking Narváez's harsh treatment of natives. Chroniclers later learned of the conquistador's deeds from other sources, including stories passed down from those who endured his savagery.

Cabeza de Vaca, the orphan of a hidalgo of southern Spain and a New World virgin, had signed on with Narváez in Spain as the expedition's royal treasurer. Today, a monument to Cabeza de Vaca resides in Hermann Park in Houston. The patina bust on top, which seems a fair rendition, has him in ringleted beard, fluted shirt sleeves, morion (the classic conquistador helmet), and a chest-puffing breastplate, with a stare more inquisitive than stalwart. The state recognizes him as the patron saint of the Texas Surgical Society (he excised a projectile point lodged in an Indian's chest), first European merchant of Texas (he coordinated trade among Indian groups), first ethnologist (he recorded descriptions of hunter-gatherer societies), and first historian (he chronicled his time on the coast)—activities that followed the demise of the Narváez expedition.

Cabeza de Vaca also made note of indigenous plants and animals. New World nature for the Spaniards was on one level fascinating, and on another, repellent. Absent from his observations was evident exuberance for the verdant wild. Nature was less likely to get the attention of a conquistador when it was unthreatening than when it was menacing—a notable hindrance to conquest. Cabeza de Vaca described the Gulf coast as a "land so strange and so bad and so totally lacking in resources either for staying or leaving." Yet, at minimum, 350,000 Gulf-side natives thrived on that land, most of them beside an estuary.[7]

Upon arrival at Tampa Bay, the expedition mounted to colonize, explore, gain wealth, and take revenge soon began unfolding into a hellish saga that would drag on for eight years and expose Narváez's cruel nature and flawed leadership. It also revealed how two cultures, native and European, can take the same environment and turn it into different things: friend of one and adversary of another.

FROM THE NATIVE VIEW around Tampa Bay, the five anchored ships swinging with the tides were a loathsome sight. The natives were probably the sun-worshipping Tocobaga, who tattooed their bodies with snakes and birds and geometric shapes. They neither attacked nor opened their arms to the sea-weary and lost Spanish.

To conquistadors, no wild coast was more dangerous than that populated by Indios, as they called the inhabitants of the "new founde lands." From the Spanish perspective, which primed that of other Europeans, the natives lacked the ambitions and accomplishments of Western civilization. God had created them, yet they had not accepted His grace and instead worshipped, as one Dominican friar wrote, "their natural lords." A reality in interactions between Gulf natives and Europeans that historians rarely account for is that the natives' relationship with nature, as much as spiritual practices, reinforced European images of Indian inferiority and the righteousness of conquest. People who had failed to exploit their surrounding abundance for commercial purposes were artless and lazy, in the judgment of the Spaniards, who therefore felt justified in taking the God-given gifts of nature and enslaving heathens to aid their quest. It seemed the Indios lived simply—half-naked and impoverished—as idle subordinates to nature, and in failing to dominate it, they had become as wild as it. They were savages born of a savage land. For a time, they could be useful to the Spanish as guides, slaves, and providers of food. Otherwise, like thorny underbrush, the Spanish wanted them cleared out of the way.[8]

When the expedition made contact with the Tocobaga, Narváez expected them to hand over food to his heavily manned enterprise and to guide him to gold or silver. Gripped by ambitions of wealth and power, he could not accept that deposits of neither existed around the Gulf outside Mexico. Patience was not one of his virtues either. According to an early source, during a quarrel with the Tocobaga he lopped off the nose of a cacique and loosed mauling war dogs on his mother. Eager to rid themselves of this bearded tyrant, the Tocobaga pointed north and assured Narváez that what he desired could be found in a place called Apalachee. Narváez sent his ships to search the coast for Rio de las Palmas, the intended destination, while he marched overland toward the fantasy of wealth, leading three hundred men, forty malnourished horses, and an uncertain number of friars, who, no matter their plight, were to Christianize the natives. The plan was to rendezvous at some point with the fleet, though no one was clear about when or where. Narváez was decisive at crucial moments, but not always right in his decision.

For two-hundred-plus miles, Narvácz's party followed native pathways. It also laid down fresh European footprints through cypress swamps and hardwood and pine woodlands, axmen opening the way. By the time they lumbered into Apalachee, near present-day Tallahassee in north Florida, every man and horse was in a weakened state, and they found neither riches nor respite. The Tocobaga had deceived the Spaniards. Warned of the approaching conquistadors, the peoples of Apalachee had vacated their villages, and from the camouflage of woods and swamp they discharged random bursts of cane arrows tipped by fish boncs, crab claws, or chert, hitting Spanish targets time and again.

Food and escape quickly replaced the quest for gold and silver as the expedition's main objective. The Spaniards withdrew to Apalachee Bay on the coast, where they prayed for a rendezvous with the ships. None occurred.

The stranded Spaniards resolved to rescue themselves. By now, they had figured out they were on the wrong side of the Gulf. Their best option, they decided, was to build log rafts to take them to Spanish territory in Mexico—easier to imagine than to do. No one within this rough cross section of Spanish society seems to have had skills in shipbuilding, yet the desperate endeavor became a high point in an expedition in need of intelligent direction.

The men, now numbering 250 or so, worked together to build seaworthy craft—an undertaking inspired by the area's endowments. The shore was thick with tall, straight pines. In centuries to come, many would be extracted with mechanical ease for the paper pulp industry. But with no tools for sawing or chopping, the Spaniards improvised a bellows from horsehide to melt down spurs, armor, swords, cutlasses—any metal in their possession. They forged makeshift axes, which felled roughly 150 mature pines, thirty per raft. Each would have to carry four tons of human and material cargo. Ultimately, the rafts were crude but eminently sturdy—models of resourcefulness in the use of imported and local materials. Cypress wood made paddles. Sails were a patchwork of stitched-together clothing. To seal gaps between the logs, the novice shipwrights fashioned a mixture of stripped palmetto leaves and pine pitch.

They also had Apalachee Bay at their disposal, which sits at the top of the Big Bend, a two-hundred-mile coastal estuarine region between Tarpon Springs in the south and Ocklocknee Bay (pronounced "oh-CLAHK-nee") in the north, including the Homosassa basin that in 1904 would delight Winslow Homer with the best fishing he knew. The water of the Big Bend is shallow and almost pool-like, making conditions right for the expanse of tidal marshes, cordgrass, and needlerush. The gentle water, combined with the sunlit shallows, encourages the growth of sea grasses, primarily turtle and manatee grass, which sprawl out to a twelve-hundred-square-mile underwater prairie. In the warmer months, manatees come up from the south to graze. Some people call these large mammals sea cows; Columbus allegedly mistook them for mermaids. Eighty-five percent of the eastern Gulf's fish spend part of their lives foraging in Big Bend grass, where scallops, shrimp, crabs, sea horses, and sea stars hide from predators. For ages, this estuarine environment has fed people.

But it did not feed the Spaniards. There was plenty to be had in the late-summer months when they were on the bay. Oysters were ubiquitous, their beds feasting grounds for black drum, sheepshead, and blue crabs. The raft building overlapped with the last month of the stone-crab spawning season, when the meaty-clawed crustaceans migrate into shallow water, and the beginning of redfish spawning, the only time the monastic species gather in schools. The self-taught raft builders seemed to have little aptitude for learning how to harvest seafood. To survive, they slaughtered a horse every other day, consuming the last just before pushing off on their log vessels on September 22—just about when throngs of mullet would have been coming to inshore water until winter spawning. Underway, the rafts carried a store of commandeered Indian corn, which was rationed at a handful per man per day.

THE WIND AND LONGSHORE CURRENT drove the Spaniards in the desired direction, west. The tenuous fleet initially stayed between the shore and barrier islands, careful to avoid oyster beds. Indigenous people valued oyster beds as a year-round food source; the Spaniards could see them as little more than serrated shoals threatening to rip apart their hard-won vessels, which quickly swelled with the hunger of the passengers. They resorted to custom and raided Indian settlements on their route, a danger of another sort. The confiscated food, Cabeza de Vaca wrote, was a "great help for the necessity in which we found ourselves." They could hardly disparage the diet of the various oyster and mullet fishers from whom they stole. "All the Indians we had seen are a people wonderfully built, very lean and of great strength and agility." From a "distance they appear to be giants."[9]

Leaving the protection of the inland waterway, the raftsmen drifted into bad weather. Rough seas loosened the lashings around the logs, but they held, a testament to the craftsmanship of novices. The men fared less well. Freshwater and food remained in constant shortage— "our bones could easily be counted"—and natives often attacked when the vulnerable flotilla made land for food stores. Nor'easter season replaced hurricane season, and chilling winds and the opaque winter

sea routinely battered the rafts. Narváez declared every man for himself, following a maritime protocol of last resort for occasions when
acting as a group jeopardizes individual survival. Cabeza de Vaca
believed instead that his commander had turned cowardly.[10]

Soon after, on a frigid November night, the surf breaking "loudly in
the dark," waves tossed the rafts one by one onto the beach. The Spaniards were in Texas, strewn between Galveston and Corpus Christi.
Natives ambushed the raft that washed ashore at the southernmost
point. Those aboard had survived the harrowing sea journey, only to
meet death at its conclusion. To spare himself the same, Narváez exer-
cised the privilege of rank and took two men to spend the night in
the presumed security of his raft anchored offshore. At some point,
the wind came up and carried the sleeping party out to sea and their
demise.[11]

NARVÁEZ'S BAD LUCK AND EGO had left behind Cabeza de Vaca
and some forty survivors, staring wearily into a new ordeal on land.
Many crouched on the beach naked, having lost everything since
Apalachee. Winter on the upper Gulf, the raw north wind a constant,
was not a season that engendered a spirit of providential salvation.
Exposure was only one concern. The barrier islands were the restless
winter residence of migratory hunter-gatherers. Utterly defenseless,
knowing nothing about their haven from the cold sea, the survivors
resigned themselves to the mercy of the natives.

Cabeza de Vaca later named the island *Malhado*, "Island of Misfortune," something of a misnomer, since the island's natives saved him.
They took him and the others as slaves, yet gave them food, shelter,
and their lives. They also left unharmed five who decided to fend for
themselves for fear of falling to human sacrifice or cannibalism. It
turned out they had no one to fear but themselves. Out of either ignorance or apprehension, they forfeited the goodness of the estuary and
met a terrible fate. They "ate each other up," wrote Cabeza de Vaca,
"until only one of them survived." The Christians committed the very

unthinkable act they regarded as custom in a savage land. Stories of aboriginal cannibalism were fodder for European chroniclers eager for sensational tales of the New World. No lesser figures than archaeologists of latter-day American universities refused to let the myth die. One historian, writing in 1959, called Texas's Indian shores the "cannibal coast." Yet no one's field studies ever uncovered unimpeachable evidence of the practice, ritualistic or culinary. To the contrary, Cabeza de Vaca reported that the natives were appalled by the desperate appetite of the cannibalizing strangers.[12]

The Spaniards were marooned on the island province of the Karankawa. Although Cabeza de Vaca's report contains not a single ill word about his captors, history would treat the Karankawa as bloodthirsty terrorists. For centuries, whites trembled at the thought of being shipwrecked on the Texas coast, so allegedly quick were the natives to torture, slay, and eat outsiders. No nostalgic statements accompanied the passing of the last Karankawa sometime around 1830.

A hundred years later, Texas's coastal natives were still remembered coldly in stories of old-timers. They also became a subject of scholarly interest when Edwin Booth Sayles, a founder of the Texas Archeological and Paleontological Society, completed a preliminary survey of the state's aboriginal past, while accompanied by his Jack Russell mix named Happy. Many researchers followed, reconstructing the aboriginal culture one spear point, shell mound, and dig site at a time. Like the Calusa, the Karankawa were forceful and dominant. For centuries after European contact, they fiercely defended their territory and way of life against multiple aggressors coming at them by land and sea—the Spanish, French, Mexicans, and Americans. To stereotype the native defenders as "hostile" (a descriptive that Anglo-American society still today reserves for indigenous peoples), says Texas archaeologist Robert Ricklis, condemns them for behavior exhibited most profoundly by the invading aggressors.[13]

Ricklis is among the latest researchers in the line descending from Sayles. The Karankawa, he maintains, were not a mere tattered group of scavengers randomly scratching out a survival. That image is no more accurate than their reputation for bellicosity and cannibalism. Succeeding from ancestors who had arrived on the coast eight to ten millennia earlier, they were a people of physical and societal integrity endowed with a traditional knowledge of the earth. Accepting nature as the sacred force of human life, society, and culture set up fateful distinctions between aborigine and European.

Differences might begin with something as seemingly irrelevant as native mosquito repellent, commonly a confection of alligator fat and shark oil, with a pungency that failed to convince European visitors of native humanity. Said one student of the Texas coast, "You might be able to smell a Karankawa before you see him." They decorated their bodies with tattoos and favored necklaces of conch shells, coyote teeth, and carved bison-bone danglers, which, unlike their Calusa counterparts on the other side of the Gulf, reflected their semi-nomadic existence. They quit the islands in spring, vacating their encampments of hide-covered oval huts to escape the mosquitoes and irritating midges, and continued to gather oysters and clams on inland waters before following white-tailed deer and bison across grazing territory until fall, when the natives returned to their island places. On the coast, where the harvest was dependable, they ate more heartily.[14]

The Karankawa were physically impressive like other Gulf coast natives, and better fed than peoples of the interior. "All witnesses from earlier and later epochs are unanimous," commented a nineteenth-century ethnologist, "that their men were very tall, magnificently formed, strongly built and approaching perfection in their bodily proportions." Ricklis writes that the "possibility that physical stature resulted in part from dietary factors rather than strictly from a culturally maintained gene pool must be kept in mind."[15]

The 367-mile Texas coastline of bays, back bays, bayous, tidal passes, and sounds that the Karankawa controlled is an arcing series of estuaries, luxuriant and supple. Many took shape after aboriginal settlement on the Gulf and had a prior life in another form, like estuaries everywhere. Chesapeake Bay and Narragansett Bay were once river valleys that flooded during glacial melts. Some estuaries, like Tampa

Bay, began as lake bottoms. Other systems are located on what was once solid land before collapsing during tectonic or volcanic unrest. San Francisco Bay came from the former. Puget Sound has estuaries of this origin too. It also has fjord-type estuaries that were once deep-walled valleys cut by glaciers before ice-cold water filled them. The Texas coast is modestly low-lying and riven with no bold valleys or fjords. It has, instead, flooded river deltas, including Galveston, Matagorda, and Corpus Christi Bays. They converge with a lagoon breed of estuaries, formed as sand piled up off the coast into barrier islands.

The largest estuarine lagoon in Texas is Laguna Madre. On a map, it appears as a narrow blue line between Padre Island and the mainland. The three-thousand-year-old mother lagoon runs from Corpus Christi Bay in the north to the Rio Grande delta in the south, 115 miles (the same distance from Cuba to Key West). A second half, Lower Laguna Madre, separated from the Upper Laguna Madre by tidal flats and the border between the US and Mexico, extends the same distance along the shore in the state of Tamaulipas. This is where Narváez's ill-fated fleet was supposed to make landfall after leaving Cuba.

Back on Upper Laguna Madre at the middle is Baffin Bay, named for its distant Arctic cousin. Like Corpus Christi Bay, Baffin joins a drowned-river-delta estuary with Laguna Madre's arterial lagoon estuary. The absence of substantial fresh river water, combined with the lagoon's shallow depth and slow flush rate, has made it one of the saltiest bays or lagoons in the world—saltier than the Gulf. Too salty, as it happens, for oysters, a historically important comestible on the Texas coast. Still, three-quarters of the state's sea grass meadows range across sixty-five percent of the lagoon, and along with sprawling tidal flats and cul-de-sacs of black mangroves, they give vegetative residency to crabs, fish—mullet, skipjack, sea trout, redfish, and more—and young brown shrimp and pink shrimp, all of which are major contributors to Texas's contemporary commercial fishery. Over seventy percent, roughly one million, of North America's redhead ducks winter on Laguna Madre—an embarrassment of riches that sportsmen discovered in the early nineteenth century.

Most of the raft-wrecked Spaniards were beached north of Laguna Madre on island shores adjacent to Galveston Bay or one of its minor water bodies—Christmas, West, or Drum Bay. A confusion of sub-bays are cordoned behind the islands of Galveston, Follet's, and San Luis, where historians believe Cabeza de Vaca landed. Galveston Bay is the largest bay on the US Gulf coast, two hundred square miles more expansive than Tampa Bay. It is part of the Trinity–San Jacinto Estuary, the amplest estuary in Texas, the seventh largest and among the most bountiful in the nation, with a trifling seven-foot average depth. Thirty-three thousand square miles shed freshwater to it via overland runoff and the Trinity and San Jacinto Rivers, supplying enriching sediment and a brackish mix. When the Spaniards landed there, the bay was alive with oysters, not to mention shrimp, crabs, and fish, black drum and redfish in particular.

During their increasingly despairing journey across from Apalachee Bay, some of the wan refugees had fumbled with harvesting shellfish. In Texas, the survivors learned how to forage in an estuarine environment from their captors, who expected the Spanish to gather food for all. A century and a half later, when the French expedition of Robert de La Salle was marooned at Matagorda Bay, a hundred miles down the coast from the Spanish landing, its members were grateful for the estuary as a source of protein. The "water was agitating and boiling with fish darting from one side to the other . . . and we made an enormous catch," expedition member Henri Joutel noted in his journal. "This type of catch was made often and contributed much to our subsistence."[16]

One conspicuous yet furtive source of carbohydrates for the natives, comparable with corn and rice, was the cattails that colonized the wetlands. Cabeza de Vaca ate Indian bread made from the starchy pulp pounded and then scraped with clamshells from cattail root mass. During the mainland months, he dug up assorted edible roots and cut prickly pear cactus, and he joined in the fall gathering of pecans at wild groves along the Guadalupe River valley, a festival-like harvest that drew bands of natives from great distances. The Indians also hunted white-tailed deer, a staple of the woodlands and riparian corridors around the Gulf, as well as bison. The Narváez refugees were likely the first Europeans to taste bison flesh, and Cabeza de Vaca imagined a future in which European cattle would graze on the amber grassland that supported North America's largest beast. Bison accounted for a sizable portion of aboriginal meat consumption, according to Ricklis's research, but not as sizable as the "estuarine aquatic fauna." Not one of the Spaniards was apparently envisioning an empire of commercial fishing.[17]

DESPITE HIS SALVATION, Cabeza de Vaca remained malnourished much of the time. For years, he was passed as slave from one family to another, finding himself in the position the Spanish readily imposed on indigenous peoples of conquered lands. Still, Cabeza de Vaca was constantly plotting escape. Finally, he and two Spaniards and one enslaved Moroccan who had belonged to another expedition member slipped away in an attempt to reunite with their countrymen in Mexico. Walking fragments of the Narváez quest, they groped inland across sun-scalded land and northward through the stiff range of the Sierra Madre Oriental. It was the final link in an extraordinary journey. On the coast, they had acquired a reputation for healing the sick. Word traveled the indigenous networks of communication, and at villages and encampments on their route, their services were demanded in return for continued passage. Usually, a prayer and sign of the cross over the ill secured the four safety and food. By mid-1535, they had reached north-central Mexico and began moving southwest on ancient trade routes over the Sierra Madre Occidental and down through the Sonoran Desert toward the sunset.

Nearly eight years after being tossed up on a frigid Texas beach, four ghostlike survivors, the only known of Narváez's original overland party—emaciated, sun bruised, clad in skins, three unrecognizable Christians and a foreign slave—reached their countrymen at San Miguel de Culiacán near the Pacific coast.

ON HIS EVENTUAL RETURN to Spain, Cabeza de Vaca defied a brush with French privateers and, once again, the awful winds of a hurricane. The report he read to the imperial court offered a studied understanding of the Gulf, its indigenous people, and its estuarine environment. But many continued to think of New World resplendence only in the form of glittering metal, ignoring the fact that hundreds had perished without producing spoils.

Hernando de Soto was one who believed that returns would outweigh the risks of another Gulf expedition, and that he could succeed where Narváez had failed. Having recently filled royal coffers with Peruvian silver, he persuaded the Crown to grant him the rights to the Narváez territory with all the requisite titles, including a bonus: governor of Cuba. A partnership was discussed with Cabeza de Vaca, but the two could not reach an agreement, which saved Cabeza de Vaca from additional travails.

Soto's Gulf campaign ultimately reprised Narváez's naked brutality and defeat. Conceptually, the reprise began with the phoenixlike notion that Gulf lands were brimming with precious metals. Soto bet all his money on it, and borrowed some too. Even relatives of Cabeza de Vaca invested in the phantom gold rush. Physically, the reprise began in Havana in May 1539, this time with sails unfurled in good spring weather and Tampa Bay as the intended destination. Soto reached it a week after embarkation and named it *Bahía de Espíritu Santo.*[*]

Natives saw nine ships come over the horizon from the southwest and enter the bay, and Spaniards saw smoke trails rise above the tree

---

[*] Historian Robert Weddle disagrees with consensus that Soto made port at Tampa Bay. He instead calculates Soto's landing to have been in the area of Charlotte Harbor. Robert S. Weddle, *Spanish Sea: The Gulf of Mexico in North American Discovery, 1500–1685* (Texas A&M University Press, 1985), 214.

line. The smoke lasted for days as coastal dwellers continued to signal to inland villages the changing position of the strangers. Soto made camp at a recently evacuated village atop shell mounds at the mouth of Little Manatee River, estuarine pantry of the local Uzitans. Donning ceremonial regalia, the governor-general stood shoreside and, for the Spanish Crown and himself, took possession of all he could see and more, dispensing, observed historian Marjory Stoneman Douglas, "salutes and banners, music, Masses served by priests in gold vestments, and with proclamations to the Indians." It was all very orderly, and replete with different meaning for the two sides. Soto had more than five hundred soldiers to back up his, and twelve friars to do the requisite proselytizing. He gained an interpreter too, Juan Ortiz, who had been an eighteen-year-old member of the Narváez entrada, captured by natives and spared his life by appeal from the cacique's wife and daughters—an incident that inspired John Smith's latter-day Pocahontas tale. The Soto entrada put ashore two women, 237 horses, numerous servant slaves, pack mules, greyhound war dogs, and a drove of long-legged Iberian pigs. Unlike Narváez, Soto would have fresh meat walk beside rather than under his mounted contingent.[18]

The natives met a leader who was different in appearance from his red-bearded predecessor but his equal as a bloody tyrant. If posthumous portraits are to be believed, Soto had brown hair (either wavy or straight), a brown ducktail beard, and placid brown eyes hawking over an aquiline nose. His bearing was lofty. A descendant of minor nobility, he was a man with too much "thunder and passion," says one of his many biographers, and too much ambition for conventional life.[19]

The king had instructed Soto to observe "good treatment and conversion" of the Indios, even as they were to be enslaved and their possessions taken. The new *adelantado* also received the contradictory order to "conquer and settle" the land and "reduce [it] to peaceful life." Soto relied on familiar practices. After a few weeks, he and the soldiers and friars set out toward Apalachee, his contingent swollen by scores of Indians that the well-armed Spaniards forced into servitude as porters, shouldering not only the matériel of an army but the trunks of Soto's lavishness: wardrobe, fine bedding, china, olive oil, and wine. Heaved into motion like a single living force, the great column of men and beasts—stretching several miles—cut a wide swath through the wilderness, except the wilderness was occupied land, threaded with foot trails and stamped with growing fields, the face of the land altered by other humans. Progress of the procession was announced by a piper; the whack of machetes; the trampling of men, horses, and pigs; and the shackles of the enslaved. There was so much discipline in the march, and in the reprise: the foreigners commandeered food, took more slaves, and cut off hands and noses of uncooperative natives.[20]

Soto's expedition reached Apalachee in October. Archaeological evidence suggests that the Spaniards observed Christmas there. If they did, it was likely the first observance in the present-day United States, and likely conducted without much celebration. After Soto's army ransacked an Apalachee village, confiscating food and destroying homes, the natives struck back, as the Spaniards should have by now expected of Gulf Indians. They ambushed patrols and attacked Soto's encampment, often with bows as long as a man and using arrows that, according to the Spaniards, could pierce a horse lengthwise. Near the bay, a Spanish scouting party discovered remnants of Narváez's raft-building camp, including the bones of slaughtered horses. They were an omen. After ten months in Florida, under constant siege the last six, the Soto expedition moved into Georgia, carrying the inevitable fighting and suffering well beyond the Gulf.

The gradually dwindling and increasingly fatiguing procession continued its feeble reconnaissance for gold and silver as it picked its way into the Great Smoky Mountains. It then turned west and eventually crossed the muddy father of all rivers, the Mississippi, into Arkansas and Louisiana, coming upon one native group after another. Three years to the month after his expedition left Cuba, Soto took ill near the river. Some modern-day researchers say a tropical fever killed him. Yet that conclusion seems off target. Malaria and yellow fever were the maladies in question, but both originated on the other side of the Atlantic, and neither had a presence in the northern Gulf that predated Soto. Eyewitness accounts record no rampant fever following along with the expedition either. They do, by contrast, mention influenza. The virus's spread requires no insect carrier, as do yellow fever and malaria, but only a cough, sneeze, or touch, and it can be passed between humans and animals, wild and domestic. Another possibility is typhoid infection, easily contracted from an extended winter encampment when offending fecal bacteria have opportunity to multiply. Undisciplined sanitary practices can devastate a sedentary force. Soto's was coming off winter bivouac when he died.

When the Spaniards slipped their leader's body into the Mississippi from the west bank, the once grand expedition had shrunk to about three hundred hungry survivors in rags or skins and a few withered horses. The integrity of their expedition had at least fared better than Narváez's. They had not been taken as slaves of Indians either, and they had traveled into regions never before seen by Europeans. Yet they were an expedition of conquest that had conquered no lands, produced no bounty, and mapped no new territories. Their plight was such that it was time to abort the mission and find a route to Spanish Mexico. When an overland attempt failed, they reprised Narváez's expedition one last time by building seven sailing crafts to return them to Mexico.

On a midsummer night in 1543, the Mississippi's current floated the makeshift fleet out into the Gulf. The Spaniards were uncertain at first of their arrival at sea. One of the survivors remembered that after evening prayers, the Christians noticed they had exited the river banks but were still on a current of fresh, muddy water "very distant from the shore." Soto's remnant sailed west, trying to keep the coast in sight, hit one bad storm, survived, and reached Texas. The boats were leaking badly, but the Spaniards discovered, as one of their officers later wrote, a black "scum which the sea cast up and which resembles pitch," and they used it to seal their boats. They were unaware that they had seen a vision of the future: oil, the eventual dominating story of the northwestern Gulf.[21]

From Texas, Soto's remaining compatriots pushed on to the mouth of Río Pánuco, where the Gulf's first mapmaker, Álvarez de Pineda, had perished a quarter century earlier. Lasting four years, the Soto enterprise covered four thousand miles through ten US states and Mexico. In the end, Soto had accomplished no more than Narváez. The "Eldorado" of his dreams, as the late historian Francis Parkman put it, had "transformed to a wilderness of misery and death."[22]

Yet the leader of the doomed expedition has survived as an exalted icon in white American culture. Standing outside the standard Anglo Plymouth and Jamestown narratives, Soto represents equal-opportunity apotheosis (if, of course, we ignore native perspectives of the past). Only select Founding Fathers, a few presidents, and Martin Luther King Jr. succeed him as a namesake public figure in America. Cities, counties (in Florida, Louisiana, Mississippi), schools, golf courses, streets and avenues, state and local parks, a national park, a national forest, a federal fort, a US naval ship, freshwater springs, a waterfall, and a record company all bear his name. Chrysler Corporation operated the DeSoto automobile division from 1928 to 1961 (no car has been named after a Founding Father, although Ford has the Lincoln Motor Company, and GM had the Pontiac). Hood ornaments featuring a miniature bust of a helmeted Soto from 1950s models are now collectors' items, and in the rotunda of the US Capitol hangs a portrait, commissioned in 1847, of his discovery of the Mississippi River. Even that was a hollow achievement. No one at the time took note of the river's geographic location; Europeans had to rediscover it.

Soto scholars tend to be protective of this most celebrated conquistador's place in history. For some, chasing down every loop, turn, backtrack, and switchback in his wanderings is equivalent to the search for the origins of the universe. Most, however, don't whitewash Soto's murderous ways. A recent biographer calls his a "savage quest in the Americas." Four firsthand accounts generated by his expedition give a rare glimpse into the demographic layout of the time. Placing them beside archaeological evidence reveals a landscape crowded by numerous native groups of the flourishing mound-building Mississippian culture, overlain with earthen structures and crop fields, and etched with traces and trails. A century later, when French explorers were following some of those same pathways and colonizing Louisiana, native resistance was no longer what it had been. Many fewer aboriginal villages existed. Soto's military march had unsettled intertribal power structures. Yet his battling, food stealing, and village burning were less abidingly virulent than the invisible pathogens that typically shrouded his incursions.[23]

Smallpox, measles, influenza, and other infectious diseases foreign to North American immune systems likely traveled from village to village along Soto's historic trail and beyond, mounting up into an efficient killing scourge that left millions dead. Those black-and-russet-colored pigs he brought, and left behind—including the original razorbacks of Arkansas—became an unexpected legacy of his journey. Today, their descendants are a feral menace that roots up native plants and disrupts species succession. Back then, infected pigs likely triggered outbreaks of tuberculosis, trichinosis, brucellosis, anthrax, leptospirosis, or cysticercosis, or transmitted viruses to the wild game that natives ate, such as deer and turkeys. If Soto had simply traveled in peace and taken the hands of villagers in his, rather than cutting them off, he still would have planted a genocidal time bomb that helped clear the way for future colonization.*

The Apalachee, Tocobaga, and Calusa in Florida, Karankawa in Texas, Mobilian in Alabama, Biloxi in Mississippi, Houma in Louisiana, and all other Gulf aborigines stood up to Spanish swords and missionaries for more than two hundred years. But they could not resist the diseases, and their once-powerful chiefdoms collapsed. In the case of the Calusa, Indian slavers, prompted by the Spanish, came down from northern territories, raided the depleted villages, and took the remaining Calusa away. Baptismal records in Havana indicate that a few ended up in Cuba when Spain gave up Florida to the British in 1763.

"History begins for us," wrote William Carlos Williams of America

---

* The Spaniards were much aware of how their diseases facilitated conquest.

and conquest in the Gulf, "with murder and enslavement, not with discovery."[24]

NO ONE HAS FIGURED OUT why conquistadors starved on the Gulf. Some historians say that in coming primarily from inland Spain, they lacked a taste for seafood. Yet surely they cringed at the prospect of eating their horses and own kind. Most likely they defaulted to pillaging native food stores because that strategy was more familiar to them than harvesting native waters. The critical point is that they starved, where Gulf aborigines had thrived and grown tall in the estuarine environment. It was sheer irony that those who did not thrive conquered those who did.

In all their improbable centuries on the Gulf, the Spanish never took full advantage of the lavish plenty of the estuaries. Despite their firsthand observations, they weren't inclined to the same conclusions as Frank Hamilton Cushing, digging his evidence out of the past, lauding the native way of life. No less inclined were the French or British, who, coming to the Gulf after the Spanish, endeavored not to find gold and silver, but to establish a more conventional economy while making better sense of the geography.

Four

A MOST IMPORTANT RIVER, AND A "MAGNIFICENT" BAY

A busy Pensacola Bay and harbor in the 1760s, as depicted by
British geographer George Gauld.

*This survey has opened a new Light to us, both respecting the
Nature of the country, and the Importance of it, which exceeds
the most sanguine Expectations.*

—BRITISH WEST FLORIDA GOVERNOR
GEORGE JOHNSTONE (1766)[1]

THE DELTA OF THE MISSISSIPPI RIVER IS ONE OF NORTH
America's most impressive alluvial plains and one of the Gulf's most
expressive geographic features. Every year, the Mississippi, the conti-

nent's largest riverine system, draining lands across the Midwest and beyond, once sent perhaps as much as 400 million metric tons of sediment down its course, inspiring the river's nickname "Big Muddy" (its major tributary, the Missouri River, is also called the Big Muddy). Reaching the end, all that mud disperses from the river's mouth, and much of it gathers into marsh and shoreline—mud that was land elsewhere building into new land. Where the channeling water sluices into the Gulf, the mud creates the delta, singularly vast and constantly in flux, with up to five water passes connecting to the sea. The delta can be vexingly indiscernible, especially during spring flood, even when one stands or floats in the middle of it. That's why Soto's men, escaping their travail on the vernal rush, couldn't tell at one point whether they were still riding the river or deposited into the Gulf.

In sorting out geographic priorities, European explorers emphasized the placement and location of certain features—a bay for safely harboring ships, a stout bluff on which a fort could stand, and a river to grant access to the continent's interior reaches. Deltas like the Mississippi's were not places that enticed settlement. Their "shabby and scanty vegetation," their muckiness, Joseph Conrad observed generally of river deltas in a poetic but little-read book, *The Mirror of the Sea*, conveyed the "impression of poverty and uselessness." The Mississippi's was nonetheless fated to geopolitical affairs. Whoever controlled this biggest of rivers controlled much of the continent's commerce and trade.[2]

To get to the river from the Gulf, you had to find your way through the delta's confusing geography and one of its passes. Soto's expedition stumbled onto the river, but no one mapped it, and the Spanish did not return to look for it again. Despite the river, the upper Gulf region, between the Rio Grande and the Florida peninsula, without gold or silver, frequented by hurricanes, fell low among Spain's New World settlement priorities.

In that vast of Spanish indifference, the French saw opportunity. Ever protective of their fur-trading empire in Canada and the Great Lakes, they were eager for an alternative to their traditional export route through the Northeast, where British colonists were amassing in growing numbers. In pursuit of that objective, René-Robert Cavelier, Sieur de La Salle launched a descent of the Mississippi River in December 1681 with fifty-four Indians and fellow countrymen. A hard winter had already set in when they pushed off from Fort Miami (in present-day Ohio) with bark canoes that they slid along the iced-over Illinois River. By the time they advanced to the confluence with the Mississippi and began paddling the cold currents south, two months had passed.

Finally, in April, they reached the delta. In the mud beside a makeshift post marker, they buried a lead tablet engraved with the arms of France. La Salle claimed the land—wetland, dry land, river, bayous, feverish swamps, and all—the land of seventy thousand natives—for his king, Louis XIV. Paying proper tribute, he named the lower river valley Louisiana. Then, with supplies running low, the canoes turned back upriver against the churning spring swell and returned to Illinois.

Descending the river in canoes was one matter, and accessing it from the sea with ships to reach French trading posts another. Two years later, La Salle was on the Gulf to locate the Mississippi again. He had convinced the Crown to support his expedition by reporting that the river's mouth was in present-day Texas and near Spain's silver mines of Mexico, which he pledged to seize "for the glory of our King." Historians have long called La Salle's misplacement of the river his grand hoax, but that may be extreme. On his original descent, he had carried a broken compass and faulty astrolabe, so perhaps ineptitude has been confused with deception. Whatever the case, his four-hundred-mile error fooled cartographers into sketching the river terminating on the Texas coast into a large bay. The bay was another La Salle blunder. Those unfortunate to be in his company on the second expedition—soldiers, artisans, women, and children—suffered for it.[3]

After crossing the Atlantic with four ships and losing one in the Straits of Yucatán to Spanish galleys, La Salle's little fleet entered the Gulf. "Not a man on board knew the secrets of its perilous navigation," wrote the late historian Francis Parkman, referring in part to the Gulf's tricky currents. La Salle struck north toward the river's mouth and apparently reached it. But he didn't see it. Not knowing to look for a delta, he was looking for the nonexistent bay. A leadsman cast a line and didn't know the sediment-clouded water he was sounding was the river's deposit. La Salle took a longboat to shore and didn't know the muddy land he was standing on was the delta. The French were directionally and environmentally challenged, argues historian Christopher Morris, unable to "comprehend the delta's size, shape, location, and mechanics." La Salle insisted they were in Apalachee Bay, which was in the far eastern bend of the Florida panhandle, and he ordered his ships to sail west, unwittingly moving away from the river.[4]

The expedition eventually installed itself at Matagorda Bay, where La Salle's erroneous map placed the Mississippi. The bay lay behind a peninsula, which hid the French from a passing Spanish patrol ship looking for them. Tidal marshes and oyster beds engorged the shoreline, alligators sunned on pushed-over reeds, and Indians migrated in for seasonal stays. The Mississippi was nowhere about.

Another disappointment was La Salle himself. He was grave, haughty, self-possessed, and given to violent mood swings. The titled Frenchman, "Sieur de La Salle," demanded respect but encouraged the opposite. The captain of the supply ship ran aground in the bay's entrance, destroying his vessel in an apparent attempt to sabotage the venture and force its abandonment. A second ship defected and returned home to France. The last was lost. The wilderness-defeated colonists now had no choice but to find the "fatal" river and make their way north to French territory. "Fatal" was the word expedition member Henri Joutel used for the Mississippi, and historian Francis Parkman used for the expedition. For two years, its leader continued to look west before Cenis Indians drew La Salle a map with the river lying to the east. He set off with seventeen of the stronger survivors, many of them shoeless, while the weaker, a few more than twenty, stayed behind. He was going in the right direction, finally. But before the party realized the river, "vengeance and safety alike," as Parkman put it, prompted mutiny and La Salle's murder. In the end, a handful of men succeeded up the river to Illinois.[5]

La Salle was an insolent trespasser, as far as the Spanish were concerned. Since taking his ship in the straits, they were intent on evicting him from the Gulf. Five patrols went out, four by sea and one by land. Over the course of several years, they found no French to expel. Yet the prospect of rival activity put territorial Spaniards back in touch with the upper Gulf. Their pursuit of La Salle, notes historian Robert Weddle in a scrupulous study of early French activities in the Gulf, edged up into the "most intensive exploration of the Gulf of Mexico to that time." They located Galveston Bay, Matagorda Bay, Choctawhatchee Bay, Mississippi Sound, Mobile Bay, and numerous barrier islands.[6]

In all their scouring, the Spanish never found the Mississippi. One search party sailed right into the delta but failed to grasp the river's entrance. They, too, were looking for La Salle's make-believe bay. Thirty-three major rivers flow into the Gulf, and Europeans had learned to access most, yet not the grandest river, not the tenth largest in the world.

PROVOKING SPAIN ONLY REINFORCED France's commitment to establishing a riverine thruway between the upper continent and the Gulf.

In 1698, Pierre Le Moyne, Sieur d'Iberville, sailed from Brest with three thirty-gun frigates to find the river, once and for all, from a Gulf approach. The thirty-eight-year-old commander, son of a prominent Montreal family, brother of several distinguished soldiers of New France, and a proven and gallant one himself, did not put his trust in the maps of the day. When he arrived in the Caribbean, he asked pilots about the location of the river. No one knew precisely.

So Iberville took a chance, sailed up to the northern Gulf coastline, staying to the east so he could run a thorough reconnaissance, and met Pascagoula Indians who gave him the clearest idea yet of the river's whereabouts. Satisfied that he was close, Iberville anchored his ships off the Mississippi coast in the lee of a barrier island. He, his much younger brother, Jean-Baptiste Le Moyne, Sieur de Bienville, and several others then set off in two shallops and two bark canoes in search of the river's contrary access. At the end of the fourth day, they came upon a rush of freshwater sending forth dead trees and other vegetative debris. This time, the Europeans knew they had found the river's mouth—having been lost seventeen years since La Salle's descent. "It is jolly business," a buoyant Iberville wrote, "discovering the sea coasts."[7]

Indeed, he still needed to explore the mouth and the surrounding shoreline, and secure a permanent presence. The delta was too wet and transitory to settle, so the French looked back where the ships were presently lying at anchor near the Pascagoula River. But the Pascagoula's shallow water and hull-gashing oyster beds turned them away. Three leagues' sail to the west, Iberville sounded suitable depths at Biloxi Bay. On the east, the water touched a solid wedge of land locked between the bay and a picturesque back bayou. There were freshwater streams and springs, and familiar food to gather and hunt (oysters, plums, turkeys, hares, and partridges) and some unfamiliar wildlife (raccoons and opossums), all of which had sustained Biloxi and Pascagoula peoples for ages. Running to the edge of the water, the woods were heavily timbered with pine for a fort's construction. The French called the settlement Biloxi and the fort Maurepas. Both afforded a lookout's view across the sound between two barrier islands, Ship and Horn. So much depended on geography.

Even though their countries had become allied through royal familial ties, the Spanish were not happy with the French installing themselves on Gulf shores. In response to the Biloxi settlement, the Spanish assembled a permanent colony at Pensacola, and entertained themselves with the notion that nature might drive the French out, as a hurricane had done to the Spanish at Pensacola the century before— the main reason they had initially abandoned the upper Gulf. France's Louis XIV had a different role in mind for nature. He instructed

Iberville to "breed the [native] Buffalo at Biloxi; to seek for pearls; to examine the wild mulberry with the view to silk; the timber for ship-building, and to seek for mines."[8]

Iberville was familiar with New France's economic tie to nature. He had earned his soldiery stripes in an undeclared war in the 1680s defending fur-trading interests against the encroachment of the Hudson's Bay Company, a British concern. But Louisiana didn't deliver what Louis XIV had hoped. The pelt of southern otters and raccoons wasn't the quality of cold-country beavers. If Europeans lusted for anything as much as fur, it was silk, an expensive import from China that traveled a long distance and required silver in trade. Although Louisiana's mulberry trees were the perfect habitat for silkworms, the industry failed to get off the ground. Drought and Indian hunters were pushing the bison westward, and pearls could not be found among all those oysters.

Biloxi's natural setting also wasn't quite right for the French. In 1702, they abandoned Fort Maurepas and moved the administrative capital to Mobile Bay. It had a navigable access to the interior, which Biloxi lacked. Yet sometimes a good lie of the land turns bad. When sand washed in and fouled harborage at Mobile, the French retreated to Biloxi. When a hurricane that year altered the watercourse in Biloxi Bay, they moved—with name—to the west side. Louisiana's capital was becoming something of a game piece on a board of changing geography.

The French had hardly begun to settle in at Biloxi the first time, when an unwelcome third party appeared. Six months after Iberville accessed the Mississippi River, a ten-gun British corvette slipped sixty miles upstream. It was the first oceangoing vessel to navigate the Mississippi, which was insulting enough to the French. But now the appearance of the English, who would soon be at war with France and Spain over trade disputes and over the Spanish throne succeeding to Louis XIV's grandson, threatened to upset the balance of imperial power on the Gulf. Iberville's brother, Bienville, only nineteen years old and at the command of two canoes, managed to chase the brazen corvette off the river. To safeguard against future interlopers, he took charge of building a fort down on the delta, and then as backup he established an outpost in Natchez Indian territory to the north on a grand bluff with a clear view of unwanted downstream activity. The port capacity beneath the brow of Natchez was barely adequate, however, and the fort in the delta constantly flooded. Bienville then turned his interest to a broad bend between the two. One hundred miles from the coast, it had backside access from a large lake he named Pontchartrain. Its curving shore and the river's bend gave the eventual city a crescent shape and future nickname. The French officially designated the settlement New Orleans, after Philippe II, Duke of Orléans. Bienville moved the capital there in 1723, convinced it would withstand both invading forces and hurricanes.

DURING THE SPANISH REIGN, the Gulf was little more than a conveyance for gold and silver coming out of Mexico. After the French rediscovered the Mississippi's entrance, glittering metal shared shipping lanes with up-country skins and pelts. Then the Seven Years' War (known in North America as the French and Indian War), an Atlantic-wide conflict over colonial and trade interests, with Britain and France as principal rivals, upset power shares. The Gulf was spared the guns of war but not the reshuffling of colonial possessions by peace ministers in 1763, who seemed to take joy in testing the sorting skills of geographers.

France ceded Canada and Louisiana east of the Mississippi to Britain. France kept western Louisiana and New Orleans but gave both to its former ally, Spain, and temporarily wiped its hands clean of Gulf territory. Spain lost Havana during the war to the British and traded Florida to get it back. Cuba had a lucrative sugar industry; Florida had nothing lucrative. Near the war's end, a fortune seeker struck the mother of all mother lodes in the silver-rich Sierra Madre range, and Havana's role as guardian of the Gulf treasure fleet became more important than ever. Adding to Spain's fortunes was New Orleans, a dirty thumbprint on the edge of British territorial maps. One loyal subject huffed, the "free navigation of the Mississippi is a joke whilst the Spaniards are in possession of New Orleans."[9]

So here's how to picture the redrawn map of empires. Spain controlled the Gulf coast west of the Mississippi, and Britain, east of it, save for New Orleans. Indians be damned.

The attraction of Florida to the Brits was that it completed their control of the North American Atlantic coastline. The Crown divided its new possession into two colonies, West Florida and East Florida, adding them to its existing fourteen colonies, which included Nova Scotia. It should be said that when the Patriots revolted in 1775, Great Britain had fifteen colonies that would eventually become part of the United States, two of which American history textbooks have faithfully ignored. They were the only Gulf colonies, though the real difference was that they remained loyal to the king during the Revolution— anti-American, in other words.

In the twenty years that they belonged to Britain, they were royal provinces, as opposed to those founded as private enterprises. On East Florida's Atlantic side, the temperate climate and soil fathered a plantation landscape of indigo, cotton, rice, sugarcane, and oranges. The economy wasn't terribly robust, but the Crown hoped English virtues of industry and thrift would duplicate the commercial setting on the Gulf.

Gathering geographic data was paramount. Although the Mississippi, with a delta instead of a bay, had been in the correct place on maps since 1701, some geographic details remained elusive. Cartographers continued to draw the Florida peninsula to look like a stubby stalactite and the Yucatán as a top-heavy desert rock formation. Maps and nautical charts, which showed navigational directions and distances, were "shamefully defective," said England's superintendent of Indian affairs in the Gulf region. Many of the old Spanish maps had been drawn by workshop cartographers who had never been to the places they rendered, but instead toiled at a table inside a building in Spain using information culled from ship logs. The British, by contrast, put their mapmakers in the field using the latest survey-ing equipment, such as the sextant, which more accurately measured latitude, and the latest mathematics and techniques of projection to account for the curvature of the Earth. They also began meticulously measuring the depth of navigational waters.[10]

Reflecting either bureaucratic redundancy or Britain's interest in the Gulf enterprise—probably both—three men obtained separate commissions to undertake the task of thoroughly mapping and chart-ing the upper Gulf from the Mississippi River to south Florida. All future members of the American Philosophical Society, they gave the world an enlarged geographic vista of the Gulf.

A Scotsman educated at King's College in Aberdeen, George Gauld landed on the coast the year after peace had been settled. He was coming from the Mediterranean to what people were calling its American equivalent. Appointed coast surveyor of the admiralty, he spent seventeen years in the Gulf, often aboard worm-eaten ships, some pulling a draft too deep for efficient surveying. A talented pencil artist, Gauld left behind a little-known and wonderfully descriptive drawing of the nautical scene on Pensacola Bay—ships under way and at anchor transferring men and matériel, a long pier identified by the conspicuous flying of the king's colors, and a line of hip-roofed build-ings attending permanent residency at bay side.

Thomas Hutchins was a native of colonial New Jersey who had fought in the French and Indian War. A twenty-year military career followed, with assignments as engineer, surveyor, and cartographer. A dedicated scientist who "measured much earth," said a contemporary publication, Hutchins mapped the colonies of the mid-Atlantic and upper South, and the courses of the Ohio River and the upper Missis-sippi. Appointment to Florida came next. Surveying the spoils of war was a fitting commission for one who had helped win the war. Work he completed on the Gulf led to his writing *An Historical Narrative and Topographical Description of Louisiana and West Florida*, published in 1784 at a brisk ninety-five pages.[11]

Bernard Romans was similarly a "man of action," according to one source, and the most vivid of the three British geographers. Dutch born, he emigrated to the colonies from England three years into the French and Indian War. Whether he took up arms is unclear. He was capable. In his forty-three-year life he was a sea captain, privateer, surveyor, cartographer, botanist, and scholar, a reader of history, poetry, anthropology, and politics, in Dutch, Spanish, French, and Latin. In the 1760s, while captaining a load of tropical mahogany from Cuba, he ran aground on the Florida Reef off the Keys. This and a subsequent voyage that sank his sloop were his introduction to the "mazy navigation" of Gulf waters. Given the natural tendency to learn from mistakes, there was some logic in his securing an appointment as deputy surveyor of the Southern District. He assembled surveying data and both favorable and hapless experiences, including sinking another boat, this one on Tampa Bay, into a book, *A Concise Natural History of East and West Florida.* The title was deceptive. With text, appendices, and maps, its conciseness "swelled imperceptibly," he said, to some eight hundred pages in two volumes. It contained reams of good information, much of it borrowed from Gauld's unpublished work.[12]

Charting the uncharted was challenging. Nothing took a front seat to sounding the Gulf's notoriously shallow water. This was painstaking, wholly mechanical work using a lead line with a plummet at the end. Over and over again, the plummet was dropped to the bottom, and each time a seaman called out to a recorder depths indicated by measured marks, or knots, in the line. The floor was virtually all sand and shells, and a mariner need not worry about running up on rocks or, outside the Keys, a coral reef. Yet nowhere was the bottom a constant deep or a constant shallow. Many ship's captains, including the thrice-shipwrecked Romans, learned of the perils of a sandy shoal, which lay in wait not just near shore, but miles out. Even more treacherous were oyster beds, found just about everywhere a river met saltwater. Hutchins warned of one bed at the mouth of the Pascagoula River that was an astonishing four miles long. The three surveyors ultimately sprayed their charts with countless sounding numbers, heaviest in potential shipwreck areas.

Aside from shallows, cartographers kept their eyes peeled for good natural harbors. The best by everyone's reckoning was Pensacola Bay, westernmost in the Florida panhandle. When Gauld took his assignment and arrived on the coast from England, the ship that brought him, HMS *Tartar*, passed through the Straits of Yucatán and pressed on for the favored port. The *Tartar* ended up far to the east—a not surprising reach, given the still-sketchy navigational charts and, more crucially, the inability of navigators to measure longitude. Even if the pilot had followed the correct compass track, navigation lacked an instrument to determine east–west positioning, and the Gulf's currents urged sailing vessels to the east, no matter the wind direction. Correcting, the *Tartar* followed the coast westward. Close to shore, the Gulf was a shining jade and turquoise, clear at forty feet to a sand bottom, at times a rippling mirror reflecting the frigate's classic long lines. When Santa Rosa Island, a serpent-slender barrier fifty miles long, with "Sandy Hummocks . . . all as white as snow," appeared off the starboard bow, the *Tartar* had reached familiar water. The mouth of Pensacola Bay lay at the island's west end. Before entering, the *Tartar* dropped anchor to wait for high tide and a harbor pilot.[13]

Pensacola was West Florida's capital. On its northwest side, beyond Gauld's view, the mainland shore trended toward a near hundred-foot rise several miles long. The shade of rust-red clay bleeding down from inland hills, the bluff was Pensacola's signature feature, supreme to any on the upper Gulf, and a smart place to raise a fort. The Spanish had done that, though theirs had been a "trifling little" one built of logs, as an officer on board the *Tartar* later sniffed. The British would rebuild it in brick, using the local clay. Eight years hence, the capital had 180 houses, by Romans's count, constructed "in a good taste, but of timber," with many roofed impracticably with palmetto fronds.[14]

Pensacola was not the genial tropics. Soldiers complained about winter winds probing the roofs and thin boards of the houses. But no one complained about the bay, apparently not knowing that ten storm-wrecked Spanish ships lay at the bottom. Their grave was the work of the hurricane that had discouraged permanent Spanish settlement in the area in the sixteenth century. The British officer who belittled the fort declared the bay "magnificent." Romans delighted in its spaciousness, thirteen miles long by two and a half wide, and sounding thirty delicious feet or more. It was the "best watered of any I know on the continent." The bays at Tampa, Apalachicola, Mobile, Biloxi, Pascagoula, and Port Charlotte fell short of this measure. So did those in Texas.[15]

Despite the bay's nautical advantages, a bar made navigating into it risky. That's why the *Tartar* waited at anchor for a pilot. Standing between a battery of guns on the salt-sprayed upper deck planked with North American oak, and looking toward the not-distant but presently unattainable bay, Gauld must have envisioned his first task: to develop a chart of the bay's entrance. The Brits' proper harbor had another deficiency. The Escambia and Blackwater Rivers reaching north from it could take watercraft only a short distance into the interior.

NOTHING BEAT THE MISSISSIPPI. That's what made limited access beyond Spanish New Orleans so maddening to the British. They were convinced, though, that the days of foreign control were numbered. Claiming the Mississippi's east pass at the mouth as theirs, they dispatched Gauld to decipher the delta. Uniformed and regimented, he made scrupulous soundings and stippled his chart with hundreds of tick marks to warn of shallows. His rendering of the delta's splay of five passes resembles a tree's searching roots wriggling far into the soil. When Hutchins later surveyed the area, he noticed that wherever Gulf water was a "clayey colour," the Mississippi was "not far distant," delivering "vast quantities of mud, trees, leaves &c. brought down by the annual floods" (if only La Salle had known this).[16]

Romans spent his time on another river, the Tombigbee, corkscrewing into the top of Mobile Bay. Perhaps eight hundred Europeans and Africans lived in Mobile. Romans most certainly ran into Jews, newcomers drawn to Britain's policy of religious freedom who, with fellow Israelites in Pensacola, were the Gulf's first Jewish settlers. He mentioned and rather liked a hardy bunch of French holdovers from the time when Mobile was their empire's most significant Gulf-front settlement. The Brits never cared much for Mobile, a swampy and fever-plagued place. With that and a painfully shallow bay and "barren miserable" seacoast, it seemed to have little going for it aside from its "fine river." Romans thought it might be hiding a water route that connected to the Mississippi above New Orleans, bypassing the irksome Spanish. He searched for it in vain. He found, instead, sixty Choctaw and Chickasaw villages, remnants of the Mississippian mound builders, which he listed on a map of the river. The Choctaw population was about seventy-five hundred; the Chickasaw, twenty-five hundred; and their more prosperous Creek neighbors, twenty thousand. Romans was filling in the cultural contours of a continent that British policy sometimes treated as officially empty.[17]

Upriver, Romans turned ethnographer, asserting himself in another quarter of the gentleman scholar. Native relationships with the land, he surmised, might suggest ways the environment could benefit British commercial interests. In addition to gathering nuts, acorns, berries, and wild oats for consumption, the southeastern Indians were also "esteemed good hunters" who took meat from deer, bears, bison, turkeys, and feral hogs, the latter of which had come down the line from Spanish swine abandoned by early explorers. The Indians raised cattle too—the old Iberian breeds and English ones that had wandered into their territory.[18]

Before European contact, Indian gardens produced mostly corn, beans, squash, sunflowers, and tobacco. Now, virtually every village had sweet potatoes, a South American native plant that journeyed east to Europe and then back west with the Gulf's early explorers. A quenching vine fruit, watermelon, introduced to Europe by invading eighth-century Moors before its passage to the Gulf, was a favorite of the Indians, as a century later it would be of southerners, who ritualistically sold watermelons in the spring at town squares and on rural crossroads from the backs of wagons, and who dreamed up watermelon festivals (with beauty contests), pickled rinds, and seed-spitting competitions. Indians, said Romans, "carried the spirit of husbandry so far as to cultivate" leeks, garlic, and cabbage, all of which had been part of the biological invasion across the Atlantic from Africa.[19]

Romans keened for what his countrymen could not grow in the sandy soil near the coast. Beneath the Indians' "noble and fruitful country" was a substructure of material that had begun forming in the Gulf fifty million years earlier. When the earth was much hotter and the sea's rustling edge reached a hundred miles inland, dead planktonic algae sank to the floor, where their calcareous skeletons bit by bit solidified over eons into a dense limestone bed known as the Selma Chalk. This same process created, beneath the eastern Gulf states, a subterranean structure that a hydrologist in the 1950s named the Floridan aquifer. Charged by rain and wetland, the aquifer reaches beneath the lakes and ponds and springs of the entire Florida peninsula and the islands and dunes across the upper coast to the pedestal of Mississippi. It supports the underside of the scrubland and pinelands of lower Alabama and Georgia, and as far as South Carolina. Here and there, this ancient limestone aggregate breaks through to sunlight, and Romans probably saw it, yellowish and mold stained, pitted and potholed.[20]

Most limestone stays secreted in the dark below—as a vast permeable rock full of tunnels and chambers and chinks, a pocked honeycomb, a hardened sponge abraded by quadrillions of gallons of freshwater. It is the primordial underground source of bubbling springs that feed rivers and lakes, springs that natives visited for millennia for drinking water and bathing and that thirsting European sailors sought for replenishing empty casks—the very springs that inspired the Fountain of Youth myth. The Selma Chalk beneath Romans's Indians is the solid hem at the Floridan aquifer's northernmost fall. After the Gulf withdrew to the modern-day coastline and farther, decaying organic plant matter, mainly prairie grasses, piled up into phenomenally fertile soil atop the Selma Chalk.

Romans resented the "savages" occupying this luxuriant land and predicted that a "civilized people in the future will enjoy all the earth sweets they can wish for." (After removing the Indians, those "civilized people"—white Americans—would use enslaved humans to realize those "earth sweets," cotton primarily.) As for the Gulf's role, he wrote, "In a word, I foresee [it] will become the seat of trade and its attendant riches in North America." How right he was. British traders were already sending nature's commodities down the Tombigbee.[21]

It was they who birthed the region's industrialization, though only outside the sea itself. Indians routinely gathered in Pensacola with merchants to exchange crops for blankets and a few metal utensils and knives, plus a little rum or whiskey. For the Indians' bear and deer skins, the English were willing to trade rifles. They managed to extract plenty of resources on their own too. Local cypress made durable clapboards. Cedar was turned into shingles, posts, and barrel staves. Brickmaking cropped up out of the red dirt of the Pensacola plateau, and saltworks at the edge of the Gulf, for preserving meat.

Their French predecessors had found a utility for the muddy Mississippi delta and Mobile's marshlands in growing rice. That environment, Romans wrote, produced the grain "very willingly." Propagating a chain of plantations, the French, longtime users of rice in soups and breads, including beignets, relied on the West African experience with wetlands systems. Many of their enslaved hailed from the Niger and Gambia River deltas, environmental twins of the Mississippi, where inhabitants had been raising the alluvial grain for three thousand years. It gave Louisianans a culinary icon: gumbo. After the French, the Spanish and British carried on rice production. They also exported indigo, hemp, and citrus, and Romans hoped to see a lively industry in silk, figs, raisins, cotton, and sugar, as well as rum making and winemaking. Only cotton persisted. Alongside it was a naval-stores trade in pitch, rosin, and turpentine. The naval-stores industry survived into the twentieth century, until it and timbering depleted the prodigious pine forest that dressed southern lands from Virginia to Florida to Texas, around the edge of the Gulf.[22]

The British all but ignored the resources of the sea and stuck to products of the land and their native trading partners. The arrangement was a bad one for Indians. Crippling pressures of European disease and aggressive encroachment drew natives into a commercial enterprise absent from aboriginal cultures before contact. They became supply-side hunters in a Faustian exchange, devastating animal populations and the wilderness ecosystem that had sustained their people for thousands of years. Hunting the woods near empty, they racked up huge debts to traders. Worse, they began starving in places once of plenty. Squeezed by British Carolinians pushing west and Gulf coasters pushing north, defaulting their land to British creditors, Choctaw, Chickasaw, Creek, Cherokee, and others moved down into the Florida peninsula in search of food and skins. The British lumped them into an undifferentiated collective they called Seminole.

Ultimately, thanks to Indian trade, Pensacola's economic importance surpassed that of Spanish New Orleans, rankling the Louisiana governor and exacerbating already strained graces between Spanish and British settlers. Before anything could be settled, war broke out between Great Britain and its unruly North American subjects.

THE AMERICAN REVOLUTION changed the three geographers' lives—and their beachhead. When Spanish grenadiers supporting the Americans captured Pensacola in 1781, they took Gauld prisoner. He died a year later, still loyal to the Crown.

Romans traded sides to the Patriots, initially volunteering his engineering skills to the construction of a fort on the Hudson River. A military commission denounced it in a report to General George Washington: "Mr. Romans has displayed his genius at a very great expense, and to very little public advantage." Fired, he joined the southern campaign as a field officer. En route to Charleston he was captured by the British navy and mysteriously disappeared.[23]

Hutchins was a hesitant Loyalist before authorities threw him in an English prison for trumped-up charges of high treason. Engineering a release, he appealed to Benjamin Franklin for a commission in the Continental army and secured appointment as geographer of the

South. After the war, Congress made him the first geographer of the United States.

When the Floridas were returned to Spain at the peace table in 1783, closing Britain's short Gulf chapter, Hutchins was an instant loud voice for their US annexation, along with Louisiana. He believed that the new republic's destiny lay in the West, and that this abounding region, the Gulf of Mexico, and the Mississippi River were inseverable and rightfully American. Important people would listen.

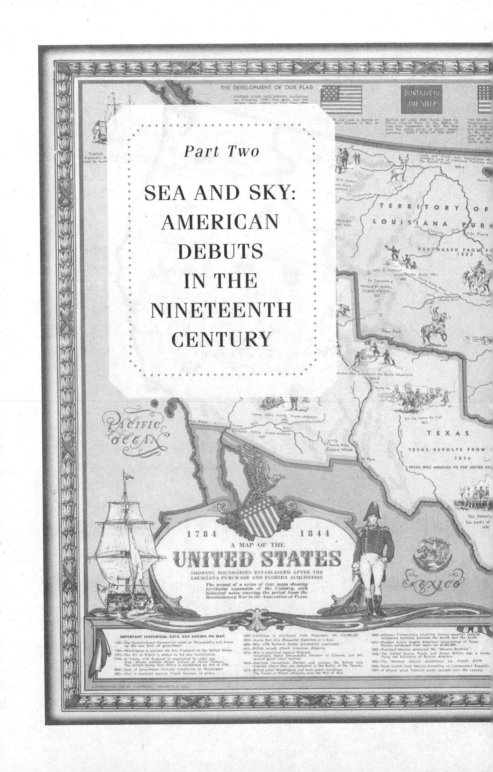

Part Two

SEA AND SKY: AMERICAN DEBUTS IN THE NINETEENTH CENTURY

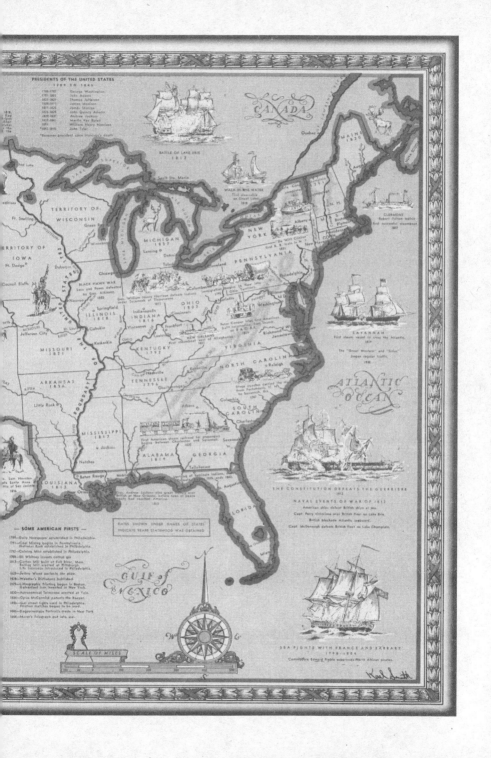

PRESIDENTS OF THE UNITED STATES
1789 TO 1845

1789-1797	George Washington
1797-1801	John Adams
1801-1809	Thomas Jefferson
1809-1817	James Madison
1817-1825	James Monroe
1825-1829	John Quincy Adams
1829-1837	Andrew Jackson
1837-1841	Martin Van Buren
1841	William Henry Harrison
*1841-1845	John Tyler

*Became president after Harrison's death

CANADA

BATTLE OF LAKE ERIE
1813

WALK-IN-THE-WATER
First steamship on Great Lakes
1818

CLERMONT
Robert Fulton builds
first successful steamboat
1807

TERRITORY OF WISCONSIN

TERRITORY OF IOWA

MICHIGAN
1837

NEW YORK

PENNSYLVANIA

SAVANNAH
First steam vessel to cross the Atlantic
1819

The "Great Western" and "Sirius"
began regular traffic
1838

BLACK HAWK WAR
Sacs and Foxes defeated by Gen. Atkinson
1832

ILLINOIS
1818

INDIANA
1816

OHIO
1803

Gen. William Henry Harrison defeats Indians under Tecumseh at Tippecanoe
1811

Peter Cooper tries first American-built locomotive on B. & O. line, "Tom Thumb"

NEW ORLEANS
First steamboat west of Alleghanies
1811

MISSOURI
1821

KENTUCKY
1792

VIRGINIA

NORTH CAROLINA
Raleigh

ATLANTIC OCEAN

ARKANSAS
1836

TENNESSEE
1796

First American steam railroad for passengers running between Charleston and Savannah
1830

SOUTH CAROLINA
Columbia

Charleston

THE CONSTITUTION DEFEATS THE GUERRIERE
1812

MISSISSIPPI
1817

ALABAMA
1819

GEORGIA
Tallahassee

Natchez

LOUISIANA
1812

FLORIDA

Gen. Andrew Jackson wins great victory over British at New Orleans, before news of peace treaty had reached America
1815

NAVAL EVENTS OF WAR OF 1812
American ships defeat British ships at sea.
Capt. Perry victorious over British fleet on Lake Erie.
British blockade Atlantic seaboard.
Capt. McDonough defeats British fleet on Lake Champlain.

DATES SHOWN UNDER NAMES OF STATES
INDICATE YEARS STATEHOOD WAS OBTAINED

GULF of MEXICO

— SOME AMERICAN FIRSTS —

1784—Daily Newspaper established in Philadelphia.
1791—Coal Mining begins in Pennsylvania.
National Bank established in Philadelphia.
1792—Coining Mint established in Philadelphia.
1798—Eli Whitney invents cotton gin.
1813—Cotton Mill built at Fall River, Mass.
Rolling mill erected at Pittsburgh.
Life Insurance introduced in Philadelphia.
1819—Jethro Wood perfects the plow.
1828—Webster's Dictionary published.
1829—Lithographic Printing begun in Boston.
Railroad Iron first invented in New York.
1830—Astronomical Telescope erected at Yale.
1836—Cyrus McCormick patents the Reaper.
1836—Gas street lights used in Philadelphia.
Friction matches begun to be used.
1840—Daguerreotype Portraits made in New York.
1844—Morse's Telegraph put into use.

SCALE OF MILES

SEA FIGHTS WITH FRANCE AND BARBARY
1798-1804
Commodore Edward Preble supervises North African pirates.

Five

MANIFEST DESTINY

Great Blue Heron on Florida Coast.

When the US Gulf states formed in the nineteenth century,
the coast was still a wild place that was a challenge to
US Coast Survey mapping expeditions.

*[I am] fully conscious of the great importance which you attach
to the uninterrupted continuation of our beautiful system of
triangulation, chaining together the coast of the Union from
section to section.*

—FERDINAND GERDES, US COAST SURVEY (1853)[1]

"TROUBLES APPEAR TO FOLLOW YOU," JOSEPH SMITH
Harris read in a note penned by his supervisor in Washington during
the Civil War, "but you just surmount them all." Harris received the
crisp praise aboard the Union gunship *Sachem*. Weeks before, exposed
to "shot and shell," he had scaled the ratlines to the topgallant mast-
head to direct mortar fire at Confederate forts Jackson and St. Philip,
twin sentinels positioned on either side of the Mississippi River. Seventy miles upstream lay New Orleans, queen city of the South.[2]

Prior to the Confederacy's Stars and Bars, three national flags had
flown over New Orleans. Its population of 160,000 reflected the layer-
ing of previous imperial occupiers and the international composition
of a port city. The signature architecture of wrought-iron balconies in
this French-founded city with its elegant French-sounding names was
primarily Spanish Colonial, even in the old French Quarter. The overall look, taste, and sound of New Orleans was an uninhibited fusion
of European and West African influences—apparent in the cuisine,
dress, music, art, worship, and lingua franca, itself a lithesome creole
of English and French with Spanish, Senegalese, and native Musk-
ogee stirred in.

As to the purpose of war, the South's most fluid city was one of the
Confederacy's few industrial centers. Factories shipped out munitions
and the gray uniforms of Confederate troops, and shipfitters launched
state-of-the-art vessels: ironclads and submarines. New Orleans was
also home to North America's largest slave market, and the city's
eventual seizure would be a tremendous moral victory for the aboli-
tionist rear guard, including, especially, the enslaved. As important
as anything, the great river fronting the city was a relentless mover of
domestic and global commerce that made New Orleans the South's
busiest port city; that, in turn, made it a key target of the Union's Gulf
Blockading Squadron, commanded by Flag Officer David Farragut.

At the outbreak of war, no one doubted that the Union would, in
time, draw New Orleans into its sights. But Confederate leaders were
convinced that an attack would advance from the north with infan-
try forces. A report leaked to the *Washington Star* disclosing details

of an impending assault from the other direction hardly nicked this steel-hard conviction. Confederate warlords scoffed at the idea of a southerly approach as simply too foolhardy, even for the Yankees. For one, lower Louisiana's swamps and bayous would turn back the best of infantries. For another, the river's mouth was not a single yawning, beckoning entryway, but five arcane passes, fingers on a hand, a perfect gauntlet, with shifting muddy shoals that would block enemy warships. Forts Jackson and St. Philip, of earthen walls double sheathed with red brick, and with a wire-cable-and-cypress-log barrier strung across the river between, were mere backup for what nature promised to throw in the way.

Nature played its hand all right, but in favor of the aggressors. The river's spring rise allowed Farragut's fleet to enter the passes. It also pulled apart sections of the barrier. Thirteen Union ships made it past the forts' cannons, and on to New Orleans. The stately levee of America's nether city was a bulwark against the river in flood, but not against a determined enemy. New Orleans fell quickly. Eleven US sailors received congressional Medals of Honor;[3] and Farragut, a promotion to the rank of admiral, created expressly for him.

As for Joseph Smith Harris, who had helped direct mortar fire, praise would have to suffice. He was not regular military. His applauding boss in Washington was the superintendent of the US Coast Survey, the agency charged with mapping the wet edges of America. When war broke out, the skills of its surveyors became a military asset. In the New Orleans campaign, Harris volunteered to ascend the river with the navy to map the exact locations of the enemy forts and determine the placement of mortar boats for the most effective assault. His work was completed with such preciseness that one gunboat captain said he would "never undertake a bombardment" without Harris or another surveyor "at my side."[4]

Apart from the hazards in war, charting the Gulf—fixing it to lines on a map—presented plenty of challenges to men of Harris's profession. As the Spanish, French, and British had previously learned, where water and land met was rarely a certainty. You couldn't approach the Gulf as if you were mapping the rocky, fixed coast of Maine. The Gulf's was a living coastline, in perpetual motion. As a line, it naturally turned, twisted, bulged, and receded. It even circled, and constantly tested one's sense of direction. The sun logically rose in the East and set in the West, over land and behind sea. Or did it?

Americans were still learning the geography of the Gulf three and a half centuries after Europeans got their first inkling of its existence. The Spanish found the Gulf, the French made its connection to the Mississippi, and the British began charting it. Finally, after Americans assumed control in the nineteenth century, after Joseph Smith Harris descended the *Sachem*'s mast and the smoke of war cleared, coast surveyors captured the Gulf in geographic detail—where it lapped against sand beaches, slipped into reedy marshes, and snuck behind islands up in coves, bayous, and bays. America's sea.

THE PERSON WHO GOT IT ALL STARTED, Thomas Jefferson, had once been a surveyor himself. When president, he cheerfully signed legislation creating the Coast Survey in 1807. He appreciated the value not only of national expansion, but also of geographic exactitude. That's why he sent Lewis and Clark out west in 1803 to discern the land acquired in the Louisiana Purchase. Authorizing the Coast Survey four years later came from the same imperative. Water was no less a crucial consideration than land. That's the hidden story behind the Louisiana Purchase. Jefferson had been listening when Thomas Hutchins— British royal geographer, first geographer of the United States, and fellow surveyor—argued that the Gulf was geographically and justifiably American. In his brief arguing for the Louisiana Purchase, the president cited Hutchins's work.

The proverbial narrative of this pivotal moment in American expansion goes something like this: in the land deal of the century made with Napoleon Bonaparte and the French, Thomas Jefferson doubled the size of the nation, opening the way for his countrymen to march across the continent unimpeded, a few Indian wars and snowy mountain passes notwithstanding. This is true. But settlement and trade in new western lands had greater chance of success with secure access to the sea. What made the deal especially enticing was New Orleans and the control of the Mississippi River, with the Gulf of Mexico as its vestibule.

Jefferson paid Napoleon $5 million for 800,000 square miles of land reaching to the Rocky Mountains. He paid him double that for New Orleans and the riverine security of America. Although Jefferson never set foot on Gulf shores, a map was enough to show how the sea was a missing letter in the name "American." It would significantly enlarge the water communication of national commerce and shift the boundary of the country from vulnerable land to protective sea. When he was secretary of state, Jefferson had advised President John Adams that Cuba, as a natural citadel at the entrance of the Gulf, was "indispensable to the continuance and integrity of the Union."

National security was a valid concern before Jefferson acquired Louisiana. British West Florida had fallen to the Spanish during the American Revolution, and peace negotiations had awarded East and West Florida not to the United States, but to Spain. Spain also continued to hold Louisiana, as it had since the French and Indian War. Then, in 1800, Napoleon secretly pressured Spain to return Louisiana to France, hoping that the Floridas would eventually come into his possession. The Americans barely tolerated the relatively quiet Spanish neighbors in their backyard, and the boisterous Napoleon would have been insufferable. Jefferson was president by this time, and although a Francophile to the core, he made clear to his minister in Paris that if Napoleon came to possess New Orleans, France must be regarded as "our natural and habitual enemy."[5]

As it happened, enslaved Africans revolted in the French colony of Saint-Domingue (Haiti), forcing Napoleon to reconsider his North American ambitions. In need of cash to put down the unrest, and "capable of the grand gesture," as Florida writer T. D. Allman notes, "putting on, then throwing off, Louisiana as though it were a magnificent cloak," Napoleon was ready to unload the outsized province. He didn't know that in a plot to end France's trans-Mississippi presence, the United States had been secretly aiding the ultimately successful Haitian revolt.[6]

With the Louisiana Purchase, Jefferson closed on the nation's first Gulf-front real estate. The transaction conveyed the present-day Louisiana coast, just under four hundred miles, but there was a snag. The US claimed that the parcel included another two hundred miles of a portion of Spanish West Florida, from the Mississippi River to the Perdido River, the current Alabama-Florida state line. The Spanish protested, of course. While negotiations dragged on, American settlers calling themselves the West Florida Dragoons sacked the Spanish garrison at Baton Rouge, founded the Republic of West Florida, drew up a constitution, and elected a president—Fulwar Skipwith, a Virginia tobacco and wine merchant, failed Louisiana cotton planter, and distant cousin to Jefferson, not to mention a negotiator in the Louisiana Purchase.

At the new republic's capital on the Mississippi, St. Francisville, the patriots hoisted national colors, a single white star against a blue background. Theirs was the original Lone Star Republic, though it was short-lived. President James Madison saw an opportunity and stepped in with a proclamation of annexation to bring the patriots and their territory, in the words of an unhappy President Skipwith, into the "bosom of their native country."[7]

The US was sprouting like a rambunctious teenager at a time when elder European nations were scaling back their North American ambitions but not quite ready for full retirement. Right where the young nation was seeking to stretch its legs, Spanish Florida was in the way. Its presence wasn't the sole annoyance. There were the Indians who were living in it, and the enslaved Georgia blacks running away to it. At the center, bringing all together and literally igniting an Indian war, later known as the First Seminole War, was the so-called Negro Fort. Rising on the east bank of the Apalachicola River a fifteen-mile sail from the Gulf, in Spanish territory, the Negro Fort was built by the British during the War of 1812, when it was called simply the

British Post. It wasn't long before they realized they could use it to entice slaves to run away from US plantations and, along with Indians, take arms up against their enemy. When the war ended and the defeated Brits pulled out, they bid the Americans adieu by leaving the river redoubt fully armed and in the possession of blacks and Indians.

To stop the persistent hemorrhaging of plantation labor, the Americans built their own fort upstream on the connecting Flint River in Georgia. As commander of US military affairs in the South, Andrew Jackson insisted on using the Apalachicola River to run supplies to the Flint River garrison. When the fort's occupants ultimately fired on an American patrol, as Jackson had apparently hoped would happen, he was quick to retaliate. Ten days later, a lucky shot from a US gunboat found the Negro Fort's powder magazine, obliterating the munitions and killing most of the fort's occupants.

The explosive event didn't stop Georgia slaves from escaping to sanctuary promised by Florida Indians. Jackson had zero tolerance for both groups outside their expected places—Indians confined to reserves, and blacks to white ownership. The Spanish weren't among his favorite people either, and in his opinion it was high time they decamped from North America. So it's easy to imagine him taking leave from his Tennessee plantation, as he did, mustering a military force, and marching south to bring Florida to submission.

The extent to which his campaign was consistent with orders from President James Monroe is unclear. Jackson's actions in the field seem largely born from Old Hickory hubris and previous military conquest. Having sacked Pensacola and New Orleans during the War of 1812, the lean, tall major-general, with a malicious shock of hair and piercing eyes, arrived in Spanish Florida feeling secure in his supreme authority. Near St. Marks, he accused two British citizens of conspiring with Indians against American security, summarily determined their guilt on the flimsiest of evidence, and—on foreign soil—executed them. Looking west, Jackson moved on Pensacola, the capital of West Florida, beat his chest with a few warning shots, and sent Spanish officials fleeing to Cuba.

No sound logic could support Spain's continuing to hang on to its faltering possessions. There was no longer a flush treasure fleet sailing the Gulf Stream, requiring protection from the peninsula. Moreover, the Florida colonies had never covered their operational costs. Trying to put its liabilities in the black, Spain had parceled out generous land grants to American settlers. The newcomers helped stimulate the Florida economy but also came to constitute the majority of white residents, as well as a cheerleading majority for Jackson's exploits. His war down on the Gulf raised a firestorm, in Congress and the national press, between those who believed Jackson had overstepped his authority and those who defended his actions. But in the end, his aggression paid a major dividend. In 1819, the US acquired Florida, and 770 more miles of Gulf front, for the nominal price of unpaid debts.

If anything, the public controversy steeled Jackson's nerve. He told Secretary of War John Calhoun to give him the guns, men, and go-ahead and he would take Cuba too. Removing the Spanish at the gateway to the Gulf, which Americans were increasingly seeing as their sea, was enticing. Watching intently from Monticello, Jefferson wrote to President Monroe, saying that control of Cuba would "give us over the Gulf of Mexico" and "fill up the measure of our political wellbeing."[8]

Monroe resisted temptation and left Cuba alone, yet Jefferson was confident that another Gulf parcel was fated to enter the country's coastal portfolio. "Techas," he assured Monroe, will be the "richest State of our Union, without exception." Texas was soon entangled in the successful Mexican bid for independence from Spain. A free Mexico then made the mistake Spain had made in Florida by inviting Americans to settle Texas. Jefferson had been dead a decade, but it should have surprised no one that men from the country that sired the Declaration of Independence would organize and fight for separation. Succeeding, "Texians" created the second Lone Star Republic. For nine years, they sustained their sovereignty before President John Tyler and his successor, James K. Polk, maneuvered approval of annexation through Congress. In 1845, the US picked up 367 more Gulf miles.[9]

That wasn't enough for some. None other than southern planters, gripping tight to their controversial labor system, held out hope for acquiring Cuba. Steeped in its own slave tradition, it was to be an archipelagic extension of the power of slave interests in Congress. Polk, a Jackson protégé from Tennessee, made Spain a generous, $100 million offer for its island. The president might as well have been asking the Pope to give up the Vatican. Profitable, loyal, symbolic, and nicely positioned geographically, Cuba had always been a sacred possession. Spain said it would sooner see it "sunk in the Ocean" than sold to the Americans.[10]

Southerners in the US House of Representatives couldn't contain themselves. The rebuff was not only insulting; it potentially dashed dreams of expanding southern political influence. With little haste, the southern congressmen took a report that Pierre Soulé, a former Louisiana senator, had written as US minister to Spain and adapted it into what became known as the Ostend Manifesto. The gist of their twenty-five-hundred-word document was this: after the blasphemous dismissal of the president's friendly and honorable offer, the US was "justified in wresting" Cuba from Spain.[11]

That was fall 1854, when sectional cordiality in Congress was faltering under the stress of westward expansion, shackled as it was to the slavery question. Southerners wanted new slave states in the West; northerners wanted only free ones. Conflict between sectional groups in what became known as Bloody Kansas broke out, and Americans killed Americans. National pride was wounded. In Cuba and the Gulf, removed from the volatile West, white southerners saw an alternative preserve for their labor/caste system. Florida senator and Gulf-side plantation owner David Levy Yulee called the Gulf a "common basin of expansion." Southward, then, southern society might go— even beyond Cuba to Venezuela, perhaps on to Brazil (where, after the Civil War, many southern slaveholders did end up) with its vast slave-labor force, to build an empire of commerce, and, as the *Richmond Inquirer* put it, "control the power of the world."[12]

NONE OF THAT HAPPENED. But mapping America's new coastline on the upper Gulf after the Civil War was like putting a national stamp of proprietorship on the sea. That was the job of the Coast Survey.

Its most immediate predecessors—the British geographers Hutchins, Gauld, and Romans—had made good maps. They were patrons of the Enlightenment upsurge in science, attuned to the notion that the truth of the natural world could be discerned through disciplined observation. Into field, wood, and marsh, they freighted the considerable lading of their profession: surveying chains, transits, quadrants, reflecting telescopes, plain tables, theodolites, gold-plated or brass surveyor compasses. What they lacked was the ability to calculate longitude, east–west locations.

One of the most important developments in navigation and cartography of their day was the perfection of the marine chronometer by a powder-wigged British clock maker named John Harrison. Conducting tests around Barbados aboard the *Tartar*, in the year the ship delivered George Gauld to Pensacola, Harrison perfected an instrument that precisely measured the time of a fixed location against that of celestial bodies, and thus established longitudinal position. Unfortunately for Gauld, Hutchins, and Romans, the practical and affordable use of the chronometer didn't arrive on the Gulf before the twenty-year occupation of the British came to an end.

A luxury in time and availability of new technologies permitted the Coast Survey to plot lines that did not exist on British maps—and to reduce the staggering number of shipwrecks. With Alexander Bache as superintendent, a post he assumed in 1843, the Coast Survey emerged as one of the federal government's largest agencies and the country's most important organization of science. Bache was a former army engineer and professor of natural philosophy, the first president of the National Academy of Sciences, and the father of "red, right, return" (the channel-marker placement that endures today). Following the navigational lead of his great-grandfather, Benjamin Franklin, the whaler-bearded superintendent had overseen the precise charting of the Gulf Stream.

Like Franklin, Bache was a stickler for scientific exactness, which he applied as a standard for his surveyors: to be proficient in astronomy, meteorology, physics, mathematics, optics, and geodesy. They had to know how to hoist and trim a sail, how to tack and jibe in the wind, and, since their vessels were hybrids, how to perform general boiler and screw maintenance and repair. Bache's "assistants," the official classification of their rank, were arguably the best of the breed. He was the boss in Washington who sent the letter commending Joseph Smith Harris for a job well done in Farragut's capture of New Orleans.

Born and raised in backcountry Pennsylvania, Harris might have seemed ill suited for surveying a seacoast. Not so. He and his older brother Stephen, siblings among nine, were graduates of a science-and-math-oriented high school of which Bache previously had been president. Duty in the Coast Survey was also made for men who squirmed for the outdoors, as did the brothers. Though only eighteen, Joseph was groomed and ready when he followed Stephen in joining the agency, in 1854. He spent almost a year at Pascagoula, six weeks of it recovering from typhoid fever, before taking an assignment surveying the forty-ninth parallel in the Northwest. Returning to the Gulf in February 1862, by way of captaining the USS *Uncas* down the Potomac River from Washington, he witnessed the Battle of Hampton Roads between the ironclads USS *Monitor* and CSS *Virginia* (USS *Merrimack*). In two months, he would be on the Mississippi dodging cannon fire himself. Slender, agile, twenty-six years old, Joseph Harris was an able one for ascending a ratline, and for surveying a coast.

Despite the expertise and equipment at the disposal of the exuberantly funded Coast Survey, the fugitive Gulf shore surrendered stubbornly to nautical charts and maps. "More or less difficulty will be found in many parts of this coast," Ferdinand Gerdes, Harris's imme-

diate supervisor, reported from the field to Bache, "and these difficulties will increase as the investigation becomes more detailed." Gerdes
had been in the Gulf since 1848 as lead surveyor. By the 1850s, he was
heading up the agency's biggest project, and focusing efforts on high-
traffic areas in maritime shipping and commercial fishing: Key West,
the upper coast, and newly annexed Texas.[13]

The Gulf was exotic duty, but not in the way of a plum assignment.
There were the Gulf summers, for one—the "unhealthy season." Mosquitoes and micro-sized midges, the latter of which locals took to calling "no-see-ums," were merciless. According to one assistant under
Gerdes's charge, their density was "beyond description." Midges were
pure nuisance; mosquitoes were that and more. Their eggs thrive in salt
marshes, freshwater wetlands, and the damp floor of forests. They can
survive freezing temperatures and hide out for months in dry places
until water comes and they hatch and metamorphose into airborne
killers. Those tiny bodies—not all or always, but many and often—
carried ferocious diseases that worried every surveyor. Two—malaria
and yellow fever—had wracked the coast for centuries and would do
so for half of another. No place was repeatedly hit harder than New
Orleans. Thousands perished during an 1853 scourge.[14]

The weather wasn't great that year either—at least not for mapping the coast. In May on the Texas waterfront, Bache noted, a "violent hurricane suddenly came up, which prostrated the camp and . . .
continuation of work was rendered impracticable." Storms could blow
up anytime, anyplace, without notice, and send a surveying crew
scrambling to higher ground. The assistant in Texas, James Williams,
revealed his frustrations in a report to Bache: "The stormy winter, the
short twilight, and intense heat of cloudless summer; the frequent,
almost constant, high winds; the hazy, misty air—all battle against
progress."[15]

Maybe Williams was a complainer by disposition, but he had a point.
Storms frequently stalled the work of crews. Along many stretches
of the Gulf's phantom coast, marshes and mangroves obscured the
meeting place between land and water. Granite geodesic monuments

sunk in the ground ostensibly for the duration of time sometimes disappeared because the land they were marking disappeared. Islands vanished and materialized on a regular basis, river passes silted and cleared, and the edge fluxed between periods of erosion and building.

In spite of itself, the geography had a stable and constant side too. The Survey revealed to America not only the shoreline, but valuable physical descriptions of the land—its contours and what grew on it. Harris found an expressive side to the geography in green-growing things—most prominently, trees. Their species were few but their numbers many, some truly ancient provocateurs dismissing the threat of shoreline change. The grandest were live oaks, most overt along the forty-four-mile Mississippi coastline that Harris measured with his surveying chains. Forming maritime forests of hardwood, live oaks were cut by the US Navy for framework timber in United States gunships. Although not the most prolific of the coast trees, they were a vernal landmark, living hundreds of years, and witnesses to history. Harris no doubt encountered live oaks that had been around since Soto, Narváez, and even precontact mound builders.

Live oaks are arguably the region's most poetic trees. They are "lusty" and "joyous," wrote Walt Whitman, with wandering limbs longer than the trees are tall, offering residency to birds and squirrels, and Spanish moss, a wispy, hanging epiphyte that clings to a warm, humid climate, and as regionally expressive as the trees themselves. Planted in line, live oaks lent a canopied aesthetic to streets, boulevards, and grand plantation avenues. An evergreen, they drop their leaves for a brief period in winter and their acorns in fall, like pelting rain, feeding squirrels, raccoons, deer, bears, ducks, turkeys, and jays, and giving native peoples a source for cooking oil. Live oaks populated the coast down from southern Texas around to the Florida cape, seeking habitation in hammocks, inland enclaves of slightly raised, peaty ground that they helped build with their leaf fall. They are more sensitive to the poison of intruding saltwater than are most coastal trees, but they withstand storm winds the best, with roots burrowed deeply in the ground and region.[16]

In Texas, Coast Survey assistant Williams produced some of the first accurately detailed charts of the state's amorphous coastline. He also provided descriptions of dry-land features. Unfolding out from numerous look-alike marshlands, and from around every bay and lagoon, prairie loped inland far and wide. The wind was tenacious on the Texas coast. On rare still days, it appeared in the lean of seaside and salt-stunted oaks and mesquite trees and in the sculpture of their canopies. Some bent defiantly into it; others surrendered and bent with it. None seemed to stand straight up. Although green and wide, the coastal tree canopy was short in stature. The sky was big like the desert, leaving all on the mean flat land to look small and stark. Clumps of oaks occasionally interrupted the uniformity, often standing with sabal palms. The latter are comfortable as either hermits or neighbors, welcoming congregation with any community of trees, sometimes gaining a toehold in a small space between another's roots and joining in a bispecies relationship—palm and oak, palm and pine, or palm and magnolia. No tree abides the Gulf's wavering cold-hot, dry-humid, salt-fresh environment as well as the sabal palm.

As readily as palms grew on the Texas prairie coast, they grew on Louisiana's coast, nearly every inch of which surveyors determined to be saltwater and brackish marshes, appearing as much a part of sea as land. In Mississippi, the assistants found solid footing and a gentle sandy rise along the state's brief waterfront, carved out of West Florida in 1817 when Congress granted statehood. Pine trees ran the edge, longleaf primarily, the monarch of the southern pine forest, with other varieties thrown in (sand, slash, spruce, and loblolly), sharing pockets of geography with less-dominant but well-established trees that can handle sandy alkaline or acidic soil (magnolias, cypress, and live oaks), each articulate in its own way. Magnolias are strictly dry-land trees with scented white blossoms and turtle-shell-like leaves; and cypress, a poised swamp species with fluted trunks and upward-growing roots, called knees. Above, from the cypress's short limbs, festoons of Spanish moss usually hang as heavily as on live oaks.

At the approach to the border of Alabama, which had obtained statehood in 1819, while taking fifty-three miles of West Florida's coastline, the surveyors were once more mucking it through wetland. Much of the state's edge, particularly around Mobile Bay and adjoining bayous, was persistent marsh. The sylvan contour continued too, pines dominant, through Alabama and on into Florida. Across the panhandle, long stretches of beach were a white line between Gulf and woodland. Hidden behind camel-hump sand dunes, some forty feet high, was scrubland—expanses of low-lying saw palmettos and yet more pines, their plentitude foreshadowing the sweeping exploitation of woodland and labor, mostly black, by timber, turpentine, and, eventually, pulp-paper industries.

Farther east and around the underarm of the state from panhandle to peninsula, along the Big Bend, the beaches disappeared momentarily and yielded to coastal marsh of the like in Louisiana. Here the water was shallow above the continental shelf rising gently up to a surfless edge. Scientists call it a low-energy coast. The current is too mild to carry much sand for beach or sand-dune making, and in fair weather the Gulf merely laps against the grassy shore.

Farther south, sand glistened again, though dunes were not as repetitive and high as on the panhandle, and mangroves took command of inner shores. One assistant called mangroves "among the most formidable difficulties." They could run for miles, forming impenetrable seaside forests miserable with mosquitoes and midges. The upper Gulf's average winter temperatures in the fifties were ten or more degrees cooler than south Florida's. Below Tampa, the coast wandered into a subtropical zone with little "winter effect," as Romans had put it. Tropical botanical varieties—coconut palms, mahogany, gumbo-limbo, orchids—grew, but not north of there or across the Gulf outside Mexico.[17]

The Survey mapped the Florida peninsula with tight precision; no longer would it look like a stubby stalactite. The assistants sailed around the Florida Keys, a coral-cay archipelago that coils down and away from the southeastern tip of the peninsula to the west into the Florida Straits like a knotted line pulled by the current, except the current in the Straits moves in the other direction. The uninhabited Dry Tortugas, where Ponce de León had found all those turtles three centuries before, are the final knot in the line, lying seventy-two miles out from Key West and longitudinally in line with the peninsula's westernmost protrusion. On the Atlantic side of the Keys, the Survey had to sail gingerly along the 170-mile-long Great Florida Reef, the US's only living coral barrier reef.

HARRIS LEFT THE US COAST SURVEY in 1864, before the Gulf mapping was complete. He took a position in the railroad industry, putting himself on a trajectory to the presidency of the Reading Railroad. The Survey carried on its work into the next century, civilizing the Gulf, sizing up a natural place by breaking it down into rational parts. That's what putting lines and sounding-data on charts and maps did. Assessing the lie of the land and water, beginning with the Spanish, was an early step toward rejecting original form before changing it. Little time was spent reveling in the natural scenery. Order and system, not wildness, was beauty to the mind of conquistadors, cartographers, engineers, and American settlers.

If Jefferson's West was the land of the nation's manifest destiny, the Gulf was its sea. And while it would be easy to make slavery the primary propellant of national expansion southward (a direction most historians have forgotten), we should keep in mind that nature was the kindling that allowed manifest destiny to burn as an idea—that very American idea that the nation was ordained to take dominion over the continent. Nature in this context was nature commodified: natural resources sought by commercial interests and a government that regarded those interests as essential to national and economic security. The dreamers of an American Empire imagined the advance of agriculture, mining, timber, and, as long as it would last, the skin and pelt trade. None of this was possible without land, which geographer Donald W. Meinig calls "that great, exhilarating American feature." It was the principal commodity on the continent, the commodity that begot the storied American homesteader, and it was the guarantor of storied American individual freedom.[18]

The Gulf coast had land, yes. But it offered bounteous harvests of another sort, and better in some ways than those delivered by soil. If, across hill and dale the pioneer saw limitless tracts of cropland, pastureland, and timberland, then across crest and swell the Gulf fisher saw limitless sea life. There were testimonies of mullet roiling at the surface like "distant thunder" pulsating "day and night," and of other finfish passing beneath boats and brightening the sea in endless silver rivers, often chased by sharks and dolphins and, overhead, by birds, their flocks known to black out the sun. Such density in the sky depended on an even greater density in the sea. The Gulf was, simply, fabulously rich with fish. "The most marvelous stories are told," wrote poet Sidney Lanier of the Gulf in 1875, "of the hosts of fish, even to the stoppage of vessels that have sailed into shoals of them."[19]

Fishing people became the American Gulf's frontiersmen and -women, full of yearning and determination, with dreams of unlimited opportunity. Fishing villages were frontier towns, faithful equivalents to those raw-board towns in the fabled West. Both open land and sea embodied the promise of equal stakes and equal status central to Jefferson's vision—free people of a free nation—behind territorial acquisition. If the soil was to surrender to the ax and plow, fish were to surrender to nets and lines. An ox, a boat—each was a means to self-reliance. Yet, unlike the homesteading grids and fences that eventually cordoned pasturage and field, Gulf waters remained mostly open range; and unlike finite land in the West, the natural resource of the Gulf seemed self-replenishing. A lack of rain never worried the fisher, and the specter of failure did not haunt; the Gulf was too damned giving.

Six

A FISHY SEA

Commercial fishermen off the Mississippi coast in the days
the work was done from sailing schooners.

There seems to be literally no end to the oysters, the fish, the sea-
birds, the shells, the turtles, along these waters.

—SIDNEY LANIER (1876)[1]

HISTORIANS HAVE YET TO ASSEMBLE THE LARGER HIS-
tory of commercial fishing on the Gulf. If they do, they will talk
about Cubans, Indians, and New Englanders; shrimp, mullet, oysters, and red snapper; and the Gulf's confirmation as an American
sea. Research might also lead them to a particular gravestone, a white

marble obelisk blemished by a spray of black mold, which has settled in the chiseled birth and death years, 1813 and 1884.

The seventy-one years between represent Leonard Destin's time on earth—and water—extending from New London, Connecticut, to East Pass, Florida. There is but a single surviving image of him, probably in his forties, from the chest up and in the soft carbon etchings of a pencil drawing. While likely a Yankee at heart, he would have been living on the Gulf coast for some twenty years. Trim and stiff, he wears a plain dark suit coat and vest, with an understated bowtie tucked beneath white shirt collar. His hair is raked back from his forehead and falls like curtains over the ears. On his narrow, clean-shaven face is an expression that is just this side of severe. It would do justice to a fiery sermon on the sinful body or the evils of drink. Destin commanded not from the pulpit, however, but from the helm of a fishing smack. Twelve years after his death, the little whitewashed post office at East Pass recognized him and the prosperous fishing village he founded by changing its designation to Destin.

Leonard Destin arrived on the Gulf in 1835. Texas was an independent republic; Louisiana, Mississippi, and Alabama were US states; and Florida was a territory, ten years from statehood. Indians still lived in the region, and within a month of Destin's arrival they were at war with the United States. Getting to this coastal frontier by sea, as in getting to western lands on trails and passes, could be treacherous.

Twenty-two years old, Leonard had sailed out of New London as one among a crew of five, which included his younger brother, Nathan, on the *Gallant*, a sloop-type vessel forty-two feet from stem to stern. His father, George, and older brother William were aboard a second smack, the *Empress*. They were planning to spend the fall and winter catching fish off Key West for the Havana market, and to salvage cargo from ships that frequently wrecked on the coral reef along the Florida Keys. The New Londoners had set off in late August, a season of storms and unfriendly seas.

Off Cape Hatteras, North Carolina, fog separated the two boats. Down off the Florida coast, they encountered worse. A hurricane roared in from the south and turned the New Londoners' vessels into bounty for the salvage industry that was supposed to enrich them. The storm took the *Empress* and Leonard's father and older brother. Somehow, the five aboard the *Gallant* survived when they lost their boat. All washed ashore a deserted barrier island. For two months, thirst and exposure tested their diminishing luck before a fishing crew found them and took them to Key West.[2]

Tragedies of the sea were common in Leonard's day, and he did not give up on southern waters. Eventually, he acquired his own fishing craft. For several years until 1851, he worked out of Key West, Mobile, and New Orleans before permanently settling on a neck of land on the east side of an inlet at the east end of Santa Rosa Island he named East Point. The Connecticut fisher would remain an "easterner."

If Destin experienced survivor's guilt, the beauty of his new surroundings likely contributed to it. The point where he would construct a clapboard house, sire seven children, build a commercial fishing business with a fleet of boats (including the thirty-ton schooner named *Jack 'a Don't Care*), spend time in a Confederate prison for allegedly spying for the Federals, and quietly meet his maker was a blast of sand and grassy dunes. It was most striking for the juxtaposition of three dominant tones: the blue encircling sky, the immaculate white beach, and the Gulf water, as bright emerald and vividly crystalline as the gemstone itself. The water got this quality from sunlight reflecting back from the clean seafloor, an extension of the white beach, through microscopic algae and billions upon billions of other microorganisms.

Around in the pass and into Choctawhatchee Bay, the bottom was grassy with intermingling beds of oysters, and the water tinted by organic materials from inland wash. It was vibrant with crabs, shrimp, and a curious jumping fish called a mullet. Twelve miles out into the Gulf, Destin and other fishers from Alabama and Mississippi discovered the one-hundred-fathom curve, a sharp six-hundred-foot plunge where grouper, mackerel, and snapper could be caught. Two hundred miles more over toward the peninsula was one of the largest sponge habitats in the world. And feeding on sponges were sea turtles, riding on invisible currents to and from every corner of the Gulf. Each corner was as splendidly alive as the other.

Biologists say that the Gulf's fish biomass density and species diversity is among the highest in the world. Avoiding science speak, poets of an earlier year came to a similar conclusion. In the 1930s, a pithy Wallace Stevens called the Gulf "the fishy sea." When Sidney Lanier visited from Georgia sixty years earlier, he inventoried the marine life as would the lyricist he was: "Here are the black-fish, white-fish, yellow bream, blue bream, silver bream, grouper, porgy, barracooter, trout, perch, eel, mullet, herring, flounder, gar, sheep-head, bass, grunt, yellow-tail, jew-fish, king-fish, pompano, amber-fish, angel-fish, red-snapper, drum, whiting, sturgeon, whipperee (whip-jack), skate, and one knows not how many more." Lanier's contemporary and emotional opposite Edward King, neither poet nor scientist, all business and chamber-of-commerce staid, wrote that along the coast from Florida to Texas, "there is such a multitude of oysters, fish, and game, that enterprises for supplying the market from that section should be very successful." A century earlier, when that rather clumsy British surveyor of Gulf geography, Bernard Romans, ran his boat aground, he may have been distracted. "Sea fish," he wrote, "are in such Innumerable Quantity's as exceed even Imagination."[3]

In Destin's time, the Gulf emerged as a miracle of supply in the world seafood market. The trade was expanded by industrious New Englanders, many of whose ancestors all but invented American commercial fishing up in the northern sea. Some came south for the winter to secure a season's take from the Gulf, and some relocated permanently. They landed fish and turtles; started harvesting crabs, oysters, sponges, and shrimp; and sold their stock at New Orleans and Havana or took it back to New England. Commercial fishing was the Gulf's first industry of real importance. Citizens of the United States did not initiate it, but they seized it, while affirming the transition of the Gulf from a Spanish to an American sea.

BERNARD ROMANS HAD WANTED the British to seize it. The Gulf's potential in commercial fishing, he wrote, "Requires and Merits a Serious Consideration." Consideration never came. The diet of the colonizing British (as, too, of the Spanish and French) consisted mainly of beef and pork and locally grown vegetables, rice, and harvested nuts—rarely of fish. Europeans were intent on exploiting products of the soil, not of the sea. The bureaucrats and the adventuresome who led early exploration and settlement were typically from landed classes. Land was what they understood, and though they were not ones to get their hands dirty, they knew what the land could and might deliver, so they stuck with what was familiar and directed others to cultivate and pluck its resources. Those scruffy, fish-smelling salts who hauled in the sea's harvest had no official voice in the direction of empire, which is not to say they didn't lend texture to the experience.[4]

Romans had seen the potential of a major industry in makeshift fish camps he encountered while surveying the Gulf. "The whole of the west coast of East Florida," he noted, "is covered with fishermen's huts and slakes." The huts were actually house-sized buildings, hewed-wood framing covered in shaggy, grayish-brown palm thatch, resembling, in an odd way, woolly mammoths that had roamed long-ago Gulf lands, but without the mammal's sturdiness. Lopsided, sagging—it seemed a whisper would blow them down. Hammocks to sleep in swung inside and out. Pit fires for cooking and abating the bugs remained clear of the palm thatch. Slakes were hand-built racks used for drying fish in the sun before salting it for preservation, which allowed it to keep during transport to market. Occupants of the camps were like industrious cobblers at workbenches, constantly cleaning, salting, and drying what they had caught and sold. The disciplined fishers that Romans saw weren't English; they were Cubans—to wit, Spanish subjects of mixed Old World and New World lineage.[5]

Havana had an insatiable appetite for fresh and dried-and-salted catch. The latter was transported over green hills and mountains to plantations to feed enslaved Indian and African workers. Cuban waters met the need for a period, but with its growing importance and population, the island looked increasingly to Calusa, who made for the Florida Straits in tandem canoes laden for trade. Along with fish, the natives bartered oil rendered from the rich fat of West Indian seals and manatees, desired by Spaniards for greasing the bottoms of their ships. Often the Calusa offered a delicacy, mullet roe, which Europeans compared to caviar. Native canoes returned home with coffee, tobacco, sugar, cloth, and liquor. It was clear to the Cubans that the Calusa had a bounty in Florida. Spanish fishers endeavored to reap it and ventured north into the sea that they claimed as their own. At first, they fumbled ineffectively with hook and line; then they turned to the Calusa way of making nets from grass twine and learned how to use them in inshore waters. Eventually, experienced fishermen from Spain brought over cotton nets.

"Cuban fishermen made use of Florida waters," writes folklore and fish scholar Michelle Zacks, "as a kind of backdoor larder, proximate and accessible." In time, camps arose along the shore for fall and winter fishing. Cubans devoted the spring to restocking meat-preserving salt and then prudently sat out the summer hurricane season. The camps persisted into the British occupation of Florida, when they became well known as fish ranchos. Romans urged his government to emulate them, calculating that twice each season, Cuban fishers delivered "One Thousand Tons Weight of dry'd Salted Fish" to Havana.[6]

Initially, Romans's superiors paid the ranchos no mind. Quick with criticism, he chastised them for "supinely, not to say stupidly," allowing the Cubans to "run away" with the "extensive fisheries in the power of these colonies." They were selling, he said, Gulf pompano at Cuban markets for a higher price than anything English fishermen were sell-

ing in Newfoundland. Only after their hand was forced did complacent authorities decide the Cubans had to go, though not to make
fishing opportunities available to their own countrymen. Customarily,
the ranchos employed Indians. Many in the early days were undoubtedly remnants of the disappearing Calusa. Later, Creek and Yamasee
retreated southward from Carolina's aggressively expanding Anglo
population. When American radicals in New England began raising
shot and powder for national independence, Florida's colonial leadership feared the fish-camp Indians would side with the Americans, as
did Spain. So, Loyalist Florida expelled the Cubans and closed down
the ranchos.[7]

Yet as quickly as the fishers departed, they returned. American
victory and the peace settlement restored East and West Florida to
Spain. By the 1810s, more than a half dozen ranchos between lower
Pine Island Sound and upper Tampa Bay were back in business on the
sparsely populated coast, and remained so after Florida's transition to
US territory. In 1831, a customs officer sailed up from Key West on his
usual tax collection run and counted some two hundred people working out of four ranchos in the Pine Island Sound area, some of whom
invited him to share their Cuban bread, coffee, and cigars.

The journalist John Lee Williams met many of them while writing a book on America's newest southern territory. He was particularly taken with an old-timer named José Maríe Caldez. Ninety years
of age, Caldez was a "stout, healthy, old white-haired Spaniard, very
industrious," who for three decades had been the proprietor of ranchos in Tampa Bay and Pine Island Sound. In the latter he located his
home base on an island he called Joseffa. It was small, an islet, though
favored by an eighteen-foot ridge on which Caldez could secure his
operations above storm waters. In Spanish tradition, he had released
hogs years before for propagation and eventual consumption. When
Williams visited, their offspring overran the island.[8]

Half or more of Caldez's workers were Indians, whom Americans
identified indiscriminately as Seminole. Intermarriage and common-
law arrangements between Cuban men and Indian women were as

routine as the moon tide. The American frontier had always been and would always be a cultural potpourri. Customs officials had no qualms with the social fluidity of ranchos, as long as their operators paid their duties, which they did faithfully. The rancho operators also contributed to the Key West economy by buying salt used for preserving dried fish. And they sold cigars, pineapples, oranges, and more to soldiers of Fort Brooke, semi-isolated at the top of Tampa Bay.

New Englanders arrived soon after Florida came into US possession. As did Leonard Destin, they traveled in fishing smacks, a name given to their boats for the sound of the circulating seawater that smacked the wooden sides of the live fish wells built amidships. Caldez might have seen as many as thirty Connecticut fishing schooners sail past his island in a given season. The two groups at first got along as friendly counterparts. The Cubans specialized in salted-and-dried fish; the Yankees, fresh. The latter off-loaded great heaps of fish, grouper for the most part, onto Havana wharves, and in May they would press home to work for the New York and Boston markets through November. Eventually, the New Englanders started drying fish and competing head-to-head with the Cubans. There had always been some scattered protectionist grumbling about the prosperous alien fishers. While trouble was bound to escalate, other pressing problems intervened. Either way, the Cubans were the losers.

Things took a sharp turn in 1835, the year Destin arrived on the Gulf. A cholera outbreak in Havana temporarily shut off the market, and a duty war raged between the US and Spain, reaching deep into the pockets of rancho operators. Then, in December, armed conflict broke out in Florida between the US and the Seminole, catching the ranchos in the cross fire. As far as the military was concerned, an Indian was an Indian, and all, including peaceable industrious rancho Indians, were targeted for removal to the West. In addition, rumors circulated that the Cuban fishers were smuggling in arms to the warring Seminole, even though Indians had routed some of the ranchos.

At the same time, the Americans feared that fugitive slaves were using ranchos as escape portals to Cuba, where conversion to Catholicism could bring freedom, or to the Bahamas, which had ended slavery the year before. Enough runaways were fighting beside the Seminole to suggest that the war was a slave rebellion as much as an Indian uprising. In 1836, the year American settlers broke Texas away from Mexico, the secretary of the navy ordered his Gulf fleet to rid Florida of the Cuban ranchos.

By then, the island of Cuba survived as the only colonial possession on the Gulf. It was no longer a Spanish sea, and no longer merely a travel lane for products of the land. New England fishers would soon turn it into an industrial sea, and an American one. A number of Gulf-side places assumed the aspects of a New England fishing port— no place more so than Pensacola.

ANGLO PENSACOLANS WERE FOREVER GRATEFUL to Andrew Jackson for sending away the Spanish in 1817 during the First Seminole War. One local publication grandly claimed that the general's Pensacola triumph had opened the nation's "eyes to the 'manifest destiny' of the United States." The claim was spun from hometown pride, but Pensacola had reason to feel especially relevant. For a short time, it was US Florida's territorial co-capital, sharing honors with St. Augustine (Jackson served as provisional governor). On the mainland at Pensacola, the federal government located a navy yard; and on Santa Rosa Island, a fortress, using slave labor to lay 21.5 million bricks fired from local clay. The lumber industry boomed, culling longleaf pine for building construction and live oak for naval timbers (southern wood had proved its worth in the USS *Constitution*).[9]

Federal forces occupied Pensacola throughout the Civil War, and northerners sustained their influence during Reconstruction and after. They did so mainly with regard to the natural features that suited the bay for harboring a fleet—not a naval fleet like those of the Spanish and British, but a fishing fleet. Equally ideal, the bay lay within easy range of the hundred-fathom curve. Many unreconstructed local southerners resented the northern carpetbaggers, but the damn Yankees knew a damn thing or two about the sea, and they built one hell of a fishing industry in Pensacola, premier in the upper Gulf.

Andrew Fuller Warren had something to do with that. Another New Englander lured to the Gulf by sea life, he bore unimpeachable Yankee credentials. His father's ancestors had arrived in America on the ship *Arabella* with John Winthrop; his mother's, on the *Lyon* with Roger Williams. Warren was sent to Brown University in Rhode Island. The only member of the 1863 class to move to the South, he went to Pensacola in 1871 at age twenty-nine. Before settling in Florida, he worked in Boston for a bank and a large maritime shipping firm. The smell of fish, hemp rope, and pine pitch and tar were all familiar, as were the sounds of creaking and chafing mooring lines, clunking lanyards, flapping canvas, and gulls cheering from atop fishhouse roofs and dock pilings. This was the scene on Pensacola's crescent bayside with its dozen wharves branching into a woodland of masts, sails furled neatly on their yards. Vessels were registered under Canadian, British, Russian, Austrian, and other national flags. Near the quay was a Norwegian Seamen's church.

At the end of Commendencia Street Wharf was the Pensacola Ice Company, the city's first such concern, founded by a Connecticuter named Sewall C. Cobb. His ice operations doubled as a fish house, and Warren went to work for him. Along with his experience in maritime trade, Warren brought some knowledge of ice. The use of ice in keeping meat fresh in storage and shipping had been developed in Boston earlier in the century, cut from New England's iced-over lakes and rivers in winter with long, gap-toothed handsaws. It was then packed tightly in ship holds with sawdust as insulation for delivery as far away as India. Harvesters sawing the ice-skating surface of Walden Pond into large chunks of global commodity prompted Henry David Thoreau to quip, "Thus it appears that the sweltering inhabitants of Charleston and New Orleans, of Madras and Bombay and Calcutta, drink at my well." Frozen New England gave the South one of its symbols of hospitality, ice tea.[10]

Before ice, Gulf fish like grouper that came from cooler depths and traveled in smacks didn't always survive passage in the warm, crowded wells. Fresh bay and river water flowing through them was the death knell. Captain Silas Latham, another Connecticuter, claimed he was the first to remedy this problem. In spring 1868, he sailed south with eight tons of ice, for which he paid $200, and fished his way from Tampa to Mobile. When he brought his catch in on ice, the wharves began buzzing with stories of the "crazy Yankee." Soon enough, craziness became brilliance. Reefer ships with airtight compartments made regular runs to Havana, Key West, New Orleans, Mobile, and Pensacola. Ice boxes aboard fishing boats enabled captains to hawk their cargo as "fresh" as opposed to dried and salted. Then, from New Orleans and Mobile, where much of the catch came in, ice-packed fish proceeded by riverboat or train to inland restaurants and fishmongers.[11]

Cobb's Pensacola Ice operated one fishing boat and contracted with several Connecticut vessels in port for the season. Warren, of "naturally quick and adaptable mentality," as one contemporary described him, helped expand the fishing operations, and the company soon changed its name to the Pensacola Ice and Fish Company, and then later dropped "Ice."[12]

Feeling good about his prospects on the Gulf, Warren returned north to marry Fannie Clarke Stearns of Bath, Maine, a fishing and boatbuilding port on the coast. They settled into the old Spanish colonial city with the welcome familiarity of a New England fishing village and watched it grow tenfold, to over thirty thousand residents in Warren's lifetime, which had a generous forty-six years left.

In those years, national rail companies came in and linked the city without a deep inland river to more people and markets. Pensacola was also graced with the Louisville and Nashville Passenger Station depot, a showpiece of orange and yellow brick combining Prairie School, Spanish Mission, and Italianate architectures. Complementary buildings flanked the town streets, many with Spanish-style balconies à la New Orleans and Mobile, running directly down to the wharves.

The city's businesses and those engaged in them—from laborers to proprietors—seemed to pile up on the restless bayfront. Smacks brought their catch to fish and ice houses daily. There were packing-houses, warehouses, boathouses, boardinghouses, bathhouses, the harbor master's house, and the customs house; ship chandlers, ship-builders, and sail lofts; boiler, machine, repair, blacksmith, junk, and coffee shops; gin, shingle, and planing mills. Rafts of cut timber floated in the harbor around the clock, queued up for sawmills. Ships came in, off-loaded ballast rocks—left at the edge of the waterfront and soon covered with formations of black spider-like grapsid crabs—and loaded milled lumber that exited the Gulf and crossed the Atlantic. There were billiard parlors, bars, and bordellos—an excess of them, according to high-minded locals, who said their most devoted patrons were thirsty and rutty crew members off the cargo ships and fishing schooners. Too often, they swaggered in payday-rich and stumbled out stone broke, though presumably gratified.[13]

Among the straitlaced and wary was Warren's brother-in-law Silas Stearns. Two years after Andrew married Fannie, her sixteen-year-old younger sibling came down from Maine to join them. Stearns served an apprenticeship at Pensacola Fish, proved himself an able clerk—a number cruncher and details man—and then joined his brother-in-law to start up Warren Fish Company on the Baylen Street Wharf. For a while, Pensacola Fish and Warren Fish were the main houses in town. Later, two New Englanders—one from Rhode Island and the other from Connecticut—operating the E. E. Saunders Company on the Palafox Street Wharf, bought the boats and equipment from Pensacola Fish. At its peak in the 1880s, the local fleet of thirty-three boats prospered mainly with one fish, red snapper.

PENSACOLA FISHERS HAD BEEN DEALING in red snapper ever since the 1840s, when Connecticut captain James Keeny intro-duced the fish to the market. Keeny had been heading in the direction of New Orleans to sell a haul of sheepshead, pompano, redfish, and others—what he called "beach fish"—when his schooner sailed into breathless air and lay becalmed several miles offshore. According to an agent with the US Fish Commission, who wrote down the story, when the cook threw table scraps over the side, fat, red-colored fish appeared—"strange looking" and "eagerly feeding" on the refuse. So the captain and his crew baited hooks and ultimately pulled in two hundred. In New Orleans, the snapper "sold like hot cakes."[14]

Boats typically had to make deep water to catch red snapper. Prolific in the Gulf, with a splotchy ruddy complexion across their scales, red snapper are most comfortable in depths of thirty to two hundred or even three hundred feet, and around reefs, banks, and ledges, where they gorge themselves on crabs, crustaceans, and juvenile fish. If an old Spanish galleon rests in a deep seafloor grave, the western Atlantic native is surely haunting it. Along with other snapper—mangrove, lane, mutton, and dog—the red, as a contemporary of Stearns put it, "is a large chunky-built fish." It has a classic fish shape—one a child might draw with a line arcing sharply up from a frowning open mouth around and down from a spiny dorsal fin into the flourish of a fan-shaped tail, and then into a less-exaggerated curve back to the protruding lower jaw, set with needlelike teeth. The drawing would have pointed pectoral and pelvic fins, uneven red coloring, and—a final touch for personality—an eye as round and shiny as a black pearl button.[15]

Dragging a net through the snapper's jagged habitats would be disastrous, so fishers used a hook and line. Typically, they rigged the line with two codfish hooks on separate snoods, and a two-pound sinker five or six feet above. Menhaden, a little fish plentiful in the Gulf, was the preferred bait. "When the fish are hungry," wrote Stearns of red snapper, "they bite as fast as the lines are lowered. . . . From this habit they have gained the name of snappers." On those tarred-cotton lines, fishers pulled in snapper that averaged twenty-four inches in length and, in Stearns's day, weighed between twenty and sixty pounds.[16]

Any fish caught on a hook commanded a higher price than netted fish, with shipping on ice adding to the cost. In New York, Gulf red snapper was going for eighteen cents a pound in 1883, eight cents more than live lobster and three times more than cod—the first trapped, the second netted—but three times less than pompano, another hook-

and-line fish. Pan fried or oven baked, Creole style, the red snapper became an instant favorite of the lower South. Once full train service opened to Pensacola, snapper started selling up the line in Alabama, Tennessee, and then the Midwest. The Gulf fish were written up in national magazines and newspapers, and presented on warmed plates at women's club luncheons and in railroad dining cars, most often with a lemon garnish. A piece in the *New York Times* called red snapper a "highly prized luxury and valuable article," predicting it would exceed the popularity of cod. It didn't, but Warren and Saunders were selling all they could put on ice.[17]

Red snapper and Pensacola became synonymous, and both got the attention of the US Fish Commission, established in 1871 to help develop and improve commercial fisheries. The commission also noticed Silas Stearns, who was making a reputation for himself as *the* ichthyologist of the Gulf. The historical record contains no photos or paintings of him. We don't know if he was tall or short, slim or portly, bewhiskered or clean shaven. He was always young; he didn't make it past thirty. But we don't know the cause of death. And we don't know what fired his interest in fish. Had it been something back home in Bath? Or in Pensacola? We know that his father's death interrupted his schooling, and that after his move to Pensacola, when he was trying to convince ichthyology's patriarchy in Washington, DC, of his abilities as a naturalist, he was initially dismissed as a mere amateur.

Expressions of humility probably didn't help. "I am young and not so well informed," he wrote to the curator of the Smithsonian Institution. The rejection seemed to motivate him, though. With the Gulf as laboratory, as well as a sharp mind and eyes, the exceedingly earnest young man identified more than fifty new species of fish, four of which bear his name. The Smithsonian finally sought him as a consultant, and he landed an appointment as special agent to the US Fish Commission, earning the praise of the country's premier ichthyologists.[18]

One was George Brown Goode, assistant secretary and head of fish research at the Smithsonian. When he decided to compile a comprehensive study of the fishing industry for the US Fish Commission, which he would soon head, Goode asked Stearns to prepare a contribution on the Gulf. It was the assignment of Stearns's life. Studying fish was in his bones, and it would become his legacy.

He traveled the Gulf from Key West to Brownsville, meeting with fish-house operators, boat captains, and crews, meticulously gathering all the details on vessel types and tonnage, harvest quantities and value, and income, including crew wages. He spoke to people with German, Italian, Greek, Portuguese, Swedish, Norwegian, Nova Scotian, Yugoslavian, and Newfoundland accents. He met immigrant Chinese shrimping and crabbing on Louisiana's Cajun coast. If he had stopped over at St. Bernard Parish, he would have encountered Spanish speakers, Isleños emigrated from the Canary Islands, who worked the bayous Terre aux Boeufs and La Loutre. Gulf-wide, he counted 5,131 persons employed in the industry in 1880 alongside 1,449 fishing craft. He seemed to count everything except the number of hooks and sinkers.

Florida dominated the trade. Three-quarters of the US Gulf's indigenous craft worked out of its ports. It had 1,936 fishers to Texas's 290; they landed 8.3 million pounds of fish compared with Texas's 3.8 million, which ranked third among the Gulf states. Florida occupied half of the US Gulf front, so its reign would not have been surprising. More impressive, though, was Louisiana. Although its coastline extended only half the distance of Florida's, its catch weight amounted to eighty-five percent of what Florida fishers pulled in. With a haul of 3.5 million pounds, fishers working out of Alabama's little toe of a waterfront nearly equaled Texas. Mississippi weighed in at 788,000 pounds; eventually, it would have one of the most productive fishing ports in the country.

Stearns opened his section in Goode's study by acknowledging the venerable American fisheries in New York, Massachusetts, Maine, and Oregon. Each on its own outperformed all 1,550 miles of the US Gulf coast—for the time being. It went without saying that the East Coast grounds were worked more efficiently by larger fleets and fishers with generations of the salt life in their blood. Stearns's acknowledgment, though, seems to be merely an obligatory prelude to his high-lighting, with understandable pride, the Gulf's merits: the "endless variety" of "delicious fish and mollusks." For such generosity, he credited "beneficent nature"—the "benign influences of the tropical sun" and "genial habitat."[19]

A veteran ichthyologist at the commission, Joseph W. Collins, who came from Maine fishing stock, was less enamored with the Gulf. It is "not probable," he wrote in an obscure government publication in 1885, that the Gulf "will ever reach an importance at all comparable with such fisheries as those of New England, simply because there are not the enormous resources to draw from." He added that "these southern species are not likely to fill so important a place in cured food as do the staple production of northern seas."[20]

Collins's superior Yankee attitude toward the "southern species" surely would have elicited a sharp retort from the native-born still smarting over the lost war. His fellow Mainer in Pensacola, a convert to southern waters, harbored his own biases, but then Stearns had a fish-eye view of the Gulf, including its nurturing estuaries. And few better recognized that the Gulf's promise went beyond red snapper. The fish that kept Stearns and Warren's business afloat wasn't even the American Sea's most economically important product. Oysters claimed that honor, followed by sponges, grouper, mullet, shrimp, and, finally, red snapper.

Traveling around Texas in 1950, naturalist Roy Bedichek noted, "There remains the unimpeachable evidence of ancient oyster production along the coast which staggers the imagination." More than two centuries earlier, French explorer Pierre de Charlevoix had anointed the Gulf coast the "Kingdom of oysters." Both men were referring to the mounds upon mounds of weather-bleached shells that were the dietary remnants of the Gulf's original peoples.[21]

Up north, where the principal domestic market in shellfish emerged, people thought of oysters as a gift from the waters between New York and Connecticut, with supplemental imports occasionally coming in from Chesapeake Bay. In all those places, thanks to Indian charity, oysters had saved starving white settlers unable to fend for themselves. In its fecund unspoiled prime, the lower Hudson River estuary supported some 350 square miles of beds, maybe half of the world's oysters, with shells measuring up to ten inches.

New Yorkers turned the succulent bivalve into a defining staple of the nineteenth-century urban culinary culture, much in the way they did pizza and bagels in the next century. Delicatessens and street wagons sold oysters on the half shell. Restaurant menus included oyster patties and pies; oysters fried, scalloped, pickled, and fricasseed, with cocktail sauce, roasted on toast, cooked with bacon, or stewed in milk or cream; and dishes with fancy names like Oysters Pompadour, Oysters Algonquin, Oysters à la Netherlands, Oysters à la Newberg, and Oysters à la Poulette. There was a downside, alas, to what Charles Dickens called the "wonderful cookery of oysters": overharvesting. It had been a problem since the early eighteenth century, exacerbated by the ballooning metropolis's sewage sloshing into bivalve habitat.[22]

What turned foul in New York was still sweet in the Gulf. North American oysters are of one species; presumably, Gulf oysters would make a felicitous substitute for New York's dwindling local supply. But, "as with wine," Mark Kurlansky writes in a fascinating book on the city's oyster history, the size, shape, color, and even taste vary according to upbringing. Water temperature, salinity, and nutritional content, the configuration and density of the bed, and age of the oyster make a difference. Although oysters grew in nearly every Gulf estuary, not all tasted the same, and none quite like a Hudson River oyster. New Yorkers could be snobbish about their preferences, but they loved oysters, period, and the ones they came arguably to appreciate most from the southern sea grew in Florida's Apalachicola Bay. Stearns said there was "none better in any part of the Gulf."[23]

It was the bay's estuarine salubriousness that gave Apalachicola oysters their zest. It had the ideal balance between seawater and nutrient-laced freshwater, coming from the river of the same name, itself watered by two other rivers, the Flint and Chattahoochee. Four barrier islands fronting the bay sequestered the river's freshwater and let in just the right amount of saltiness from the sea. Island fences of this sort exist at Pine Island Sound, Bayou La Batre, Bay Batiste, and Matagorda, Galveston, Biloxi, Caminada, Mobile, Pensacola, and Boca Ciega Bays—all succulent oyster habitats.

Thanks in part to its oysters, Apalachicola was a good place for fishing, crabbing, and shrimping. Oysters are filter feeders, each sifting about two gallons an hour and consuming algae and plankton. The 214-square-mile bay stayed clear as a result. Its sunlit bottom encouraged the growth of sea grass, which generates oxygen and makes a nursery for other marine life. It's all part of a cyclical routine. Once grown, fish eat floating oyster larvae and spat, which are young oysters beginning to form their shells. Mature oysters aren't in the clear of predators either. Their fully developed shells are knife-cutting sharp and will cruelly slice open the skin of a foot that steps on them or a hand that reaches for them. But they aren't impenetrable armor. Sea stars and crabs eat oysters. Raccoons ferret them from the shallows. Oyster drills, which are shell-dwelling snails, bore holes and suck out the animal.

For a while it looked as though Apalachicola would become a major cargo shipping port. The river ran deep enough to transport cotton from Alabama and Georgia, and timber from all three states. The railroad's arrival in 1907 redirected much of the shipping trade to other ports, though it ran the "oyster express," carrying the tasty shellfish on ice directly to burgeoning Atlanta. Economically, Apalachicola in the end didn't need to grow into a major cargo port; it instead became the Gulf's big oyster. A man could make a fair living on the bay, and it was almost exclusively a man's world out there. In 1915, one-third of the town's male residents, four hundred of them, worked on 117 oyster boats.

Tongs were the tool of their trade. They consisted of two ash or oak handles—eight to sixteen feet long—pinioned like scissors with a steel rake-like head on the lower ends. Among fishers, oystermen stood out with broad backs and shoulders from handling tongs day after day. Often, their wives, daughters, and sisters worked as shuckers—mindlessly repetitive work requiring a single tool, a shucking knife, to pry open the shell and cut out the meat. Oyster houses in Apalachicola employed 250 shuckers, many of them children. One of their employers was among the town's wealthiest citizens, John G. Ruge. He was known for his big waterfront Victorian home, and his crustiness (he was once fined for calling the postmaster a damn fool). He and his brother George, sons of a German immigrant, established Apalachicola's first oyster cannery at the mouth of the river. By then, 1884, local commercial oystering was fifty years old.

Folks did a fair bit of oystering around Biloxi and Bayou La Batre too, and down at Galveston. Louisiana estuaries would eventually outproduce them all with a million-dollar harvest in 1912. It didn't matter that they were mere "kitchen oysters," as many Louisianans conceded, not as tasty as those from Apalachicola. If you had one bushel of oysters or a hundred, you could always sell them in New Orleans, three to four dollars a barrel (three bushels) in the 1890s. By then, diners were spicing up their shellfish with Tabasco-brand pepper sauce made down in bayou country where oysters resided. Three-quarters of the Gulf's beds were scattered across Louisiana waters, in Chandeleur and Breton Sounds and in bayous with those distinctive bayou names: Caillou, Dularge, Lafourche, Teche, Terrebonne.

For the most part, the bayous, freshened by the Pearl, Atchafalaya, and Sabine Rivers, had been "seeded" with oysters taken from the natural beds east of the big river. Within months they reached market size with shells less elongated than round, the shape that fussy restaurant-goers preferred. This delicate task of moving spat from one place to another began in the early nineteenth century largely with immigrant Croatians from the Dalmatian coast, cultivator of oysters for 125 years. (Stearns wrote, "Hardly a word of English [is] spoken in the whole gaily painted oyster fleet of Louisiana.") Larvae need to attach to a hard foundation, or clutch, at the bottom of a river or bay to grow into spat and mature oysters. The best thing a processor could do was throw old oyster shells back in an estuary to give larvae that clutch.[24]

Oysters also need lime in their diet, and discarded shells are full of it. The worst thing processors could do—the self-defeating thing, but the thing they did most often—was have their shells crushed for fertilizer, hauled away for roadbeds, or hoarded in forgotten piles, laced with black mold like Leonard Destin's headstone. When the automobile came along, road builders got so greedy for bedding material that they quarried ancient shell mounds, horrifying antiquarians. Morgan City, Louisiana, had two shell-crushing plants in the 1920s, selling the remnant not only for roads but for poultry feed and lime used in chemical plants. A quarter of all crushed-shell product came from the Louisiana coast.

Louisiana also gave birth to oyster canning. Apalachicolans like to say that the brothers Ruge operated the first oyster cannery on the Gulf. But two brothers from New Orleans—George and Frank Dunbar—deserve that credit. They studied culinary arts in France during the Civil War (in part to avoid the war) and built a cannery near Grand Terre Island in 1867. A decade later, someone opened a cannery in Pascagoula, and a few years after that, in Biloxi—all before the Ruge outfit.

The Mississippi coast became the canning center of the Gulf, little different from the sardine district of Monterey, California, described in the opening line of John Steinbeck's novel *Cannery Row*. Both were a "poem, a stink, a grating noise, a quality of light, a tone, a habit, a nostalgia, a dream." In 1900, Biloxi plants employed twenty-five hundred people, nearly half the city's population. As in northern factories, the labor force depended on immigrants—Poles mainly, same as Steinbeck's sardine workers—who migrated seasonally between oyster canneries in Maryland and the Gulf coast.[25]

Predating zoning ordinances, Biloxi canneries edged up to and over the bay on just about any weedy lot; they were a mixed bag of job creation and eyesore. Machinery clanged and creaked around the clock. Discarded shells rained noisily down chutes running outside bleak, rusting, and dented corrugated-metal buildings, piling up mountain high on the premises. The canneries infused the air with the signature musk of dead sea creatures, and workers went home in their rubber boots and stained trousers perfumed with it. Biloxi's town fathers in time adopted an odor ordinance and forced at least one cannery to relocate downwind.

SHRIMP, TOO, ADDED PUNCH to the air around canneries, and to the oyster fisher's wallet when the crustaceans were running in summer and fall. The Gulf was so saturated with them that their molts collected on the beaches like mats of seaweed.

Commercial shrimping in the Gulf began with two guys and a seine net, in French Louisiana in the eighteenth century (one source says 1735[26]). Each man took separate ends of the seine, pulling it across a sea grass bed, gathering food for their table. Greeks and Romans and Gulf aborigines were all shrimping the same way thousands of years earlier. Eventually, the two guys began selling shrimp to their neighbors—to be boiled, stewed, and fried, stuffed with rice or bread crumbs, tossed in gumbos and jambalayas, and served with grits. Others added length to the net, until it reached up to two thousand feet and required twenty men to drag it. They sometimes rigged lines to horses or mules to assist. Then they figured out how to deploy the net behind a schooner, making their sweep farther out in bays, bayous, and sounds.

That way of shrimping continued for some time. Then, a Massachusetts fishing captain named Billy Corkum experienced a headscratching moment in 1913 while working at Fernandina, on Florida's east coast. He was never happy with the conventional seine. Too much manpower, not enough shrimp. So he rigged up a modified otter trawl used for cod fishing, essentially a bag-shaped net with wooden doors at the front that gaped open like the large mouth of a hungry fish. He paid it out from the stern of his schooner and began hauling in shrimp, and using a smaller crew to do so.

It took Gulf shrimpers nearly four years to catch on, and when they did, their yield soared. Louisiana fishers were easily outshrimping everyone. They included Croatians and Chinese, "foreign-speaking peasant folk," and coastal Cajuns, who also hunted alligators for the leather market, living "by the rising and falling of the tides," wrote a New Orleans *Daily Picayune* correspondent, Martha Field. "The fisheries of Louisiana," she added, "are one of the chief, most picturesque and remunerative industries." Field was more right than she probably knew. Fronting her state was forty percent of the country's coastal wetlands—incubator, home, and food trough of sea life.[27]

Shrimp have been around for as long as about any sea creature, and eaten by numberless many, from whales on down. The ancient Roman cookbook *Apicius* includes shrimp recipes, and in the 1860s, Chinese immigrants—in camps that resembled the Cuban ranchos of Florida—started exporting dried Louisiana shrimp to China, Hawaii, and the Philippines. Americans in the Northeast once used shrimp for not much more than arranging in tulip glasses and serving as a fashionable edible cocktail. That was before the otter trawl made shrimp more available at cheaper prices.

The trawl and a growing demand for shrimp hit at the same time boats started using gasoline engines to propel them up and down the coast, out into and across the Gulf, and back again. Becoming less dependent on fickle wind power represented yet another break between humans and the natural world, and yet another way they became enslaved to a finite natural resource—refined fossil fuels in this case. Refrigeration then came aboard in the 1920s—nature's ice no more—in near perfect concert with Clarence Birdseye's mastering of the quick-freezing process for seafood. Sales were poised to take off.

To cash in, shrimpers disappeared for several days at a time. They pushed farther out into the Gulf, the classical music of a wind-driven sea passage drowned forever by the heavy metal of internal combustion and snorting exhaust. Fishers discovered that if they worked past sunset, their trawls were filling with a new kind of shrimp, browns, which rose near the surface at night, adding to the whites they'd always caught in inshore waters. Then, in 1949, at dusk on the Gulf side of Key West, a trawler winched in nets full of another species, pink shrimp, its existence first revealed in the bellies of grouper and snapper, with meat tender and sweet.

"Hundreds of tons" of this pink gold, observe science writers Jack Rudloe and Anne Rudloe, ultimately eighty-five percent of the national harvest, the making of a winter fishery, were taken from the west coast of Florida. Next, royal reds came up from two hundred fathoms out from Alabama, putting Bayou La Batre on the map of major shrimping ports. Then, yet another kind, rock shrimp, appeared off Apalachicola. New net designs came along to work best in all the new environments—"flat nets, balloon nets, skimmer trawls, butterfly and mongoose nets," write the Rudloes, each "to outsmart the minuscule brain of a shrimp." According to writer Bern Keating, a shrimper in the 1970s could buy an eighty-five-foot steel-hulled trawler for $150,000 and pay it off in five years.[28]

It was the serendipitous cascade of innovations—gasoline and diesel engines, the otter trawl, refrigeration, frozen food—that changed shrimping and fishing and opened the Gulf to unlimited commercial access. And what of the boats to accommodate the new drive power and nets?

The answer to that question begins at the end of Crawford Street in Biloxi, at the shipyard of a Croatian immigrant named Jacob D. "Jacky Jack" Covacevich. For seven decades, until his death in 1962, he launched hundreds of new boats into the flat water of the Back Bay, vessels designed and crafted watertight by him in milled local longleaf pine, live oak, and cypress—cut, planed, joined, lapped, and bent by his deft hand, around sturdy frames and keels. He had the help of apprentices, who in the 1890s earned seventy-five cents for a fifteen-hour workday. That was after a hurricane in 1893 sank or smashed almost every boat around. Biloxi was the epicenter of Gulf boatbuilding, and its half dozen or so yards worked round the clock to restore the fishing fleet.

Like his competitors, Covacevich turned out "white-winged

queens," pet name of the hallowed schooner, but unlike them, he introduced a smarter working boat, dispassionately christened the Biloxi lugger. Built thirty to sixty feet long, it bore a Mediterranean influence, which Covacevich said came to him from Italian fishers in Louisiana. The lugger had a squared aft deck, low waist, and high-sweeping bow, and drew a mere three-foot draft. The pilothouse lay astern and the working deck forward. The first to come off the skids were fitted with mast and sails; later ones, with engines and propeller shafts, absent the sail rigging. They were used around Mississippi, Louisiana, and Alabama.

Another innovation was the so-called Texas trawler, which was the same as the Florida trawler. The superstructure was the reverse of the Biloxi lugger: working deck aft and pilothouse forward. The trawlers succeeded as the favored boat, and around midcentury they came equipped with outriggers that unfolded like dragonfly wings to pull nets from each side, two or more to an outrigger. By then, Gulf fishers were catching most of America's shrimp, and shrimp trawlers became the signature working boat on the water, the ones that artists standing at easels captured crossing a sunset—sway-bellied, low-riding, imparting forthright prow and pilothouse, nets gathered and suspended astern, rust stains on white paint, a deep swelling wake trailing behind en route to the horizon or returning from it.

THE BOAT IS NEARLY AS IMPORTANT as the catch. It reveals who the fisher is to a large degree. It proclaims the fisher's profession, even heritage. Near the end of Stearns's unjustly short life, boats similar to shrimp trawlers began sailing out from Anclote River on the Florida peninsula. They had no outriggers, and the swooping line of their hull was more pronounced. The geometry was Greek, the crews were Greek, and their home port of Tarpon Springs was largely Greek. Their catch, sponges, was embedded in Greek tradition.

Not until a turtle fisher caught his net on a squishy snag in the 1870s did people realize the extent of the sponge grounds in the Gulf.

They turned out to be nine thousand square miles and unrivaled in the US. Although sponges look like plants and fasten themselves to a place like plants do—some even putting down roots—they are animals. As are coral, sponges are invertebrates, and they come in different sizes, shapes, and colors, and live in colonies and build reefs, as do coral. They tolerate almost any water temperature, from polar cold to tropic warm, but prefer it clear and calm. Although some grow on rocks, most Gulf sponges root themselves in the sedimentary bottom. They lack circulatory or digestive systems, and instead absorb nourishment and expunge waste as water passes through their pores. Fish and shrimp are partial to the living spaces that sponges create, and sea turtles like how they taste.

For decades, Gulf Coast dwellers cut sponges from their moorings in shallows for personal use before realizing, in the 1840s, their full commercial value. Key West and Cuba were initially the hub of the Gulf sponge trade and remained so until the end of the century. By then, the industry had begun a permanent shift up the coast to where that turtle fisher had snagged his net and where yellow, grass, wire, glove, and sheepswool sponges grew. Hospitals used the grass species as surgical sponges, while everyday folk used sheepswool sponges for bathing and for washing carriages and, later, automobiles. Before the turn of the century, Apalachicola served as an important port for these two.

At the time, everybody thought Tarpon Springs was destined to be little more than a cheerful winter retreat for northeastern snowbirds. Its resort-worthy climate, bowering oaks, amiable river with bait-hungry game fish, and bathing springs that remain the same temperature year-round were enough to keep a lot of people content. But the sponge beds were a straight shot out from Tarpon, and they were a natural underwater treasure trove. Stearns reported sponges selling for a dollar a pound. Nothing from domestic waters approached their value. Tops, pompano might get fifty cents. In 1890, according to local histories, the beds delivered to one Tarpon firm a million dollars in sales.

The possibilities encouraged John Cheyney, a Philadelphia native and owner of a processing house, and John Cocoris, a Greek native and Cheyney's buyer. They came up with a plan to recruit experienced spongers from the Dodecanese Islands, where harvesting sponges dates to free divers in Plato's time or before. The Gulf beds were a good place to go to work, Cheyney might have proclaimed when making his recruitment pitch to Greek divers. The waters were calm and shallow, as "transparent as crystal springs," noted a writer in *Scribner's*, with "such a bewildering profusion" of "nature's beauties and novelties" that would "arouse the keenest enthusiasm of a naturalist." Five hundred Greeks emigrated the first year, soon followed by hundreds more.[29]

In the 1940s, the Anclote River harbored 150 sponge boats. They were designed from an original thirty-foot imported Mediterranean model with an upsweeping bow and stern. Each rode the water, said a writer for the Works Progress Administration, "like a crescent moon." Before the fleet put to sea for two- to four-week trips, the priest of St. Nicholas Greek Orthodox Cathedral blessed each boat.[30]

Every fishing port likes to claim it is the capital of this or that fish. For two or three decades into the late 1940s, Tarpon Springs truly was the world's most prolific sponge port. Its natural product washed America.

ALTHOUGH TARPON SPRINGS'S ECONOMY latched onto a sedentary aquatic animal, the town's name came from an animated one, albeit by way of mistaken identity. Northern newcomers to the Anclote River thought fish jumping in the water were tarpon. They probably saw the steely-gray mullet instead. Tarpon jump only when stressed. Mullet do so seemingly for the hell of it, maybe for the joy of living in the sea (researchers have yet to determine their motivation). "Mullet Springs" would have been an accurate but entirely disagreeable name for the winter resort. Aside from its airborne tendencies, the mullet is a plain-Jane fish next to the grander tarpon. You don't mount one if you catch one, as you might a nice tarpon. And you won't get one to bite your baited hook; they're unwavering vegetarians. Mullet had no sport in them until anglers came up with a seductive flora-type fly. Their station is also without prestige. They're common, living in every Gulf bay, sound, cove, bayou, and river mouth with a patch of sea grass.

Nonetheless, one edge that mullet have over tarpon is that they're edible. People for eons have been consuming these worldwide warm-water fish that tolerate fresh- and saltwater. The *Daily Picayune*'s Martha Field called them "that Acadian luxury," referring to how they had become an inviolable palate pleaser of working folk, more or less exclusively. In her superlative dissertation on the mullet, Michelle Zacks says the fish was "generally eaten not by white, urban epicures but by ordinary people of many shades of skin." Mullet never made the menu at New York's Delmonico's restaurant.[31]

But that didn't matter to the fish's connoisseurs. "There was no way to starve to death," said a multigenerational fisher from Cedar Key, Mike Davis, as long as mullet were leaping. No matter the condition of the economy, no matter how well or poorly fish or shrimp were selling, there was food in the water. The many North Carolina families who relocated to Cortez, Florida, in the 1880s, bringing skiffs they called skipjacks, dubbed their bay the "kitchen." Mullet always jumped out there—striped ones common to the Gulf, bluish gray in color, elongated with two small dorsal fins, filling out at about eighteen inches to two feet and several pounds. They were as plentiful as oysters or shrimp. Cast a net off a dock or the stern of a skiff—sail furled—pull in the fish, sever the head and tail of one, slice open the belly, slide out the guts, butterfly the meat with the backbone on one side (leaving the eater rather than the preparer to deal with the toothpick-like bones), and cook. Add grits and hush puppies, and you had a meal that stuck to the ribs—"three times a day the year round," wrote a *New York Times* correspondent in 1876 of the mullet. "Above hog and hominy, he is the staple article of the diet of the 'crackers.'"[32]

As a meal, mullet embodied the days of the fish ranchos and Cuban slavery. They usually went to table and market salted rather than iced, loaded on oxcarts rattling through rural areas and on trains shuddering into southern depots rather than charging up to cities in the Northeast and Midwest. Untold tonnages of minnow-sized mullet were used for baiting the hooks of Yankees who, in a sportfishing mania, came south.

That was about as far as the outsiders' interest went. Even with the railroad and ice, there was no erasing long distance. Mullet taken from Texas waters typically were eaten by Texans; those from Alabama, by Alabamians; from Florida, by Floridians and Georgians. Southern planters, like Cuban planters, bought mullet for their slaves and, after emancipation, for their sharecroppers. There was penny-wise logic in buying a reliable food selling for two cents a pound. Nothing from the local sea was as available and nutritious, or as cheap (grouper went for seven cents a pound). When Stearns was counting fish and fishers, mullet accounted for fifty percent of the Gulf's seafood take but only twenty percent of the value.

Mullet was the codfish of the South, woven into the regional economy and into the image of those who netted the fish, though with a little Yankee prejudice cast upon them. Up North, cod fishers were idealized as clean, sober, hardworking people, made of the stuff that ensured the nation its greatness. Down on the Gulf, it wasn't typically New Englanders on leave from their overfished grounds who pursued the lowly mullet; it was locals who didn't cut such a favorable impression. The US Fish Commission estimated that three thousand Gulfsiders partook of the mullet trade. Sixty percent were white, twenty-five percent black, and the rest Bahamians, Cubans, and the usual Cajun, Chinese, and Croatian suspects in Louisiana. Because mullet were caught in inshore waters, their fishers didn't go to sea, where they might prove their mettle under the scrutiny of a New England shipmaster. Mullet fishers tended to work independently. Many revived the old fish ranchos, sometimes complete with the woolly-mammoth shelters in remote areas where you could go for days and weeks without seeing a stranger.

These places affirmed life in ways that offended the sensibilities of outsiders. One was an inspector for the Freedmen's Bureau, Colonel George F. Thompson, who was disgusted by mullet fishers at Sarasota Bay—especially their breakfast, "stinking salt fish and bread!!!" Apparently, the exclamatory Yankee colonel had not suffered the privations of the Civil War as had the many upon whom he cast harsh judgment. Yet even Silas Stearns, true-blue Gulf defender, the seeming innocent, but still with the suggestion of old Puritan in him, called mullet fishers a "wretched lot of men."[33]

The top species was not the only consumer. Nearly every fish eats mullet. That's why their meat is such good sportfishing bait. Birds eat them; turtles and crabs do too. Somewhat sympathetic to the fish's plight, though known for hauls in the thousands of pounds, Gulf fisherman-restaurateur-writer Leo Lovel calls mullet the "basis of the food chain in the sea."

> *Poor ole mullet. Everybody and everything in the sea, air and on land love 'em. . . .*
> *By far the porpoise's favorite food. . . .*
> *Pelicans dive on 'em when the mullet are trying to run up the river.*
> *Eagles and osprey snatch at every one that gets close to the surface.*
> *All your fish in the ocean eat mullet. From trout feeding on the finger mullet in the estuaries to the marlin eating three-pound mullet offshore.*
> *Cormorants chase 'em underwater.*
> *Seagulls pick up the small fry in the grass.*
> *Gators eat 'em.*[34]

The mullet's biological inclination to all this taking has been to produce far more eggs than the number of offspring expected to survive. The late conservation biologist Archie Carr called this behavior a response to "predator glut." Many species take the same measures—for example, frogs and horseshoe crabs (a single female might disperse 100,000 eggs at a time). The only time mullet go offshore is to spawn, away from the estuarine rivers and bays and sounds, where, in unfath-

omable numbers, they have fed all summer on the bottom fall of plant
and animal remains. In late autumn and winter, when the females
are full of roe, the fish make their exit to the open Gulf. The air has
turned crisp and the water chill, stirring migration instincts.[35]

A mullet run in flashing thousands was a site to see. Fishers were
often there to watch and catch and be amazed, trying to stay warm
in heavy clothes, some wearing flour sacks over their heads like ski
masks, "pints of dark whiskey" coming out of coats and cubbies, says
Lovel, "mullet so thick they're beating the sides of the boat like a
drum." Fishers would chase nets hundreds of yards long across a river,
or gang their boats up side by side, the water churning and stirring
with jumping mullet, countless many hurdling to freedom over the
cork line, and still literally tons to be taken. Says Lovel, "Mullet don't
like to be caught."[36]

NOTHING DOES, AND SOMETIMES fishers don't want what
they catch. Every now and then, a Gulf net fisher would pull in a sea
turtle. The first time Jack Rudloe saw that happen to a shrimper, he
heard, "Goddamn, there ain't nothing I hate worse than catching a
big old stinking turtle!" Experience had taught fishers that turtles can
do considerable damage to shrimp and fish nets. Dolphins were the
same, and even less wanted. With a turtle, though, irritation would
soon accede to the reality that the net had just spilled onto the deck
one of nature's most handsome spoils. Worldwide, the sea turtle's
shield brought good money for making expensive tortoiseshell combs,
brushes, and jewelry boxes. Julius Caesar's triumph in Egypt, despite
yielding near-empty coffers, produced the happy surprise that Alexan-
dria's storehouses were stacked high with tortoiseshell. Mostly, turtles
were prized for what they put on a plate and in a soup bowl. "They
say a turtle got seven different kinds of meat in him," the shrimper
who caught the goddamn turtle told Rudloe. "Some tastes like pork,
some like veal, chicken, and I don't know what all. But it's damn sure
good!"[37]

Rudloe's shrimper pulled in two loggerheads. Of the world's nine sea turtle species, they are one of the five that make a home of the Gulf. Local people used to say sea turtles were so many that you could walk across water like Jesus by stepping on their backs. Their messianic-like proliferation prompted Ponce de León to name that little gathering of islands southwest of the Florida Keys *Los Tortugas*. The 160 that his crew plundered were probably loggerheads and Kemp's ridleys.

Loggerheads are vagabonds of the sea, wandering all parts from deep to shallow. They usually forage inshore for mollusks, crabs, and crustaceans. Kemp's ridleys do the same, in waters where trawls tend to cross to swallow up shrimp, making these two turtle species the likeliest to land belly-up on the deck of a boat. Green turtles, little sleek guys, have powerful swimming muscles and can usually outrun a voracious trawl. Leatherbacks, also known as trunkbacks—the fourth heaviest reptile and largest turtle with the largest flippers, distinguished not only by size, but by their teardrop shape—are rare and stay far out at sea, where they feed on jellyfish. Hawksbills frequent jagged net-tearing environments. Yet the elaborate, brilliant patterns on their shells were, and still are, most prized by tortoiseshell collectors.

Turtles didn't end up in nets solely by cursed happenstance. They were once a major Gulf commodity hunted intensely. For thousands of years, coastal aborigines sought them for food, and later to trade down in Cuba, and the skin from their necks and legs made durable water vessels. When John James Audubon toured the Gulf in the 1830s, he noticed whites painstakingly running nets across the entrances of small rivers. He learned they were using gear with a large mesh that would let fish through while trapping those coveted seagoing reptiles. When swimming, turtles reminded him, "by their celebrity and the ease of their motion, of the progress of a bird in the air."[38]

The gifted painter and ornithologist was on track for celebrity himself, though he did not use his fame to generate sympathy for the wildlife so valuable to his work. In the prevailing mood of the day, life on Earth revolved around the interests of humankind, and wildlife numbers seemed far too excessive to worry about the killing of a turtle here and there. If Audubon admired their grace in the water, he admired more so those "accomplished turtlers" who harpooned them. Still, as a commodity, turtles were worth more netted and kept alive on board boats, eyes blinking. They were then sold to dealers, who in turn corralled them in kraals and waited for an attractive market price.[39]

Turtles were hunted all over the Gulf. Greens were considered the best eating. One dealer boasted, "What champagne is to other wines, green turtle is to other meats." Stearns reported that twenty-four thousand pounds of greens, at three to four cents a pound, were caught and sold in Texas in 1879. A boat pulled into Pensacola one day with a bounty of five hundred live turtles. Facilities that converted turtles into canned meat and soup circled the Gulf. Some of the best turtling grounds for a while were around Cedar Key and southward, where the bottom was covered with sea grass.[40]

Down in the latitudes of Key West, turtling went on year-round. At the urging of a New York wholesale grocer, a French chef named Armand Granday opened a cannery on the tropical island at the foot of Margaret Street. His was the busiest and most famous around. He sold turtle soup in a 1.4-pound can, wrapped in a paper label that claimed the turtles were caught in the "neighborhood," though the label's image includes two men turning a green on a beach in front of mountains, despite Key West's being sandspit flat. The caption proclaims, "*Direct from Sea to Kettle.*" Yes, by way of a slaughterhouse, which was not to be spoken of in the many fine New York restaurants that served Chef Granday's specialty. Except when soup was cooking, his cannery had the marine stench of death. It was no model of appearance, with its bare-board siding, guano-splotched corrugated metal roof, and crowded turtle kraals out back. At any given time, Granday had a hundred turtles crawling and swimming in each other's way, confused by their impoundment. People were fascinated by them, so he started charging ten cents for a look at the big, curious, soon-to-be-soup reptiles.[41]

Canneries were a mere adjunct to the widespread turtling that went on. You didn't need to call yourself a turtler to be one, and you didn't even need a boat. Anybody, and it seemed like everybody, who lived on or near the coast removed turtles from the environment. From late April to midsummer, during nesting period, when turtles hefted themselves out of the Gulf and up onto the beach—as ungainly as half-drowned sailors—people would be waiting. After a turtle laid its eggs, covered the nest, and lumbered through the sand back toward the water, someone would come along to turn it on its back, flippers helplessly fanning the air. A turtle's back was its greatest protection and greatest liability. Turning the heavy leatherbacks, loggerheads, and hawksbills required two or more able-bodied individuals or the assist of a leverage bar. Once the turtles were stranded on their backs, hunters went for the nests, filching every last egg, up to 250 per clutch. After the folks back home got their fill, the dogs and hogs got theirs, a bounty not squandered—but then again . . .

Plundering nests was a reversal of nature's fortune that even Audubon could not abide. He called the stolen eggs "ill-gotten ware" that threatened species regeneration. In addition to invasive humans, turtles had to contend with other wildlife. Raccoons, bears, wolves, and wildcats raided the buried nests. When hatchlings dug out and raced to the sea—their haste instinctual—birds rained down on them and ghost crabs dragged them away, and once in the breakers, fish snatched them. Turtles compensated as did mullet, by overproducing. Providing forage to wildlife was burden enough without having to feed humans, especially when they took both the progenitor and offspring without regard to future generations.[42]

Stearns did not list turtles as a major Gulf commodity. They were disappearing. Granday opened his cannery in 1890, a year after Stearns's death, when their absence was already noticeable in the northern and western Gulf. Where once several thousand turtles could be had, only a few thousand pounds of their meat was reported. Granday had been hardly ten years in business when his suppliers were no longer bringing in turtles from the "neighborhood" and instead were going over to Central American and Caribbean waters—where mountains do rise in the backdrop.

THERE HAD ALWAYS BEEN waste in the fishing industry. Eternal abundance was the worldview of fishers, who surmised that fish would swim in from somewhere else to fill the holes their nets left in the sea. A Naples, Florida, resident once saw fishers lash seines together a quarter of a mile long and drag in fifty-four thousand pounds of mullet headed out to sea to spawn. Nearly the entire school was wiped out. It was more fish meat than anybody could want. The historical record contains numerous testimonies of other phenomenal catches. The Fish Commission calculated that, in 1896, fishers took 500,000 pounds of mullet out of southwest Florida waters, with an untold percentage never making it to market. Some hauls were so big that fishers couldn't prepare and dry them fast enough, or acquire enough ice to keep them from spoiling.

Not long after, in 1904, Texas fishers shipped 200,000 barrels of oysters—the peak before a permanent decline. Apalachicola and neighboring St. Vincent Sound generated nearly 300,000 pounds of meat a decade later but would never do so again. Mississippi officials established a harvesting season as early as the 1890s, yet oystermen routinely violated it. In Louisiana and Texas, fishers did themselves and undersea environments a major disservice when they adopted the oyster dredge as their modus operandi in the 1880s. During the hunger years of the Great Depression, Mississippi conservation laws approved the use of the dredge, which had a big maw something like the shrimp trawl, with a rake-style lower lip. It enabled fishers to oyster in deeper water, but it dragged along the bottom, leaving a gouged trail that no fish would follow. The oyster fishers in Apalachicola could never understand why their counterparts took this destructive path. The Marco Island clams that William Collier harvested with a dredge of his design were gone by 1910.

Shrimpers were bottom-trawling by the second half of the twentieth century, and long before then they took inspiration from mullet fishers and ran net blockades across a river or bayou. The shrimp couldn't endure the roundups, and the inshore population plunged. But no lessons were learned. Shrimpers kept saving themselves by finding fresh grounds with new kinds of shrimp, going as far as Mexico, deeper into what they treated as a bottomless well. Numbers in their harvest trended upward, from about ten million pounds in the 1880s to twenty-four million in 1905.

Red-snapper fishers navigated similar waters. Stearns reluctantly reported that 1883 had been a miserable year for them. The red-snapper population was either overfished, he speculated, or had moved elsewhere. Fishers preferred the latter explanation, making a remedy simple: they would go elsewhere too. Ice opened up time and distance. Two hundred miles out from Pensacola, to the southeast, they hit the mother lode of red snapper in 1885, at the Gulf's so called Outer Banks. The habitat ran down to the Dry Tortugas and lay fifty or sixty miles from Florida's west coast, luring fishers from Cedar Key, Tampa, and Sarasota, as well as the North Carolina families from Cortez.

The windfall turned out to be a whirlwind lasting only until about 1910. But it didn't matter. By then, fishers were finding red snapper off Louisiana, and commercial boats from Port Aransas and Galveston joined in. By the mid-twentieth century, with refrigeration and engines—power on demand—fishers were running down to Campeche Bank, drawing complaints from the Mexican government. Disputes over maritime boundaries festered beyond the millennium.

The birth of commercial fishing on the Gulf was indicative of its "beneficence," to borrow Stearns's word, yet even in his day, human excesses jeopardized that generosity. Remarkably, the Gulf's claim to fame as the Lower Forty-Eight's best fishing hole still lay ahead. The fishery would expand and then surpass the volume in weight yielded by the East Coast fisheries combined, even as the bounty was declining. But it was all relative. The bounty was declining in every fishery. The year 1971 marked the start of the Gulf's reign, when it produced forty-two percent of the nation's total catch.

Exactly a hundred years earlier, Congress had passed a joint resolution expressing concern about the "public injury" incurred from the nation's overwrought fisheries—meaning those of the Northeast. The resolution had produced the US Fish Commission, while New England fishers responded by following the fish and going south. Doing as Leonard Destin had done decades earlier, they set a course to the Gulf. And they repeated mistakes, as did those who joined and came after—predator glut, Archie Carr called it.[43]

As careless marine harvesters, they weren't alone. Recreational fishers were coming to the Gulf too—growing numbers of them at the time Stearns was earning his ichthyologist credentials. Theirs was a different world of taking from nature—one of leisure, sport, and privilege. They weren't working folk either; they were the sporting set. The vanguard among them were bankers, lawyers, architects, business leaders, and their wives and widows. Some revolutionized the American economy. A century after their entrada, a fishing-guide-turned-fiction-writer dug into the past and learned how they, too, helped open the Gulf to the nation, and how they, too, plucked spots in the aquatic garden bare.

Seven

THE WILD FISH THAT
TAMED THE COAST

Christine B. M. Hawley in 1914 with her 154½-pound tarpon. Well-off men and women from the North went to the Gulf beginning in the late nineteenth century to catch such fish, igniting Gulf tourism.

*Then he would diplomatically bring the conversation around
to deep sea monsters, and the innate possibilities of a vacation
at Useppa Island, or Long Key, or Aransas Pass, or even far off
Tampico.*

—RICHARD SUTTON (1924)[1]

YOU COULD EASILY MISTAKE RANDY WAYNE WHITE FOR a professional wrestler. He had the muscular, triangular torso of one, topped by a head shaved in the fashion of a contender created for the televised emporium of the sport. All bulk and brawn, you might think, until you looked into his eyes. They were bright-blue windows into a literary mind. White wrote popular crime fiction, producing two-fisted titles such as *The Heat Islands* and *Tampa Burn*. He set most of his books on the late-twentieth-century Gulf coast. Before becoming a best-selling author, he spent thirteen years as a fishing guide on the same historical waters that Frank Hamilton Cushing explored nearly a century earlier.

Guides typically knew a little something about the backstory of their trade, and White knew practically everything. He was especially obsessed with the history of Gulf tarpon. Stallion sleek, possessing the stamina of the same, often weighing over a hundred pounds, a hooked tarpon is a glorious fighter, a trophy hunter's fish. After thousands of charters, White never tired of its backward-vaulting midair acrobatics. Each performance was a new thrill. He got another thrill when he dug into the history of how this wild fish fired up the sport-fishing world back in the nineteenth century and changed the Gulf coast forever.

This fascination for a saltwater animal did not seem preordained when White was a wispy-haired farm boy growing up in Ohio and Iowa. In high school, he was far more interested in baseball, football, and springboard diving than fishing. He otherwise filled his land-locked solitude with reading—among his favorites, Twain, Steinbeck, Conrad, and Doyle. Graduation was followed by his postsecondary education, the road. He lit out for places never seen, getting by on his wits. At one point, he worked on the small farm of a well-traveled couple who "raved about" Sanibel, a Gulf barrier island of tropical hues and wildlife, not to mention excellent saltwater fishing. White hit the road again, in 1972. He was twenty-two years old, a free spirit on the verge of anchoring himself beside a sea he had never seen before.[2]

Driving down to the Gulf coast in a 1968 GMC three-tone

pickup—red, white, and rust—he found his way to Fort Myers. On San Carlos Island, wedged up against Fort Myers and across the bay from Sanibel, he rented a house that was a bit tattered, like the shrimp yard in which it was located, and liberally scented by the yard's marine smells. The midwesterner who was raised in a sea of land had become an island dweller surrounded by salt marshes, mangroves, bays, a river, a sound, a pass, and the Gulf. He signed on as a beat reporter at the daily mullet wrapper, as locals called the Fort Myers *News-Press*. It was a crucial apprenticeship, and grist for the imagination of a budding crime-thriller writer. So were the marinas he haunted.

White was always looking for a way to get on the water and, more ideally, to get his own boat. He passed the grueling three-day Coast Guard exam for a charter captain's license and scraped together the money for a used twenty-foot skiff with "sweet lines" in the polish of white fiberglass. By 1977, he had begun guiding, putting in three hundred days a year on his boat and doubling his income. He worked out of a marina beside Tarpon Bay, a fish-jumping estuary more the size of a cove than a bay, off Pine Island Sound and near the southern end of Sanibel Island. Between charters, White wrote. All around him, in the past and present, he found material for the books he would produce.[3]

If he had been living on the Chesapeake or on Cape Cod, he could not have avoided the venerable history of Jamestown and Plymouth, the Powhatan and the Wampanoag, the Virginia Company and the Puritans. But high school history textbooks, even those in Florida, said nothing about the Calusa who had lived around Pine Island Sound where Ponce de León had tried to unpack the Gulf's first European settlement. White learned unexpectedly that this sunny, fish-leaping water had an exceptional history, and that his clients were a thread in it. They wanted to catch tarpon. The infatuation for this particular fish went back some ninety years, and it aroused White's curiosity. He began collecting scientific studies, old magazine and newspaper articles, and selections from forgotten memoirs—anything about tarpon—blowing dust off the past.

It turned out that the first tarpon of record caught with a rod and reel had been boated on the sultry little bay where he took his clients, on March 19, 1885. This was the year commercial fishers discovered red snapper out from Pensacola. Fewer than eighty thousand people lived on the US Gulf coast at the time. Houston and Galveston accounted for half that population, but Tampa, the largest city on the sunset-viewing side, had only 2,375 people. Fort Myers didn't appear on the US census. Two weeks earlier, Grover Cleveland, who would become a Gulf-coast tarpon angler himself, had been inaugurated the twenty-second US president.

When it comes to the making of the American Sea, the tarpon, like the red snapper, is a fish to remember. It brought people to the coast— not New Englanders so much as New Yorkers, and not new residents so much as tourists, who were among the Gulf's first.

A THIRTY-YEAR-OLD GOTHAM ARCHITECT who designed big ornate churches and Carnegie libraries hooked that historic fish. A premier largemouth bass angler—some said no one caught more— William Halsey Wood was determined to capture a tarpon. He did it in a little rowboat using a five-foot single-piece bamboo rod, a reel of his own design, 250 feet of twenty-one-thread line, a large cod "O-hook" (circular and similar to the hook that commercial fishers used for catching red snapper), a strip of mullet, and disciplined patience. Instead of instantly pulling back when the fish took the bait, Wood let the line pay out 250 feet. That turned out to be the trick: give the fish time to gnaw on its would-be meal before trying to plant the hook. The lining of a tarpon's mouth is steel-like and nearly impossible to penetrate. The second the fish feels a tug, it will try to discharge the offending object. The hook needs to snag the gills or reach the gut. We don't know where the hook ended up in Wood's fish. But we know it fought for twenty-six minutes, weighed ninety-three pounds, and measured five feet nine inches.

When Randy Wayne White learned this origin story, the New

York architect was not the one who jumped out as the hero. It was the guide, Captain John Smith, a tan, wiry, hardworking boatman. He was the same John Smith who, ten years later, would run the frail artifact collector Frank Hamilton Cushing down from Punta Gorda to Marco Island in his sloop, the *Florida*. The exacting Cushing had little regard for Smith's competence as charter captain, perhaps unfairly, but Wood sang his praises as a guide. Wood took a second tarpon on March 25, and a third, fourth, and fifth on the thirty-first—all with Smith's peerless assistance.

Sources describe Smith as a Finnish seaman who was shipwrecked in a storm at Key West before making his way up the Gulf coast to Punta Rassa, a flat corner of land at the marshy mouth of the Caloosahatchee River. Just across from Sanibel, Punta Rassa had been many things since Spanish settlement: the site of fish ranchos, a US military provisions depot, and the dusty, sometimes muddy, end of the south Florida cattle drive. It was as untamed as any cowpunching town in west Texas, and it looked like one, except it had a cattle dock. Otherwise, it was occupied by stock pens, stables, boardinghouses, saloons, and, presumably, brothels. It clamored with voices from around the world, and cracked with the leather whips of sun-browned Cracker cowboys fresh off the scrub. You smelled the cattle and heard the money; transactions were conducted with hard coin. During the Civil War, cattlemen preferred the risk of running the Federals' Gulf blockade to sell their cows to the Cubans for gold or silver rather than to the Confederacy for worthless paper currency. Punta Rassa made many Florida men into big, western-style landowners.

It was also the original beachhead of Gulf angling. Unless you were driving cattle, you got to Punta Rassa by boat, and the first thing you would see was a warehouse-sized wooden structure clinging to the edge of the water. Built during the Second Seminole War and raised on piers, it had a cedar-shingle roof in the ironic shape of an Indian mound. More recently, it had housed a telegraph station of the International Ocean Cable Company. It also shared space with northern sportsmen on fishing and hunting trips. Visitors who slept there knew

it as the "Barracks," a name that suggested the state of the accommodations—spartan but orderly. Smith worked there. While guides usually moonlighted as commercial fishermen, Smith was a cook for the
cable company (Cushing appreciated his culinary skills).[4]

After a hurricane nearly pulverized Punta Rassa, Smith moved out
to Pine Island, an elevated barrier that the Calusa had built up with
shell. Not long after Randy White got into the guiding business, he
followed his predecessor's example and also moved to Pine Island, into
an old house situated on the remains of an Indian mound. He liked
knowing that people had been telling stories on that hump of land for
thousands of years.

The one about Wood's triumph spread quickly. Before his first
tarpon, the saltwater game that excited American sportsmen and
-women were Atlantic salmon, pompano, snook, and black bass. Any
one of them reeled in at one-quarter the weight of a tarpon was a
prize. While Wood's ninety-three-pounder was on the smallish side,
big ones can go to a leviathan 280 pounds and eight feet. All sizes put
on a show. "Most world-ranging anglers agree," wrote the author of an
angling guide, "the tarpon is the ultimate light-tackle fish for its aerial
displays, its power, and its heart."[5]

Although you could catch bigger fish offshore in open water—
bluefin tuna or marlin—the sport in Wood's day for the most part
left the deep-sea prospects to the commercial fishermen. Offshore
fish of all sizes would not become desired game until the widespread
use of powerboats, and they never excited as many people, because
they were never as accessible. Tarpon came into bays, sounds, passes,
and rivers in the spring through summer. Catching one was like
going deep-sea fishing without going out to the deep sea.

And it was all for sport. The flesh is full of small, hard-to-clean
bones that make the tarpon virtually inedible. There was, though, the
adrenaline rush of a battle royal with a vigorous opponent, a victory
pose next to a big fish hanging by its gills for the camera, and the
legacy of the moment preserved in the handsome creature mounted
and displayed on a wall, bragging rights beyond dispute. "I hated to

see the great silver monsters lying in the dust of the wharf," wrote John Dos Passos, who often fished with Hemingway in Key West. "Sheer vanity catching tarpon."[6]

Early on, what people knew about this coveted game fish they knew only from the sporting set and its guides, and some of that was fairy tale. Everyone thought instinct spurred it to inshore waters to spawn. When biologists finally got around to studying this 130-million-year-old species, their research showed that Gulf tarpon spawn in open water, mainly at Campeche Bay and off the coast of southwest Florida.

Like the eel, a cousin once or twice removed, tarpon spend a number of years in the larval stage, when they also look like eels, finger long, thin, and translucent. Storms and currents conveniently transport the larvae into estuarine waters, where they take cover in the grass and around mangroves and transform into juveniles that are miniature versions of adults. Tolerant of a broad salinity range, adults leave the deep between spawning cycles for inshore grounds, traveling even up rivers, to forage on smaller fish. Generally bottom-feeders, they favor shrimp but will also pick up crabs and a nice chum of mullet lying on a bed of grass concealing a hook. They have a fantastically large, mechanical-looking mouth and protruding jaw—an anatomical assembly that could inspire design in earthmoving equipment. The mouth opens to the full diameter of the body, itself long and cylindrical, bluish green on top and chrome metallic on the sides. Its pectoral fins look like clinging gossamer butterflies.[7]

With its sheen, speed, and majesty, the tarpon acquired the nickname "silver king." Its scales are the shape and polish of silver dollars and were removed and kept as souvenirs and sometimes sold as costume jewelry, or stamped with name and number and used as fancy calling cards. At a number of fishing lodges, anglers pinned them to lobby or dining-room walls with their name and the date of catch written on each until the mass acquired the density of wallpaper. In Texas, there is one that reads, "5 ft 1 in. 77 lbs. Franklin D Roosevelt May 8-1937 Port Aransas." Behind the tarpon's scales, inside the body, is a unique component, a swim bladder webbed with blood vessels, the same as the lungs of a land animal, that seconds as an oxygen feeder. Biologists call the tarpon an obligate air breather, meaning it must on occasion come to the surface for oxygen. When it does, it rolls. If around, sportfishers know where to cast their line.[8]

The tarpon runs the Atlantic from Virginia to Brazil, and the West African coast from Senegal to Angola, and it worries the shallows and depths off Southeast Asia, Japan, and Australia. "Its real home," wrote an English angler in the 1890s, expressing the prevailing opinion of his sporting class, "is undoubtedly the Gulf of Mexico."[9]

MANY PEOPLE CONNECT the historical origins of sportfishing, which began exclusively as a freshwater activity, to another Englishman, Izaak Walton. A London businessman, Walton cultivated his passion for angling after retiring to a thatched-roof farmhouse in the English countryside, bounded on one side by the River Meese. He fell into writing as a second career, eventually penning a series of short biographies that influenced the literary form. His first book, *The Compleat Angler, or Contemplative Man's Recreation*, published in 1653, earned him recognition as sportfishing's paterfamilias.

If a best-seller list had existed then, *The Compleat Angler* would have been on it. The book would eventually run through three hundred printings, and it or Walton would make cameo appearances in the works of Coleridge, Dickens, Jules Verne, Thomas Hardy, Zane Grey, Norman Maclean, and countless others. *The Compleat Angler* is a timeless exposition on the stratagems of fishing, which Walton wrote as a reading man's manual of the sport. It includes verse, prose, and parables; it even has a protagonist, Piscator, the voice of angling authority.

The word "angle" means "fishhook" and dates to Old English. When William the Conqueror stormed across the English Channel from Normandy in the eleventh century, he gave Britain castles, feudalism, and fly-fishing. One of the earliest books on recreational fishing, and the first by a woman, appeared in 1498: Juliana Berners's *Treatise on Fishing with an Angle*. Berners's background is something of a mystery, a confusion of reliable and not-so-reliable sources. Some say she was one of England's earliest poets, and others, the cloistered but worldly prioress of a nunnery. The more alluring supposition is that she was a beautiful and intelligent woman whose apprehensions toward love drove her to field sports. She may have been none of these things, and she may have been all. It's also possible she was the first woman published in the English language. Of the known books of field sports, hers are the earliest in English, and about hunting, hawking, and fishing.

These activities were expected pursuits of gentlemen, many of whom, as it turns out, were informed by a nun or female poet whose obligatory place fell outside their masculine privileges. One hundred and fifty years older, Berners was an invaluable source for Walton. Her *Treatise* explains how to build a rod and tie a fly, and which fly to use for which fish in which season. It elevated angling to the level of importance of other field sports, such as fox hunting and wing shooting.

Berners also conceived an enduring foundation for sportsman and conservation ethics. "When you have a sufficient mess you should covet no more," she wrote, and "nourish the game in all that you may." Five centuries later, the International Game Fish Association called her principles of conservation "startlingly modern."[10]

Angling was primarily for those who had the social standing and time to "do nothing but angle, and talk of fish and fishing," wrote Walton. Great Britain's landed gentry, a minority who controlled the woodlands, made hunting foxes and stags a recreational preserve of their class, to the exclusion of the peasant and laborer who would otherwise, but generally wasn't allowed to, hunt for the pot. The gentry also more or less determined who could fish in which bodies of water. For British subjects across the Atlantic in the American colonies, settled largely by those not of the old landed class, freedoms once denied became freedoms tenaciously defended. Recreational fishing and game hunting in America ranked with private landownership and voting as a sacred democratic expression. Casting a lure, in other words, was an unceremonious rejection of hereditary privilege. Guns and rods erased rather than drew social divisions; the English nobleman's sport was the sport of all Americans. Not least of all, the rivers and lakes in the land of liberty were hopping with fish.[11]

Still, the appeal of angling was more than a full stringer of fish and testing the angler's skills at outwitting fish. Some referred to their engagement as an art. Walton compared it to poetry. His alternate title, *or Contemplative Man's Recreation*, revealed a cherished truth: fishing, like art, was an emotional escape, an opportunity to freshen the spirit and withdraw into inner thoughts. It was meant for solitude, even when in the company of another. Two anglers in a boat or standing in a stream made not a voluble pair. "All that are lovers of virtue," wrote Walton, "be quiet and go a-angling." For one outdoorsman writing home to Philadelphia from the Gulf in 1878, angling was like a patent medicine that worked. "Success at fishing is a source of great contentment to the mind, dispels corroding cares, excites within a feeling of profound enjoyment, invigorates exhausted nerves and promotes digestion."[12]

Virtue was also found in the quality of the setting—the immersion into outdoor scents and sounds, the glinting sky and water, the undying momentum of a stream, a lake in glassy repose, the transported moment when the connection to the immortal world seemed acutely real and personal, in perfect beautiful harmony. Well into the nineteenth century, angling rarely crossed beyond the thresholds of freshwater streams and lakes. To gentlemen anglers, saltwater fishing smacked of net haulers with crude tattoos on ropy arms. Eventually, the liveliness and spirit of the fish in bays, bayous, and sounds won them over. Many referred to their newfound activity as blue-water angling.

The nominal father of the saltwater sport was another Englishman, Henry William Herbert. Exiled in 1831 for uncertain—some say scandalous—reasons, Herbert emigrated to New York at age twenty-four. His acquaintances and associates knew him as self-absorbed, pompous, and hopelessly attached to his distinguished lineage (an earldom). He had a temper that seemed to add curl to his collar-length hair and imperial mustache. It doomed him to divorce, social ostracism, and suicide. Still, he was not without some qualified level of accomplishment. He founded the *American Monthly Magazine*, though his contrarian manner led to his early departure from its offices. Within three years of arriving in the States, he published a novel, followed by several others, none of which the domestic literati awarded much merit.

At some point, Herbert began fishing in New York Harbor and the surrounding estuaries. The water was starting to show the burdens of the metropolis, and he became an early voice for fisheries protection. Still, he managed to pull in some sizable salmon, herring, and striped sea bass. On occasion, Theodore Roosevelt's uncle Robert joined him on piscatory outings. True to character, Herbert had a superior attitude about his avocation, insisting that saltwater fish were, "without any exception, the strongest, the boldest, and, as such, afford the best sport of their tribe." After a day catching his fill, he would affix himself before a drink at his favorite tavern and crow about getting the better of the strong and the bold.[13]

There was something legitimate about Herbert's fish tales, though. They became the basis of his legacy, *Fish and Fishing of the United States and the British Provinces of North America*. Published in 1849, the first of its kind in the US, more of an instructional guide than meditative tract, the book was mainly a taxonomy compiled through correspondences with saltwater anglers from different parts of the country, explaining what they caught and how they caught it. Like *The Compleat Angler*, Herbert's *Fish and Fishing* was a testament to the future of sportfishing.

Surprisingly, Herbert included no reports about the Gulf, although it had sometime before welcomed its first anglers. Always on the hunt for new fishing holes, sportsmen in the Northeast devoured reports coming off packet steamers and trading schooners of seamen who had dropped an angle over the side in waters elsewhere. In his 1826 journal, kept during a voyage from New Orleans to Liverpool, John James Audubon observed the crew of the *Delos*, including the captain, with hook and line pulling in scores of rudderfish and dolphinfish, the latter of which "glided by the side of our vessel like burnished gold."[14]

Indeed, the first recreational angler on the Gulf may have been a sailor. Perhaps it was a shoreside squatter who fished for the table and realized from it an element of fun. Maybe a midwesterner visiting the mineral bathing springs on the Mississippi coast and opting for a go at snapper and mackerel. Or it might have been an Alabamian spending contemplative time on the emerald waters enveloping the tongue of sandy land where Leonard Destin had introduced commercial fishing. So many fish struck in those waters that by the mid-twentieth century, the town of Destin had amassed one of the largest recreational-fishing fleets in the country and took to calling itself the "World's Luckiest Fishing Village." It made perfect sense for a commercial port to diversify. Biloxi, Tarpon Springs, Galveston, Port Aransas, Port Isabel, and Sarasota had the boats, the expertise, and the fish. All they needed were anglers.

CHARLES HALLOCK—a patrician, not a sailor—was as responsible as anyone for getting anglers to the Gulf. A rod-and-gun adventurer from the urban canyons of New York City and author of seventeen books and hundreds of magazine articles, he had few equals in promoting outdoor sports. In August 1873, he launched *Forest and Stream*, with the mission "to inculcate in men and women a love for natural objects." Innovations in the printing industry had made producing serials more cost-effective, and railroads opened up a wider market for the distribution of magazines—not to mention anglers. An expanding class of leisure takers wanted recommendations on where to go for hook-and-bullet escapades, and when unable to go themselves, they wanted stories to take them there. Hallock made introductions with a readership that soon enough invited additional serials: *Sports Afield, Outdoor Life, American Angler, Field and Stream*.[15]

A descendant of British colonial stock with family money, Hallock had the means to fund his adventures. He fished the trout streams of the East and Midwest and the salmon rivers of the Pacific coast. He dropped a line through the ice in the Arctic and packed his rod and gun on trips to Florida. He hunted and fished throughout the sparsely settled peninsula, where the game, according to a contemporary, was "so abundant as to make good cheer for the sportsman." The Gulf coast captivated him. It was, he said, "one of the choicest of the delectable lands," with "estuaries without end, with open sea beaches and rocky coral harbors." He said as much to Charles Kenworthy, who had recently moved to Jacksonville from the North to be closer to wild playgrounds. Hallock asked Kenworthy to explore the sporting opportunities on the Gulf while sending the magazine dispatches. In the first, Kenworthy made his objective clear: "We have long maintained that the south-west coast needs but to have its advantages known to be appreciated."[16]

The correspondent threw himself into the assignment. He purchased a twenty-one-foot sloop in New Jersey, shipped it to Savannah, and from there sailed to Fernandina, where he loaded the boat on a flatcar bound for Cedar Key, on the same rail that a few months later would conduct Sidney Lanier on his travelogue project. Cruising the bays, inlets, and islands from Cedar Key to Key West and back, from March to June, yielded twelve dispatches. Kenworthy was sure the "disciples of Old Izaak Walton" would rightly be satisfied with the Gulf. It was, he concluded, a "sportsman's paradise."[17]

The place most responsible for that description was the last he visited, Florida's Homosassa Springs. "We spent a week at Homosassa, and found but one thing to annoy," he reported, "that being the fact that we were compelled to leave." About halfway between Cedar Key and Tarpon Springs, a village of five hundred beside the spring-fed river of the same name, Homosassa was sheltered by live oaks and silver-gray veils of Spanish moss. It brought wilderness and civilization together in an untroubled coexistence. People got from place to place on wildlife paths, and wildlife left footprints on wagon roads. Old Spanish citrus trees grew in the scrub, where locals raised peaches, pears, figs, and guavas.[18]

Just before Yankee sporting-types came down, whooping cranes arrived to winter among a bustling community of pelicans, herons, ospreys, cormorants, cranes, and anhingas. The presence of fish eaters was always a promising sign. Bring a "full supply of strong hooks and lines," Kenworthy advised; the "piscator" would find "cavalla, red-fish, bass, sheepshead, weak-fish, and red and black grouper in thousands leisurely swimming about the basin." Kenworthy could have added tarpon, but "knights of the rod" had not yet learned the secret of snaring this elusive opponent.[19]

By the turn of the century, Homosassa would become one of the most popular fishing destinations in the Southeast. Kenworthy's dispatches played no small role in giving it national exposure. He was one of a growing number of guide and magazine writers who were talking up its "home comforts, excellent accommodations, superior table, perfect cleanliness, and an admirable climate." Grover Cleveland built a retreat on the river for himself and his rod-and-reel confederates, and Winslow Homer's name appeared on the register of a local boardinghouse.[20]

That was in early 1904. Come winter, Homer would depart his home in Maine for tropical islands in the Atlantic. He went as much for a chance to hook a bluefin as for artistic muse. In December, he was immersed in the warmth of Key West when he got a hankering to try the fishing up on the Gulf coast, where amusement and work would converge. Homosassa inspired eleven watercolors in Homer. The best known is *Black Bass*. At the center of the piece, a beautiful specimen convulses in midair, trying to throw off an angler's fly, a scarlet ibis blazing the color of the bass's dilated gills. The water is limpid and the back shoreline close and deep-shadowed, framed by native sabal palms and other "jungle" vegetation. Floating overhead is an eagle or osprey, the Gulf's most common birds of prey, or perhaps a turkey buzzard, a signifier of inevitable death, so common in Homer's work.

Black Bass is a sportsman's pastoral. "Delightful climate here," Homer wrote in a letter to his brother, Arthur, back on snowy Prouts Neck—"about as cool as our September." He stayed a month and returned the next year, and again in 1908 and 1909, the last time after having suffered a stroke. He never painted on his subsequent visits. He was a sportsman only, engaged in what he believed to be the best fishing in America.[21]

Similar remarks by others described fishing retreats across the Gulf from Florida to Texas. Anglers returned home with news of blue-water remoteness, tropical serenity, paradise islands, and David-and-Goliath combat. Big-fish stories weren't altogether tall tales. You could just about drop a rusty hook in the water and get a bite. When Wallace Stevens was on the Gulf, locals told him the waters teemed with "big 'uns thick as minnows." Like Homer, Georgia poet Sidney Lanier had been an Atlantic man when he first visited the Gulf. The blue-water multitudes astounded him, and he not a rod man. "For mere variety these fish are wonderful."[22]

The most wonderful to Gulf enthusiasts was the tarpon, not yet reeled in for the first time when Lanier was writing in the 1870s. Blue-water anglers were hooked, though. They were very much aware of the metallic-bright fish. They dreamed of what it might be like to fight one with a rod and reel. Some believed that "no man is strong enough to hold a large tarpon." Others had seen the sporting potential from catching a few—although not with hook, but harpoon, often thrown by the confident hand of a guide, with the harpoon tied to a long line fastened to a floating wooden cask. A rowboat of giddy spectators would follow as the harpooned fish shot repeatedly from the water fully airborne and, after a half hour or more, tired itself. Sometimes the line was secured to the bow, as outdoor author James Henshall witnessed near Marco Island. "The great fish tows the boat around like a cockle-shell . . . until his fierce struggles and grand leaps begin to tell on him."[23]

Then William Halsey Wood landed a tarpon, recounted the miraculous event in *Forest and Stream*, and displayed his mounted catch with rod, reel, and line at J. R. Conroy & Co. fishing and tackle store at 65 Fulton Street in New York City, four blocks from the polluted East River. Much down on the pristine Gulf was about to change.

RANDY WAYNE WHITE made the tarpon a regular feature in his crime novels: "Six feet long, most of them, rolling and diving in a frenzied carousel, gulping surface air before ascending, blowing bubbles, their huge horse-eyes vivid with life but devoid of emotion; primeval fish that were wild with purpose but as mindless as rays of light," says the narrator, speaking in *Sanibel Flats*. The protagonist is Doc Ford, a marine biologist who is also an ex-CIA agent. Ford studies tarpon when he's not trying to rescue the son of a dead friend from Central American terrorists.[24]

Along with lacing his fiction with fish facts, White found a nonfiction outlet for the tarpon. With his consent, a friend, Carlene Fredericka Brennen, a silver-king enthusiast and author, pulled together the materials he had collected over the years and, with some of her own, published *Randy Wayne White's Ultimate Tarpon Book*. They filled 406 pages with newspaper and magazine articles from the late nineteenth and early twentieth centuries, and well over two hundred black-and-white photographs, all led with an introduction by White. They selected essays and quotes by some of the great names connected with the sport: Zane Grey, Thomas Edison, Ernest Hemingway, William Halsey Wood. They found a gem attributed to Baseball Hall of Famer Ted Williams, who once made a film about tarpon fishing and founded a tarpon tournament down in the Florida Keys, and then won it several times. "A dynamic, eager, tackle-busting—well, just a sensational, spectacular fish," said Williams, who cowrote his own book about tarpon fishing. Few game fish have been the subject of as many books.[25]

The first, by Frank Pinckney, appeared three years after the sport was born. But the best known of the period is *The Book of the Tarpon*, published in 1911 and written by Anthony Weston Dimock. The slim, bushy-mustached Dimock was the WASP archetype of the Gulf angler. Attendance at elite schools had given him a head start to early success on Wall Street, where he made a fortune in the gold market.

Read his books and you hear a man who is a bit proud of himself. He understood his advantages and used them to travel the world in search of adventure. He ran bison with Comanche, tracked grizzlies with Shoshone, hunted crocodiles and manatees with Seminole, and cruised and camped "among other creatures and peoples of the wild." His son, Julian, a uniquely talented photographer, usually came along with a cumbersome view camera and dry gelatin-bromide glass plates, with thousandth-of-a-second exposure time that could capture wildlife in motion. The tarpon book includes ninety-two of Julian's black-and-whites.[26]

It is the only book that Dimock devoted to a single animal. He opened with the story of a tarpon that he hooked three years before Wood hooked his. Trolling where the "current sweeps" into the Gulf from the Homosassa River, Dimock had employed a guide, a black man whom he referred to as only Tat. Black guides in southwest Florida were common. Many were commercial fishermen who knew how to tolerate the color line drawn by their clients (including the Yankees), and Dimock, for one, treated Tat like his man Friday. The tarpon that took his fly ultimately got away. When Dimock gaffed it, the fish knocked him backward out of the boat—a wet misadventure for which he scolded Tat. The prideful Dimock wrote, "I believe the tarpon then on my line was entitled to the credit for being the first of his species captured with rod and reel."[27]

Dimock or Wood—the name of the honoree didn't matter. The bourgeois rod-and-reel community had been waiting for anyone to show that hooking—and boating—a tarpon was possible. After it happened, a *Forest and Stream* correspondent made the case that if Izaak Walton had caught a silver king, he would have devoted a chapter to the fish, and *The Compleat Angler* would be "not simply complete, but perfect." Alerting ever-intrepid British anglers, the *London Observer* predicted that "sportsmen may yet go to Florida for the tarpon, as they now go to the Arctic zone for reindeer, walrus, and musk-ox."[28]

The fish's coronation as silver king was immediate. *Webster's* added "tarpon" to the next edition of its dictionary, and outdoor writers began exalting it with honorific titles: "peerless monarch," "his excellency," "lordly fish," "big, gamey silver king," "El Sabalo" (which means "the tarpon"). Just as quickly, the new game fish became, as one outdoor writer put it, "perhaps the world's greatest angling target." It was all hyperbole, of course. Or was it?[29]

As the cod inspired New England's working waterfront, the "peerless monarch" inspired the Gulf's leisure coast. Railroads and steamship lines zeroed in on their own target: the new tarpon angler. They ran ads devoted to travel schedules and rates to tarpon retreats. Transportation and shipping mogul Henry B. Plant made it easier to get to them—much easier than getting to reindeer country in the Arctic. In carpetbagger fashion, the silver-haired Connecticut Yankee for years had been snapping up struggling and bankrupt rails around the region and laying new track across the state from Jacksonville and down the peninsula's west side, while Henry Flagler pushed another down the east. Both lines were following the southward expansion of citrus and winter-vegetable growing, but the two magnates, rivals and friends, also built resort hotels along their routes for winter-weary northerners—wealthy ones. By sheer coincidence and with good timing, Plant opened the first line to Tampa in the year Wood set the angling world on fire. He was also building a $3 million hotel with Gilded Age comforts, including an elevator, electric lights, and telephones (all firsts in Florida), private baths, bowling alley, horse track, and casino. Six silver-gray Moorish minarets, the first thing you saw approaching Tampa by boat or train, announced the hotel's opulence.

Then, not so coincidentally, Plant began cutting a new route southward through the subtropical scrub and wetland to Punta Gorda. This time, in 1888, when steam power first rolled in, coming to a stop with a release and a sigh, he had accommodations awaiting the angler crowd. All 150 rooms in his Queen Anne–style Hotel Punta Gorda looked over Charlotte Harbor. Guides were waiting too. Prime tarpon fishing was a few hours away by steamer or sloop. Plant himself, the *Fort Myers Press* observed, was a "master in handling a fish line as well as a railroad line." At the Tennessee Centennial and International Exposition in 1897, he displayed a 150-pound silver king he had boated that April on the Caloosahatchee River.[30]

He caught it from the yacht of Standard Oil millionaire Ambrose McGregor and his wife, Tootie. The McGregors were seasonal residents who had a house in Fort Myers on the Caloosahatchee River. Their next-door neighbors were Thomas A. and Mina Edison, and next to them was the winter estate of Henry Ford (whose name White borrowed for his serial protagonist). In the year of Wood's fish, the Edisons began construction of a house and laboratory on thirteen acres purchased from a Punta Rassa cattle baron, and named the estate Seminole Lodge. Behind it they added a dock that ranged out into the flush, crystalline river. The Edisons were agog over tarpon. They kept rowboats and an electric launch on hand, with a boatman on call, and plenty of fishing rods and tackle for guests. The tarpon rods they reserved for themselves. "The finest tarpon fishing in the world is right in front of my house," Thomas dictated in a reply to a Texas businessman inviting him to hunt the same over on the other coast. "So many tarpon and other fish come up the shallow river that it raises it—11 inches every season."[31]

"Everybody talks tarpon," wrote a *Forest and Stream* correspondent of southwest Florida. "Tarpon" was painted across the transom or on the bow of countless boats, including a twin-screw steamer in the Plant fleet, which connected points along the Gulf from Mobile to Havana. There was Tarpon Bay in the Everglades, not to be confused with the Tarpon Bay where Wood caught his fish, and up the coast there was the village of Tarpon Springs, incorporated two years later. The Barracks at Punta Rassa adopted a new official name, Tarpon House. Other lodges would soon compete with it.[32]

There were plenty of guests to go around, thanks to Wood, Smith, and their ninety-three-pounder. Nearly all were from the UK, Canada, and the northern US. Coming south, the men traded their woolen suits for linen jackets and slacks, while the women shed a third or more from the weight and yardage of their dress. Across the bay from the Tarpon House at the lower end of Pine Island, where John Smith's guiding business was flourishing, a group of investors from Maine and Canada laid out the boundaries for St. James City. They imported key lime and lemon trees, pineapples, bananas, guavas, and thousands of coconut palms as part of a planned enterprise in agriculture. The plantings had a secondary purpose in giving the scrub island a tropical aura.

At the end of a white shell drive, the proprietors built the Hotel San Carlos. It had three stories, fifty guest rooms, a wine room, and a dining salon that would seat a hundred. On the long, shaded porch spanning the first floor, the staff lined up rocking chairs where guests could smoke, read, or trade business cards and tarpon stories. "Everyone talked of that fish," said one lodger, "hoped, longed, expected to, or feared he wouldn't capture it." Anglers who wanted to be on the water around the clock could lodge at the Hotel Captiva, a twenty-one-room floating annex of the San Carlos. Its anchorage alternated between Captiva and Boca Grande Passes, the "Greatest Tarpon Grounds in the World," the proprietors claimed.[33]

That's what John M. Roach thought when he bought Useppa Island in 1894. The president of a Chicago streetcar line, Roach knew a thing or two about location. Useppa had a bit of a history as José Maríe Caldez's former fish rancho island, then known as Joseffa. More important to Roach, it had convenient access to both Boca Grande and Captiva Passes. The three-story, white-painted Useppa Inn he built, commanding a bluff view over Pine Island Sound, with the Gulf in the distance, and proffering fine accommodations and an excellent chef, was instantly popular. An advertising millionaire named Barron Collier, who bought and sold ad space on Roach's streetcars, and who had once employed F. Scott Fitzgerald to write ad copy, acquired the inn in 1911 for $100,000. He expanded the third floor and added a columned entrance that communicated the wealth and exclusivity to which its clientele was accustomed. Lest anyone worry that the resort was losing its center, he changed the name to Tarpon Inn. The tongue-and-groove paneled walls in its club room flashed the round scales of the enshrined fish caught by guests.

Their days on Useppa began early, with the staff rousing guests before daybreak for a sumptuous breakfast of eggs, bacon, and grapefruit. Down on the hotel's dock, one of the wood-burning steam yachts, the *Valima* or *Adroi*, waited to take them to one of the passes, thoroughfares for tarpon headed to estuarine feeding grounds. Wading birds positioned along the shallows were already fishing by the time a boat got under way with the rising sun. The scene was a picture for the camera: black boiler smoke drifted from the toy boat–like stack, a wisp trailing over a surprisingly large Union Jack saluting a flotilla of empty rowboats towed behind.

The snaking assemblage was a creation of tarpon fishing. After the steamer dropped anchor, each guest with guide climbed into one of the boats, eight to eighteen feet long, and was set adrift. Guides rowed to a school of rolling silver kings or to a place where they might be loitering around mangroves. The client cast bait or fly tackle and waited, usually not long. There was nothing quite like riding in a boat pulled around by an alarmed, hooked tarpon, sometimes for miles, or being on the water as the fish shot skyward—"in the shape of a crescent," wrote Zane Grey of his first catch, "to straighten out with such marvelous power that he seemed actually to crack like a whip."[34]

Useppa guests caught a lot of tarpon. The patron who pinned up probably more scales than any other, with name, hometown, date, and weight of catch on each, was Edward vom Hofe from New York. The dates of his catches range over thirty-three years, their weight from under a hundred pounds to well over. He was a friend of John Roach and, more important, he manufactured high-end fishing tackle and reels. His reels were custom-made to the fish—highly engineered, elegant works of art, as fine as a jeweled watch, said one aficionado— with black side plates of hardened Brazilian rubber and a contrasting nickel silver frame, spool, and crank arm. (Hemingway fished with a vom Hofe.) Beginning in 1888, vom Hofe traveled to the Gulf every season until his death, staying three to four months. Technically, he was engaged in product testing and research, and the old man's lengthy stays may have stirred grumbling back in his New York offices, but never from tarpon anglers. He developed a special drag reel for catching their fish: the Universal Star, patented in 1896. The best cost $70, about $1,700 in today's currency.

Two years later, vom Hofe justified that expense. He caught a record 210-pound tarpon at Captiva Pass. In a smudged photo of the record holder standing next to his trophy, hanging by mouth and gill from a rafter of the Useppa boathouse, the fish bigger than the man, vom Hofe wears a coat vest over long shirt sleeves, a dark hat with the brim rolled up, like a Vaudevillian jokesmith, and a lure hooked to the band. His right hand grips his rod fitted with a Universal Star reel, while his left lights a celebratory cigar in place of his usual pipe. He is jubilant, transported, practically dancing a jig.

IF VOM HOFE SEEMS TO BE OVERREACTING, he might be forgiven. Tarpon fishing was an antidote for the perceived emasculation of his generation, linked to the disappearing American frontier, urban expansion, and a nation at peace. Sons of the bourgeoisie were gripped tightest by this crisis of manhood. Managing a trust fund didn't require physical exertion, and while one could demonstrate his masculinity in the dog-eat-dog world of high finance and business, he could still be weak in body. A flabby physique, once a mark of status that distinguished the manager, owner, and heir from the sinewy-bodied worker—a fishing guide, for example—was falling out of fashion. A country led by effete men—"with shoulders that slope like a champagne bottle," as Theodore Roosevelt put it—allegedly jeopardized national security.[35]

Competitive sports, western adventure, and war were the beneficiaries of the national-masculinity zeitgeist. Boxing's image evolved from brutish senselessness to manly art. Football replaced rowing as the most important intercollegiate sport. Theodore Roosevelt, who epitomized and valorized American masculinity, maintained that gridiron play steeled future leaders with grit and self-discipline, and the imperative of winning. He also believed in the transcendent power of an errand to the badlands, mountains, or canyons of the American West giving passage to manhood. He went west countless times. He also went to war, in Cuba against Spain in 1898, for the good of American manhood—a war staged out of Tampa. His famous ascent of Cuba's San Juan Hill was an exhibition of both American victory and virility.

Hunting big game was chief among Roosevelt's masculine endeavors. He usually went after four-legged terrestrial prey and left the contemplative art of fishing to enthusiasts. But in March 1917, the former president took a trip to Captiva Island. Congress was a week away from a special session to consider entering the Great War in Europe, and as a fan of the most masculine sport of all, he would be there lobbying for US involvement. A suitable warm-up to engagement in the political wilds of Washington was sparring with a wild animal fighting for its life. TR arrived at Punta Gorda with his usual entourage, and shook hands with local muckety-mucks for the usual corps of press photographers. At Captiva, he rented a fifty-foot houseboat, literally a white clapboard house set on a floating barge, flying the American colors from the stern. Tarpon mania had given rise to a trade in houseboat rentals that catered to weekend bachelors on cigar-and-bourbon retreats.

TR wasn't on the Gulf for bourbon, or to devote much time to tarpon. The most famous outdoorsman in America—in history—set trends rather than followed them. He went to tarpon country to harpoon devilfish, known today as devil rays. He called them "great sea brutes," ignoring the reality that devilfish, despite their name, are among the most graceful and passive creatures of the sea. Upon one victory, a photographer captured him shoreside in triumphant mode, posing gladiator-like with seven-foot harpoons crossed before his chest, a bandanna around his neck, left foot triumphantly atop a slain devilfish, with Gulf waters washing its lifeless sixteen-foot wingspan. Five male companions stand with the Rough Rider. Cowboys of the sea, the group could have been posing with a dead bison on the plains or a bear in the rocky badlands.[36]

William Halsey Wood's disciples referred to themselves as tarpon hunters and tarpon slayers. Their big game added something more to the adventure than did an elephant or hippo that dropped in unison with the delayed report of a rifle. Tarpon challenged you. That was its appeal. Going up against a fish that matched or exceeded your weight and height and fought like heavyweight champ John L. Sullivan, leaving you bathed in sweat, spent and sore, with bruised knuckles and burned thumb (from the line), renewed a faith in your physical self. At the same time, there was an element of excitement in landing a large, powerful, agitated fish in a small boat. Even exhausted, a "live" one on board was like a lunatic madly swinging an oar. People got hurt. A guide was killed when a tarpon, in a final burst to survive, knocked him cold and over the side. "Beside the tarpon," wrote Henry Wellington Wack, author of yet another book extolling the saltwater angler's toughest contender, "all other quarry of the sea is tame."[37]

Big-game fishing, says Paul Hendrickson, who has written fluently about Hemingway's salt life, "wasn't a competition so much as a passion undertaken for its own sake." It was man against fish first, and against man second—and then woman. Confining Victorian womanhood was on the wane, and in no place more so than on the water. Women rejected any notions of tarpon hunting as exclusively male—though happily ceded the lubricated frat-boyish houseboat weekends to the other sex. Mina Edison's love affair with tarpon fishing was as intense as Thomas's. She encouraged her infatuation in their children and generated a stream of letters back north with fishing reports, knocking tarpon that rebuffed her bait as the "sauciest things." Women hunted tarpon in the company of their husbands and on their own, decorated the club-room walls with proof of their passion, and posed with some mighty fish.[38]

Christine B. M. Hawley had her picture taken at Useppa on May 6, 1914. A widowed thirty-one-year-old New York socialite with a fancy for bridge playing, she was a strikingly small woman. In her trophy shot, she squints into the sun from behind prim eyeglasses and wears a billowy ankle-length walking skirt (standard attire among her fishing contemporaries) topped by a mock navy-style white jumper with bib collar and neckerchief. The mouth of the hanging tarpon is gaping as broad and round as a basketball hoop. The fish looks big enough to swallow her. Hawley was the first woman to receive a silver button, awarded by the inn's anglers club to guests who landed a tarpon weighing 150 or more pounds. Hers tipped the scales at 154½. Recognition of an arcane sort survived a century later. The inn's restaurant served an eight-ounce Angus-beef burger, "grilled to your liking," named the C. B. M. Hawley.

Hawley had used a vom Hofe. When the reel designer caught the tarpon that made him dance, he broke a record held for seven years by another widow, Mrs. George T. Stagg. The historical record leaves a virtually barren trail to her life, not even a sign of her own name; such was the state of American womanhood when women lacked the vote and, when married, personal rights and a separate identity. The trail leads through her husband, a Kentucky whiskey distiller on his second marriage, and to little more than a single platitude within the documents: "Mrs. Stagg" possessed the "charming modesty of her sex."[39] She caught her 205-pounder on the Caloosahatchee from the family yacht and, beyond charming modesty, exhibited it at the Chicago World's Fair in 1893.[*]

UP UNTIL AROUND THEN, tourists visiting the water-surrounded state gravitated to the interior rivers and freshwater springs, those mystical fountains of youth that supposedly inspired Ponce de León. Every year, fifty thousand excursionists went to Silver Springs—as many as went to Niagara Falls—from Jacksonville on paddle wheelers that navigated jungle-shrouded rivers through the state's watery heart.

---

[*] The US census indicates that the first Mrs. George T. Stagg was named Elizabeth and died around 1877. George may have remarried before the 1890 census was taken, but the manuscripts were burned in a fire. He died in about 1891, around the time the second Mrs. George T. Stagg caught the record tarpon. If she appears in subsequent census records, she cannot be identified.

They came to see exotic wildlife—birds feeding, turtles sunning, alligators basking, otters playing. A century later, they would have been called ecotourists. Beach bathing eventually supplanted the attractions of the interior, but not before tarpon tempted the tourists away from it, when islands and shorelines of dune grass and scrub were turned into resorts of clapboard and shingles for fishing enthusiasts.

As noted earlier, Henry Plant perceived the trend toward the coast. The year he showed off his taxidermy tarpon specimen at the centennial exposition, he opened a hotel, the Belleview, on the Gulf side of Tampa Bay. It was located at the end of a spur across a peninsula named, centuries earlier, *Punta de Pinal* for its stands of tall pines. Plant sacrificed the heartwood of the natural landscape to build the Belleview, ultimately sprawling to 820,000 square feet beneath a green Swiss-chalet roof. Billed as the largest wood-frame structure in the world, it was soon to become another angler's rendezvous.

Not long after acquiring the Plant railroads in 1902, the Atlantic Coast Line Railroad opened service to Boca Grande on Gasparilla Island to carry out phosphate excavated at the Peace River and to carry in anglers. Intentionally or coincidentally—certainly fittingly— the name Boca Grande (big mouth) matched the anatomy of the fish responsible for the resort's national recognition. In Dimock's view, there was no "better tarpon fishing in the world than can be had at Boca Grande."[40]

Two years later you could take the train to Fort Myers. After the decommissioning of its military post, Fort Myers had little reason to exist. Then tarpon stirred life into the place, made it into the eastern Gulf's fishing headquarters, bricked its streets, erected its houses, capitalized its businesses, made it the county seat, and landscaped its boulevard with eighteen hundred royal palms transplanted from the Everglades. "Every branch of its trade," *Forest and Stream* wrote, "is, more or less, influenced by the fishing industry." On April 14, 1898, when news of imminent war in Cuba against Spain plastered the front page of every daily in the country, the *Fort Myers Press* highlighted instead the year's "Official Tarpon Record."[41]

A town had its priorities. Fort Myers boasted the best selection of lodging on the Gulf coast, from basic to luxury, and a night life, which included the twenty-four-hour Tarpon Restaurant, and the Silver King Bar and Billiard Hall. It had the Heitman-Evans Company, reputedly the largest outfitter south of New York's Abercrombie and Fitch. If you forgot something in your tackle box or needed—to wit, wanted—new equipment, Edward Evans would set you up. Zane Grey said that Evans stocked the largest selection of fishing tackle of any store. By some accounts, Fort Myers had the best guides, who charged up to six dollars a day (twice the rate over on the Texas coast), and townspeople thought of the visiting anglers as "walking gold mines." Someone calculated that for every tarpon taken—389 in 1894—local businesses made $500. That "someone" was probably Evans, who kept catch records for the chamber of commerce.[42]

A tad down the coast, at Naples, remotely beyond the reach of locomotive service until 1927, a T-shaped fishing pier reached several hundred feet into the Gulf. On any given day, anglers and fish-panhandling pelicans went elbow to elbow on it; at night, moonlit dances and cocktail socials projected music and the thrum of melded conversation and laughter across the water. Storms routinely wrecked the pier, and once, someone's smoldering cigarette butt set it afire. Neapolitans, the main of whom were relocated Kentuckians, always rebuilt it. The pier was the mainstay of the economy. Nearly three decades before the train came, when anglers arrived twice weekly on the Plant steamer *Tarpon*, the *New York Times* said the "watchword" in Naples was "are they bitin'." This was in a two-column feature expressing concern about fishing tourists bypassing New York for the Gulf coast.[43]

To Texas and Mexico they also went—not only skirting New York, but coming from it. They came from St. Louis, Duluth, Billings, Wichita, Cleveland, Boston, Toronto, London, Newark, Baltimore, Louisville, Pasadena, Long Beach, and Chicago. In 1891, the Lone Star State Show rolled into the Windy City aboard the Santa

Fe Railroad. It was a chamber-of-commerce lollapalooza, with three handsome coach cars converted into a traveling exhibit of the state's offerings. Tightly scripted representatives claimed Texas had the biggest and best of everything, except taxes—still the best, but in this case, of course, the best meant *not* the biggest. Come to live or come to play, they were saying, and to prosper either way. Amid the hype, the exhibit's show-and-tell articles were pretty standard fare, if not uninteresting: building-stone, timber, meats, fruits, grains, and corn. But there was one standout, a mounted 110-pound tarpon.

The Texas coast turned into a silver-king mecca practically before anyone knew it was happening, and through an odd turn of events. Northern sportsmen had long traveled to the coast to shoot ducks. Favored hunting grounds lay near Aransas Pass, the name the colonial Spanish gave to a Y-shaped natural waterway connecting Corpus Christi and Aransas Bays to the Gulf. Sometime after 1890, when the state contracted an engineering firm to build a rock jetty to improve navigation, engineers and crewmen, many of them Croatian immigrants, noticed the fish activity in the water. They hired some of the local commercial fishermen to row them out into the pass, where they caught tarpon. Before long, sportsmen were turning their hunting trips into fishing trips. The late start behind Florida in angler tourism didn't discourage the Texas coast from advertising itself as the realm of the silver king.

Chambers of commerce were keen to cash in on tarpon fever. In 1892, when someone caught the sleek game fish off Cumberland Island, Georgia, the *Atlanta Constitution*, calling tarpon fishing the "greatest of all sports," was certain the Georgia coast would divert traveling anglers away from the Gulf. The East Tennessee and Western North Carolina Railroad, traditionally a grimy hauler of iron ore, put the Cumberland trophy on tour to increase passenger service. Although wayward tarpon have ventured up to Nova Scotia, their warm-water druthers tend to keep them south. Coastal Georgia was never able to cash in like the lower Gulf. Even up around Mississippi and Alabama, anglers usually snelled on tackle used for speckled trout, mackerel, redfish, and snapper. These are tamer species, but good eating. And few complained about their luck. "One day's fishing," wrote *Daily Picayune* journalist Martha Field of Louisiana, "landed us nearly twenty, dozen fish from eight lines"—enough, she said, to lure Izaak Walton from the grave for a day on the water.[44]

In southern Texas, you didn't have to accept a trade-off. The waters offered the spectrum of both edible and strictly sport fish. To get to tarpon from interior Texas, you could ride the San Antonio and Aransas Pass Railway from San Antonio, home of the state's number one tourist destination, the Alamo, 260 miles to Rockport. A schooner would then run you down to Aransas Bay and out to Mustang Island, two hours on a steady wind and ebbing tide, six under unfavorable conditions. If your tastes were the least bit discriminating, you would likely stay with the Hatfields, pleasant and accommodating mother-and-son hosts of the Tarpon Inn at Tarpon, Texas, the former barracks of the jetty builders. Its reception room walls were covered with silver dollar–sized scales. Many had been pinned up by Mary Hatfield herself, who once took four tarpon in two hours—the smallest, six feet and 125 pounds.

An alternative route to the good fishing came up from Corpus Christi, connected by train to New Orleans. A lot of anglers stayed south and fished around Laguna Madre or went on down to Port Isabel for tarpon that were chasing baitfish running up the Rio Grande. At the Tarpon Inn, newly arrived guests would keep watch from the cupola for silver kings jumping around the guide boats, each flying an identifying pennant, and decide which boat to hire the next day. Guides charged three dollars an outing—"pretty good wages," said one—and came with names like Pompano Red and Pontoon Mack.[45]

In late November, mullet drew *el Sábalo* up the Río Pánuco and anglers to Tampico, Mexico. This was the hallowed river on which Alonso Álvarez de Pineda, the first European to round the Gulf, had met his final fate. Indians still traveled in hand-hewn canoes, often laden with oranges and great bunches of bananas, sharing the broad waters with pink flamingos and white wintering whooping cranes.

"Under the rosy dawn the river quivered like a restless opal," wrote Zane Grey, who had fished these waters more than once.[46]

The same crowd from the north—described snippily by Martha Field as "those New York millionaires"—fished at Tampico. They practiced their Spanish on tolerant guides, and puffed on cigars and traded lies around diminishing bottles of tequila at cafés full of south-of-the-border atmosphere. Perhaps a little greedier than most anglers, the American in Mexico was often looking to get a head start on the Texas fishing season.[47]

Tarpon hunting in Texas and Florida lasted roughly from March to August. Some blue-water anglers swore the sport was better in Texas, and the tarpon, of course, bigger. One said that fishing Aransas Pass was like floating "at the end of a rainbow." Someone landed a 234-pounder in 1894—a catch that should have smashed Stagg's record but one that, apparently, never received official confirmation. Like everything else, big specimens and big numbers came out of Texas. A dozen delivered to your hook in a week's time was nothing. They were combative too, supposedly more so than those Florida fish. One angler claimed that a Texas silver king fought him for five hours.[48]

Texas had a lot of stories that keepers of tarpon lore loved to tell—two in particular, about angling presidents. The first involved Warren G. Harding. An opportunity for a holiday on the Gulf came up just after he won the presidential election in 1920. He and the First-Lady-to-be, Florence, were invited by a campaign donor to play golf at Port Isabel near the Mexican border. Harding's schedule allowed mornings to tarpon fishing, a new sport for him, and afternoons to golf, his keenest obsession. Caught on film during one outing, he is wearing dark trousers, white shirt, and tie, with canvas shoes and straw sun hat. As he hams it up for the camera crew trailing him, his movements are twitchy on the old 35 mm celluloid. He declared Port Isabel his "favorite fishing spot at the end of the world." He was charming the locals, but his declaration didn't lack sincerity.[49]

Eight years earlier, when Harding was languishing between political offices, the *New York Times* had noted, "Society is giving up its golf

clubs for the tarpon rod." When Harding was later at the top of his
political career and in Texas, he made a profound statement by cancel-
ing two afternoons on the links, truly his favorite place outside home,
to try for a trophy on the water. A seven-footer snapped his line—the
big one that got away. Luck delivered him a four-footer the next day.
Florence, whooping and crowing, then landed one that came in at
two hundred pounds and just under six feet. It turned out to be the
year's record tarpon. The president-elect got the headlines, the imminent First Lady got the bragging rights, and Port Isabel got priceless
publicity.[50]

After Harding, voters elected two more Republican presidents
before choosing an avuncular Democrat to pull the country out of
the Great Depression. Franklin Roosevelt's son Elliot was a regular
visitor of Aransas Pass. In spring 1937, Elliot persuaded his father
to order the presidential yacht *Potomac* to Texas for tarpon fishing.
Barney Farley, owner of a local tackle shack, got the call to be the
president's guide. Later in life, Farley would have two memories of
Roosevelt. In one, imprinted in his memoir, Farley said the president
was unfailingly gracious, excited as a boy to catch a fish, and eager
for Farley's instructions on how to handle a hooked tarpon. In the
other, recorded in an interview for a sportfishing book, he described
the president as deaf to angling advice, unteachable, thrashing his rod
around like the baton of a possessed orchestra conductor. Either way,
FDR caught fish. It's all on a Movietone News reel—the president
strapped in a fishing chair, his crescent-moon jaw and indelible smile,
tarpon after tarpon gaffed for him at the side of the little powerboat
bobbing in choppy water. He fought one for an hour and twenty minutes, obliging him to miss a press conference. That was okay. The press
boys were out there in their own boats bobbing around, and the public
too. People cheered every time the Gulf served up a writhing prize.

THERE IS A MESMERIZING black-and-white photograph, circa
1900, of a solitary man on Naples's six-hundred-foot fishing pier.

Wearing a dark, casual suit, he is wielding a rod two and a half times his height, his feet open in a batter's stance, left hip against the dock rail for support, left hand gripping the rod, right arm akimbo with hand on right hip, the weight of his upper body pulled back to offset whatever might hit his line. We don't know the extent of his luck, but we can guess that it was excellent. The Gulf was generous in that way. Around the same time on the other side in Texas, a Denver man took eighty tarpon at Aransas Pass in twenty seven days.

People took, and why not? The tarpon bit, and anglers piled up the numbers. Fishing clubs were formed to promote the sport. At Useppa Island, Barron Collier and others founded the Izaak Walton Fishing Club, predecessor to the Izaak Walton League of America, which devoted itself to conservation. That wasn't the Useppa group's goal—not at first. It was the same as the Aransas Pass Tarpon Club, headquartered in a town called Sport. It had organized "in the interest of a higher standard of the sport." Weight took favor over volume, the club pledged. Numbers were the goal of the common market fisher, not the dignified angler. "A true sportsman will never boast the quantity he bags." The club gave out gold and silver buttons to those who caught trophy-sized specimens, the same as the silver button that Useppa's Izaak Walton Fishing Club awarded Christine Hawley for her trophy. Still, everyone who talked tarpon talked numbers. Newspapers tallied daily and seasonal "kills"; this was their word, used without compunction. *Forest and Stream* reported catch numbers, hotels gave out prizes for the most fish caught, and there were all those tarpon scales on club walls.[51]

It was a contest: who could make nature tender the most. In a single day in 1889, the founder of Naples, Walter Haldeman, publisher of the *Louisville Courier-Journal*, caught ninety-four fish. The next year, a New Yorker at Punta Rassa landed 199 tarpon from January through March. Dimock once caught 334 in fifty-two days, or so he said—sixty-three on a single fly. Tampico's 1906 season included 1,287 tarpon. At what point did the sport lose its meaning? As early as 1895, the *New York Times* reported, "So many Northern sportsmen now annually visit the tarpon fishing grounds of the Gulf States that the big fish are becoming scarce and shy in some of their first discovered haunts."[52]

A decade into the next century, anglers had a problem and knew it. They had ignored Juliana Berners's timeless prescription: "When you have a sufficient mess you should covet no more." Tarpon stock was dwindling. During some seasons, that stallion of a fish seemed to forget to come inshore and play its expected role as game. At Aransas Pass, part of the issue was a shifting emphasis toward water commerce. The village of Tarpon was renamed Port Aransas, and the jetties were reconstructed to deepen the way for cargo shipping, with the result that the monarch of game species snubbed the pass. The dual damming of the Rio Grande in later years had the same effect near Port Isabel, where anglers once had caught tarpon from the shore at the river's mouth. That happened south of Houston to the Brazos River, dammed and fouled with industrial waste. Where estuaries no longer existed, starved for freshwater and smothered by pollutants, the tarpon no longer rolled.

Early on, the main problem, everywhere, was silver-king mania. The fish were caught, killed, photographed, occasionally mounted, and thrown away. It was a waste. The Izaak Walton Fishing Club took initiative and called for a practice of catch and release, making the tarpon one of the first game fish targeted for conservation—albeit, save-the-sport conservation. Hawley introduced, and may have designed, a special hook, the circle hook, that usually stuck before going down into the gut where it might tear apart the innards.

These were noble measures, though ignored by most anglers. If one season was bad, they waited for the next. When the tarpon returned, the killings resumed, increasing in number as more anglers crowded passes, coves, and river mouths. Paradoxically, tarpon tournaments, with huge prize money, sprang up around the Gulf: Aransas Pass, Port O'Connor (Texas), Grand Isle (Louisiana), Sarasota, Boca Grande, Veracruz. Randy Wayne White lent Doc Ford's name to a tournament at Boca Grande Pass—and then withdrew it.

The killing was the one part of the history of tarpon fishing that bothered White. When he was a guide, his clients released most of their tarpon. But he "winced" when he thought of those kept and hung for a picture, or caught legally but unethically by the technique of snagging: using a bottom-weighted hook to literally snag the fish, with death the likely outcome—fishing's "dirty little secret," he deemed it. A century after the Izaak Walton Fishing Club's initiative, White stopped sponsoring the Boca Grande Pass tournament because it permitted snagging to continue under a different name. He also urged the Florida Fish and Wildlife Conservation Commission to designate the tarpon a catch-and-release species, and it did.[53]

Americans had cultivated an industry in sportfishing while developing a remarkable skill for capturing a remarkable fighting fish. It was a testament to their ingenuity and perseverance and their love of sport. At the same time, they were ominously inclined to leave their imprint on nature, as did many others not among the sporting class.

Eight

BIRDS OF A FEATHER, SHOT TOGETHER

Mother and baby egrets on Avery Island, Louisiana, where they
received protection from hunters acquiring feathers
for the women's hat industry.

In French it is long-beak; *and of such a nature it is,*
When it comes to its young birds, and they are great and handsome,
And it will fondle them, cover them with its wings.

—Phillipe de Thaon, "The Pelican,"
translated by Thomas Wright (1841)[1]

AT DUSK IN APRIL ON THE FAR SOUTHERN SHORE OF Argentina, a bird standing in the surf readies to follow its instincts. It's a small bird, less than two ounces, lighter than a couple slices of bread. Its beak is straight and narrow, and dark with a hint of orange, a flute that peeps and squeaks. Its belly is white, and on top, replacing winter gray plumage, snowy feathers lace warm-brown ones. Pivoting its head on a barely discernible neck for a final preening, the bird reveals more white above the base of its tail, and thus its name. The white-rumped sandpiper has been in Patagonia since December, gorging on marine invertebrates. Its reserve of fat will soon convert to fuel. Once dark descends, the sandpiper will rise on a seventeen-inch wingspan, nearly three times its body length, orient its direction by the stars, and draw toward a destination its species has known for millennia: the American Arctic.

This bantam bird is one of the pluckiest migrators in the world. By the time all is said and done, it will have flown seven thousand miles, staying aloft for up to sixty hours a stretch. The entire length of South America passes below before its first stop at Venezuela. After rest and replenishment, it again travels under a starlit ceiling, with its companions—each a mere foot apart—beating wings over the western Caribbean and the Yucatán, and then, without stopping, across the Gulf. When the sandpipers make landfall between Texas and Louisiana, they drop into a Spitfire dive straight toward earth, still in winged formation, and touch down gently at water's edge. For a week, they will feed at the surf on marine worms, mollusks, and crustaceans before pointing their compasses north again.

In spring 1915, an article in a Honduran newspaper discussed birds crossing the Gulf as a matter of common knowledge. American ornithologists claimed otherwise, insisting the aerial feat was beyond the animal's capacity. When Wells W. Cooke of the US Department of Agriculture's Biological Survey, who kept scrupulous migration records, tried to dispute them, they scoffed. They scoffed even though they knew about the writings of William Bullock, an English horticulturist who, in 1824, was joined on a schooner north of

Campeche by hundreds of alighting birds migrating "from the north side of the Gulph of Mexico to the coast of Yucatán." They knew about Martin Frazar, who, fifty-seven years later, was pitching in a spring storm thirty miles out from the Mississippi River when more than a hundred birds of two dozen varieties—warblers, flycatchers, swallows, and snipes among them—appeared out of the south and sought refuge on his boat. They knew about navy seaman W. T. Helmuth, who recorded crossings by land birds while patrolling the greater Gulf during the First World War. And it was true that John James Audubon and learned correspondents, among them John Bachman (of Bachman's sparrow fame), spoke of Gulf passages, including that of hummingbirds, as accepted fact.[2]

Twice a year, a billion birds passed over the Gulf and the heads of doubting ornithologists. The book of Job and Jeremiah make references to migrating birds; and Homer, Herodotus, and Aristotle tracked seasonal flights. Yet modern science cracked the code for nuclear fission before it accepted the validity of a trans-Gulf avian execution.

The scientist who set out to see who was right—the believers or the doubters—was George H. Lowery Jr. A zoologist from Louisiana State University, he hitched a ride on a Norwegian freighter sailing out of New Orleans in April 1945. The ship steamed directly across the epicenter of the Gulf. Lowery could not have been farther from shore when he spotted birds flying overhead at all hours of the day and night. He also identified twenty-one species of land birds that came aboard to rest. Once the freighter was berthed on flat water at Progreso, Yucatán, he set up a telescope and observed silhouettes silently winging across the moon—north, he wrote, in the direction of Louisiana. Fifteen years later, when scientists began using storm-tracking radar to study bird migration, everyone was a believer. Ultimately, they learned that more than two hundred species from dozens of families clear the Gulf twice a year. The sea, it turned out, accommodates the Mississippi and parts of the Atlantic and Central Flyways, three of North America's four migration routes.[3]

Their travelers are winged pilgrims, and North America is their

Mecca, where their ancient annual rituals ensure the future of their species. Among many many others, Baltimore orioles and ruby-throated hummingbirds journey from Central America; indigo buntings and American redstarts, from the West Indies; bobolinks and chimney swifts, from South America. A south-to-north Gulf hop is about six hundred miles; circling around the coast would just about double the distance, so most birds fly direct. The Yucatán Peninsula is an ideal staging platform, a geographic godsend for the migrators. They use it as a rest stop, munching on tropical insects and sipping on tropical blossoms in preparation for the long haul. When the time comes, thousands rise to treetops at twilight and, like the sandpiper, take off when the stars come out. They will fly all night and into the next morning or afternoon before landing in the northern Gulf—twenty to thirty hours in the air, depending on conditions. Theirs is the longest open-water migration of land birds in the world.

Besides being a shortcut, the Gulf crossing has other advantages. For one, the migrators are troubled by no predators; the sky belongs to them. For another, they've been doing this for thousands of years. They devote the off-season to fattening themselves—what scientists call hyperphagia. A gram of fat will yield a warbler 125 miles in the air. Finally, they ride the seasonal winds that begin sweeping in toward the northwest from the Bermuda High over the tropics. Not all make it. Some late in age fall exhausted from the sky. Some encounter storms that can be disastrous for thousands. Scientists have opened the bellies of sharks and discovered unlucky songbirds. Yet the majority avoid mishap, and most of those end up on the coasts of eastern Texas and western Louisiana.

While they're in flight, surface water currents prepare for their arrival by pushing seaweed ashore packed with scrumptious invertebrates. This is the way nature works. Spent sandpipers, plovers, sanderlings, gulls, and other surfbirds will devour the provisions like the famished marathoners they are. For the exaltation of incoming land birds, spring warmth has brought out insects in trees and shrubs and under last autumn's leaf fall.

Every April and May, it seems as if the entire avian kingdom is endeavoring to Gulf shores. Tens of millions arrive daily. Some will travel an extra thirty- or forty-mile leg to inland forests. Chimney swifts are usually the first to come in, and hummingbirds soon follow. The migrants appear in every size, shape, and color—plumage aglow for the approaching nuptial season. Thousands make the approach together, drop as a cascade out of the sky, and then a wave breaking over the greenery, until trees are inundated with busy noises and song. The feeding begins straightaway, "without preamble," writes the naturalist Scott Weidensaul, "without stretching or relaxing or preening." Birders refer to this type of phenomenon as a "fallout"; in the American Sea, they call it the Gulf Express.[4]

"Happy birds!" John Muir wrote during a short stay on the Gulf in 1867. "It is delightful to observe the assembling of these feathered people . . . gracefully taking their place at Nature's family table." Because the Gulf shore is a food factory, it sees so many birds—ocean, wading, surf, land, and island birds, the passers-through, seasonal visitors, and permanent residents. There even come the blue-faced booby and the red-throated loon. A meeting ground between temperate and tropical zones, the Gulf is the northernmost migration point for fair-weather species and the southernmost for cold-weather counterparts. Ducks, sparrows, and hawks—as, too, the loon—migrate no farther south each winter than the Gulf. Sieges of egrets, herons, spoonbills, wood storks, and ibises fly no farther north in the spring, joining the infinite multitudes that stay year-round.[5]

In late July, migrators begin to feel the pull to return south to winter homes. Of those that summered on the Gulf, surfbirds leave first, along with birds passing through from the north. Soon after the terns, oystercatchers, and black skimmers that nested on Florida's St. George Island depart, warblers by the tens of thousands from the Northeast replace them. Some are only a month or two out of the nest. None will stay long. The barrier islands are way stations for the retreating hordes, their colors no longer so radiant. Fall migration continues into October, a time of year when the seasonal airstreams tend to lead the birds along the eastern side of the Gulf. The white-rumped sandpiper shows up from the Arctic in September. Crossing hemispheres, it will soon be back in Argentina.

It was a September hurricane that sank the fifteen-ton *Flower of France* between Aransas Pass and Galveston in 1886. A salvage crew discovered six hundred bird carcasses. They were *not* migrating victims of the storm that had alighted on the schooner for protection. Also found on board were several hundred dollars' worth of guns and ammunition.

The cargo of the ill-fated *Flower of France* affirmed what William Earl Dodge Scott had learned earlier that summer. One year, one month, and twenty-four days after William Halsey Wood caught the tarpon that changed the Gulf coast, Scott was on a schooner scouting the same waters. He wasn't after fish, as was almost every other person in a boat. He was an ornithologist, recently turned thirty-four, on a collecting expedition for Princeton University's museum of biology.

In those days, the observation phase of natural history occurred primarily in the laboratory, with scientists going outdoors to gather specimens for study indoors. The distinguished progenitors of American ornithology, Alexander Wilson and John James Audubon, carried two wooden boxes into the field—one with paints and brushes, and the other with powder and shot. A gun was Scott's most important field instrument. Although a bad leg from childhood had left him dependent on a cane, he could deftly negotiate the snarl of woods and mangroves to get off a shot.

On his 1886 Gulf expedition, however, he rarely fired his gun. In terms of collecting, the trip was a bust. Something was horribly amiss.

Seven years earlier, Scott had seen this grim future, confirmed in the exotic interior of Florida. He had traveled then on the Ocklawaha River, the principal artery of Florida's popular "jungle" cruises. Wildlife was the main attraction at the time, but the jungle was quiet. The riverboat crew explained that previous excursions had turned into impromptu hunting safaris. Armed passengers—a common lot—amused themselves by using red-bellied turtles, otters, alligators, herons, and ospreys, anything living, for target shooting. The tourist trade was now suffering for the want of viewable wildlife, though the crew blamed timid creatures rather than gun-happy excursionists.

Scott knew better. So did Harriet Beecher Stowe, who had enjoyed the river cruises on the Ocklawaha before witnessing the killings, described to her as a sport. "Certainly," she wrote with a heavy heart in her book *Palmetto-Leaves*, published in 1873, "this is an inherent savagery difficult to account for. Killing for killing's sake." If the shooters had been traveling by train on the Great Plains, railcar windows would have been blazing like a warship's gunports, and a line of dead bison would have been left ghosting the tracks across the prairie. From the Dakotas to the Gulf, nonhuman life in the late nineteenth century didn't stand a chance against the casual toxicity of human indifference.[6]

Scott's latest Gulf expedition would expose infinite barbarity. His hired sloop, the *Tantalus*, competently captained by an old sponger named Baker, shoved off from the docks at Tarpon Springs in May and headed down the winding Anclote River. Scott was traveling with his wife, Marian; their dog, Grouse; and an assistant. They saw anglers everywhere. The water was full of excitement, though not for the ornithologist. On Scott's earlier trips to the Gulf, great flocks had blotted out sun and sky, but now anglers outnumbered birds, and avian colonies that had once pulsed with life were dead-still. The entire coast had become a slaughter zone. The killing had not been random and recreational like that on the Ocklawaha River; it had been methodical and industrious. And yet it was the same—complete.

Behind it all were forces radiating in from afar, up north and abroad, and from an unlikely source, the women's hat industry. The straw sun hats women favored to screen out the intense light when tarpon fishing weren't the problem. Those worn to socials, dinners, and church were. Some were as big as a bird bath, blooming with long, airy feathers; and you might not even see the bonnet, for the bouquet of plumes. Preeminently fashionable in Victorian society, feather hats were expensive, significantly more than the price of a top-end vom Hofe reel. Still, they were a must-have adornment of the cosmopolitan well-to-do in America and Europe.

Designer favorites in feathers were long, lithe ones, like those of egrets, herons, ibises, wood storks, spoonbills, and flamingos—any of the large wading birds. The product was not merely picked up from the ground, where it might have been shed, as the industry liked to say. Fashion and money generated catastrophe in every known corner of the world. A handful of fine mating plumage from snowy egrets earned a commercial hunter the same as an ounce of gold. So it's little wonder that killing birds for hats amounted to one of the bloodiest crimes committed against wildlife in modern times, equal to the destruction of North American bison and beaver. In those better-known episodic carnages, pelts and hides at least provided warmth to those who demanded them. Even that fabled symbol of forced extinction, the passenger pigeon, blasted out of existence in an eyeblink, ended up in food markets and restaurants. Feathers for hats amounted to nothing more than vanity.

Gulf wading birds were a primary target. Had they not come under the protective wing of Audubon groups, women's clubs, a US president, and the king of Tabasco sauce, representing the birth of conservation on the Gulf, they might have been wiped off the map.

THE EXTENT OF THE KILLING JUGGERNAUT was made plain when Captain Baker took the *Tantalus* into Tampa Bay. At the entrance was Maximo Rookery, historically one of the most productive bird colonies in the entire Gulf. Once the roosting home to nearly 100,000 birds, a clamor of hyper wing-flapping, squawking, and nest building of twenty-five species, Maximo was no longer a rookery. The lonely brace of mangrove islands had been left in a state of avian undress, with the white stain of guano and tumbledown stick nests the only evidence of the rookery's former preeminence.

Scott and company were witnessing the handiwork of the "Old

Frenchman." His real name was Alfred Lechevelier, or it might have been Jean Chevelier. No one knew for sure. Like a wandering gull, he just appeared on the coast one day. He spoke a curious type of pidgin English and apparently came from Montreal, although he referred to life in Paris as if it were home. In 1881, he bought 120 acres on Pinellas Point, within striking distance of Maximo. Fifty years earlier, another Frenchman, Count Odet Philippe, had introduced citrus to the point, and for a long while a handful of settlers caught fish, raised cattle, and grew oranges. That changed overnight after the *Journal of the American Medical Association* in 1885 declared the point the "healthiest place . . . of any portion of Florida." Consumptives and asthmatics from the North converged on the area, and many others came across the bay whenever yellow fever and other diseases struck the port of Tampa. The healthiest spot on earth was anything but that for birds.[7]

After dispensing with Maximo, the Old Frenchman and his two assistants shot their way down the coast to the Ten Thousand Islands. In the Everglades, where Chevelier accidentally put a bullet through his right hand, he adapted by learning to shoot with his left, and he continued the blitzkrieg, leaving his assistants to skin and pluck the birds and store the feather bounty aboard his schooner. Somehow the ruthless feather hunter became the namesake of a creek in Pinellas, a bay in the Ten Thousand Islands, and the construction company that built the first highway to traverse the Everglades. Many years hence, he lingered in Burl Ives's portrayal of a manic plume boss in the 1958 B movie *Wind across the Everglades*. Gruff and rotund, wearing a persistent sheen of sweat on his bald head and bearded face, he was addicted to violence, an outsized character in Technicolor.

Scott followed Chevelier's bloody trail from one rookery to another. There were hardly any birds on the bays at Sarasota, and at Gasparilla Island, but a pair of reddish egrets, two white ibises, and three herons that had somehow escaped the plundering. The few living specimens that Scott happened upon he described as frightened. And then— "Charlotte Harbor!" Scott's exclamation appeared in a report he sent to *Auk*, the journal of the American Ornithologists' Union (AOU).

Before Scott mailed the dispatch, the postmaster at Punta Gorda told him that hunters had annihilated local heronries in two swift seasons.[8]

Scores of plumers competed with the Old Frenchman. Feather agents advertised in newspapers and by word of mouth to recruit native "gunners" (as Scott called them) with the promise of easy money, and responses poured in. New York agent Joseph H. Batty contracted with up to sixty hunters. There was a time when Batty had sought feathers for nothing more than camouflage for wildlife traps and for museum collections and laboratory research. Those less lucrative endeavors remained a sideline as long as he could sell plumes to milliners.[9]

Ever the innovative huntsman—he wrote an instructional book on shooting, trapping, and poisoning wildlife—Batty armed his associates with breech-loading shotguns designed with a combination twelve-gauge barrel and a less-destructive and quieter .22-caliber barrel. The latter was used for small birds and close-range shooting. His forty-five-foot sharpie schooner was a cargo vessel and a familiar one calling at ports, islands, and fishing-boat piers to take delivery of feather consignments. At Gasparilla Pass, Scott watched Batty's hunters row to shore from the anchored schooner, and for the next few hours, until dark, the pap-pap-pap of gunshots crossed the sky. They were using the .22's. Investigating the next morning, Scott learned they had shot terns and sandpipers.[10]

In late June, Scott returned to peaceful Princeton. If he had extended his travels to other parts of the Gulf, he would have learned about the six hundred bird skins that went down in the Texas storm with the *Flower of France*. The hurricane that sank the schooner most likely preempted the killing of thousands more. Diminishing dividends on the nearly shot-out Florida coast sent plumers to better their prospects on the barrier islands and coasts of Louisiana, Texas, and Mexico.

Feather agents had put the word out that they would pay top dollar for the now-scarce egret plumage. Biologically, the egret's white feathers lacked pigmentation yet possessed a silky purity that designers coveted. Three years later, an AOU reconnaissance of the Texas coast revealed that the "snowy product" could hardly be found. By that

time, agents had resorted to taking whatever was available: terns, avo-
cets, willets, pelicans, herons, gulls. One plumer apparently delivered
a thousand of a mixed lot, representing a week of gunning. By the late
1880s, Texas islands of yucca and cactus were dreadfully quiet. In the
pages of *Science*, the highly respected curator of birds at the American Museum of Natural History, Joel Asaph Allen, lamented that the
"havoc . . . as wrought in Texas prevails all along our coast-lines."[11]

Not far from Allen's Upper West Side Manhattan office, New York
dealers had recently taken delivery of feathers from seventy thousand
birds shot around a single village on Long Island. Plumers blasted
away at nesting colonies in Australia, Africa, the Middle and Far East,
South America, and southern Europe, shipping their spoils across
regions, continents, and oceans. In 1902, commercial salesrooms in
London, a vast fashion market in itself, reported an inventory of fifty
thousand ounces of feathers. In number of birds, that weight equaled
192,000 adults and two to three times as many nestlings and eggs
lost—all from the US, and most from southern coasts. Four egrets
made a mere ounce of plumes. It was not unusual for someone like
Chevelier and Batty to deliver a shipment from 100,000 kills. An
Audubon Society member said birds were "taking their last meal."[12]

In the winter just before Scott went to the Gulf, the ornithologist
Frank Chapman spent two afternoons walking Manhattan's uptown
retail district. He counted 542 feathered hats representing 174 species,
from sparrows to ostriches. Some hats had whole birds—wings, head,
beak, feet, and all. The most flamboyant headgear flaunted feathers
from wading birds, and many, undoubtedly, had previously been part
of the Gulf's natural flourish.

Before the slaughter, wading birds were central to the exotic that
attracted tourists, like ocean sunsets and palm trees. Memoirs, journals, and letters back home rarely failed to mention an egret, heron,
wood stork (old ironhead), or neon-pink spoonbill. Some long-necked
waders stood to a man's chest, stiff in posture and almost mechanical in
the way they stepped about on stick legs with inverted knees. Ending
a day of fishing, their twilight ritual easily captivated any onlooker.

Passing overhead, author Marjory Stoneman Douglas wrote, "they would move in their white thousands and tens of thousands, with the sounds of great stiff silk banners, birds in flocks, birds in wedges, birds in wavering ribbons, blue and white crowds, rivers of birds pouring against the sunset back to the rookeries."[13]

Wading birds tend to be solitary—except ibises, which are partial to feathered company—and all are vivid. Their nests in mangrove and cypress trees (wood storks prefer the latter domicile) are strikingly visible, as are their daily labors in shallows or wetland. Disciplined fishers, some of these waders remain improbably still, like living statues performing in a public square, until something edible comes within reach of their swift beaks. Others, including the snowy egret, shuffle through shallows to stir up prey.

Belonging to the heron family, snowys hatch from baby-blue eggs in low-hanging nests built from twigs and reeds. As adults, they reach to about twenty-four inches and three-quarters of a pound, making them medium-sized. From birth, their feathered center of gravity remains flawlessly satin-white above long, strikingly black legs and yellow feet that you would swear had been dipped in a bucket of paint. The colors repeat on a beak the length and shape of a small saber. In breeding season, the yellow turns orange-red, and nuptial plumes emerge billowy and sheer white. George B. Sennett, a specialist in Texas-coast birds, thought snowys were the "prettiest of all the herons." Their range spans wetlands across the globe's midriff, and their bloodline dates to the Pleistocene, when on the Gulf they lived with mammoths, pre-European horses, camels, llamas, and giant three-toed sloths, fauna that failed to survive geological and climatic changes and the crude weapons of early humans. Egrets, more flexible and adaptable, did. But they could not endure the modern hunter's gun.[14]

NOTHING APPALLED Edward Avery McIlhenny of Louisiana more than people gunning down egrets. The act assaulted his southern gentleman's sensibilities, not to mention his affinity for birds.

He developed his empathies in the environment of his youth, a wooded and wildlife-crowded island ensconced in Louisiana's marshy coast. Birds love it there. It gives them the basics of life: food, nest-building material, protection, and respite during migration. Ned, as McIlhenny was called, was born on the island among wintering avian hordes in 1872, the year Yellowstone became the country's first national park. He never left, save for college, business trips, and adventures to the top of the world. As a blue-eyed, blond-haired boy, he would go fishing with his father and uncles and sit in the skiff bored by their sport and conversation but fascinated by the "egrets and herons stalking along the edge of the flats." Once old enough, he would row out on his own to watch and study. He drew and painted the birds and wrote poems. He devoured works on ornithology and, many decades later, wrote a young readers' book titled *The Autobiography of an Egret*. It wasn't long before he realized that the wading-bird population around the island was suffering. He heard the guns and saw the discarded bloodied, feather-stripped bodies. The mutilation had to be stopped.[15]

McIlhenny was amply prepared to do just about anything he wanted. Whether it was creating an expansive flower garden, experimenting with bamboo cultivation, or running the family business, enterprise inspirited him. He was also born into privilege. The McIlhennys owned the island, named Avery after the family of Ned's maternal grandfather, Daniel Dudley Avery. It was a quiet paradise scented by wisteria, cypress needles, and magnolia blossoms; shaded by those trees, too, as well as live oaks and tupelos; rained on sixty inches a year; wet with ponds, coves, and creeks harboring turtles, fish, and crawfish; brilliant with planted azaleas and camellias; animated by parakeets, ivory-billed woodpeckers, and an assortment of wading birds. Three miles long and two and a half wide, Avery is so hemmed in by marshy cordgrass (*Spartina alterniflora*) that it doesn't look like an island. It rises a stunning 162 feet above sea level at its highest point, like a mountain in horizontal bayou country 140 miles west of New Orleans. Before the Civil War, the island and slave labor afforded Daniel Avery elevated status as a successful sugar planter.

Salt went with that sugar too. Avery Island is over a subterranean dome of rock salt—hence its elevation. The first to mine it were the island's original white settlers, Irish immigrants with a Spanish land grant parceled out to good Catholics in the New World. Rock and sea salt were valuable as a spice and food preservative. Saltwater distilling—essentially boiling seawater in a large kettle above a wood fire— was one of the Gulf's oldest industries, dating to the colonial period. During the Civil War, the Confederates got most of their meat from Texas and Florida cattle; and sea salt to preserve the meat, from Gulf water. As part of the supply blockade, Federal gunboats patrolling the coast fired shells wherever wood smoke and steam rose together through treetops—a sign of a distillery. Mining a salt dome eliminated the distilling process and served to the advantage of whichever side controlled the mine.

During the Union siege of New Orleans, the Avery family was in self-exile in Texas. David Farragut's forces took control of the island and reopened the rock-salt mine to supply their commissary. After the war, Daniel Avery rounded up former slaves, now paid laborers, and returned to sugar growing. He also took a lesson from his former enemy and partnered with a firm to mine the salt. Royalties from the operations secured his family's financial security after his death in 1879.

Salt was a lucrative legacy, but Edmund McIlhenny, Ned's father, left a spicier one. Heavyset with a thick black beard, he had the look of a well-fed parson or a banker. He had been the latter in New Orleans before the war, when he married Daniel Avery's daughter Mary Eliza. The postwar economy, arbitrarily controlled by Yankee carpetbaggers, left him without a job. He and Mary returned to Avery Island, where they had a roof over their head and Mary's salt royalties. But Edmund needed a purpose.

That's when he started experimenting with Tabasco peppers brought in from Mexico or Central America. A descendant of Spain and the Columbian Exchange, the bright-red finger-shaped peppers under his care were growing robustly on the island by 1868. He worked tirelessly in a brick-and-clapboard outbuilding, grinding ripe ones into pulp. He aged the rubicund mash in stoneware jars, covered in Avery Island salt to seal in the flavors, mixed in vinegar, and continued the aging. Weeks later, he poured the spicy results into cologne bottles ordered from a New Orleans glassworks, and on each he stuck a label, "McIlhenny's Tabasco Brand Pepper Sauce."

His creation was soon adding zest to steaks, stews, soups, gumbos, and a lot of those oysters and shrimp taken from the bayous. Without the local seafood diet, he might not have been inspired to create his sauce. Its culinary contributions notwithstanding, the country was in an economic depression when McIlhenny died two decades later, and the company was struggling. Tabasco making fell to his eldest son, John. Despite laudable efforts to turn things around, the brand was faring little better when he joined the Rough Riders during the war against Spain in Cuba, and climbed San Juan Hill beside Theodore Roosevelt. The next son, Ned, stepped in to run the company. He streamlined operations, downsized product offerings, and, to achieve a fuller flavor, extended the aging process in repurposed Jack Daniel's white-oak whiskey barrels. Kicking new life into sauce making, Ned slowly turned the family business into a profitable operation.

Its success was, in some ways, a reflection of McIlhenny's abounding personality and appetite for adventure. According to family lore, he wrestled alligators and shot the largest on record, nineteen feet; sparred with Gentleman Jim Corbett, holding his own just before the contender KO'd heavyweight champ John L. Sullivan; and rescued two hundred stranded seamen, among them Jack London. McIlhenny probably never traded jabs with Corbett, and never threw a lifeline to London. But he was undeniably an intrepid adventurer who once helped save the crews of ice-bound whaling ships.

He was twenty-five at the time, and handsome in youth. His hair, then parted in the middle, would in later years be combed back from his forehead, and a trimmed mustache would be gone. The projection of virility, however, would endure. He always wore his social advantages like a pair of comfortable old shoes, walking in them wherever it struck his fancy. In 1897, he left his rock-salt island for ice country on a self-funded expedition—he and two assistants—to collect prized specimens of Arctic wildlife, including the white-rumped sandpiper. The trio established a base camp at Point Barrow, Alaska's northernmost reach. Besides wildlife, only natives and Christian missionaries lived there, with the whaling fleet passing through in summer until early fall.

This wasn't McIlhenny's first time in the frozen north. Three years earlier he had been in Greenland with Frederick A. Cook (who would claim to be the first explorer to gain the North Pole) when their ship sank and they required rescue. Point Barrow, Alaska, brought back memories of that experience when several whaling vessels carelessly lingered into late summer. "Getting worried about them," McIlhenny wrote in his journal on September 6. Within days, slabs of pack ice formed around the ships, threatening the stranded crews with starvation. McIlhenny joined in a rescue effort launched by the US Revenue Cutter Service to hunt food for the marooned. In a book chronicling the event, John Taliaferro writes that Ned exhibited the skills of a "winged shooter extraordinaire," acquired in his youth on fall days spent hunting waterfowl. To save the whalers, he shot several thousand ducks, one day killing 430. All told, his deadeye tack secured nine thousand pounds of meat.[16]

It turns out there were some birds McIlhenny wanted to shoot and some he wanted to save. In a southern latitude four thousand miles from Point Barrow, a parallel rescue was in the works. It involved McIlhenny's benign passion for avian life, and he pursued it virtually singlehandedly. He came up with a simple but not-so-obvious solution to save overhunted egrets: a birdcage. Between the Alaska and Greenland expeditions, he and hired help enlarged a pond on Avery Island and, beside it, built a huge aviary framed in bamboo and covered with wire mesh. Next he located two egret nests, fragments of Avery's vanquished bird kingdom, and pilfered their eight juveniles for the birdcage. He took over as parent, feeding and interacting with them daily. They were soon, he said, "evincing real pleasure in being near me."[17]

In late fall, when the young were able fliers, he had the birdcage dis-
assembled, expecting its occupants to migrate south. Two nights and a
frost later, they were gone. Come March, he walked the grounds daily,
hopeful of a homecoming. On the eighteenth, he discovered that four
of his snowys had returned to a bushy area where the aviary had stood.
Two days later, another couple flew in. In no time, two nests were
under construction, stick by stick. Eight birds hatched that spring.
Thirteen egrets flew south in November, and in March, all returned.
By summer, Avery Island was nursery to twenty hatchlings, and as the
years rolled on, the population doubled, tripled, quadrupled. Before
long, cousin birds joined the egrets. When the new century arrived, so
did some two thousand winged breeders.

McIlhenny did not fully blame local hunters for the crisis he was
combating. He saw them as victims of a changing environment, even
if it was change they helped precipitate. Shooting and trapping wildlife had always been a way of life in Louisiana. Alligators, for one,
had been hunted in fresh and brackish waters around the Gulf for
centuries, ever since the 160-million-year-old cold-blooded American
reptile captivated European explorers. Around the time he rediscovered the mouth of the Mississippi River for the French in 1699, at
the birdfoot delta, Iberville wrote in his diary, "I killed a small one,
8 feet long." Cotton mills and riverboats used alligator oil to lubricate machinery, and the Confederates turned the hide into saddles
and boots, and the meat into rations. In McIlhenny's time, alligators
passed into a second life as purses, satchels, and shoes. Teeth, eggs,
feet, and baby alligators, live and stuffed, were widely popular novelties of nature.[18]

Between 1880 and 1933, Louisiana surrendered 3.5 million alligators to the market; Florida, twice as many. The alligator and egret
populations went into tailspins simultaneously. The difference was
that hardly anyone cared about the welfare of alligators; their one
salvation was the plume market. Once it opened, alligators became a
comparatively low-paying dangerously pursued prey. The only salable
part of the hide, the belly skin, went for ten cents a foot. One young

hunter questioned why anyone would hazard infested waters when "a day's wages of plume-hunting" was equal to a month's of "gator hunting."[19]

Other wild populations faced worse. White-tailed deer recovered from the skin trade intensely executed by native and European hunters, but bears, beavers, and more did not. By the time of the feather trade, hunters and the market had settled for raccoons and muskrats. Enter the raccoon-skin coat craze of 1920s collegiate life, and yet another population tumbled. To keep Louisiana active in the fur economy, someone hatched the idea of developing nutria farms. Semiaquatic rodents, nutrias might be the result if you crossed an otter with an eager beaver. They are like feral hogs of the wetlands, nuisance creatures that multiply as if on fertility drugs. Within a couple decades, twenty million were setting their grossly large incisors to indigenous vegetation, clearing areas that locals called "eat outs." In the twenty-first century, when the fur market collapsed, the multiplying rodents chewed up as many as forty square miles of wetland vegetation a year.

McIlhenny had one of the first nutria farms, and for a long time, the historical record blamed him for importing the giant rodents from Argentina and unleashing them on the Louisiana coast. Yet other nutria farms predated his, which he began with a start-up population purchased from a New Orleans dealer. After the market could no longer sustain the ventures, farmers released their nutrias.

Birds weren't an environmental nuisance like nutrias and didn't bite your arm off like alligators. And their feathers fetched princely sums, which drew local hunters out in force. Among the bird-snatching enthusiasts were people who had, up to that time, fired a gun for nothing other than table food. The money, observed an Audubon warden, was a "terrible temptation to many real fine fellows." Before, when locals were killing wading birds only for food (in the Ten Thousand Islands, they called egrets "Chockoloskee chickens"), guns had hardly nicked the population. According to the AOU, the hat trade consumed five million birds annually, leaving the Gulf by century's end with ten percent of its original plume-bird population. Chapman said it was nearly impossible to find a bird for a photograph. At the height of the slaughter, more bison survived on the Great Plains—eight hundred, tops—than snowys on the Gulf. It seemed the egret was on the verge of becoming a memory and museum piece.[20]

Market hunters typically didn't look toward the future, but many ultimately couldn't stomach a complete serving of their vocation's violence. The best time to shoot the birds was after their eggs hatched, when the adults were still wearing their valuable courtship plumes, and the rookeries were full and occupied around the clock. At the sound of gunfire, instead of scattering, the parents shielded their young. Orphaned nestlings were left to wild prey, or to perish in the sun. Guilt set in when one hunter couldn't reconcile killing mother egrets with "doing God's service." The young man who was drawn to the wages of plume hunting over alligator hunting ruined himself for the trade: "I couldn't stand it, hearing those hungry little birds."[21]

Sympathy for wildlife was an occupational hazard. If you worried yourself over killing, you wouldn't have a job. Whether slaying for the market or just living off the land, being tough on nature seemed a necessity. Birds suffered for this compulsory callousness and not just in giving up feathers. At Pelican Island near Galveston Bay, George Sennett, the Texas ornithologist who liked snowys so much, made a shocking discovery: "Every square yard of the island," someone told him, had once flapped and chattered with nesting pelicans. That was before a few "enterprising men" landed on the beach with a venture scheme: kill and boil down the birds for oil. Within a few years, Pelican Island had no pelicans. But the exhausted supply was of little consequence, financially speaking. The would-be capitalists never found a market for the oil.[22]

You didn't have to be in nature to be hard on it. Your impact could come from a sheltered distance, and with the wrenching of a single object from its domicile. To use the passenger pigeon example again, borrowed from Jennifer Price's wonderful book *Flight Maps*, patrons of Delmonico's of New York weren't giving a thought to the origin of the bird on their plate beyond the restaurant's steaming kitchen, or to their personal role in its imminent expiration. With birds on hats, there was the same disconnect from the pandemic slaughter.

In urban, industrial society, turning to nature for standards of dress and personal expression had become common. Looking down on London streets from her apartment window, Virginia Woolf wrote, "Plumes seem to be the natural adornment of spirited and fastidious life, the very symbols of pride and distinction." Birds had a feminine quality, so people thought. Converting feathers—ample, dramatic, and frolicsome—into women's fashion made aesthetic sense, if not for the one fatal ecological twist: natural beauty encouraged borrowed beauty, while borrowed beauty decimated natural beauty.[23]

Feathers on head, blood on hands; that's how McIlhenny saw it. He condemned the "barbaric love of adornment." The national press and the science and conservation communities vilified female vanity. "It is a barbarous taste that craves this kind of ornamentation," wrote the famed naturalist John Burroughs in *Century Magazine*. FASHION HAS NO SOUL, screamed the top of a four-deck headline in the *Washington Post*. The article beneath it could not abide "Madame," who "is but resting on her guns before looking about for other fields to exploit." Endless appeals went out to maternal tenderheartedness: mother birds were being killed by the millions. *Can't you see this!* Burroughs, Chapman, McIlhenny, and others were shouting. The president of the League of American Sportsmen said women had forsaken the moral high ground upon which to castigate male recreational hunters "for being cruel to animals."[24]

Woolf had equally harsh words for the "tinted and powdered" woman who offset her "stupid face" with a feathered head. The writer, however, was too perceptive to let men off the hook. Critics of women's bloody fashion sometimes ignored the fact that it was a man's world. Men shot the birds, and they owned the millinery concerns and the stores that displayed feather hats in their windows. Men ran the newspapers that, year after year, printed page after page with headings proclaiming: LEADERS OF FASHION ARE WEARING . . . , SMART WOMEN

ARE WEARING . . . , FASHIONABLE GIRLS ARE WEARING . . . , PARISIAN BEAUTIES ARE WEARING . . . , and so on. The *Washington Post*, the same gazette that proclaimed fashion without soul, used the words "poetry" and "grace" in a full-page spread on the latest plume-wear. Female journalists typically edited the fashion pages, and women retained some control in dress choices, but, as Woolf recognized, they made them in a social context largely dictated by men. The dominant sex was no stranger to vanity either. With tidy mustache and canted bowler, men put much stock in being seen with an elegant woman on their arm, feathers and all.[25]

McILHENNY LEANED TOWARD the camp that held women accountable for the demand in feathers. At the same time, he knew that women, custodians of social standards and organized in clubs, led in making bird killing a moral issue. Among their most immediate concerns were boys with BB guns taking aim at winged targets, and the proliferating cat population "slinking about" bird feeders. To deal with the former, they launched education campaigns and wrote letters asking juvenile magazines to stop selling ads to air rifle companies. More extreme measures were deployed against what a newspaper writer called feline bird slayers. In St. Petersburg, a club woman named Katherine Tippetts persuaded the city commission to adopt an ordinance to exterminate "all tramp cats."[26]

Tippetts had the tribal influence of her local Audubon Society behind her. Bird-loving club women channeled their passion into Audubon; in some places, society rosters were a carbon copy of women's club rosters, amended with a few male names. Nationwide, female Auduboners outnumbered males sixteen to one. Organized conservation, whether coming out of Audubon or women's clubs, was part of the late nineteenth-century rise of American Progressivism, a social and political response to the economic and social problems related to rapid industrialization and urbanization—problems such as political corruption, monopolized corporate power, the exploitation of factory labor (including child labor), and the senseless destruction of wilderness and wildlife.

Famous people were associated with American Progressivism: Theodore Roosevelt, William Jennings Bryan, Alice Paul, Jane Addams. A major push for reform came from women's clubs, whose agendas included multiple causes, ranging from mandatory school attendance and public libraries to prohibition and woman suffrage—the usual back-burner issues for men. Club memberships were made up of socially prominent women with the time to devote to public and human interests, and although they lacked the vote, as the popular *Picayune* columnist Martha Field wrote, they were a "power in the South of fearful force when they organize."[27]

Connections and networking meant everything to someone like Katherine Tippetts, a widow unhampered by wifely duties, a hotel owner and property manager, published author, consummate civic worker—active in two dozen groups—who ran for public office the moment law allowed. She helped launch the local women's club and duplicated its membership into the St. Petersburg Audubon Society, over which she presided for thirty-three years. She also served terms as president of the Florida Federation of Women's Clubs and Florida Audubon Society.

Young Cecile Seixas of Galveston seemed on a similar trajectory when she organized the first Texas Audubon Society in 1899. Tragically, the next year, fate swept her, her mother, two sisters, and more than eight thousand others away in the Galveston hurricane. In 1903, Millie Eva Lamb and Hope Turhune assembled a new group in La Porte, on the mainland side of Galveston Bay.

Women often seized the initiative and then, strategically, convinced effective men to work for them. The chief lobbyist for the female-dominated Texas Audubon was a genuine gunslinging former Texas Ranger named Mervyn Bathurst Davis. Davis, who had Wild Bill Hickok long hair and mustache, wore a six-shooter on his hip. Presumably, the gun remained on his hip when he went to Austin to persuade legislators to pass the AOU's model law.

Drafted in advance to ease legislative adoption, the model law could be tailored by legislators to their liking. Pretty typically, the Texas law prohibited the sale of wild-bird feathers and the taking of eggs belonging to shore and wading birds—a festering problem. While visiting the Dry Tortugas in 1832, where roosting birds swirled in a "cloud-like mass," Audubon witnessed Cuban egg hunters using sticks to knock thousands of birds out of the sky. They ultimately "laid in a cargo of about eight tons of the eggs of the tern and the noddy," which they sold in Havana and Key West for twenty-five cents a gallon.[28]

Decades later, Gulf-side dwellers looked ravenously to wild eggs as a seasonal food source, and not unreasonably. For the first time since the previous nesting season, skillets would sizzle with eggs and pork bacon. Still, the homey smells of this spring jubilee masked the foulness of improvidence: egging was effectively sterilizing a race of birds. Townspeople converged on nesting areas, overlooking hardly an egg, smashing each with celebration. This was a precaution against taking home partially developed embryos. A day or two later, after newly laid eggs appeared in the same nests, the hungry human phalanx returned to rob again, this time carefully filling tubs and barrels with fresh takings.

New York was the first state to pass the model law, in 1886, although its essence had appeared in the statute books of a Gulf state nine years earlier. Remarkably, in a year when Florida was mired in a presidential vote count scandal that tainted the election's outcome, state lawmakers had the presence of mind to outlaw the destruction of plume birds and their eggs. Elsewhere in the region, legal protection lumbered along slowly. Thirty years passed before the last of the Gulf states, Alabama, embraced the model law.[29]

State and federal bird protection was an Audubon Society priority. As a national organization, Audubon had two births, the first in 1886. George Bird Grinnell, a naturalist with a most appropriate name, not to mention a beak for a nose, founded the Audubon Society at the very moment Chapman was counting bird hats in upper Manhattan and the AOU introduced its model law, and just before William Earl Dodge Scott discovered ghost rookeries on the Gulf. Grinnell was editor of Charles Hallock's *Forest and Stream*, based in New York. A man in the know, Grinnell was in the position to publicize his new organization. Membership quickly exceeded fifty thousand. Caught off guard, he was too overwhelmed to run both a magazine and an organization, so he reluctantly dissolved the latter.

The good intentions survived, nevertheless. Chapman founded *Bird-Lore*, a bimonthly magazine, to monitor the plight of birds, and McIlhenny built his birdcage. In Boston, a city with milliners and feather agents, Harriet Hemenway read about the avian pogroms with strong emotions that she transformed into constructive deeds. Hemenway came from an affluent family (John Singer Sargent painted her portrait) that believed social privilege obligated one to altruistic endeavors. Her ancestors had agitated to protect hunted runaway slaves; she would agitate to protect hunted birds. In 1896, she recruited her cousin Mina Hall and, plucking names from the social register, they organized the Massachusetts Audubon Society. Nine hundred women formed its core membership. Others elsewhere followed their example and started state and local societies—Cecile Seixas in Texas, for example. On the Gulf's other coast, nine women and six men organized the Florida Audubon Society in 1900.

Several state groups began meeting annually in New York City before incorporating the National Association of Audubon Societies in 1905. Its mission, said its newly elected president, William Dutcher, was to place a "barrier" of wise laws, bird sanctuaries, and wardens between wild birds and "selfish people."[30]

As states fell in line with the model law, the national association piloted an aggressive lobbying effort for federal bird protection. Five years earlier, Congress had passed the Lacey Act, which authorized federal prosecution of anyone killing birds in violation of state laws. The first case prosecuted under the act had involved a shipment of gulls and terns from Brownsville, Texas, to New York. Then, responding to some 200,000 letters and the barrage from Audubon lobbyists, Congress added a ban on imported plume fashions to the federal Tariff Act of 1913.

Commercial bird hunters were now *poachers* operating outside the law. Yet good law is little good without enforcements. The Gulf states employed no wildlife officers, and the US Department of Agriculture, charged with enforcing federal bird protection laws, posted agents at shipping ports but not at killing grounds. Where it could, the US Lighthouse Service pitched in, with its keepers watching out for poachers. Birds prospered under the care of the keeper at Matagorda Island Light in Texas, and his counterpart on Timbalier Island in Louisiana shooed eggers away like so many cats. Troubled by the enforcement gap, New England artist Abbot Thayer raised money for employing wardens and handed it over to Dutcher, then head of AOU's Committee on the Protection of Birds.

One of the first wardens Dutcher hired was thirty-two-year-old Guy Bradley. He was assigned to watch over the lower Everglades, Florida Bay, and the Keys. Reared in the islands and wetlands, Bradley knew well that he was policing a domain habituated to its isolation and against outside authority. He also knew that when he pinned on his warden badge, though deputized by the county sheriff, he made himself no less fair game than a plume bird. A fractious poacher named Walter Smith, who had known Bradley since he was a boy, shot him during an attempted arrest and left his body adrift in his patrol boat, *Audubon*. It was a depressingly low moment for bird saviors when a Key West grand jury refused to issue an indictment. Weeks later, National Audubon was incorporated.

A brother was down—the first; then justice was denied, deterrent withheld. Wardens had every reason to reassess their safety, to quit even. The wolves had taken the shepherd to get to the flock. The other wardens stayed on their watch, nevertheless, including Columbus MacLeod, guarding volatile Charlotte Harbor. He lived alone and exposed in a tiny, tidy wood-frame house shaded by a single scrub oak and sabal palm fronting a sturdy little two-plank dock. He surely knew the wolves were circling. Every year birds returned to reclaim roosts, and every year hunters came for them. In November 1908, they came for MacLeod, and he went missing. Having been sunk with sandbags, his patrol boat surfaced with clues of his demise. Inside was MacLeod's hat, holding shards of his skull. His body was never found. The wolves took down a third shepherd that year in South Carolina.

Implicated in the violence, the National Millinery Association, keeper of the industry's public image, defended itself on the public relations front. Feather fashions were legal and hatmakers honorable, it assured consumers. Taking the offensive, the association accused Audubon and Chapman, who pitched public denunciations in arena after arena, of smear tactics that threatened not only a multimillion-dollar industry but the economy, healthy again after the long depression of the 1890s. Hardworking people could lose their jobs, industry spokespersons claimed, shaping the issue into a choice between people and birds.

In a funk since the murders, Chapman chose people, although he wasn't siding with the industry. He advised against putting new wardens in the poachers' crosshairs, while a dispiriting cloud settled over Audubon headquarters. Dutcher, mourning the loss of his recruits, inelegantly suggested that integrating bird colonies with leper colonies would be more effective than laws or wardens.[31]

DESPITE THE GLOOM, bird sanctuaries were flourishing—apart from leprosariums. The success of McIlhenny's Bird City had not gone unnoticed.

In 1903, Dutcher and Chapman took a request to President Roosevelt at his Sagamore Hill, Long Island, home. Roosevelt had tremendous respect for his solicitors: the idealistic Chapman, who believed everyone was "born with a bird in his heart"; the entrepreneurial and always meticulous Dutcher, who had catalogued every bird known to inhabit Long Island. They wanted Roosevelt to declare Pelican Island on Florida's east coast a bird reserve. He agreed, and met the request by executive order. The two-and-a-half-acre dollop in the fish-filled Indian River was the first federal set-aside initiated for the sole purpose of sheltering wildlife. The Gulf was next in line.[32]

Roosevelt had long before established his bona fides as a bird lover. His interests were studied and deep, dating to when he was a boy. He could whoop like one too, whenever he identified a bird that an outing companion could not. As governor of New York, he signed bird protection laws, and as president, he kept a running list of feathered creatures on White House grounds. More Audubon groups elected him an honorary vice president than he probably knew. The Gulf's birdlife first caught his attention when he was hunting wolves in Texas and bears in Louisiana and Mississippi. In 1904, it was apparent that his characteristic bully pulpit verve was not reserved solely for trust-busting. He turned it against plumers, "sordid bird-butchers," and eggers, an "unprincipled minority wasting the heritage of unborn generations." With another stroke of his pen, he made the Breton and Chandeleur Islands off Louisiana a federal bird reservation.[33]

The reserve was one salvo in the Roosevelt revolution: the setting aside of hundreds of millions of acres of protected federal land. Previously, the government had given away land like beaded necklaces at Mardi Gras to predatory moneyed interests, which believed the resources of the public domain—minerals, fur, oil, water, timber—were an entitlement of free enterprise. TR gave life to fifty-one bird reservations.* Eleven of those were in the Gulf, including East Timbalier Island in Louisiana, a stopover for Arctic-bound white-rumped sandpipers; Passage Key, once shot out by the Old Frenchman, Chevelier; and three around Charlotte Harbor. Roosevelt had explored Passage Key while waiting in Tampa to be shipped out to ride against the Spanish in Cuba, and he would hunt devilfish around the Charlotte Harbor reserves years later. In 1915, after he was out of office, he toured Breton Island, the only one of his bird reserves that he visited.

Tagging along, a motion picture crew recorded him on film. A black-and-white former president, his midsection grown round, wears long sleeves and trousers, buttoned up tight, his socks pulled over the cuffs, and a softened campaign hat pulled low, all guarding against

---

* Some sources say he created fifty-three reserves.

mosquitoes and no-see-ums. He walks across stippled celluloid frames, gingerly in stocking feet through sand and dune grass. Tern nests lie everywhere and must not be damaged. Later he would argue for the government to exterminate pillaging raccoons to preserve the nests of birds and green sea turtles. The man in the stocking feet, nevertheless, bends over his bulge to dig up a clutch of eighty-four turtle eggs. A companion later said they made a "real delicacy for our table."[34]

Breton is one of the northern islands in the Chandeleur group, a major wintering roost for travelers of the Mississippi Flyway, and summer breeding ground for roughly thirty-three species. Some nest on the ground, some on scrub, and some in mangroves. The Roosevelt film predates sound technology, but, watching it, you know the former president is stepping through an aural season of high-decibel cheering, screeching, and squawking mixed with low-decibel chattering, quacking, and fluttering. There is plenty of nourishment in the sea, in bayous, and onshore for adults to quiet complaining broods. Dashing around and overhead, they wheel, soar, crisscross, veer, careen, swerve out and up, and in and down. A chaos of flight to Roosevelt was perfect aerial performances in nature.

TR wrote about the trip in *A Book-Lover's Holidays in the Open*. He praised McIlhenny as the mayor of Bird City. That single accomplishment—the birdcage and restoration of the egret population—was enough for people to start calling the pepper brewer an ornithologist, and for Louisiana Audubon to elect him president when it organized in 1902. He soon began engineering new projects. He and a friend, Charles Willis Ward, a wealthy New York businessman who moved to California to open a nursery, conceived a plan to buy swatches of coastal real estate to retain as a patchwork of sanctuaries. Ward helped McIlhenny cultivate camellias and develop what became Jungle Gardens on Avery Island, and one can imagine their plans for sanctuaries taking shape as they prepared the garden.

In 1911, Ward and McIlhenny bought a large tract of marshland and donated thirteen thousand acres to the state of Louisiana to create a waterfowl refuge (where in later years it had to exterminate runaway nutrias). That same year, they approached the extravagantly wealthy Olivia Sage, philanthropist widow of Russell Sage, a Gilded Age Wall Street titan. They asked her to buy Marsh Island, a seventy-six-thousand-acre insular haven of ducks and geese. It was an easy sell. A bird lover, Sage scooped up the island and dropped it into the lap of the state, with the requirement it be made into a wildlife sanctuary.

McIlhenny in the meantime purchased eighty-six thousand acres of wetland near Avery Island, using donated money supplemented with his own. Much like a conservation land trust of later years, he was looking for a benefactor. Sage introduced him to John D. Rockefeller, and the billionaire's foundation bought the property. The Louisiana Conservation Commission managed it for five years before the foundation transferred title to the state, which created the Rockefeller Wildlife Refuge and Game Preserve.

In Florida, sanctuaries were popping up in local communities like spring crocuses—beautiful ones in the eyes of club women and Audu-boners who cultivated them. Tippetts was responsible for eleven in the St. Petersburg area. In Texas, the state land office leased Green Island on the southern coast to Audubon for a dollar a year. The organization's warden, R. D. Camp, successfully fended off poachers, despite his "disagreeable" rheumatism. It helped that the island was a citadel of thorny acacias, with diamondback rattlesnakes holding down the fort. "You don't come to Green Island for your good health," one of Camp's successors told wild-bird photographer Ted Cross decades down the line. For twenty-seven springs, Cross traveled from Princeton with camera and snakebite leggings to photograph the island's reddish egrets, a "sensational heron of great beauty, rarity, and comic charm," as Cross described it. The sanctuary and its wardens had ensured that birds would be around for future generations.[35]

For Roosevelt and McIlhenny, that's what conservation was about: the future. Looking ahead, the president of the Florida Federation of Women's Clubs wrote to McIlhenny. She was seeking counsel on the "proper means of attracting wild life" to the Everglades state park that her organization was developing. The ultimately long road to Everglades conservation began with saving egrets. Two years later, in 1918, McIlhenny counted twenty thousand nesting birds on Avery Island. He was feeling good about the egret's future.[36]

Mercifully, the future arrived, and the carnage slackened. It shifted to Europe, from man against bird to man against humanity. The Great War between nations redirected resources away from civilian markets and fashion. Women's outfits shed several yards of cloth, and hats grew smaller, in part to complement the latest bobbed hairstyle and accommodate new enclosed automobile designs. When women working the red-light districts, which were booming around military installations, took a fancy to feather-wear, women of proper society boxed up their plume hats for fear of mistaken identity. Vanity once again succeeded where moral persuasion had not. Still, bird laws, wardens, refuges, Auduboners, and E. A. McIlhenny introduced a meaningful spirit of conservation to the Gulf.

AT THE TIME PEACE WAS RETURNING to rookeries around the globe, new gunfire was shattering the air over Gulf waters. A visitor could have shouted, "They are shooting the pelicans!" The shooters were fishermen.

The Gulf sees two of the world's eight pelican species: the brown and the white. Whites fly in for the winter and muster on barrier islands, while browns are year-round locals. Someone a long time ago described pelicans as "grotesque," and others, including ornithologists, repeated the insult across the years. Frank Chapman came to their defense, saying they deserve our respect. "Pelicans," he wrote, "became pelicans before man became man."[37]

Around the mid-twentieth century, renowned Gulf artist Walter Anderson drew them as if they were the most handsome birds on earth. Indeed, they were long an icon of the region. Aborigines replicated them in carvings and masks, and their headlong aerial dives repeatedly captivated early European visitors. When Iberville returned to Louisiana in 1704, he captained a ship named the *Pelican*. In 1887,

New Orleans's minor-league baseball team adopted the name Pelicans, and Louisiana chose the brown as its state bird, emblazoned on its seal and flag. St. Petersburg's city logo featured a pelican perched on a dock piling—a position the birds have taken for as long as docks have existed. Finally, there is Dixon Lanier Merritt's catchy limerick:

Oh, a wondrous bird is the pelican!
His bill holds more than his belican.
He can take in his beak
Enough food for a week.
But I'm darned if I know how the helican.

"Enough food for a week," however, was the offense that led to the bird's execution during the war. Entering the conflict in Europe in 1917, the US faced a food shortage. Fish prices soared, and fishermen enthusiastically cashed in. Stuffing fish into its three-gallon throat pouch, the largest of any bird, the pelican stood accused of eating into the fisherman's income. Louisiana's French settlers had endeared pelicans with the name *grand gosier*—"big throat"; that sizable gullet later implicated them in their alleged crime as robbers, thieves, and pirates. Their classic crashing dive into the water for food was a disquieting reminder to American fishers that their competition was at large. So they shot the birds and smashed their eggs.

To their detriment, pelicans are a gregarious lot. Comfortable around humans, they are unabashed panhandlers, fearless. Why not? They outlived dinosaurs. They also have the protection of Leviticus chapter 11, which declares them a forbidden meat. Anyone who has ever fished off a pier or boat knows that doing so is not a solitary experience. Even if you're alone, you're not. A brown pelican is invariably trying to get chummy with you. They'll blithely drift up to a trawler, boat landing, dock, or quay looking for handouts.

To market fishers, pelicans were not chums, but bums. Gulf fishermen complained loudly to their legislatures and governors about the feathered fish filchers. They wrote US Food Administrator Herbert

Hoover, petitioning for eradication. Quoted in a Tampa newspaper, one of the aggrieved said, "Give the fishermen the right and we'll quick clean 'em out." Said another, "I have seen one pelican eat enough fish in 20 minutes to last any family a week." A shrewd legal advocate for the fishers could have found amicus material in the journals of John James Audubon; the spiritual forebear of bird protectors claimed that the number of fish "destroyed" by a single pelican was "quite extraordinary." Absent Audubon, the complaints had a patriotic ring. Fishers were feeding a country at war while pelicans were a "menace of no small proportion."[38]

Aside from disgruntled fishers, no one wanted another bloodbath. Chapman and others insisted that the beef against pelicans lacked merit. To settle the matter, the US Food Administration asked T. Gilbert Pearson to investigate. Pearson had grown up near the Gulf, but he would not have been the fishers' choice for the assignment. He was an executive officer in National Audubon. Collaborating with the conservation committees of Texas, Louisiana, and Florida, he had hundreds of pelicans shot and sent to Washington, DC, for stomach dissection. Not a single food fish was found. The Gulf states determined that pelicans were innocent of all charges and should be left unharmed. That year, 1918 (four years after the last surviving passenger pigeon keeled over in the Cincinnati Zoo), Congress passed the Migratory Bird Treaty Act, which protected several hundred species, including the pelican.

To THE RELIEF OF BIRD LOVERS, federal legislation superseded what Audubon Society historian Frank Graham calls the "crazy-quilt pattern of local laws." Yet even after poachers went home, even after fishers remembered that pelicans were really their chums—that wherever they plunged from sky to water, fish could be had—the Gulf would never be allowed to rest quietly. The persistent noisemakers were sportsmen and -women.[39]

The grassy tidal flats, rice fields (often abandoned ones dating to the

French), seaweedy beaches, and freshwater inflows were both salvation and death for migrators and sojourners. Paradise had its dark side. Of coastal Louisiana, naturalist Henry Kopman said with intended irony, it was "one of the most picturesque hunting grounds on the continent." As soon as birds set down, they became proverbial sitting ducks—those geese, coots, cranes, and more than twenty-five varieties of ducks that wintered on the Gulf. And the rushes of little birds chasing and chased by the frothy edge of the in-and-out surf weren't exempt.[40]

The *Picayune*'s Martha Field was another faithful observer of the loveliness and the ruination: "The delicate friendly little sandpipers stood in the salt water shallows. . . . Pierre's gun banged forth. Two of the little creatures fell. The others clustered curiously around. I wondered how he had the heart to load again." Imagine the emotional texture of her observation, had she known of the aerial commitment of these gutsy little birds, leaping the Gulf—for species survival.[41]

The rendezvous with armed sporting men and women, many themselves from the North, was older than tarpon fishing. Schooners and launches took hunting parties on excursions that lasted weeks at a time, with daylong shooting marathons, followed by festive dinners of roasted wildfowl with decanters of spirits. At Sabine Lake between Texas and Louisiana, hunters walked behind grazing steers trained to act as screens while circling in on birds. The iron horse led hunters to more birds more quickly and in more places. On the Gulf and Interstate Railway between Galveston and Beaumont, the engineer made unscheduled shooting stops for sporting passengers and crew when a raft of waterfowl was spotted. On the San Antonio and Aransas Pass Railway, hunters could lease a private Pullman car, the *Izaak Walton*, outfitted for their indulgences, including a chef who specialized in preparing wildfowl. A Houston railroad agent once organized a hunt-by-rail expedition that traveled the entire Texas coast.

By late fall, this major migration stop was fat with ducks, and everyone was a great hunter. At Aransas Pass in 1894, a tarpon angler took time away from his rod and reel and picked off 160 snipes (cousins of sandpipers) in three hours, as well as 251 ducks in two days. You might brag about having bagged such a lot, except the next guy could usually brag the same. This was play, not sport. Didn't killing over and over the same way become boring?

Despite the obvious waste, plenty of recreational hunters saw themselves as members of the conservation creed. There was no more resolute devotee of blood sports than Roosevelt, the first conservation president, just as the hook-and-bullet serial *Forest and Stream* was the first conservation magazine. The lineage between game shooters and the namesake of bird protection, John James Audubon, was more direct than that of Chapman or Tippetts. The inspirations for two of Audubon's most familiar paintings, the roseate spoonbill and the egret, came from Texas and the Florida Keys, respectively, and required the shooting of several birds for a pose. Yet Audubon killed far more Gulf birds—thousands— à la the sportsman. He confessed once to shooting with companions so many "winged creatures" in the Keys that the dead piled up like "a small haycock." At the same time, he conceded that birds deserved a reprieve from guns—just not his own.[42]

Still, the earliest conservation laws adopted in the Gulf states were supported by sportsmen. In the 1820s, legislatures outlawed firelighting—hunting at night using a torch to light the eyes of quarry. Next came closed seasons around reproduction cycles, protection for game species in danger of collapsing, and bag limits to sustain populations. Hunters paid for licenses and stamps that funded the purchase of habitat land, and they lobbied for game preserves, albeit to ensure the continued existence of their sport. But as did the unarmed conservationist, armed ones looked to the future.

Few people looked farther down the line than McIlhenny, and few better enjoyed sitting in a duck blind in the autumn dawn mist. He was the duck-and-geese-hunting personification of his state's future nickname, "Sportsman's Paradise." Yet George Lowery, the perceptive zoologist who proved the existence of cross-Gulf migration, said that as a conservationist, McIlhenny was ahead of his time. When Louisiana Audubon chose McIlhenny as president, a state newspaper described him as a "fit successor in the field of ornithology to Louisiana's great son, Audubon." Having banded some 200,000 birds (which Lowery said was eminently important to revealing migratory routes), having written a score of articles for ornithology journals, and having all but invented the bird sanctuary and brokered the establishment of three, he earned the esteem of bird lovers everywhere.[43]

Then he lost it. He wanted to set up a fourth preserve, but it turned out to have problems. By the early 1920s, he had acquired some eighty thousand acres to protect 120 bird species, and the national press awarded him the expected "attaboys." He advertised for a dredging crew to expand wetland area and anticipated employing up to seven wardens at the new preserve. When enough financial backers failed to come forward, he pulled out from deep in the sportsman catacombs of his mind a somewhat desperate idea: he would get the money from recreational hunters by opening the preserve to their sport three months of the year. He named his venture the Louisiana Gulf Coast Club. It was to have four thousand members, each paying $1,000 in dues. He immediately signed up US senators and congressmen and the postmaster general.

Critics screamed hypocrisy, duplicity, treason. They said the newly demarcated habitat, sandwiched between the Sage refuge and the original Ward-McIlhenny refuge, was to be a happy hunting ground for the elite. According to the *Chicago Daily Tribune*, the revelation "raised a perfect storm of complaint." Perhaps the most upsetting condemnation came from William T. Hornaday, director of the New York Zoological Park (Bronx Zoo), savior of the American bison, and esteemed grand old man of wildlife conservation. He accused McIlhenny the bloodletter of masquerading as a conservationist and using the neighboring sanctuaries to lure birds into a death trap.[44]

Navigating the storm, the club's supporters pointed out that the land in question was now open to a year-round hunting free-for-all, while the club would institute seasonal hunting. It would also limit the number of hunters and leave a sizable parcel off limits to hunting, including a demilitarized flyway between the existing refuges.

T. Gilbert Pearson, who succeeded Dutcher as president at Audubon, exploded. Apparently trying to legitimize his club, McIlhenny held Pearson up as an early supporter. Although a reformed sportsman, Pearson was often criticized for being cozy with the pro-hunting crowd. Backpedaling to save his reputation and potentially his job, he went after McIlhenny in full fury. He hit the speaking circuit with a film he had made of birds at the Louisiana sanctuaries—the legitimate ones—with the intent to destroy McIlhenny's Gulf Coast Club. He succeeded when he went to Grace Rainey Rogers, the sister of the late Paul J. Rainey, who had owned a portion of the proposed club land. Pearson convinced her to turn it into a wildlife sanctuary that would be run by National Audubon.

McIlhenny lost his club but got a sanctuary. Still, it hurt to be misunderstood and lose the respect of those he had long admired. He never forgave Pearson for turning on him in such a volatile manner. Years later, he slipped an arrow into the quiver of Pearson's enemies within Audubon: He let it be known that since taking charge of the Rainey land in 1925, the organization had been violating the terms of the deed of gift by allowing fur trappers to operate in the refuge and to shoot its birds to use as bait. Moreover, a portion of the fur money went to Audubon. The revelation was another leg kicked out from under Pearson's weakening throne, and his enemies eventually deposed him.

THE SQUABBLING DID NOT leave birds in the lurch. They got seventy-five miles of protected coastline in Louisiana, and refuges and sanctuaries around the curve of the Gulf coast. Their numbers increased with each passing decade. National Audubon assembled eighteen sanctuaries of its own. Hunters remained a permanent fixture, although committed to wildlife conservation. And the birds were joined by another gathering crowd, people on the seashore, which in the long run wasn't necessarily a good thing.

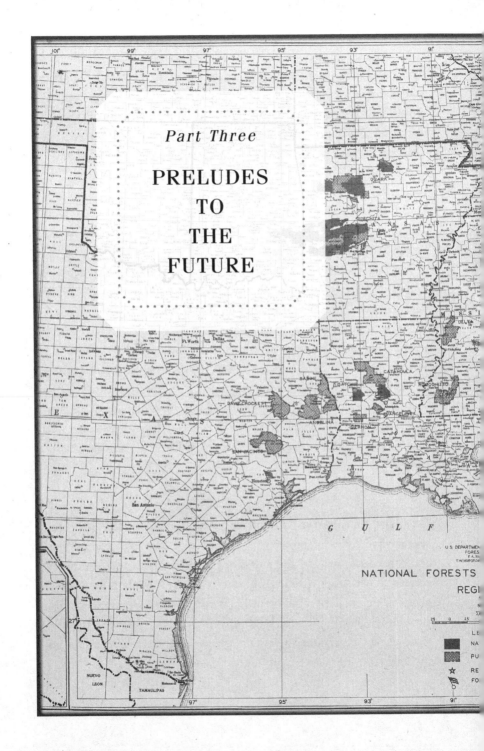

Part Three

PRELUDES
TO
THE
FUTURE

NATIONAL FORESTS

REGI

Nine

FROM BAYSIDE TO BEACHSIDE

Beachgoers on the Gulf in the 1890s.

The edge of the sea is a strange and beautiful place.

—RACHEL CARSON (1955)[1]

TARPON MIGHT HAVE LAUNCHED THE GULF'S TOURIST trade, but to visitors arriving in expanding numbers in the twentieth century, and increasingly without rods and reels, the American Sea had more to offer than a fighting fish. Even the fixated sportsman

Anthony Dimock took a moment to note that his activities had never been "carried on amid natural surroundings more healthful and beautiful," where the "flora of the country is . . . more flourishing, the fauna more numerous and active, the sky bluer, and the gorgeous effects of clouds and color are beyond compare." And the best place from which to take in this splendor was the beach, the "beautiful, breezy beach." Some of the Gulf were so flawlessly white or handsomely sculpted by the wind and water that they truly left you gobsmacked. By the mid-twentieth century, these gifts of nature had become the center of Gulf tourism and one of the region's most important economic assets.[2]

And from where exactly was this natural asset, or more precisely the stuff of beaches—sand—delivered? Probably the most common answer heard outside of scientific explanation, and offered as long as people have been going to the seashore, was a simple one: the sand washed in from the sea and built a beach. That explanation is only a small part of what really goes on. "Each grain on a beach," said Rachel Carson—who called sand both "beautiful" and "mysterious"—"is the result of processes that go back into the shadowy beginnings of life, or of the earth itself."[3]

On some parts of the Gulf, sand is newly arrived, like that in Louisiana, which comes from the Mississippi River as sediment drawn from the thirty-one states in its watershed. Dirt that some kid kicks up in North Dakota can end up on Louisiana beaches, which, incidentally, bear the unmistakable look of the Big Muddy. The sand is typically dark like soil, and the beach flat, "smooth and hard as asphalt," said the nineteenth-century *Daily Picayune* correspondent Martha Field. This is the reason Louisiana never achieved world fame for its beaches. When people began taking an interest in tanning under the sun and walking barefoot in the surf, beaches with softer, foot-massaging, whiter sand appealed most.[4]

Sand on most Gulf beaches has been around for a long time. Rivers, rain, wind, and the rising-and-receding continent-washing sea of ages transported it. Even if yesterday's arrival, no grain is new; each is millions of years old, the creation of eons' worth of scouring, polishing, tumbling, and traveling. Erosion makes the sand that makes the beach that makes beach tourism.

Tens of thousands of years ago, when the ocean was far inland, pounding and wearing away at rocks, it was creating infinite grains of sand. Then the Earth turned cold and glaciers solidified, and the ocean withdrew from the chiseled mountains that now stand above our world. The withdrawing waters carried down the manufactured sediment to the Gulf, depositing it across terra firma and into the sea. Then the ocean swung back slightly to current levels. The modern-day beach does not stop at the surf; it reaches far out into the Gulf to the submerged edge of the continental shelf.

Once the ocean backed off the mountains, glaciers and then rain took over as industrious agents of erosion. Each drop of rain on the solid aggregate of minerals is a hammer blow, minuscule but mighty over time, chinking rock into granules; and each drop is a transport, parlaying granules down over land to ocean, or to rivers and streams to the sea. Every river that runs or ran to the Gulf was once clouded with mineral sediment, and some, like the Mississippi and the Rio Grande, remain so. Mountains are more than exoskeletal spines on the Earth; their wash is the soil-sand skin that covers it. Their sediment flow is the lake bottom, ocean floor, and seashore.

So when you walk on a beach, you walk on mountains. You walk on sea life too. Often mixed in with mineral sand are the pounded-to-dust remains of coral, fossilized marine life, and mollusk shells— the "she sells seashells by the seashore" kind. The beaches of southwest Florida are a mishmash of mineral sand and granulated marine residue, known as carbonate sand. The Florida shelf is up to three-quarters carbonate. Drifts of shell lie on the beach, future sand on top of existing sand.

Sand never stops moving. Whether in Florida or Texas, the beach is different from one day to the next—subtly, and not always to the eye, unless a storm has visited. Sand is shifted and thrown about by wind, currents, and the moon tides pressing and pulling against the shore. A single nondescript wave along its full course—from sea to breaker to thin sheet racing out front and soaking into the existing sand—will move thousands of tons more. As geologist Michael Welland puts it, sand's journey is eternal, "up the beach, down the beach, or along the beach," back out into the water, forming into offshore bars, from which it is likely to return at some point to the beach.[5]

In the 1950s, Professor William Armstrong Price Jr. of the Agricultural and Mechanical College of Texas (now Texas A&M University) returned to his state's beaches time and again. He put in a lot of hours scrutinizing Texas's aeolian coast, named for Aeolus, the Greek god of wind. Geologists mainly studied Aeolus's puff-cheeked impact on desert landscapes, particularly after the black dust storms of the 1930s changed the land and demographics of the Great Plains. But the bespectacled Professor Price was interested in wind-rippled beaches and wind-built dunes. Lighter per granule than Louisiana's, Texas sand, which is nearly all mineral material, runs in shades from white to sandstone to pink. The colors match the terrain in the floodplains of the Brazos and Colorado (of Texas) Rivers, as well as the Rio Grande, all the way up to the latter's rise in the snowcapped Rocky Mountains. Borne by the Rio Grande, kaolinite, used in ceramics and toothpaste, varies from gray to reddish brown. Hematite, a form of iron oxide, and often the pigment that gives sand ripples their pinkish blush, travels the Colorado and Rio Grande. All the rivers convey quartz, the maker of white beaches.

Quartz is the second-most-prevalent mineral on Earth, harbored in nearly every type of rock. Certain varieties have been used in jewelry making since antiquity. It's always been the chief particle in beach sand, reflecting the light that blinds your eyes on sunny days. Florida's long coast is mostly quartz, nearly pure in some places, and dates to the Pleistocene. The sand on the panhandle and west peninsula coast came from the Piedmont and Appalachian highlands, when the mountains stood in the clouds nearly twenty thousand feet taller, as tall as the Himalayas today. Erosion's spoil washed southward into the peninsula and down the Apalachicola River, which now runs clear, and the Tennessee River, which once reached the Gulf. The longshore currents distributed the mountain-made sand across the panhandle as far as western Santa Rosa Island in Pensacola.

Florida's Gulf beaches might be the whitest in the world, with a "special sparkle and glitter," wrote Carson. The dry sand squeaks—some say, chirps—under bare feet. The beaches are another world—warm, drowsy, and white, yet filled with color, unequivocally inviting—which is why, in recent times, they have been awash in human history.[6]

THE HISTORY OF THE MODERN GULF BEACH, another unfamiliar story of the past, could begin with the following quote: "I wondered how the summer visitors could leave so lovely a summer land . . . when the sunshine was softest, the sea breeze saltiest, the fishing at its best, and a surf bath was worth a whole course in athletics and hygiene."[7]

The passage dates to the 1890s and comes from an article in the New Orleans *Daily Picayune* by Martha Field. Her lilting descriptions don't sound like typical newspaper writing in the day when every page was hopelessly crammed with text boxes in tight columns filled with bare-bones copy. Field worked for Eliza Jane Poitevent Holbrook Nicholson, the country's first female publisher of a major daily newspaper in the United States.

After taking the helm of the *Picayune* in 1876, having succeeded her husband on his death, Nicholson proved to be an innovator who wanted to elevate her newspaper above its inconvenient name ("picayune" means "petty"). She lit up its offices with electricity, installed telephones, and converted the press to linotype, at the same time that ink bottles and blotters made room on desktops for bulky new machines called typewriters (shunned by pen-and-paper traditionalists). As for the page itself, she revamped the Sunday edition, traditionally treated by the industry as the week's throwaway sheet, by adding sections on a range of subjects, from travel to children's fiction to household concerns, offering something for every family member.

To open up those tight, boxy columns with a wider variety of interesting subjects, she assembled a stable of women writers at a time when female journalists had few opportunities beyond editing the social page. Under the pen name Pearl Rivers, Nicholson wrote her own opinion column, titled "Nature's Dumb Nobility," which was devoted mostly to the subject of animal cruelty. She brought in Mollie Evelyn Moore Davis, a well-known writer and poet from Texas, to weigh in on progressive issues of the day; Dorothy Dix, who, with Nicholson, introduced the advice column; and Kate Chopin, whose fiction, deploying self-emancipated women as protagonists, gained a national audience. Their talents, along with that of Martha Field, helped Nicholson triple the newspaper's circulation.

Hired in 1881, Field contributed a regular column under the pseudonym Catharine Cole. Female journalists generally adopted pen names to shield their husbands from the social embarrassment of a working wife, and even though she was widowed, Field followed the practice. Born in Missouri, raised in New Orleans, and educated at Macé Lefranc Institute, she was employed by three papers before being enticed to the *Picayune* by Nicholson and her exciting vision.

Like her boss, Field was small and dainty, with resolute feelings about the intellectual capacity of her sex. She was equally a fearless interviewer and traveler whose most popular pieces were about Louisiana. Although sometimes swelled with Victorian flourish, her writing was full of life, whether the topic was a Cajun fisherman or the bayou that gave him a living. She introduced readers to Louisiana's ethnically diverse population (black, white, Chinese, Croatian, Italian, Spanish, and Creole) and similarly diverse landscapes (pine forest, swamp, bayou, coastal marsh, and dune).

In 1891, Nicholson sent Field out on an eighteen-hundred-mile statewide assignment, to all thirty-nine parishes. A buggy drawn by "wiry little Creole ponies" and driven by a "small colored lad" took her over land, and schooners and pirogues (a Louisiana-vernacular hand-built canoe-like boat) drew her along the coast, through two years of fitful movement. She was ambushed by rainstorms, threatened by lightning, bogged down in mud, and turned back by washed-out roads, alligators, and insect swarms as thick as confetti. The experience energized her. Although you can sense stiffening in essays that mention cruel bird hunters—including the Pierre who shot sandpipers on the beach—she otherwise met no disagreeable person. Similarly, she encountered no disagreeable landscape. With its marshy edges, beaches, and surf, the coast tugged hardest. She referred to herself as "more or less amphibious."[8]

Only in recent decades had Americans become drawn in the same seaward direction. The constantly expanding cities of the nineteenth century were growing woefully loud, confining, and insalubrious, where the downy green of parks was not yet common. People increasingly craved escape from the dull slabs of gray and brick, at least temporarily. Initially, they took a breather in the pastoral countryside. Gradually, oceanside sandy spots gained appeal as attitudes about modesty and the body, and about relaxation as recreation, began to change—but especially, as deep-seated fears of the sea dissolved.

Before leisure seekers were beachgoers, they were surf bathers; that is, they flocked not to the beaches facing the open sea, but to those along inshore waters—a bay, sound, or lagoon. The summery seashore as an altar of vacationing escape had to evolve in apprehensive minds. As beach historians Lena Lenček and Gideon Bosker put it, the beach we know today—where people lie in the sun, play in the surf, and look out to the infinite sea horizon—had to be invented. Centuries of attitude adjustments were required, as were aficionados like Martha Field, to push things along.

ACTUALLY, AMERICANS WEREN'T INVENTING something new; they were reprising something that had been lost amid centuries of emotional debris. Ancient Romans and Greeks had been mad for the beach. Although the gods vented their moods across sea and shore, and assorted sea demons reared their heads in Homeric tales, citizens put fears aside to frolic in the surf of the Mediterranean and Adriatic Seas. Romans learned to escape stultifying urban centers for the silky air and vistas of the seaside, while Greeks appreciated exercise. That included aquatic sports and even a Greek version of Muscle Beach, millennia before southern California's. For the philosophers and poets—Plutarch, Sophocles, Cicero, even Homer—the seashore evoked Elysian bliss. But when the Greco-Roman world collapsed, so did favorable impressions of the beach.

After the fall of the Roman Empire in AD 476, as population centers drifted northward into the European continent and Christianity's influence expanded, the seashore lost its luster. For one thing, as Lenček and Bosker tell it, the outdoors lacked Mediterranean felicity. Skies of the north were grayer and the sea colder; plagues entered through seaports. People believed immersion in water opened pores to infection, and they shunned bathing. Cleanliness was for clothing, not for the body, and in a Christian world, the body was not to be worshipped or exposed, as it had been in Greek art and water, where activities of the ancients had amounted to a "vanity among vanities." For another, the sea was the setting of Old Testament horrors. Christianity's reign demanded a fear-ridden worldview, bowing toward the Dark Ages and away from the sunny beach. In Genesis, no sea or oceanic vista graces Eden. The Old Testament sea is the "great abyss"; God commands it into an epic flood to wash away the wickedness of man. In the book of Revelation—the Apocalypse—the seven-headed beast rises from the abyss; and in the book of Daniel, it releases four others to persecute the saints.[9]

Even if Westerners desired to take cues from Mediterranean antiquity, the material evidence of Greek and Roman pleasures—beaches, baths, and resorts—had been lost in the rising seas of a warming globe. Engulfing water was yet another reason to avoid the coast.

For centuries, Europeans carried around a lot of emotional baggage associated with the beach. As the wilderness in early Western myth sheltered trolls and wood sprites, the sea harbored serpents and dragons and such, and it had the dropping-off edge of the Earth (an idea supported more by popular belief than by scholarly consensus). Apart from myths and suspicions, frightening realities were plentiful. Even more so than woodlands, the sea teemed with wild things—oversized ones, and man-eaters many. In *Toilers of the Sea*, Victor Hugo did oceans no favor by having his protagonist, Gilliatt, engage in battle with a giant among octopuses, creatures the narrator condemns as the "chosen forms of evil. . . . They are as the darkness converted into beasts . . . phantoms as much as monsters."[10]

The beach was a step away from the perilous sea. It was the threshold over which titanic storms crossed, sometimes without warning and always without welcome or compunction. Tsunamis crossed less often, yet they all had the power to crush defenseless villages. At times, they arrived when conditions—a calm, pale-blue day—were an inconceivable backdrop to catastrophe. The sun did shine fairly often, and birds did sing plenty. It was just that moods were dark and humanity paranoid. A gaze turned to a momentarily wondrous sea was likely to be seized by an old albatross appearing as a question: what danger lurks on the horizon?

That question had not haunted Gulf coast aborigines—not before hostile Europeans showed up on the beach. In North American cosmology, the sea was a reverential place, the birthplace of terrestrial Earth and what lived on it, including humans. It was full of creatures for sure, but instead of monsters, they were edible creatures, and of the kind whose bones, teeth, and skin could be fashioned into ornaments and useful tools. Storms were routine and prepared for, probably more so on the Gulf than in other places; many aboriginal peoples, such as the Karankawa, purposely lived away from the coast during the stormy season. Natives regularly bathed too, pinching their noses to offensive odors when they met the unwashed Christians from Europe.

After a long passage at sea, a sandy coast could appear to early European travelers as a welcome green-and-white gateway to a new land. Yet it was often a bloody meeting place between foreign invaders and native defenders. Remember, Ponce de León's day on the beach included a poison dart in the thigh. If you survived a shipwreck, the beach was the mesa of salvation you were washed up on—except you might be captured by natives and enslaved, as Cabeza de Vaca had been, and you would likely prefer drowning at sea to becoming the object of human sacrifice. A worse fate than slavery awaited a party of six from La Salle's expedition sounding the Texas shore in a longboat. When night fell and they bivouacked quietly on the beach, natives rushed out of the blind and slaughtered them. Centuries came and went before playground replaced battleground.

Even after foreign pathogens thinned native numbers and opened up the coastal frontier to Europeans, the beach suggested cold isolation and danger, not rest and relaxation. On the eve of the American Revolution, Bernard Romans had few kind words for Gulf shores. He talked about "dreadful squalls," "bleak winter winds," and thunder and lightning. He knew from his shipwreck experiences that the coast also remained vexing geography for the explorer and cartographer. Its presumed suitability was limited to ports pressed into the safety of bays, and to hardy working people who made their living on the sea and knew the risks. The beach was for digging up turtle eggs and scavenging driftwood and ship wreckage. Otherwise, it was to be no one's bother.[11]

IN KEEPING WITH THE TIMES, Martha Austin made the bay-shore, not the Gulf shore, her interest in 1850 when she lobbied her husband, William, to build a tourist home in East Biloxi. A fishing village on the corner of Mississippi Sound and Biloxi Bay, East Biloxi had been the original capital of Louisiana, when the French called it simply Biloxi. They eventually relocated their settlement and its name to better water across the bay, giving the original capital a false off-spring identity as East Biloxi, and confusing the actual geographic lineage of colonial settlement.

The decade before the Austins pursued Martha's suggested venture, a Mississippi minister was scouting the area for baptismal water when he discovered mineral springs along the back bay of the wedge of land that was East Biloxi. The aquifer beneath the coastal plain mixing with subterranean infusions of marine salt created spa-like mineral springs across the Mississippi Gulf coast. Indians had once bathed in them, and white Americans took an interest in doing the same.

The Austins were from New Orleans, where William practiced medicine. East Biloxi was relaxed beneath live oaks and lightly criss-crossed by paths and narrow roads of crushed oyster shells. Martha and William built a white clapboard tourist home on three hundred feet of oak-shaded bayfront. It had up- and downstairs wraparound galleries and eventually room for 150 guests. Out in front of the hotel's picket fence, you could climb into a waiting carriage and clop down Jackson Avenue to the sound in one direction and the springs in the other. The Austins named their establishment the Ocean Springs Hotel. Townsfolk liked the name so much that they appropriated it in 1854 to replace East Biloxi.

The Austins were relative latecomers to the spa trade that sprang from Mississippi's springs. Across the bay in Biloxi, though support-ing fewer than a thousand residents, six hotels were operating. Some had been there for a decade or more. They were all very similar, with wood floors, Persian rugs, gleaming staircase handrails and balus-trades, golden chandeliers, wallpaper and wainscot, velvet upholstery and curtains, amply fortified by recreational amenities: bathhouses, billiard rooms, barrooms, ballrooms, and separate family suites. Prom-ising good results, fishing piers jutted out into the sound, and guides were available to take you beyond them in a boat, even bait your hook. Visitors who came on private craft organized a yacht club and then started racing each other, making their regatta the must-attend event of the summer.

But it was the springs that enticed visitors to Biloxi and Ocean Springs, and to Bay St. Louis, Pass Christian, Pascagoula, and Mis-sissippi City (which became Gulfport). Each, according to an early chronicler, was "fully endowed by the natural gifts of climate and location." Dubbed the Six Sisters, with Biloxi known as "Queen of the Watering Holes," Mississippi's spa resorts had a relaxed Victorian charm that coexisted with the working waterfront. Guests could do without the smell of the local canneries, but fishing schooners skirting the horizon were a vaunted part of the scenery. Hotel dining rooms of linen tablecloths served locally caught fish, oysters, and shrimp, soon to be spiced by a newly conceived Louisiana-brand pepper sauce called Tabasco. Steam packets made regular stops, taking away seafood to the Mobile and New Orleans markets, and dropping off merchandise, food staples, mail, and holiday visitors. Ocean Springs made use of discarded oyster shells from canneries to erect a tower topped with a beacon to guide packets scheduled to arrive at night—insurance against being bypassed for the next resort.[12]

The tourist homes were seasonal establishments marketing to a tradition. It had long been the fashion of southern planters to flee the stifling fields of summer to hunker down on the inshore coast in second homes of wide porches and tall windows—a leisure time that, much like that of the ancient Greeks and Romans, was undergirded by slaves. Nearly as soon as Spain ceded lower Mississippi and Alabama to the US in 1811, planters built the first seasonal residences. The patriarch of their culture, former Confederate president Jefferson Davis, came to join them near Biloxi in the centennial year of the nation's birth. Woeful in defeat, the penniless hero moved into a cottage on the grounds of the Beauvoir estate.

His accommodations were provided by Beauvoir's owner and a sympathizer of his lost cause, Sarah Dorsey. She would help the emotionally needy Davis write his memoir, in the hope of restoring his reputation and finances. Outside one window of his humble lodging was the signature natural feature of the 608-acre estate: a freshwater bayhead swamp fed by an artesian spring. Out another was the estate's main structure, a raised Louisiana-style plantation house. Nine-foot French doors and windows opened to a white-columned portico that looked out to the vitality of the sound. Three years later, Dorsey bequeathed Beauvoir and its view to Davis.

City folk, many from New Orleans and Mobile, built summer houses on the coast too. The springs, as well as Greco-Roman-style public baths that piped in mineral water through bamboo plumbing, were inviting enough on their own. Still, the summer heat and humidity of urban places was a major reason people packed their bags for the coast, and nothing chased them out of the city like an epidemic.

Cities, plain and simple, were a health risk. Although they helped clean up fly-covered food scraps tossed in street gutters, pigs ran as freely about as roving street gangs. "Necessary" men, as they were artlessly known, hauled away wagonloads of horse manure and human waste cleaned out of privies and cellars. Not surprisingly, cities were cauldrons of diseases: cholera, smallpox, typhoid, tuberculosis, influenza. Yellow fever—a.k.a. yellow plague and yellow jack—was the scourge of the Gulf and especially ugly: a fading pulse, bleeding gums, bloody urine, fever, and black vomit preceding welcome death.

Specialists on southern maladies attributed most epidemic diseases to poisonous air. Unfamiliar with or skeptical of the concept of germborn and viral contagions, they believed a miasma wafted up from a city's common filth—open cesspools, and streets of rotting garbage and animal carcasses. The hotter, wetter, and more stagnant the conditions, the more potent the miasma, supposedly. During an outbreak in Corpus Christi, Texas, a worried resident wrote her parents back home in Prussia, "Yellow fever appeared in the streets where the water had no outlet, thus producing contagious matter."[13]

When it came to holding water, no place was a more efficient catchment than New Orleans. Bienville and the French had built their new capital in a swamp, after all. Worse, flooding is the natural way of the Mississippi—a boon to wetlands, a bane to cities. Just as soon as the town had begun to take shape, the river invaded. Bienville ordered a levee built, and ominously reversed normal land and water elevations, while subverting horizontal perspectives. From the streets, you looked up and saw ships freakishly above you passing by on the river. He managed to thwart the river—sometimes—but when clouds burst over the city, water shedding from rooftops had nowhere to drain. Gathering pools encouraged mosquitoes and yellow-fever outbreaks, a future inglorious hallmark of the Crescent City.

As a matter of course, the poor—scorned for living in squalor and in the dankest parts, as if by choice—were blamed for breeding citywide contagions. Before the Civil War, New Orleans's per capita income was among the highest in the nation, conspicuously displayed in the opera houses and theaters and in the Garden District's Queen Anne Victorian and Greek Revival homes. The elegant city of wrought-iron balconies also had its share of slums. They housed much of the free-black population (the largest of any city) and immigrants, Germans and Irish mainly. Poor neighborhoods, with inadequate stormwater drainage, were often an epidemic's first target.

Yellow fever visited summer after summer, none causing as much grief as that of 1853. In the worst yellow-fever epidemic in US history, ten thousand fell ill in New Orleans. The streets were shrouded in black smoke from barrels burning creosote, a common—and poisonous—wood preservative used in railway crossties and dock pilings. Public officials held to the mistaken belief that the acrid smoke would cleanse the air of the miasma. It didn't. The *New York Times* kept a running tally of the daily deaths. Nearly eight thousand succumbed in the end, accounting for half the city's mortality that year.

No one understood that it was not an invisible, nonexistent pall, but a brazen mosquito, *Aedes aegypti*, that spread yellow fever, a viral disease, from infected human host to unsuspecting new host. The mosquito and yellow fever both arrived in the Americas from Africa, transported as unintended cargo on Spanish ships delivering slaves, who hosted the virus in their blood. Africa is also the likely place of origin of malaria, another troublesome affliction on the Gulf. Its mosquito, *Anopheles*, was a pesky but innocuous native before it lifted malaria off an infected newcomer from the Old World and passed it on to the human population in the New. Like almost everything else foreign, diseases usually made entry through seaports.

The Gulf's were busy exchanges, where ships arriving from Central and South America, Cuba, and the Caribbean off-loaded tropical products: mahogany, rubber, rum, coffee, pineapples, bananas—and tropical diseases. New Orleans was a world leader in the importation of illnesses. A single infected sailor in from the tropics on liberty, bound for bars and bordellos, could prostrate the entire city.

One particular natural condition determined the extent of the scourge: rain. The year that brought so much death, 1853, also produced a bumper sugarcane crop. When fields looked robust in the summer, New Orleans could expect tragedy, although no one could say why. As it happens, *Aedes aegypti* preferred not swamp for its breeding habitat, but rainwater, collected in streets, rain barrels, livestock troughs, even plant pots. The same rainwater that swelled crops bred mosquitoes that, tragically, rose like an invading force from the thousands of vases of flowers that family and friends placed at the graves of yellow-fever victims.

New Orleans's susceptibility had always been a given. Ships and sailors streamed through the port as steadily as the big river sidling past it. At two miles, the wharf was the longest in the world, stacked forever high with crates, hogsheads, and cotton bales. Only in New York and Boston did stevedores move more freight. Shipping temporarily fell off during the Civil War, and then recovered afterward to make New Orleans the country's fourth busiest port, although it couldn't sustain the ranking. Near the end of the century, it dropped to the number twelve spot. Railroads stole away some of the freight business, but more than anything, New Orleans's feverish conditions discouraged traders and travelers.

Locals could hardly blame them. Every summer, those of adequate means vacated New Orleans. Typically, they went to the Six Sisters, comforted by wholesome Gulf breezes, respite waiting at the springs. Physicians like William Austin commonly prescribed time away from the city at a health resort; conveniently, he could also recommend accommodations: William and Martha opened their Ocean Springs Hotel the year after the 1853 yellow-fever summer.

Sometimes, though, the prescribed respite could be laced with death, as was the case in 1878, when yellow fever quite unexpectedly invaded Ocean Springs. The Louisville and Nashville Railroad sent the stricken resort ten barrels of creosote from its nearby tie plant. Smoke billowed day and night, and maybe it helped keep down the mosquitoes, the unknown culprits, but thirty people died anyway, among them the manager of the Ocean Springs Hotel and some of his guests.

Infection came again in 1897, when sanitary inspectors at first thought the consumption of bay oysters, contaminated by the town's sewage release, was the cause. Then they realized they were dealing with another full-fledged yellow-fever epidemic, and they traced its source to a recent arrival from Guatemala. Unfortunately, before the army could establish a quarantine, visitors fled for home and passed the pestilence up the rail lines to Macon, Atlanta, Memphis, even Chicago. More than five hundred died.

If a resort could no longer promote health benefits, it could still offer escape. Some years before, the Six Sisters had added a winter season to their schedules. There was a certain logic in it. If you lived in Chicago, for example, where the frigid wind whipped off Lake Michigan well into spring, the Gulf could seem like a tropical paradise by comparison, and only a train ride away. Local historians say the Mexican Gulf Hotel at Pass Christian, a 250-room affair that opened in 1883, was the first to cater to winter tourists. With rates at three to five dollars a night, it remained packed with midwesterners fleeing the frostbitten plains until fire destroyed it in 1917.

To the east, Ocean Springs turned into a little Chicago in the winter. One Windy City escapee was famed architect Louis Sullivan. In the 1890s, the master of steel-frame skyscrapers built a single-story wood-frame house on the bay. He called his winter hometown "a village sleeping as it had slept for generations with untroubled surface." He apparently knew nothing about the yellow-fever outbreaks.[14]

IRONICALLY, THE PLACE that was most frightening, the Gulf front, with its steady winds, might have provided greater protection against infectious mosquitoes. As tourists continued to linger around inshore springs and barrier island–protected sounds and bays, scientists out on the Gulf were investigating the mysteries of the sea, and dispelling a few. Mapping the coast, discerning its line, helped make it more familiar. What lay in the deep, monsters or otherwise, was yet another matter, and to find out, the Coast Survey launched a major underwater biological study of the Gulf in 1877—a first of its kind.

A handful of years earlier, a number of scientists had still subscribed to what was known as the azoic hypothesis, or the idea of a lifeless deep sea. British naturalist Edward Forbes introduced the hypothesis in the 1840s, maintaining that the cold, light-starved depths below three hundred fathoms (eighteen hundred feet) could not support life. Forbes was a naturalist, although he was best known as a pen-and-ink caricaturist who drew whimsical man-eating sea creatures, monster-sized flying fish, and post-Jurassic marine dinosaurs for magazines and newspapers. Was it sheer irony that scientists embraced the hypothesis of a man whose special talent was making cartoons? There was plenty of evidence to contradict his hypothesis too, including accounts of Portuguese fishermen who had been bringing up sharks from fathomless reaches since "time immemorial." The learned community, however, was generally unwilling to legitimize the empirical knowledge of inarticulate fishermen, and for decades, professional arrogance sustained a false assumption.[15]

Skepticism, questioning, and dissent, though, are the vital organs of scientific investigation, and some practitioners disagreed with Forbes. One was Louis François de Pourtalès, who believed the truth lay below three hundred fathoms and that science needed to go there. Pourtalès had been a student of Harvard scientist Louis Agassiz, one of the country's foremost naturalists and an important force in the development of marine science (he founded the Museum of Comparative Zoology, of which Pourtalès would become a custodian, and later set up the first marine laboratory on the East Coast, the predecessor to the Woods Hole Oceanographic Institution).

To test the azoic hypothesis, the Swiss native Pourtalès went to the Gulf. As an assistant with the Coast Survey, he had helped triangulate the Florida Reef, but his expertise was in marine zoology. In 1868, he was atop deep water in the Florida Straits when he lowered a dredge off the stern of the Coast Survey's *Bibb*, a 160-foot side-wheel steamer that three years earlier had been running blockades in the Gulf against Confederate supplies. Sounding at 517 fathoms, the dredge was trolled behind the *Bibb* for a short distance before the crew winched it back on board. When they opened its collection bag, a consommé of sediment and live invertebrates spilled onto the deck. No matter how far the dredge went down, living things kept coming up.

Pourtalès's expedition had come at the urging of Louis Agassiz's son, Alexander. After emigrating to Cambridge, Massachusetts, with his father in 1849, the Swiss-born, American-raised Alexander was groomed for science from an early age. He earned multiple degrees, studied ocean life around the globe, published numerous books on marine biology, and served a term as president of the National Academy of Sciences. He was also a founder of fisheries science, a discipline that worked toward improving commercial fishing. Although his interests were many, oceanography was Alexander's studied passion, and indeed, he would die at sea at age seventy-four. Coast Survey superintendent Benjamin Peirce thought Alexander Agassiz was the right man to lead the 1877 biological study in the Gulf.

Recently returned from an antiquities expedition in Peru, Agassiz was forty-two, balding, and entering his intellectual prime. He had also recently been part of the team investigating the collection of specimens gathered from around the world by the first oceanographic expedition, undertaken on the British HMS *Challenger*. On the Gulf, the Coast Survey put the *Blake*, a sail-and-steam schooner custom built for hydrographic work, at his disposal. Agassiz benefited from the expertise of the boat's commander, Charles Sigsbee, who a few years before had innovated the use of piano wire to replace weaker and elastic hemp rope for depth soundings. The hybrid schooner enabled Sigsbee to furl the sails and maneuver by propeller to his desired point. He did that more than three thousand times, detailing the entire Gulf floor. The expedition produced the first realistic bathymetric (underwater) deep-sea chart. On it, Sigsbee drew sinuous terraces in tints of blue green roughly paralleling the contour of the coast. The bluest shade identifies the nethermost section of the Gulf, west of center, surpassing two thousand fathoms, subsequently named the Sigsbee Deep.

Agassiz and Sigsbee traced an exploratory triangle from Key West to the Yucatán and up to the Mississippi River and back. In two years' time, they completed some three hundred dredges that confirmed the biodiversity of the Gulf.* The resulting collection required several years of study before Agassiz wrote up his findings in a two-volume work. In fine illustrative and written detail, it describes deep-sea flora and fauna that include crustaceans, worms, sponges, mollusks, rhizopods, gastropods, cephalopods, brachiopods, crinoids, actinoids, alcyonoids, and much much more. Sigsbee's bathymetric chart, Agassiz's specimens, and the innovations in dredging and sounding pushed oceanography deeper into the modern realm of science. Erasing the sea monsters from maps of lore, it made the Gulf more knowable, rational, and perhaps less intimidating. More specifically, it showed that while some strange creatures lived in the deep, and many of them were slimy and spiny, no serpents or demons were to be found.[16]

To THE PROSPECTIVE BEACHGOER, scientific breakthroughs could be an arcane matter. What was more responsible for bringing attitudes around and people to the beach was art and literature born on American soil and water, extolled by Romantic painters and writers: the likes of James Fenimore Cooper, Henry Wadsworth Longfellow, Walt Whitman, Thomas Cole, Thomas Moran, and George Catlin. As the continent opened up to white settlement and the country fixated on the West, these early lights of brush and pen developed a distinctly American art form on nature's grand canvas. Wildness became romantic, strangeness beautiful, immenseness rev-

* A subsequent separate cruise was undertaken to explore the Caribbean.

erential. Natural America was wondrous America. While the trapper, trader, and pioneer out on the borderlands might quibble with the Romantics—urban sophisticates who avoided the unceremonious job of taming wilderness—the dreamers and idealists seemed to be onto something. In unspoiled canyons, gorges, geysers, peaks, waterfalls, high and low deserts, arched rocks, cathedral-like forests, and long and leggy shorelines, Americans recognized a national aesthetic unrivaled by European countries.

Most of the artists who ventured across America drew toward the setting sun and beyond the Mississippi River. Though the list is short, those who went south were an impressive lot: William Bartram, Ralph Waldo Emerson, Harriet Beecher Stowe, Henry James, Stephen Crane, John Singer Sargent, Martin Johnson Heade, Winslow Homer, Laura Woodward, Martha Walter. Typically, they rode the train to Florida's upper east coast and then booked a ticket on a scenic excursion on the St. Johns River.

The list of those who went over to the Gulf is even shorter. William Faulkner's bride, Estelle, on the couple's honeymoon, tried to drown herself in the Gulf, and Hart Crane succeeded when he jumped from the stern of a tramp steamer out of Mexico—his one poetic expression, sad and misguided, related to the American Sea. Their despondency was unrelated to the Gulf, which most often inspired wonderment. In the 1930s, Wallace Stevens went to New Orleans and the coast of the Six Sisters, and wrote a poem, "Some Friends of Pascagoula." The friends were two locals and an eagle, "Spread on the sun-bronze air."[17]

Stevens spent decidedly blissful moments at Key West. It was tropical and bright and gay, and its masses a little besotted—Hemingway lived there after all. There, too, Stevens composed a poem, one of his most acclaimed, "The Idea of Order at Key West." You can read it as a revelation story. The poem's speaker, unsuccessful in a search for order in sea sounds, as in the meter of a singing human voice, finally accepts the visceral quality in nature's haphazardness.

Oh! Blessed rage for order, Pale Ramon,
The maker's rage to order words of the sea[18]

Poet Sidney Lanier did not compose verse when he was at Cedar Key in the 1870s. Yet, thumb through his travelogue, and inspiration and reverence appear throughout the chapter he devoted to the Gulf. The natural world for him was lyrical and transcendent, in the way it was for Emerson and Thoreau. Lanier called the loblollies and long-leaf that populated the coast "stately pillars of a temple . . . religion carven into trunks and branches and cones." On arrival at Cedar Key, his train came to a stop atop an elevated terminal reaching into the tidewater. The Gulf opened out from his window, and the "vast sweet visage of space" moved him. "To the tourist and sportsman desiring a mild flavor of adventure," he wrote, "this portion of Florida offers a charming field."[19]

John Muir had a similar response seven years earlier when he arrived at Cedar Key. In 1867, while he was working in a wagon wheel factory in Indianapolis, self-reflection had summoned him on a thousand-mile walk to the Gulf. En route to becoming America's foremost guardian of nature, the leggy, auburn-bearded young man of twenty-nine entered Florida at Fernandina, above Jacksonville, and walked across the state along the railroad tracks that would later convey Lanier. Muir could not keep himself from occasionally sauntering into Florida's garden of anonymous plants and birds and sounds. Saw palmettos fanned into legions; he called them "dazzling sun-children." From juniper and pine woods, he walked out into a panorama of coastal marshes shushing like the wheat fields he knew in the Midwest. He saw a group of small palm- and cedar-inhabited islands, "arranged like a tasteful bouquet, and placed in the sea to be kept fresh."[20]

Four outfits in the town of three hundred were milling local red cedar into pencil slats. They were shipped, sometimes alongside feathers bound for hat factories, to New York and Europe to be turned into final product. By 1890, the mills were consuming 100,000 cedar logs a year and producing enough pencil blanks to circle the globe five times. Locals would later say that an 1896 hurricane crushed the factories and economy. In truth, the industry's fatality was self-inflicted, caused by an overconsumption of the local wood.

Muir witnessed these factories in action, even working in one for a day. It was December, but mosquitoes were biting nonetheless, and malaria knocked him flat. Muir scholars like to highlight the Gulf malady but tend to ignore what came of his month-long convalescence. Incapable of remaining idle, he dragged himself out of bed to sit like a stone beneath a live oak, contemplating the birds feeding in winter's broad tidal zone. After gaining a little strength, he went from island to island exploring in a borrowed skiff, and he began to reassess the human place on Earth. Routine encounters with "venomous beasts" and "thorny plants," combined with his illness, convinced Muir that positioning humans above nature was one of Western society's greatest conceits. "Nature's object in making plants and animals," he confided to his journal, "might possibly be first of all the happiness of each one of them, not the creation of all for the happiness of one."[21]

In no way was Muir discouraging peaceful interactions with the nonhuman world. For him, nature was divine, and to preach fear would smack of his Calvinist father's detested fire-and-brimstone teachings. Nature was hospitable, inviting, vitalizing—"immortal truth" and "immortal beauty." Humans were "earth-born" and nature was their home; life in the outdoors, not in the church or circumscribed by Calvinist doctrine, cleansed and strengthened the body and soul. A year before being absorbed by California's Yosemite, the outdoor home he would be eternally identified with, Muir was on the Gulf forming the sensibilities that would steel the conservation movement he came to lead.[22]

Unlike Muir, a founder of the Sierra Club, most Romantics were not nakedly Pied Pipering the American people off into the woods and water. The idea that nature should be accepted on its own terms and engaged with was implied in their artistic reverences. This was true with Winslow Homer's Homosassa watercolors. The tranquility in his paintings is a seduction beyond the art, even in the one work with a wild panther at its center and titled *In the Jungle*. Set in a swampy scene, the painting depicts two dead trees, gray and bare, cast horizontally in the foreground. Sabal palms stand at varying angles in and beside the water. The panther straddles the trunk of one, climbing up and looking away from the viewer. No danger here. Quite the opposite: reflections on water, green tones across the spectrum, and sunlight filtering through woodland shades—without eerie shadows—lend a three-dimensional depth that opens the painting like an *Alice in Wonderland* portal. Through it, the viewer might wondrously step.

WESTERN CIVILIZATION BEGAN STRIDING toward the beach, tentatively, in the mid-eighteenth century—not in America, where the Sons of Liberty were still to throw politically laden English tea into Boston Harbor, and where the Spanish and French continued to control the Gulf—but at the English seashore.

Beachgoing in Western civilization opened with gray wintry weather, an aquatic form of immersion therapy, and an odd contraption known as a bathing machine. A horse-drawn wagon bearing a cabana would maneuver into the surf until the water reached just below the hub of its wood-spoke wheels. This was the machine. A patron, or patient, would emerge from it dressed in an ankle-length smock and descend steps into the grip of an attendant, known as a dipper, waiting in the water. The patron was then dunked several times. The terror aroused by the sea, along with the cold water and alarm over drowning, was supposed to revitalize one's core by restoring harmony with the soul. After losing the American colonies, King George III suffered acute bouts with mental illness and underwent this treatment. In the end, the baths did not save him.

When the machines were at the shore, spectators would gather. In time, people began coming as much for the beach and water recreation as for the voyeuristic pleasure of witnessing the bathing-machine rituals. These early beachgoers were called surf bathers. The elite began moving their inland spas to the seashore, and both therapeutic and pleasure bathing leaped the channel and spread across the continent's northern shores. Down south, farming and rural folk had for some time engaged in the pleasures of the seashore, Cassandras be damned (and clothes too), and revived the bathing traditions of the Mediterranean coast.

Americans followed the aquatic lead of the British and French, by the mid-nineteenth century growing accustomed to the notion of a day at the seashore. The lakeside initially remained the more popular and safer vacation spot, but by the 1880s, increasing numbers were leaving the stale confines of Boston, Philadelphia, Newark, and New York on commuter rails for July-through-August weekend day trips to Revere Beach, Rockaway Beach, Coney Island, and the Jersey Shore. The latter had a hundred miles of sandy coast and half as many beach towns. There were grand pavilions of restaurants, shops, and bathhouses, and enormous boardwalks. Hundreds of people on a given weekend day queued up at bathhouses to change into beachwear: bloomers or flannel smocks for women, and drawers and waistcoats for men.

Magazines gave advice on how to properly frolic in the waves and simultaneously declared surf bathing a frivolous trend soon to pass. *Atlantic Monthly* editor William Dean Howells proclaimed himself to be repulsed by bodies "lolling" and "wallowing" on the beach. It was not "picturesque, or poetic, or dramatic," but "queer." Yet on both sides of the Atlantic, the work of impressionist artists—Claude Monet, William Merritt Chase, Maurice Pendergast, John Sloan— romanticized a day at the beach and painted the future. Robert Henri asked, "Why do we love the sea?" His answer: "Because it has some potent power to make us think things we like to think."[23]

It's anyone's guess what bathers were thinking in 1835 when Mary Austin Holley was shocked to see a clutch of them near the Brazos

River. She was traveling the coast by schooner at the time Texians were literally gunning for independence from Mexico. For the moment, all was quiet at Velasco, where her cousin Stephen Austin fourteen years earlier had settled his first "colonists." Fellow passengers, including "lady passengers," took leave to "bathe in the surf." It was an unexpected scene that anticipated a coming recreation. Six decades on, Velasco was both a deepwater port and a beach resort, anchored by the newly opened four-story Surfside Hotel. Boldly facing the open sea as it did was a rare thing. The local newspaper offered assurances that "there is positively no undertow whatever," and half a mile out the "water is only shoulder deep."[24]

One barrier island to the north, the Galveston Beach Hotel occupied a similar Gulf-front berth. Ready for guests in 1883, the hotel existed as an exception that didn't last. Guests coming great distances stayed in one of its two hundred rooms on one of its four floors, each room with a saltwater bath and each floor wrapped by an eighteen-foot wide veranda. On the manicured lawn out front, they were serenaded by musical ensembles and a bubbling water fountain, and thrilled by fireworks and high-wire walkers. Having visited, Stephen Crane said, the "principal floor to this structure is the sea itself, to which a flight of steps leads." The grand hotel with its signature red-and-white shingled roof mysteriously burned down in 1898 after the city health inspector ordered it to stop piping its sewage into the Gulf, near where bathers swam. Standing directly in front of the Gulf, the hotel had been ahead of its time, but it was a wood-frame structure and architecturally not ready for the future. Two years later, the famous Galveston hurricane of 1900 would have demolished it—every rafter, stud, clapboard, and red and white shingle.[25]

Most holiday locations continued to play it safe and stay behind an island bulwark or within inland waters. The Grand Hotel at Point Clear, Alabama, had been around since the late 1840s, when guests could lounge at water's edge and raise a mint julep to the source of their wealth crossing Mobile Bay on riverboats. More than 400,000 bales of slave-picked cotton a year came down the river from up-country plantations plowing toward the Gulf, still several miles away. Upon the footfall of the next century, Corpus Christi had nearly eight thousand residents, a half dozen hotels, and a reputation for being a "land of balmy sea breezes, sunshine and flowers" where the *bay* promised the "safest" surf bathing. The Tarpon Inn at Tarpon, Texas, protected on Turtle Cove, no longer catered exclusively to the rod-and-reel crowd; it advertised "Surf Bathing Unexcelled" a carriage ride away on the pinkish-white beach of the Gulf. When Barron Collier acquired the tarpon resort on Useppa Island, he responded to expanding recreational desires and built a beach, sequestered safely within Pine Island Sound, where northern tourists leisured beneath big umbrellas stabbed into the sand.[26]

Louisianans were different. They had no choice but to be bold. Their mainland options were coastal marshes and more coastal marshes. If they wanted a beach, they had to go to the islands. The most popular were Grand Isle and Last Island. Martha Field considered Grand Isle the "bouquet" of Louisiana's barriers, and most Louisianans agreed. Six miles long and a half mile wide, a leisurely hundred-mile boat ride down the river from New Orleans, Grand Isle was tucked behind the eastern toe of the state. A ridge ran along its middle with a brow of oaks bending to the sea wind, worshippers with arms stretched singing hallelujah. Island dwellers, "deep-stained with the gold of the sun," had been growing cotton, sugarcane, and blackberries, and fishing and crabbing, since the French. Cauliflower and shrimp were more recent market additions. And for as long as anyone could remember, wrote Field, the island had been a "camping ground for all manner of the sportsman," the waterfowl hunter and angler.[27]

The resort tradition more or less started with a Grand Isle cauliflower grower named John Ludwig and known as the terrapin king. In and amid his crop rows, he always wore the same outfit: work trousers and shirt with a black derby and brown cigar, fixed inside his cheek. Through coke-bottle spectacles he saw wealth in raising diamondback terrapins. Thousands crept around his pens until orders from New Orleans boiled down the chosen into turtle soup, or from New

York, where they appeared as an expensive meat entrée on Delmonico's menu, alongside passenger pigeon. Years before, a moment or two ahead of war breaking out, the entrepreneurial Ludwig had converted a plantation house into the island's first inn and invited paying guests. Newspapers called it an American *pensione*. His timing was rotten, but his idea catching.

After the conflict, former Confederate naval captain and Virginia transplant Joseph Hale Harvey gave the idea an improbable twist. He and a partner refitted the slave shacks of another Grand Isle plantation into cozy guest cottages. They were popular enough to justify regular steamer service between the island and New Orleans. The water shuttle, in turn, prompted French Creole families, the top of Louisiana's social strata of courtly men and genteel women, to build summer houses on the island. Through the season, their patriarchs commuted from the city at the end of each workweek. The season Field visited, 1892, the $100,000 pièce de résistance, Ocean Club Hotel, lit at night by 320 gas lights, opened its 160 rooms to a beachfront Gulf view.

The surf bathing out front in the saltwater was "absolutely unequaled," if not miraculous. Field claimed to know a severely paralyzed man who was given regular baths in the saltwater and within three weeks walked aboard the boat that took him home. She undoubtedly stretched the truth. "The voice of the sea is seductive, never ceasing, whispering, clamoring, murmuring, inviting the soul to wander in abysses of solitude." But one reality was the loosening of southern and Victorian formalities. You did not need the excuse of health to stroll the beach barefoot or jump into the surf.[28]

Still, habit, convention, fright—or whatever was causing apprehension—was not so readily forsaken. Field knew the prevailing temper of the island's guests. A "great many" failed to take advantage of all the offerings.

They never chased a yellow sand crab . . . to its lair under the sea drift of ship timbers and forest trees. They never broke up barnacled beer bottles in the hopes of finding that letter from the sea that never comes. They never made a collection of the quaint, carved images done in driftwood by the waves, nor joyed over finding lucky sea beans, or mildly tortured a jellyfish in the interest of amateur science.[29]

Even after ocean fears calmed, stories and realities came along to stir them up again. For one, there was the unseeable undertow that would drag bathers out to sea. And if exhaustion didn't drown you, there were stingrays, jellyfish, and sharks that maimed and killed. "Closer and closer," wrote Field, "crept the stealthy fin of a waiting shark." Mythic sea monsters did not altogether die. There, for one, was the harmless devilfish, Theodore Roosevelt's brute of the sea, damned with its very name, which was inspired by its spiny tail and protruding eyes resembling horns. Field listened to a lighthouse keeper who warned, the "horrid devil fish . . . haunts the Gulf and sometimes drags a schooner or a lugger away out to sea, and then down, down to the bottom of the ocean." He was repeating lore, perhaps taking it from a popular youth novel of the time, *Young Marooners on the Florida Coast*. Making a cameo appearance, a devilfish initiates a plot turn after tripping a skiff's anchor line and pulling the four young main characters to a deserted island.[30]

The physical composition of the seaside was also sometimes unstable. Grand Isle's leisure sibling, Last Island, also known as Isle Dernière, exuded precariousness. A narrow, twenty-four-mile-long bacon strip of an island slightly southeast of Edward McIlhenny's bird preserves, it rose so minimally out of the water that it defied its nominal status as a barrier. You could stand on the grassy mainland side of the island and see waves breaking on the other.

Despite all, merchants and doctors from New Orleans, sugar and rice planters from up the river, and state political leaders from the governor down made Last Island their favorite retreat—"To seek in summer ease divorce from care," wrote a visiting poet. Days had no urgency, fading one into the next and then the next until it was time, alas, to return to the city or plantation. An annotation on an 1853 Coast Survey chart read, "Isle Dernière may be readily known by the numerous houses on the beach." Three years later the houses were gone.[31]

Just before the summer season opened that year, bloody conflict broke out in Kansas between pro- and antislavery firebrands. On the holiday islands, over cigars and bourbon, there was surely talk of coming sectional conflict, but Last Island, suffused in summer tranquility, might have been a million miles away in 1856. The rooms were full at Muggah's Hotel; energy filled the bowling lanes, billiard room, card tables, and dining salon. The auspicious seasonal residents sat on the porches of the summer houses, offering a kindly "good day" to passersby, while servants brought refreshments. For the free men, the beach offered moments of contemplation, and in the salty, tame breakers, some partook in the novelty of bathing. You could walk out five hundred feet and still be only shin deep. Beneath covered galleries, women with their desirable milky-white skin shied away from the sun and waited for the promenade. All gathered on the hard-packed beach for this sunset ritual: "sober-sided gentlemen" on foot with walking sticks, and crinoline-attired women riding on horses or in carriages—everyone dressed in finery. When night fell, they attended an event at Muggah's or returned to their houses, disrobed with the aid of their body servants, and climbed into beds tented by fine-mesh insect netting. Night air came off the water, bringing with it felicitous slumber. This was their summer, lustrous, grand, idyllic— before it took a turn.[32]

When they woke on the morning of August 10, they might have wished to be in Bloody Kansas, had they known how the next twenty-four hours would unfold. The night before, they had attended a ball at Muggah's Hotel. Outside, unseen waves pounded the beach, and the black wind leaned heavily against the elevated structure. It rattled and shuddered; still, everyone went on dancing. The restless weather seemed more of an annoyance than a threat. Besides, if the "roughness of Neptune's greeting" became too much, remembered William Pugh, Louisiana speaker of the house on holiday, a river steamer was ready to take them to a protected bayou.[33]

The next morning, the wind was approaching gale force. The surf thundered, the rain came hard, and the wind, mixed with debris, tore houses apart. The two-story hotel collapsed. The storm tossed the steamer, the intended lifeline, up on the beach. Then the Gulf was upon the island sojourners. At the time of day when they normally would be partaking in their promenade, the island vanished beneath a twelve-foot storm surge.

Days earlier, an Atlantic hurricane had churned through the Florida Straits and advanced northwest, building strength. Last Island took the full blow. The sea swallowed the narrow strip and carried away 198 people. Survivors numbered 203. All had been a vanguard of an accepting attitude toward the seashore, and even if the storm had not broken the spirit to return, it had broken up their playground into eight tattered islets.

Martha Field toured the coast almost forty years later. She had convinced herself that Grand Isle's superior elevation, such as it was, meant the island would "never be washed away," as had Last Island. The next year, 1893, a hurricane lifting a sixteen-foot surge demolished the Ocean Club Hotel. Every eight years, Grand Isle suffered a direct hit. On a visit between storms during a lull in island bustle, the novelist and upriver midwesterner Charles Tenney Jackson fretted over the "unfortunate day Grand Isle will be discovered and muddled over with hotels and tourists." He was unaware of the island's resort tradition but prescient about its days ahead.[34]

When people discarded medieval trepidations about the seaside, they simultaneously threw caution to the wind. Half of them forgot storms come and gone, and half barely acknowledged the likelihood of recurrence. On the eve of the country's deadliest hurricane, the 1900 Galveston storm, the Texas island city was inundated by beachgoers from Houston who were taking advantage of a weekend special that transported them there by rail. Charging five cents a ride, mule-drawn streetcars made regular runs to the Gulf beach, which people shared with portable bathhouses. They were a more recent incarnation of the old horse-drawn bathing machines of England, with a different purpose: to keep the patron's feet from getting sandy. There were plenty of shod and barefoot strollers too, and bicycles.

Galveston was on the cutting edge of genuine beach culture, and then devastation. Despite death and destruction, eleven years after the 1900 hurricane engulfed the island, local investors opened the million-dollar, 226-room Hotel Galvez with the hope of reviving the tourist economy. Texans called it the "Queen of the Gulf." Seven stories of elegance, it stood only feet away from the city's new hurricane-defying seawall, hedging bets against another storm, daring nature to do it again. In 1927, the state teachers' bulletin said the island's commercial port and thriving tourist economy "justify the faith of those heroic men of 1900 who refused to accept failure." Because of them, Galveston had much to recommend it, with the "finest" Gulf-front surf bathing "in the world."[35]

AROUND THIS TIME ACROSS THE GULF, Florida beaches had much to offer. That's what Thomas Rowe was banking on when he began inviting his first holiday guests to accommodations that he had built out next to the breakers. Rowe was a Cambridge, Massachusetts–born son of Irish parents who loved opera. Trim and solemnly handsome, he also loved the enchanting leading lady, Lucinda, in a London performance of *Don César de Bazan*. They fell for each other. She was his Maritana and he her Don César. They planned to elope to America, before her parents intervened. Reluctantly, he set sail alone with an empty heart.

Eventually, Rowe married someone else, but the emptiness persisted. He consoled himself with the pursuit of wealth. When everybody seemed to be going to Florida in the 1920s to get rich quickly in the building boom, he joined them. It appeared that all roads to Florida—and new ones were being built to accommodate the stampede—led to riches. Newspapers said it was 1848 and the California gold rush all over again, or 1897 and the Alaskan Klondike. Except gold wasn't the hot commodity. Real estate was—the hottest in the country, hotter than molten gold. Investors were doubling, tripling their money in a week's time.

South Florida was a dream, a dubbed version of southern California—ceaseless sunshine, hypnotic sea breezes, dancing palm trees (many of them imported California date palms), with Mediterranean architecture to match—but still an opiate of its own. Real-estate offices in Sarasota tallied $11 million in sales in October 1925. John Ringling brought his train of circus clowns, acrobats, big cats, and elephants to town and established winter quarters; bought a big bayfront lot; and built a private art museum and a Venetian Gothic mansion for himself and his wife, Mable. Some press person dubbed winter sojourners "snowbirds," and the name stuck.

Sarasota's year-round population nearly tripled during the boom decade; Tampa's nearly doubled; and across the bay, now spanned by a two-and-a-half-mile poured-concrete bridge, St. Petersburg's population more than doubled, to forty thousand. Nonnative residents in St. Petersburg far exceeded native-born ones—by something on the order of twenty-five to one among business and civic leaders. They made the city into their version of Shangri-la. There were long domains of bayfront parks, neighborhoods with winding streets (one with concrete streets dyed pink), rows of planted palms, and Mediterranean Revival creations everywhere—the yacht club, country club, women's club, YMCA, arcade, and public restrooms, each hooded with a barrel-tile roof, white or terra-cotta.

The city centerpiece was the million-dollar fourteen-hundred-foot municipal pier, wide enough for two auto lanes and a streetcar line, domiciling a two-story Mediterranean Revival casino with an open-air ballroom and observation deck that looked out toward Tampa Bay and back at the city's skyline, rising with the same signature architectural expression. St. Petersburg would have 140 hotels by decade's end. The world champion New York Yankees set up spring headquarters at the posh Soreno Hotel. Babe Ruth and Lou Gehrig leased twin roof-garden penthouses atop the Flori-de-Leon apartments, with bay views. The Babe fished for tarpon, caroused for women, and thumbed his bulbous nose at Prohibition. Speakeasies with names like the Gangplank Nightclub sold liquor by the boatload smuggled across the Gulf from Cuba and the Bahamas. The twenties roared with pleasure-seeking passion. There was even a city-owned solarium where one could sunbathe au naturel.

On the artless side were the binder boys, slick-haired men dressed in knickers and two-tone shoes, standing on downtown corners atop wooden orange crates hawking real estate. This is a stereotype, but only slightly. Selling contracts on home lots for ten percent down, they personified the era's Babbittry. The assumption was that the binder could be resold at a profit many times over before full payment would be due after thirty days (Florida's original Ponzi scheme). And they were sold and resold, until the market imploded at the end of 1925.

Rowe got rich in the boom, rich enough to pay a princely $100,000 for eighty acres on Long Key, a two-hundred-yard-wide barrier connected to St. Petersburg by a bridge—one of the few such assets on the Gulf. The bridge and automobiles were a boon for real beachside development, and Rowe sensed correctly that the times were expanding from bayside to Gulf-side. He divided most of his island property into home lots and then spent $1.2 million to build a six-story, 220-room, Moorish-style hotel with arched openings, balconies, and red barrel-tile roof. Instead of the nail-and-board construction common to other Gulf hotels—the ones that blew away stick by stick in hurricanes—Rowe chose concrete and stucco. He completed the project with twelve thousand gallons of custom-mixed pink paint, and on January 16, 1928, the public attended a twilight gala grand opening.

Did Rowe long for the presence of Lucinda, his Maritana? *Claramente*. He named his new showpiece the Don CeSar Hotel, and its setting was appropriately romantic and abiding. Guests began their evenings watching the setting sun dropping orange before ebbing into pink. The hotel's matching luminance slipped into shades of dying light, and guests went to sleep to a lullaby surf.

Rowe placed his hotel just a few hundred feet from the Gulf. To ensure its stability on shifting sand and against storm surges, his construction engineer designed a floating concrete foundation supported by deep-set concrete pyramid footings. The design made possible a new conquest of the outer beaches. Rowe built the Don, as locals took to calling the hotel, to endure the weather of time as had his heart endured for Lucinda. Rising between dunes, it stood pink and palatial, a monument to the Gulf-side's ultimate and lasting annexation into the realm of holiday leisure.

BY THE ERA OF THE DON, "vacation" was the word increasingly spoken in place of "holiday," and more so now in pursuit of recreation than for spiritual, physical, and mental self-improvement. Gulf-side wasn't a new playground just for the moneyed set either. For every high-end resort newly anchored in the sand in the 1920s and after, there were many more unpretentious lodges and cottages for regular folks. The automobile was changing the vacation landscape too, shifting the tourist infrastructure—meaning overnight lodging and related attractions—away from steel rails to asphalt ribbons.

The Good Roads Movement encouraged three federal highway aid acts, in 1916, 1919, and 1921. A beneficiary was the Old Spanish Trail, which went under construction in 1915 and eventually stretched from St. Augustine to San Diego. It hugged the Alabama and Mississippi coast and linked the Six Sisters by paved road. The Dixie Highway had eastern and western routes from Canada to Florida by 1927, while expanding automobile ownership drove a growing number of Americans on vacation. And not all booked a room for the night.

Interestingly, the modern convenience of the automobile got people itching for vagabond adventure. According to the *New York Times*, half of America's newest mode of transportation in the mid-1920s were used for auto camping. The newspaper was likely overstating the case, but a phenomenon was surely sweeping the nation. It took in thrall those who could not afford the cost of a hotel room and those who simply preferred to sleep under the stars. They proudly wore the moniker "Tin Can Tourists," which derived from the type of food they cooked over campfires. They identified their allegiance with an empty soup can pushed over the radiator cap of their Chevrolets, Oldsmobiles, and Fords (Tin Lizzies). Some simply stowed gear in or atop their car and unpacked at each camp site, and the more creative converted cars and trucks into auto campers that looked carpenter-built in a home garage. Fashioned of plywood over the rear half of the chassis, they were stained and varnished rectangular boxes with trimmed corners and windows, and doors you knocked on to be invited inside.

Tin Can Tourists traveled east and west, north and south. Thousands went to Florida each year, avoiding the binder boys and urban ruckus, staying in tree-shaded parks, a farmer's fallow field, out in the scrub, or in specialized Tin Can Tourist camps, for a buck a week. They chartered a national association at Tampa, played shuffleboard at Dade City, carved Thanksgiving turkey at Arcadia, assembled a brass band at Sarasota, square-danced at Melbourne, hunched over bingo cards at Zephyrhills, and barbecued everywhere. And they went to sections of Gulf beach still wanting for hotels. Tents pitched and staked, they swam, sunned, fished, and stoked the embers of driftwood cook fires to panfry their catch. Come sunset, blissful day slipped into blissful night.

The boom and the Tin Can Tourists bypassed the Florida panhandle, although for no lack of an exquisitely quartz-white beach. What the panhandle did lack was easy access in the days of modern transportation. No highway forded it yet, and a train line snaked through agricultural country in its northern corridor away from the coast, aside from a connection at Pensacola. This exception apparently left a local newspaper editor with the hedging belief that Santa Rosa Island and its broad alabaster beach across the sound would soon "become the Coney Island of the South." That was 1887, and while a few bathers graced its immediate future, neither roller coaster nor hot-dog stands did. When an automobile bridge opened in 1931, the island became a weekend beach for Pensacolans, and when hotels went up, Alabamians were bidden to come down. A casino for dancing and dining opened too, as did the requisite fishing pier. There were now hot dogs, but still no roller coaster. "It was a start, albeit a slow one," writes historian Harvey Jackson in an engaging book on panhandle beaches.[36]

At the eastern end of Santa Rosa Sound at unincorporated Fort Walton (which had no fort but did have an Indian mound in the middle of town), the less than one hundred locals and a handful of Alabama visitors built houses and cottages on the sound and on Choctawhatchee Bay. Some would boat or swim across the sound and hike over the Gulf's lofty sand dunes to bathe in the Gulf. The dunes rolled out like foothills of an absent mountain range. Where not covered in grasses of sage and brown, they shone impossibly white. They sloped down against sculpting wind to a thick cushion of beach continuing to the watercolor sea. The magnificent beachfront would one day draw hordes of tourists, and that's apparently what Thomas E. Brooks, grandson of the town's nominal founder (an Alabamian), predicted. He put up forty cottages, an observation tower, and a casino out on the island beach in the 1920s. Nobody spent the night the first year, says Jackson, but still it was a start.

East across the inlet to the bay, Leonard Destin's legacy charter fishing fleet remained as busy as ever, taking tourists out to the hundred-fathom curve to catch trophies for their photo albums. Despite the sugar-sand swath fronting gemstone Gulf waters, the beach languished in near desertion. When US 98 opened east–west along the coast in 1933, at points mere feet from water's edge, where it had plowed through dunes but opened up vistas, it got more Alabamians to drive down to the coast. The tourism stream was still little more than a summertime rivulet, but it was flush enough to irritate shrimpers, oystermen, and longleaf woodsmen who lived in isolation for a reason, which, in part, had to do with annoying city folk.

Some of the latter drove east of Destin to Grayton Beach to stay at a Gulf-front hotel built in the 1880s, either by the area's namesake, a bearded Civil War veteran named Charles T. Gray, or a timber company that used it as a barracks for tree cutters. Someone with a waggish sense of humor named it the Washaway Hotel. That's what chunks of the beach did in these parts—wash away. A best-kept secret of the area were coastal dune lakes, tannin brown and dirty-looking, yet clean and inviting. Separated from the sea by sand dunes, they are features in a hydrologic system found in a few places in Australia, New Zealand, and Madagascar, but nowhere else on the Gulf. Routinely, as rain and stream water fills a dune lake to capacity, the building water weight breaches a vulnerable strip of beach sand. When this happened, locals and vacationers got a carnival-ride thrill in bodysurf-ing the swift outflow into the Gulf, and then hauled themselves back across the dunes for another ride. A storm or, eventually, Gulf cur-rents would seal off the lake again until the next breakout.

On down the road was Panama City, the largest panhandle city next to Pensacola, with about ten thousand inhabitants in 1930. Like Pen-sacola, it was located on the north side of its bay. The same as Pensacol-ans, residents seeking a respite from their daily lives (which, for many, meant working at the local paper mill) started crossing the bay to the beach. Cottages, a dance casino, and hotels soon went up Gulf-side. A Birmingham developer bought four thousand feet of oceanfront next to Highway 98, sectioned his parcel into lots, and sold thirty-seven in the first week of the offering, all of them to Alabamians.

Floridians on the peninsula hardly paid attention to the panhan-dle, apart from its majority reign in the legislature despite its minority population size. As Harvey Jackson points out, a state promotional pamphlet distributed in 1937 didn't bother mentioning the beaches at Pensacola or Panama City. Floridians were less intimate with their panhandle than were Alabamians. From early on, panhandle folk ini-tiated serious agitating for secession from Florida to join Alabama's cradle of "southernness." These were, for the most part, middle-class, Protestant, white people. They kept the beaches segregated, but for that matter, so did white Mississippians, Louisianans, Texans, and, indeed, the transplanted Yankees down on the Florida peninsula.

Maintaining white-on-white beaches made little difference to the development of the panhandle. Long, lonely sections of Highway

98—pine-wooded on the north side, and Gulf- and bay-scenic on the south—waited for the day when condominiums and strip malls would draw across its edge.

All of that arrived well after the next world war, eventually with the rolling intensity of the accompanying amusement park ride that finally elicited screams on Pensacola Beach. Almost no part of the US Gulf coast was overlooked. Back in her electric-lighted *Picayune* office, writing columns, Martha Field sometimes wished for civilization's keener interest in Gulf beaches. If she had lived beyond her forty-three years and into her eighties, she might have taken back her wish. By then, nothing could keep people, businesses, and developers away—not racial integration, high real-estate and construction prices, environmental degradation, crowded beachfronts, traffic-racked highways, not even hurricanes.

It is unlikely that those who went were familiar with the primordial link between the beach that lured and the fossil fuel that delivered them, between an industry that tended to brighten the world and one that darkened it.

Ten

OIL AND THE
TEXAS TOE DIP

Goose Creek Oil Field, site of the first over-water oil wells
on the Gulf, and of the first Gulf oil spill.

*It may be tentatively assumed that the Gulf of Mexico is a
potential source of salt-dome oil.*

—ORVAL L. BRACE, GEOLOGIST (1941)[1]

A BRONTOSAURUS STOLE THE SHOW AT THE 1933 WORLD'S
Fair in Chicago. Most of us know brontosaurus as the dinosaur with
a smallish head serenely held high on a long neck, counterbalanced by
a long tail dragging behind a hummock-shaped body on stubby legs.
The two-ton, greenish-gray mechanical replica at the World's Fair was
part of a dinosaur exhibit sponsored by the Sinclair Oil Corporation.
An average of twenty-four thousand visitors toured the exhibit each
day, by the company's count—a half million over Labor Day weekend.

They took photos of each other standing small beside reptilian giants. There were three, a sharp-fanged tyrannosaurus, a heavy-horned triceratops, and the friendly looking brontosaurus, which people started calling Dino. Seeing an opportunity, Sinclair adopted him as its official mascot.

It was a public relations coup (which the company badly needed after founder Harry Ford Sinclair had been implicated ten years earlier in the Teapot Dome bribery scandal). Dino put Sinclair in the forefront of the industry's explanation for the origin of oil, albeit false, and simplified for popular consumption: fossil fuels came from the fossils of dinosaurs. Emphasizing ancestral lineage through the popular Dino lent Sinclair fuels an authenticity that competitors could not claim in quite the same way. A company ad at the time asserted, "By and large, the oldest crudes make the best motor oils."[2]

There was no mistaking the new Sinclair filling-station signs put up after the World's Fair: white with green trim and red lettering, and a green profile of Dino front and center. Customers who bought a tank of Sinclair gas got a free collectible miniature brontosaurus. In 1964, Sinclair took its exhibit back to the World's Fair with the name Dinoland. That same year on the main highway running down the Florida Gulf coast, the company built a service station in a three-dimensional form of Dino (the maintenance bays were housed between his legs). It was one of a kind. In cars passing by out front, fingers pointed and little faces pressed against the windows. Children loved the Sinclair mascot. Eager for an inflatable Dino for the Gulf beach, they pestered parents to fill up at the dinosaur sign.

Years later, critics denounced the McDonald's Corporation for trotting out Happy Meal toys and storefront PlayPlaces as a marketing ploy targeting children. But Sinclair had deployed the strategy long before: "Children are as fascinated with the pre-historic uniqueness of the dinosaurs as are adults," noted a company document, "and the correlation with Sinclair therefore begins at an early age."[3]

The innocent Dino had a hidden dark side. He was a forebear not only to Ronald McDonald but to R. J. Reynolds's cigarette-smoking icon, Joe Camel. Dino was a feel-good brand image for a product that polluted the water and filled the air with greenhouse gases and poisons—some obvious, like the smog-producing particles belching from refineries and automotive tailpipes; others insidious, like the exquisitely fine and poisonous lead oxide produced by burning leaded gasoline (until the federal phase-out of lead additives in the 1970s). Unlike the cigarette giant's infamously banned prince of cool, however, the dinosaur ambassador of oil's origin story has yet to go extinct.*

That origin story has problems too. First, brontosaurus never existed. The best-known dinosaur was the creation of an ambitious, if also careless, paleontologist rushing to trounce others in the so-called Bone Wars of the late nineteenth century. Brontosaurus is really apatosaurus with someone else's head. It seems supremely apt, then, that a fictional dinosaur came to represent another falsehood: oil comes from dinosaurs. According to geologist Paul Mueller, the deception is a case of mistaken identities among fossils. Yet, even after scientists realized the truth, the original story lived on as clever product marketing, bestowing on fossil fuels an agreeable *Jurassic Park* image. As does any good myth, this one hides an unpalatable reality, which is the messy business of taking oil from the earth.

THE FACTS BEHIND PETROLEUM'S geological beginnings are comparatively tame. Even the most creative marketing genius is unlikely to find a lovable mascot in oil's actual primordial DNA—decayed marine algae and zooplankton. (Shell Oil Company has its yellow scallop-shell logo, but it holds no candle to a green Dino.) On ancient seafloors where organisms had lain dead long before Jurassic megafauna lived, bacterial decomposition consumed oxygen, nitrogen, phosphorus, and sulfur and left behind matter of mostly carbon and hydrogen. The process went on for millions of years. Millions

---

* As of this writing, Sinclair operates some twenty-six hundred filling stations in twenty states, in the Midwest and West.

more passed as, in the case of the Gulf, sediment from the Appalachian chain washed down to the sea—the same sediment that made
beaches.

Layer upon layer built up, thousands of feet, mountaintop turning
into sea bottom, producing cauldrons of heat and pressure. (Some scientists believe that volcanic ash from the Rocky Mountains was part
of this process.) Deep inside, in a remarkable fusion of biology and
geology, the decomposing plants and animals transformed into crude,
the future bonanza of oil drillers. "Now, if I can reach down there and
bring up the results of all those millions of years," says a wistful James
Stewart playing a Gulf oil hunter in the 1953 film *Thunder Bay*, "and
make them work for the present and future, then I've done something.
Haven't I?"

The Stewart character's real-life predecessors, working around the
Gulf in the late nineteenth century, initially concentrated their search
on land in Texas. Since the Gulf was once much larger than it is today,
deposits of the benthic sludge—that is, oil—were left beneath dry
ground after the seawater backed off. Calling themselves wildcatters,
early oil hunters were ruthless stalkers of the land. Their search methods were unsophisticated at best, though consistent with the science of
the time. They relied on surface geology, essentially determining—or
guessing—what lay below by reading the contours above. Sharp eyes,
a good set of legs, and sometimes multiple pairs of shoes, dust-caked
and tread-worn by the end, were required to divine crude in Texas—
vast, dusty, swampy, rocky Texas; mosquito-, wildcat-, rattlesnake-
bedeviled Texas.

Prospectors looked for oil seeps, mineral springs, paraffin dirt,
and sedimentary rock, and sought testimony from locals. If fortunate
enough to come upon smelly gas hissing from a rent in the ground,
they would strike a match and hope for it to flare. It was a matter of
"pitting man's skill against nature's obduracy," proclaims a midcentury industry history, "and applying human intelligence to solving the
riddle of where oil and gas are stored in the recesses of the earth."
Individual oil hunters went broke trying to solve the riddle, partner-

ships went bust, and investors went elsewhere. Then, as quick as one could strike a match, the answer—and wealth—might reveal itself.[4]

It happened that way in 1901 near Beaumont, Texas, at a place called Spindletop, named by Spanish explorers for the area's spindle-shaped cypress trees. About twenty-five miles from the Gulf as the crow flies, a gusher as never seen before exploded from a newly drilled well. It was the first on the Gulf coast, and so impressive that it turned heads in the industry. Pennsylvania, Ohio, and more recently California had been the lucrative centers of oil. Few thought the South had potential, even though in Texas people had been aware of sur-face oozes for centuries. Natives and colonial Spaniards, including Soto's retreating expedition, used the pitch-like substance from black springs, or seeps, to seal their boats. The seeps were like seams break-ing open on an earthen container bulging with crude.

That was more or less the suspicion of Patillo Higgins, a one-armed former logger turned brickmaker with a fourth-grade education (he lost his arm in a logging accident), who was also a cop killer. In his wild youth, he fatally shot a deputy trying to arrest him for bombing a black church, apparently because he hated the color of its congre-gants. He got off scot-free after convincing the court he had killed in self-defense. As with many erstwhile murderers, religion ultimately saved the square-jawed young man. Getting right with God, he had his long, lean body washed in baptismal waters and described his sal-vation as the "silent, supernatural working of the Holy Spirit." He started teaching Sunday school at a Baptist church, enjoying best taking his classes on picnics up to Sour Spring Mound, south of town at Spindletop.[5]

This was hill country growing out of flat country, rich and peaceful with none of the drudgery of town and farm. It was shaggy country with ankle- to waist-high grass and hypnotically brushing wildflow-ers, where the sky could be high and empty or low-slung and saturated, where the air on a west wind was dry and on a Gulf wind humid. It wasn't always pure, though—not to the nose. The stench of sulfur often moved across the knoll. Yet this, too, was part of the allure. The

Sunday school teacher would delight the children by puncturing the ground with a stick of bamboo to release gas; methodically, he'd pull out a lucifer matchstick and ignite the remarkable torch.

As the name suggests, Spindletop's Sour Spring Mound had mineral springs. The medical corps of the Confederacy used them to treat yellow-fever patients during the war. Afterward, entrepreneurs turned two of them and a place known as Sour Lake into health spas. Spindletop's surface features, which included oil seeps, were transparent clues to its subterranean tissue. Geologists determined that Sour Spring Mound had risen on a salt dome. Higgins knew this. Amid everything else, he was an amateur geologist, and he believed a salt dome and the caprock above it were natural lids on repositories of oil.

Vestiges of primordial evaporating seas, salt domes are briny boils that have thrust upward through the layers from vast salt reserves that lie beneath fifty thousand feet of sediment. More than five hundred domes are scattered on- and offshore around the northwestern Gulf, making the American Sea one of the most replete salt-dome regions in the world.

Edward McIlhenny's Avery Island owes its remarkable 162-foot elevation to a salt dome. It is deeper than Mount Everest is tall, and will never be mined out. Tabasco, Mexico, home of the pepper that lent its name to the McIlhennys' famous sauce, has a major salt dome. Around the time the family was launching its spicy condiment, snapper fishermen discovered three reefs a hundred miles out from Texas covered with plants, sponges, and corals. The reefs are unique in the upper Gulf (the corals are ten to fifteen thousand years old and likely loop-current migrants from Mexico). The fishermen named them the Flower Garden Banks, unaware that the underwater beauty was attached to the summits of salt domes coming through the Gulf floor.

Hardly anyone at the time understood the nature of salt domes. Their own knowledge limited, geologists seemed certain that salt domes had no connection to oil. When Higgins organized an oil company in 1892 and sought investors to start drilling on Spindletop, the local newspaper wondered whether he wasn't selling snake oil. Townsfolk talked about him behind his back, calling him "rather peculiar." He took penance for his past to a holier-than-thou extreme by policing the morality of others, loudly condemning alcohol, dancing, theater, swimming, beach resorts, and preachers who forgave the sins of repeat offenders. He raised plenty of eyebrows for being a longtime bachelor who lived with his mother, and raised them highest when he began adopting teenage girls—even, at the age of forty-five, marrying one, who gave him a trio of children. After three years of drilling for oil, he came up with nothing more than validation for his detractors.[6]

When his company went broke, he advertised for new investors. Local interest remained indifferent at best, and then a promising inquiry came from a Croatian immigrant over in Louisiana named Anthony Lucas. Lucas was a native of the Dalmatian Coast and a former officer in the Austrian navy. He emigrated to the US in 1879, donned the title "captain," though he had advanced no higher than lieutenant in Austria, and eventually found work as a mining engineer and superintendent of the salt mine on Avery Island. He and Higgins were equally convinced that where there was salt, there was oil. In addition to Avery, Louisiana had four other salt-dome islands: Jefferson, Weeks, Belle, and Cote Blanche. Lucas had investigated them all and found evidence of oil.

In the summer of 1900, he began drilling at Spindletop. He employed a Christmas tree–shaped wooden derrick, or "rig," to position and stabilize a rotary drill bit powered by a steam engine. Assembled in sections, the bit was hollow, enabling the crew to run pressurized fluid, often called drilling mud, through to the bottom to wash away debris as the bit's toothy end bore into the earth. At 575 feet down, Lucas ran into difficulties and out of money. A trip to Pittsburgh and a meeting with experienced oil developers secured a group of financial backers, which included banking millionaire and future treasury secretary Andrew W. Mellon and his brother, Robert B. Mellon. The new investors forced the pietistic Higgins out, believing he had nothing to contribute to the venture, but left Captain Lucas at the helm. They also brought in an experienced crew from Corsicana, between Houston and Dallas, where six years earlier the state's first commercially viable, though modest, well had been established.

Before operations at Spindletop resumed, the 1900 hurricane struck, drowning the island city of Galveston, less than a hundred miles southwest of the drill site. The compassionate citizens of Corsicana sent ice, water, and a thousand loaves of bread to the storm victims. The new oil crew boarded a train that carried derrick timbers and drilling equipment to Beaumont and relief supplies on to Galveston. While hurricane survivors dug out from the rubble, roughnecks on Sour Spring Mound soon raised a derrick to house a new rotary rig. Its twelve-inch drill bit began boring through sediment rock in October.

On January 10, 1901, with drilling at 1,139 feet, the rig began to shudder. Thinking the bit had dulled, the crew pulled it from the ground to replace it. When they did, mud exploded from the drill hole, propelling six tons of four-inch steel pipe through the top of the rig. Workers dove for cover. No one was hurt, and things settled. Then, before anyone could catch his breath, mud shot up again and everyone hit the deck a second time. Gas hissed and sighed, and the air grew foul. Quiet trailed, though everyone remained cautious. The sound of bubbling rose from the drill hole. Oil pushed slowly to the top, spilled out, gained momentum, and burst upward into a roaring stream of crude that seemed enraged by the disturbance from its million-year slumber. One hundred and fifty feet it raced, twice the height of the derrick, before doubling into a shower over dancing roughnecks.

TEXAS HISTORIES SAY THAT SPINDLETOP brought oil into the modern age. That's not an exaggeration, although timing was, as they say, everything. Before Spindletop, illuminating streets and buildings with kerosene lamps fueled the oil industry. Hitting the market at three cents a barrel, Spindletop crude encouraged a new energy source for heating, war, and transportation. Once fired almost exclusively by coal, electrical plants were expanding across the country and into oil use. The railroad industry developed petroleum-powered locomotives to replace coal burners (by 1905, the Santa Fe Railroad, which serviced the Texas coast, operated 227 of them). Coal got jilted by the US Navy, too, in 1910 (the coal payload was heavier than oil). The British had recently converted their navy, and the year before, Theodore Roosevelt's Great White Fleet—mobilized to show off the country's sea power—had returned to port from its world tour blackened and unsightly with coal soot.

Gasoline was still little more than a waste by-product of the process for refining kerosene, which was used mainly for treating head lice and removing grease stains from clothing. Refineries dumped most gasoline into rivers. It was on its way, though, to becoming the most important derivative of Gulf crude. Within a decade of Spindletop, the automobile revolutionized American transportation, travel, and shipping, creating one of the greatest commercial demands ever for a natural resource. Automakers initially considered many different fuels, including alcohol and ethanol, before settling on less expensive gasoline upon the development of octane-boosting tetraethyl lead.

By 1918, the US was producing seventy percent of the world's petroleum. Research-and-development laboratories were constantly coming up with new applications. Petroleum "lubricates the wheels that it turns, helps to pave roads, and furnishes synthetic rubber for tires," notes a history of Humble Oil, homegrown on the Gulf. "It heats buildings and also roofs and paints them, waxes their floors, and cleans their windows. It supplies the basic ingredients for the manufacture of synthetics, plastics, and chemical products—literally numberless—for uses of peace and war."[7]

Beaumont was poised to have its variously muddy and dusty streets surfaced in asphalt, and why not? Asphalt is a petroleum product, and the town had plenty. Before the Spindletop strike, Beaumont had been a workaday lumber town and rather plain and listless. Overnight, it turned into what some dubbed the "City of Gushers." Oilmen and speculators, men and women looking for work and fortunes, coming off farms and ranches and from northern cities, descended on the town. By 1902, five hundred oil-related businesses were operating. The population of nine thousand tripled in three months and never stopped growing. It spun off three new towns: Spindletop, Gladys, and South Africa (where blacks and Mexicans lived). Real-estate prices shot up like Lucas's gusher. "Pig wallows sold for $35,000 and cow pastures for $100,000," says one history of Texas oil. "Land 150 miles from Beaumont sold for $1,000 an acre." At Spindletop, an acre could cost $900,000.[8]

Oil derricks grew on Spindletop like tulips in a Dutch garden, though colorless and unsightly. Leases were as small as twenty feet square, barely room enough for a single derrick, some running multiple wells. By 1904, a blizzard of twelve hundred derricks blanketed 170 acres. A man could step from one derrick to the other and cross the field without touching the ground. Every inch of it—every structure and walking, talking person—wore a grimy sheen of crude. Even when the sky was blue, the place was gray. Three million barrels of oil floated in an enormous open pit carved in the ground, a great black shining mirror of prosperity. Three future giants in the industry—Gulf Oil, Mobil, and Texaco—grew out of Spindletop. The Mellon brothers reportedly reaped $40 million from their investment. Though forced out of their arrangement with Lucas, Higgins was soon wearing expensive suits. He had founded a new oil concern and leased out property he still owned, eventually selling his interest for some $3 million. Celebrants at the silver anniversary of Spindletop hailed the man once dismissed as a fool as an oil-finding savant.

The hill yielded more than seventeen million barrels of crude in 1902. A glut pushed oil prices to an all-time low. But they soon rebounded, just as the dome started going dry. As quickly as the boom had happened, Spindletop began sputtering out. "The cow," said Lucas, "was milked too hard." In 1904, the well pumped only 100,000 barrels.[9]

The Spindletop bust made no difference in the grander scheme. Derricks soon pumped the Texas earth at Saratoga, Sour Lake, Batson, and Humble, at West Columbia, Barbers Hill, Hull, and High Island. The state's coastal region was the industry's new wonderland, and not simply because of men with guts and fortitude. Nature favored success, putting forward decidedly agreeable conditions. Texas weather was mild, and the ground soft. Unlike hard rock in other oil regions, the Gulf's sedimentary layers for the most part eliminated complications in drilling. And there were the Gulf's five hundred salt domes. The hunches of Higgins and Lucas were right. After Spindletop, wildcatters spread out across the region, going from dome to dome in Texas and Louisiana. Then, they looked to the water at a place called Goose Creek.

KARANKAWA AND ATAKAPA had once made seasonal visits to the banks of Goose Creek and Tabbs Bay in Texas for the oysters, clams, and fish. Colonial Spanish and French apparently paid the area little mind, although Goose Creek lies where the San Jacinto River enters Galveston Bay. Americans began showing up in the 1820s after Mexico liberated itself from Spain. They ranched and farmed, covering the area with rice fields, using slave labor and West African ingenuity in rice cultivation.

In 1834, Mary Jones sold a small peninsula at the confluence of Tabbs Bay and Goose Creek to the Chubb brothers of Charlestown, Massachusetts. They built fishing and shipping schooners on the site and, in the fight for independence from Mexico, served with Sam Houston and the Texians, with one brother as fleet admiral. They smuggled slaves from the African Gold Coast, and when sectional hostilities erupted, the Chubbs turned against Yankee brothers, establishing a Confederate naval yard at Goose Creek that built shallow-draft blockade runners. Within a few years of war's end, Thomas B. Gaillard bought the Chubb property and brought his wife and eight children down from Natchez, Mississippi.

In 1903, around the time Spindletop lost its verve, one of Gaillard's grown sons, John, was fishing on Tabbs Bay at the mouth of Goose Creek. He was floating over a salt dome, something he didn't know, when he noticed bubbles rising to the surface. He thought they were coming from buffalo fish and prepared to cast his line. But then he had a mind to strike a match. By now, virtually everyone around the Texas coast knew this as a trick of oil geologists. If the bubbles burst into red-orange flames and black smoke, they were natural gas, and oil likely lay below. John Gaillard was not a geologist, but a rancher, owner of a small, 262-acre spread—and soon he would be a rich man. His match flared.

Or did it? The Gaillard story could be another fictional origin tale on the order of Sinclair's dinosaurs—the story of oil's discovery offshore in Texas. It pops up in a dozen or more online sources. Each is a verbatim copy of the others, and not one cites a source, which means each is plagiarizing the original, either directly or indirectly through one of the other copycats. The original, it turns out, is an article in the *Handbook of Texas*, posted on the web in June 2010, in the midst of the *Deepwater Horizon* oil spill. The article cites four sources. Two mention Gaillard; both are books. One misspells his name and claims his fishing adventure occurred in 1916, rather than 1903. The other gives no date, though it gets his name right. In a black-and-white photograph on page thirteen of the latter, four men before a rig stand squinting into the south Texas sun. The one in the middle with a handlebar mustache curling up to high cheekbones is Gaillard. He is small, the size of a boy. He wears a Stetson Boss of the Plains, the crown uncreased, the brim saucer-flat—a small rancher in a big hat. Neither book says anything about a match.[10]

The confusion doesn't end there. According to a field guide published by the Houston Geological Society in the 1950s, the Tabbs Bay bubbles were spotted in 1906, and not by Gaillard. Three other weekend anglers were out on the water, quite probably fishing for tarpon and passing about fortification in a glass bottle, a matchstick in one pocket ready to light a celebratory cigar from another—or to light anything that might pop up. One of the men, Lovic P. Garrett, had a degree in geology and worked for the Rio Bravo Oil Company. He would know to strike a match. After it flared, his companions, Robert A. Welch and R. T. Rue, organized the Goose Creek Production Company the next year and started drilling test wells on Gaillard's ranch.

The author of the field guide entry worked for Gulf Oil Corporation and in an industry that wrote the earliest histories of oil exploration. They have a proprietary texture and form a documentary of sorts with a standard narrative—one that credits the industry's own with brave discoveries that transported the country into the modern age. Gaillard is a shadow character, if mentioned at all. Maybe he did light that match in 1903, only to be shunned by official chroniclers. He makes lousy copy for them. Although he leased his land to oil companies, he remained a rancher at heart, evident by a controversial clause in his leases allowing him to boot roughnecks off his property if they failed to keep gates closed and let his cattle wander off. In the legacy narrative, the early wildcatters were all oilmen, and courageous visionaries with unassailable qualities. They were "ultracompetent," says one source, "marvelously well-informed," positively endowed with an "aggressive spirit." It's a boring portrait of stoic heroes without flaws, quirks, or dark secrets—an exclusive club of white men, wealthy or on the way to becoming so.[11]

Regardless of who struck the match or whether it was struck at all, the first good oil from Goose Creek did not come in until 1916. The front-page headline of the August 24 *Houston Chronicle* reads: 10,000 BARREL WELL IN AT GOOSE CREEK. The American Petroleum Company had brought in a good producer, and just in time. In eight months, Woodrow Wilson would ask Congress for a declaration of war against Germany. The great conflict in Europe was the first war run on oil; eighty percent of that used by Allied powers came from US fields.

Soon after Congress authorized Wilson's declaration, Sinclair Oil and E. F. Sims Oil (Edward Sims was on Sinclair's board of directors, and wealthy enough to employ eight gardeners at his Houston estate) unleashed a gusher from their well "Sweet No. 11," again in August, on a plot leased from Gaillard's neighbor, and dubbed "Sweet Evangeline." Reaching three thousand feet, the bore yielded thirty-five thousand barrels a day. An oil company seeking investors to fund new Goose Creek wells advertised in the *Pittsburgh Gazette*, "Gusher makes $33 a minute." The year before, Goose Creek yielded 400,000 barrels; the year of Sweet Evangeline, it turned out 7.3 million. It wasn't Spindletop in 1902, but the industry was calling Goose Creek the country's new sweet spot, and the rancher Gaillard found himself herding leasing offers.[12]

Ultimately, this hallowed history and the subsequent enterprise in crude erased the land's identity as a serene little notch in the grandest estuary in Texas, the Trinity–San Jacinto. Before blockade runners and oil, Goose Creek had been a winter haven for avian life, inviting migratory birds such as merganser and bufflehead ducks and white pelicans. Under John Gaillard's stewardship, it invited fortune seekers. Sweet Evangeline brought heavy timbers, framing brackets, rotary tables, Kelly pipes, and the new twin-cone roller bit designed by Howard Hughes Sr. of Houston; boilers, steam engines, and sooty smoke; forty-two-gallon steel barrels, earthen reservoirs, and roughnecks bathed in grimy sweat making $5.20 for a ten-hour day; and a city of cook wagons, privies, and canvas tents that crowded out the stick-and-brush roosts of year-round brown pelicans and roseate spoonbills.

The changing scene, noted the *Houston Chronicle*, "burst upon you . . . from behind a screen of verdure." The vegetative screen was disappearing quickly. More than forty derricks hastily appeared on Gaillard's ranch. If not for what they were—noisy, smoky, wet with oil—they might have doubled as roosting platforms for opportunistic ospreys and eagles. Other landowners began leasing and selling their property too. Hardly two years passed before fifteen hundred wooden or steel structures towered over the region that the industry and press called the Goose Creek Oil Field. All this industrial production supplanting an estuarine environment, itself a major producer in nature's economy, registered little public or scientific concern. When the demand for defense oil spiked barrel prices, development was bound to trump all else. "Progress is not without fault, my friend," says a truth-speaking government conservation officer in that James Stewart movie *Thunder Bay*.[13]

It was inevitable that derricks would migrate from avian territory to marine territory—to wit, into coastal Texas's poshest resort for shrimp and oysters. Though connected to land by wooden docks, these wellheads were the Gulf's first over-water oil rigs.

JOSEPH ISAACS, AN ENTERPRISING MAN, plied the muddy thoroughfares of the Goose Creek Oil Field in a converted platform wagon drawn by a pair of mules, both black and tall. A steel tank lay horizontal on the wagon, and on top of that, at the front end, Isaacs had rigged a seat where he sat, feet dangling, and held the reins to his obedient beasts. The tank carried water from an artesian well, potable water that he sold to Goose Creek households for thirty-five cents a barrel. Business was brisk. The oil industry had contaminated home wells.

Foul water was the unintended yet ineluctable legacy of an idea that had come to light decades before. In the midst of the country's first oil rush, incited by an 1859 strike in northwestern Pennsylvania, Thomas Rowland had filed an application with the US Patent Office. Rowland was fairly well known for his innovations in metal fabricating. He had built the shot-proof steel hull of the celebrated USS *Monitor* at his Continental Works on the East River in Brooklyn.

Changes were coming to the economy at the Civil War's end, and Rowland stayed on top of them, even ahead of them. Ten years after the Pennsylvania oil strike, he received the patent for his "submarine drilling-apparatus." It was an early version of an offshore oil rig, and remarkably prescient. It consisted of a stand-alone platform above telescoping legs that could extend fifty feet to the seafloor. Unfortunately for Rowland, his apparatus remained a concept on drafting linen until long past his death. While he went on to develop giant steel storage tanks for natural gas, the oil industry started going offshore. Except it didn't do it Rowland's way, and it went in the opposite direction from his factory, to the other side of the continent.

The first step into ocean water happened at the edge of the Pacific in front of the white bluffs at Summerland, California, near Santa Barbara, in 1896. There was no fanfare; no brass band, ribbon cutting, or speeches; no submarine drilling-apparatus—just a wooden derrick, like any derrick, although this one was at the end of a short pier, a couple strides from shore. Five years later, piers spanned the length of the bluff coast, each supporting two or three or even several derricks—totaling some four hundred oil rigs on piers. None extended out more than a few hundred feet. It was both an eager and a timid reach.

Over-water drilling was limited not by design or technology, as historians and oil industry aficionados have claimed. Independent producers were, at the time, drilling on Ohio's seventeen-thousand-acre Grand Lake reservoir, built as part of the Erie Canal system, and a puddle compared with the oceanic Great Lakes a hundred miles to the north. Oilmen drove wooden piles into the reservoir bottom to build stand-alone platforms, known as cribs. They were individually crowned by a conventional cable-tool derrick. Roughnecks changed shifts by boat and went to work on constructed wooden islands on the constructed reservoir, sharing their water-encircled space with a rackety steam engine and boiler. The only tether to land was a pipeline to shoreside storage tanks—no connecting dock or pier or even catwalk. In 1913, the *New York Times* reported "more than 100 wells" going at it. One historian believes that the earliest ones predated the California wells by as much as five years.[14]

That possibility would addle the community-spirited people down in Mooringsport, Louisiana. In 1994, they dedicated a roadside historic marker making claim to the country's first freestanding "offshore" oil well, at Caddo Lake (once known as Ferry Lake). Straddling the interior border of east Texas and northwest Louisiana, Caddo is a big lake of smaller lakes and uncounted bayous where the water coils around the fluted trunks of old cypress trees. Texans call Caddo their only natural lake—or only "honest" one, as they say (all lakes in Texas are artificial). A future First Lady of the United States, Claudia Alta Taylor, was born on the Texas side in 1912. When she was later known as Lady Bird Johnson and appreciated for planting wildflowers along interstate highways, people traced her sensibilities to the lake's biological treasures, altered though they were.

Early in the century, after a production foreman from Gulf Oil set strings of gas bubbles in flame, he convinced his employer to lease eight thousand acres of lake bottom from the Louisiana levee board. The Army Corps of Engineers authorized a dam on the east side to control the water level (that's how Texas got its honest lake). Oilmen cut the cypress to build platforms, and Howard Hughes Sr. brought his new twin-cone drill bit, the "rock eater," up from Houston for a successful trial run. The year before Claudia Taylor was born, a Hughes bit opened the lake's first productive over-water well. (Hughes was destined to great wealth, and Howard Jr., to name his first film company Caddo Productions.) When Claudia was a toddler, tugboats pushing oil barges crossed the lake, itself an outdoor theater of more than 250 derricks. The lot of them were the picture of a meticulous surveyor's commission, aligned in a grid that resembled the headstones at Arlington Cemetery.

When it came time down at Goose Creek to venture into the water, crews followed both California's dock-and-pier and Caddo's standalone models. Yet, if Caddo was precise and geometric, Goose Creek was slapdash. There was no orderliness to it, in part because going off land in Texas had followed the hurried needs of war. The onshore oil fields teemed with derricks in as much as they teemed with leaseholders, and everyone was after the same pool of oil—cutting up the same hog, as they said in Texas. So you put down as many wells as your inches allowed before the guy next door sucked you dry. If you held a shorefront lease, you could buy yourself free real estate by crossing over the line between land and water. Goose Creek's peak years, delivering nine million barrels, came between 1917 and 1919, when fifteen hundred derricks stood on land and marsh and over creek.

You can split hairs and say that putting a derrick over water close enough to swim or wade to land—two to ten times closer than your drill hole was deep, the water shallow enough for the diminutive Gaillard to stand in—wasn't really offshore drilling. Except, these rigs on creeks and bays were the precursors to the far-flung rigs on the large sea. And they had some of the same taste, look, and feel.

That was especially true with regard to oil spills. Production fields were dirty, ugly, smelly places. People living on or near the grounds watched balefully as one oil rig after another went up and turned their world soggier and blacker. Raised wooden walkways crossed over greasy mud, relentlessly present, even when rain was a distant memory. Puddles and pools of crude on pervious ground, stored in pervious reservoirs, were everywhere. More oil seeped back into the ground or sluiced off into creeks and streams and bays than went into barrels. "Oil spill" wasn't even part of the vocabulary. A "gusher" was the closest thing to the concept.

When gushers were still novel, there was cause for celebration, an adrenaline rush, in letting an active well flow like an uncorked bottle of champagne. The Spindletop gusher lasted nine days, discharging 800,000 barrels before the crew was able to cap it. You shut down a gusher in the interest of economics, not because you cared about fish and birds or even the groundwater. That's why there were men like Joseph Isaacs with a pair of mules delivering good potable water in virtually every boomtown. You shut down a gusher to keep peace with neighboring drillers who didn't need your good luck raining on their bad. Still, operators occasionally opened controlled wells to gauge their flow rate, and some gave in to the temptation to show off a sky-high fountain of black. Waste was a sign of success. Blackened land had the shine of gold.

Still, Sweet Evangeline was not so sweet for everyone. That August 1917 gusher started out as a 250-footer that turned into a three-day downpour. Thirty-five thousand barrels were lost, enough to heat twenty-one hundred homes for a year. The lost oil created a ten-acre lake two inches deep, and not all of it pooled. The wind carried showering crude for miles. Trees were left dripping, roads slick, and clean laundry hanging on lines stained. What was left of the Goose Creek rice fields was ruined. Families living beside the derricks packed up their houses and their schoolhouse and moved inland, many to the township of Goose Creek, organized a few years earlier by others who had fled the daily subjection to foul air and water. (The relocated school's yearbook would later be named *The Gusher*.) That was about the time Gaillard moved his cattle across the bay to Hog Island, which he bought for $900 (he would later sell it to Humble Oil for $250,000).

In 1918, people wondered whether a big gusher would blow in August for the third year in a row. Days, then weeks, passed in dulling heat and routine. Finally, on the thirty-first, Sims-Sinclair Sweet No. 16 exploded at waterside, so loud you could hear it in the next county. The derrick burst into pickup sticks, and an upward stream of green-black sprayed for nine days, ten thousand barrels in all. This time the renegade oil went not inland, but out into Tabbs Bay. If your well was on solid ground, you could contain a deluge in a temporary sump or by digging canals to a permanent one. Oil fields over water or its marshy edge were different. A gusher could spoil a swamp or estuary before anyone gave it a thought—not such a good thing from the vantage point of wildlife or duck hunters and sportfishers who regarded Goose Creek as their playground. The spilling oil rode the current down to Galveston Bay and into the open Gulf, in the direction of the future.

Eleven

OIL AND THE LOUISIANA PLUNGE

In 1953, James Stewart and *Thunder Bay* dramatized actual events in Louisiana associated with the drilling of the first offshore oil well.

Keep drilling, Johnny, keep drilling.

—JAMES STEWART AS STEVE MARTIN, *THUNDER BAY* (1953)

IT WAS SPRING 1953, AND THE POSTWAR ECONOMY WAS in a recession, but the slump would not last a year. Americans were feeling prosperous, and the consumer engine was revved up. They were purchasing homes and having lots of kids, booming the birth rate to an all-time high. They were buying cars, big cars with big engines—ten-to-fifteen-miles-to-the-gallon cars—but that was okay. The decade's drivers were more interested in horsepower and zero-to-sixty acceleration than fuel efficiency, and gas was cheap. For twenty cents a gallon, they were hauling all those boomer kids around, commuting to work from the suburbs (if the car owners were white), and steering blissfully toward summer vacations. Every week on prime-time television, the popular Dinah Shore sang, "See the USA in your Chevrolet."

Americans were buying TVs too (more than fifty percent of US households had one). The kids plopped down in front of *Romper Room*; *Kukla, Fran and Ollie*; and *Winky Dink and You*. The entire family gathered for *I Love Lucy*, *The Adventures of Ozzie and Harriet, Amos 'n' Andy, Arthur Godfrey's Talent Scouts*, and the *Texaco Star Theater*, one of television's first successful programs, with a remarkable run from 1948 to 1967.

Despite this new competitive medium, enthusiasm for the movies remained strong. Americans bought an estimated forty-three million tickets for the big screen that year. In May, at the Times Square Loew's State Theatre in Midtown Manhattan, a crew made the movie screen three times the average size, and panoramic. It was preparing for the gala premier of *Thunder Bay*, starring James Stewart and presented in color and three-speaker stereophonic sound (which some critics would find distracting).

On the evening of the event, the night air serene and seventy degrees, a crowd formed outside the theater. People were there to see who would emerge from the procession of shiny black limousines pulling up under the bright marquee lights. The president's daughter, Margaret Truman, a singer and radio personality, was one of the first, followed by the Boris Karloffs, Xavier Cugat, and the "too sexy for Italy" Abbe Lane. Crowd-control police tightened the line when glamour couple Tony Curtis and Janet Leigh stepped out into camera flash and a gauntlet of microphones. Then Stewart arrived, and spectators jumped over each other for a look at the loose-limbed, all-American icon. He was accompanied by his longtime wife, Gloria, who in heels was nearly as tall as he, and wearing a mink stole on that seventy-degree evening.

There was heat in *Thunder Bay* too, an adventure film billed at the time as the saga of the beginning of offshore drilling. It's about a pair of unwavering wildcatters who overcome doubters, hostility, and monetary constraints to sink the first oil well too far from shore to see land, Louisiana land, and it was based on the real event of six years before.

The director, Anthony Mann, liked to make movies with an epic struggle, settled by the fists of a tough good guy—the type who kisses the girl who doesn't want to be kissed until she's kissed. Mann's style lent itself to westerns, and Stewart was his ideal leading character— laconic and anguished, yet rock solid, prepared to throw a punch or draw a gun to defend the law, the weak, or himself. They made five westerns together—two that year (one costarring Janet Leigh), both forgettable. Universal-International Pictures wanted them to move on to fresh pastures, and that's when they settled on *Thunder Bay*. Stewart, who knew something about the oil business from profitable investments in Texas wells, suggested the project to Mann. Stewart would play Steve Martin, an ex-GI engineer who has designed a rig with telescoping pilings, à la Thomas Rowland's patented design, and who is bound and determined to find oil under the Gulf. "There's enough oil down there to lubricate the universe," Martin insists with a wide-eyed expression on that widest of movie screens.

Mann liked to have everything big and bold in his pictures, so he would film on location under natural light, where he could capture raw, vivid scenery. For *Thunder Bay*, he chose the place where the real action happened: Morgan City, Louisiana, which skirted a grassy oxbow near the mouth of the Atchafalaya River. Intrepidly flat Louisiana had no buttes, canyons, or painted rocks, but Mann made good use of the southern light and immense Gulf sky, not to mention gentle sea breezes furling the hair of his actors. If the water was calm or choppy on the river or out in the Gulf, he made sure moviegoers saw that too, in Technicolor blues and greens—and in grays, when a hurricane brewed.

Critics were distracted by the film's oil rig, though, to the point of complaining that Mann had sacrificed the natural panorama to highlight the steel structure. "Visually," the "most distinctive aspect of *Thunder Bay*," according to a *New York Times* reviewer, is the "complex off-shore drilling apparatus." In a proud-papa's voice, Stewart's Steve Martin calls the rig his "baby." Mann's film biographer, Jeanine Basinger, says the director portrayed it as a thing of "beauty and majesty."[1]

Perhaps he was doing so metaphorically. The film's offshore job site is pretty much a giant greasy Erector Set splattered with drilling mud and cluttered with the industrial gray and rust of Kelly pipes. The critics failed to see the big picture beyond the box office and Mann's art. None of them confronted the rig as a symbol of changing America and assaults on the Gulf waterscape, aesthetically and ecologically, or as an industrial takeover of the region, already amassing on shore and inland waters. The rig instead represented economic betterment and a higher standard of living, promise and goodness. Like Dino's genial profile, it stood in front of reality. To be fair to the critics, this was the 1950s, and asking for ecological foresight is asking too much. But the potential to read and see the broader future was there, between the lines of dialogue and the celluloid frames. It was there in the mud, grease, and rust.

To UNDERSTAND THE GENESIS of this made-for-the-movies offshore oil rig, we need to go back to Spindletop and 1901, when a man named Walter Scott Heywood made his way over from Texas to the Louisiana coast. Heywood was an oil wildcatter, born in 1872 in Cleveland, Ohio, the original headquarters of Standard Oil, founded two years before. His mother was a schoolteacher, and his father taught at Hiram College when future US president James A. Garfield headed the institution.

Young Scott learned to play the cornet well enough to join a concert company touring the western states when he was still in his teens. In the midnineties in California, he took his last bow as a professional musician, married, began selling insurance, and directed a school band. Then in 1897, the year his only child was born, he succumbed to gold fever. He and his three older brothers, all of them clean-cut, musically talented, and deeply devoted to each other, joined 100,000 hopeful other miners lugging pickaxes in improbably long lines winding up snowy passes of the Klondike, between jagged rocks and beside death-drop ledges. Heywood called it "sheer torture." The brothers were among the very few who worked a profitable claim, though barely.[2]

Back in California, Heywood caught the oil bug and began drilling on leases in San Benito County. When news of the Lucas gusher reached the West Coast, he packed his grip and boarded a train to Texas, and again his three siblings joined his venture. He was the kid brother but the leader of the tribe. They were not rival siblings, but a quartet, happy and harmonious, who formed the Heywood Oil Company. As drilling superintendent, Scott released four gushers at Spindletop within months. It was clear he had a knack for getting precious commodities out of the ground.

That's what a group of investors was banking on when it invited him to Jefferson Davis Parish, Louisiana, where, as in Goose Creek, gas bubbles had been the telltale. Near the town of Jennings, a rice grower named Jules Clement had been curious about the bubbles rising to the surface whenever he flooded his fields. He took a stovepipe and placed it over an effusive spot, stepped back, lit a match, and tossed it in. Oil geology wasn't rocket science, but sometimes it could look and sound like it. The stovepipe boomed and shot out a red flame. After hearing about Clement's experiment, five local businessmen acquired leases adding up to two thousand acres, keeping things quiet so as not to attract competition and send land prices soaring.

Heywood came out and looked over the rice field. In another month he would turn twenty-nine. He had a neatly trimmed mantle of hair and the soft, pleasant features of a choirboy, or grade-school band teacher. But if you looked closely, you could find dirt under his fingernails. Someone once took a photograph of him and four diligent companions standing on a pile of oil well sand, a gusher sprouting to the rear, all of them slick and shiny, looking like a troupe of minstrel performers in blackface (looking, in fact, like his brother Alba, a popular minstrel performer).

Clement's property turned out to be over a salt dome, and it offered enough promise for Heywood to make a deal with the five Louisiana businessmen. After shipping one of his rigs over from Texas, Heywood and his crew reassembled it in June heat. The work was tough going that summer. Several times, the well began to discharge oil, raising everyone's hopes before quickly clogging with sand. Clearing it was laborious and time-consuming.

When one particular stream kept running, a neighboring farmer hustled into Jennings and spread the word that a gusher had been sprung on the Clement place. Texas and Louisiana newspapers got wind of the fresh oil. The *Dallas Morning News* put up a four-deck headline: JENNINGS HAS BECOME GREATLY EXCITED. But the enthusiasm was premature; the cantankerous well fouled again. The roughnecks made such a mess with their oil and sand that at one point Jules Clement padlocked his property. Some of the investors pulled out, and on the streets of Jennings, said Heywood, "I was pointed out as that crazy guy drilling for oil in rice fields." He forged ahead anyway and, in the end, had to let the well go.[3]

Failure was no damper on the spirit of possibilities. Other wildcatters had rushed in, and straightaway, southern Louisiana was pumping oil. Heywood shifted to a new site, and success. He bought a house in Jennings and moved his family out from California. Living there until his death in 1950, as a one-term state senator, member of the state mineral board, and recognized father of Louisiana oil, he witnessed the unfolding fate of the salt-dome coast. Before century's end,

181,000 oil and gas wells had been drilled on Louisiana land and in its waters.

By the 1920s, prospectors had discovered eight salt-dome oil fields, all onshore, or on those islands, like Avery, that were briny humps bounded by marshland. The industry wanted access to more exploration sites, and the state obliged, as it almost always would, leasing out huge tracts of coastal wetland—tens of thousands of acres to a lease in some cases. Oil money was a drug to rich states and poor states, but especially to a poor one like Louisiana. "It was pitiful," Heywood at one point told Governor Huey Long, "the way some of our people had to live and the sacrifices they had to endure." Oil meant jobs, development, tax revenue, and a little palm greasing for those in power. Said Long, a.k.a. the "Kingfish," a state with a valuable commodity desired by many was a state with leverage.[4]

But that wasn't the whole story. Louisiana had been eager to reclaim or develop its submerged lands even before the Swamp Land Act of 1849 transferred possession from the federal to the state government. (The greatest beneficiaries of the three Swamp Land Acts—1849, 1850, 1860—were Florida, gaining twenty million acres of new real estate, and Louisiana, gaining nine million.) In the official dictum, wetland was wasteland—even that forming the ecologically divine Louisiana coast. Exploiting it for hunting and fishing and rice growing was a good and proper thing; for oil, an even better, more lucrative, thing.

New technology in geological investigation came along that coaxed explorers into marshlands and bayous. The gravity meter, torsion balance, and, especially, seismograph gave petroleum geologists the tools to peer through the water into the mysteries of the Earth. They found deep-seated domes, oil on their flanks and hidden in faults. During their explorations, geologists learned that the Gulf's nearshore bottom was a long extension of the coast, running a hundred-plus miles out in front of Louisiana, rarely deeper than twenty feet, and they predicted there were domes and oil out there. Scientists would later count 204 in the state, with eighty fully beyond dry land.

THE OUTFIT THAT SANK the first legitimate offshore well was formed by Superior Oil and Pure Oil, independent companies that no longer exist (the former absorbed by ExxonMobil and the latter by Chevron). In the 1930s, the two partnered to make an unprecedented leap a mile and a half out from Cameron Parish to a "stick" platform of 140 creosoted piles of southern yellow pine. The Creole Oilfield was in a mere fourteen feet of water, yet a two-hour boat ride out, where a head turn back revealed the mainland as a distant sliver of terra firma. The new well went active on March 18, 1938 (the same day, half a world away, that Standard Oil of California discovered the first oil in Saudi Arabia).

Down the coast a short piece, the year before, FDR had been reeling in tarpon at Port Aransas with his trademark grin. The year before that, Wallace Stevens had called the Gulf a fishy sea. Others were already thinking of it as a giant oil field waiting to be pumped. An industry magazine spoke of the new imperative of Louisiana crews: they must not only "know oil" but have a "workable appreciation of what it means to be a sailor."[5]

Looking back from the present, we can see portentous signs of shifting industrial priorities on the American Sea. Shrimp boats were converted to oil crew boats, sallying forth with a new purpose, diesel fumes overpowering remnant fish smells, carrying rig workers on a four-hour commute to and from the Creole platform, which had no sleeping quarters as did later offshore facilities. The years ahead revealed the irony in the Creole field's name, opening a steady migration away from the family fishing boat to an offshore platform, from fish-house paydays to company paychecks, joined by a general loss of the traditional Creole way of living by the sea. This is not to say that commercial fishing was passing to a bygone era—not yet at least. Its best years were still ahead. By that time, however, a new power in oil would reign on the Gulf and in the centers of political authority.

After the success of the Creole Oilfield and with the coming of war against Germany and Japan, oil's unprecedented ascension seemed certain, in part because war is a boon for those who provide the resources that run it. As with the previous war, the Allied demand for oil pushed the industry to explore new territory to drill more wells to fill more barrels than ever before. The number of dots designating discovered salt domes began to crowd geological charts, and with the watery frontier cleared by Superior and Pure, other oil companies clamored to cash in on the offshore wealth. Except events didn't come to pass that way—not entirely.

DURING THE WAR, the Gulf lurked with evil that delayed this future. Within weeks of Adolph Hitler's declaration of war against the US in December 1941, he unleashed his best naval weapon, *Unterseeboots*—a.k.a. submarines, U-boats, wolf packs—on the US East Coast. They swarmed in on merchant marine ships swollen with war supplies and oil. The US Navy was both ill prepared for the onslaught and initially hesitant to provide escort convoys, for fear of losing ships from its still minuscule fleet. The Atlantic seaboard turned into a carnival shooting gallery, though it was harder to hit a rigged target at a carnival. The Germans couldn't believe their luck, or how careless the Americans were, leaving their shore lights on at night, giving the enemy a silhouetted bull's-eye on merchant ships, unescorted and woefully vulnerable. Between January and August 1942, Hitler's U-boats picked off nearly four hundred vessels transporting one-quarter of that year's Allied cargo. "Happy time," the Germans called it, the "American shooting season."[6]

For Americans, the opening months were the bleakest of the four-year conflict. Army chief of staff General George C. Marshall said the assaults "threaten our entire war effort." It was a worrisome moment in American history—more worrisome than Pearl Harbor. Remarkably, few people today know about it, despite all the civilians at the time who stared into the face of the enemy. Beachgoers, vacationers, and coastal residents from the Jersey Shore to Miami Beach were haunted daily by explosions at sea, domestic security going up in great billows of smoke. Pitch-black meant an oil tanker had been hit, and most often, what stained the sky was pitch-black. All Americans felt the fallout when the government rationed domestic gasoline use.[7]

In May, when the US Office of Price Administration issued the first ration books for fuel, U-boats slipped through the Florida Straits past the naval station on Key West. Throughout the summer, from below the surface and out of sight, the enemy took control of the American Sea. As many as twenty-four U-boats trolled the Gulf, most of them lying in wait along the sea-lane emerging from the Mississippi. The Americans destroyed only one U-boat to the fifty-six Allied vessels the enemy sent to the bottom (where they still rest, now as archaeological sites for the maritime studies program at the University of West Florida).

When the British journalist Alistair Cooke was traveling to the Gulf Coast in 1942, he chatted with a fellow airline passenger who operated a fleet of tankers out of New Orleans. Three months earlier, the man had lost twenty boats. That morning he had a dozen left, and by evening he expected to be down to "eight or nine maybe." Cooke asked about signing on crews for the tankers, and the response was sobering: "Might just as well advertise for suicides." It wasn't a good time to drill in the open water either—not when U-boats crept close enough to see people on the beach. The New Orleans man said he'd about reached the point of saying, "The hell with oil."[8]

But the war couldn't be won without it. By late summer, with 380 ships torpedoed out of the water, the navy's hand was forced. Blackouts went into effect. American production of warplanes and ships, many of the latter at Biloxi, quickly reached historic rates, enabling the navy to provide air and sea convoys to merchant lines. Air protection flew out of Corpus Christi, Biloxi, Pensacola, Tampa, St. Petersburg, and Key West, over from Miami and up from San Julian (Cuba). The navy shut down the enemy's shooting gallery.

THE WAR WAS EIGHT YEARS PAST when *Thunder Bay* premiered; another, in Korea, would be over in two months. The oil rig used in the movie, and that which distracted the film critics, was the genuine thing. Mann found it not on the studio back lot, but standing twenty-five miles out in the Gulf, operated by Kerr-McGee Oil Industries. There was a powerful allusion in that fact. Kerr-McGee was the outfit that had punched the world's first distant offshore well (the one behind the *Thunder Bay* story) in 1947, eleven miles south of the Atchafalaya River, with not even a sliver of terra firma in sight.

As oil companies go, Kerr-McGee was a relatively small Oklahoma independent, "chronically short of working capital," said Tom Seale, the man who more or less was the model for Stewart's Steve Martin. On top of that, Kerr-McGee was a land driller with no over-water track record. No one had ever sunk a well beyond the horizon, but everyone knew seaward was the direction to take, whatever the risks. "If there was nobody to gamble," says the agreeable Kermit MacDonald, head of the firm funding the vision of *Thunder Bay*'s Steve Martin, "the oil business would stop."[9]

Kerr-McGee was, in part, forced to gamble offshore because the big oil companies dominated the best land leases. The firm's number two man, Dean McGee, a geologist whose father had been a short-term and unlucky wildcatter in Kansas, said, "We decided to explore areas where the really potential prolific production might be—salt domes—the good ones on land were gone." There was no rest in that exploration.[10]

From the beginning, the enterprise seemed to function like an eleventh-hour scramble. A crease in the state's seismographic map nearly let McGee overlook a most promising underwater lease. Then a snag with bid money for a lease wired to a Western Union office in Baton Rouge led to a desperate phone call to the governor to release it. A speeding taxicab ride to Louisiana's thirty-four-story-qua-phallus state capitol building followed, with McGee in the backseat filling out the bid paperwork. He beat the filing deadline by minutes, though the legality of the lease was questionable. The federal government had recently won a court decision in California in which the mineral rights of states had been determined to extend no more than three miles offshore. McGee was potentially leasing federal territory from the state; all the same, Louisiana issued a permit on August 13. The company had one month to start drilling or face a monetary penalty, and McGee still had important logistics to figure out so that his engineer, Tom Seale, could get started.

Out on the job site, McGee—stocky, with a sturdy center of gravity, who sometimes wore a black fedora shading his eyes and a khaki work jacket and work pants—looked like a cross between a crew boss on the cargo docks and the mob boss who controlled the docks. His biggest challenge was how to support operations that were a three- to four-hour boat ride out to sea. An idea struck when he toured the New Orleans harbor and spotted mothballed World War II vessels berthed in retirement.

He acquired two LSTs, tank-landing ships, 382 feet long, lacking in any elegant aspect yet uniquely suitable for multipurpose functions. McGee started with one, had it refitted, and gave it a second life as a floating tender for well site Kermac No. 16. It had enough space to provide crew quarters and a mess hall, and to store supplies and drilling mud. Kerr-McGee painted its name on an exterior bulkhead in big letters crowning a mural of airplanes in flight over oil wells. The offshore tender and living quarters were another first in the business, but the mural couldn't disguise what looked makeshift to many. Some said the company's venture "took courage," remembered McGee; "others just said we were foolish."[11]

Once the LST had steamed to the designated location, anchored in eighteen feet of water and a circle of sea and sky, Seale and his crew erected a steel rig on steel pilings. In *Thunder Bay*, Jimmy Stewart's character looks up at his "baby" at one point and declares that it will withstand any hurricane nature can throw at it. Seale's was put to the test a week after drilling started (before the penalty deadline) when a tropical storm stirred to life in the western Gulf, cut eastward toward the Florida peninsula well south of the drilling area, but then made a clockwise loop and took a Murphy's Law aim at the rig, stirring up winds to seventy miles per hour. Seale's baby withstood.

Not three weeks later, it proved its viability too. On a shimmering October morning, Kermac No. 16 began delivering oil. The crude rose from fifteen hundred feet, much shallower than anyone had expected. Seale had intended to push to ten thousand feet, to a "different geological age," someone said, and into the flank of a dome. He had unwittingly run through its cap and hit a sweet pool of crude. (It would flow for decades.) Oilmen well knew the value of good luck; back at the Oklahoma headquarters, the place was all smiles and backslaps. The next company newsletter would report, "Everybody shook hands with everybody twice."[12]

Somehow the significance of the strike escaped the attention of the national press. There wasn't a peep about it in the big dailies. To oilmen it was like nectar, and the industry was abuzz with the excitement of new possibilities. One of its leading journals compared the Kerr-McGee milestone with the original Pennsylvania well and the Lucas gusher. It "definitely extends the kingdom of oil into a new province." Seven years later, forty rigs reached fifty miles offshore. People were predicting that by the end of the century, the Gulf would be one of the world's most productive oil provinces. They were right.[13]

"There's oil out there," insists *Thunder Bay*'s Steve Martin. "Somebody's gotta get it." You can hear the urgency in his voice, in his belief that for the good of humankind, the oil must be rescued from nature, from those millions of years.

SIMILAR CONVICTION, SAME GENERAL PLACE, several years earlier, different director. His name was Robert J. Flaherty. His film *Louisiana Story* is about the oil industry's interaction with the backcountry population of the Louisiana coastal swamps. It wasn't the same as in Texas, where the industry was native-born. Oilmen were mostly outsiders. Flaherty filmed on Bayou Petite Anse and made acquaintance with the king of hot sauces. McIlhenny opened up the hemmed-in salty circle of Avery Island to Flaherty, pressing one condition: no wildlife could be harmed. Flaherty complied, though in truth he wanted his lead to shoot an alligator.

For *Louisiana Story*, Flaherty cast no one from the Hollywood list. That would have been disingenuous. He was making a documentary, or so he called it, and he wanted locals. He was touched, patronizingly so, by how they were "gentle, gay and picturesque." To play the lead, a barefoot Cajun boy, he hunted down a genuine barefoot Cajun boy, Joseph Boudreaux, a mop-haired fourth-grader from Cameron Parish, who had flunked a grade because he spoke only Louisiana French at the time. His character's name is Alexander Napoleon Ulysses LaTour. The film's voice-over narrator refers to him as merely "the boy."[14]

Boudreaux didn't have to worry much about his English when in front of the camera. His character spends most of the time in his pirogue fishing and hunting with his pet raccoon, Jo-Jo. He's either mute or monosyllabic for most of the seventy-eight-minute movie. None of the characters say much of anything. Flaherty and his wife, Frances, kept perhaps two dozen lines of dialogue in the final cut (and still received an Oscar nomination for writing, now called original screenplay). Upon its release, *Variety* described the film as a "documentary-type story told almost purely in camera terms."

Back in 1922, Flaherty had established his credentials as the father of film documentary with the production of *Nanook of the North*, the story of an Inuk family of Arctic Canada. *Louisiana Story*, which debuted in major theaters in 1948, has that formal aura of a documentary, but in truth it's fiction (so is *Nanook*). It had to be, to deliver its intended message: as a steward of civilized progress, the oil industry is equally a steward of a pristine environment and, in particular, the primitive culture that depends on it. If he had been forthcoming, Flaherty would have included a disclaimer in the credits disclosing that he had taken $200,000 from Standard Oil of New Jersey to make the film, which the oil corporation wanted distributed to mainstream theaters.

Moviegoers came to Flaherty's message through the boy's healthy curiosity. For several minutes in the opening scene, he explores the wonders of his backyard bayou before hearing explosions not far off. Alarmed by them, he paddles home to tell his mother and father, only to be surprised upon finding a brightly varnished motor launch slipped up on the landing next to his father's unburnished johnboat with a little kicker outboard. Home is a cabin in the mossy woods, with drying skins of nutrias and alligators nailed to the clapboard siding. The skins are the family's way of life. Inside, an amiable oil representative is sliding a lease agreement across the kitchen table to the father that will permit the representative's employer to drill on the bayou. The father (played by McIlhenny's private game warden) signs his name in tight cursive, and soon after, a crew barges an oil derrick into the next scene.

Years earlier, Spindletop-born Texaco developed a rig on a tug-drawn barge that could be floated into the bayous and partially submerged once in place. During a location scouting trip, the Flahertys saw, above a brow of cordgrass, the top of one of these barges skirting past without a whisper. The image was transporting. "Poetry," Robert later remembered, "its slim lines rising clean and taut above the unending flatness of the marshes." Knowing they had to re-create the scene for the movie, they got a loaner rig from Humble Oil. Just as Anthony Mann would do with the Kerr-McGee rig, Robert Flaherty had his cinematographer shoot it from below. The 35 mm Arriflex camera becomes the eyes of the barefoot boy. The rig is no less a marvel to him than if he were standing shod on the streets of New York before the Empire State Building.[15]

In the film, civilization in the form of the barged rig enters the monochrome swamp. The two mesh as do cypress and bayou, despite an unfamiliar din that saturates the days and nights: metal chafing against complaining metal, and the reciprocating sigh and thump of a steam engine piston and pushrod. Rather than repulsing the boy, the industrial restlessness piques his curiosity, drawing him into friendly interactions with the oil crew, full of smiles and affability. He shows them how he catches fish by spitting on his bait, and they show him how they drill with racing-wire cables, spinning wind-lasses, slinking chains, and threading pipe—the speed and efficiency of an advanced culture. Later, the operation suffers a setback from a blowout of water and gas. The boy reaches for a pinch of magical salt he carries to ward off evil spirits and throws it down the drill hole. Then he spits into it—a primitive but profitable ritual. Soon after, the crew strikes oil.

Flaherty then cuts to an important scene: he's delivering his message. Back in the cabin, it's like Christmas. The LaTours unwrap store-bought food, a double boiler and patterned dressmaking cloth for mother, and a new hunting rifle for the boy—all the fruits of having signed the oil lease.

In the scene that follows, the crew caps the wellhead for the time being and barges away the drilling rig, leaving no trace of their visit other than the silenced wellhead. No gusher was allowed to poison the home and playground of the Cajun boy with the grand name. In the film's closing moment, shot from below, he sits atop the well-head, clean and sterile, hugging it with Jo-Jo, waving to the departing roughnecks as he shouts, "Well done!"[16]

THIS WAS THE MYTH that Standard Oil paid for. The industry needed a positive narrative. There was trouble on the water at the time, centered on the kind of explosions that Alexander Napoleon Ulysses LaTour heard. They were part of the geophysical exploration that the industry adopted after a Gulf Oil crew on the Texas coast successfully ran the first seismic surveys offshore in 1924. In a method known as refraction, petroleum geologists used dynamite charges to chase sound waves deep into the earth. If they hit a salt dome, the seismometers would show the waves' travel time increasing. As bad as the explosions were on land, they were even worse in the bayous. They shot up plumes of water, mud, and plant life, left huge craters in sea grass and oyster beds, and killed fish, crabs, and shrimp.[17]

Flaherty never explains the explosions, or suggests the consequences for the quaint bayou. In *Thunder Bay*, Mann doesn't get into the nitty-gritty detail either when Steve Martin sets up a string of eruptions in the Gulf, yet he introduces controversy when one of the locals cries, "Don't they know they're killing the shrimp?" The central conflict in *Thunder Bay* is not between humans and nature, as reviewers maintained. When Mann switched genres, he resorted to habit and turned out a western in different melodramatic duds. Stewart conceded as much, and the image is clear in the movie poster. He's in a gunfighter stance, a pose he knows from having affected it a hundred times before. The difference boils down to props: his sweat-stained Stetson is now a scuffed hard hat, and his drawn six-shooter is a charge of six dynamite sticks. Instead of renegade Indians or ruthless outlaws looking down his barrel, Louisiana Cajuns confront his burning fuse. In a tense standoff scene, teeth clenched, Martin tosses a stick of dynamite to beat back a mob of locals who have accused him of blowing up Gulf shrimp.

Through a modern lens of social sensibilities, there's something untoward about the leading man fighting hardworking, law-abiding Americans, ethnic Americans included. It was 1953, however, and the Cold War was hot. Americans kept close watch on fellow citizens who might interfere with economic progress and leave America to fall behind the Soviets. Besides, Stewart had street cred. He was a genuine decorated World War II veteran who had seen action piloting a score of bombing missions in Germany. In the pictures, he always plays the sensible, exceptionally farsighted, though sometimes troubled, good guy who gets it right. He's the unfailingly compassionate George Bailey who has an angel on his shoulder to ensure a wonderful life; he's the dutiful Mr. Smith who goes to Washington to stand up for the little fellow. Those Cajuns who are trying to impede Steve Martin's progress, and who seem too Frenchified and behind the times, need a little sensible Americanization. Who better than apple-pie Jimmy

Stewart to set them straight? He was more iconic than the iconic Dino, and a similarly effective propagandist. Oil PR folks might have kissed him for this line delivered to his Cajun accusers: "Those shrimp can withstand ten times the blast."

Offscreen fishers in Louisiana and Texas, having seen too many crustaceans blown to bits, knew better, and they filed complaints in their states. Just about the time Dean McGee was racing to file for his drilling permit, a *New York Times* headline read, FISHERMEN IN GULF OF MEXICO IN CONTEST WITH OIL MEN. Fishers sought relief from state officials, who were sympathetic to a point. In Texas, off-shore seismic testing could proceed only with the permission of local county judges, yet few were inclined to stand in the way of prog-ress and jobs. Louisiana allowed only detonations suspended off the bottom, and a state conservation officer had to be on hand, ostensibly to protect sea life.[18]

Offshore dynamiting continued into the 1960s and, said one plain-spoken Louisianan, "That was not environmentally good." Seismic air guns came along to replace the dynamite, and the new technology relieved two industry headaches: accidental detonations on the job site and the liability wrapped up with the loss of human lives. There weren't the same liability concerns around marine life, as the air guns showed. They were cannons really, with as many as forty-eight guns in one, and they released an acoustic explosion 100,000 times more intense than a jet engine. They didn't make craters, but they killed fish and did irreparable harm to the biosonar of whales and dolphins.[19]

There were other problems in bayou country too, including oil spills and brine pollution (a by-product of drilling). In 1932 and '33, Louisiana oyster fishers filed nineteen lawsuits against Texaco. Oil slicks and brine constantly vandalized their oyster beds in Terrebonne and Lafourche Parishes. After an eleven-year legal battle, the state supreme court ordered the industry to pay $211,000 in damages— essentially the price of a Flaherty propaganda film.

As there was no real link between dinosaurs and oil, there was no clean drilling entrance and exit into and out of the bayous as por-

trayed in *Louisiana Story*. In the southern parishes, the industry's
arrival felt like an invasion. It was the magnitude, breadth, speed,
relentlessness, and completeness of the invasion; it was the footprint,
the first inevitably followed by a second, and a third by a fourth; it
was the unavoidability and permanence; and it all said that Flaherty
was pouring Louisiana cane sugar over it.

Whether you welcomed, hated, or feigned indifference about oil,
you were possessed by it. The native population indiscriminately
denounced its agents under the single category of *les maudits Texiens*,
"those damn Texans." Theirs was an invasion of big trucks, airplanes,
barge rigs, and giant rubber tires. Those tires were the amphibious
treads of yet another loud, newfangled contraption, designed for Gulf
Oil to use in wetlands for seismic surveys, and appropriately called a
marsh buggy. The first of the breed was featured on the cover of *Popular Science* in March 1937 with custom Goodyear Terra tires, ten feet
high and three thick, said to be the largest in the world. They threw
up muddy rooster tails nearly as high as a gusher and forded swamps
as if Moses had parted the cordgrass, crushing everything in their
path—yet another extreme.

Les maudits oilmen had an intense way of doing business, employing a git-'er-done-yesterday impatience, corporate-lawyer persuasion,
and a no-trespassing sense of proprietorship—though, someone said,
they "didn't know an oyster bed from a flowerbed." And they didn't
seem to care about trampling either one. They invaded with pipes, not
just those Kelly drilling pipes, but big steel pipes (some forty-eight
inches in diameter) welded together and routed through the water and
ground. Worse than humping along in swamp buggies, they invaded
with dragline dredges to dig the channels or canals where the pipes,
crew boats, and barges went. They originally built wood-plank roads,
but that consumed too many wage-hours and millions of board feet
of native cypress, and once more, the muskrats and nutrias ate the
vegetative foundation that supported them. First they dredged tens of
miles of canals. That expanded to hundreds, then thousands, through
oyster beds, rice fields, wetlands, and wildlife habitat. By 1982, they

had secured seventy-three thousand miles of pipeline right-of-way. One line, the Muskrat, didn't quit until 355 miles, passing over bayou, bay, river delta, and barrier island, and like the rest, its canals uprooted vegetation, altered water flow and salinity, and contributed to the inundation of the most precious of southern Louisiana commodities: dry land.[20]

Cajun country, with its traditions of fishing, farming, and hunting, was becoming less Cajun country and more outsider industrial country. It was indisputable in a place like Morgan City, where the shell roads bend with the Atchafalaya River and the economy once flowed with the estuary. Before industrialized oil, Morgan City had been little more than a quiet bayou-and-swamp setting, which, upon Acadian French settlement in the eighteenth century, had given rise to sugarcane growing followed by the installation of a live-off-the-land-and-water Cajun culture. Come the nineteenth century, that meant trapping, fishing, shrimping, oystering, and logging the cypress swamps.

Wildcatters and big oil companies entered—invaded—the surrounding bayou country in the 1930s and set up storefront offices at Morgan City. From industry representatives, locals undoubtedly heard the line countless times long before Steve Martin spoke it in stereophonic sound: "Oil is going to do good things for the place." Morgan City was an ideal location from which to service the wells on landside salt domes, four within the parish. By way of the Atchafalaya, it gave easy access to the Gulf, and it had plenty of shrimp boats at the fishing docks to rent or buy for the commute to the rigs. Kerr-McGee set up its shore headquarters there before its monumental oil strike, and, learning of this, Anthony Mann trucked in Hollywood and used those shell roads for his opening scene.

By the time of *Thunder Bay*'s 1953 premier, seventy-five percent of the land that Louisiana leased to oil and gas companies was in the coastal zone and pumping most of the crude. The state, said one observer, "issued oil and gas permits like orders at McDonald's: how many would you like today?"[21] No place was sacred or spared. The

Muskrat line crossed Grand Isle, the "bouquet" of Louisiana's barriers that had charmed Martha Field, which also served as the Louisiana headquarters of Humble Oil. Other companies sank wells on Marsh Island, which housed the Russell Sage State Wildlife Management Area that McIlhenny had helped set up to save birds. The National Audubon Society kept its Paul J. Rainey Wildlife Sanctuary off limits to the public but not to natural-gas extraction (from thirty-seven wells). It was too much to resist. The gas drilled at the Rainey sanctuary eventually netted Audubon $25 million, and at the Sage State Wildlife Management Area, lease payments and oil royalties funded the operation many times over.*

Despite the intrusion, domination, and pollution, local resistance waned. No matter how much hostility Steve Martin encountered at Thunder Bay, he could always find a shrimp boat to hire. Ferrying big-wigs, a boat owner could make as much as a sumptuous catch without having to break his back. A regular job with a company paid unheard-of wages—ten times what a man or woman could make hauling in nets all day. And it was a steady paycheck, not subject to the vaga-ries of nature. Eventually, it also came with medical benefits, vacation time, and a pension. You could buy a house already built—not build it yourself from scrounged-up materials—pay it off and retire in it, send your kids to the state college that oil money had helped build. Even if you wanted to take a stand to save the traditional way of life, you likely had a brother, sister, cousin, aunt, or uncle who worked in the indus-try, and you let it go. The McIlhennys eventually had to stop growing most of their peppers, when better wages lured their field hands to oil jobs. The loss withered a quaint connection from Tabasco's treasured past. But the family had to accept some of the blame: they let Humble Oil drill on their geologically rich island.

---

* In the 1990s, when Audubon opposed oil drilling in the Arctic National Wildlife Refuge in Alaska, an op-ed in the *Wall Street Journal* accused the organization of hypocrisy. "PC Oil Drilling in a Wildlife Refuge," *Wall Street Journal*, September 7, 1995.

LABOR DAY 1937 was the beginning of the road to imperfect harmony between Louisianans and the industry. Morgan City residents kicked off the first annual Louisiana Shrimp Festival that day. Each year from then on, they'd eat bowls of gumbo and jambalaya, play fiddle music, and bless the homeported fleet of trawlers. Thirty years later, the petroleum industry wanted to be headlined in the community celebration. It was a controversial proposition, but some compelling facts stood out. Forty-four St. Mary Parish residents had worked in oil and gas production at the beginning of the Great Depression; more than four hundred, before the end. That said something to folks.

When it asked for recognition in the festival, petroleum employed 2,352 parishioners. Its payroll annually pumped $7 million into the economy—more than any other single industry—giving the local working class a per capita income that ranked near the top in the state. The 1,474 wells bored offshore the next year promised even more good times. Unlike the situation in many other fishing communities around the Gulf, young people stayed around after coming of age—some sustaining the family's fishing heritage, yet an increasing number of others starting a new one in oil work, carried on by their children and grandchildren. In the 1980s, a Morgan City resident told the writer John McPhee, "When you're fishing in the bayou, you're out in nature with the oil industry all around you."[22]

As for the environmental impact of spills, pipeline canals, and marsh-buggy thoroughfares, a 1977 report written for the US Department of Commerce by researchers from the University of Southwestern Louisiana claimed that the "advantages" of converting "swampland to industrial site . . . far outweigh the disadvantages." Since none of the researchers was a biologist, their findings were highly suspect. But whenever the industry reached for its wallet, it flexed its bicep. Money was muscle, and it was used to change the festival banner. Since 1967, it has read, "Louisiana Shrimp & Petroleum Festival."[23]

For a long time, the balance between drilling and fishing seemed to work. Whenever the industry faced criticism, its spokespersons could stand up and say, "Yes, we drill more intensely off Louisiana's shores than any other coastal area in the US, and it is now the Gulf's most commercially successful oil and gas region"—then add the qualifying "but" statement, supported by government data: "But our success has not come at the expense of commercial fishing. Louisiana fishermen have been consistent leaders nationwide in volume and value of fish landed, ranking at the very top by the 1980s." It was all true, and it allowed the industry another claim in the form of a question: "Who said oil and water don't mix?"

MANN AND STEWART were saying the two did. The way they settled the conflict between the outsider Steve Martin and the shrimpers can be seen as an unintended cautionary tale. In the final scene, a group of boat hook–wielding Cajuns, prepared to shut down Martin's enterprise once and for all, confront him on the rig. But this time Martin doesn't draw a stick of dynamite from his hip. He's got a better weapon of defense: golden shrimp. It's the elusive prize the fishers have been hunting for generations, and Martin has found them. The shrimp have been clogging the water-cooling pump to his drilling apparatus, and he has learned that they are attracted to the rig. It's an artificial reef! Martin can have his oil, the Cajuns can have the elusive shrimp, and the sun can set pleasantly on this Hollywood ending.

Here was more grist for the real-life oil drillers, gratis this time. The industry would eventually get a lot of mileage out of that artificial-reef trope, driving it into the next century when Big Oil persistently trumpeted it—more mileage than Dino and the dinosaur origin myth got. It made the banner design of the Louisiana Shrimp & Petroleum Festival, which features a giant shrimp in a yellow hard hat embracing an oil rig, the very image evoked by Mann's movie, and one that Flaherty suggested in his film with the young protagonist hugging the wellhead.

Now fast-forward to 2006—maybe too fast for that skinny Cajun boy and onetime movie star who's peeking into his eighth decade, and who's possibly eaten too much jambalaya and gumbo. Joseph Boudreaux walks like a man with a bad back or hip, and his mop is silver gray. Down on the coast in Cameron Parish, on a day in spring, he takes film students from the state university down memory lane, talking about hurricanes, his movie, and the oil and gas industry. He had worked in it for several years, knows that his people depend on it, and is careful not to say anything critical.

But then he sits down in front of a laptop watching the last few minutes of the movie, talking about it, and there is a truth that wants to come out. "Now, in that innocent scene," he says, pointing to the young Alexander Bonaparte Ulysses LaTour perched on the capped wellhead with Jo-Jo and giving his smiling farewell to the drilling crew. "I tell you go back 20 or 30 years later, that's when the erosion's going." He is referring to the flip side of good jobs and artificial reefs—the side the industry doesn't like to see turn up, revealing the phenomenal erosion of the Louisiana coastline, and with it the erosion of Cajun culture, caused in part by the canals that the industry has cut through the marshes.[24]

As it pulled taut the economic lifeline, the amassing petrochemical industry in Texas and Louisiana slackened emotional ties to nature— Gulf nature.

Twelve

ISLANDS, SHIFTING SANDS OF TIME

A 1948 sketch of pelicans by Walter Anderson.

It is the outermost place that becomes the innermost place in the spiral of creation. I will always carry a bit of Horn Island deep within my soul.

—JOHN ANDERSON (2009)[1]

IF ANYTHING WAS CERTAIN ON THE GULF, IT WAS THE inevitability of change. That was the understanding of Walter Anderson, who had nothing to do with the oil industry, wanted nothing to do with it, and hardly ever used its product—except on his bicycle chain, maybe a dab on his oarlocks, sometimes in his paints, though he preferred working in watercolors. In his lifetime across the mid-twentieth century on the Mississippi coast, living mostly in Ocean Springs, he saw a lot of change. He kept his eyes always alive to it—mostly outside of human influence, though: in the wind that pushed his skiff to and from islands, the forms taking shape beneath the tracking sun, the "conflict" between shifting seasons, new growths replacing old in the scrub and on the dunes. He once highlighted the word "change" in his logs and said it was "magical." For him, the best place to be enchanted was on islands.[2]

Never did they have to compete for his attention, not even with his family. His wife, Agnes, conceded that as father and husband, Walter was missing in action most of the time. Each of their four children had been born in his absence. Patient and understanding by nature, Sissy, as Agnes was known to most, quietly accepted Walter's self-involvement as the fire and ice of artistic genius. Gulf wildlife was the fount of his expressive being. He needed to be with his subjects, to study them before he translated them into art. The barrier islands—"those white spines of land," she called them—skirting the coast from Florida to Mexico, especially excited his curiosity. He wanted to know "what winds, what currents built them up . . . the deaths of how many animals, how many vegetables allowed the slow growths . . . what birds or waves deposited the seeds of trees, of grasses, or sea oats." He painted it all; he was simply island struck. One particular barrier preoccupied him most, Horn Island, the "back of Moby Dick, the white whale."[3]

This is Walter's metaphor, and it seems right. Horn was a mile wide and ten long, a vertebrate of white dunes. It ran lengthwise to the Mississippi coast, and you got there only by boat. In his, Anderson was Captain Ahab approaching the white whale, except the island did not resist and Anderson sought no vengeance.

Aside from the visiting artist, Horn was unburdened by human habitation. For about thirty years in the nineteenth century, it had had a lighthouse and keeper before a hurricane washed both away in 1906. A family had lived there too, tending small herds of cattle and hogs, likely descendants of Spanish transplants. The family left in 1920. The struts for supporting life still existed, though. In the average year, about sixty inches of rain fell, sweetening the island's many lagoons and ponds, which turned brackish during dry spells. The island had one freshwater spring, Rabbit Springs, named for Horn's most abundant fauna. There were lots of raccoons and nutrias and feral hogs. Wild horses ran on the island until the military removed them during World War II. Waterfowl, shorebirds, and songbirds were a given. Vegetation was of the scrub variety: wax myrtle, dune rosemary, and yaupon holly, all somewhat exaggerated in size for lack of fire. Slash pines grew in woods disturbed by neither timber worker nor developer. On nearby islands, plant life was much the same, except oaks gathered in large numbers. Horn had only two.

The island was *uninhibited*, too. That's why Anderson liked it. "All of the fauna of Horn Island seemed out yesterday," he recorded in his journal, "marsh hawks, snipe, teal, mallard, great blue herons, rabbits, and, just at dusk, a coon." He named the raccoon Inky. From the end of the war until his death in 1965, Anderson was a frequent visitor, staying for a week or two at a time. When in residence, he regarded himself as nature's "privileged spectator."[4]

Horn lies eight miles out from Ocean Springs across Mississippi Sound. Anderson made the crossing in leaky skiffs of some vintage, either borrowed from his brother or salvaged from a Gulf storm, his budget of food and art supplies secured amidships in gunnysacks and a metal garbage can. "My light little skiff was a cargo barge. I rowed and bailed and rowed and bailed." Beneath a salt-stained, workingman's fedora, he poled as well as rowed, and when the wind was up he sailed, catching it sometimes with nothing more than an old blanket rigged between mast and boom. On good days, the crossing took six hours. He liked to set out around sunset, "the magic hour" of light and color, and then become wrapped in the night, when the wind was steady but gentle, when Orion traveled too and the stars were his guide. The "moonlight water was like glue at times, and I ate apricots and rowed." He watched for spectacles of bioluminescent marine life in the unsleeping sea, and he listened for the invisible flight of birds overhead, guessing their kind from their vocals or beating wings. "And after the morning star had danced with me on the water the dawn came and the sun rose."

On those mornings when he and the first light arrived on the island together, he would secure his boat, make a bed on the beach or the amber grasses, and sleep until afternoon. He often woke looking up at two, three, or four man-o'-war birds, on seven-foot wingspans riding a thermal, the most aerial of waterbirds waiting to snatch nourishment caught by some other avian party. He sketched them with their long, forked tail feathers, giving attention to what moved him. "The beauty was there. I have never seen anything more dramatic than the effect of man o'war birds." He was familiar with all the bird species of the islands. Pelicans, first cousin to the man-o'-wars, he knew best. He knew their habits and their multiple stages of maturity. He knew if you lifted a fledgling by its wings, you were likely to break them. The islands exposed him to many such realities, and much death and dying.

He accepted it all, including the risks to himself. Snakebites, stingray barbs, and the toxic burn of jellyfish, drifters of ocean currents for five hundred million years, were always a threat. Even the protected sound could turn against him. More than once, a boater came upon Anderson quietly swimming his swamped skiff toward shore, yet miles away. Sometimes he accepted offers of a tow. Other times he responded politely from beneath his soaking fedora with a "No, thank you, I'll make it," and a kindly tap to its brim. Solitude had no price.

It was the same once he was on Horn Island. In 1965, he traversed the sound in a green-painted skiff on September 1, the day an Atlantic storm, Hurricane Betsy, pivoted west across Florida into the Gulf. "Never has there been a hurricane more respectable, provided with all the portents, predictions, omens, etc., etc.," Anderson observed to his log. "The awful sunrise—no one could fail to take a warning from it—

the hovering black spirit bird—only one—(*comme il faut*)." The wind rose around the island, and the sea tossed hard against the beach. A rescue boat with the Coast Guard's familiar red-and-blue hash mark against white hull came out to take him home. He knew his family had sent the help. But he remained hunkered on the beach beneath his overturned skiff, his island shelter in foul or fair weather. The boat "finally went off," he recorded, "her running lights showing in the water." Betsy entered the Gulf as a category 4 hurricane and peaked just below a category 5 by the time its center reached Anderson, winds blowing around 150 miles per hour.

If the storm were to take Anderson, so be it. He was a month shy of his sixty-second birthday: strong, mentally sharp, wildly talented, emphatically reclusive, and, at times, stubborn. He was where he wanted to be, with the wind and rain, the thrashing sea, and the island's creatures.

HORN, SAY SCIENTISTS, has been around roughly forty-five hundred years. The same is true for its closest sibling islands to the east and west—Dauphin, Petit Bois, Ship, and Cat Islands. Like all the Gulf's islands, they are barrier islands, which are different from sea islands. For one, only sea islands function as the sole landmass of countries, such as those in the Caribbean. By average size, they eclipse barrier islands, which can be "no larger than a ship at sea," wrote Martha Field in the days before cruise liners, and most sea islands are rock-sturdy creations of long-moribund volcanoes. They are archipelagos in the strictest sense, associated with no mainland, and they can crop up anywhere in the sea. Sail across the Gulf and you'll bump into no island out there in the middle.[5]

Barrier islands remain close to the mainland; they are the median strip between the ocean on one side and a bay or sound on the other. They exist in service to the coast, armoring it against destructive weather launched from the sea, and impounding nearshore the stirring union of sea saltwater and river freshwater that gives life to estuaries. The five sibling islands that include Horn form a ninety-mile bulwark between the Gulf and the mainland, from Mobile to western Mississippi. The Pascagoula and Pearl Rivers feed a constant flow of freshwater into the sound in between.

Horn may have been attached to another island at one time or to the mainland before ice melts lifted sea levels. Or it might have materialized on its own, originating as soil and rock coming off the Appalachian Mountains, down the Tennessee River, and into the Gulf, way back when the Tennessee reached Mobile Bay (today, it loops westward through northern Alabama and up again to confer with the Ohio River). Reaching the Gulf's shallows, the sediment would have trekked along with the currents to some anchorage and piled up at an evolutionary pace into dry land. Barrier islands are literally giant sand piles, beaches surrounded by water, many large enough to provide catchments for rainwater, a resting spot for acorns and pinecones set adrift by the mainland and lighter seeds sent airborne. Animal life— the fliers, strong swimmers, and castaways on driftwood or boat— eventually finds its way to the islands.

Simultaneous with making new Gulf islands, rising seas drowned old islands. In 2001, a team of scientists from the US Geological Survey and the University of New Hampshire spent two months aboard the 210-foot research vessel *Moana Wave*, sonically mapping the continental shelf off northwest Florida. They wanted to learn whether the deepwater reefs that lie off Mississippi and Alabama, charted the year before, continued to the east. What they found was evidence of six ancient river deltas and numerous barrier islands that had existed when seas were low. If the scientists had been exploring on land, they would have found on high ground remnants of barrier islands that had existed when seas were high.

That's when the Florida Keys started taking shape, during the Sangamonian Stage, approximately 130,000 years ago, when the sea was perhaps twenty-five feet above current levels. The keys are coral islands rather than sand islands, made when corals started building reefs along the submerged Florida plateau, following a westerly arc down from the peninsula's eastern edge to present-day Key West and the Dry Tortugas. A hundred thousand years ago, the capricious sea began to withdraw again into glaciers, and the keys appeared. Only the upper ones, from Key Biscayne north, guarding Miami, are technically barrier islands. Tropical hardwoods—mahogany, gumbo-limbo, pigeon plum, Jamaican dogwood, and buttonwood—grew behind each island's perimeter of mangroves. White-tailed deer adapted by growing smaller to penetrate the dense vegetation. The miniaturized subspecies came to be known as Key deer. Hernando d'Escalente Fontaneda, marooned in Calusa territory in the sixteenth century, remembered them in his memoir as looking "like a fox, yet is . . . fat and good to eat."[6]

Barrier islands are a distinct part of Gulf geography, an all-consuming feature on much of the coast, as, especially, in Texas. Remarkably, they did not begin showing up on maps until after 1700. In some ways the prior omission is understandable. Barrier islands can be elusive. Their exact number depends on who is doing the counting, and when. They are impermanent, precarious places, at the mercy of wind and washing water—making, shaping, and destroying them. Texas, Louisiana, Mississippi, and Alabama have twenty or so barrier islands currently in residence. The Florida panhandle has nine and the peninsula has forty-one, many of which are limestone rock formed from the bottom of an interglacial sea and more secure than the standard sand barrier.

These numbers don't include the Ten Thousand Islands. This curious congregation of islands in southwest Florida, which beguiled and confused early mariners, stands apart from those elongated barriers that are front bumpers for most of the Gulf coast. Numbering in the hundreds rather than thousands, they are mangrove islands—mostly small, bushy, vegetative clumps that sometimes secure no more than a shovelful of dry sand. From the air, wrote Rachel Carson in *The Edge of the Sea*, they look "like a school of fish swimming in a south-easterly direction—each fish-shaped island having an 'eye' of water in its enlarged end, the heads of all the 'fish' pointing to the southeast."

Most of the islands have their origin in red mangrove trees taking hold on oyster beds and growing tall and thick on prop roots.[7]

People are speaking anthropocentrically when they say the Ten Thousand Islands are uninhabited. They reek of excrement and half-eaten fish carcasses. Nearly two hundred species of birds spend part of the year among them, some year-round, nesting in the snarl of trees and feeding themselves and their broods on purple-clawed hermit crabs that scuttle about the shallows. Humans have staked out only a few of the larger islands, like Chokoloskee, kingpin of the group, with maybe four hundred residents. Those islands left alone make up a ninety-nine-mile wilderness waterway and national wildlife refuge of clear water, narrow beaches (where they exist), and the largest expanse of mangrove forest in North America, from Marco Island to Lostmans River. The islands are a confusion of hidden bayous, bays, and tidal inlets. A boater can be floating behind a blind of mangroves, mere yards from open water, and be lost for hours.

Scientists say that islands move or drift. Some that are merely masses of vegetation literally float. Barrier islands don't, but they still migrate. "You just can't argue with a barrier island," says archaeologist Cheryl Ward. "It's going to go where it's going to go." Wave action generated by prevailing winds along with shore drift lifts sand from one side of an island and carries it around to the other. In 1848, Petit Bois was anchored east of the Mississippi-Alabama border; a century later, it was one mile west of the border. The entire Horn group has slowly edged westward over the years. "Everything," wrote Anderson, "seems conditional on the islands."[8]

Hurricanes expose their conditional nature, often inducing dramatic, overnight change. With passing storms, islands have historically appeared and disappeared repeatedly, shoals instantly turning to land and land to shoals. Galveston, the best-known island in Texas, was two islands before a huge storm in 1820 closed a severing pass to make one. In 1969, Hurricane Camille split Ship Island in half. When the British geographer Thomas Hutchins surveyed Mississippi Sound in the 1770s, he measured Horn at seventeen miles long; a century later, Coast Survey assistant Joseph Smith Harris measured twelve miles. Anderson knew a ten-mile island.

ISLANDS CULTIVATE MYSTERY, romance, and the idyllic; they suggest paradise, freedom, and sanctuary from the babel of everyday life. The physical setting is one reason *Robinson Crusoe* has endured as one of the most popular books in history. Readers are drawn to the exotic possibilities of island escape, no matter the challenges to survival. Daniel Defoe needed insular geography to segregate his protagonist fully from civilized society. A forest or mountain range, retaining continental connections, would have denied complete removal. An ocean must lie between Crusoe and his home for the book's intended validation of Western culture to work.

Although Horn removed Anderson from the conventions of mainland living, he was no Crusoe. He was never a castaway, and he never tried to replant to the island some semblance of mainland imperatives, as Crusoe, the one-man colonist, does first in his solitude and then with Friday, converting him to be the good servant of an artificial order—to wit, civilization. Horn's denizens of feather, fur, and scale were to Anderson the essence of a natural order that deserved the respect and admiration of humankind. He would have violated all his beliefs to give an island, as Crusoe does, the name Despair.

Horn and the other islands were hopeful places. We know of Anderson's love for them from the trove of drawings and watercolors he produced, almost all on inexpensive typewriter paper—sheets sometimes burn-scarred from his mangrove wood campfire or ripple-dried after rain, flood, or swamped boat. And we know from the expressive passages he "wrote up" with pen or pencil in bound notebooks and on loose pages, accumulated in some eighty-five logs. "Through them blows the fresh island wind," wrote Sissy. "When I read them I tasted the salt and squinted my eyes against the glare."[9]

On the mainland, Anderson was a heavy drinker and smoker; on the islands, he was as abstemious as a monk (he occasionally took along a carafe of wine). He needed no escape, no relief, no construction of a false reality. Read his logs, and you will be struck by the completeness of his contentment. "I left Ocean Springs about six," he recorded on January 4, 1959. "The black posts at the entrance of the harbor slipped past. Filled with the spirit of their forms—pretty brutal spirits possibly. I was not uplifted until I saw the sun shining on the Ocean Springs water tower, when I was halfway out to Horn Island."

Few so fully assimilated the Gulf of Mexico, or, as Anderson rightly put it, accepted "identity with the countless thousands clamoring for existence and present consciousness." Note in the following passage the awareness of the impact of his presence: "Last night I built a fire and had boiled potatoes. I used up a good deal of nest materials in doing it. Dried mangrove wood is almost the only fire wood on the beach." One might be tempted to compare Anderson to Thoreau at Walden. But Redding S. Sugg Jr. cautions otherwise. He pored over Anderson's logs while editing them back in the 1970s, observing that Anderson's solitary Ocean Springs cottage, in which he resided alone, "was already the equivalent of Thoreau's cabin at Walden Pond," which was steps away from Emerson's house, and from clean laundry provided by his mother. When Thoreau ventured beyond Walden to Maine's north woods, his wilderness counterpart to Anderson's barrier islands, he clumsily invoked the established order's language and pronounced the wilderness "savage and dreary." He felt, he said, "more lone than you can imagine."[10]

Never did Anderson feel lone on an island. He was family in nature's house. He would not cast judgment against any of its members—not snake, stingray, or Portuguese man-of-war. He did not squander nature's revelation by attaching anthropomorphic descriptions to it; no matter how threatening, the sea was never an *angry* sea. "All things exist in themselves," he wrote, "have integrity of their own, the grass and the little animals that move through the grass."[11]

People in town said that the middle of the three Anderson brothers was a bit peculiar. He was smart, even a genius in a creative way, handsome with a firm jaw and full mane of wavy hair, something of a Bohemian type in his dress and behavior but quiet and withdrawn, a stranger in commonplace society. He spent time in three mental hospitals between 1938 and 1940. From two, he escaped. From one of those, he shimmed down bedsheets tied together and thrown over the sill of a second-floor window. He lived hermit-like in a cottage on the Anderson property, twenty-four wooded acres that accommodated the families of the three brothers and their pottery business.

Walter's interaction with the others, including Sissy and their four children, grew less frequent over the years. When landside and unable to escape by boat, he did so on a fender-rattling bicycle, the mechanical equivalent of his leaky skiffs. He pedaled everywhere. Without a word to anyone, he would disappear on extended trips to Texas, south Florida, and New York. Grinding the eighty-three miles to New Orleans along the Old Spanish Highway, the sound off his left shoulder, was a mere jaunt.

HIS WANDERLUST ASIDE, Ocean Springs was a perfectly acceptable Gulf-side town, a village really, of less than two thousand residents. Sometimes called East Biloxi or Old Biloxi, it was semifamous for being the site of the first European settlement in the lower Mississippi River valley. It began when Iberville located the mouth of the Mississippi River for the French in 1699. Ship Island, west of Horn, served as the staging ground for his discovery.

If Iberville's Gulf journals are an accurate reflection, the islands released in him no inner compulsion to know nature as an intimate. He was a man of neither art nor science. Sailing the Gulf of Mexico, he sought not to collect new specimens or to encounter the sublime. His journals make no references to nature as an entity and only a few to natural objects—and then, solely in detached utilitarian terms. What mattered to Iberville were the exigencies of exploration, the success of his mission, and the survival of his men and himself. He was a loyal soldier of empire. That was the lens through which he viewed barrier islands, and he saw little that impressed him.

The barriers were for the most part water-bound wastelands, "unwooded" and prone to inundation during foul weather. Not least, they were mosquito haunted and crawling with raccoons, furry creatures that the French mistook for *chats sauvages* ("feral cats"), giving genesis to the name *Isle aux Chats*—Cat Island in the Horn group. Although Iberville found little in the way of freshwater and food on most of the islands (the raccoons were unappetizing), they were important landmarks that helped him navigate the coast and ultimately map parts of it. And more than once their lee provided shelter in foul weather. He gave Ship Island its name for its deepwater access, which he used as the fleet's anchorage before settling down beside Biloxi Bay.[12]

When the Andersons moved to Ocean Springs in 1923, it was still a resort, one of the Six Sisters. But more than fashionable visitors of means kept the local economy afloat. Ocean Springs always had a working side, exhibited by the wide-beamed shrimp and oyster boats that berthed at the local docks. The most expansive oyster beds in the northern Gulf lay in Chandeleur and Breton Sounds, an easy tack out of Biloxi Bay. Biloxi was shipping more than ten million pounds of shrimp and oysters a year by the turn of the century, and it had begun calling itself the "Seafood Capital of the World," and Ocean Springs's fishing fleet figured significantly in that boast, its contribution evident in the streets surfaced with oyster shells.

Altogether, they were quiet streets. They had "no anxious faces," wrote winter resident Louis Sullivan, "no glare of the dollar hunter, no land agents, no hustlers, no drummers, no white-staked lonely subdivisions." Cattle still roamed freely. Save for a few canneries, Ocean Springs had no factories, though it had products of the soil: satsumas and grapefruits, pecans, and on a secondary level, wool. In three months between 1915 and 1916, local nurseries shipped 200,000 pecan trees. Tourism remained important to the village, with continued ties to the Midwest. In 1927, brothers Wilbur and Harvey Branigar of Chicago developed Gulf Hills, a $15 million, eighteen-hole golf resort across the back bayou with exclusive homes for well-heeled, out-of-state residents. Greens fees were $1.50. During the Great Depression, *The WPA Guide* to Mississippi, which targeted tourists with spending money, gave Gulf Hills a blurb: "one of the show places of the coast."[13]

The guide featured only one other Ocean Springs establishment: Shearwater Pottery, which belonged to the Andersons. The recognition undoubtedly excited them, especially older brother Peter, who built the pottery on the family property in 1928 with money borrowed from his father. Peter banked it on the talent of the three brothers: he himself, Walter, and youngest brother Mac. Their mother, Annette, who had studied at Tulane University's Newcomb College, renowned for its art program, lent her own potter's hand to the family business. Peter took the name for the pottery from the shearwater, a wave skimmer given to beautiful aerobatics and endowed with long wings, long-distance flight, and longevity. Peter liked to keep things local; that included his clay source. He routinely sailed a twenty-six-foot schooner towing a skiff, to carry the clay, to the top of Biloxi Bay and several miles up the muddy Tchoutacabouffa River, where he quarried the high banks. This was the same clay dug by the late abstract expressionist George Ohr, styled by himself as the "Mad Potter of Biloxi" and later, by others, as the "Picasso of Pottery."[14]

Walter's job in the family business was to decorate the pieces fired by Peter and his mother with carved patterns and painted designs. He also created whimsical clay figurines he called widgets. His stylized birds and fish were an important influence in establishing the pottery's regional signature. But the island lover was an undependable business partner. Bursts of productivity for the pottery competed with bursts devoted solely to his personal art and to island sojourns. He patterned his family life with similar swings of attention and neglect, mostly the latter. "He was a painter always," wrote Sissy, "a lover at times, a husband and father never."[15]

His temperament followed the rhythms of the sea rather than the obligations of domestic life. To the "dominant mode on shore," to the company of his own species, he yearned for that of the longleaf and loblolly pines and goldenrod of Horn Island, and that of sheeps-head, gar, stone crabs, owls, grackles, gulls, pelicans, herons, coots, purple gallinules, redhead ducks, the thieving raccoons that burgled his camp, and the island's feral sow, who lived to old age, beating pathways that Anderson walked, before it drowned in Hurricane Betsy's deluge. They were the brilliant animation of the Gulf of Mexico, and the main subjects of Anderson's drawings, watercolors, and block prints, which were themselves striking in colors and sinuous brush strokes, almost hypnotic in the way they simulate the contour and motion of Gulf nature. "When a wave comes in, magic!" he exulted. "What glowing sequences of color, what strange convulsions of form."

Some well-meaning critics have made Anderson heir to the style of better-known artists before him. One is Audubon, who spent his share of time around the Gulf. But the assertion slights Anderson. He could not think of killing his subjects and forcing them into a pose, as did Audubon, who shot several birds and ran positioning wires through their bodies to render the image of a single subject. Anderson painted the dead as well as the living, but the former came to their end by natural causes. And Anderson's canvas was significantly more diverse than Audubon's; he painted all the things the Gulf presented him.

Other observers have invoked Cézanne, Matisse, Van Gogh, and Picasso. Again, the comparisons fall flat. They minimize, as Anderson biographer Christopher Maurer writes, his "manner of pursuing 'realization'—both of himself and of nature—[as] uniquely his own." He used warm to cool colors in chromatic variations and strokes to show feeling; his lines are vivid, limber, and alive. They are the lines of the Gulf of Mexico and its wildlife. They transpired from his search for wholeness in nature, a "significant form" that he sought to discover not merely from the visual form but from the biological, by touching, feeling, listening, and even tasting. "1 single beautiful image is practically inexhaustible," he noted in his log. Yet, typically, "Man begins by saying 'of course,' before any of his senses have a chance to come to his aid with wonder and surprise." That is what Anderson's art translated: wonder and surprise.[16]

He found it by setting aside the "categories of mind" and the "prejudices of human interest," says Redding Sugg, and answering to nature's lead. Anderson wrote, "It is extraordinary to observe how a fish radiates from the eye as a center, how almost anything is possible when it is brought into proper focus, that the proper relation of two things produces a third which is completely satisfactory—and that third thing is a miracle." He never took a powerboat to the islands. That would have been imposing himself and civilization on nature— better to be seduced than to subjugate. "The butterfly here stamps its feet. Nature does not like to be anticipated, but loves to surprise." So he sailed, rowed, and, when necessary, swam his boat. "I survived the terrors of the sea and saw the red sun go down to come to this place to paint—all nature appreciates my courage and love."[17]

That love probably saved him from himself, and it probably saved Sissy too. The artist who thrived on the extremes of the sea had an interior that was much the same. During those years when he was escaping from mental hospitals, he suffered from transitory delusions and hallucinations. That was a relatively short period. More common and persistent throughout his adult life were alcoholic rages, apparently set off by self-doubt and feelings of confinement. In her memoir that is both loving and honest, Sissy discussed his dark side. More than once, he threatened her life and the lives of their children, who nevertheless, like their mother, never stopped loving him. He denied having sired the oldest two, and disavowed parental obligations. In December 1946, he announced in a fit of temper that he was moving out. "I can't take it anymore," he said. "I am an artist; I have to be." That's when the islands stole him away. He had to be an artist, but in a more crucial sense, he needed nature to be an artist.[18]

Anderson is *the* artist of the Gulf of Mexico. The Atlantic has its many famous painters: Monet, Seurat, Signac, and, most intensely, J. M. W. Turner and Winslow Homer. Anderson is different from these Atlantic artists, in part because the Gulf is different. His sea does not crash and thunder. It is instead an undulation of sprightly waves in cheerful hues. He was not particularly interested in the struggle between humankind and the sea, as was Homer, whose paintings often feature heroic figures, sometimes a single determined individual, symbolizing the "loneliness" he saw in the Atlantic.[19]

There was nothing lonely about the Gulf to Anderson. It had its many busy, scuttling, flying, diving, jumping, skittering creatures— his company and his source of happy fascination. They are the heroic figures in his work. He had studied in New York and Paris and traveled to Costa Rica and as far as China to observe and compare natural forms and colors, but he always returned home for his art. Mississippi has that kind of pull on its people, with a sense of place that is profound. Faulkner crafted his literary career around it. The pen of Eudora Welty was loyal to it. Anderson might have painted somewhere else, but it is hard to imagine somewhere else with a grace of color and motion and life equivalent to that of the Mississippi Gulf coast and its islands.

ASK A FIRST-GRADER TO DRAW islands in the sea and she is apt to create them in shapes of circles. That geometric simplicity tends to persist even when the maturing mind learns that islands come in all shapes and sizes. Each of the Gulf's is unique (a few are even round), although some are more striking than others.

One is two-thousand-year-old Padre Island in Texas. The island formed out of granules of mainland soil carried by rains into the Rio Grande and down to the Gulf. The longshore current conveyed sediment northward, the Mississippi sent sediment southward, and together they built the largest barrier island in the Gulf, giving fodder to the Texan assertion that everything in Texas is bigger. Not quite, though. Padre is only the second-largest barrier island in the contiguous United States. New York's Long Island is bigger, and the most populous. Fewer than three thousand people in 2010 lived in South Padre, the sole incorporated area of the island. Yet, physically, the New York island's name is better suited to Padre, the longest barrier island in the world—more feed for native crowing.

Less than three miles wide, Padre Island parallels the Texas coast for 113, fronting five counties. It traces the shoreline's sweeping contour flawlessly. On a map, narrow, long Padre looks as lithesome as Anderson's brushstrokes. In 1920, the *Washington Post* pronounced its thirty miles of unbroken beach the "finest natural beach on the gulf coast." It has marvelous, wind-sculptured sand dunes, constantly building and eroding and rebuilding, much like the island's shoreline, and always striking to the visual artist. Photographer Geoff Winningham describes the general terrain as "roughly half desert and half grass flats"—the makings of a landmass that ship's captains were wise to give a wide berth.[20]

Padre was the site of the first shipwreck of the Spanish treasure fleet, three laden carracks in 1554 caught in an April nor'easter and likely in the strong eddy swirling around Devil's Elbow, a bight at the island's southern end. Thereafter, the inexorable terra firma waited to claim the timbers and cargo of innumerable storm-trapped vessels. Four national flags—Spain, Mexico, the Republic of Texas, and the US—have flown over the island, and its physical features more or less wrote its history with Western culture.

The first Westerner to install himself permanently on the island was José Nicholas Balli, a Mexican priest. He was also its first owner, by an early nineteenth-century Spanish grant, later validated by the independent republic of Mexico. Balli was both enterprising rancher and padre, the founder of a mission to dispense gospel to the island's wintering and withering Karankawa and to the whites he recruited to settle on it. He and his nephew Juan José Balli established a profitable rancho on which they raised cattle, sheep, and horses. The mainland across Laguna Madre was turning into a country of far-flung cattle ranches. Eighteen dominated the landscape, each over 10,000 acres; the largest, 600,000. Juan José survived his uncle by twenty-five years. When he died in the 1853 yellow-fever epidemic that devastated New Orleans and parts of southern Texas, his heirs showed no interest in the island.

John V. Singer did, as an accident of fate. Harboring plans to enter the shipping trade in Texas, he and his wife and four children set sail from their home in New York in 1847, Singer at the helm of their three-masted schooner. Crossing the Gulf, they steered unwittingly into a storm that tossed them into the shoal at Devil's Elbow and stranded them on the long, austere island. The Singers played out Padre's version of *The Swiss Family Robinson*, yet another island adventure story, published thirty-five years earlier and still hugely popular. They salvaged wood from the splintered schooner and built a house for themselves and corrals for the horses and cattle that Balli had left behind. In the best years, they were branding fifteen hundred head and salvaging jewelry, gold coins, and various valuables from wrecked ships delivered by Devil's Elbow. John accumulated enough wealth to fund the start-up of his brother Isaac Singer's sewing-machine company and, according to his oldest son, to bury $80,000 in hard coin in the dunes before the Confederates expelled the Union sympathizer from the island. After the war, the Singers made a fruitless search to recover their money. Local historians say the changing dunescape foiled them.

Padre's next primary occupant, Patrick Dunn, never found the money either. He earned his money, as had his predecessors. A veteran cattleman of the mainland, Dunn could have been played in the movies by Audie Murphy—they looked so much alike—and Murphy, a Texan, liked to play the westerns. Dunn came of age as a rancher with the invention of barbed-wire fencing. He chafed at its use. It closed the open range and gave advantage to the big cattle outfits. But unlike a Murphy character, Dunn did not holster up and fight for a cause. He moved to Padre Island, where natural fences—Laguna Madre and the Gulf of Mexico—would corral his cows.

He was onto something. Other ranchers turned three other Texas barrier islands—Matagorda, San Jose, and Mustang—into cow pasturage. There were additional benefits too. Unlike those sprawling ranches on the mainland, Padre had little brush in which to lose cattle. Freshwater for the herd was accessible anywhere on the island by digging a few feet into the sand. Gathering drift lumber on the beach,

Dunn built a modest two-story house, which he furnished with pieces salvaged from Devil's Elbow's spoils. Then the island began to attract others, who talked about developing it.

In the last decades of Dunn's life (he died in 1938), Padre was becoming less and less secluded. Sportsmen had discovered the good fishing—pompano, redfish, deep-sea bass, and tarpon. President Harding came to try his luck in the 1920s, and he brought the national press. Investors made plans for a resort town with hotels and fishing outfits. A causeway connecting the island to the mainland opened it to automobile tourists, and plans for development continued to circulate. So did plans to turn the northern portion of the island into a protected wildlife area. While some valued Padre's expanse for its natural existence, others saw it as an island desert. That was the US military's take. During World War II, Padre made the list of possible test sites for the first nuclear explosion. The navy was already using parts of it and Laguna Madre as a bombing and gunnery range. Mainland newspapers warned bathers to stay out of the water, for fear they would be strafed during a training session.

Each Gulf island has its individual history, with some, like Padre, serving double duty as nature deemed and as civilization demanded. Many of these natural protectors of the mainland were commissioned to protect the US from its enemies. Collectively, they supported ten fortresses at one time or another, yet not one was ever exposed to battle. The first was Ship Island's Fort Massachusetts, a redbrick redoubt that, from a bird's-eye view, resembles a capital **D**, in serif typeface and full block, like a letter on a varsity jacket. During the Second Seminole War, the army used the fort as a transient facility for Florida Indians it was removing to an Oklahoma reservation. It was from there that Farragut assembled his fleet of gun- and mortar boats to ascend the Mississippi River and capture New Orleans. Union forces used several Gulf islands to aid the blockade of Confederate supplies in and out of Mobile, Galveston, and other ports. During the Spanish-American War, with Tampa as the embarkation point for the invasion of Cuba, engineers constructed Fort De Soto on Mullet Key and Fort Dade on Egmont Key, both of concrete with an aggregate of imported rock and local shells.

Never seeing action, the island forts were somewhat cushy duty for roughly four hundred occupying troops. The beaches were breathtaking, the water turquoise, and the Gulf sunsets exquisite. Almost paradise, save for the blasted mosquitoes. A local historian claims, they "were the fiercest foes Fort De Soto ever fought," and truly a military concern. The chief surgeon of the Department of the Gulf, a careful and discerning man, said that if this "post is to continue as a station, life for those concerned should be, at least, made bearable." Lacking an effective means of mosquito control, the commander interpreted "bearable" to mean making beer and wine available to the troops. Was it by mere coincidence, then, that when national Prohibition began, garrisoning the vinous island ended?[21]

Many Gulf barriers had neither troops nor booze nor people. The Mississippi group supported little, if any, human habitation, and never consistently. Some Gulf islands ended up as parks or preserves, with birds as the primary tenants. Those islands near enough to make a mainland connection by causeway or bridge economically practicable were fated to the promiscuous sprawl of civilization. Others, such as Padre, ended up supporting both people and abundant wildlife, in part because it became a divided island—literally. The Army Corps of Engineers finished cutting a thirty-mile boat channel across Padre in 1962, two years after bombing practices had stopped. That year, as development continued at the southern end, President Kennedy signed legislation to turn eighty-one miles of Padre Island into a national seashore, the fourth in the National Park Service's inventory.

IT COULD BE THAT PADRE never returned that hidden cache of money to John Singer because someone else found it. For years, hopeful treasure hunters chased rumors that Gulf pirate Jean Lafitte had hidden contraband somewhere on that long barrier. To imaginative minds, islands existed for the burial of pirate booty that some latter-day lucky soul would find. Exploiting such fantasies, a couple of clever real-estate investors on an island off the west coast of Florida early in the twentieth century dug up fake treasure chests they had secretly planted to promote land sales. Their bluff got the wanted publicity and a name for their insular parcel, Treasure Island. Up the coast, residents of Fort Walton Beach scavenged the alpine dunes on Santa Rosa Island for the chest of prizes that the chamber of commerce buried every spring. The ritual was part of the Billy Bowlegs Pirate Festival, begun in the 1950s.[22]

Billy Bowlegs was fictional. The inspiration for his creation was real, in the man of William Augustus Bowles, a Maryland-born Brit who, after the American Revolution, lived with Lower Creek Indians near the upper Gulf. Bowles, handsome and positively Anglo in a Thomas Hardy portrait for which he posed wearing native ceremonial adornment, founded a short-lived Indian state in Spanish Florida before he commanded a swift fleet of two schooners and turned to raiding cargo ships on the Gulf. The Spanish captured him twice. He escaped the first time, and after the second, he died on a hunger strike while imprisoned on an island, Cuba.

Islands and pirates, mystery and romance, truth and fable: the lore of one is the lore of the other. John Gomez was a seaworthy sort of half-truths, who may or may not have been freebooting on the Gulf in Bowles's day. He was genuinely bowlegged, though—at least in old age, which seemed to have encompassed half of his life. He lived most of his days on Panther Key, near Pine Island, and was said to be a "compound of Spaniard, Indian, hunter and fisherman," born in either Portugal or Spain in 1778, 1781, or 1791, ending up in St. Augustine at an early age, and either orphaned or kidnapped soon after. Fable has little certitude.[23]

It was then that Gomez allegedly began an adventurous engagement with piracy as the cabin boy of the legendary but apocryphal José Gaspar, a former Spanish naval officer turned indomitable freebooter. From his buccaneer's den, a lair of debauchery and concubines, on an island now called Gasparilla, at the top of tarpon-shadowed Boca

Grande Pass, Gaspar hunted ungainly cargo and treasure ships. Until his spectacular death in 1821. Under attack by the USS *Enterprise*, his brigantine in flames, he wrapped himself in the anchor chain and leaped into the Gulf, proclaiming, "Gasparilla dies by his own hand not the enemy's."[24]

In 1904, Gaspar was resurrected in the first annual Gasparilla Parade in Tampa, something of a grimy port and cigar-making city eager to promote itself as a winter resort. There was one problem with the Gaspar narrative (aside from its glorifying piracy): it was all lies. Jolly Roger, Polly-want-a-cracker legend was the kind of color many tourist communities added to their history. Unfortunately, authoritative books on pirates bought into the Gaspar fable, and Tampa even named its NFL team the Buccaneers.

Gomez was the chief pitchperson for this fibbery, and likely its inventor. At the time he was supposedly pirating, he was, in reality, provisioning the Coast Survey crew charting the Gulf. He had valuable geographic knowledge to offer too. During the Civil War, he had served as a pilot for the Federal blockade. Said his commanding officer, Gomez knew "every shoal, rock, oyster bed, creek, inlet, mud bank, fishing ledge, roosting place for birds, deer track and channel from Key West to Pensacola." Not surprisingly, blue-water anglers later sought Gomez for his littoral acumen. He was renowned for his guiding services, and his sea stories, delivered in the salty tongue of an old mariner. On Panther Key, he lived with his wife in a hut shingled and shaked with sun-browned palm thatch. It fit his persona. Always dressed "tropical and free" and properly barefoot, he wore a long, grizzled beard with a head of brush-thick white hair. *Forest and Stream* made him a familiar figure in its pages. He died in 1900, from accidental drowning at the age of 119, or so the magazine reported—thus in death living up to his tall tales.[25]

Jean Lafitte was the real deal, even born with his splendid buccaneer name—either in France or Saint-Domingue, maybe in 1780. He started out as a run-of-the-mill smuggler operating out of New Orleans, which had plenty of his kind, more so after President Jefferson enforced the 1807 Embargo Act's prohibition against trading with Britain and France. When local authorities gave Lafitte the boot, he moved operations down to Barataria Island, west of the Mississippi's passes and superlatively positioned for intercepting cargo ships. Before long, he, his brother Pierre, and their den of thieves, along with several lean ships outfitted with cannons, made Barataria into a booming port. Their activity was unwanted by Louisiana officials, who arrested the brothers. They promptly skipped bail. When war with Britain broke out in 1812, they momentarily redeemed themselves by protecting New Orleans from invasion, earning commendations from Andrew Jackson.

Afterward, the pirate-patriots went to Galveston to aid Spain in its efforts to preserve Mexico. There, they reverted to habit and preyed on cargo and slave ships. In 1821, the USS *Enterprise* sailed to Galveston to expel the Lafittes. The *Enterprise's* appointment with the pirates was later reprised in the tale of Gaspar's sensational end, with one major difference: the Lafittes departed without a fight. Jean ended up in Cuba but quickly wore out his welcome. From there he went to Colombia, where the independent government gave him a commission and a gunboat. He began raiding Spanish ships as a state-sponsored privateer. Off the coast of Honduras in 1823, while trying to intercept silver shipments, he lost his life in a battle against two Spanish warships. "Thus fell Lafitte," wrote the president of the Louisiana Historical Society in 1919, "a man superior in talent, in knowledge of his profession, in courage, and in physical strength."[26]

Louisianans would give the Lafitte name to a festival, streets, fishing villages, and a national historic park and preserve. People scoured Grande Isle for Lafitte gold. Fantasy also led them to draining Indian Bayou, where they recovered but a native canoe—treasure enough for Indian scholars.

EARLY ONE SPRING, Walter Anderson became interested in drawing the dead and dying animals on Horn Island. He was obsessed with their changing colors. An expiring turtle "identified itself with all the precious substances of the Chinas," he penciled in his log, "old gold, jade, copper red." The artist in him would not "allow all that form and color, that order, to go to waste."

He had good reason for having death on his mind. The spring before, he had been sloshing around an oyster lagoon on the island's north side when he spotted a bittern's nest in a high bush. Wanting to investigate color at the front end of the life spectrum, he reached blindly into the nest for an egg and received a sharp pain. As he yanked his hand back, he saw a "startled" moccasin slide away. He had no sharp edge for incising the bite and bleeding the poison, so he hurried the three miles back to camp. Finding only a butter knife, he boiled water to soften the skin of the swelling hand, then passed out before doing anything more. When he came to, the stove fire had spread. "It seemed to be devouring the island," he wrote, "and it was all my fault. I wept and howled and was powerless to save a single tree, a single little bird or bunny." He fought the fire for hours, then collapsed again. Exerting himself was the wrong thing to do; it was circulating the venom, but he'd been thinking about how Abel in William Henry Hudson's *Green Mansions* survived a snakebite by keeping active.

When Anderson woke, the wind had turned the fire back on itself, and the flames had died. Two boys in a small motorboat found him and took him home to Sissy. His doctor said he was lucky to be alive. Anderson never felt animosity toward the snake; countless others, he reasoned, had let him pass without a bother. Sissy nursed him back to health, and he promptly returned to Horn Island.

He always seemed to be making up for lost time, as if he had come to the discovery of his passion late, or was trying to recover the years when World War II denied him the island. The conflict abroad intervened in domestic peace with demands for supplies, training bases, and big and little sacrifices in personal routines and expectations. At the outset of US military involvement abroad, German submarines torpedoed more than two dozen merchant ships not far disgorged from the mouth of the Mississippi River. For Anderson, the veracity of war was everywhere evident in the oil slicks in the water and the tar balls and refuse washed ashore. He also had to sacrifice Horn. The military took control of several Gulf islands. Florida's St. George Island and Mullet Key, like Padre Island, served as bombing ranges. The army used Cat Island for training combat-ready attack dogs, using stray mutts taken from the streets. As if confirming the joke, the sound of shellfire turned the would-be war dogs into frightened kittens.

With similar clumsy military dispatch, the army's Chemical Warfare Service (CWS) secured Horn Island to set up an elaborate biological-weapons lab. One of its first priorities was to abate the mosquito population by spraying creosote as a larvicide over the island's ponds. Navy Seabees then laid 7.6 miles of narrow-gauge train track, and barged over from the mainland two fourteen-ton locomotives and twenty wooden freight cars. The Army Corps of Engineers built barracks for two hundred personnel, separate recreational facilities for officers and enlisted men, a basketball court, movie theater, mess hall, headquarters building, motor pool garages, storage sheds, machine shop, sewage system, power plant, weather station, animal corrals, and test laboratory. The contrast to this horizontal assemblage was the redbrick chimney stack standing over an incinerator, for burning the chemicals and the expired test subjects—which were expected to range from mice to horses.

According to science writer Ed Regis, the military intended Horn to be the "workhorse site for American biological weapons trials." But before refitting the island, army engineers realized that Horn did not meet the required criterion of remoteness. Commercial fishing boats motored to and from the Gulf past the island daily, close enough for their yawning wake to roll up on the island's shore. Even the mainland population was too close. Worse, it was downwind. Still, the funding had been appropriated, the money would be spent, and testing would begin, if only to fulfill a fraction of the CWS's original agenda. In the end, the army exploded sixty-seven four-pound bombs filled with botulinum slurry, an agent that was supposed to cause botulism. But, of hundreds of test subjects of varying species, only one succumbed from inhaling the toxin, a guinea pig, and in the operation's single wise decision, the army declared botulinum unsuitable as a killing agent and ceased all testing.[27]

But operation Horn Island had one more task at hand before shutting down: disposing of three thousand tons of captured German grenades, rockets, and bombs, some of which were mustard gas munitions. The army cast an initial thirty-thousand-pound bomb and three five-hundred-pound bombs into the Gulf. It then took the chemical weapons to Horn Island and burned them in a bonfire. For days, people on the mainland heard explosions and saw flaming plumes rising into the southern sky. Once the fireworks were over, the ordnance experts barged the bomb cases, some of them unexploded and leaking mustard gas, out into the open water and deep-sixed the lot between Petit Bois and Horn. The navy was doing the same with weapons that had been stockpiled in New Orleans. Finally, the army dismantled its island laboratory and left in 1947, bequeathing to Horn a litter of abandoned buildings overseen by the incinerator chimney.

For the island-happy Anderson, the chimney was a towering insult to a natural place. "I investigated the army camp, found it in ruins, and decided to move in," he wrote in his log on a cold March day in 1950. But his residency in the old buildings was brief. He didn't go to the islands to seek shelter in civilization's habitat—moreover, in the remnants of a military takeover that offended him. He had previously shared this view with the island's uniformed occupiers.

Near the end of the war, they found him washed up on the beach. He had been sailing out to Louisiana's Chandeleur Islands when his boat capsized. Before reaching the shore at Horn, swallowing lots of water, he gave himself up for lost. The sound of a train whistle, an "utter impossibility" on the island, convinced him that he was crossing over to the other world. Then he saw the actual train, along with a big, barking military dog defending the beach on which he lay, and two soldiers with guns approaching him. "I realized, with a shock, I was the enemy!"

He later confessed to Sissy that at first he felt weak for requiring rescue. Gradually, he grew angrier toward the reality revealed to him. The soldiers took him on the train across the island for interrogation, and he got a fuller look at the military operations. Before the probing had hardly begun, Anderson turned the questioning back on the officer in charge. "Why did you come here?" Anderson asked. "You have ruined the most beautiful place in the world. I can never forgive you." It was then, he told Sissy, that his interrogator "spotted me for a 'crazy'" and he knew he would be released.[28]

That was all it took: to describe a Gulf barrier island as having no aesthetic equal to a man who thought his billet there was the south end of rotten duty. The captive, of course, had no knowledge that his rescuers would soon pollute the Gulf with dirty munitions. He never did know. The ordnance dump between Petit Bois and Horn remained a military secret until five years after Anderson's death. (In 2012, the National Park Service discovered containers of mustard gas on the island.)

OUTSIDE THIS ONE OCCASION, the accidental visitor steered clear of Horn Island during the military's occupation of it. Until he could come back to it, Anderson went to the Chandeleur Islands, the fifty-mile chain that Theodore Roosevelt had declared a federal bird refuge the year after Anderson's birth. Throughout the war, they were his refuge too. Due south of Biloxi, the Chandeleurs were twenty-five miles out beyond Horn. In 1772, a five-day hurricane had cut channels across the crescent assemblage of islands, giving them the dental display of the Cheshire cat, each island a tooth in an impish grin. Part of St. Bernard Parish, they are the easternmost boundary of Louisiana, yet they seem to hang out in the Gulf as their own autonomous realm. The islandscape is more or less salt marshes, scant trees, and low dunes with beach grasses and shrubs (wax myrtle and groundsel bush). The islands appeared on Iberville's horizon on February 1, 1699, the eve of La Fête de Chandeleur, and the good Catholic christened them in recognition of the feast day.

"On Chandeleur," Walter explained to Sissy, there is "the feeling of being released into a new dimension." He was referring not to the vanishing of the islands, a circumstance few people were noticing back then. He was experiencing "that dimension occupied by the free-flyers, the free-swimmers." That's what the islands were to him—freedom, delight in aloneness. Once, while he was sleeping blissfully in his tent out on the Chandeleurs, the tidal current wrested his boat from its beach anchor and took it to sea. When he told the story to his daughter Mary, she shrieked, "Daddy, you were marooned!" "Yes," he replied. "and it was lovely."[29]

Yet, it wasn't always. On another occasion, he had been island dwelling for a week, drawing and painting, cavorting with the birds, before he saw another human being—a skiff with two fishermen, "strong, sunburned, blond, with the wellbeing that people get from exposure to the sun and wind." He chatted with them. They gave him a redfish to cook and then went on their way. That evening, the reclusive log writer expressed disappointment: "One of the charms of the island is gone. At least I had seven days."

Anderson had been going to the Chandeleurs since boyhood, when he and his brothers would head out on great adventures. Later, he went as a solitary adventurer. But the Chandeleurs did not give him the isolation he relished on Horn Island. Here's the log writer again, the time he was joyed to be stranded: "I just saw a boat go past. Last night there were the lights of three boats around the island; for a marooned person I have plenty of company." The shallow bays and lagoons around the islands—flush with turtle grass, manatee grass, widgeon grass, and shoal weed—meant fish; fish meant fishing people.

Still, fish and the wild grassy dunes and the black mangroves (their northwesternmost reach is the Chandeleurs) also meant birds—feeding birds and nesting birds—and birds meant Anderson. Log date, July 25: "The flat with the tide out was full of wading birds, white egrets, little blues, Louisiana herons, rails, pelicans, laughing gulls, shearwaters." Horn Island may have been his preferred barrier, but the avian life on the Chandeleurs was hard to beat, thanks in part to ink from TR's pen. Anderson made some of his most expressive log entries there, and hardly a one fails to mention birds. July 29: "After lunch I took the skiff and went in pursuit of man o'war birds. . . . I drew some on the wing. . . . Driven home by rain about 2:00 where I wrote up the log and drew pelicans from the front of my tent." July 30: "It was an embarrassment of riches. While I was painting pelicans with white bodies against the dark clouds of the squall, first a terrapin, then a crab and last a king rail came tiptoeing out between the mangrove tubers." July 31: "There were herons and the sky was patterned with man o'war birds."

As soon as the army finished its business on Horn, Anderson packed his skiff and returned to his favorite green, white, and amber insular precinct, stepping up the regularity and length of his visits. The birds were not as plentiful as on the Chandeleurs, but this was not a bad thing. A diversity of life divided his attention and gave him more to write about in his journal: a sea horse, "the reconciling agent in time— *motor magna*—between the horrible monotony of the machine and the bomb of poetry. . . . My perfect rapport with nature"; shrimp, "bright vermillion with a dragon's body," captive in a tide pool at the low and valuable end of the Gulf food chain; a frog, "green and gold and black and copper—magnificently dressed," borrowed for an artist's model and coveted by a moccasin; a "Barrel of Monkeys"—as he called an octopus—washed up on the beach and rescued from a pecking herring gull, its curvilinear anatomy ideally suited to Anderson's expressive brush.

As with any log keeper, a ship's captain or a farmer, reports on the weather filled much of the space of daily entries. Islands know every subtle or pronounced and instant change in Gulf conditions, and Anderson was consummately attuned to it all. January 1959: "It is wild weather. The sky has been moving since yesterday evening." Absent from his logs are complaints about freezing temperatures or hard-driving rains, or about the wind that blew away his canopy or sent sand into his camp. It was all the continuing business of the island, varying conditions under which to paint and observe his subjects, the world coming to him in new ways.

That's why he could not accept rescue from the Coast Guard during Hurricane Betsy in early September 1965. He had to experience the storm as did his fellow island dwellers, and like them, he scrambled to survive. Betsy's raging winds forced him to abandon his camp for higher ground. The sea reached him again, and he retreated again. After his third move, he looked for "suitable trees to tie to if the water kept rising." Ultimately, the hurricane let him be.

When it passed and the water receded, Horn had survived, but not without impact. His camp "—the place where I had nested snugly for years—was gone, simply sliced off by the waves." The east end of the island's long, sandy point was now a "short bar with waves breaking on it." Familiar dunes were gone too; "great high" interior ones, which had protected him in the end, were "still there," but more vulnerable for their lost shoreside defenses. For miles, the salt spray and sand blast had turned pine trees to a coarse brown and "hurt" the balsam and goldenrod. By contrast, the island's north side had a beautiful new beach, and birds were everywhere feasting on half-buried sea fleas and the dead.

Renewal had begun instantaneously. Here is another value of the logs: the firsthand account of the storm-recovering barrier. Ants returned to Anderson's camp in no time; rafts of ducks reappeared almost instantly. "I saw my usual curlew in its usual place on the outside of the west point," he wrote the day after barely escaping the surging waters. "The y c [yellow-crowned] night heron has come back to the same place at the mouth of the little bayou. . . . I'd like to know where it had been." The islander took his time getting back to Ocean Springs. "Change," he reflected, "is magical."

SURVIVING BETSY MARKED ANDERSON'S last escape to Horn or any island. A month after his return home, he was coughing up

blood. His doctor found a tumor and diagnosed lung cancer—a consequence of cigarette smoking, an affliction of the "dominant mode." The
end came quickly. He died from complications of surgery on November 30, 1965, in a New Orleans hospital, not on a Gulf island—in
civilization's grip, not in nature's embrace.

After his death and with her sister, Sissy entered Walter's cottage for
the first time in years. It was dust caked and disheveled, she remembered in her memoir, but "bursting with treasure." Piled and strewn
about was the lifework of a prolific, intense, and enlightened nature
artist: thousands of watercolors, block prints, and drawings—pencil,
pen, crayon—some whole, some ripped, some discarded and burned
in the little fireplace. An old-fashioned floor safe, its door open, held
his island logs from nearly twenty years, no better organized than
the artwork. Within them were the sensibilities of a man spiritually,
intellectually, and unconditionally connected to nature, reflecting an
earthly wisdom from which larger, changing society might benefit,
though wisdom from which society in his lifetime and after was turning away.

Through the cottage to the other side of the clutter was a padlocked
door to a second room. Sissy had the key and walked in. She gasped.
The room was an expansive tribute that Walter had paid to the wonder
that became his artistic muse. Across the ceiling and three walls, his
lithe and luminous brush strokes followed a full day's movement of the
sun and the wildlife "upon the Gulf Coast." Sissy's sister immediately
had a name for it: "Creation at Sunrise."[30]

Thirteen

WIND AND WATER

Despite the repeated assault of hurricanes, such as the 1919 storm
that wreaked this devastation on Corpus Christi, Texas, Americans
continued to expand their presence in harm's way.

> *God didn't want me. He took the ones he wanted and left us to
> tell this story.*
>
> —Laura Dupuis (2009)[1]

⁕ ──

"They are called typhoons," Joseph Conrad's Captain
MacWhirr explains in a letter to his wife, to which she stifles a
yawn, uninterested in "all these ship affairs." A principal character in

Typhoon, MacWhirr is honoring the mariner's practice of referring to hurricanes in regional vernacular. His letter arrives from the China Sea in the northwestern Pacific. If he had been writing from the South Pacific or Indian Ocean he would have bored his wife with that region's nomenclature, "cyclone." A hurricane is a "hurricane" only in the eastern Pacific and Atlantic—and, too, the Gulf.[2]

It is so, in part, because of the Yucatán Maya. They paid tribute to a no-nonsense, one-legged god named Huracan, the divine source of wind and storms and, appropriately, birth and destruction. Their · neighbors to the east and southeast, the Taíno and Carib, each had a deity of similar name and disposition. From them the Spanish got a word, *huracán*, for those incomprehensible tempests they discovered in the New World—acts of God, as they saw them, that wrecked their ships and settlements.

Scientists have scoured maritime records, lighthouse logs, diaries, and newspapers to assemble a century and a half of global hurricane geography. On historical storm maps, they draw color-coded tracking lines—purple for the most intense storms and light blue for the least—wandering and seemingly whimsical lines that a child with crayons might draw, though they are precise and ever serious. The colors congeal in seven areas near, but not on, the equator. These are hurricane hot spots, or basins, as scientists call them: three around the Indian Ocean, two in the North Pacific, and one each for the southwestern Pacific and northern Atlantic.

Hurricanes are natives of the tropics, born in the swelter of evaporating seawater, eighty degrees or warmer, often on long, hot summer days. That's why those who sail the world's oceans feel safest in the southern Atlantic. The cooler water temperatures between the distant landmasses of South America and Africa rarely boil up a hurricane. Salts have been most likely to kneel and pray in the northern Pacific, the stormiest sea. It generates nine typhoons on a yearly average. The northern Atlantic is only slightly tamer.

Every now and then, in these hot spots near the equator, gathering heat energy reaches a tipping point and brings to life a tropical storm or hurricane. This happens when vaporous air rises in a column over the warm sea, causing the surface pressure to drop. More air and moisture rushes across the sea and draws, like a vacuum, into this column and up to cooler altitudes that condense the sopping air. Dark clouds build, thunder cracks, lightning stabs through the clouds, and rain begins. Low wind shear invites storms to multiply, grow, and concentrate into a single system.

When the system is expansive enough, the Earth's rotation nudges the storm into its own rotation—counterclockwise if north of the equator, clockwise if south. Primed with heat energy, the entire implacable mass is self-willed to move across the sea, throwing it into a rage, dumping rain in torrents, preying on the elements in its path. If winds stay below seventy-four miles per hour, all remains a fairly defensible tropical storm. Above that wind speed, you've got a hurricane on your hands—far-reaching but compacted power, a tightly wound colossus with its famous centered eye.

After Hurricane Katrina, Louisiana climatologists Barry Keim and Robert Muller put together numbers on Gulf storms. They published their findings in a book that is a combination of historical narrative, scientific explanation, and raw data.[3] One of Keim and Muller's most revealing charts gives 639 as the number of hurricanes stirring up the Atlantic between 1886 and 2005—slightly more than five on a yearly average. One-third of them either tracked into the Gulf or originated there—nearly two a year. Two may not sound like a lot, yet imagine Californians contending with the same number of major earthquakes every year in the span of a few months. Gulf states are struck by hurricanes fifteen percent more often than all other US states combined, and coastal dwellers in the eastern and northern Gulf, from Key West to Galveston, have to batten down their homes and flee danger more often than any other Americans.[4]

Some Gulf hurricanes travel all the way from Africa, having risen from the tepid waters beneath the Bermuda High, an expansive high-pressure area that pushes down dry, hot air and opens the skies to allow the sun's evaporative energy to reach the ocean. Developing storms glom on to the North Equatorial Current and move westward. This is the same current that feeds the Gulf Stream and that European explorers rode to the New World. The storms terrorize Caribbean islands and sometimes continue west and up through the Straits of Yucatán. Or they catch the Antilles Current branching off to the north, charging either up the US East Coast or through the Florida Straits into the Gulf. Heated by the sun and the loop current drawn up from the Caribbean, the Gulf's warm waters, hovering in the eighties during storm season, attract Atlantic hurricanes like steel to magnets, and then invigorate them.

When shuttle astronauts aboard *Discovery* photographed Hurricane Elena on September 1, 1985, the viewing public was awestruck. From space above, the hurricane was an ethereal swirl of whipped-cream white against the cool-blue Earth—graceful symmetry from outer edge to eye, big and beautiful. On the ground, however, it was terrifying. Hurricanes can expand to thousands of square miles. Elena consumed nearly three-quarters of the sky above the Gulf of Mexico. It generated enough energy in the course of a day to light up American homes and businesses for six months.

Elena was a category 3 hurricane, at the low end of the storm spectrum. A category 3's sustained winds race between 110 and 130 miles per hour. That's enough to uproot trees, blow off roofs, and disrupt electricity for days or weeks. Elena washed houses into the Gulf and took nine lives. Hurricane Katrina was physically smaller but a category 5, the highest rating—winds over 157 miles per hour, nearly 300,000 houses destroyed, twenty-five hundred confirmed deaths. Elena ran up $2.8 billion in damages (in today's currency); Katrina, $130 billion.

Adding to woes of hurricane season, the Southeast is the rainiest place in the United States, and it has the ten most saturated metropolitan areas. The majority, writes Cynthia Barnett in *Rain: A Natural and Cultural History*, get "doused by storms brewed in the warm waters of the Gulf." Four are in Louisiana; two others, on the Florida Gulf coast. Mobile is the rainiest of all. Nearly every place on the Gulf gets fifty to sixty or more inches a year. Storm season alone, says Barnett, dumps more rain than Seattle sees all year. You might think that in such a soggy place, cities would be equipped with advanced stormwater drainage systems. They aren't. Their systems are the same as you'll find in thirty-six-inch-a-year Topeka, Kansas, with one important difference: they drain into the same body of water that a hurricane pushes at them, the Gulf.[5]

Worries about flooding, destruction, and death run highest from June 1 to November 30, hurricane season. The worst storms have historically occurred in August and September. But sometimes a bad one sneaks up in June.

DOWN ON THE COAST in Cameron Parish, Louisiana, in late June 1957, thousands of crawfish were fleeing the marsh flats for higher ground. A storm was coming, a big one, and somehow they knew it. Nature or natural instinct, or both, had triggered their retreat.

Louisianans knew of weather conditions from forecasters. On June 26, residents learned that a storm named Audrey was moving up from the lower Gulf. But they weren't expecting much from it. The bad storms usually came in August or September, and no one had ever heard of a major threat so early in hurricane season. The forecasts said Audrey was traveling slowly and people living on the coast where it was expected to hit could sleep comfortably that night and wait until morning to assess the need for evacuation. "We all went to bed feeling that all was well," said Loretta Flowers, a teenager who was spending the summer with her grandparents in Cameron Parish, "and we would only have bad weather the next day."[6]

Up in New Orleans, Nash Roberts was methodically checking all the indicators. Roberts was an independent meteorologist and television weatherman. In 1957, however, most people still got their forecast information from newspapers and radio. That was unfortunate on

this occasion. Roberts was like the retreating crawfish. He felt something all the other forecasters did not, which was that the storm would
hit sooner than anyone expected. "With that thing bearing down on
them," Roberts remembered years later, "they should have never fallen
asleep."[7]

"We were awakened around 4:30 a.m. by howling winds," said
Flowers. Two hours later, "we looked out the front door and saw water
was rolling in."[8]

"Everyone saw it," said Laura Dupuis, who was a young mother
living in Cameron Parish. "You could see that wave a coming."[9]

"You can't imagine what was coming," said Jimmy Trahan. "You
could hear it before you could see it. It was a big gray wall just a
coming at you."[10]

"It looked as if the whole Gulf was coming toward us," recalled the
wife of a Coast Survey assistant.[11]

At Jerry Furs's house, the picture window exploded. "There was
nothing but a wall of water coming through it."[12]

"God help us," Marshall Brown whispered into his wife's ear, just as
the wave came crashing down on their house.[13]

Those who survived the wave, and the number is few, said it must
have been fifty feet high. Later, weather scientists, doing their measuring, calculating, and fact-finding, confirmed its vertical ferocity.
After the wave passed, flattened, and drew back, the water regrouped
and, as if to finish the job, sent in a twenty-footer. Both waves rode
the top of a twelve-foot storm surge that swept twenty-five miles
inland and extended as many across the coast between eastern Texas
and western Louisiana. Ten-foot waves were common. They were the
unrelenting yield of winds that reached up to 145 miles per hour, a
category 4 hurricane.

People who lost loved ones wished they had listened to Nash Roberts. In the future, they would. They would follow him as closely as he
followed hurricanes; they would track him, read him, practically worship him, and abide his advice without fail. For Roberts, accurately

tracking a hurricane wasn't about being right or wrong or the best forecaster; it was about lives. Audrey took five hundred.*

In the nearly fifty years between Audrey and Hurricane Katrina, there was no deadlier Gulf hurricane. But outside a handful of chance survivors, who remembers Audrey? And what about lessons that might have come from that forgotten Gulf storm? One that Roberts wanted people to learn was to think twice about living in harm's way.

INITIALLY, THE US WEATHER BUREAU (now the National Weather Service) predicted that Audrey would slam into Galveston. That wasn't an unreasonable call. The island city had seen more than its share of hurricanes; that it had even come to be and enjoyed a thriving existence is a wonder. Lying in the Gulf's storm alley, with high ground creeping barely to nine feet above sea level, Galveston had always been trouble waiting to happen. And it never happened like it did with a September storm in 1900. No so-called natural event has killed as many people—more than eight thousand, according to the National Hurricane Center. The research of Erik Larson, who affirmed the storm's epic status with the publication of his riveting drama *Isaac's Storm*, puts the number at over ten thousand. Either count is more than the combined tallies of dead in the 1889 Johnstown flood and the 1906 San Francisco earthquake. An American disaster without equal, the Galveston hurricane—more so its aftermath— defined the way the modern Gulf population would deal with storms, and not the way Nash Roberts would have recommended.

Galveston is a thirty-mile-long, two-mile-wide, cudgel-shaped island wedged between the Gulf of Mexico and Galveston Bay. It has been wintering grounds of Karankawa; lair of freebooter Jean Lafitte;

---

* Sources disagree about the death toll, with estimates ranging from 390 to over 400 to over 500. According to the National Hurricane Center, at least 416 died; NOAA says over 500.

and capital of the new Republic of Texas. Audubon visited the marvelously fecund bay and was treated to the front end of the spring bird migration, plenty to admire and shoot. Before whites began flattening the island's dunes and clearing coastal scrub to make a city, they had been busy on the mainland raising crops and cattle. There was also the Trinity River feeding vitalizing freshwater and nutrients, which trundled 710 miles down from Fort Worth and Dallas, to the bay's fish and sprawling oyster beds, harvested for market.

Michel B. Menard, a thirty-one-year-old Quebec-born Indian trader and timber cutter, settled the island in 1836 as his private enterprise. With all the easterners and immigrants rushing to farm the Great Plains to the north, more commerce was sure to come along down the Trinity River. No one seemed to doubt that Galveston's future lay in a busy port. From that point on, the island was always about money and growth. "Galveston," wrote Stephen Crane, who visited the city five years before the storm, "has always been substantial and undeviating in its amount of business."[14]

The waters around it weren't naturally suitable for a port. The bay's depths averaged seven feet—nine on a fat-water day. Galveston wanted to be another New Orleans and didn't want ambitious, competitive Houston to outrival it, so business leaders commissioned the construction of a jetty. That got them thirteen feet at the harbor entrance—not enough in an age when square-riggers were giving way to steam cargo ships. They needed closer to thirty, and millions of dollars to fund a dredging project. Islanders formed a Deep Water Committee; invited President Grover Cleveland, an avid fisherman, down for a try at Texas tarpon; and, with winning catches and a little cajoling, secured his support for a federal grant. After reaching the desired depth, the Galveston port was, for a while, one of the busiest in the country. Boosters claimed it shipped more cotton than any other. That wasn't true, but it handled four or five steamships a day. Foreign exports hit $86 million the fiscal year before the storm. Three railroad trestles and a 2.1-mile wagon bridge—wood-planked, with an iron frame on concrete piers—crossed over the bay from the mainland.

Galveston men wore Texas Stetsons, not sweaty off-the-trail ones, but clean and brushed, and as stiff edged as their starched shirt collars. Their city was no dusty cow town. It was a cosmopolitan island place of nearly forty thousand residents where you heard languages from around the world. It had churches, a cathedral, and a synagogue with architectural panache. It had a wall of elegant homes fronting Broadway Street, a sixteen-hundred-seat opera house with a foyer lined in imported marble, and multiple bordellos. It was as clean and tidy as those Stetsons—unlike muddy Houston, much of which was built on wetlands. The main thoroughfare, the Strand, was paved with creosoted wooden blocks to dampen the dust and the sound of clopping horse hooves. What escaped no visitor's attention was the broad, red-and-white, horizontal-striped roof and domed cupola of the Beach Hotel, betraying a "self-conscious grandeur" as the centerpiece of the tourist trade, and one of the state's principal holiday destinations. Writes Texas journalist Gary Cartwright, Galveston had a "Toy Town mystique that suggested that life was a party that went on forever."[15]

That the party might end should not have surprised anybody in Galveston, or anyone anywhere on the Gulf. Seven years before the Galveston storm, a hurricane had killed two thousand in Louisiana and completely wiped out the communities of Oyster Bayou and Chenière Caminada—just as completely as the US Weather Bureau botched its forecast of the storm. Indianola, Texas, got hit just as badly, in stages, with a first blow coming in 1875 and the finishing one in 1886. Obliterated into the sand—the whole town simply gone.

The hero in Erik Larson's Galveston story—a tragic hero—is Isaac Cline, the chief of the US Weather Bureau's Galveston Station. He wore a Three Musketeers mustache and goatee, both turning white in his forty-ninth year. His job was sometimes a stressful one, especially in a storm-prone area like the Gulf, where the wrong forecast could cost people's lives. There were no planes or radar then to track storms—only infrequent teletype messages from ships at sea and other Weather Bureau stations. Making matters worse, all storm information from the field had to be cleared through headquarters in Washington, DC.

On Friday, September 7, by official instructions from afar, Cline raised storm-warning flags on the lanyards hissing in the growing wind outside his office. It was about time. Washington had been begrudging in these instructions. It had at first said that a relatively harmless tropical storm was moving up through the Gulf and would fishtail over northern Florida into the Atlantic. East Coast stations had been put on alert, but not those in the Gulf. Then, just that morning, Washington had changed the position of the storm to south of Louisiana, though still calling it a moderate one.

But something didn't feel right to Cline. The barometer was falling, for one. For another, when he walked the beach, an unhindered wind was blowing against the tide, yet the tide was above normal and rising. Cline had been with the Bureau when it predicted light showers the day before the 1893 hurricane plowed under Chenière Caminada, and quite possibly he was witnessing another Bureau mistake.

That's essentially what Cuban weather experts thought. Thirty-six hours earlier, that same supposedly moderate storm south of Louisiana had risen out of the Atlantic and crossed over them, dumping twenty-four inches of rain on Santiago. Cuban meteorologists, who probably had more experience with Atlantic storms than anyone else, predicted this one was growing into a hurricane and moving toward Texas. But the United States still controlled the island two years after the Spanish-American War, and Washington took a superior attitude toward Cubans. Overriding their native counterparts, US Weather Bureau personnel in Cuba reported to Washington that a weakening tropical storm was entering the Gulf.

They were wrong; the Cubans were right. A category 4 hurricane was drawing toward Cline, and nobody in Galveston knew it. On Saturday morning, families went down to the beach to marvel at the unusually large and explosive surf. When breakers began pounding the bathhouses and piers into pieces, and ripping out the creosoted street blocks, turning them into floating torpedoes, horrified spectators backed away and dashed home. By 1:00 p.m., high water and wind had submerged the bridge and three trestles, minutes after the train from Houston crossed over to the island and relinquished panic-stricken weekenders, disembarking onto a drowning island. Houses were breaking apart, and brick buildings collapsing, along with the 220-foot tower of St. Patrick's Church. Late that afternoon, write a pair of students of the hurricane, the storm surge was "pushing a more than ten-foot-high and miles-long wall of debris across the island . . . working like a giant bulldozer bringing down still-standing structures."[16]

Hours later, after the wind and rain and sea had calmed, frazzled survivors walked out into wholesale desolation, gathered their wits, and searched the wreckage for lost loved ones. Cline recovered his three daughters but lost his pregnant wife. One-third of all buildings were gone; hardly a one escaped heavy damage. The island looked like a rampaging behemoth had taken a hundred lumberyards and a hundred brickyards and turned them upside down into heaping piles. Funeral pyres burned for weeks.

But the people of Galveston would not let the hurricane defeat them. Instead of abandoning the island and leaving it to the vagaries of the sea and winds, they rebuilt. Americans didn't run away from nature; they confronted it, especially in the age when technological advances encouraged their domination of the natural world. They had the know-how and machinery not only to dam rivers but to move them; to drain vast wetlands; to bore railway tunnels through mountains; to span the East River with the steel-wire suspension Brooklyn Bridge; and to erect iron-frame buildings up to the clouds. Radio waves would cross the Atlantic the next year; not long after, Samuel Langley would conquer the sky with the maiden flight of a plane propelled by an internal combustion engine; and just up the coast at Beaumont, the country's first real oil gusher, Spindletop, would erupt, a sign of advanced modern times to come.

Americans had always lived wherever they wanted. In a swamp, out in the desert, at the edge of a rock, in a floodplain, on an island, and where it was bitter cold or hellaciously hot. They always brought their way of life and expectations with them, preferring not to adapt to the local environment so much as retrofit it to them. "Reclaim" is the word they liked to use, as if nature had taken something away from them and now, come hell or high water—and sometimes one or the other or both did come—they were dogged about getting it back. It might not rain in the desert much, but they would still grow market crops. They would get the water somehow, and they did.

Galvestonians would reclaim their island from the waters that took it. As they pieced back together their community, the city drew up a comprehensive engineering plan. First, under the auspices of the Deep Water Committee, it constructed a seventeen-foot-high-by-twenty-seven-foot-deep seawall of granite boulder that ran, with a promenade on top, initially three miles along the Gulf front, and over the coming years stretched ever longer. Then the city raised itself, and not simply on stilts. Engineers pumped fill from the estuarine bay, equivalent to a million dump trucks worth of marine habitat, to elevate the terra firma beneath their own habitat—five hundred city blocks of it. They hoisted houses higher or moved them and built temporary boardwalks at fence-top level so that people could avoid the filling mud. They raised sewer, water, and gas lines, and fire hydrants, power poles, and streets. No task was too ambitious. They wedged seven hundred hand-crank jacks under the three-thousand-ton St. Patrick's Church to get it five feet closer to heaven.

After a 1915 hurricane as large as the 1900 one tested the city on mud, Galvestonians said the brave men of their dominion had outengineered nature. The new Hotel Galvez, built on the seawall as a symbol of local grit, stood tall. Only nine residents died. But Louisiana, where more than a hundred people were lost, got the direct impact, not Galveston. And while the constructed environment directly behind the new seawall endured, ninety percent of the buildings outside were lost. Forty-six years later, Hurricane Carla crushed 120 buildings and killed six people. In 1983, Hurricane Alicia wreaked $300 million in property damage but took no lives. Hurricane Ike smashed into

Galveston in 2008 with a mind-boggling twenty-foot storm surge, saddling the state with $50 billion in storm damages. Eighty percent of Galveston's homes were damaged. Fed up, scared, scarred, people began leaving for good—nine thousand in the end, seventeen percent of the population.

Yet the stick-to-itiveness that came out of 1900 had not wholly disappeared. The assistant city manager, Brian Maxwell, a fifth-generation local, told a Texas journalist he "wouldn't trade our island's future with anyone's."[17]

In the history books and local museums and historical society, the memory of the phenomenal comeback after 1900 is one of triumph emerging from tragedy. The tenacity of Galvestonians said to others, "You too can make it where hurricanes blow."* That comeback and blind faith brings to mind a T. S. Eliot quote that Phil Scott chose for the opening epigraph of his book on the catastrophic 1935 Labor Day Hurricane: "All our ignorance brings us closer to death."[18]

LONG AFTER television meteorologists started announcing the weather in front of computerized images, Nash Roberts continued to use a plastic weatherboard and felt-tip markers. He never went high-tech, and Louisianans never lost faith in those squeaky markers. In 1998, after he outforecasted his professional counterparts who relied on Doppler radar and said Hurricane Georges would steer east away from New Orleans, the *Atlanta-Journal Constitution* called him "right as rain." The big-city newspaper wasn't telling the people down in Louisiana anything they hadn't known for years. Ever since Audrey, they'd been following the weather by asking each other, "What does Nash say?"[19]

---

* This was the tone of a 2013 NPR *Science Friday* episode about lessons that New York could learn, in the wake of Hurricane Sandy, from Galveston. "Galveston, Hurricanes, and Sea-Level Rise," *Science Friday*, June 15, 2013 (National Public Radio).

Balding above a cheerful face, Roberts was the next-door neighbor you'd borrow hedge clippers from and then invite over, along with his wife and kids, for burgers on the grill. Like so many other men in his New Orleans suburb, he'd been in the war, completing his tour in the Pacific theater. When he went home to New Orleans in 1946, he opened a weather-consulting firm in an office off the lobby of the St. Charles Hotel. His principal clients were commercial fishing outfits and oil companies. He built a reputation for being a spot-on forecaster, and after considerable coaxing, WDSU television, Channel 6, convinced him to go on air in 1951. He was New Orleans's first regular television weather forecaster, broadcasting remotely, from his office. "There's only *one* Nash," the station advertised, "and he's on 6."

It was doubly important now that he make an accurate call with foul weather. If oil rig workers or fishing crews evacuated unnecessarily, his clients lost money. If he made a bad call and a hurricane pounced, worker lives were at stake. As a TV weatherman, he had to expand his safety net. There was the whole viewing public to think about.

Audrey was a little tricky. Since first going on air, Roberts had had to deal with only one hurricane, Florence, a Caribbean storm that entered the Gulf in September 1953. It buffeted the Florida panhandle with eighty-mile-per-hour winds and quickly dissipated over land, as hurricanes do when they lose their heat and vapor source from water. Usually, storms announced themselves from the Caribbean or Atlantic. Audrey wasn't an Atlantic hurricane. It was Gulf-born. Gulf hurricanes stir to life less frequently, but their unpredictability keeps forecasters on their toes.

Audrey had no transoceanic course or established pattern of behavior that might give clues to probable movement, no record of its tendency to build or lose strength and speed. It simply appeared without warning, first as a tropical depression in the Bay of Campeche on June 24, three days before Trahan, Dupuis, and others saw the big tidal wave. By afternoon, a shrimp trawler reported rough seas and fifty-mile-per-hour winds: a tropical storm. The next day a navy hurricane hunter flew into Audrey's dark mass, clocked seventy-five-mile-per-hour winds, and identified a well-developed eye: a hurricane. On the twenty-sixth, Audrey slammed a seventy-eight-ton fishing boat against an oil rig and killed nine men. That afternoon, a second reconnaissance plane reported winds exceeding a hundred miles per hour.

Airborne weather chasers were invaluable for tracking hurricanes. The first storm cowboy in history lifted off from Bryan Field in Texas during World War II. His name was Joseph Duckworth, a flight instructor in the US Army Air Corps. The storm that earned him recognition as the original hurricane hunter was another Gulf native. It organized on a July day in 1943, one hundred miles south of the Mississippi coast. At the time, Duckworth was training British airmen in instrument flight using the AT-6 Texan single-engine trainer. Experienced combat pilots, the Brits hated the Texan, a decrepit airplane beneath their expertise. When the July hurricane prompted an order to evacuate the planes from Bryan Field, their disdain for the aircraft deepened. The AT-6 wasn't worth saving at the risk of British lives, the trainees said.

Coming to its defense, Duckworth set out to prove both the plane's sturdiness and the merits of instrument navigation. He wagered a highball with the Brits that he could fly the AT-6 into the hurricane and live to tell about it. Without official permission, he and a navigator, Lieutenant Colonel Ralph O'Hair, belted in, took off, and bored into the black wall of the storm, where, O'Hair later said, they were "tossed about like a stick in a dog's mouth." They discovered the eye— calm and quiet, ten miles across—and saw the ground below. After circling inside, they plunged back through the wild darkness.[20]

Back at Bryan Field, Duckworth and O'Hair collected the bet. The storm, meanwhile, zeroed in on Bolivar Peninsula across the channel from Galveston. It raked through homes and buildings on both sides. Nineteen people died.

The Weather Bureau initially thought Audrey would turn toward the same target, and it issued a hurricane warning for the area. But Audrey did not veer; it did not stray. It kept driving north, straight for

Louisiana. At 10:00 on the night of June 26, when Loretta Flowers was waiting to go to bed, the New Orleans Weather Bureau office sent out an update report, "Advisory Number 7," with a corrected course. Audrey was moving toward Louisiana. The report put the entire coast and eastern Texas under a hurricane watch. It downgraded the Galveston-area forecast to a storm warning. The surge in Louisiana could reach up to nine feet, and winds a hundred miles per hour, read the report, which located the storm 235 miles south. Audrey was the first hurricane that the Bureau tracked on radar, and the vital statistics it assembled on the storm were reliable, save one. "Advisory Number 7" listed the hurricane's movement at ten miles per hour. After doing the math, forecasters determined a strike wouldn't happen for almost twenty-four hours. No wonder they advised a good night's sleep. The report closed by saying that the next advisory would be issued at 4:00 a.m.[21]

A half hour after that specified time, Flowers was awakened by the voice of the wind.

IRRESPONSIBLE IS HOW THE LACK OF CAUTION struck Roberts. Channel 6's weatherman was the only one saying Audrey would make landfall in the night. Unfortunately, Louisianans were not yet asking, "What does Nash say?"

Roberts had a number of methods that seemed to put him a cut above. He would "lock on 'em," he said of hurricanes, "24 hours a day, seven days a week." He wouldn't leave his office, and when exhaustion set in, he'd crawl into a sleeping bag in the corner for a nap. He continued this rigorous routine into his eighties. One advantage he had over rival forecasters (and forecasters tended to be highly competitive) was access through his private practice to a steady flow of weather data coming in from oil rigs and fishing fleets. He would compare his information with US Weather Bureau reports, which he found were all too often plagued by "house thinking," meaning that perspectives were narrowed by institutionalized mind-sets. After breaking down all the facts and drawing on a dose of instinct, he would make his own call. He wasn't like Isaac Cline. He didn't have to take orders from Washington.[22]

Roberts had one more advantage over Bureau men in New Orleans and probably all other television weathermen at the time: he had flown into the eye of a hurricane, and he was the first meteorologist to do so. It happened when he was with the VRF-1 naval squadron in the Pacific during World War II. Typhoons constantly disrupted operations and sank American ships—a major frustration for fleet command. An idea emerged one evening out of "nebulous, officer-club talk," as Roberts put it, about using the tumultuous Pacific weather to US advantage. If the Americans could accurately track typhoons, the fleet could sneak in behind one moving on Japan and finish off enemy ships and aircraft left amid the storm's rubble. Roberts loved flying, meteorology, and solving problems, so when the first opportunity arrived, he and a pilot took off and flew into a typhoon. Once in the eye, he took coordinates to track its direction and speed. His reconnaissance enabled the Seventh Fleet not only to dodge the typhoon, but to follow it and launch the first carrier strike against Japan since the celebrated Doolittle Raid in 1942.[23]

Ever since then, Roberts knew that in addition to watching a hurricane, it was necessary to absorb it with all his senses. Decipher its personality, and you can more accurately predict its behavior. But you also had to see what was going on around it. The high-pressure system north of Audrey was weakening. That meant the storm's pace would pick up. Indeed, its travel speed would accelerate to nearly twenty-five miles per hour more than the Bureau had calculated, and it was pushing a lot of water.

That wind and water would change a lot of lives.

DON TRISTAN DE LUNA Y ARELLANO didn't have an instinct about weather; he was a luckless conquistador and, as such, an example of how a hurricane can alter the course of human history. A member of a distinguished family of Spain and cousin of the wife of Hernán Cortés, Luna participated in the conquest of Mexico, earning the respect of his superiors. In 1559, the viceroy of Mexico dispatched him from Vera Cruz to West Florida in command of thirteen ships carrying a ready-made colony of fifteen hundred soldiers and settlers and the requisite missionaries and enslaved Africans and Aztecs. Horses numbered 180. Food provisions included olives, cherries, peaches, hickory nuts, walnuts, almonds, goats, chickens, and cows. And there were stowaways: weasels, beetles, African cockroaches, and European rats—with rickets.[24] The project was undertaken, observed a Luna biographer, with "prefect preparedness" and "care."[25]

The Spaniards had a distinctly unfavorable opinion of *La Florida*, which expanded well north and west of the present-day state's boundaries. Ponce de León and Soto had both met their fates there; Narváez had barely escaped, but crippled and not far from his end in Texas. Survivors of previous journeys rejected Florida as "full of bogs and poisonous fruits, barren, and the very worst country that is warmed by the sun." Empire was the utmost priority, however, and King Philip was worried about rival incursions.[26]

Luna's pilots convinced him to plant the flag of empire and cross of Christianity beside present-day Pensacola Bay, which they called *Ochuse*. It had a lofty bluff and deep water, and in Santa Rosa Island it had a physical barricade against storms and the sea. Luna later wrote, "I took a good port." The pilots said it was the best in the Indies. As if to prove them wrong, a September hurricane roared through. The ships were lying at anchor in the bay, presumably safely. But the wind ambushed them from the north. Doubly unfortunate, Luna had not yet ordered the provisions off-loaded.[27]

The storm left behind a dictionary definition of disaster. Ten ships went down. The number of dead is unknown. Within a year, the frantic settlers abandoned the endeavor. The viceroy declared the storm-disheveled Florida panhandle off limits to Spanish settlement, and it remained that way for 139 years. Except for a hurricane, Pensacola would have been the first European city permanently established in the present-day United States. But, during the moratorium on colonizing the panhandle, Pedro Menéndez de Avilés settled St. Augustine, giving the first-city distinction to the East Coast.

Foul weather 163 years later deprived Pensacola of another first, the opening shots of the Civil War. When Florida seceded from the Union, Federal forces retained control of Pensacola's four clay-brick forts. President Lincoln dispatched supply ships and reinforcements simultaneously to Fort Sumter, South Carolina, and to Pensacola to prevent Confederate takeovers. An Atlantic gale delayed the convoy, and the same storm foiled Confederate plans to attack Pensacola's Fort Pickens. By the time reinforcements arrived in Pensacola, Federal forces at Fort Sumter had already endured enemy bombardment and surrendered.

Decades later, a big storm changed the direction in which tiny, anonymous Coden, Alabama, expected to grow. Huddled beside the bayou of the same name, across Mississippi Sound from Dauphin Island, Coden was an angler's retreat for businessmen and their families from Birmingham and Montgomery. Untroubled, bucolic, propitious, it had two nice hotels on a tree-shaded street and the service of the Mobile and Bay Shore Railroad. Coden was envisioning its future as a modest but world-class resort. That was before a September hurricane, one of five during the 1906 season, scattered houses, hotels, and everyone's belongings to the four winds. Along the upper Gulf coast, 134 people died. Coden reined in its resort dreams and reconciled its future as a commercial fishing village. That was okay; fishing people knew better than anyone the risks of living on the edge.

Let's look to the Florida Keys for two more examples of storms instigating human events, starting with the decade before the domestic conflict over slavery and concluding with Ernest Hemingway, the human tempest. Merchant shipping between the Gulf and the Atlantic had picked up considerably prior to the Civil War. Cotton bales on plantation wagons and timber on trains arrived at Gulf ports, where fishers had delivered their catch. Other staples and goods came down the rivers on Mark Twain–style paddle wheelers from faraway

places—Chicago, St. Louis, Minneapolis—all for transfer to outgo-
ing cargo ships, which were swapping out their holds of goods from
the Northeast, Europe, and the Caribbean. As had everyone since the
Spanish, ships had to navigate through the Florida Straits and the
Bahama Channel, gingerly around coral reefs and shoals about the
Florida Keys.

The area was a nautical nightmare. Ponce de León referred to the
Keys as *Los Martires*, "The Martyred"; the Spanish name for Key
West was *Cayo Hueso*, "Bone Island"; and the name for the two Matecumbe keys apparently derives from *mata hombre*, "kill man" (some say
it derives from the poisonous manchineel tree that grows there). An
early objective of the US Coast Survey was to develop reliable charts
for the Keys, but its work was often hampered by Washington bureaucracy, the time-consuming chore of mapping, and storms. Even as the
Survey's charts and markers began to improve navigation, the traffic
had to negotiate not only objects, but harsh weather, and when a storm
came through, "navigate" became little more than a figure of speech.
Thomas Jefferson believed this region of the Gulf to be the "most dangerous navigation in the world." It tested the skills and nerves of the
best helmsmen and pilots. Not all were up to the task. In the 1850s,
the area was delivering an average of a shipwreck a week, with ships
sometimes foundering atop another sunken vessel.[28]

Down in the American tropics, brutal weather and hazardous sailing spawned a robust economy in scavenging from shipwrecks, an
industry that Key dwellers called "wrecking." Its practitioners, known
as wreckers, lived by the creed that "one man's loss is another man's
gain," which went hand in hand with another tenet: "possession is
nine-tenths of the law." Leonard Destin and his father and brother
had intended to venture into the trade before misfortune turned their
sunken schooners into the quarry of wreckers. By the nineteenth century, salvaging furniture, silver, china, and women's and men's finery
that had been en route to auction houses in New Orleans and elsewhere made Key West one of the country's wealthiest cities.

Wrecking amounted to legal looting. In the 1850s, some fifty Key

West salvage outfits operated under licenses issued by the federal court. Law sanctioned what gonzo journalist Hunter S. Thompson later described as the "cruel imperatives of salvaging rights": whoever got to the cargo first and could defend it—with gun, knife, or brawn—had the rights to it.[29]

Benjamin Strobel, physician and editor of the *Key West Gazette*, portrayed wreckers as "hearty, well-drest, and honest-looking men." Audubon found them to be selfless and kind, disciplined sailors commanding with "regularity and quickness" the cleanest, trimmest, sleekest schooners on the water. Less kind assessments said that wreckers fed on the doom of others, and were the only people known to wish for a hurricane. The Coast Survey's Ferdinand Gerdes reported bitterly that within fifteen minutes of a ship's running up on a reef, "five or six vessels under the denomination of wreckers" would converge on it like ants at a June picnic. In turn, making navigation safer jeopardized the wreckers' lucrative vocation. Legend has it that these "honest-looking men" tore down the Survey's beacons and markers, and lit phony lighthouse signals to abet disaster.[30]

Despite the shenanigans, mapmakers forged ahead and got the job done. The number of wrecks gradually declined, even as shipping through the area increased. Eventually, most wreckers went out of business, and Key West's economy was destined to dependence on commercial fishing and shipping tropical products.

Still, the new economy was good enough to spark an idea in Henry Flagler, a tall, regal Standard Oil millionaire with a bristling white mustache and white hair. Retired from oil, he remained a conspicuous figure in American business when he ran a railway down the east coast of Florida, built sprawling resorts along the way, and reached Miami in 1896. Residents proposed naming the city after him, but he declined the honor. Besides, he wasn't finished. He wanted to go all the way to Key West. There were fresh pineapples from Cuba, and sponges and citrus from the Keys to ship north. Equally important, the leisure tycoon expected to run tourists back and forth on his rail. So he did what others said couldn't be done. In 1904, he set in motion plans to build a railroad over the ocean and across the Keys, 156 miles to the end. And why not? Engineers on the other side of the Gulf in Galveston were raising an entire city on an island—models of bold action against the seemingly impossible.

Building a railway largely suspended over water was a huge undertaking. The Overseas Railroad, as Flagler called it, would consume untold quantities of concrete, steel, and muscle power, not to mention 4.5 million gallons of freshwater shipped to the crews each month—so much of it lost to sweat cooling overheated bodies. One span of the new railway had to reach an improbable seven miles out across the sea between Knights and Little Duck Keys. When Flagler's Standard Oil drilled for crude, the risk came with at least minimal odds in favor of earning the investment back. But in this case, it was pretty clear from the start that the island-hopping railway would never pay for itself. People called it Flagler's Folly. But it was the old man's money, $6.5 billion in today's currency, and he could do whatever he damn well pleased with it. What mattered was the accomplishment.

Yet it almost didn't happen. Not for lack of money or enthusiasm, but for weather. In the eight years required to build the railway, three hurricanes barreled in, packing winds racing twice as fast as Flagler's trains would ever run. Each time, millions of dollars of equipment was destroyed. Completed sections were washed away. So were some three hundred human lives. Finally, on January 21, 1912, the train rolled down the finished line to Key West, Flagler in his private car, number 90—three bedrooms, bath, salon, kitchen, office—clattering over all those miles of trusses and causeways connecting island after island, an artificial divide between the Atlantic and Gulf.

People were now calling his railroad the Eighth Wonder of the World. Flagler had just turned eighty-two, and those old, lanky legs of his straddled two eras. His railroad was the machine symbol of the earlier age. Its monumental extension across the sea, however, was less than a felicitous projection into a new era; it was an anachronistic intrusion. Ironically, the oil that had made him rich and paid for his railroad hastened the railroad's obsolescence. Three years after Henry

Flagler clickety-clacked to its end, Carl G. Fisher, wealthy manufacturer of automobile headlights, sire of the Indianapolis Raceway,
hummed the length of his own pet project, the Dixie Highway, from
Chicago to Miami. Cars and paved roads, not water-bounding rails,
were the new age. Fisher's highway would inspire; Flagler's railroad
would soon expire.

Back then, the state of Florida was on top of its game. By the time
the first set of rotting ties beneath Flagler's rails required replacing, the
state was planning to build a blacktop-and-concrete highway to the
bottom of the Keys. Its contractors would be the twenty-three-year-
old Overseas Railroad's best and last customers. They would use the
train to carry supplies and equipment and then put it out of business—
with the help of a hurricane. Flagler's Overseas Railroad was already
in receivership, encumbered by the Great Depression. Key West, once
one of the wealthiest cities in the country, had declared bankruptcy too.
The few tourists who were traveling were doing so more by car than by
train, so Julius Stone, head of Florida's Emergency Relief Administration, reasoned that an island highway would shepherd their precious
dollars to the tropics, and Key West to solvency. So blatant was the
intended overthrow of the rails that the new street to paradise assumed
the co-opted name Overseas Highway. When construction was mid-
stride, hurricane country gave it an unfriendly welcome.

It came in the shape of a category 5 storm, the first ever recorded, on
Monday, September 2. History knows it as the Labor Day Hurricane
of 1935, though the name's relevance, with tragic irony, is greater than
the date on which it struck. The majority of its victims were people
whose labors were supposed to be recognized by the holiday—in this
case, federal Works Progress Administration relief workers building
the Overseas Highway. As was their due, they had taken the day off
and were oblivious to what was coming. The hurricane took aim at
their construction site at Matecumbe Key. Various events delayed the
departure of a rescue train from the peninsula, which finally arrived in
blinding rain and on drowning islands. But it didn't get out. A giant
wave rolled its ten cars off the track, leaving only the engine, Old 447,

upright. The overturned train ended up being not such a bad place to wait out the hurricane. Outside—that's where most of the killing happened. The rock embankment of Flagler's track and trestle impeded the storm tide and created an undertow that swept away matériel and men. In the end, well over four hundred died.

Earlier that year, the US Weather Bureau had opened regional offices in New Orleans and Jacksonville to improve forecasting. Apparently, it had not worked out the kinks in the new system. Hours before one of the most powerful hurricanes ever made landfall, the Bureau was still calling it a tropical disturbance. Weather forecasters didn't get a handle on the hurricane's correct track until 4:30 in the afternoon. The storm's full force came down on the Keys sometime around 8:30 that evening.

Forty-five miles south in Key West, Ernest Hemingway watched it from inside his two-story coral-rock home, built hurricane tough in 1851 by the slaves of a salvage wrecker. Hemingway had recently bought the house from the ailing city for back taxes. In the predawn hours on Wednesday, when the wind and water finally becalmed, the writer, sportsman, and war veteran was in a fit and under way in his boat, *Pilar*, to survey the destruction up at Matecumbe. He helped recover bodies, lots of them. He hadn't seen so much death since the war. The unlucky were tangled in mangroves, floating in the rippling water, lying on the beach bloated and stiff, blackening in the sun, rigor-mortis arms reaching toward heaven, open hands asking to enter.

Hemingway was outraged. Nearly all the relief workers were war veterans, the kind of joes he had known when he was driving ambulances across war-beaten Europe. Some of them he had drunk and jawed with at local saloons. He vented in an article he wrote gratis for *New Masses*. He wanted accountability from Washington. "Who" was the subject of the piece, which he titled, "Who Murdered the Vets?" *Who*, he wanted to know, sent these down-on-their-luck but good men to Florida to die? *Who* failed to know better than to leave them without an evacuation plan during hurricane season? They were "practically murdered," he wrote to his editor, Maxwell Perkins.[31]

Yet Hemingway never questioned the wisdom of building the Overseas Highway. Opened to traffic in 1938, it would bring many more people into hurricane country. At the time of the Labor Day storm, the population in Key West was down thirty-eight percent from its peak population in 1910. By 1950, it would more than double, to twenty-six thousand. "All our ignorance brings us nearer to death."

THAT HURRICANE AUDREY was likely moving toward Cameron Parish was well known to locals by Tuesday, June 25, 1957. And since the US Weather Bureau had given it a name, that meant the Gulf storm had worked itself up into something serious. Yet for the time being, conditions outside suggested differently. When Cameron residents looked up, they saw blue skies with billowy cumulus clouds scudding across them. Temperatures were hothouse high and the air lifeless and saturated—normal, in other words. Clothes stuck to bodies like wet paper. It was one of those limp southern days that the fewer than seven thousand residents of Cameron Parish knew well. The school year had ended, and people were at the beach with their kids, many of them speaking Cajun French and playing Cajun music on the radio.

Physically, Cameron is the largest parish in the state. It is conspicuously square-shaped and wedged in between the Gulf and Calcasieu Lake, known to locals as Big Lake, and fronted by a low-energy coast, saturated with mudflats and grass that are Louisiana's abutment with the sea. The continental shelf reaches beyond a hundred miles out, farther than at any other place on the US Gulf. A big surf is a rare event. The water is usually as quiet as a bayou, waves coming in like sheer curtains lifted by a puff of air. The parish is also low-lying, three feet above sea level on average, more than one-quarter water and swamp.

On Wednesday, cool gusts brought occasional relief. People were pretty certain the hurricane was still moving their way. That's what the newspapers warned. Cameron businesses were taping storefront windows well in advance of the storm's expected arrival, or so everyone thought. The newspapers said Audrey wouldn't hit until Friday morning, a full day later than the actual strike.

In the Gulf, oil companies evacuated crews from offshore rigs lying out from Galveston, where the Weather Bureau initially thought Audrey would hit. Ten years earlier, Kerr-McGee's Kermac No. 16 well had opened a new chapter in oil extraction, and the northwestern Gulf had turned into a city of oil and gas platforms. D. W. Griffith,* among the many boat captains ferrying platform crews and equipment to safety on shore, remembered the currents "running crazy around the platforms." He had seen a gray sky on a gray sea to the south that frightened him, he told his wife, Geneva, after arriving home in Cameron on their thirty acres of oak-studded land at the edge of the marshy coast.[32]

A big man with broad shoulders and a head of plush, dark hair, D. W. had grown up on the Gulf and was not one to treat a hurricane lightly. He had two young children, Leslie and Cherie, and his parents were visiting from Port Arthur, Texas. A first task in defense against the coming storm was to nail plywood up over the windows of their house. Geneva had already stocked up on supplies and batteries, and their Cameron Parish neighbors were gassing up their cars in preparation for possible evacuation the next day. That evening, the weather forecaster on the radio said Audrey was now expected to hit Thursday afternoon. Evacuation could still wait until morning. The evening newspapers said the same, and the family went to bed.

COMPARATIVELY FEW WERE CAUGHT in bed when Hurricanes Betsy and Camille rampaged across the Gulf in the 1960s. Betsy was such an unnervingly erratic, unpredictable storm that sleeping was hardly an option. It began as a tropical depression on August 27, 1965, north of French Guiana and followed something of a frenzied course.

---

* No relation to the film director of the same name, who some said invented Hollywood but perpetuated racial stereotypes through film.

It raged up quickly to a category 3 storm, then a category 4, eased back to a category 2, raged up again to a 3 and then a 4. Stretching to six hundred square miles from edge to edge, it was one of the largest storms in recorded history. It traveled northwest across the Atlantic, turned up and took aim at the Carolinas, but did an odd doodling loop to the southwest and nicked the upper Bahamas, punishing Key Largo—the setting and name of a memorable Bogie and Bacall hurricane film from 1948. With 125-mile-per-hour winds and a nine foot storm surge, Betsy cut Key dwellers off from access to the peninsula. It crossed Florida Bay and the Everglades and then, feeding on energy from the Gulf's warmth, spun toward the north—toward Walter Anderson bivouacking on Horn Island.

Betsy was a tough storm to call. Nash Roberts had been working it for some time in the office, broadcasting remotely from in front of a plate-glass window looking out on a darkening St. Charles Avenue, the weather growing worse by the hour. After Betsy entered the Gulf, he gave his listeners the bad news: it would come ashore around Grand Isle and plow ahead to New Orleans.

Approaching the mainland, the storm destroyed eight offshore oil platforms, though it let Walter Anderson endure on Horn Island. It wiped clean the fishing villages at Yscloskey and Delacroix Island. And there was Grand Isle, that easy mark of bully hurricanes, never cowering but always vulnerable, bruised or crushed twenty-eight times by tropical storms or worse since Martha Field described it as her summer-land favorite in 1892—eight times by hurricanes. Betsy followed convention. Its now 150-mile-per-hour winds and ten-foot surge pulverized Grand Isle's roadways and lifted almost every structure from its foundation. The entire island was swamped. The flooding unmoored caskets from their grave sites and sent them afloat in Caminada Bay. A miracle survivor was Susie, a trembling Chihuahua, who rode out the storm alone in a bucket floating around inside her family's evacuated home.

Up in New Orleans, on the outer side of the levee, the big river rose ten feet. Giant waves lifted and pitched on Lake Pontchartrain.

Roberts was still on the air. Before the power went out, when he was broadcasting live, television viewers saw a rock or brick—some heavy object—crash through that big window and hit the trusted forecaster in the back. He was all right, though—just more of a hero.

The Florida Avenue floodwall, never a comfort to live behind during storms, was not all right. As it had with past hurricanes and would with future ones, it gave in. The electricity was out by then, and the city was dark. Water poured into the already rain-drenched Lower Ninth Ward, inundating 160,000 homes and drowning people huddling in their attics. A UPI reporter captured the inadvertent yet appropriate redundancy of a police spokesman, who said, "Numerous areas are flooded, and are too numerous to mention."[33]

Thirteen people died in Florida, and seventy-five in Louisiana. Monetary damages were staggering, crossing the $1 billion threshold for the first time. An official at insurance giant Lloyd's of London confessed, "Betsy is a dirty word around here."[34]

President Johnson arrived on Air Force One the day after the storm, and the unprecedented swiftness of his response moved New Orleanians. Houses were still submerged; water was still running through the streets, and would be for ten or more days. The president walked around the Ninth Ward and talked to the locals in his trademark folksy manner, relating to them. To a gathering crowd of people, many of them among the city's seventy thousand homeless, he said, "I am here because I want to see with my own eyes what the unhappy alliance of wind and water have done to this land and to its good people." Later, back at the airport, he departed with a promise: This state "will build its way out of its sorrow," he insisted. "And the national government will be at Louisiana's side to help it every step of the way, in every way that we can."[35]

Johnson was a former New Dealer, and his own Great Society agenda was just over a year old. The federal government had an obligation to help those in need, as he saw it, and alongside the poor, disaster victims qualified for assistance. The city itself would get federal help too. Since colonial French settlement, Louisiana had been chiefly responsible for managing flood control around New Orleans. That responsibility shifted more fully to the federal government after Congress passed a new Flood Control Act in October specifying that the Army Corps of Engineers rebuild and strengthen New Orleans's levee system—a project that was expected to take thirteen years. When Katrina hurled its way through New Orleans forty years from the day Betsy was identified as a hurricane, bureaucracy, scandals, and insufficient funds had left the Corps's levee project a work still in progress.

It had hardly begun, when just before midnight on August 17, 1969, Hurricane Camille swept over the mouth of the Mississippi River, forcing the river waters to flow backward as far north as New Orleans. But the city was spared this time. The hurricane came ashore 120 miles to the southeast on the Mississippi coast. It wasn't a mere strike, but a category 5 pummeling. Winds blew apart anemometers and may have reached 175 miles per hour, maybe more. No one knows for certain.

Roberts predicted Camille's course right as rain. It began as a tropical wave coming out of Africa, crossed the Atlantic, and grew into a hurricane south of Cuba and west of the Cayman Islands before entering the Gulf through the Straits of Yucatán. From its windowless operations room in Miami, the National Hurricane Center—the federal entity now in charge of reporting hurricane courses and issuing watches and warnings—posted a hurricane watch for the Florida panhandle from Fort Walton Beach east. Thousands on the coast boarded up their houses and evacuated.

Roberts was saying something else: Camille would hit Mississippi. A day away from that truth, on the sixteenth, the National Hurricane Center raised the watch for Florida to a warning. The next morning, the Center finally extended a watch, but not a warning, to Biloxi. To the west over in Pass Christian, police chief Gerald Peralta and his small force of officers were knocking on doors urging residents to evacuate. A lot of them wouldn't, insisting that their old houses had stood up to hurricanes since before the Civil War, or their apartment building of steel-frame construction could withstand any storm. That's what people were saying at the Richelieu Apartments on US 90, the coast highway, except within its walls was wood framing, nothing but stick construction.

Around 6:00 p.m. on the seventeenth, Chief Peralta looked across the sound toward the dark Gulf. "That water was calm, just as calm as it could be," he said. "But right behind it, you could see the black coming in." A shrimp trawler crossed his view, wake furling as it motored toward presumed safe harborage.[36]

The people over in Fort Walton and Destin were still expecting Camille to smash through their front doors. But just before midnight, it thundered ashore 197 miles away at Waveland, Mississippi, two towns west of Pass Christian, thirty-two miles west of Biloxi, the place the National Hurricane Center thought would catch the western fringe. Camille was small in breadth but strong in might, the century's second recorded category 5 storm, serving up an unfathomable twenty-four-foot surge. It obliterated the three-story Richelieu Apartments (killing nine), antebellum mansions, and a Frank Lloyd Wright house in Pass Christian—all rubble. Jefferson Davis's Beauvoir survived with heavy damages (which would spur a national fundraiser to pay for repairs). A fuel barge ended up on US Highway 90; three ocean freighters were beached side by side, like huddling geese. The hurricane opened a pass through Ship Island, which locals named Camille Cut.

On the thirtieth anniversary of Camille, Nash Roberts was in Biloxi. The trimmed hair left on his head was all gray; his face was fuller, his chin lost to gravity. He was eighty-one, and would live another eleven years. He was there to give a speech, to reflect on Camille. Outside, the coast highway was buzzing with traffic and construction. It was building up, right where debris from Camille had been cleared years before. Roberts was now retired from television, yet he continued to be called in to quarterback when a hurricane was coming onto the Gulf gridiron. He left his rapt audience in Biloxi with a sobering yet unimaginable suggestion—delivered from a man who had flown through the eye of the hurricane, literally and figuratively, unquestionably the best storm forecaster around. What did Nash say? "If there is one thing we have gotten from all this is to go north—get away from the water."[37]

Soon after Audrey's wind woke Loretta Flowers sleeping in Cameron Parish, her aunt and uncle came over from next door with their three babies. Everyone was glued to the radio when the electricity blinked off, and when they looked out the door, the waves were coming. It was time to execute a plan. They floated freshwater and food on a long board and filed out the back door, stepping knee-deep into the unleashed waters of the Gulf and into sideways-blowing wind and rain, wading with the board in the direction of the barn, the water rising. Once in the barn, they climbed into the loft, handing up their provisions. The home they left behind floated up from its foundation and spun slowly away, like Dorothy's house aloft in the Kansas tornado. Who knew whether the barn would hold or, if it did, whether it would be high enough to keep them safe. "We could put our fingers through the floor of the loft and touch the water."[38]

Young Walter Rutherford's house slipped off its foundation pilings too, as did countless others. Cameron Parish was a highway of traveling wooden structures. Some collapsed under the weight and force of the water, some broke into pieces, and some remained intact but sodden. When the house was lost, Walter's grandparents disappeared. "Had an aunt and uncle together and they went off in the water," he recalled. "An aunt and a cousin and a little girl, they went off in the water." Walter and a cousin managed to get up to the roof. The water pushed their temporary raft into an oak tree, and the two scrambled onto it. By the time they got settled, the roof was gone. "Far as we knew we was the only two left."[39]

The ordeal wasn't over. The rain felt "like someone shooting you with a BB gun. In fact, it blistered my back." That's how everyone remembered it, ripping and thrashing, BBs or rocks against their arms, face, and temples, a torture like the one meted out in the prisoner-of-war camps of not too many years earlier. They never forgot the roaring wind, so loud you could hardly hear yourself think. Walter didn't know how much longer he would last in that tree. "I can't hang no longer," he said to himself. "My arms are just gonna fall off." He looked down into the water, "swirling and churning," torpedoes of debris shooting through it. "I said, well, you know what, I can probably make another five minutes before I turn loose."[40]

Jimmy Trahan was holding on for dear life too, his little hands wrapped around the belt of his father, who in turn had staked their lives on his grip around tall pondgrass. Powerful waves tried to pull them loose, and it wasn't just father and son. "My Momma had my daddy's belt, and she had my sister." Then the belt broke. "It was bad."[41]

After the living-room picture window shattered at Jerry Furs's house, the family knew its last sanctuary was about to go. It did, and everyone seized on a floating refrigerator.

The storm snuck up on Geneva and D. W. Griffith. They woke at 4:00 a.m., and outside things were relatively quiet. D. W. happened to open the door, only to get a frightening chill. Seawater had advanced while they slept. The offshore winds had pushed the Gulf above the marsh grass and onto their land ahead of the storm. Their house was an island. Worse, the water reached more than a mile inland, cutting off all roads. "My God, Geneva," he said, "we are trapped like rats." He waded out to the barnyard and released the animals, nervous and sensing danger. The wind was now whipping, and higher water was a certainty.[42]

Back in the house, the family knelt and prayed. Amens said, they were soon standing in rising water. D. W. cut a hole in the kitchen ceiling, and three generations scurried up into the attic, grandmother and grandfather too. All the furniture below washed out of the house, lined up at the door like cattle moving through a chute. The bathtub followed. The water rose to the plasterboard ceiling, dissolving it. Then D. W. cut a hole in the roof, and the family climbed out, holding tight wherever they could. It was light out now, and in every direction water stretched to the end of eyesight. Only treetops and power poles peaked above. The barn was gone.

Then the house collapsed, and the Griffiths floated off atop the roof. It swept into the woods at the back of the property, and the family climbed into trees. The storm surge in their area would rise to fourteen feet before falling back. An unbroken advance of waves crashed over them, and they held their breath. On a shorter tree, D. W.'s father struggled and then let go, not to be seen again until D. W. identified him days later in the morgue. Geneva was hanging on with a broken ankle, smashed when the roof crashed into a tree. Worse, a venomous snake had bitten her.

Not until 4:30 that afternoon did wind and water abate. The roof of the house appeared below, and the Griffiths climbed down. At one point, Geneva asked D. W. whether he thought help would arrive soon. "I don't believe anyone knows," he said. "I think everyone is dead but us."[43]

They were rescued before nightfall. A few others came through the June storm alive, but rarely without having suffered loss. The barn with Loretta Flowers and her family miraculously withstood the storm. Walter Rutherford kept his perch in the tree despite his aching arms. Jerry Furs and his family survived, except for his grandmother, who could not hold on to the refrigerator. Jimmy Trahan and his brother, Keith, escaped death, but it claimed their mother and sister, who was found in the pond, her grip still tight around the grass. Survivor Laura Dupuis lost her three-year-old daughter, June, to a rare early-season hurricane in the month of June.

Personal stories too often read like an inventory of loss and sorrow. "My grandmother and grandfather drowned," remembered Benny Welch, "and her brother and his wife and six kids drowned, and my dad's brother and his wife drowned next door, and his brother-in-law next door drowned, and my friend that was staying with me and the three people—his grandfather, grandmother, and his great-grandmother—they all drowned, and another family that lived across from

South Cameron Elementary they all drowned. Everyone. Everyone around us drowned."[44]

ON THE MISSISSIPPI COAST between Biloxi and Pass Christian, a few hundred feet from the sound, up on slightly sloping ground, stood a nearly five-hundred-year-old live oak. It was already grand when the first Spanish reconnoitered the coast, and somehow it had avoided axes and saws that might turn it into ship timbers. Someone at some point called the old tree the Friendship Oak. The name stuck, and others said that those who shared its shade shared friendship for life. Camille blew every leaf off, yet the ancient tree defied its age and survived. Its improbably long horizontal branches, bent and twisted in arthritic-like contortions, though limber and elastic, eventually budded out in green and gave shade again. They also gave renewal through the acorns they dropped.

During the first four years after Camille, volunteers planted 100,000 of the Friendship Oak's sprouting offspring along the coast from Pascagoula to Waveland. The volunteer arborists were propagating beauty, shade, even lifesavers, like the oak over in Louisiana that had protected the Griffiths from being swept away by Hurricane Audrey. The volunteers, though, were likely not to see the regrowth as symbolic of the changing demographics on the coast.

At one point when D. W. and his family were still in their own stalwart oak, he turned to Geneva with a promise: "If I ever get out of this tree, I am going to put miles between me and Cameron Parish." He broke that promise. He came back and built a new house on heavy, creosoted piers, elevated one floor above the ground on a ridge. When still in the tree, he had seen that ridge appear above the receding water before any other land.[45]

Others, including Geneva, who cried, resisted, and prayed, said they would never go back to live in Cameron Parish. They did, though—even Geneva. People initially left, but the parish's population rebounded in the 1960s and peaked in 2000 at nearly ten thousand, sixty percent above its 1950s population. Then, in 2005, two weeks after Katrina, Hurricane Rita delivered a blow, square on like Audrey. Of the thirty-five structures in the Oak Grove area where the Griffiths lived, only four withstood the 180-mile-per-hour winds and seventeen-foot storm surge. One was the house that D. W. built. He had died in 1972, and his son, Leslie, lived in it now. Having let down his guard since Audrey, Leslie had converted the bottom floor into living space. Rita gutted it and ruined almost everything on the main floor. Leslie and his family moved into a white FEMA trailer next to the house, which he began to rebuild. "I had no choice," he told Cathy Post, who was writing about Audrey. "I will not abandon my house or my land."[46]

Joseph Boudreaux, the Cajun-boy star of *Louisiana Story*, pushing into his seventies, lost his house. The carpet he and his wife had put down two weeks before still had that new chemical smell when the storm came. Afterward, they became FEMA trailer refugees too, living on their son's property in late 2006 when graduate students from Louisiana State University interviewed them. The couple said they were unsure of the future. "We gettin' a little age on us to go back and build," Joseph conceded. "Somewhere's out there there's one [a hurricane] lookin' at us." Thirty-one percent of Cameron Parish's residents chose not to return after Rita.[47]

Griffith and Boudreaux had deep roots in the parish, a rarified intimacy with the place. That wasn't the case for thousands of newcomers moving to Harrison County, the administrative home of Mississippi's central beach communities. A postmortem report on Camille, commissioned in part by the National Oceanic and Atmospheric Administration, criticized the local rebuilding effort for pursuing "unchecked growth with no regard to hazard mitigation." There was no evident shift toward getting out of harm's way—just the opposite. It seemed counterintuitive, but growth was a new major industry, and the local leadership embraced it, as if Camille had never happened, as if Nash

Roberts had said, "Go for it." A year after the tragedy, the county population was 135,000, representing no net loss from the previous decade. In 2010, it was 187,000.[48]

The main impetus was the legalization of casino gambling. The state law allowing gaming had a major ironic requirement: gambling establishments had to float on water (a ruse for circumventing federal taxes on landside casinos). In the 1990s, the gaming industry converged on the area like a storm surge. Giant gambling palaces on barges were maneuvered shoreside, prompting hotel room and single-family housing starts to just about triple. Tourist dollars plunked down in Biloxi more than doubled, and people called the new economy the Mississippi Miracle. Mayor A. J. Holloway liked to cite how the little regional airport had gone from a modest concern serving 185,000 passengers a year to a sleek new facility serving one million.

What did change across the years was preparedness and evacuation. With improved forecasting and communication technology and the centralization of storm tracking to the National Hurricane Center, and with increased public pressure, forecasters started to move into Nash Roberts's league. Authorities erred on the side of caution when it came to calling for evacuation. If the people had learned anything, it was to get out when danger was coming. When Rita visited Louisiana, hardly anyone remained in Cameron Parish to greet it. By the end of the twentieth century, far fewer people were dying in hurricanes.

Still, Americans were on the move, and they might as well have been the mariners of the Spanish treasure fleet, mindlessly sailing into hurricane season. Roughly between Audrey and Katrina, the US coastal population expanded by seventy percent, with the rush to hurricane country the greatest. The Gulf coast population swelled by 150 percent, to fourteen million. To accommodate the arriving hordes, more houses, businesses, shopping centers, restaurants, and sprawling infrastructure had to be built. The number of housing units soared by 246 percent, double the national increase. Architecture is the most expensive accoutrement of civilization, and intense Gulf weather was an omen for its destruction and replacement, conjuring images of Spanish gold spilling across the seafloor. Eight of the top ten costliest (adjusted for inflation) hurricanes in the US struck after 2000. Seven were Gulf hurricanes, all colliding with a society intent on building, growing, staying put, and building some more.[49]

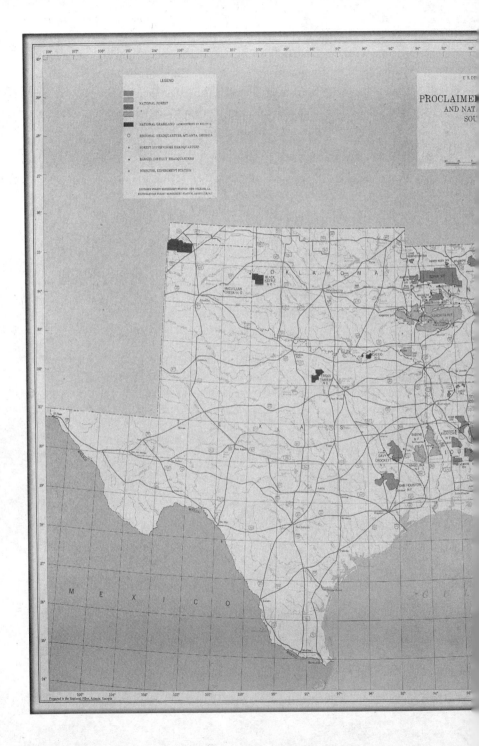

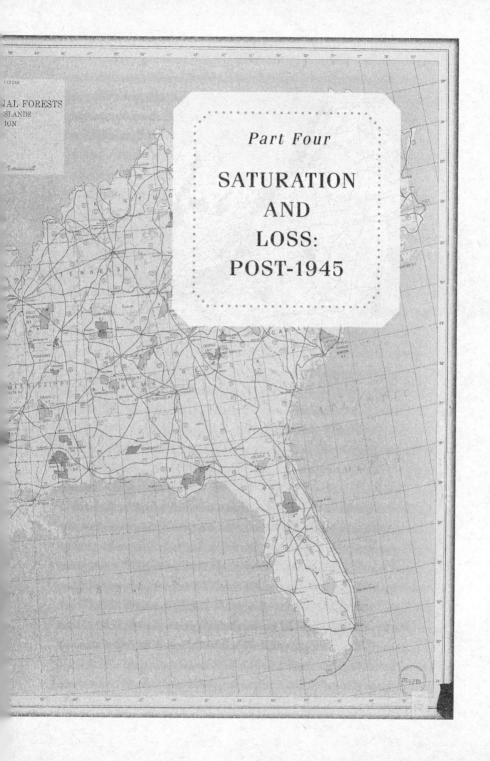

Part Four

SATURATION
AND
LOSS:
POST-1945

By the post–World War II period, roadways heavily webbed the US
Gulf states, contributing to and reflecting massive population growth.

Fourteen

THE GROWTH COAST

Condominiums on Marco Island, 1983. What many called southwest
Florida's Mangrove Coast as late as the 1950s turned into a growth
coast, with houses, hotels, and condominium towers replacing vital
natural vegetation in less than two decades.

mangrove
noun
1610s, mangrow, *probably from Spanish* mangle

mangle
verb
1. to injure severely, disfigure, or mutilate by cutting, slashing,
or crushing

—Dictionary.com

THE OLD CONCHS DOWN ON THE KEYS USED TO SAY, when a hurricane blows, head to the mangroves. The leggy trees succumb to only the most violent storms and possess the strength to both preserve and shape a coast. The naturalist Archie Carr once mused, "There is no telling what southern Florida would look like if mangroves had never flourished there."[1]

Mangroves live on the edge. They are continental outliers, sentinels of the intertidal zone. Their tolerance of saltwater and salt air puts them in a special class of trees. Proof is in the briny crystals that seep from their leaves.

Like humans, mangroves are on a relentless march. They seize territory, expand fiercely, and dominate. Natives called red mangroves "walking trees" in reference to their long prop roots. The name is also an apt description of their rapid propagation. Their seedpods can ride the currents to new shores thousands of miles away, or to nearby shoals, where they may take root and grow into woody islands. Black mangroves often then join them. "Sea becoming land," an admiring Rachel Carson wrote, "almost before our eyes."[2]

The tropical forest that mangroves create is one not of stunning heights, but of emphatic density, such that, wrote Frank Hamilton Cushing, "naught of their inner contours could be seen." Their canopy hangs low and heavy, embowering a forest floor of unruly roots that claw into wetness. Their tangle invites no easy passage.[3]

"Freaks." That's how one pioneering mangrove scientist referred to them. Maybe he had been reading *Heart of Darkness*. Conrad's Charles Marlow calls mangroves "contorted" shoreside invaders, keepers of an understory "rotting into mud . . . thickened into slime." They set the stage for Marlow's quest up the Congo River into the alien interior, where he finds the stricken Kurtz, whose gratuitous violence represents the jungle's horrors internalized. The mangroves, Marlow recounts, "seemed to writhe at us in the extremity of an impotent despair."[4]

Historically, humans have despaired of the mangroves' existence. On the Gulf, they were a parapet between indigenous peoples and conquerors arriving by sea. Their forest frustrated early mapmakers wanting to draw a clear line between land and water. They were and continue to be the disagreeable neighborhood of ferociously biting bugs.

The ecological truth is that mangroves are giving trees. Their outlandish roots calm tidal water, take delivery of washing-in sediment, and build a shoreline. Their forests are the provider and protector of life in the estuary. Florida mangroves give residency to 18 mammal, 24 reptile, 181 bird, and 220 fish species, from little fish to eventual big fish, including the goliath grouper, which sticks close to the trees its first five or six years. They also serve as way stations of rest and replenishment for trans-Gulf migrators, including the endangered Barbados yellow warbler.

The Gulf's mangroves predated Ponce de León's visits by as much as two thousand years. Cabeza de Vaca saw mangroves in Texas. Sidney Lanier glimpsed them at Cedar Key, the northernmost reach in Florida of these tropical trees. William Halsey Wood hooked the first documented tarpon while surrounded by them near Sanibel Island. Cushing dug for artifacts next to them on Marco. And Tin Can Tourists camped in their shade. The mangrove forests between Homosassa Springs and Key West had no rival in the Americas, and few across the globe.

In a book on the region, Karl Bickel, a former president of United Press who retired to Sarasota, popularized the name Mangrove Coast. He was writing in 1942, which is to say that there were enough of the native trees around to inspire him. But there would not be for long. Bickel called mangroves the "dominant construction crew all along the coast." That was the rub with those who came south, soon after Bickel published his book, to do their own construction, to dominate in place of mangroves. Like the disapproving Charles Marlow, they were tragically indifferent to the tidal forest's geographic and ecological service.[5]

When Rachel Carson wrote *The Edge of the Sea* in 1955, she wondered, "What is the future of this mangrove coast?" She was sensing the assembling march of postwar America. Perhaps she had seen mud-splattered bulldozers, or heard the apocalyptic toil of dragline dredges.[6]

THAT WAS THE YEAR machines were poised to start two major private dredge-and-fill projects in St. Petersburg, where Carson had undertaken research. Developers regularly dredged up fill from a bay bottom and piled it up and out from land's edge to enlarge their real-estate holdings, sometimes creating hundreds of new acres. Wherever they wanted more waterfront, they called in a bulldozer and chainsaws to indiscriminately clear mangroves, and a dredge to build the land. During the prosperous decades after World War II, the machine noise of ripping out native growth grew louder as the pace of expansion turned more aggressive.

Nineteen fifty-five was also the year land builders got a shock. What traditionally had been standard practice in waterfront development now faced opposition. The US Fish and Wildlife Service and the Florida governor commissioned a biological study of a proposed project area on Boca Ciega Bay in St. Petersburg. The governor wanted to silence the machines, something unheard of in growth-obsessed Florida, and on the Gulf.

It wasn't so much that developers over the years had been taking a mile when given an inch. The state had invariably given them a mile to begin with. In 1856, lawmakers passed the Riparian Act, which recognized a landowner's prerogative to fill swampland. They renewed the act in 1921 during a growth boom and extended the prerogative to tidal land, proclaiming, "Waterfront property [should] be improved and developed." The state owned all submerged land, and the board controlling it, comprising the governor and cabinet officers, was eager to sell it to private interests who would reform it into dry productive land.[7]

After World War II, Florida entered another building boom, which was characterized less by the sale of swampland than of bay bottom. One county, Pasco, extended its boundary two miles out into the Gulf in anticipation of real-estate expansion. Making new land began with a simple procedural step: "You just went up there [to Tallahassee, the state capital] and paid them the money for what you wanted to dredge," explained an attorney for one development company, "and they gave you a permit." Newspaper headlines trumpeted the permitted results: BAY-BOTTOM SAND TURNS INTO FLORIDA'S SILVER COAST; HOW TO MAKE A BRAND NEW ISLAND; BEACH PROJECT READY FOR DREDGING; LOWLY MANGROVE SWAMP IS TURNED INTO "PARADISE ISLAND".[8]

Albert Furen followed the protocol in 1953. Although he owned only six acres of Boca Ciega Bay mangrove shoreline in St. Petersburg, that was enough for the state board to allow him to buy and fill 504 acres of the bay. The final go-ahead had to come from Pinellas County commissioners, but he anticipated no obstacle in getting it. Local developers had already manufactured thirty-seven miles of new waterfront, and the commissioners had never rejected a fill project.

Boca Ciega Bay, which lies lagoon-like off the mouth of Tampa Bay between the St. Petersburg mainland and Long Key, where Thomas Rowe built the Don CeSar Hotel, was an underwater garden spot. You had to be from another world not to know it was a gift of nature. Red and black mangroves encircled thirty-eight square miles of luxurious turtle grass. In the year that Furen ran his permit through Tallahassee, the bay contributed more than 1.6 million pounds, or forty percent, to the total catch of commercial fishers in Pinellas, itself the top producer among Florida counties. The pungent smell of more than twenty-five bait shops around the bay declared its popularity among recreational fishers.

While Furen awaited county approval, a group of local citizens organized an alliance to try to prevent the project. They got the ear of *St. Petersburg Times* publisher Nelson Poynter, an important ally. For one, his newspaper was an influential voice; for another, he lived on Boca Ciega Bay and, over the years, had watched fill projects rise up in his sunset view. There was an unsavory paradox between the pleasantry suggested in names such as Paradise Isle, Capri Isle, and Isle of Palms and how these developments had turned the clear bay pale and muddy, and threatened the good fishing and business of the bait shops. Poynter had met Rachel Carson when she was briefly on the Mangrove Coast conducting research for *The Edge of the Sea*, picked up a lesson or two from her about the ecological importance of estuaries, and passed them on to his readers.

There were so many bays and lagoons around the Pinellas County peninsula that residents easily took them for granted. To a similar degree, few understood how all this manufactured land was impoverishing the marine environment. The only drawback to fill projects "is that nebulous thing about 'view,'" said one waterfront owner eager to expand, as if she were talking directly to Poynter. But "as this view is of [mud] flats and mangroves, we don't feel changing that would be a loss."[9]

Then, as the ink was drying on Furen's application, a second fill request came before the commissioners. Detroit developers Hyman and Irving Green were seeking to dredge nine million cubic yards of Boca Ciega Bay for a project that would connect fifteen "lowly mangrove" islands into a single landmass. One was Mullet Key, the home of historic Fort De Soto, where soldiers once had endured mosquitoes with a ration of beer and wine. The brothers called their concern the Green Land Company, and their development Tierra Verde, taking inspiration from their surname rather than from the terra firma vegetation. Poynter's paper called the dual grab for the bay "distressing." Pinellas citizens were once again potential victims of the county's "ill-conceived planning philosophy."[10]

Watching these developments, the US Fish and Wildlife Service and the state's conservation board (the latter founded in the plume-hunting days and headed by the governor) commissioned a study to determine the prospective biological fallout of the two projects. It was the first time scientific research was used in Florida and on the Gulf to control development. A rarity anywhere, the study was a predecessor to the environmental impact statements that the EPA would make common practice in the 1970s.

Robert Hutton, a retired University of Miami marine biologist, headed the research. For years, St. Petersburg had disposed of sewage indiscriminately, Hutton and his team wrote in their report, leaving many areas of the bay "grossly polluted with organisms typical of the intestinal tract of man." The Army Corps of Engineers had simultaneously done major damage by digging a fifteen-foot channel for the Intracoastal Waterway—too deep and turbid for light to penetrate and sea grass to grow—while piling dredge spoil on several hundred acres of thriving habitat. More dredging and filling would "result in a considerable loss of fish and wildlife," the scientists concluded, and jeopardize the area's annual $150 million tourist industry, generated by 600,000 visitors.[11]

Despite the report's revelations, the county commissioners did as expected and approved the Furen project. Governor LeRoy Collins then sued to rescind the state permit. "When and where is that local board down there," he asked, "going to draw the line against further filling of Boca Ciega Bay?" Collins came into office just after the state sold Furen his piece of bay bottom. Forty-five years old, salty haired, a passionate freshwater angler, Collins hailed from comparatively undeveloped north Florida and, like Poynter and the *St. Petersburg Times*, took a grave view of the swift permitting practices.[12]

A governor with environmental sensibilities was a rare commodity in the 1950s—and virtually nonexistent in the South. Maybe Collins wasn't a flesh-and-blood environmentalist, but he was known to say that "no state has a greater stake" in protecting its natural endowments. At the time, ecological science was only just coming into its own as a legitimate field of study at American universities, yet here Collins was taking Hutton's research along to court to try to stop the dredge-and-fill free-for-all. He wasn't arguing permitting technicalities or zoning violations; he was arguing environmental destruction.[13]

By that time, Furen had sold his land and bay-bottom permits to Leonard Ratner, a multimillionaire rat poison manufacturer from Chicago always in search of a tax shelter. Ratner hired an attorney who was as aggressive as one would expect of a former aide to the communist-hunting Senator Joseph McCarthy. In court, with Hutton on the stand, Ratner's lawyer tried to impeach the scientist's credentials, competence, and intelligence. Though the composed Hutton proved his integrity, a lower court and appellate court determined that Ratner had the prerogative to improve and develop his waterfront property. Then the state supreme court refused to hear the case. The county had also permitted the Green brothers' application, and the two projects went forward.

The equivalent of a four-lane highway to New York—that's what the combined fill for the new land could cover—and a foot deep. Boca Ciega Bay lost half of its sea grass meadows and half of its mangroves. Several islands lost all of both. The developers suburbanized the bay with houses and condominiums built so close together that sunlight had to squeeze its way between. The plug of new fill land at the lower end of the bay constricted circulation and flush, leaving the water stagnant and polluted—hardly worth the effort of casting a line or net. Commercial fishers and bait shops deserted the place. Poynter's newspaper said shortsightedness passing as wisdom had "ruined" the bay.[14]

Bay defenders walked away with one victory, however. Poynter and the *Times* convinced the commissioners to turn Mullet Key into a county park, preserving Fort De Soto—originally built to secure civilization's advancement on the Gulf.

IN 1957, WHILE DREDGES churned and growled around the clock on Boca Ciega Bay, Collins put a submerged land bill before the legislature to reform the permitting process. The bill emerged from an extended session weighted with so many amendments that it hardly changed traditional practice.

That was good news to Jack and Leonard Rosen, who broke ground that year on their 103-square-mile master-planned community, down near Fort Myers in tarpon country, behind a blind of mangroves. The brothers were creating Florida suburbia. That meant adopting proven Levittown essentials: cookie-cutter house lots, architectural sameness and simplicity, and affordability. Unlike the New York development and its innumerable postwar copycats, theirs wasn't built with the nine-to-five commuter raising 3.2 children in mind.

The Rosens' advertising ballyhoo—and there was a lot of it—targeted the retiree, the semi-retiree, and the seasonal resident looking for leisure in paradise. Standard amenities in the Rosens' development would come courtesy of nature: warm weather, sunshine, and good fishing. Jack and Leonard incorporated one more amenity, "planned to match your fondest dream." Nature had not fully come through on this one, so they would create it themselves. They promised that every homesite would have either a waterside or water-view location. That blind of mangroves, in other words, had to go.[15]

When all was said and done, you could fault the brothers for a lot of things, but not their timing. Barely three million people lived in Florida in 1950. In two decades, the state population escalated to a solid seven million. Only Nevada surpassed Florida's growth. The Baby Boom was driving up numbers all over the country. But it wasn't so much newborns as it was new*comer*s who were booming the Sunshine State. Grown-ups dominated the population, and virtually everyone was from somewhere else, mostly from the Northeast and Midwest. Even the developers were transplants. And everyone seemed to have migrated around the same time. Historians attribute their mass arrival to effective mosquito control (in the form of DDT) and the introduction of residential air-conditioning. The absence of a state income tax was an especially juicy carrot.

Most were drawn to ocean's edge, which developers ensured would expand to make more room for more people. Population growth along the Mangrove Coast outpaced the rest of Florida, multiplying sevenfold, from 600,000 to 3.5 million. It morphed into the densest region of the US Gulf. Housing units across Florida increased from less than one million to seven million; roadway miles, from eight thousand to eighty thousand. A strange continuum materialized: native Floridians complained about planners and developers paving paradise so that new people could move to Florida, and those new people complained about paving more of paradise so that newer people could come, and the newer people complained about . . . and before long, no one knew what paradise was anymore.

Whatever one's version of the ideal, southwest Florida still had expansive tracts of undeveloped land available to transform into it. Redfish Point, where Jack and Leonard Rosen were preparing to roll out blacktop, was a wildland corner of the Caloosahatchee River and Matlacha Pass. Fort Myers and Punta Rassa lay southeast across the river, and Pine Island, west across the pass. Living on the point had not historically been easy. In 1836, Seminole, restricted by military rule to a designated area on the peninsula, attacked the white man's trading post and fort on the point, killing fourteen soldiers and escalating the Second Seminole War.

Congress then facilitated Indian removal with the Armed Occupation Act of 1842. In return for a grant of 160 acres, the federal land office expected homesteaders to clear, enclose, and cultivate five of those acres. It also assumed the settlers would bear arms. To deal with a different kind of adversary—mosquitoes—some of them burned smudge pots of cow manure, which wasn't hard to find. The Matlacha Cattle Company raised stock on twenty-five thousand acres, fattening its herds on nonnative Bahia grass, imported and planted specifically as fodder.

At the onset of the next century, Franklin Miles, a mail-order-medicines millionaire out of Elkhart, Indiana, retired to seventeen hundred acres on Redfish Point he had bought for seventy-five cents each. He grew winter vegetables, fruits, and ornamental flowers.* He also ran an agricultural program to show homesteaders how to get the best out of their sandy land. Among them were a few colorful characters, most especially William T. Belvin.

---

* Some histories say that Franklin Miles was the inventor of Alka-Seltzer. It was, however, a chemist named Maurice Treneer, employed at the Dr. Miles Medical Company, who developed Alka-Seltzer in the year of Miles's death, 1929. Miles had long before left the company (renamed Miles Laboratories in 1935) in the charge of others, and he had nothing to do with Alka-Seltzer, which was first marketed in 1931.

A widower and former minister from Georgia, Belvin arrived on the point with his two children. They took up residence in a thatched-roof house, which was too primitive for William's daughter, who moved in with a family in Fort Myers—though apparently not primitive *enough* for her dad. In 1929, Belvin walked off into the scrub buck naked to prove that a man could survive off the land and estuary as had the Calusa. "Only his eyeglasses and false teeth," writes Nick Foreman, who has studied the Rosens' development (and grew up in it), "connected him with the material world." A year later, "Wild Bill" emerged sporting a beard, a vesture of Spanish moss, and ten extra pounds.[16]

When the Rosens acquired Redfish Point three decades later, someone with a mind to could have reprised Belvin's stunt. The brothers became the owners of sixty-six thousand acres of wetland, pineland, wire-grass prairie, oak hammock, and Bahia pastureland, all as flat as a tabletop, etched by a few wagon roads and horse paths that were sandy or mucky or both. The point still domiciled panthers, black bears, and burrowing owls, each an ill-fated inhabitant of peninsular Florida, and mangroves had long before sprouted along the point, most heavily around its chin. Those life-giving trees had generated the bounty that gave countless pleasurable hours of fishing on the Caloosahatchee to Thomas and Mina Edison and that encouraged Captain John Smith to guide his clients to Matlacha Pass.

Tarpon hunters might have answered Rachel Carson's question about the fate of this raw mangrove land by leaving it alone. In the proverbial American mind, however, nature invited humans to intervene—to improve nature, do it better, bring it into the fold of civilization. Even the most magnificent places were in need of refining—the removal of an unacceptable native species or introduction of a complementary alien one. Redfish Point was the opposite of magnificent; it was desolation, good for little by the measures of modern society.

You could not leave the land to lie as is—not in growing, expanding postwar America. That would be unconscionable—rather wasteful. Remove something, add something, tame it, tweak it—and this thatch of ground could be good for much more than cows. No value-added benefit would accrue from preserving its indigenous ecological wealth; indeed, removing the burden of mangroves was integral to improving the property's real-estate value and ensuring a handsome payoff for Jack and Leonard. Wild Bill's big adventure wasn't so much a stunt as an adieu, a final expression of a wilderness place.

AFFIRMING THE COMMON ORIGIN STORY of Florida's population, Jack and Leonard came from a brimming northern metropolis. "Back home," as people phrased it, was Baltimore. Mother Rosen was a widowed Russian Jewish immigrant who raised a brood of four while running a small grocery. Leonard made it through the sixth grade; Jack took a few classes at Johns Hopkins. They occasionally worked as pitchmen on the boardwalks of Atlantic City and the midways at carnivals and county fairs. They enjoyed the hell out of persuading people that this product or that amusement would excite them. And they were good. Leonard was a natural.

Soon, they were selling furniture and appliances for the Rosen Home Equipment Company, a business they started in Baltimore. Recalling their mother's practice of extending credit to her customers, they offered installment plans to theirs and began moving a lot of stoves and refrigerators, which were in big demand during the postwar housing explosion. With partner Charles Kasher, they launched a mail-order business for lanolin hair cream, Charles Antell Formula No. 9.

Mail order was pretty traditional, but in the new medium of television, the Rosens saw a kind of boardwalk on which to pitch their merchandise. They bought a few minutes of cheap airtime on New York's WOR-TV at the end of the broadcast day, just before the national anthem played and the picture tube bleeped to the Indian-head sign-off pattern. They were pioneering infomercials—and getting rich. You could see Leonard on the box saying "pull up a chair" because he was about "to tell you a hair-raising tale." Sometimes they'd call Mickey

Mantle in from center field to pitch. On other occasions they used seven-year-old actor Patty Duke. She was a bang-haired unknown, but you knew she was on her way to an Emmy or Oscar (she won both). The brothers were on their way too—to their biggest venture.[17]

It happened like this. While on vacation in palmy Miami, Leonard observed agents for development firms selling home lots on subdivided parcels of land. They sat in their offices and waited for walk-in customers—no advertising to speak of, no binder boys hawking on sidewalk corners as in the hullabaloo days of the 1920s. Leonard reported back to Jack, and the two wondered about using television to move Florida real estate. As a test, they bought eight acres near the center of the state, and Leonard sold them on a Baltimore station in no time. He might have sold all of Florida, had they owned it.

Leonard took off on a scouting trip to buy at least a chunk of the state. He glimpsed Redfish Point during an aerial reconnaissance in a single-prop cloud hopper, grabbed Jack, and went into negotiations with the heirs of Franklin Miles, the medicine man. The brothers set up the Sandy Investment Company, and in July 1957, they closed on the Miles parcel. "I had no intention of doing anything else," Leonard later said, "except . . . buying this land for a dollar and selling it for ten." That wasn't exactly true. They bought more land and intended to build a whole city with streets, electricity, running water, streetlamps, shopping centers, rose garden, golf course, yacht club—the works. They'd call it Cape Coral.[18]

They were in their midforties and their prime, with plenty of hard-knock experiences behind them—successes too. That didn't stop their mother from famously telling Leonard, "You can't build a city. . . . You can't even clean your room." Of her two sons, Leonard was the sloppy one, which seemed somewhat at odds with his neatly cropped hair, yet consistent with his lopsided, horn-rimmed glasses. Less mindful of decorum than his brother was (he once showed up for a business meeting shirtless), he was excitable, impetuous, a little too quick with comments better kept to himself. He was the extrovert of the two, the consummate salesman and handshaker, the point man for public presentations and media interviews, though full of bravado and sometimes crude language. He was also a womanizer, which disturbed Jack—wavy-haired Jack, a "sweet man," said a company vice president, reserved, coolheaded, savvy in business, always dapper, and partial to silk ties. With Leonard out beating the bushes and pressing the flesh, Jack stayed behind to mind the store and check his brother's excesses, while trying to follow through on Leonard's better ideas.[19]

Despite mother Rosen's pessimism, by the 1960s her sons were running the largest land sales business in the US: the Gulf American Land Corporation. Their venture was about selling a dream and making it affordable. That's where the tried-and-true installment plan came in. Their crack sales force liked to say that twenty dollars down and twenty dollars a month would reserve you a sunny spot in paradise. Indeed, a New Yorker on a mailman's pension could retire to Cape Coral, dock a little motorboat on a Rosen-built canal behind his $10,990 Rosen-built two-bedroom home on a $1,990 lot, and spend his golden years hooking big ones. Riverfront lots were comparatively pricey, at $3,390; water views without waterfront were a $990 alternative.

The Rosens gave away homes on *The Price Is Right* and created publicity-generating extravaganzas around visiting celebrities, Bob Hope among them. In 1961, an average of 125 couples toured the development each day. The Rosens gave them free boat outings, lunch, and a bird's-eye view from one of a fleet of Cessna Skyhawk four-seat planes. The scraped-clean land below wasn't much to look at. This was paradise? Where? To the west, where Matlacha Pass, Pine Island Sound, and the blue plain of the Gulf shimmered in the tropical light. If you picked out your spot in the promised wonderworld, the pilot dramatically dropped a sack of white flour to mark it. For those couples hedging, a useful strategy was to keep them around to catch a radiant Gulf sunset. By the last sunset of the year, the Rosens had sold twenty-eight thousand homesites.

Many did not yet exist. The brothers needed all those twenty-dollar down payments to keep the bulldozers and dredges running to carve them out. They invested in $100,000 of earth-moving equipment and forty tons of dynamite. The equipment filled in wetlands over here using refuse from borrow pits dynamited in the coral-rock substratum over there. Yellow machines on tank tracks pushed native palmettos, oaks, and pine trees out of the way, leaving hardly a vertical object of nature's own. This was the tropics, and they bulldozed the shade!

Machines spread out crushed limestone and shells to elevate the cape, burying hundreds of indigenous gopher tortoises alive in their burrows. Home owners couldn't get grass or ornamental shrubs to grow in the humus-barren ground around their twenty-dollar-a-month houses. Years later, a wildlife biologist equated Cape Coral with the Sahara desert. "Every time the wind blows the dust flies. They've completely denuded the land of every bit of vegetation."[20]

But there was luxury, the brothers insisted, in the abundant sunshine and endless recreation of Gulf-side living. Besides, they were creating not a green dell, but a waterfront wonderland. That's why you couldn't have trees. Unless they were correctly placed—a job too important to leave to nature—trees blocked the water view. So did houses as they went up. There were only so many riverside lots to sell, so the Rosens made new waterfront. They cleared thousands of acres of mangroves. "Obliterated," was the word Charles Lee of the Florida Audubon Society would later use. And they dug canals, lined them with concrete seawalls, and lined those with houses. Four hundred miles of canals eventually coursed Cape Coral—more miles than any city in the world, more than twice those of Venice, Italy, half as many miles as the Florida Gulf coast, more miles than the Texas coast.[21]

For more than seven thousand years, people have been digging canals to facilitate irrigation and transport, as did the Calusa not far from Cape Coral. The Rosen canals were not thruways, though. The majority were short, lateral canals that branched off main canals into clusters, with each stopping at a dead end. People in the business called them finger canals. But those built by the Rosens were too hard-edged and geometric to be fingers. From the air, some clusters resembled teeth on a comb; some, tines on a fork; and others, the nine or seven branches of a menorah. Waterside lots were small and backyards tight, and the docks were built sideways instead of outward because the canals were narrow. It seemed you could step over from your dock to the neighbor's directly across. You could certainly see all that went on in the other's backyard. The canals conveyed boats to the bay or river, though you were like a rat in a maze trying to find your way through them. Transport wasn't their primary purpose—this was not Venice. Making waterfront property was.

So, in the Rosens' wonderland, "waterfront" in most cases meant canal front. That's how the retired New York mailman could afford that kind of living. But the economical waterfront came at huge ecological costs. The canals flushed poorly, trapped lawn fertilizers and pesticides, and encouraged little to live in their murkiness. Each mile of Cape Coral's dredged-through and filled-in wild habitat was an artifact pilfered from the region's fishing past, another quantity of natural heritage removed from the visual and mental landscape of the amassing newcomers.

Two hundred and eighty of them lived in Cape Coral in 1960. Eleven thousand, in 1970. In twenty years, the population would be striking toward 100,000. It is a safe bet that those who lived on Cape Coral's Wildwood Parkway knew nothing of the wild woods of Wild Bill. And that those who lived on Bayshore Drive, Coral Drive, Riverside Drive, and Nautilus Drive knew nothing about the ecological vitality of the mangroves that once had thrived where their concrete-block homes now squatted. And further, that those who lived on Flamingo Drive, Palm Tree Boulevard, Chiquita Boulevard, and all the other kitschy- and not-so-kitschy-named streets knew nothing about the Rosen boys' shady business practices and slapdash excavation.

The financial success of Cape Coral by the early 1960s had given the Rosens the means to buy 175 square miles down in Collier County on the western apron of the Big Cypress Swamp in the Everglades. That ambitious development, named Golden Gate Estates, eventually amassed eight hundred miles of roads, mostly limestone, and 183 miles of drainage canals, mostly ineffective—although they dropped the groundwater table four feet and increased wildfires. In 1962, the *Miami Herald* ran an exposé of the high-pressure tactics of the Rosens' sales force, and the next year the *Saturday Evening Post* published a portentous article titled "Land Frauds." Gulf American, a member of the national Better Business Bureau—by invitation—was a featured chiseler.[22]

Among the alleged offenses were promising water access from Golden Gate Estates to the Gulf (not a realistic proposition) and selling homesites still underwater (back during the 1920s this was wryly called "selling land by the gallon"). The Rosens responded to the bad publicity by placing a sensational sixteen-page ad in the *New York Times*, as if all were normal. To quell Wall Street and stock investors, Leonard reported that sales contracts were up thirty-two percent from the year before, and that the company had topped $13 million in earnings from $111 million in sales in 1965–66. An article in the *Chicago Tribune* asserted, "What makes [Florida's current] land boom different from the house-of-cards land boom of the 1920s is the stability of the companies in the land development business." Among the stable companies, said the *Trib*, was Gulf American.[23]

The newspaper might as well have called the Chicago Cubs stable. Finishing dead last in the National League that season, the baseball team had lost sixty-four percent of its games. Down in Florida, Gulf American was dead last in customer satisfaction among land sales companies, targeted by sixty-four percent of the complaints filed with the state. Using evidence gathered from undercover agents, who taped sales pitches from inside car trunks, the Florida Land Sales Board charged Gulf American with deceptive tactics, including making misleading claims about the location, value, and future appreciation of property; replatting land without state approval; surreptitiously switching lots to as far as seven miles from the originals after selling them (as many as thirteen hundred); and failing to show property reports to buyers.

In 1967, the board ordered the suspension of sales for thirty days, beginning December 10. Gulf American pled guilty and agreed to a fine. Then the Rosens changed their minds. They went to court and more or less won. Sales spiked initially, and then plummeted, after charges of attempts to blackmail Governor Claude Kirk surfaced. In July 1968, Leonard stepped down as chairman of the company, saying he wanted to devote his time to philanthropy. The brothers made a deal to sell their company to General Acceptance Corporation for more than $200 million. Jack and Leonard each received $100,000 cash and approximately $63 million in General Acceptance stock with an annual dividend payment of $544,000 for each of the first three years, $1.64 million per year thereafter. (The Cubs had a winning season too.)

The payoff far exceeded Leonard's original design for a ten-to-one return on investment. It was more like one hundred to one. You can argue that the brothers profited at the expense of others, to say nothing of getting richer by leaving the Mangrove Coast ecologically poorer. One of the main complaints the land board filed against Gulf American was related to its fill projects. At Cape Coral, Gulf American dredges had shoveled up 3.6 million cubic yards of fill from the bottom of the Caloosahatchee River, six times as much as had been permitted. The legal issue at the time wasn't so much with wrecking sea grass and mangrove habitat as with stealing from the state. The pilfered river bottom belonged to Florida, and the state wanted fair compensation.

There was, as well, an alternative, less institutional perspective of the dredging. Charles Lee of Audubon called Cape Coral an "environmental tragedy." The nonprofit research group INFORM confirmed Lee's assessment in a 1977 study of nineteen US subdivisions. It concluded that Cape Coral had the worst environmental record of the group. Sea grass and mangroves were wrecked, thousands of acres of each gone. Birds and fish were no longer plentiful. Gopher tortoises were dead. The water was silted and contaminated by lawn and street runoff. Houses aside, the land was fleeced.[24]

Jack and Leonard on the Gulf amounted to an ecological catastrophe, but there was an upside to that. By their pillaging, they inspired to action people who cared about the future of the Mangrove Coast.

ONE OF THOSE PEOPLE was the writer John D. MacDonald. He lived between the Cape Coral and St. Petersburg onslaughts in Sarasota, where many locals feared for their mangrove-trimmed bays. During the legislative undercutting of Governor Collins's submerged land bill, a concerned local legislator asked, "Isn't it possible Manatee County bays will end up as bad as Pinellas County bays?"[25]

Ever since moving to the Gulf coast in 1950, John and his wife, Dordo, had seen a lot of what John identified as hit-and-run development. As far as he was concerned, nobody was more to blame than elected and appointed officials and their reckless planning. The author of crime and detective fiction, he would bang out his irritation with them on his typewriter. "This is instant Florida," says the momentarily severe narrator in one of his novels, *The Dreadful Lemon Sky*, "tacky and stifling and full of ugly spurious energies."[26]

Most of MacDonald's books qualify as poolside and air-travel pulp, but they are edgy and smart, and not nearly as sexist and bawdy as genre contemporaries. The popular demand for them made him one of the most successful writers in the second half of the twentieth century. He put in eight hours a day at his beige IBM Selectric, laying down twenty thousand words a week and publishing seventy-eight books in a thirty-eight-year career. By some estimates, more than seventy million copies have sold in a dozen languages.

MacDonald developed his workday regimen as a paper-pushing intelligence officer in India during the Second World War. Afterward, he earned a Harvard MBA and took a nine-to-five. The white-collar world quickly bored him, and the cold, gray weather in New York, where he grew up and worked, pushed his mind to warmer places. On vacations to Florida, he and Dordo (real name Dorothy), fell in love with the Gulf of Mexico. He found it "bright and fresh and handsome." They rented a house on Clearwater Beach, where he shed his woolen monkey suit for an open-collar California shirt and gingham pants that didn't need to hold a crease. He wrote two books and fifty-some-odd stories before the first year's lease was up.[27]

By then, the MacDonalds realized that Clearwater had been discovered. The population would more than double in the 1950s. Rather than renew their lease, they packed their car, steered south, and took the ferry across the mouth of Tampa Bay, churning past elliptical mangrove islands off the starboard side, which in another few years would become the Green brothers' Tierra Verde. They drove on. Out their rolled-down windows, shore mangroves banked the shoulder of the road for miles. They ended up in Sarasota, bought a house, and never lived in any other town.

Sarasota was a relatively unspoiled hamlet of eighteen thousand residences. The 1920s land boom and bust left it a legacy of Mediterranean architecture, including John and Mabel Ringling's thirty-room Venetian Gothic mansion and 150,000-square-foot Italian-villa-style museum, which held their growing collection of Baroque art. An art school bearing the Ringling name opened a few years later. The little Gulf-side community had culture, which attracted a number of writers, among them Erskine Caldwell, Carl Carmer, and MacKinlay Kantor. They formed a Friday luncheon group that counted MacDonald among its prime members.

On the eastern fringe of the city, ranchland spread deep into the interior, out where Franklin Roosevelt's Civilian Conservation Corps had built the beautiful Myakka River State Park back in the thirties. A bunker of quiet barrier islands—all named keys (Longboat, Lido, Bird, St. Armands, and Siesta)—lay to the sunset west and encased resplendent Sarasota Bay and a group of lesser bays (Palma Sola, Roberts, Little Sarasota, and Blackburn). Bottlenose dolphins romped around them, and mullet never stopped jumping. MacDonald was smitten with the "softness of the air, the blue of the water, the dip and cry of the water birds, the broad beaches."[28]

The city tried to do something smart in 1925. It commissioned the talents of landscape architect and urban planner John Nolen, who was known for integrating the natural and built environments. Cities from coast to coast incorporated his ideas. He gave Sarasota a series of waterfront parks and scenic drives that followed the outline of the bay, the same as he had done recently in St. Petersburg. Then, three years later, state and federal road engineers routed US 41, a.k.a. the Tamiami Trail, built on crushed shells from excavated Indian mounds, along one of his winding drives and through the center of town. Follies of the sort prompted Nolen's opinion that "man is the only animal who desecrates the surroundings of his own habitation."[29]

The Sarasota that John and Dordo first encountered still had the enduring quaintness of summertime lake towns that they had known in upstate New York. Except, Sarasota would not remain consigned to the quaint past. Three years after they arrived, their new home came out of semi-isolation. The state replaced the Tampa Bay ferry with a double-span bridge, tall enough to let freighters pass under and ambitiously named the Sunshine Skyway. Boom; Sarasota County's population exploded by sixteen percent.

The composed landscape descended into motion and noise. Snarling bulldozers never stopped. Nolen's scenic drive qua US 41 turned into a strident speedway that scattered city pedestrians. Wetlands were soon fender-bender parking lots, rooftops replaced treetops, and air conditioners rattled in the windows of houses. When neighbor took neighbor to court over noisy units, judges told plaintiffs to shut their windows if they didn't like the sound of the new age. Damn if all these people and all their din, drowning out the singing birds and frogs and thrumming palm fronds, people who came for Florida's natural vitality only to trample it and hide inside from it, didn't annoy the hell out of MacDonald.

Getting out on the water was an easy escape to quietness. When he moved to the Gulf coast, he took to sailing and fishing, and wearing a yachting cap. And then noise came out of nowhere. He'd be spincasting from the shallows on a "gray silent morning," working his lure back and forth, drinking in the moment, and the wail of a dredge would come up on the wind. The mangrove fringe meant nothing to developers, and it meant everything. That it was wildlife habitat and a storm barrier was irrelevant; that it was abutment for new value-laden manufactured land was exceedingly relevant.[30]

MacDonald saw mangroves yanked out by heavy equipment, piled up, and burned as refuse with other trees. He saw his fishing luck turn bad. It was all connected, a disquieting rippling outward—the "fast-dollar philosophy," the conquest of land, the loss of nature, the diminished quality of life. He complained to friends and vented in the *New York Times*, the *Sarasota Herald Tribune*, and his books—the personal feeding the creative, the creative capturing the changing reality. "Florida is constantly growing," reflects the lead character in *Dead Low Tide*, a 1953 Fawcett paperback, "not in the normal fashion of other places, with more houses going up on existing land, but the land itself is growing."[31]

In 1966, MacDonald built a large bayside house on Siesta Key on his own growing land. He had to bring in thousands of yards of fill—"trucked in, not dredged," he assured family members who had heard his rants—and he had to buy a "small hunk of bay bottom" from the state before his contractor could erect a seawall. You saw this sort of duplicity back then—people who had gotten their slice of paradise and didn't want others cutting into it. That wasn't quite MacDonald. He wanted to shut the floodgates only enough to save the coast from drowning in newcomers, and he opposed only growth that was a "hypnotic insistence on quantity against worth." He would have appreciated a planner like John Nolen, and could sound like him. "Man is a part of nature. God help him, he cannot survive in a world where the order of nature around him has been destroyed."[32]

As for developers, MacDonald preferred to impound the breeds that he labeled fast-dollar buckaroos, money-grubbers, zoning busters, antiplanners, and keep all others on a short leash. "And after they are dead," he wrote in his last novel, invoking the seventh-generation concept, "the damage they do goes on and on, visited on their descendants forever. Their great-grandchildren will live in a world that is drab, dirty, ugly, and dangerous . . . sick and stinking."[33]

MacDonald was paying attention when Nelson Poynter and the citizens' alliance in St. Petersburg were trying to stop the Boca Ciega Bay developers. MacDonald mounted his own fights in Sarasota and turned into the "Resident Big-Mouth" of groups he helped found: the Committee for a Better Sarasota and the Non-Partisan Citizens Committee. And he joined the local Society of Conservation.[34]

When an application to fill part of Little Sarasota Bay came forward, MacDonald shouted in a full-page editorial. Developers take it as their "function," he wrote, "to make a buck by creating waterfront properties that nature curiously neglected to provide." He demanded that the county commission deviate from convention by taking the "firm and very brave stand that there will be *no* more permissions granted for bay filling." The only stand that elected officials considered was the usual one. Commissioner Glen Leach called the shoreline in question "unstable tidal flats" that were "gas-producing, debris-producing areas [that] should be eliminated." But this ancient dogma hardly squared with his assurance that "nobody is more opposed to bay filling than I." As pathetic as his claim must have sounded to fill opponents, it was an implicit acknowledgment of their position, even if revolution wasn't in the air. The commission approved the application.[35]

Then came a bigger fish that threatened to swallow all the minnows in the bay. Arthur Vining Davis, crusty former chairman of Alcoa Aluminum and third-richest man in the world, decided, at age ninety-one, that he didn't like retirement. So he founded Arvida Corporation in 1958 to do something with 800,000 acres of land he owned in Dade County at the southeastern tip of the Florida peninsula. It took him only a few months to discover the Gulf Coast and buy two thousand acres from the Ringling estate. He wanted to build hotels, commercial outlets, and four thousand homes—to manufacture a lifestyle instead of humdrum aluminum, in part by manufacturing land. MacDonald wrote to a fellow conservationist, "Obviously they plan to do their best to fill the bays." Indeed, the 3.5 miles of waterfront in the Ringling parcel wasn't enough to satisfy Arvida's plans, which included fill projects on Bird and Longboat Keys. "Public vistas should not become car ports and boat docks," MacDonald declared in an editorial before breaking out heavier firepower.[36]

A lot of trees ultimately fell for MacDonald's pulp, but at least it was pulp with a conscience. Within eighteen months after Arvida disclosed its plans, he completed a draft of what writer Jim Harrison would call the "first and best of all novels with an ecological base." Titled *A Flash of Green*, it appeared in bookstores in 1962, two months before Carson's *Silent Spring*, the book that many argue kickstarted the environmental movement. But MacDonald could not have written *Flash* without the movement already under way. His dedication page is a salute to fellow activists "opposed to the uglification of America."[37]

MacDonald set his thirty-eighth novel in the bayfront town of Palm City on the Gulf Coast, a fictional place that geographically and temperamentally resembles Sarasota. There are hints of Boca Ciega Bay and Cape Coral, and MacDonald's own experiences. The narrator says early on, "As the quiet and primitive mystery of the broad tidal bays disappeared, as the mangroves and the rookeries and the oak hammocks were uprooted with such industriousness, the morning sound of construction equipment became more familiar than the mockingbird" (the state bird).[38]

The thriller plot revolves around Save Our Bays, a citizens' group that prefers the defiant acronym SOB. The group tries to stop Palmland Development from filling eight hundred acres of Grassy Bay fronting Sandy Key (the main drive on Sandy Key is Mangrove Road). The developer, it turns out, has the county commissioners in its pocket. "It's going to be a steamroller operation, Kat," MacDonald's protagonist, newspaperman Jimmy Wing, tells the SOB's Katherine Hubble, his would-be lover, "and it's going to run right over anybody who stands in the way." The SOB's archnemesis, Commissioner Elmo Bliss, is hoping the steamroller will pave his way to the governor's office. He ultimately corrupts Wing and uses him to undermine the credibility of a marine scientist that the SOB recruit to testify against the project.[39]

The title of the book was obvious to MacDonald early on. Green flashes are natural events that sometimes occur when a glint of green appears in the final second of sunset, as the light disappears behind the watery horizon. MacDonald would have seen them from the porch of his house. In his mind, they were a metaphor of the fast green money to be made in the Palm City real-estate scheme. Another metaphor, not explicit in the book, relates to MacDonald's artistic context: the natural green of the Mangrove Coast disappearing in a flash. Like the fictional SOB, the conservation groups in Sarasota failed to stop their nemesis, Arvida—the first time.

DOWN ON MARCO ISLAND, nobody stopped the Mackles either—not before they gave the island a makeover that even the most stalwart of land sculptors, the Army Corps of Engineers, questioned. Like the Greens and the Rosens, the Mackles were a brother development team, except they were three: Elliot, Robert, and Frank Jr. In 1908, Frank Sr. founded a Jacksonville construction company, which gave his sons a head start to launching the General Development Corporation (1954) and the Deltona Corporation (1962).

By the end, the family had built thirty thousand houses. They popped up in Mackle developments at Deltona, St. Augustine, and Biscayne Bay. The Mackles put up houses, condos, and hotels on Tierra Verde, and on the north end of Charlotte Harbor they turned eighty thousand acres into the sprawling Port Charlotte. Inside New York City's Grand Central Station and the Mandel Brothers Chicago department store, they built model homes and passed out promotional brochures with cups of orange juice. The next year, 1958, General Development Corporation sales hit $45 million. Nineteen fifty-nine was even better.

Around that time, the state refused an opportunity to buy the bulk of Marco Island for a wildlife preserve from the Barron Collier family for $1 million, and the Mackles followed with a $7 million check for essentially the same property. The purchase would ultimately yield eleven thousand homesites. The brothers proved that they were among the best at doing what MacDonald hated most: making new land.

A comparison of before and after aerial photographs of their island transformation explains MacDonald's loathing. On the eve of construction's start in 1964, Marco looked virtually the same as when Cushing had visited seventy years earlier—fist-shaped, six miles long and four wide, residence to a population of 550. William and Maggie Collier's Marco Inn was still there and operating, its white clapboards nestled in dense vegetation. Wetlands, pine barrens, native palms, and tropical hardwood hammocks remained untroubled. A thin white line of beach, a perfect crescent shape, drew three miles along the Gulf side. Mangroves fortified the rest of the island's outer edge. A "panorama of verdant splendor," a state tourism film called Marco in 1965.[40]

What was safely frozen in a photograph was not in time. In the year of the promotional film, MacDonald prompted his protagonist in *Bright Orange for the Shroud* to lament, "Marco Village saddened me. The bulldozers and draglines had gotten to it since my last visit." What catches the eye in the later aerials is the island's gray-brown, nature-smothered makeover. Its completeness is stunning. Finger canals poke everywhere into the misshapen island's interior, adding eightfold to the waterfront from before. Lined up in precise domino fashion, rooftops hugging each other wind between blacktop roads and ninety-one miles of nearly lifeless canals. Backyard docks berth a fleet of private watercraft that range from "gin-and-tonic" pontoon boats to cabin cruisers. On opposite sides of the island is the carpet green of two golf courses. The sliver of beach on the Gulf is a longer, broader gleaming belt of white before a fortress of resort accommodations.[41]

The built environment by the 1980s had arisen implacably indifferent to the idea of the waterfront as a public common. It was not unusual, as elsewhere on the growing Gulf coast, for one trying to glimpse the seascape to be stranded in a car or on a sidewalk behind hard-edged architecture. Upscale hotels and condominiums stood like crowd control against those who arrived without a reservation or guest pass. Alternatives were few. Marco's two public beaches had pricey parking fees, yet lines of waiting traffic. They occupied a token thirty-two acres of the island's nine thousand.

So much natural growth venturing forth, once hemmed in only by the island's perimeter, hampered only by storms and drought, was gone. Rainwater gathered into wetland and pond, lapped up by tongues and beaks and soaked up in roots, was routed into stormwater systems. Nests and burrows—and shell mounds—were turned under for houses, condominiums, and real-estate offices. Berries, leaves, and roots were ripped out for supermarkets and convenience stores. Pathways of clawed and padded feet gave way to roads and canals. Bird music was smothered by traffic drone and powerboat wail. Leading up to this state of affairs, the Mackles launched a worldwide advertising campaign, complete with the offer of installment plans, touting Marco as a "Primitive Paradise."[42]

SEAWALLS WERE THE ARMOR of that paradise. They've been with civilization for a long time. The ancient Greeks and Romans made them out of poured concrete. Many times over, a cut-limestone seawall protected Constantinople against the sea and invading forces, though not against the Ottomans. The most celebrated Gulf seawall is arguably Havana's Malecón, across the harbor from the Spanish Colonial Castillo del Morro, and recognized less as a bulkhead than as a breezy twilight esplanade on which lovers stroll hand in hand. Its construction began in 1901, during the four-year US occupation.

West across the Gulf, Galvestonians began raising their island that year behind a long, granite-boulder seawall, which by 1962 reached ten miles. Mississippians liked to boast that their twenty-six-mile Dutch-design, stair-step concrete seawall, built to secure the new coastal highway, which was dubbed the Old Spanish Trail, was the "world's longest." After the seawall was completed in 1928, property values shot up tenfold, according to the local press, and boosters were doubly pleased to see more people building vacation homes.[43]

No one has counted how many mangroves on the Florida Gulf coast have been lost to seawalls. All the concreted twists and turns around islands and finger canals and the straight lines along artificial edges add up to well over a thousand miles of construction and destruction. As late as 1969, the year Congress passed the National Environmental Protection Act, Harold J. Humm, director of the Marine Science Institute at the University of South Florida, around the bend from Boca Ciega Bay, inelegantly called mangroves a "form of wasteland."[44]

Scientists then and now emphatically reject that notion. This is not to say that seawalls create ecologically sterile environments. Algae and barnacles grow on their hard surfaces. Small sea creatures live and shuttle around the debris from their construction and detritus that collects at their base. You can comfortably perch yourself on one, bait and cast a line, and catch fish. But you won't catch as many of them or specimens as big as you would floating in a boat next to mangroves.

Developers maintained that seawalls protect existing and new shoreline. This isn't always the case. Seawalls can actually contribute to erosion. They prevent the sea from distributing fresh replenishing sand, and as the energy of the water bounces off a seawall, it scours the base, even reaching underneath and behind it. "The sea wall stood," MacDonald wrote, in 1956 in *Murder in the Wind*, "until the solid water, cresting over it, sucked the fill from behind the wall. . . . Soon, without backing, the sea wall twisted and crumpled."[45]

It was hard to slow or stop the proliferation of seawalls when someone like Professor Humm, an expert on estuarine sea grass, was telling state officials that replacing mangroves with an artificial bulkhead would not reduce marine productivity. It was hard when the undisputed number one industry in your state was growth, and waterfront real estate generated the highest property tax revenue, and seawalls made the expansion of that prime real estate possible. It was hard when a big outfit like Arvida, with paid lobbyists, was promising to enlarge the tax roll and not just with single-family houses, but with concrete residential towers that would fit many times more the number of people than houses would accommodate on the same square of waterfront.

If MacDonald hated anything as much as the unfurling of seawalls (beyond his own), it was condominiums. The term "condominium" is a legal, not an architectural, invention of medieval Europe. It provided the guidelines for multiple interests occupying a single residential structure. As buildings, modern-day condominiums became attractive in places where the population had outgrown the availability of land, and among a demographic wanting to escape the responsibility of maintaining a patch of green—such as pensioners seeking warm-climate retirement. Puerto Rico, where condominiums had served the crowded island commonwealth since the 1950s, exported its building ideas to south Florida. When Congress allowed the Federal Housing Administration to insure mortgages on condominiums, construction took off. By the late 1960s, so-called supertowers were stacking humanity as high as fifty stories. To Florida developers, condominiums were an ingenious way to sell a single waterfront lot to fifty, a hundred, or more buyers.

MacDonald saw condominiums as a guarantee of traffic congestion, overburdened potable-water sources, and disrupted water views. Readers got full disclosure of his contempt when in 1977 he published *Condominium*. His sixty-sixth book was his first hardcover, nongenre novel, but still classic MacDonald fare. Its cast of characters includes unscrupulous businessmen; corner-cutting builders; defrauded senior citizens; a couple of smart-cookie retirees; and a mammoth hurricane that bears down on the vulnerable structures and their occupants. He meant the book as a screed against what Floridians called "condo canyons," the emerging hardscape on mainland shorelines and barrier islands.[46]

ARVIDA WAS A PIONEER in canyon building. When it moved toward a new development phase on its Sarasota properties, site plans included condominiums. The opposition moved into its own new phase. It gave an undisguised nod to *A Flash of Green* and organized Save Our Bays. The real-life SOB partnered with the Sarasota County Anglers Club, which filed a lawsuit against Arvida, the state, and Longboat Key—the proposed site of a new Arvida fill project—maintaining that selling public land, in this case bay bottom, "to private interests for private gain" was a violation of the "public trust."[47]

MacDonald remained ever the "common scold," writing letters to President Lyndon Johnson, Interior secretary Stewart Udall, and an unsympathetic Senator George Smathers of Florida. MacDonald also helped organize a "bay fill conservation fund dinner" to raise money for the lawsuit. In December 1964, the state tabled Arvida's proposed purchase of bay bottom around Longboat Key indefinitely. "We have driven Arvida stock down appreciably," a cheery MacDonald wrote to the vice president of the Save San Francisco Bay Association, with whom he was trading war stories.[48]

Arvida tempered the euphoria when it came back requesting a permit to fill more than 170 acres around Otter and south Lido Keys. The SOBs remained similarly relentless, and they could not have predicted how things would unfold. Help came from Tallahassee, in the form of a new attitude midwifed by Nathaniel P. Reed, the governor's "dollar-a-year" environmental adviser. "It was rape and run, avarice and greed," Reed once said of Florida's construction practices, as might a character in one of MacDonald's books. In 1967, he persuaded Governor Claude Kirk to sign a law requiring a biological survey—à la LeRoy Collins—prior to official consideration of permits to alter tidal and submerged lands. The law's sponsor was state representative Ted Randell from Fort Myers.

Randell liked spending time on the Caloosahatchee and had personally experienced the impact of Cape Coral construction, when fish stopped biting at his line. In January, he and Kirk were in Sarasota for a legislative weekend, which included a lunch with Arvida president Brown Whatley at Bird Key Yacht Club. The SOB knew about the lunch and launched a "boatacade" of some two hundred craft that "formed ranks in the bay." The shrill of whistles, bells, and air horns sounded their presence. Kirk reportedly turned to his lunch companion with a one-liner that MacDonald could have written: "I see your navy out there, Brown." The next month, the Sarasota County commissioners voted unanimously against permitting the new Arvida development.[49]

It was not isolated bravery. Down the coast a stretch, Sanibel Island existed as an insular repudiation of the development hypertension. Crab-leg-shaped, it has an east–west lie that hinges northward before connecting to Captiva Island by a short bridge. From the right spot on Sanibel, you can watch the sun swing out of the Gulf in the morning and back into it in the evening. Across the sound you can also see the tip of Pine Island and St. James City. After the tarpon fishers' Hotel San Carlos burned to the ground and a hemp rope factory closed down, St. James City retreated into an island slumber. In the 1960s, developers awakened it by digging a veritable confusion of canals for residential housing. Looking through binoculars past St. James City from Sanibel, past Picnic Island, Merwin Key, and Starvation Key, past Big Island and tiny Bird Key—all unoccupied—you can make out the outer edges of heavily populated Cape Coral. To do so, you'd be standing in or floating in front of protected Sanibel mangroves.

Ecologically, the five-thousand-year-old barrier island is a tropical and temperate mix, and more intact than not. Postwar residents wanted to keep its sand dunes, dune grass, beach sunflowers, sea grapes, and mangroves. They were lucky to have the option. Their island had been part of one of the oldest US-based development concerns in the state, the Florida Peninsula Land Company, organized by New York investors in 1837. Its overseers plotted a town of fifty homesites surrounded by farm tracts, and marketed the island as a garden spot, only to have legal issues force its dissolution and the Second Seminole War halt settlement. By the late 1870s, after the Civil War and a major hurricane, settlers began arriving again, mainly to farm sugarcane, citrus, avocados, eggplants, and tomatoes.

In 1926, a storm powerful enough to crush Miami and its building boom raced across the state and put Sanibel underwater. The island survived, although the saltwater bath ruined the soil for future farming. The islanders had a fallback, however. A modest economy had taken hold around tarpon fishing and winter vacationing. Two years later, ferry service opened and boosted the number of visiting birders, naturalists, and shell collectors.

A critical wintertime retreater was Jay Norwood "Ding" Darling. A midwesterner, he discovered Sanibel and Captiva with his wife, Genevieve, in 1935. The year before, President Franklin Roosevelt had appointed Ding chief of the Biological Survey (soon to be reorganized as the US Fish and Wildlife Service), though he seemed an odd choice. Neither bureaucrat nor scientist, Darling was a Pulitzer Prize–winning syndicated editorial cartoonist and loyal to the other political party. His qualifications lay in his outdoorsmanship, as well as conservationist ideals that were compatible with many New Deal programs.

As director of the Survey, Darling ushered in the Federal Duck Stamp Program to expand the government purchase of wildlife habitat, and he lent his artistic talent to the first stamp and designed the blue-goose logo of the national-wildlife-refuge system. When would-be obstructionists moved against the Survey's new conservation initiatives, it occurred to Darling that ducks, geese, bears, wolves, moose, and the rest had no voice in Washington. So, in late 1935 he resigned his post to organize a voting constituency to advocate for them. Within months, he was the founding president of the General Wildlife Federation (later renamed the National Wildlife Federation).

Once back in Florida, he joined with Sanibel-Captiva residents to organize the Inter Island Conservation Association. Darling wintered in a house on pilings over the water on the sound, which he called his fish house, accessible by a drawbridge that he could raise when he wanted privacy. Keeping the island quiet satisfied personal desires, but more than that, outside his windows the wetlands that sidled up to the sound for the entire length of the island quivered with birds day and night. He could not imagine the island any other way. In 1945, he and the association convinced President Truman to create the Sanibel National Wildlife Refuge. Renamed the J. N. Ding Darling National Wildlife Refuge in 1967, the original green idea of residents made an emphatic statement for Sanibel's future.

The majority were cold-weather refugees from the North and, for the most part, decently educated, wealthy, and politically conservative. A legitimate green streak ran through their numbers, fortified by a major not-in-my-backyard complex. Virtually the moment the first causeway and bridge to the island opened in 1963 (against many islanders' wishes), developers drove over with blueprints and big ideas. Dredging and filling got started near the causeway, and the county's new comprehensive plan revealed a future of condominiums towering over Sanibel's shell-strewn beach.

Islanders quickly got their own ideas. They founded the Sanibel-Captiva Conservation Foundation and, in 1974, incorporated the island as a city. Then, acting on the initiative of Erard Matthiessen—a retired New York architect, aquaculture pioneer, twenty-year board member of National Audubon, founding member of the Sanibel-Captiva Conservation Foundation, and father of writer Peter Matthiessen—they commissioned a study for the island's own land use plan. Sanibel's first mayor, Porter Goss, guided the plan through a phalanx of developer opposition to successful adoption.[50]

No more dredge and fill, no more uprooted mangroves, no over-scaled condominiums; resorts, yes, but buildings no taller than forty-three feet and hidden behind lots of protected vegetation, accessed by nothing bigger than two-lane roads, with speed limits set at thirty-five miles per hour, and paved bike paths stretching twenty-five miles, all in a lavish showcase of wildlife habitat. Between preserves established by the Sanibel-Captiva Conservation Foundation and Ding Darling refuge land, some two-thirds of the island was protected from development.

IN 1987, THE DING DARLING refuge expanded its boundaries to include Tarpon Bay. The Department of the Interior shut the bay down to fishing, forcing the marina where Randy Wayne White based his fish-guiding operations out of business. White read the tea leaves, closed shop himself, and started writing books full-time. He never looked back, except to the local roots of his former profession. He prospered as a writer and eventually moved from Pine Island to the bucolic luxury of Sanibel, joining other residents who were from somewhere else, including Porter Goss, who had become a national figure as a US congressman and director of the CIA.

On Sanibel and Captiva, there was also Robert Rauschenberg (who bought Darling's fish house), Willard Scott, and R. Tucker Abbott, the country's premier conchologist. Avian photographer Ted Cross bought a house across the water from the refuge. Although he traveled the globe—including the South Pacific and Soviet Siberia, as well as rattlesnake-infested and reddish-egret-happy Green Island, Texas—he considered Sanibel one of the best places in the world to shoot birds, with nothing more lethal than a Nikon and a super-telephoto lens.

By the end of the century, Sanibel's population had reached six thousand, fulfilling local ambitions to control growth, although the wintertime population could swell to more than twenty thousand. The birds at the refuge and the shells on the beach drew nearly a million visitors a year. The main roads turned into long snakes of idling cars. Tourists pedaling beach cruisers, provided by their hotels and inns, were grateful for the bike paths. The average age of a Sanibel resident was sixty; the average annual income, $80,000; the average price of their home, $500,000 plus. The wage and salaried staff at the hotels, shops, and restaurants, and the uniformed traffic directors at the main intersections, could not afford to live on the island. They crossed the bridge from the mainland at both ends of the work shift through the six-dollar toll booth. Nature had become a rare and coveted commodity on the growth coast, and, alas, an unaffordable one for many.

In the parlance of the Rosens and virtually every other developer who helped turn the indigenous coast into something rare—adherents all to the principle of supply and demand—nature was never so good as when it was a salable item. The economic value acquired by untouched waterfront gave little wiggle room to those who wanted to preserve it for ecological reasons. But then, against the backdrop of a national awareness of environmental imperatives conveyed by the first Earth Day, in 1970, local and state officials began to rethink coastal development. Environmentalists celebrated a decision of the Army Corps of Engineers to deny the Mackle brothers' permit application to convert additional Marco mangroves and sensitive land into thirty-seven hundred presold homesites. In the 1980s, the Department of the Interior created the Ten Thousand Islands National Wildlife Refuge, later expanding it to thirty-five thousand acres, of which two-thirds was mangrove forest.

Around the same time, Florida lawmakers adopted legislation recognizing the ecological value of mangroves by severely limiting their trimming and removal (although violations by waterfront property owners were common). State, local, and federal authorities and private interests set aside eighty percent of Florida's surviving mangroves expressly for preservation or conservation. The state did not end dredge and fill, but it did designate many Gulf areas as "outstanding waters" or "aquatic preserves," including Boca Ciega Bay and three other sections of Tampa Bay. Sarasota Bay, Charlotte Harbor, Pine Island Sound, and Matlacha Pass made the list too, acquiring special protection against future dredging and filling, as well as seawall construction. Where the state deemed shoreline protection appropriate, it often recommended or required riprap rock barriers—loose boulders—as an environmentally friendly alternative to seawalls. The days of making estuaries into housing developments were past.

Still, powerful tensions between protection and growth remained. You just couldn't stop people from moving to Florida's Gulf coast. At many places, the line of condominiums and hotels ran down along sandy stretches into the hazy distance. At the millennium, Cape Coral was the fastest growing US city, with a population of 100,000 or more.

Pricey Sanibel had an untaxing population density of 356 people per square mile, allowing the coexistence of human and wildlife habitation. Affordable Fort Myers had 2,065 people per square mile and Sarasota 3,540, allowing little more than the coexistence of humans and concrete. With a population density ten times the state average, Pinellas County was completely built out. Treasure Island, on Boca Ciega Bay, had a sardine-packed 4,783 people per square mile. It was the most crowded barrier island along the most crowded part of the Gulf Coast.

Navigate the course that Cushing followed in the *Silver Spray* in 1895 from Tarpon Springs to Marco, making random ports of call along the way, and you would discover everywhere a reconfigured shoreline of inverted bay bottom—a fake, geometric, manicured, late-twentieth-century generic. That was the answer to Rachel Carson's question about the future of the Mangrove Coast.

One last thought—particularly relevant in the current age of climate change and sea-level rise. In that context, much attention is given to the dire consequences of the depleting Amazonian rain forest. Yet, in their vegetation and the peaty soil around their tangled feet, mangrove forests absorb more carbon dioxide, including that generated by combusted fossil fuels, than any tropical forest. This means less carbon in the atmosphere, and the mitigation of a changing climate and the acidification of the ocean, which is contributing to the death of the coral of the Florida Reef. The trees also build and secure shoreline, even as a rising sea wants to take it away. They are the "construction crew," as suggested by Karl Bickel at the start of this chapter, and a much friendlier, much smarter proposition than a dredge and a seawall.

Fifteen

FLORIDA WORRY, TEXAS SLURRY

Port Arthur, Texas. By the mid-twentieth century, the Texas Gulf coast had turned into a petrochemical waterfront.

> *Did [the bay] smell the coming, when before it knew only the*
> *relentless ebb and flow of a tide and the sound of gray heron*
> *feeding and the great wind at its breast and the hundreds*
> *and hundreds of years it had been silent and slept beneath the*
> *benign stars?*
>
> —DIANE WILSON (2005)[1]

FOR CONTEXT, IF YOU ORDERED OYSTERS AT A RESTAURANT or a seafood market in the mid-1990s, odds were better than one in two (fifty-seven percent) that they came from the Gulf. If you went for the shrimp, chances were nearly seven in ten that you'd be peeling a Gulf variety. The American Sea's oyster and shrimp fisheries were the most valuable in the US. They were the reason why, along with finfish—menhaden, tuna, mackerel, grouper, drum, herring, snapper, and flounder—the Gulf outperformed the combined commercial yields of the Great Lakes and Atlantic Seaboard, totaling one-third the domestic harvest outside Alaska, and why dockside receipts were $698 million. Another forty-two million fish came in on the hooks of 4.8 million recreational anglers.

Statistics can lie, of course, or conceal contrary evidence. After peaking in the late 1980s, Gulf yields declined. Comparative percentages remained impressive because the entire US fishery was suffering. In the Northeast, the Atlantic cod population, always the canary in the coal mine, had collapsed. Scientists had been piping a warning about the world's overfished, overdeveloped, and, increasingly, polluted seas for years. An article in the August 1, 1988, issue of *Time* declared, "The oceans are sending out an SOS." Illustrated with a shadowy tide of polluted water reaching out in the shape of human hands for innocent marine creatures, the magazine's cover shouted, "Our Filthy Seas." In the aquatic arena of the world, the United States had a lot to answer for. It was the biggest consumer of marine products, biggest energy user, and biggest polluter.* Dozens of other culpable nations occupied the Atlantic and Pacific coasts, so the US could shift some of the blame across these ailing waters. But within its backyard sea, it had a problem all its own.[2]

This was another face of postwar growth on the Gulf—the industrial face, not always as evident as the uprising and crowding residential architecture, but as shocking, once revealed. The first signs that

---

* China moved to the number one consumer spot after 2000. Worldwide consumption has nearly doubled since the 1960s, according to a report of the Food and Agriculture Organization of the United Nations (*The State of the World Fisheries and Aquaculture 2008*).

something might be amiss appeared around the time developers and newcomers were descending on the Mangrove Coast. A 1954 federal government report on pollution in the Gulf highlighted twenty-three trouble spots—nine in Florida (with the worst ones in the panhandle) and seven in Texas. All were estuarine bays that had been industrialized.

The report's authors, nevertheless, kept a positive outlook. There were state and federal agencies, including the shellfish sanitary unit of the US Public Health Service, which wrote the report, to ensure a cleaner future: "The accuracy of data on water pollution is necessarily short-lived," the authors claimed, "principally because progress is continually being made as more municipalities and industries take action to abate pollution." Two decades later, however, progress in clean water had yet to materialize. Industrial expansion had continued apace, with profit making leveraged on ecological deficits.[3]

FLORIDA PANHANDLE NATIVE Charles Lowery stood beside one of those pollution trouble spots on the Gulf and looked at the granite marker he called a "death tombstone." Its inscription was straightforward: "In Memory of Escambia Bay, BC-1971, Killed by Pollution." It might have been a gag of his sportfishing buddies, who acquired the slab of granite from a monument maker in Pensacola—a bunch who used to toss beer cans in the water after draining their contents. That was before the fishing buddies noticed that the bay was turning sick from industrial and human waste. They could smell it in the water, taste it in their catch, and see it in grotesque lesions on fish that they reeled in and that started showing up on the water dead. The tombstone was no gag.[4]

In 1969, there were twenty-one fish kills on Escambia Bay. Thirty-plus the next year. Five months after two hundred million Americans celebrated the first Earth Day, newspapers from coast to coast reported that hypoxia had dealt Escambia Bay a kill worthy of the history books. The experts measured it not by the number of dead on the water, but by its inconceivable expanse: seven miles of wasted marine life, bloated and stinking, lost from commercial use, recreational possibilities, and the food chain. A Lieutenant Lewis Zangas of the Florida Marine Patrol told the Associated Press that the density of fish floating with white undersides up made the water look "like snow," and then added truthfully, "but it doesn't smell that way."[5]

Pensacola was woefully unrecognizable as the city that had birthed commercial fishing on the Gulf. The old wharf district had withdrawn into the shadows of tourist hotels, a naval air station, state university, and subdivisions sheltering fifty thousand residents. The city's New England past, when commercial fishers from the Northeast had turned Pensacola into a major seafood port, was forgotten. Spanish roots remained relevant in a quaint sort of way, mainly to history buffs and the hospitality folks, yet residents identified closest with the city's or their own Confederate heritage. Pensacola was a dyed-in-the-wool southern city—politically conservative, racially segregated, and xenophobic, except when it came to welcoming military spending and industrial development.

Pensacola stepped in time with the rest of the postwar South, which shoved a hospitality platter of enticements in front of northern and foreign industries. Right-to-work laws weakened labor unions, making local wage labor cheap and exploitable. Tax incentives were doled out like ginger cookies. Deepwater navigation channels were built with federal money secured by southern congressmen. Six Gulf cargo ports rose to the nation's top-ten ranking in tonnage shipped and received, including the Port of South Louisiana (between New Orleans and Baton Rouge) and Houston to the number one and two spots. Southern hospitality to business was incomplete without lax environmental regulations and an understood courtesy: pollute to your heart's content.

And pollute they did in Pensacola. Four major bays surround the city, and two-thirds of their watershed reaches into rural Alabama. Agriculture and leaky septic tanks sent unwanted matter down the principal drainage thoroughfares: the Yellow, Blackwater, and Escambia Rivers. Charles Lowery's Escambia Bay got the worst of it. The

Escambia River and its tributaries provided receptacles to ten waste-water treatment plants, where "treatment" was a dubious outcome. Nine were in Alabama, its buttocks sitting hazardously atop the throne of western Florida. A tenth treatment plant squatted on the shore of the bay.

The Escambia River also conveyed the discharge of one power-generating and seven manufacturing plants, four of them multinational chemical producers. According to a 1977 EPA study, oxygen-consuming chemicals and nitrogen releases from industry were chiefly responsible for the fish kills. The plants also launched a weighty fleet of heavy-metal contaminants: lead, zinc, chromium, manganese, nickel, aluminum, iron, titanium, cadmium, copper, cobalt, vanadium. Lowery would drive his pickup over the Highway 90 bridge before sunrise, trailering his boat behind, bait well stocked, and he'd see metal oxide in Gulf Power's coal ash sparkling on the river in the headlights. He knew of a "whole damn island" in Thompson Bayou that his electric provider had covered with the highly poisonous ash. He might have cursed thermal pollution too. Electric utilities drew water out of a bay or river to cool their generating plant and returned it as hot water, which retains less oxygen and commonly kills sea grass.[6]

Industries used bays like slop buckets to dump refuse into the gutter of the ocean. By accident of geography—flow patterns, landmass locations, and barrier islands—the bays around Pensacola didn't flush efficiently into the Gulf. As many as forty chemicals lingered in high concentrations.

Somebody needed to act before the bays succumbed to the onslaught. The chemical producers weren't going to change voluntarily, and local officials weren't asking them to. The pro-business, pro-growth *Pensacola News Journal* defended industry like a favorite child. And the fish kills kept coming, one after another and another. The EPA estimated that the nation's polluted waters slew seventy-four million fish in 1971, eighty-one percent more than the 1969 record. Nearly a quarter suffocated on the Texas coast, and close to a half went belly-up in Florida, most of them in Escambia Bay.

For the first time, America's principal killing waters were not rivers and lakes, but coastal estuaries. The blind pursuit of economic growth had transformed cradles of life into chambers of death. After Pensacola posted the largest kill of the year, another pithy quote from Lieutenant Zangas traveled the AP wire: "At this rate, I think Escambia Bay will be dead within one year."[7]

Lowery didn't intend the tombstone as a memorial; it was a call to action.

PLENTY OF PEOPLE STILL BELIEVED that dumping into a big blue ocean was as harmless as spitting into a lake. Recall the army at the end of World War II coolly chucking captured chemical weapons off Horn Island. Companies manufacturing chemicals for peaceful purposes followed suit, routinely disposing of undiluted poisonous refuse, including DDT and PCBs, in the Gulf. In 1973, around the time the army confessed to its misadventure, the EPA prohibited the practice. Much of the unwanted material was redirected to an offshore incinerator 190 miles out from Texas. A petition signed by fifteen thousand residents, whose state was the number one contributor of hazardous discard (twenty-three percent of the national total), forced the EPA to shut down the floating bonfire in 1991.

Lone Star native Diane Wilson could cite any number of facts about hazardous chemicals "snorkeling everywhere" under the Texas sun. To stanch the flow of poison, she was willing to put her life on the line, and did so more than once.[8]

Wilson lived in a little town called Seadrift, in Calhoun County. The seat was Port Lavaca. Its name came from the first commodity shipped from there. Acting on Cabeza de Vaca's original vision, Spanish missions introduced the earliest form of cattle ranching on the Gulf, and by the 1840s it had reached Calhoun County. Pecans and cotton were other early Port Lavaca exports. Mined copper and lead came out of the area too. They were foretokens of many future heavy metals, yielded not from mines, but from local chemical processing.

Port Lavaca is on the north side and Seadrift on the south of Calhoun County, 150 miles down the coast from Galveston. Similar to
Pensacola, Calhoun County is a thumb poking into four bays: Lavaca,
Matagorda, San Antonio, and Espiritu Santo. Matagorda Island
fronts this land-water geography, and in the other direction, jackrab-
bit prairies and weedy pastureland roll out behind it to the west. Tree
lines are distant places of white-tailed deer, bobwhite quail, and wild
turkey. All of this was Karankawa country.

When Wilson was growing up in the 1950s, Seadrift had barely
five hundred inhabitants. Most breadwinners net-fished, shrimped,
or crabbed—often all three. In the 1920s, the little cow port led the
nation in shrimp production, or so local histories say. Wilson's great-
grandfather and grandfather were shrimpers, as were her father, uncle,
two brothers, and husband—a lineage that remained unbroken by
Wilson herself. Seadrift's evening rush hour occurred on the water
with boats coming home to fish houses. The waterfront was a habitat
of rust, splintered wood, chipped and faded paint, derelict boat motors
in weedy lots, and "tore-up" nets piled in heaps.[9]

Wilson preferred the natural surroundings that obliged the refuse.
As she remembers in her memoir, there were the "long-billed waders
and the red-winged blackbirds, and the finger mullet schools and blue
crabs gliding in the silt, and the flatfish and the flounders and the rays
moving ethereally across the muck." Shrimp boats peppering the bays
seemed to float on the presumed security of this ecological blessing.[10]

Wilson started going out to work with her father at age eight. She
bought her first boat when she was a tall, sun-darkened, and black-
haired twenty-four-year-old; her second, when she was twenty-eight.
It was a good boat with a tight keel that she named the *SeaBee*. Wilson
could navigate across a dark bay before dawn as easily as she could
walk through her house. She could drag nets behind her boat solo,
mend those that others gave up for ruin, and smell a storm coming off
the horizon. Along with running the *SeaBee*, she managed a shrimp
house (two things a woman wasn't supposed to do) while simultaneously raising five children (the thing a woman *was* supposed to do).

The bays around Calhoun County were big and billowy, in a near-constant state of windy agitation. Sunken fishing boats left a maritime imprint. Some rested half-submerged, specters of hardworking crafts with many stories. Most of the fishing took place on the bays, and every captain knew the risks of losing a boat. The choppy waters hid broken dock and marker pilings, abandoned gas wells, and recklessly discarded oil field equipment.

Wilson learned of another, greater peril when the EPA issued its first Toxics Release Inventory (TRI) report, for 1988, the year of *Time*'s "Our Filthy Seas" cover. Louisiana and Texas accounted for nearly a quarter of all reported chemical releases in the US. Half of the top thirty counties on the TRI had Gulf access, including Calhoun County. Not Pittsburgh, Youngstown, or Detroit, those big-fisted industrial cities, but Wilson's home, that bucolic paint-by-numbers fishing village, led the nation and all its 19,278 factories in land-based toxic emissions.

The poisons came from five backyard plants: Alcoa, Union Carbide, Formosa, DuPont, and British Petroleum Chemicals (a subsidiary of BP). BP casually discharged two carcinogens: acetamide and acryl-amide. Union Carbide puffed out butadiene, one of the most nox-ious air pollutants. Alcoa's bauxite plant, opened in 1948, dumped so much mercury-laced waste on an island in Lavaca Bay that the Texas health services closed part of the bay to fishing. Formosa planned a $1 billion expansion of its plastics operation, as well as an increase in its untreated-waste discharge, which included vinyl chloride, ethylene dichloride, and other chlorates.[11]

Calhoun County wasn't a lone Texan on the TRI. Four of the state's Gulf coast counties were in the top ten, seven in the top thirty, eight in the top thirty-one—joined by no inland Texas counties. Spindletop in 1901 not only sent America down the road to oil addiction; it turned the Texas Gulf coast into a leading manufacturer of petroleum-based products. A century later, nearly forty percent of the US petrochemical industry was "anchored in the wetlands," as Wilson put it, from Port Arthur to Corpus Christi, once a grand tarpon-fishing coast.

Everywhere, flare stacks at chemical plants burned like torches amid a shower of white lights, stabbing the night with a brilliant confusion of Hades and Christmas.

Whereas postwar home builders found open opportunities on Florida's Mangrove Coast, industrial America found a haven on Texas's salt-marsh coast. The eastern Gulf pursued a leisure economy; the western, an industrial one. As condominium towers rose on one side, distilling towers rose on the other. People inundated one coast; chemicals, the other coast. Florida's growth was intoxicating in a fantasy-world way; Texas's, toxic in a real-world way. Industry defenders said they were creating jobs and tax revenues. This was true. Equally true was what environmental defenders were saying: that which poisoned birds and fish would poison people.

Anyone traveling or living down in Texas would not have suspected that the Clean Water and Air acts were nearly twenty years old. The state's coast was the nation's leader in unauthorized toxic releases, chemical spills, ozone pollution, clean-water violations, and carbon dioxide emissions. Some sixteen million pounds of Texas industrial waste a year streamed down the Brazos River into the Gulf, and nearly seven million from the Houston Ship Channel and Galveston Bay.

The channel was first dug at the turn of the twentieth century between Houston and Galveston to convey cotton and cattle and other agricultural products. After Spindletop, it resolved into a maritime highway for the petrochemical industry, with a slurry of heavy metals, dioxin, and PCBs, to name a few—all headed for Galveston Bay. The overall saturation of carcinogens grew so dense that people took to calling Texas's curving coast the Cancer Belt. With morbid humor, Calhoun County residents said that if someone had liver or brain cancer, asbestosis, or a pulmonary disease, you could guess by the illness in which polluting plant that person worked. At one time you could see silver beads of Alcoa's mercury running into Lavaca Bay. If you miscarried, well, Wilson lumped the sum environmental and public-health offenses under the label "baby-aborting chemicals."[12]

Government officials claimed they cared, but seemed to do nothing about the pollution. If you walked into a factory and sabotaged the machinery or onto a farm and shot the livestock, you'd be called a terrorist and be arrested. Not those industrialists who sabotaged the estuaries that provided people a living. A letter to the local newspaper said, correctly, "Chemical plants can pollute and still remain within environmental laws."[13]

The EPA had bought into the industry philosophy of "dilution is the solution." Disperse the offending pollutant into the air and water in small-ratio doses and no one need worry. Worse, regulators routinely offered exceptions to "safe" discharge levels. Doubly worse, the industry regulated itself. The polluters measured and reported their own pollution—both allowable discharges and illegal ones. They invariably called the latter accidental, and many "accidents" stayed off the books entirely. When people were sleeping at night, factories secretly cranked up their emissions, and bulldozers buried drums of poison in secret earthen graves (common practices nationwide). Everyone knew these sorts of things went on.

After Formosa announced plans to enlarge its operations, Wilson demanded that regulatory agencies follow environmental and public health laws, and their own rules, before allowing the expansion. Public officials seemed no more eager to enforce regulations than the Taiwan/New Jersey–based plastics manufacturer was eager to comply with them. That's when Wilson turned into a self-identified "unreasonable woman."

AFTER ESCAMBIA BAY TURNED SNOWY with dead fish in 1969, Charles Lowery organized the Bream Fishermen Association (BFA). This was more than a sportsman's group; it was modeled on the Izaak Walton League, created to promote, as its mission statement reads, "the conservation responsibilities as well as the recreational enjoyment of fishermen, hunters, campers and related outdoorsmen." The BFA's original membership came from Lowery's fishing and beer-drinking companions. Hardworking, red-white-and-blue patriotic types, some with only a high school diploma and some called "doctor," they were, said Lowery, a "small bunch of rednecks."[14]

Lowery had been fishing around Pensacola all his life. He did a lot of it with his best friend since sixth grade, Gilbert McGhee, a Poarch Creek Indian. They lived in piney-woods country north of Pensacola, but the fishing was good enough on the Escambia River or one of the bays to lure them on long predawn drives.

J. D. Brown was a friend too, and a founding BFA member. He grew up on Bayou Grande, at the bottom of Pensacola Bay, below Escambia Bay. There had been a time when he'd pull four or five dozen blue crabs from traps on a single run, or walk the shore with a cast net and, after a few throws, have enough mullet for a big fish fry.

Another pivotal BFA member was Ernie Rivers, who was home-grown on the red bluffs peering over Escambia Bay. He would some-times look down on a hundred bottlenose dolphins chasing a run of mullet in tightened ranks a half mile long. He could also see fields of lush sea grass in dark shadows across the bay bottom. During the Great Depression, nobody starved, he remembered. "We had all the fish and oysters and shrimp that you could eat."[15]

Rivers joined the navy in 1943 and became a career officer and pilot. When he returned to Pensacola in 1964 for his last assignment before retiring, the sea grass was still there, although the beds had started to recede. The water in the bay wasn't as healthy as before, and it was killing the grass. The beds continued to recede, and then they were gone—ninety-five percent throughout Pensacola waters by 1980, the greatest loss of all Gulf bays. The shrimp disappeared as a consequence. The mullet left. And the dolphins no longer came. Nor did commer-cial fishers. A beleaguered class now, whose local history no longer carried clout, they either quit fishing or worked strictly offshore. Even before getting involved with the BFA, Rivers wanted to end the forced privation of the bays. An instructor in aerial photography at the naval air station, he would send his students up with instructions to fly over industrial and sewer plants and take pictures of their discharge.

While Rivers ran an aerial reconnaissance, J. D. Brown led the marine forces. He developed a monitoring system for BFA volunteers to take water samples in the bays and bayous. The two men were compiling a record of abuse. The BFA went to the state board of health and the EPA time and again, turning the screws with their evidence. At the federal level, Congress and the EPA established rigid national pollution reductions and compliance schedules. By the late 1970s, Pensacola-area industries had established holding systems for their effluence, where it awaited disposal through deep-well injection. In some cases, they reduced bay discharges by as much as ninety percent, as reported to the EPA by the industries. This brought welcome newspaper headlines: BAY RECOVERS. THE FISH ARE BITING AGAIN.[16]

This is not to say that the BFA was ready to close up shop and go fishing. Pensacola's sewage infrastructure was a pigsty. Providing nothing more than primary treatment, it did not remove biological content, including nitrogen and infectious bacteria. Leaks, accidents, and overflow discharges were common. This was pretty much a Gulf-wide norm. A map in the 1954 Gulf study conducted by the US Public Health Service uses building-shaped icons to show the placement of wastewater treatment plants in the region. They're all on bays and rivers. Black icons indicate plants dumping poorly treated waste, and from Corpus Christi to Naples, they are bunched up like flies on an outhouse.[17]

The study also mentions red tides, natural warm-water algal blooms that discolor the surface with a veneer of red, brown, or green. In that pivotal decade of the 1950s, scientists were noticing more of these noxious events in the Gulf. Red tides irritate people's eyes and lungs and leave heaps of dead sea life on the beach. Manatees are especially hard-hit. Cabeza de Vaca may have seen outbreaks in Texas, and Diego Lopez de Collogudo, a Franciscan monk, chronicled what was likely a red tide striking Yucatán in 1648: a "foul odor" and "mountain of dead fish." Experts regard an 1844 event on the Florida panhandle, near where Leonard Destin fished, as the first documented red tide, although no one knew what it was. "Poison water," people called the events. A 1935 outbreak off South Padre Island that killed two-inch mullet, eight-foot tarpon, and everything in between left researchers flummoxed.[18]

Then, after a 1947 red tide devastated most of the sponge beds, from which Tarpon Springs never fully recovered, microscope-peering scientists determined that the malicious rafts of algae discharge a toxin that paralyzes the respiratory system of marine life. But they didn't know how or why, or from where exactly the red tides originate. To control red tides, scientists tried dousing a few with copper sulfate. This only killed more fish. In the 1980s and '90s, off the south Florida and south Texas coasts, red tides bloomed in higher numbers.

As it happened, ranchers in Texas were raising more cattle than ever, and slaughterhouse capacity doubled. In Florida, the exploding residential population ignited a chain reaction in lawn fertilizer use, facilitated by ambrosial garden centers at big-box stores like Home Depot, Lowe's, and Wal-Mart and monthly lawn treatment service provided by companies like TruGreen and Scotts. Some scientists were connecting the intensity of red tides to green grass, purgative cows, and gushing sewer pipes, vexing some of their colleagues, who claimed that evidence didn't exist to confirm the connections. The press reported algal blooms as one of nature's cruel mysteries, and sometimes falsely identified pollution-induced fish kills as red tide, incriminating nature instead of the actual offender.

Red tides rolled into Pensacola on occasion, usually mucking up the Gulf beaches and tourist season. It was flush toilets that chronically plagued the bays. Ernie Rivers was constantly on the phone to the city manager, Frank Faison: "Frank, you're dumping shit into my bay again." Rivers had pictures. "You're gonna have to get the hell out." But Faison never did. He said the city couldn't afford a new system. So it made patches and repairs, installing new pipes to send the same old shit someplace different. Up to twenty million gallons of effluent a day went into the water.[19]

What perplexed Pensacolans as much as anything was the location of the main treatment plant at the edge of downtown, rising in clear view on a bayside point, an amphitheater of excrement. Retail shoppers risked a good whiff coming off the right wind. Locals dreaded storms as much for the wind and flood damage as for the sewage overflowing into streets. The nadir occurred in 2004, when Hurricane Ivan left human feces in cars and buildings. Defiling the bays was one thing; people's homes, quite another. They demanded a fix; enough was enough.

Aided by a FEMA grant, the utilities authority subsequently built a $316 million, zero discharge plant fifteen miles north of the old one. It recycled fully treated water to the local International Paper plant and Gulf Power, which used it for cooling and water-intensive scrubbers. The treatment facility won national and international sustainability awards. Instead of generating embarrassing news headlines about streets of sewer and wafting stench, Pensacola had taken a prideful leap over most other municipalities to a cleaner future.

Still, in other ways it continued to stumble, badly. Lost in the glare of glowing headlines were seven industry-derived Superfund sites. Among Gulf Coast counties, only Houston's Harris County had more (sixteen). One of Pensacola's was American Creosote Works, which poisoned the ground and water for eighty years before shutting down in 1981. Mobile had a polluting creosote plant too. So did Bogalusa on the Mississippi, and Beaumont and Houston each had one. Those wooden street blocks in Galveston that floated away in the 1900 hurricane had been creosoted at a local plant. Walter Anderson rowed his skiff in Mississippi Sound through contaminants from a nearby facility, which treated wood for the Panama Canal. Railroads owned many of the plants to make creosoted ties for their tracks. The region's pine forests supplied the raw material for not only ties but power poles, and dock and early oil-rig pilings, all treated with chemical preservatives.

Runoff from American Creosote oozed into Bayou Chico and Pensacola Bay. J. D. Brown remembered that some of those mullet he netted for fish fries tasted like dock pilings smelled. Bayou Chico was a dumbfounding irony. Unswimmable and undrinkable, hosting a broken-down wastewater lift station and the creosote plant, it was a favorite place to dock boats because barnacles couldn't live in the oxygen-starved water.

BFA members thought Escambia Bay should be on the Superfund list too. On several occasions, they tried to restore sea grass beds, spending thousands of private and public dollars, but the grass always died after a few months. The blame fell on a ribbon of residual PCBs, banned by the EPA in 1979, that laced the bay bottom. The party likely responsible was Monsanto, the company that clean-bay supporters loved to hate, and for good reasons. It had a lousy environmental track record worldwide, and as an occupant of Escambia River it was a known PCB discharger.[20]

No one knew this better than Pensacola-raised Linda Young. When she was in grade school, her mother got a phone call one day that put her in tears. Linda thought someone had died. But it was news about the big fish kill in 1969. In weeks and years ahead, the phone kept ringing with reports of the continuing apocalypse. And it did seem as if the world was coming to an end. That's how central the bay was in people's lives. Young remembered them wondering, "What's going to happen to us?" What, in other words, was Monsanto doing to them?

Thirty years later and an activist, Young was at the wheel of a van outside the plant. With her were a friend and their four kids, not entirely voluntarily. Young got behind a delivery truck and slipped through a menacing-looking gate decorated with no-trespassing and hazardous-material signs. She'd heard about an open cesspool of chemicals venting into the air, and likely finding their way into the bay. She climbed a berm and looked out over a seventeen-acre lake of lung-searing waste. She snapped photos, escaped the compound, and subsequently published the evidence in her environmental newspaper, *Pro Earth News*. More bad publicity for the trustees of Pensacola's public and environmental health. Its hand forced, Monsanto built a storage tank, and drained and bulldozed over its cesspool.

The bay might have looked pretty again, but what good was that if PCBs kept sea grass from growing back? Hypoxia remained a persistent issue, and scientific studies showed high concentrations of PCBs in fish and crabs. The health department posted no-fishing signs. But the signs weren't going to prevent fish from feeding on the contaminated bottom, poison seeping into their tissue, and then swimming off and being caught in other waters. Since the EPA and Florida Department of Environmental Protection weren't doing their jobs adequately, Young, now director of the Florida Clean Water Network, a nonprofit environmental and public health group, began ringing doorbells of bayside residences. She rounded up fifty plaintiffs and secured legal representation, and in 2008 they filed suit against Monsanto and successor companies at its site, requesting a cleanup of the residual PCBs.

Fourteen years earlier, residents had filed a similar suit on behalf of Perdido Bay, Pensacola's lone west-side bay, and a troubled one. It collects the flow of the Perdido River and Elevenmile Creek, and that's where the trouble was, up the creek at the discharge pipe of a paper mill. Papermaking was another industry people loved for its payroll and loathed for its pollution—the latter brought to mind with downwind drifts that smelled like rotten eggs. After chemists figured out how sulfuric acid could reduce resinous wood from southern pines into usable pulp for brown paper, a Pensacola firm, in 1903, made the first attempt to manufacture the product. It failed. But a few years later, a Texas plant, on the Sabine River, succeeded.

Mills popped up like mushrooms across the pine-rich northern Gulf, giving a regional toehold to one of the most poisonous industries in the world. Along with the sulfuric stench that carries for miles through the air, pulp wastewater has a low biodegradability that inhibits purification. Things did not augur well for the environment when chemists perfected a bleaching process to turn the brown paper white using chlorinates, which produce the by-product dioxin, a pernicious carcinogen that the EPA inexplicably failed to include on the TRI before 2000. In 1931, International Paper Company built the country's first mill employing the new process in Panama City.

The plant on Elevenmile Creek opened in 1941. The impact was immediate. The creek and bay turned reddish brown. Bathers in the upper bay came out of the water covered in pulp fibers, which gave them rashes. Fish, mollusks, and sea grass perished. Foam accumulated at water's edge. In the 1960s the state board of health ran tests and concluded, "Eleven Mile Creek is grossly polluted chemically and biologically, by the discharge waste from the St. Regis Paper Company operation." Yet the state did nothing. Then, Alabama, which borders the bay's west bank, complained, prompting a federal study, which inferred the same as the tests run by the state board of health. Still, St. Regis kept relaying waste down Elevenmile Creek.[21]

The more bayside resident Jackie Lane turned this reality over in her mind, the more it disturbed her. Lane moved to Pensacola with her husband, Jim, in the early 1980s. He was returning home, to where Perdido Bay had given him an idyllic childhood. He and Jackie built a house in the upper quadrant of its eastern shore to create a similar experience for their children. Though she thought the bay beautiful, Lane suspected something wasn't quite right. She'd know; she had an advanced degree in marine biology.

She started studying the clams in the bay, and then most of them died. That was in 1986. The next year, the current owner of the paper mill, Champion, applied to renew its permit to discharge effluent that failed to meet state standards. Lane and another bayside resident, Jo Anne Allen, founded a grassroots organization to demand a state administrative hearing. Ultimately, officials allowed Champion to delay compliance until 1994. The designated year came and went with little improvement as the company applied to renew its discharge permit. Lane and her group spearheaded a class action lawsuit representing bayside residents who could claim standing and harm. Champion ultimately paid the plaintiffs $5 million, yet admitted no wrongdoing, since it was operating legally under the state's permit. Lane and other class members used a portion of the award to start the Perdido Bay Foundation, while the paper mill continued to pollute the water and sky.[22]

———

LANE AND YOUNG SWAPPED war stories with another clean-water comrade, Joy Towles Ezell, who lived in Taylor County in the upper part of the peninsula. Dixie never died in Taylor County (the local Klan picketed a kosher deli in the 1980s). This was gritty, rural country, sparsely occupied by fewer than twenty thousand people, with a history of racial violence and convict labor exploited by logging and turpentine camps. It was twice timber country—the first time until thousand-year-old cypress trees had been harvested out by the early twentieth century for use in building construction, and the second time when a new generation of cypress matured in the 1980s and went into plastic bags as landscaping mulch, dyed red or black. That was also when some of the locals, including a deputy sheriff, smuggled drugs in through the largely undeveloped Big Bend coast—and got themselves arrested. For a man or woman with a high school education, if that, an honest day's work was hard to come by. If you were lucky, you had a job at Buckeye Cellulose, which at times employed nearly one-tenth of the county population.

Owned by Ohio-based Procter & Gamble, Buckeye had been operating since 1954. P&G built the plant even after the US Geological Survey warned that Taylor County's soft, permeable, sinkhole-prone ground was woefully unsuitable for an industrial site—that the aquifer would end up contaminated (that did happen); and that effluent settlement ponds would collapse (that happened too). And there was the Fen, the Fenholloway River, which wound through the county to the Gulf. Florida officials declared it an industrial waterway in the 1940s and, dangling that soon-to-be-tarnished jewel, invited P&G to come to the Sunshine State and pollute at will.

The state, in other words, took a favorite fishing and swimming hole away from the people and gave it to the manufacturer known for its household cleaners, which turned out to make messes it didn't clean up. Buckeye rendered pulp into cellulose for use in sanitary napkins, cigarette filters, and Pampers disposable diapers; as a filler in ice cream and other foods; and for sausage casings, the low-end variety. It poisoned its handout river to the point that little could live in it or an oxygen-depleted area off its mouth, a ten-or-more-square-mile permanent fixture. Ezell said Buckeye rewrote H_2O on the periodic table to represent "two parts Horrible and one part Odor."[23]

She got her first taste of horrible at her grandparents' house in 1981. Standing at the kitchen tap, her grandmother shrieked, "This water's got Buckeye in it!" Their drinking well was twenty miles from the plant, and it turned out that private wells all over the county smelled like cellulose effluent. Within five years, Ezell had gone active. A smart and tireless champion of good public health, who knew a thing or two about chemicals for having worked in the business, she hounded the plant in public meetings and demonstrations and in the press. She even went up to Ohio, knocked on the front door of the home of P&G's CEO, and chatted with his wife, who offered a sympathetic ear, about raising children in a poisoned world. The Buckeye-friendly local newspaper called Ezell a "radical environmental terrorist." People threatened her life because they said she threatened their jobs.[24]

But her husband worked at the plant, twenty-six years, and few people had roots that went as deep in Taylor County's sandy soil as she had—five generations, to the nineteenth century. Like Diane Wilson, Ezell had the people's interest in mind. Everybody was affected when you couldn't drink from your well and had to use bottled water. (Eventually, the county piped in treated water.)

The EPA regarded the Fenholloway as the most polluted place in Florida, in part because people were eating dioxin-contaminated fish that they caught at the river's end. After Ezell and others, including Linda Young, got the state to redesignate the Fen a recreational river in 1997, Buckeye, under new ownership, claimed it was investing some $30 million to clean up its discharge. But it wouldn't stop bleaching its product (mothers wanted white diapers, it insisted).

Ezell would take anyone interested to the river above the plant and have them fill a bottle with water as clear as a mountain brook, and then take them below the plant and fill another with water the color of brandy. The darkness wasn't tannins from tree bark, and one didn't dare drink it. She would drive them the length of the river and show them the chemical stream where only fish that gulp air survived. Some had mysteriously changed sex. "Bearded Ladyfish," biologists called them upon their discovery in the 1970s. The air over this classic meandering, tree-shaded waterway, which by all rights should have been a scenic river, hung pungent for twenty-five miles to the Gulf. Buckeye's final proposed remedy was to run a pipeline directly into the Gulf. In 2005, the Sierra Club sued to bar the company from simply pumping its privately owned waste, which failed federal standards, straight out to the original destination. Dilution was not the proper solution.[25]

Five years later, the *Deepwater Horizon* blowout was spilling 2.6 million gallons of oil into the Gulf a day, for eighty-seven nightmarish days. Buckeye was spilling discharge greater than that, and had done so for over five decades. And it continued after the BP oil stopped, in a nightmare without end.

DESPITE THE SUCCESSFUL LAWSUIT, Jackie Lane continued to know such a nightmare on Perdido Bay. In 2000, International Paper, which everyone called IP, acquired Champion's Pensacola facility. It increased production and went to a hundred-percent-white product. The company burnished its reputation slightly when it piped in the new wastewater treatment plant's reclaimed water to control dust and to soak its mountain-sized piles of logs to prevent fire. But this did nothing to stem the chemical discard. Lane's group initiated tests and found that the bay's few remaining clams harbored dioxins and arsenic at levels unsafe for consumption.

A new DEP discharge permit in 2010 required IP to develop an "experimental" wetland treatment system, which it did, with a $60 million bond, on some fourteen hundred acres that it called its effluent distribution site. IP planted 180,000 trees, maintained a bird count, and developed a promotional video of the site, through which it directed two-thirds of its discharge. The wetland provided IP with more than favorable PR. Although treated, the mill's release was still high in nitrogen and phosphorus. When the upper bay turned brown and foamy, and starved for oxygen, IP could argue that bad water from the wetland was not technically point-source pollution and that the system was officially designated experimental. After the bay indeed turned foul in spring 2015, IP tried to finger increased discharge from a local wastewater treatment plant as the new delinquent on the block.[26]

The bays were prized assets, the natural feature that had given Pensacola its original reason to exist. Lane longed for Perdido's lost oyster, clam, and sea grass beds, just as Lowery, Brown, and Rivers, now in their twilight years, and Young longed for grass to grow in Escambia Bay.

SEA GRASS WAS DYING in Lavaca Bay too. And in the early 1990s, so were bottlenose dolphins. Enough of them for wildlife biologists to launch an investigation. Enough of them to reinforce Diane Wilson's unreasonable womanhood. These were three-hundred-pound, top-of-the-food-chain animals that one might expect would absorb contamination more easily than smaller life-forms. Wilson heard one investigator say, "They're eating what we're eating."[27]

She had already contacted a lawyer she knew up the road in Houston about the Formosa expansion. Jim Blackburn was a native of Louisiana who grew up in the Rio Grande Valley. He and Wilson were spiritual siblings. Having a developed sense of place, each had adopted Texas's grassy bays as their higher power. In the 1970s, Blackburn decided to become an environmental lawyer when the species hardly existed. Bushy-haired and mustached, he devoted a workaholic's temperament to litigating polluter permits, wetland destruction, and Army Corps of Engineers fiascos, such as tossing dredged spoil any convenient place.

That issue came up in a campaign of the newly formed Galveston Bay Foundation against the widening and deepening of the Houston Ship Channel, which ran into Galveston Bay. The bay had suffered hundreds of oil spills since the 1918 Sweet No. 16 gusher, and its watershed received more than half of the entire state's wastewater discharge. The opposing sides came to a fairly good compromise for the bay. There had been and would be plenty of defeats. Blackburn was philosophical about them, saying that those who profited from destroying nature were put on notice that vigorous opposition awaited their freewheeling ways.

More and more people were willing to fight for the environmental cause. Quite a few were women, philosophical descendants of early club women and Auduboners who strove to keep the world better for all. There was Wilma Subra, an environmental chemist who would win a MacArthur "Genius Grant" for taking the petrochemical industry to task along the lower Mississippi. Closer to Blackburn was Terry Hershey, who became a major force in the 1960s while working to prevent Harris County from turning Buffalo Bayou into a flood control and sewage ditch. A *Houston Post* headline once read, BAYOU WATER . . . "JUST SEWER WATER". Hershey took inspiration from Anella Dexter and Sarah Emmott, who in the 1950s, by invoking precedence in an 1815 royal order by the king of Spain, induced the state legislature to pass open-beaches legislation, which prevented petrochemical companies from buying up the shoreline and denying public access.[28]

Formosa was one of the freewheelers. The company had an environmental record that even its business-friendly home government in Taiwan loathed. But Texas regulators seemed oblivious. They put up no walls when Formosa began construction of its expansion before receiving discharge permits. Workers planted ornamental shrubbery and military-straight saplings around a new plant entrance intended to give Formosa a good-neighbor, eco-friendly appearance. Wilson saw right through the façade to the polluter it decorated.

What irked her as much as anything was the EPA. The agency was wavering on requiring an environmental impact statement (EIS) for the expansion. So, Wilson and Blackburn filed a request for one. Wilson organized the Calhoun County Resource Watch and did her best to sign up members. She and her closest friend, Donna Sue Williams, were about the only active ones. Environmentalists were persona non grata among working people—by some accounts no better, if not worse, than a common criminal, a communist (for those who still feared Reds), or an Islamic terrorist, and as unwelcome in the neighborhood as a sex offender. Tulane University Law School professor Oliver Houck once heard a woman take the microphone at a public meeting in Terrebonne Parish and proclaim, "When God made environmentalists he should have had an abortion!" She raised the roof.[29]

The Calhoun County board of commissioners and chamber of commerce painted Wilson as an antiprogress and antiwork agitator. There were three explosions at the Seadrift Union Carbide plant in March 1991, after the self-regulating Texas Chemical Council named it the safest facility in the state, and still it was better to be a polluter than an environmentalist. Sure, the polluters destroyed some livelihoods, like fishing, but brother or uncle could dock his boat and go to work in the factory. People knew that the polluters weren't good for their health, but they hoped cancer wouldn't get them, and if it did, maybe it was just their lifestyle, like the industry lawyers said—their smoking and drinking and waistline.[30]

The fishers weren't crawling all over themselves to join Wilson's group either. Their plight was already bad, and they didn't need people accusing them of being job busters. They were always the scapegoats when fish populations plummeted. There was a worldwide crisis, and the press and politicians, even the UN, stuck to the default explanation: overfishing. Scientists said the fishers' bycatch was a principal factor in the crisis. At one point in the 1970s, Gulf shrimpers were discarding and destroying ten pounds of marine life for every pound of shrimp brought on board—up to a billion pounds of senseless killing a year. Beginning in 1987, the federal government made shrimpers use turtle excluder devices, essentially escape hatches, because environmentalists claimed they were murdering dolphins and turtles that became tangled in their nets, some of which were big enough, said *Time* magazine, to "swallow a dozen Boeing 747s."[31]

Market fishers got flak from recreational anglers too. The commercial guys were emptying the oceans and ruining their sport, the anglers were saying. Look what they've done to the red snapper, starting way back (in Silas Stearns's time). Now they were doing it to redfish. Some experts said it was Paul Prudhomme's fault. The New Orleans celebrity chef started a blackened-redfish craze in the 1980s, and the commercial fishers found themselves swimming in new riches. They couldn't catch enough redfish quickly enough. Some even hired spotter planes. The redfish catch shot up from fifty-four thousand pounds in 1980 to 5.4 million pounds five years later.

The problem was that the redfish was a favorite of the anglers. They sped across the water in powerful boats sporting twin outboards, the latest fish-finding electronics, and three or four rods to set for every angler on board. The duplication, horsepower, and high-tech sophistication were necessary. Fishing fortunes weren't what they had been in Christine Hawley's and Florence Harding's day, and trophy fish were growing smaller. Anglers came up with a solution to the problem. In Texas, they put their collective mind and considerable resources to banning commercial net fishing. It wasn't so much about saving fish as about who got the fish.

The commercial contingent didn't stand a chance. By the nature of their trade, market fishers were solitary and independent types, and they couldn't unite and organize to save their souls. Those who took a lead on the issue lamented that getting their people to come together was like herding cats. The Texas assemblage couldn't raise the money for TV advertisements and lobbying that came so easy to the better-organized sportfishing multitudes, who had the advantage of wealth and middle- and upper-class networking. A recreational fishing license was tucked in the wallet of an uncomfortable number of state legislators of the same social class. Nobody had ever heard of a commercial fisher holding elective office outside the occasional city council post.

So, the anglers won. Texas banned commercial net fishing in 1988, declaring redfish the exclusive trophy of recreation. In 1994, Florida voters, many thinking they were doing right by the environment (not by sportfishing), approved a constitutional ban on gill-net fishing with a seventy-two percent majority. Louisiana outlawed gill nets the next year, and Alabama put a rigid cap on net-fishing licenses. It was like taking hammers away from carpenters. Commercial fishers couldn't use the basic tool of the trade, and generations-deep fishing heritages came to an abrupt, inglorious end. There was one bit of poetic justice for the ex-netters, though: with Gulf waters hosting record sportfishing trips, twenty-two million in 2011, and with critics complaining that powerboats were crowding bays and rivers and dropping too many hooks in the water, anglers took the heat alone for any new fish declines.

In the meantime, the defeated fishers turned their nets over to the state for a few compensation dollars, and they sold their boats, let them rust and rot, or ceremoniously sunk them. Too old to bother with a job-training program, some submitted to taking an unemployment check. A lot of them had to sell their houses because the victors, enjoying their fishing monopoly, were driving up property taxes with another predatory lust—that for waterfront property where they could moor their sleek fishing machines. Some former net fishers managed by going into aquaculture. Some went to work for a polluter.

The polluters fixed themselves outside the cross fire of the fishing wars. Anglers knew it would be easier to get rid of the net fishers than the polluters, to whom many had ties. Looking for their own scapegoats, commercial fishers misdirected their anger at fisheries experts, whom they said didn't know how to count—there were more fish out there than the pointy-heads with their degrees knew.

The commercial-fishing lobby might have been more effective if it had cited studies that said ninety-five percent of commercial Gulf fish depended on healthy estuaries and that pollution penetrated virtually every Gulf estuary. That no other US fishery had as many sources of nutrient overload as the Gulf. That low dissolved-oxygen levels were a problem in a quarter of Texas's estuaries and a quarter of Louisiana's. That bad water had forced the closure of thirty-five percent of

Louisiana's oyster beds. That in the past two hundred years, the Gulf, which was home to ninety percent of US coastal wetlands, had lost about half of its wetlands. That seventy percent of grass beds had succumbed in Mobile Bay, eighty-five percent in Tampa Bay, ninety percent in Galveston Bay, and ninety-five percent in Pensacola bays. Or they could have just pointed to the poisonous algae that scientists had tracked drifting out of the Gulf of Mexico on the Gulf Stream and up to North Carolina.[32]

Even before the net-fishing ban in Texas, Wilson understood the clutch that commercial fishers were in. When she argued that the polluters were destroying the habitat that supported the fish and the fishers, county officials and a local judge blamed overfishing. Wilson watched wildlife agents aggressively enforce the Endangered Species Act against illegal fishers but not illegal polluters. Where was the justice of throwing a hardworking man in jail for using his net while Formosa executives were free to kill animals with their poison? It wasn't that overfishing wasn't a reality. But when industry was destroying marine habitat, the fish were fewer, and nets swallowed a larger portion of the diminishing population.

After the EPA disclosed that it was considering exempting the Formosa expansion from an EIS requirement, Wilson in the spring of 1990 starved herself Gandhi-style in protest. "I hated the hunger strike," Blackburn recalled. But as she wasted away, Formosa surprised them. To get her eating again, the company agreed to allow union organization, comply with clean-water regulations, and submit to independent analysis of its plant conditions and its waste discharge. All along, Wilson had been supporting the workers and the environment, showing that the two weren't separate. Maybe that was a bit too much for Formosa, because almost as soon as she bit into a hamburger, ending her thirty-day protest, the company reneged.

When the EPA subsequently agreed to require an EIS, Wilson thought its actions came too late. Construction was well on its way, and everyone knew the EPA wouldn't deny a permit at this point, and it certainly wasn't going to demand that Formosa dismantle its seductively landscaped addition. Texas officials weren't either. The state air control board didn't blink before issuing a permit, even though Wilson and Blackburn showed that the company was in constant violation of state regulations.[33]

Wilson had to step back and assess the latest luckless developments. That's when she learned about zero discharge technology, which involves ultrafiltration, reverse osmosis, and electrodeionization. Deploying this inscrutable technology, the process eliminates liquid discharge and reduces the use of clean water, meaning it had the potential of protecting a bay or sound from flowing pollutants. She also learned that no one on the Gulf had adopted it. When she went public with the idea, Formosa held town meetings to say that zero discharge technology was a hoax.

Wilson's next move was to organize a protest march, for which she had to draw on local Vietnamese crabbers, war refugees who, viewed as intruders from foreign soil, were once hated as much as environmentalists. The march of two hundred peaceful demonstrators turned out to be a prelude to a wild new plan: she would sink the *SeaBee* at the Formosa discharge, a thirty-inch steel pipe with the company name stenciled in green, belching effluent, as she wrote, "into a watery cradle meant for shrimp and fish and crabs." After she had off-loaded everything from her boat, including the engine, her brother towed her out to the designated site with his, only to have the Coast Guard descend on them with sirens, flashing lights, bullhorns, and the threat of eighteen-year prison sentences and $500,000 fines. Wilson didn't miss the irony in the "militia" being sent out to stop her from stopping the industry that was killing people with chemicals.[34]

She never got to sink the *SeaBee*—not at the polluting pipe. But later, ceremoniously, the boat was submerged in another spot to become a reef. By then, Formosa had had enough of the bad publicity and, in 1994, signed what Blackburn calls the "Wilson-Formosa Zero Discharge Agreement." The company initially reduced its liquid waste by more than thirty percent; this wasn't exactly zero discharge, but it more or less offset the expansion, and the plastics manufacturer continued to reduce its watery footprint. After settling with Formosa, Wilson promptly marched over to Union Carbide, DuPont, and Alcoa, demanding similar agreements, and convinced the county commission and Seadrift city council to adopt resolutions for zero discharge. She called it the "only common-sense approach that can stop destruction of our bays."[35]

A CLEANUP OF LAVACA BAY proceeded in the new century with some $110 million of Alcoa money. The EPA had declared Alcoa's mercury-contaminated area of the bay a Superfund site in 1994—a pronouncement far too delayed for Wilson's comfort. As part of its settlement, Alcoa recovered twenty-three hundred pounds of mercury from the bay bottom. It constructed a seventy-acre marsh next to the Aransas National Wildlife Refuge (a major waterfowl area) and donated slightly more than a square mile of land to the refuge. The company also developed an eleven-acre oyster bed and built a public-access fishing pier. State officials reopened part of the bay previously off-limits to recreation. People were fishing again. Alcoa had demonstrated a spirit of cooperation, which it talked up in the media, setting itself apart from other historic polluters.

Lavaca's restoration was a great success story, aside from a couple qualifying factors. Wilson pointed out that the settlement included no provision for assessing the physical health of bay residents. Blackburn opposed simply moving the contaminated bay sediment to a location no farther away than a containment facility on a bay island. Lavaca was a public asset, yet it remained Alcoa's "own disposal site," he argued, and he questioned whether the containment facility would withstand a major hurricane. He had a point, given that storms eliminated islands with regularity. An Alcoa spokesman offered assurances: "We live" here too. "If there is a problem, we can't walk away from it."[36]

And there could be a problem. Hurricane Katrina was coming later that year, 2005. Although Katrina lashed out at Louisiana instead, it exposed the heightened vulnerability of a built-up, industrialized coast. It took islands away too, and people began talking more about the emerging threat of sea-level rise. No shoreline and islands were more at risk than the Gulf's.

Sixteen

RIVERS OF STUFF

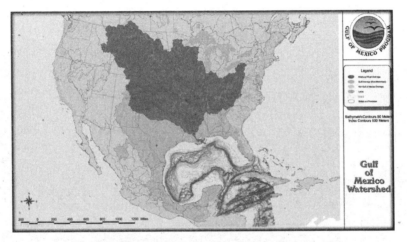

Thirty-one US states and two Canadian provinces are part
of the Mississippi River watershed, which drains
contaminated runoff into the Gulf.

*There once were men capable of inhabiting a river without
disrupting the harmony of its life.*

—ALDO LEOPOLD (1940)[1]

RIVERS NEVER SLEEP. THEY ARE PERPETUAL STRIVERS.
Some 116 insomnious rivers reach for the Gulf of Mexico, driving
megatons of freshwater toward saltwater every second. Some pursue
their endeavor for thousands of miles, some for only a few, and many

have not rested for millions of years. Removed from conventional structures of time, revealing no accord with duration or succession, they consort with infinity.

In *Siddhartha*, Hermann Hesse's classic story of humility and self-discovery, the wise ferryman Vasudeva explains, "The river is everywhere at once, at the source and at the mouth, at the waterfall, at the ferry, at the rapids, in the sea, in the mountains, everywhere at once." There "is only the present time for it, not the shadow of the past, not the shadow of the future."[2]

In their timeless way, rivers are geography's most persistent architects. The eighty-four that drop down to the Gulf from the US collect runoff from sixty percent of the lower forty-eight states and part of Canada. If not for them, North America would be mush. They cut canyons and gorges, and make green valleys and wetlands. Their waters shimmer blue, green, tan, brown, gray, even midnight—sometimes multiple colors, depending on sunlight, shade, bottom cover, and reflection.

On maps, they always appear blue, as stark, inked lines often in service to society's divided ground. The boldest line is the Mississippi, separating continental East from West. In history, that sinuous blue ink represents the epic ford of national expansion; in fable, the storied water of Mark Twain and Huck Finn. Map-drawn rivers also appear as formal borders between federated and nation-states. On the Gulf, there is the Perdido River separating Alabama and Florida, the Mississippi and Pearl Rivers demarcating Louisiana and Mississippi, and the Sabine partitioning Texas from Louisiana. The Rio Grande famously divides Mexico and the US.

Convenient borders but not always ideal, rivers have been the catalyst of many territorial disputes. They are restless wanderers disposed to changing course, taking land away from one territory and adding it to another, but more important, reminding us of their independent nature.

This tenacious spirit is the sort we humans admire in ourselves. Rivers give us metaphors that signal our own strivings. We emulate their freedom, power, and self-assurance, and seek their persistence. We put their song to music, their streaming patter into verse, and their movement and color on canvas. We wash away sins in their baptismal waters. All the same, when we make spiritual and creative connections, we come to rivers from a human point of view. Rarely does the preacher or poet plunge in to see what the river is apart from ourselves, to see the stream of life within it.

There is much to regard from the river's perspective. Sweep a specimen-collecting net through floating leaf fall or beside a snag at the water's edge and you'll come up with a sampling of biodiversity that no ecosystem on Earth exceeds. A river is an ever-moving communal link between habitats and inhabitants upstream, downstream, and across stream, and with the perennial visitors to its basin. Along Texas's Brazos River, a link between waterway and flyway, you can hear, if you know your list, the songs of more than a hundred bird species. You might also encounter thirty-seven kinds of snakes, seven of them venomous.

Older rivers, a million or so years of age, tend to saunter across gentle gradients. Younger ones, thousands of years young, often beat along as wild, white water on descending terrain not yet worn to flatness. Ignoring its age, the ten-million-year-old Rio Grande, in parts, struts like a frothy youth down through limestone rift valleys before retiring to level mesquite and yucca country, and relaxing around curving oxbows to the Gulf.

Most Gulf rivers are narrow and move over sandy rather than pebbly bottoms, leaving few stones to skip across the surface. Narrow rivers push little sediment, and their water tastes sweet and freshens the ambient air with fullness and purity. Some rivers rise from springs jetting out from the ancient Floridan aquifer, and some disappear underground along part of their flow. Their water is often invisibly clear, unless the river wanders between banks of rampant plant life where rotting leavings darken the flow with tannins. The Suwannee River, with its broad-leafed canopy, gets its name from an indigenous Timucuan word that means "crooked black water." Others similar to it are called black-water rivers, and around the Gulf people liken their transparent tint to ice tea.

Where sunlight touches the bottom, a broad path of aquatic plants—strap-leaf sagittaria grass and tape grass in particular—often shadows the river's course. The leaves, or blades, arc with the current for a foot or more (tape grass, several feet), and both bloom long-stemmed, white, floating flowers that collect waterborne pollen in dimpled petals.

Grassy bottoms are rich in dissolved oxygen. For aquatic animals, they are what fresh mountain air is for us land creatures. The dragonflies, damselflies, and mayflies that zip along the surface begin life as darting larvae beneath it. As nymphs, they forage and hide in the grass, and they breathe. Through adaptation, they have developed flattened heads to resist the twisting current. Among underwater riverine crowds, fluted bodies are common, and some species have developed anatomical hooks, suckers, and sticky undersides to anchor themselves.

The flathead catfish, which exhibits the same evolutionary resourcefulness that characterizes the nymphs on which it feeds, navigates the river bottom and finds food using whisker-like sensory organs (barbels) on its chin. Another fish, the sturgeon, wears similar bristles between a toothless mouth and a pronounced ski-slope snout, or rostrum, which leads a body that suggests the etymology of the word "streamlined." In this dynamic community of under- and above-water interrelations, the two whiskered fish have expansive palates open to mussels, crawfish, juvenile fish, and insects; and they themselves fall prey to alligators, turtles, water snakes, birds, and bigger fish. If we think of the river in terms of a story, as did Hermann Hesse, the food chain is its plot and narrative arc. Here are characters, syntax, synergy, and succession—yet timelessness.

For its setting, the catfish prefers silty water, which is more common among wide rivers. Their muscular currents swell with sediment that, when a river is in flood, nourishes bottomlands beside their channel like no factory-made fertilizer can. People say the alluvial soil in the seventy-one-hundred-square-mile Mississippi delta between Memphis and Vicksburg—not the one at the river's end—is the richest west of the Nile. Down on the sea, the silty transport creates barrier islands, beaches, and vacation pleasures.

At the end of clear and muddy rivers alike is the Gulf's ring of ecological wholesomeness: estuaries. Their bustle is a celebration of the nutrients and oxygen carried in the cumulative freshwater deluge, 280 trillion gallons a year. Without these infiltrating rivers, one of the world's great estuarine systems would not exist. Eighty-five percent of the river water coming to the Gulf spills out of the US. That's why estuaries concentrate in the Gulf's upper region. That's why, aside from everything else, the Gulf is an American sea.

Never-sleeping rivers and their estuaries have sustained humans on the Gulf for as long as they've been around it. People lived beside rivers for thousands of years without disturbing their peace, and then modern society changed that. We've insisted on more from rivers than natural sustainable offerings—we take their water in excess and use them to carry away our waste—and while we admire their strength, we don't always tolerate it. If rivers are imperious by nature, we are more so. Acting from the river-like qualities we believe ourselves to possess, we sin in baptismal waters. We are fugitives of Vasudeva's wisdom: we cast the shadows of our past and our future over rivers, and upon ourselves.

TIME's 1988 "FILTHY SEAS" cover story noted what it called dead zones. There were a few in nearshore waters around the US, all modest in size compared with one, which was three hundred miles long and ten wide and "adrift in the Gulf of Mexico." Over the next few years, this lifeless region, fronting the coast of Louisiana, reaching to eastern Texas in one direction and to Alabama in the other, would grow to the size of New Jersey. It lingered as more or less a giant underwater vacuum chamber sucked clean of dissolved oxygen.[3]

While the descriptive phrase "dead zone" suited the media, scientists preferred the technical term "hypoxic" to define the water's depleted state. To the naked eye, the water looked clear and whole-some. But fish could no more breathe in it than could Jacques Cousteau without his patented Aqua-Lung. Commercial fishers had to motor out past it to get their catch. "Drop a line in the water," said a charter captain, "and your bait rots." All manner of sea life that didn't get out when conditions turned stale met the same suffocating fate. The bottom was littered with the dead—a tragic wasteland of crab, mollusk, and sea worm remains. It was an eerie oceanic version of nuclear fallout. The toxic plume at the center of it blasted from the Mississippi River.[4]

The experts didn't know that at first. A young scientist named R. Eugene Turner puzzled it out after first putting the pieces together back in 1974. A trim, clean-shaven, newly minted PhD and recent addition to the marine sciences department at Louisiana State University, Turner was "poking around" at the time, getting to know Louisiana's coast. Another scientist told him that the water sometimes registered very little oxygen. Curious, Turner accepted the invitation of a state Department of Wildlife and Fisheries officer to go offshore from Terrebonne Parish to investigate. Seesawing in choppy water a few miles out in a fifteen-foot boat, he slipped the probes of a handheld oxygen meter, one of his own fabrication, over the side. The needle barely twitched. He'd never seen this happen. Thumbing subsequent rides on NOAA boats, Turner got low readings almost everywhere, and he suspected that human behavior was behind them.[5]

That bothered him. Turner's New England childhood, especially summers at camp in Maine, had instilled an ethical outlook on nature. "We are not appreciating our natural human condition," he said years later, "if we do not have a respectful relationship with healthy environments." In Louisiana, he took an interest in what the delta meant to the livelihood and culture of local fishing communities. He was aware of the oil and gas industry, as employer and intruder. You could hardly take in the marshy coast without platforms coming into view. At first he wondered if they were leaching something that caused the hypoxia. That idea didn't go far.[6]

One that did was looking at the Mississippi, as closely as the river is long. Its basin is America's kitchen sink, and the river itself, the drainpipe. It breaks out of northern Minnesota and runs through or beside ten states, over twenty-three hundred miles. From Montana in the West and New York in the East, its watershed engulfs forty-one percent of the continental US. That's thirty-one states. Add to that parts of two Canadian provinces. Only the Amazon and Congo Rivers form out of larger watersheds.

The Gulf is no passive sump at the drain's discharge, though. In the summer, evaporating seawater rises into a counterclockwise-moving atmospheric mass that travels northward over the continent. Approaching the Midwest, it often collides with high-pressure systems from Canada and delivers the daily forecast, forty percent of the time from May to September. Humidity on sweating summer days comes courtesy of the Gulf. More important to Turner's research, the rain that falls on the heartland is often Gulf water. It runs off into the Mississippi and its nearly one hundred tributaries, and flows back to the American Sea.

Turner decided to "crawl up the watershed," to see what it contained and sent downstream.[7]

FOUR HUNDRED MILES to the east, Vince Raffield was never compelled to crawl up the watershed of the Apalachicola River. Although not nearly as expansive as the Mississippi's, the Apalachicola's drainage basin extends well into Alabama and Georgia. At the other end is the magnificent bay of the same name. That's where Raffield, a fit young man, with muscled shoulders and forearms, tall and buff and tan, was content to stay. It gave him peace and earned him a living. He was a multigeneration oysterman. No one ever got rich oystering, but few independent fishers dreamed of going to work for a company boss, and no factory floor or big-windowed office could beat the workplace ambience of the bay.

Decades later, after Raffield was no longer able to oyster, he sat down before a camera and discussed the perks of his laboring days. Southern voiced and articulate, wearing a mariner's cap, a puffy gray beard brushing his big chest, he refers at one point to a particular moment when he was in his hand-built plywood skiff on the bay. The air, the water, everything was still.

> I had sat down to have my lunch. I heard a clicking sound coming from underneath the bottom of my boat, and I got real quiet. I could hear the oyster shells opening and closing on the bottom of that bar magnified through the bottom of that boat. It was my epiphany. I realized right then that I was doing something that my daddy [had] done, my granddaddy had done, and I was a part of something—nature. You get attuned whenever you are working that kind of oystering and fishing. You read nature and you learn. You just become a part of it.[8]

Raffield had been simultaneously pulled and pushed to his haven. His father had been an oysterman on St. Andrew Bay in Panama City. The local leadership sometime earlier had felt a "pressing need"—jobs and taxes—to bring a paper mill to town, the first in the country to use chlorinates to turn pine pulp white. By 1971, effluent had shut down oystering on the bay. Before the end of the decade, bad water would close one of every ten acres of Gulf estuaries to shellfishing, twenty-one percent of those in Texas.[9]

Raffield's father was forced to take a job in a boatyard, where he worked with hazardous material and developed asbestosis. His disease eventually killed him. That's how Vince ended up in Apalachicola. Aside from his dad's death, that was okay. He and the nearly two thousand other fishers, who pulled almost ninety percent of the state's oyster harvest, thought their plump bivalves, exposed to an optimal blend of fresh- and saltwater, sweet and spice, were the best-tasting around. Restaurant chefs from New Orleans to New York agreed.

Alas, Apalachicola wasn't immune to every other bay's maladies. Whenever a hurricane walloped the oyster beds, they eventually bounced back. But after the Army Corps of Engineers completed work to give shrimpers and sportfishers a shortcut across St. George Island to the Gulf, the newly created channel let out much of the river's freshwater before it could wash thoroughly around the bay and invigorate oyster growth. The beds endured, although they could less effectively handle drought. When dry weather harried the country in 1988, the volume of the river fell off. Saltwater entered the bay in its place, and the beds went into a tailspin.

The state rushed in scientists and fisheries personnel to rescue its premier oyster fishery. The experts brought bureaucracy to the bay, determining which beds should be open to harvesting and when, right down to the days of the week and hours of the day—and they provoked the epithet-expressed infuriation of fishers. If there is anything fishers hate more than a busted engine or a thirty-knot wind, it's the government. And government wasn't the worst of it. The 1988 events revealed that the bay had a bigger challenge than the drought—a perpetual one—and it lay far upstream with big-city single-mindedness.

Raffield's days being a part of nature were numbered.

IN HIS SEARCH FOR the dead zone's principal source, Eugene Turner went far up the Mississippi, tracing a historic course that defined the great water. Gulf rivers are natural links to landlocked America, a web of conveyance to and from the middle, and at one time used primarily for freighting people and trade. There is fine efficiency in this, and all would be acceptable if rivers were asked to transport nothing more.

In an 1837 book of travels through the US, British sea captain Frederick Marryat called the Mississippi a "vile sewer." He also described Washington as ugly and New York as corrupt. His candor incensed Americans, who refused to buy his book. But he had a point, at least with regard to the river. Where did affronted readers think the night workers of riverside cities dumped the sludge from privies and cesspits? Where did the unmeasured tons of household rubbish and street sweepings disappear to? And what about the toxic blood, bile, and unrendered parts from slaughterhouses, or the poisonous effluent from manufacturing plants? A century and a decade later, contributors to a massive 1954 government study titled *Gulf of Mexico: Its Origin, Waters, and Marine Life* allowed Marryat to endure. The Mississippi was fouled all along its course, the study's authors wrote. But they checked their negativity, and instead concluded that the "effects" of the "pollution upon the Gulf are not significant," that "natural purification" would eliminate those effects.[10]

When the study came out, the dead zone's offending source, which Turner later uncovered, wasn't fully formed or as obvious as a sewer plant, or as repugnant. What he found was deceptive on the surface: lovely, welcoming, rejuvenating spring rains—every plant's and farmer's yearning. They did more than replenish, though; they washed the farmer's nitrogen- and phosphorus-charged fertilizers into the river. Fertilizer broadcast for corn in Iowa, for beets in Minnesota, for soybeans in Illinois, for wheat in Kansas became a nefarious hitchhiker on the currents to the mouths of the Mississippi and Atchafalaya Rivers, the former's lowermost distributary, and on into the Gulf. A plume supercharged with nutrients stimulated convulsive algal growth. The algae died, sank to the bottom, and decomposed. Oxygen, the fuel of decomposition, eventually ran out in the stratum near the bottom. Like a heat rash, the hypoxia returned every summer.

Another scientist, Nancy Rabalais, soon joined Turner on the Gulf. Her interest in biology had begun with an eighth-grade science course in Corpus Christi. During high school, she certified as a scuba diver and dove sites offshore of south Texas and Mexico. She went to college and graduate school and wrote her dissertation at the University of Texas on the reproductive biology of a species of fiddler crab. "Chasing fiddler crabs across south Texas," she would later say, "did not prepare me for congressional testimony." That came after she took a position at the Louisiana Universities Marine Consortium, where she was eventually paired with Turner to study Gulf hypoxia. In 1988, they married.[11]

Usually in July, one or both of them would take a pod of graduate students out on the Gulf to measure oxygen levels. They didn't measure much in 1987. Heavy rains and floodwaters carrying tons of fertilizer lasted into the fall; hypoxic water on the Louisiana coast suffocated an estimated 187 million fish, more than twice the record nationwide kill sixteen years earlier. As if in retribution, Gulf water refused to rain down on the Midwest the next year. Nineteen ninety-eight was the driest year on record for Yellowstone National Park. In the heartland, crops withered and died. The upshot was that Gulf marine life didn't—at least not nearly to the usual extent.

The dry weather, though, also left Apalachicola Bay thirsting for river water, and Raffield wanting for a decent oyster take. Drought was a hell of a fix for the Gulf's problems, and not the kind that Turner and Rabalais were looking for.

No river has ever been asked to carry as much of civilization's refuse as the Mississippi, and few for as long. To get a historical reading of oxygen levels, Turner began studying core samples from the Gulf bottom dating back two hundred years. Slicing into the cylindrical specimens of the Earth's below-sea crust was like turning through the pages of a US history text. Other scientists were doing the same or similar, and all detected something interesting: the density of the remains of marine organisms that were considered high-level oxygen users increased abruptly in the 1950s, suggesting the beginning of a hypoxic era.

The timing made complete sense. The 1950s was a decade of shifts. Especially notable was the production of prepared and processed foods, and of babies. Between 1954 and 1965, the national birth rate added four million mouths to the American population each year. The baby boom was both a ravenous eating machine and a market. Tapping into it, fast-food restaurants began multiplying along main drags across the country. Heartland farmers got busy raising more cattle and wheat for burgers and buns, and more corn and soy for cattle feed. Adding a cola and fries to a burger order completed a popular ensemble in the baby boomers' diet, and connected to it were four of the nation's top potato-growing states huddled in the Mississippi basin.

A parallel to the fast-food counter was the grocery store cereal aisle. The boomer appetite and clever advertising—enlisting cartoon tigers, bears, bunnies, toucans, leprechauns, a chocolate Dracula, and a wacky sea captain—grew store shelves higher and longer with improbable varieties of the boxed breakfast staple. Midwest production in dairy milk, grain, and corn expanded proportionally. Corn went into making both cereal and the high-fructose corn syrup that sweetened the cereal and the fast-food colas that boomers drank. Who could have imagined that a cheerful bowl of cereal in the morning and a simple burger and fries in the evening would give the Gulf a respiratory ailment? As the boomers grew to middle age, passing their diet on to their children, overall American per capita caloric intake increased twenty-five percent.

To keep the grain and corn growing, fertilizer use spiked, and increasing volumes of runoff flowed fast and sure toward the Gulf. Federal farm programs—in particular, those setting aside idle land in return for government subsidies (allotments, they're called)—encouraged farmers to grow more on less land. Fertilizer was the magic potion in swelling per-acre yields. In the 1990s, farmers were spreading an average of 130 pounds of fertilizer per cropland acre annually. Nitrogen levels in the Atchafalaya and Mississippi sometimes ran four times the 1950s levels.

In a 1991 *BioScience* article, Turner and Rabalais called for a "fundamentally sound management approach" to controlling fertilizer runoff in the Midwest. Forty-two percent of the nitrogen fertilizer and thirty percent of the phosphorus fertilizer used in the US, they reported, went down on ground wholly or partially within the Mississippi watershed. Close to half of the nitrogen and more than a quarter of the phosphorus reached the Gulf. They weren't even factoring in the nearly one billion tons of manure that cows and cattle—to wit, milk and hamburger producers—dropped each year, or the 2.3 pounds of pesticides distributed per acre (the US spent $1.4 billion to control pesticide pollution).[12]

BACK IN APALACHICOLA, the bay's salt- and freshwater imbalance was similarly complicated by an upstream source, although in a different way. Following a fish's downstream passage from the top of the watershed might offer the most effective illustration. The fish—let's say a striped bass—starts out from an elevation of thirty-five hundred feet in the Blue Ridge Mountains in north Georgia, at the spring-fed, tree-hidden head of the Chattahoochee River. Beginning its descent, the fish swims through clear water over a bottom of multicolored pebbles. "Chattahoochee" is the native Muskogean word for "river of painted rocks." For the phalanxes of fly fishers trying to hook the journeying bass, and the kayakers, rafters, and tubers cluttering its course, the river is simply "the Hooch."

Three dams challenge the finny migrator before it enters expansive Lake Sidney Lanier on the outskirts of Atlanta. This is the Sidney Lanier who wrote eloquently about Gulf fish in the 1870s, just a few years before composing a poem about the Chattahoochee. His namesake water turned into one of the busiest recreational lakes in the country, with twenty-three thousand watercraft in residence in the early twenty-first century. There our fish contends with house, ski, and pontoon boats, to say nothing of bass boats tricked out with the latest fish-finding technology. Escaping downstream, it has thirteen more dams to hurdle on the way to the confluence of the Chattahoochee and Flint Rivers, which flow into the Apalachicola River. All in all, eighteen power-generating plants have shadowed the bass's travels.

Environmental journalist Cynthia Barnett says that, given its size, the Chattahoochee "may be the hardest-working river in America." Peanuts, corn, and cotton grown on ten thousand acres in lower Alabama and Georgia depend on Hooch water, while hundreds of industries and municipalities lawfully dump effluents into the river. Atlanta, that ever-amassing metropolis, works it hardest. The Hooch provided drinking, grass-growing, and toilet-flushing water to not quite three million metro Atlantans in 1990, and then two million-plus more in 2010.[13]

The oxygen-consuming matter in urban runoff bound for the river was three times the discharge of the regional sanitation system. For its part, the sanitation system exchanged 250 million gallons of treated wastewater daily for 300 million that metro waterworks withdrew. The drinking water came by way of Lake Lanier, which is really a thirty-eight-thousand-acre reservoir that the Army Corps of Engineers built when it put the Hooch behind yet another dam. The reservoir is the hoggish bane of Apalachicola Bay. The Corps has overpowered nature in distributing all that impounded freshwater—laterally toward its perceived principal, Atlanta, and downstream to the estuary. The water directed south, in increasingly restrictive flows, brings invisible menaces, from nitrogen to fecal coliform bacteria.

Sprawling Atlanta's water consumption exacerbated the 1988 drought conditions in the Apalachicola Bay. True to form, the Corps designed new infrastructure to hold back more of the river, and Alabama sued. Its farmers needed Hooch water. So did tupelo trees, which grew thickly in Apalachicola River swamps. The trees supported Florida beekeepers, who harvested rare tupelo honey. In the midst of the drought, and with so much river water claimed by Atlanta, Apalachicola Bay was designated a federal disaster area. Oyster fishers and their families piled into 150 cars and caravanned to the state capital to demand action, representing a rare moment of unity among commercial fishers. Florida joined the lawsuit. Linking ecology and the economy, the state maintained that Atlanta's giant Slurpee straw imperiled the survival of spawning Gulf sturgeon and the endangered fat threeridge mussel, as well as the future of the oyster industry. Florida wanted guaranteed minimum downstream flows.

In 1997, Congress approved the ACF Compact (Apalachicola, Chattahoochee, Flint), which required the three quarreling states to devise a water-sharing formula. Fourteen times in six years, Congress extended the negotiations, and then it terminated the compact for lack of agreement. That the states were left without federal water-*quantity* standards as a guide, similar to water-*quality* standards, didn't help matters. When drought struck again, worsened by Corps mismanagement of Lake Lanier (a miscalculated water gauge that it had installed), Florida went to court again.

The dogs in this kind of fight were not always competing states. They were downstream water users and upstream water diverters. Activists in Texas were concurrently lobbying the legislature for a stewardship bill to ensure that bays and estuaries would have rights to riverine water equal to those of farmers, industries, and cities. But in a portentous end, stewardship lost to growth. In Georgia, Atlantans with brown lawns and dirty cars looking at water restrictions couldn't fathom giving priority to protecting bees, a sturgeon, and an oddball mussel they'd never heard of. The court more or less agreed. Nature—not Atlanta or the Corps—the federal-district judge ruled in the dry summer of 2006, was Florida's antagonist.

The "Apalachicola River is the main artery, like the artery in our bodies," said oysterman John Richards, who took exception to the judge's exoneration of upriver urban complicity. "If that artery is cut off, we've got problems." During his fifty years on the bay, Richards had witnessed the heightened stress that Atlanta's growing voraciousness put on the oyster beds. The greenish-blue saltwater coming into the bay in place of diminishing freshwater made the oysters clam up and stop feeding. Salt also invited bivalve-eating predators in from the Gulf.[14]

Poor conditions put the bay more at risk of overharvesting, for which oyster fishers were surely blamed. They saw their working lives increasingly controlled by a growing phalanx of outsiders—extension agents and state biologists who came to Apalachicola to help save the bay and the oyster industry. To the locals, the outsiders were meddlers, one degree removed from the hated government, lumped together as an infamous "they."

They were clueless, complained fishers. *They* would come out with their notebooks, computers, sample jars, and calculations, but *they* would never really get to know the bay, not like the locals knew it. *They* would shut down beds that were prime for harvesting or open those that should be recuperating. *They* would let one area become overrun before the oysters were ripe and protect another where the oysters were ready for culling. *They* would say you can't do this or do that and drive you crazy and out of business. When beds were closed, some fishers would crab or shrimp, but *they* put restrictions on those activities too.

Most oyster fishers just quit the business. Maybe three hundred remained on the water, down from a high of two thousand. Their sons and daughters didn't follow in their footsteps, but left the county or went to work for the state prison that opened nearby in 2005. Oystering was no longer a "free life," as one tradesman put it. You were lucky if you could support your family.

Vince Raffield was one of those who had to quit the oysters. They were no longer clacking as happily beneath his skiff. Like his father, he took a job in the boatyard. Like his father, he developed asbestosis and went on oxygen. Wanting to keep active in some way, he wrote long, eloquent letters to the local newspaper defending wildlife, woodlands, clean water, and the waterfront against developers, bureaucrats, politicians, and, most of all, ignorance and indifference. Like his daddy, he died from his disease. He passed away at home, fifty-four years old, on September 28, 2011, the day federal agencies released final reports on the *Deepwater Horizon* accident, calling for tougher safety regulations on oil platforms.

AT THE BEGINNING of the new millennium, scientists counted 146 coastal dead zones worldwide. Within another few years, the number had topped four hundred and dropped a lot of jaws. The US claimed sixty-nine. Oregon, a poster child of environmental responsibility, had a dead zone. So did Lake Erie, the St. Lawrence River, Long Island Sound, and Chesapeake Bay. Researchers reported that bouts with oxygen deprivation were common for marine life in half of the nation's estuaries.[15]

One among the chronically ailing was the historic estuary of the Caloosahatchee River, where the Calusa had established their great chiefdom and where tarpon fishing got its start. As was common, the source of the sickness was upstream. The river runs down from Lake Okeechobee, sixty miles inland at the head of the Everglades, the second largest freshwater lake wholly within the continental US. But the lake and river had not always been connected.

In the nineteenth century, a wealthy Philadelphia handsaw manufacturer, Hamilton Disston, envisioned a sugarcane empire on a vast tract of submerged land he had acquired when the state of Florida, trying to bail itself out of post–Civil War bankruptcy, sold him four million acres for twenty-five cents an acre. To develop it, he planned to drain the water of the upper Everglades into the lake and direct it down a canal that he would build to the Gulf-bound Caloosahatchee River. By the time William Halsey Wood caught his milestone tarpon in 1885, Disston had dredged and dynamited his connection. In the 1930s, and again in the 1960s, the Army Corps of Engineers deepened and widened Disston's original canal, slicing arrow-straight through the old river's nearly fifty oxbows, its natural looping curves, each of which was a miniature ecosystem and filter in the water's flow. The Corps designated the waterway "C-43," conferring on it a bureaucratic name and existence detached from history and natural heritage.

The ecological repercussions were significant. Dams impeded the inflow of tidal saltwater and the upriver reach of the estuary. Controlled by water engineers, the outflow was so heavy at times that it pushed marine life seeking an estuarine home back into open water. The engineered system didn't dry up the Everglades either—not completely—but it did drain thousands of acres of pasture- and farmland, turning the river into what was essentially a giant phosphorus-loaded sewage ditch for crop fertilizers and chemicals, and cattle manure. Every summer, algal blooms clogged the estuary, the result of wastewater and stormwater. The latter carried tons of residential fertilizer from the grassy pride of the American home owner. A green lawn meant a brown bay.

In 2008, Lee County (the seat of which is Fort Myers) passed an ordinance prohibiting residential fertilizer use between June and September, after taking a cue from the Sanibel-Captiva Conservation Foundation. The organization, which four decades earlier saved Sanibel's indigenous character, had led the island city to adopt a fertilizer blackout period the year before. Sarasota had done the same, and it was seeing improvements in water quality. But Sarasota didn't have a reengineered river like the Caloosahatchee, which had no blackout period protecting it from agriculture runoff. Even if there had been, even if the dams had been removed and the oxbows restored, the once-sandy now-mucky bottoms of Lake Okeechobee and the Caloosahatchee were so thick with more than a century's load of nutrients that algal blooms would continue indefinitely. Under the leadership of Governor Jeb Bush, the state wasn't up to the task anyway. It determined that "large-scale sediment management is not a feasible option" and left algal blooms as a perennial summer event.[16]

BY 2014, SIXTY-FOUR LOCAL GOVERNMENTS in Florida had adopted fertilizer ordinances, and commercial and residential use had declined significantly from the beginning of the century. This was a remarkable development in a state where fertilizer was a multibillion-dollar homegrown industry. Tampa Bay was the nation's watery capital of its production, and it had paid the ecological price for the Midwest's constant need for soil nourishment.

One of Turner's and Rabalais's counterparts in marine sciences, Sylvia Earle, lived her teen years on the bay at Clearwater in the 1950s. Quoting family and friends in a memoir dedicated to securing the cleanup of the world's oceans, she remembers "getting enough scallops from the bay for dinner just by wading out on the grass flats at low tide"; "the red snapper we used to catch—right off the dock!"; and "fifty-two clams [gathered] in one place in Tampa Bay without moving our feet." "Now they're gone," as were the grass flats, snapper, and scallops.[17]

Sources usually cite construction, sewage, and stormwater drainage as the agents of the bay's degradation. These usual suspects, however, had a silent and much older coconspirator: phosphate, a local commodity found in ungodly quantities in the Bone Valley region east of Tampa Bay. Phosphate is a major component in the production of fertilizer. Around Tampa Bay, it originates in the bones and teeth of long-dead sea animals embedded together with mineralized sediment from the Appalachian Mountains, all buried in Florida's limestone underbelly.

A mustached geologist and civil engineer named John Francis LeBaron discovered phosphatic pebbles while surveying the Peace River for the Army Corps of Engineers in 1881. That was the same year the "Old Frenchman" Chevelier bought 120 acres on Tampa Bay so that he could shoot birds for hats. Phosphate was Florida's gold that the Spanish never found, though powdery and dull rather than glittering and, during the colonial period, without market value. That was before worn farmlands starved worldwide for fertility.

Within a decade and a half of LeBaron's discovery, two hundred concerns were mining phosphate in the area. The train that delivered tarpon fishers to Punta Gorda and Boca Grande carried carloads of phosphate away. Henry Plant extended his railroad to Tampa as much for the phosphate business as for the tourist trade. A half century later, strip-mining steam shovels and diesel-powered equipment, replacing picks and hand shovels, turned Bone Valley into the most productive phosphate region in the world, generating seventy-five percent of the US output. Nearly all of it ended up on the nation's lawns and farms, making Tampa Bay fertilizer, via the crop fields of the heartland, an indirect but major contributor to the Gulf dead zone.

There were hazards on the production side too. As one local put it, the phosphate industry turned the air in the Tampa Bay area so foul with "vicious fumes" of sulfur dioxides and fluoride emissions that shrubbery and trees died. Citrus groves wilted. Cattle turned gaunt, went lame, and lost their teeth. People's eyes watered, noses bled, and throats swelled. Many had moved to Florida for the fresh air and sunshine, only to hide indoors with windows closed. Untreated and undiluted waste from mining and processing operations, including fluoride-contaminated slurry, ran freely into streams and into Tampa Bay and Charlotte Harbor—thousands of gallons a day.[18]

The multifront assault got to be too much. By the 1970s, the remarkable estuary that was Tampa Bay was dying. Environmentalists, sportfishers, and waterfront residents began forcing the issue, going up against an industry responsible for fifty thousand local jobs. In 1991, Congress created the Tampa Bay Estuary Program, one of an eventual twenty-eight nationwide, all of which are intended to restore the water quality and ecological integrity of the estuaries. Government leaders and the phosphate industry stepped in line, and Tampa Bay, surrounded by 2.3 million people, made a remarkable comeback. By Y2K, runoff from lawns and businesses had dropped fifty percent, and scores of volunteers had replanted thousands of acres of sea grass. Forty thousand pairs of wading and shore birds, representing twenty-five species—some not seen in years—were back nesting on the bay's many islands, ones that Chevelier had shot empty a century earlier.

Tampa-supplied fertilizer that streamed down the Mississippi into the Gulf affected a sibling bay, that at Mobile. Another science colleague of Turner and Rabalais, Harvard naturalist-biologist Edward O. Wilson, had spent a good portion of his childhood in Mobile and described the surrounding area as "in the middle of the biologically richest part of North America." Bernard Romans had said virtually the same thing a century and a half earlier when he pined for Britain to exploit it. Mobile Bay's watershed drains sixty-five percent of the state of Alabama, parts of Georgia and Mississippi, and a speck of Tennessee. One or two times a year, sometimes a half dozen, in the summer, almost always in the morning, for longer than Mobile news presses were reporting the affair, the shallow bay turned naturally hypoxic. The event drove hordes of bottom-dwellers toward the surface and shore looking for oxygen.[19]

Locals christened the waters churning in a mass of panic a "jubilee." On those special mornings, neighbors called and whistled to one another, rang bells, blew horns, and raced down to the water with nets, baskets, buckets, washtubs, and gigs. Gobs and gobs of crabs, catfish, eels, and fish flailed vulnerably at the edge. Once witnessing a jubilee, naturalist Archie Carr said, "You can gig a hundred flounders and fill the back of your pickup truck a foot deep in crabs." People couldn't believe the bay held so much life.[20]

The jubilees, Carr explained, were "stirring simply as natural phenomena," the result of dead organic matter from Wilson's native greensward, accumulating and decaying on the bay bottom and gulping up oxygen. Excess freshwater from five rivers sheeted over top of saltwater—capping, some scientists call it—preventing an O_2 exchange between layers. In years of spring deluges, the same thing happens at the end of the Brazos River near Freeport. In Mobile, events have turned so severe that barnacles on vessels that plied through the bay died. Some researchers believe that, with increased nutrient runoff from farms, golf courses, and suburban lawns, jubilees began waxing more frequently and intensely. In 2014, Mobile Bay, followed by Galveston Bay, experienced the highest level of nitrogen among Gulf estuaries, mainly from manure and fertilizer.[21]

During summers when the Gulf dead zone morphed and curled around to touch Alabama's shores, fish fleeing the stuffy bay for offshore waters swam themselves into a choke hold between two threats. For some, there was no escape.

AND THEN THERE WAS THE DEEP BLUE. With the intent to pursue a globally cooperative course toward sustainability, the United Nations General Assembly declared 1998 the "Year of the Ocean." Caught up in the spirit, Bill Clinton's Washington pledged to deal with the hypoxic Gulf. Over the next decade, the federal government and private foundations disbursed a lot of money for scientific studies, which affirmed and reaffirmed the dead zone's connection to upriver fertilizer use. NOAA named Rabalais an "Environmental Hero," and in 1999 the nonpartisan San Diego Foundation presented her and Turner with a $250,000 award recognizing the value of their research.

In the playbook of conservative journalist Michael Fumento, the quarter-million-dollar "check" made the two scientists fair game. Writing in *Forbes*, he said, the "truth is that no one knows exactly what's going on in the Gulf of Mexico, or what all the causes are." He was one of many critics beginning to creep out of the shadows, not unlike climate-change skeptics, drawing on demagogic catchphrases to substitute for a deficit in meaningful logic. He called Rabalais and Turner the "environmental darlings" of the "antifertilizer crowd" driving "Hypoxia Hysteria." Defending agriculture, he argued against trying to "fix" a problem "before we know what's going on," particularly if the fix demanded "iron-fisted regulations" and a $5 billion program to return "productive farmland" to "muskrat metropolises."[22]

He needn't have worried. The government instituted no real action policy, except that which grossly contradicted relief for the Gulf. In the name of post-9/11 domestic security and environmental protection, Congress passed the Energy Policy Act of 2005 and extended it in 2007. The legislation was supposed to alleviate the country's dependence on Middle Eastern oil. It required blending biofuels with gasoline and provided tax incentives for homegrown renewable fuels, including corn-based ethanol—not exactly renewable like wind or sunshine, but nevertheless.

In 2006 and '07, taking advantage of the government-mandated demand for their product, farmers opened up fifteen million additional acres to corn growing, most of it in the Mississippi River basin. American consumers watched corn prices more than triple (and cereal prices soar), and in 2011 they shelled out $6 billion to subsidize the ethanol industry. In the third year of the subsidy, a state-and-federal environmental task force called for reducing nutrient loading in the Mississippi by forty-five percent by 2015. That wasn't going to happen. The US had become the world's largest corn producer, with a sizable percentage of its product going into ethanol. Congress let the tax subsidy lapse in 2011, but not without giving the industry a boondoggle. New federal provisions decreed that thirty-seven percent of the nation's corn crop should end up at the gas pump. They also set a goal for the US to manufacture thirty-six billion gallons of ethanol by 2022, with fifteen billion coming from corn.

Researchers estimated that nitrogen flow into the Mississippi would increase ten to twenty percent. *National Geographic* referred to the trend as the "rising tide of nitrates." "More nitrate comes off corn fields than it does off of any other crop by far," said Turner in connection with ethanol. He and Rabalais published a study showing that the Midwest was the most generously subsidized farming region in the country, and the most heavily fertilized. Nearly every year, around May or so, the national press predicted a record-sized dead zone for the Gulf. (The one exception was 2012, when another monster drought kept fertilizer on the land and out of waterways.)[23]

The upside to the ethanol boon and boom was that, by intensifying the dead zone, it made the remedy as clear as unpolluted water: contain the agricultural runoff in the basin. Rabalais liked to talk about the Black Sea, where a dead zone twice the size of the Gulf's had killed an estimated sixty million tons of bottom dwellers before the Soviet economy collapsed in the 1980s. When the government cut off fertilizer subsidies, the hypoxic sea quickly recovered and prospered again.

There was an example closer to home. The Florida Reef on the eastern side of the Keys was taking a severe beating from sewage and fertilizer runoff. From the 1980s to 2000, ninety-three percent of elkhorn corals and ninety-eight percent of staghorn corals died. The continental US was killing its only barrier reef, the third largest in the world. Across the Florida Straits off the island of Cuba, where farmers practiced organic agriculture, the Gardens of the Queen, a thirty-mile-long barrier reef, was as healthy as ever. The rest of the Caribbean, its islands enclaves of intensely fertilized commercial agriculture, had massacred approximately fifty percent of its coral reefs. "There should be little doubt," said Rabalais, "about the strong relationships among human activities, nutrient loads and eutrophication, and the demise of a coastal ecosystem."[24]

Turner referred to Gulf hypoxia as a "wicked problem." The term originated with social planners in the 1960s to denote a problem made bigger by the complicating interests of multiple parties—government, corporate, and popular. Ecologists found "wicked problem" a useful term for dealing with environmental complications—foremost, climate change. Groups such as the Nature Conservancy and Green Lands Blue Waters, an organization that Turner helped found, were trying to restore the health of the Mississippi basin, including the natural and human communities, while retaining profit-making options for farmers. Turner's group focused on reintroducing perennial crops to the heartland to mitigate runoff and on finding common ground among all parties. A key part of Green Lands Blue's model is to have communities playing a larger role in the fate of their watersheds. After the BP oil spill, Turner applied for funding from Louisiana settlement money to establish a model community. The application, he told writer Paul Greenberg, went "nowhere."[25]

The Gulf dead zone had achieved the unbecoming status of the world's second largest and best known. In 2012, Rabalais won a prestigious MacArthur Foundation "Genius Grant" of $500,000. She used the award to continue dead-zone research. Private and government funding was otherwise disappearing. The dead zone wasn't.

RESEARCHERS ESTIMATED THAT the dead zone cost $82 million in tourist dollars. Millions more were lost to pollution elsewhere in the Gulf, and millions were spent to save estuaries—when we tried to save them. American society chose cornfields and dirty water over one of the greatest gifts of nature, almost as if nature were something we should deliver ourselves from. Turner and Rabalais and all the others who tried to put us back in touch with nature's logic never saw the question—don't see it—as an either-or proposition. And they knew more was at stake than the economy.

The "Filthy Seas" article opened with a quote from Jacques Cousteau, who said, the "human species depends upon the maintenance of an ocean clean and alive." Diane Wilson had always made this point, and Sylvia Earle, after seeing the despoliation reaching the world's deepwater frontiers that she had spent a career exploring, turned herself into an evangelist of saving the oceans and humankind. She had also seen how a Gulf estuary, like Tampa Bay, could come back from the brink.[26]

Seventeen

RUNOFF, AND RUNAWAY

The once-floating Palace Casino in Biloxi, Mississippi,
after Hurricane Katrina.

*I have this fantasy. We all know the great tragedy of a child
dying when they're very young. If you believe in an afterlife,
I think there would be a special Gulf Shores circa 1930s
settlement for these kids, with a few angels overseeing them.*

—EDWARD O. WILSON (2014)[1]

BY THE TIME OF HIS LAST PASSAGE TO MISSISSIPPI'S
Horn Island, in 1965, Walter Anderson had been privy to some disquieting developments. Looking back as he rowed out to his island

retreat, he could see the tall, giraffe-like cranes of Ingalls Shipbuilding that rose above the tree line on either side of the Pascagoula River. Since opening in 1938, Ingalls had grown to employ ten thousand or more workers. Over the coming years, it built nuclear-powered submarines, more than three score destroyers, and nearly the entire US fleet of guided-missile cruisers. It was the largest shipyard on the Gulf, yet far from its worst polluter.

Being a defense contractor duly bound to federal standards had something to do with that. So did love for the Pascagoula, one of the few major US rivers that had escaped the restless compulsion to control moving water—no dams, dikes, or locks. Its nickname, the "Singing River," became symbolic of a stubborn resolve to preserve its natural harmony. In the post-9/11 era, when the George W. Bush administration announced plans to hollow out salt domes near the river to store 160 million barrels of emergency fuel for the Strategic Petroleum Reserve, loud protest erupted from several conservation groups, including an array of grassroots organizers, from wage workers to lawyers to scientists. Among them was Anderson's youngest son, John.

They pointed out that the Department of Energy's own report estimated that construction of the reservoirs would lead to seventy-five salt and nearly twenty oil spills in the river and marshes. Equally unsettling, a supply pipeline to the Gulf would intrude on fifteen hundred acres of wetland. The venerable biologist Edward Wilson pronounced the plan a good way to "screw up" the "closest thing" the Southeast "has to wilderness." Public pressure worked. The Barack Obama administration let the plan die of funding neglect in 2010.[2]

The upper river was relatively safe, but the lower continued to convey, as it had done since before Walter Anderson's time, society's burden to Mississippi Sound. Anderson's crossing to seclusion didn't pass through pristine waters. From the north beach of Horn, he could see a long stain of brownish white in the sky over the mainland. It belonged to a mill of the International Paper Company. As its smokestack splotched the sky, a drainpipe stained the water. Liquid waste went into the Escatawpa River, which fed into the lower Pascagoula River, and then into the sound.

Here was a body of water that established a scenic and recreational commonality among several cities and towns between eastern Louisiana and western Alabama. Here also was the common catch basin of black-icon designees denoted on wastewater maps in the US Public Health Service's 1954 study. After Anderson's death and the residential growth in the splintered wake of Hurricane Camille in 1969, every community increased its expurgatory contribution.

Mississippians had always been proud of their compact coastline. They embraced the state's seafood heritage, accepted the coexistence of the market fishers with the rod-and-reel set, and never banned commercial gill nets. The charter-fishing business was as robust as ever in the late twentieth century, and by some estimates the two industries supported five thousand jobs. Both were in agreement with the coastal communities' focus on the tourist trade, built beside a long walk of beach that emphasized the physical setting.

Still, there was a Faulknerian paradox in Mississippians' love of their Gulf front. In the 1990s, half of the original Six Sisters—Biloxi, Gulfport, and Bay St. Louis—left the familiar path leading from nineteenth-century resort spa to twentieth-century beach town for the expressway to gambling. Their sections of the beach highway lit up like the Las Vegas strip, with hyperkinetic marquees flashing the current stage acts and biggest jackpot. Around-the-clock floating casinos, their gangplanks hitched to ten-story hotels, blocked what had been an open view for visitors and motorists and the historic homes and businesses across the street.

As promised, the gaming industry delivered a jackpot in tourist and tax dollars, except the recipients didn't spend it on improving the sound's polluted plight. The casinoless Jackson County took a lone cleanup initiative when it constructed a sophisticated treatment system that utilized wetland technology. But the sound needed a concerted effort. In 2000, Mississippi congressman Gene Taylor tried unsuccessfully to attach an amendment to the Water Resources Development Act (best known for authorizing an unprecedented ecological restoration plan for the Everglades) that would finance revamping treatment systems across the coast. Three years after the 2010 BP oil spill, authorities were still struggling with waste contamination. In a study of thirty waterfront states, the National Resources Defense Council ranked Mississippi's neglected beachside water quality the third worst in the country.

Anderson's hometown, Ocean Springs, rejected the gambling economy for a less assuming trade in dining and shopping. Its anchor was the Walter Anderson Museum of Art, opened in 1991. The museum was significantly damaged in Hurricane Katrina (sadly, original artwork and manuscripts were lost), rebuilt and enlarged in the aftermath, and celebrated as a homegrown shining star of the coast. In a literal sense, it could not outshine those million-lightbulb casino signs across the bridge in Biloxi, loathed by so many. If you lived on the upper Gulf coast and didn't want developers calling the shots at city hall and overrunning your community with pavement and tall buildings, you brought up Biloxi as an archetype of awful, its eleven glaring casinos and never-sleeping waterfront—the pounding, growling, rat-a-tat, beep-beep-beep of perpetual building, expanding, rebuilding, and traffic detouring.

Within weeks after Katrina, the gaming lobby pushed legislation through the state capital to permit the reconstruction of casinos fully on land; no more anchoring at the dock. Next, while thousands of Mississippians remained homeless, the lobbyists convinced the Department of Housing and Urban Development to allow Mississippi officials to divert $600 million of federal emergency-housing assistance to facilitate the expansion of the gaming and cruise ship industries. The state leadership argued that the preferential treatment was essential to recovery. Others argued that the Mississippi coast was a community lost.

SAVE FOR THE CASINOS, Mississippi was in some ways copying what had grown up on part of the Florida panhandle—a bad example, some said. No community was so completely lost—stamped out and smothered—as the late Leonard Destin's historic fishing village. His namesake was an oft-invoked antimodel of growth. Behind its bull-dozed development wasn't a shrewd gaming lobby, but its own gleaming beaches and neon water. Someone came up with the name "Emerald Coast," and it became the calling card for the eastern part of the upper Gulf region, especially in real-estate sales offices.

Destin experienced the same kind of aggressive growth that had hit the Mangrove Coast, except it occurred later and in a thinner slice of time. In the 1960s, the "World's Luckiest Fishing Village" was still a fishing village, of behooving boat docks, bait shops, small wood-frame houses, lazy traffic, a couple of stoplights, a handful of all-you-can-eat-shrimp seafood restaurants, a Jitney Jungle convenience store, and a liquor store and lounge. Out front of the lounge was a curious land-mark: a giant, green-painted, armored knight. The beach was occu-pied by little more than a couple of beachcomber-style motels and lots of sand dunes. You could buy a home lot on a dredged finger canal—a one hundred percent sand lot—for $2,000. If you sold it in the early 1970s, you'd break even.

But if you waited another decade, your waterfront property would be worth tenfold, and in another, tenfold that, even as the milieu lost some of its original charm. If the lot came with a view of the Gulf, that would disappear, blocked by a condominium tower, and one next to that, and one next to that, repeating down the beach. Lost views were becoming a common theme on the Gulf coast. Housing growth in Destin expanded from an average of one percent a decade before 1960 to twenty-four percent each decade over the next four. Develop-ers tended to be from Birmingham and Atlanta rather than the Mid-west and Northeast. But like Mangrove Coast developers, their sense of space was limited largely to how they could jam-pack it.

Destin retained one of the largest charter-fishing fleets in the US, yet its famous docks were hard to find in the uprising clutter. The century-and-a-quarter-old village was chartered as a municipality in 1984, and by then had traded in its distinctive character for USA-homogenized banality with a blaze of beach tourism kitsch: two-story T-shirt shops qua surf shops, mountain-sized miniature golf courses, an oversized waterslide park called Big Kahuna's, chain restaurants out front of strip retail centers filled with chain stores, linked with one another along the spine of US 98—the Miracle Strip—and interrupted only by guard shacks and electronic gates of condominium communities, linear foot after plastic linear foot of franchised artificiality, everything landscaped with pink and white crape myrtles (heavily trimmed), all of it needing traffic lights, and so many that the city had to appeal to state engineers for a synchronization system to keep the six lanes of automobiles crawling. The green knight was gone by the mid-1990s, conquered by the blitz.

West across the bridge over East Pass, Fort Walton Beach wanted tourists but not the towers. It adopted a thirty-five-foot building-height restriction. The most precious land feature was arguably Santa Rosa Island, which was saved less by short buildings than by long stretches of beach owned by the US Department of Defense, proprietor of most of the fifty-mile island. Leaving Destin and its canyon of skyscraping condos, US 98 sliced through a white valley of undisturbed sand dunes—some exceeding the building-height restrictions—that ran the length of the island like a mountain range. Fed a scrap or two of land, eager to duplicate Destin, developers could do little more than salivate like Pavlovian dogs.

Over on Alabama's coast, writes historian Harvey Jackson, Gulf Shores "was doing its best to overtake Destin . . . in tackiness." Edward Wilson remembers as a boy riding over in a Model A from Pensacola, when Gulf Shores was little more than a few fishing shacks and summer cottages, nearly all beach on one side of the lonely state highway and woodlands on the other. "Wow, it was like magic to arrive at Gulf Shores—the big dunes, the Gulf, and the surf. There was no greater thrill for a kid my age."[3]

Development, the thrill of real-estate investors, crept in after World War II. By the 1970s, Gulf Shores had a couple of souvenir shops, a chain motel, a "nest of honky-tonks," its first condominium, and thirty thousand summer visitors. Nearly all were from Alabama, proud and possessive of their homegrown "Redneck Riviera." The year-round population was barely fifteen hundred. Growth still wasn't in a hurry—not until after Hurricane Frederic laid waste to the area in 1979.[4]

Gulf Shores became another posthurricane boomtown. Disaster relief arrived. "Then came the rebuilding," writes Jackson. "Then came the developers. Then came the change." Meaning condominiums. Within a dozen years, Gulf Shores had over a hundred condominium complexes—"not units," the director of the National Hurricane Center emphasized to Congress in 1992, "complexes." They were fifteen-, twenty-, and thirty-story towers, at the edge of high tide. If you knocked one over, its upper floors would splash into the Gulf. Developers built on top of leveled fore-dunes, the protective ridge next to the surf. To become taller, Gulf Shores was made flatter.[5]

In the other direction from Destin, high-rise complexes multiplied eastward down the beach, as if the wind had disseminated the seeds of that original invasive species. Mile after mile they popped up, until the Walton County line. There, save two midrise complexes that had snuck in early, developers hit a wall in the form of a different mind-set.

One panhandle developer of Birmingham origins went against the Destin model and earned accolades for doing so. Robert Davis came from a family of Jewish merchants who made the Alabamian's family vacation trek to the Florida panhandle. Theirs led to one of the many beaches between Panama City and Destin, including Grayton Beach, where the family owned a humble, wood-frame house across from the still-surviving nineteenth-century Washaway Hotel. Nearby to the east, on the other side of one of south Walton County's rarefied dune lakes, Robert's grandfather Joseph Smolian, known as JS, bought eighty acres in 1946, when Robert was three. He intended to develop a retreat for employees at his Birmingham store. The property included a half mile of the not-yet-nicknamed Emerald Coast's trademark beachfront, while the rest was covered in pine and saw palmetto scrub. It cost JS $8,000 and the derision of business associates, who called it a "worthless piece of sand" and refused to support the plans for a retreat.[6]

Davis temporarily left behind the beachfront family vacations when he went off to boarding school in upstate New York, college at Antioch, and business school at Harvard. He had the ability to move between Jewish and gentile, and northern and southern worlds. He soon found himself in yet another when he started teaching and working as an administrator at a black college in Austin, and when Antioch lured him back to ramp up its efforts to recruit minority and low-income students. Deciding it was time to put his MBA to work, Davis moved to Miami in the early 1970s. For a number of years, he developed low-income housing, before pursuing his own projects for the market.

An unassuming dignity made Robert Davis the kind of person you wanted to do business with. He spoke with calm and confidence, without arrogance, southern accent, or college-boy haughtiness. He kept himself neatly coiffed and dressed, with a taste for style that was neither flashy nor perfumed. Aesthetics were important—art, music, and architecture—but so was common sense. He knew what he wanted in the things he built, or at least what they should be about—people as much as objects, how humanity functioned with the physical structure, inside and out. Vision was as essential as accomplishment and result, and that's where south Florida fell miserably short. Those who were guiding its boom lacked vision outside personal enrichment. Progress was solely about getting it done, while urban planning privileged concrete over community. Davis believed a state prophesied to grow needed a smarter way forward.[7]

Looking back was one way. He considered his childhood vacations and his late grandfather's eighty acres, which Davis had acquired from his grandmother. Taking time to think out a plan for the property and to search for alternative models, he and his future wife, Daryl Rose, traveled through coastal towns of France and Italy. Back in the States, they toured the South in a red 1975 Pontiac Grand Ville convertible, which embodied both style and practicality. The Pontiac had a cushy ride and classy looks; it was also ocean-liner roomy, and with the top down, it became a rolling platform from which to take unobstructed photographs or to leap to shoot a few close details.

Robert and Daryl catalogued a record of vernacular architecture. They were interested in the layout of older walkable communities, the scale of streets, the distance from front porch to curb. Their "travels by land yacht" took them to New Orleans, Charleston, Savannah, Key West, and inland Florida towns that felt like old Florida. In the back of Robert's mind was Edgewood, the Birmingham streetcar suburb of his youth, where residents walked to the grocery store, pharmacy, schools, post office, family doctor—to all their needs. He thought about functional features of the hurricane-enduring Washaway Hotel and the house on Grayton Beach. The couple returned to metro Miami and a traditional Florida cracker house with those features, including cross-ventilation and tree shade, to test them out before making the move to the panhandle.[8]

In 1981 they broke ground on Seaside, a master-planned community on those eighty acres of scrub and marvelous beachfront. Miami architect spouses Andrés Duany and Elizabeth Plater-Zyberk signed on and borrowed the big Pontiac for their own tour of the South. They looked to Europe too, and to urban planner and architect Léon Krier's assertion that the ideal walking city limited foot travel to a quarter mile in one direction (kids start complaining "how much farther" after that). And they studied Baron Haussmann's renovation of Paris.

Haussmann's radial-boulevard design turned out to fit beautifully within eighty acres. No point would be more than a quarter mile from the town center, where there would be a grocery, shops, restaurants, and post office. Seaside's houses would be Florida vernacular, built with a "common language and grammar," Davis said, "and would differ with each other but would be sufficiently harmonious" to "create a pleasant streetscape." Every room would have natural light and cross-ventilation. The roofs would be high-pitched and metal, with deep overhangs for shading. Construction would be wood-frame on small shady lots of mandated indigenous vegetation—no turfgrass, no lawn sprinklers, no greens-keeping chemicals.[9]

Each house, painted a cheery color and different from its immediate neighbors, would have a front porch and a white picket fence. The porch was for community and the fence for aesthetics, though more than that. The line of pickets functioned as a traffic-calming device by giving the brick streets a narrow feel. No need for dreaded speed bumps. Or extensive underground stormwater plumbing. The houses would be raised on piers, which enhanced not only air circulation but also rainwater percolation. Those brick streets, comfort to eyes and bare feet alike, did the same.

Seaside departed radically from conventional mundane and impersonal subdivisions highly engineered against nature. It came to be the premier US inspiration for New Urbanism, a late-twentieth-century movement in architecture that, like Davis, cast back to old urbanism and incorporated the values of community and practicality. The professional awards piled up, and exuberant press attention befitted a rising star. Indeed, Hollywood came to town in the 1990s to film *The Truman Show*.

Seaside residents grew weary of hordes of gawking sightseers driving through their walkable community. Still, there was no shortage of home buyers, even after real-estate prices jumped twentyfold and eclipsed soulless Destin. Falling victim to its success while revealing a desire for pragmatic living, Seaside departed from original vision and Davis's affordable-housing days. More than three-quarters of the vernacular structures turned out to become second homes of high-income seasonal residents—yet a testament to a powerful human desire for what Davis had planted in nature.

Copycats came along too, calling themselves New Urbanist communities. They were adulterated versions of Seaside. Next door, St. Joe Company, an old timber and polluting pulp-paper concern, and Florida's largest private landholder at the time, built WaterColor, a five-hundred-acre resort with wood-frame homes—many of them attached condos—adorned with metal, deep-overhanging roofs and wraparound screened porches, and located a stroll from shopping. Yet WaterColor defaulted to architectural sameness and asphalt streets.

Although construction adhered to height restrictions, most buildings came close to the limit, making the scale of the built environment feel intrusive. Starting at $1 million, WaterColor's were manor-born, not cracker-style, homes. Patches of carefully arranged indigenous vegetation surrounded them, along with plenty of turfgrass, lawn irrigation, and an eighteen-hole golf course. All the new construction, much of it testing a conservation ethos that had emerged with Seaside, started people worrying about encroachment on the country's rare dune lakes.

In the 1970s, Florida, the growth state, began taking modest steps to protect its shoreline. It established a mean-high-tide setback of fifteen meters for new construction. A few years later, the rule was changed to use a hundred-year-storm-surge line, which FEMA also required.* Houses had to be built behind that line and on deep-set pilings with living space limited to levels above predicted floodwaters. Texas enacted similar measures after Hurricane Alicia in 1983, restricting construction, including rebuilding, to behind beach vegetation. A few years later, Florida's new Coastal Zone Management Act prohibited construction on sand dunes. Seaside had set the example by staying landside of the dunes, and constructing boardwalks over them to the beach.

Since beaches are inherently unstable places, and dunes are like anchors for them, it made sense to preserve dunes and the vegetation that holds them together. Logic also suggests that if you put something permanent on something impermanent, you'll create a conflict. That's exactly what happened when condominiums, houses, hotels, and tourists moved out to the beach, and to the islands. The Gulf states found themselves in conflict against nature—a conflict of their making and against the very thing people had come to love: the beach.

---

* The hundred-year-storm surge is the magnitude of a storm surge that is expected to be equaled or exceeded every hundred years, or that has a one percent chance of being exceeded in a given year.

Eighteen

SAND IN THE HOURGLASS

Beachgoers stranded poolside as a dredge rebuilds their sand playground in the 1970s. Beach erosion and expensive restoration projects were common events by the post–World War II period.

As a child I moved ten tons of sand, one plastic bucket at a time.

—RICK BRAGG (2010)[1]

❖ ─────────────────────────────────

REMEMBER WHEN MOM OR DAD SAID IF YOU HOLD A SEA-shell up close, you'll hear the sea? The naturally burnished aperture of the shell fit a small ear perfectly, and you listened. It was there, inside and around behind the shell's wonderfully formed spiral—the sound of a whole world, of wind and waves, maybe of sailing ships and pirates. You were probably also told the shell had once been the home of a small sea animal that had outgrown its house and traded up for a bigger one. Images formed again, of what that itinerant creature looked like.

Innocently enough, the popular saga of shells is myth. Years ahead, you learned or figured out that the sea is not hidden within. The shell instead resonates ambient sounds, sometimes including the listener's pulse or a twitching muscle.

The truth about its occupant is more complicated, and many of us never learn it. Only hermit crabs and a few octopi move from shell to shell, and as mere squatters, for that matter. They occupy what was once a part—a living part—of another animal. The original occupant was a mollusk and the shell was not merely its house. Mollusks are invertebrates in need of a hard, protective outer layer. A seashell is the exoskeleton they are born with and never discard. It grows with them and eventually survives them. "A shell," says marine biologist Stefanie Wolf, "is forever."[2]

Mollusks are the largest phylum of the sea, making up nearly a quarter of known marine organisms. Among their number is a tremendous variety in species, size, and behavioral traits. Demographically, southwest Florida's continental shelf is the Jakarta and Shanghai of their world. Millions upon millions—trillions—lie out there. Their numbers and the just-right shore currents have made the adjoined islands of Sanibel and Captiva one of the most popular places in the world for collecting what Wolf calls "nature's perfect jewelry." In 1880, when Americans were beginning to shed their trepidations about the beach, travel writer Abbie M. Brooks (a.k.a. Sylvia Sunshine) said of the area, "Here conchologists, and persons fond of shell-hunting, can be gratified." Ever since, more tourists have stooped over Sanibel and Captiva beaches than have sunned on them.[3]

Anne Morrow Lindbergh, married to the acclaimed aviator Charles, was one of the stoopers. Captiva is where she wrote *Gift from the Sea*, the top-selling nonfiction book of 1955. She rented a "sea-shell of a house" for the precious solitude desired in a life frayed by Charles's fame and authoritarian nature. Her time alone became a search "for outward simplicity, for inner integrity, for fuller relationship"—and for shells. On her morning beach walks, she stooped and combed through drifts of shells, jingling through her fingers, that the tide had washed in during the night. She plucked those that caught her eye. The sea's ultimate gift to her was a renewed sense of self. Its daily offering was the shells she took back to the cottage and surrounded herself with.[4]

The choices on the beach must have seemed infinite. There were whelks, cockles, scallops, tulips, cantharuses, conchs, ceriths, venuses; there was the turkey wing that looked like a smaller version of the real thing, the alphabet cone that revealed English letters, the Tampa top that might actually spin on its point, the coffee bean that spent its life in mangroves, the Fargo that could be a model for a corkscrew, the large sawtooth pen that crackled and shattered when stepped on. And there were the curlicue egg chains (or casings) of all sorts of mollusks.

The largest of the Gulf mollusks are horse conchs. As babies, a hundred can fit in the bottom of a coffee cup, shell and all. As adults, they can reach up to eleven pounds. Voracious predators, mollusks are carnivores, even cannibals. The horse conch smothers its prey. It will feed on the smaller Florida fighting conch, although not without the latter living up to its name. The lightning whelk uses the knife-sharp outer lip of its aperture to pry open a bivalve to eat the soft tissue of the animal. The beautiful alphabet cone is a stabber. It has a radula tooth, or harpoon, that it deploys for penetrating the shell of its prey and injecting venom into it. The moon snail releases an acidic enzyme to soften a spot in the shell of another mollusk before drilling through with its teeth. If you find a shell with a perfectly round hole in it or a chip on it, the distortion likely did not come from tumbling with other shells in the surf but from a predator. There is also a good chance the shell was alive some hours before washing in with the tide.

To prevent extraction by a pillager, gastropods (snails) wrap themselves around the inner spiral, known as the columella, of their one-piece shells. Shells of many bivalves—picture the half shell from which the Greek goddess Aphrodite rises—are often countershaded for camouflage, light on the underside and mottled and darker on top. Sometimes defense is successful, but given the numbers of shells on the beach, oftentimes not. Fellow mollusks are not the only enemy. Fish, such as the steel-jawed tarpon, eat mollusks. Stone and box crabs use brutally powerful claws to open shells. Not even the formidable horse conch is safe. Hermit crabs will storm one in force for its meat and a new shelter.

Humans, of course, have been consuming mollusks for as long as they've been living by the sea. And they put shells to work. When Europeans first arrived in North America, coastal natives possessed personal caches of shells polished and converted into wampum beads. They used them as currency in trade, to designate one's social rank, as articles in religious ceremonies, and in the form of belts to tell stories and keep records. As Cushing learned, Gulf peoples employed shells for tools and weapons, and to build high ground for ceremonial places and dwellings. Europeans used shells for their lime to stimulate failing soil, and quarried coquina, a shell-based sedimentary rock, for the construction of walls of houses and cannonball-impenetrable forts. To do the same, they mixed lime, sand, and water with hand-crushed shells to create a reinforced cement-like material known as tabby. Today, beneath so many Gulf-coast roads is seashell bedding, and the vehicles rolling on top are powered by fossil fuels that, in part, have their origins in the remains of ancient exoskeletons.

To protect its tourist attraction, Sanibel made it unlawful to take home a living mollusk that had washed up on the beach. But throwing one back into the surf is also the wrong thing to do. The impact can jar and wound, even kill, the creature, despite its suit of armor. Place it back in the water gently or leave it on the beach for the next high tide.

Safeguarding sand has long been another local priority. Every few years at Captiva, shoreline erosion required the state to rebuild the beach, and dredges converged offshore. They pumped in fresh sand from three miles out on the continental shelf. Mixed in with the new beach were incalculable numbers of mollusks, sucked up into the dredge, banging and clanging through the metal fill pipe, and buried alive, or by then dead, on the newly restored beach.

LIKE THE SHELLS ON THEM, beaches wash in and wash out according to the vagaries of the sea and weather. One day a nice berm of sand might exist, and the next it is gone. Artificial beaches, those made by machines and men, are even more precarious. They aren't supposed to exist to begin with, and nature must be fought to keep them from washing away.

The history of Gulf beach restoration more or less dates to 1947, when a series of tormenting storms and hurricanes set in motion a series of nourishment projects. On his bike trips from Ocean Springs to New Orleans, Walter Anderson pedaled along the edge of the breakwater drumming at the foot of Mississippi's famous twenty-six-mile seawall. Ever since its completion in 1928, erosion had been claiming the sliver of natural beach in front of it, and tourist hotels were responsible for rebuilding their sandy attractions. That changed when the "natural disasters" of '47 brought in federal aid money. Within a few years, Anderson saw dredges at work.

The compulsion to re-create the edgescape perplexed him. Soon he was pedaling past a downy new beach, uniformly three hundred feet wide and as white as an egret's plumes. The Army Corps of Engineers had taken charge of the largest beach nourishment project on the Gulf, bringing in seven million cubic yards of sand, most of it pumped from fifteen hundred feet out in the sound. Mississippians then boasted about having both the longest seawall and the "longest man-made beach in the world." They, or the federal government, also had to maintain it. Hurricane Camille in 1969 cost taxpayers a two-million-cubic-yard restoration project, and Hurricane Elena in 1985, 1.5 million. Calmer times still required several top-off maintenance projects. You dig a big trench in front of a beach you build, and the sand will want to slip back into it.[5]

Long before concern about sea-level rise, coastal states constantly contended with beach erosion. Parts of the US Atlantic and Pacific coasts have had the toughest time with it, which is not to say that the Gulf has gotten off easy. Between the early 1950s and late 1990s, the Gulf states undertook 158 nourishment projects, which ranged in size from less than a mile of a new beach built on Texas's Bolivar Peninsula to 26 miles on the Mississippi Coast.

Florida, the beachiest state, was the most gluttonous for new sand. Sixty-seven percent of the projects occurred on the Mangrove Coast, most of those in Pinellas County. Florida officials worried incessantly about the fleeting foundation of their tourism trade. Between 1950 and 1997, they authorized the relocation of forty-seven million square yards of sand, brought in by truck and pumped or shoveled in by dredges. In the 1990s, state and local governments were spending $30 a square yard for restoration, between $30 and $50 million a year—tax dollars invested to generate tourist dollars. Six to ten feet of beachfront disappeared annually. That was a lot of sand-castle building and sunbathing that needed to be recovered, for the good of the economy.

It's common to cry natural disaster when stormwaters carry away beaches. But if humans put a beach where nature didn't, it's common for nature to steal it. After looking closely, researchers discovered that human behavior was behind eighty-five percent of the theft. Dikes, jetties, causeways, passes, seawalls—all intended to solve a navigation or water problem, almost always economic related—created, in nearly every instance, a land erosion problem.

Human-made or enhanced navigation inlets, usually supported by jetties, are among the worst offenders of beach theft. In Texas, several inlet jetties, some dating to the nineteenth century, disrupt the flow of sediment that once traveled from the Mississippi delta to central Padre Island, where it met sediment moving north from the Rio Grande (an excellent seashell-collecting area as a result of this convergence). These triumphs of engineering left most Texas beaches starved for sand. The Army Corps of Engineers, the jetties' architect, made matters worse when it redirected the Colorado River and its sediment from the Gulf to Matagorda Bay in 1992.

The Corps has been the principal reshaper of the coast. One notable project is the Gulf Intracoastal Waterway, completed in 1949 after a century in the making—eleven hundred miles of channel markers guiding commercial traffic from Brownsville, Texas, to Carrabelle, Florida, and later extended to Fort Myers. Dredged at least twelve feet deep and 150 wide, cutting through bays, bayous, and sounds—slashing estuaries that had been the natural connectors between the Gulf states—the waterway incited ecological upheaval. It also subverted shorelines.

Florida legislators passed a law that required spoil dredged for navigation and of suitable condition to be thrown up on a beach for nourishment. A win-win, so they thought. But a navigation channel often changes nearshore currents. And when that happens, the channel might deposit sand on one beach while taking it away from others. Sometimes, there were simply winners and losers. In three decades, seven nourishment projects serviced Captiva Island. Sanibel needed only one, in part because Captiva's new sand, and shells, kept washing down to Sanibel.

IN 1955, THE NATIONAL PARK SERVICE issued a report recommending protection of the nation's unspoiled coastal marshes and beaches—what was left of them. "Almost every attractive seashore area on our Atlantic and Gulf coasts has been pre-empted for commercial or private development," the report maintained. "Only a fraction of our long seacoast is left for public use, and much of this small portion is rapidly disappearing before our eyes."[6]

The park service decided to include beaches in its inventory of protected places. It initially targeted parts of Cape Cod, Point Reyes (above San Francisco), the Oregon Dunes, the Indiana Dunes, and Padre Island. Texans had recently mounted an effort to preserve public ownership of their shoreline, rather than let the oil industry buy it up, and since the 1930s they had imagined a sanctuary for the coastal prairies and beaches on Padre. Texas senator "Smilin' Ralph" Yarborough, a future coauthor of the Endangered Species Act, maneuvered legislation through Congress in 1962 that set aside the majority of Padre Island as a national seashore—the country's third, after Cape Hatteras, North Carolina, and Cape Cod.

Padre was a start. A lot of people on the upper Gulf worried about the transformation of unoccupied barrier islands into remakes of the Mangrove Coast. All those lofty condos and luxury hotels down in Florida, surrounded by cookie-cutter houses hip to hip, were stacked on barrier islands, after all. Closer to home, on the west end of Santa Rosa Island, at Pensacola Beach, developers were gassing up bulldozers to level sand dunes, which remained more than a decade away from state protection. Real-estate interests were concerned, too, about the possibility of the federal government seizing salable Gulf-front land.

His novelist imagination piqued, John D. MacDonald ventured outside his usual Florida story setting to write a murder mystery involving a Mississippi builder who holds permits ostensibly to develop an island. He instead intends to fleece the National Park Service, which wants to acquire the island. The plot in *Barrier Island* wasn't a farfetched one. Padre Island landowners, predominantly large absentee real-estate syndicates, walked away with subterranean mineral rights and $18.5 million more than the federal government had expected to pay for the national seashore.

Barrier Island appeared fifteen years after Congress created the Gulf Islands National Seashore, in 1971, acting largely on a grassroots initiative that had materialized in Mississippi. The safeguarded territory, brought into the fold of the National Park Service, included parts of west Santa Rosa Island (around Fort Pickens) and Perdido Key in Florida, as well as part of Cat Island and all of East Ship and West Ship, Petit Bois, and Horn Islands in Mississippi. Alabamians were among those who most distrusted a federal presence and kept their state, including Gulf Shores and Dauphin Island, off the national-seashore agenda.

Using his old path through the dunes and scrub, national-park rangers blazed the Walter Anderson trail across Horn from the sound to the Gulf. They sunk iron posts in the sand at his campsite (although his log says that Hurricane Betsy washed it into the sea), and designated it off limits during nesting season. They named the area the Walter Anderson Crossing. It was a nice tribute to the nature artist, though a mixed blessing.

The park service established other trails and points of interest on the island, printed a visitors' map, advertised to park-goers, and at one point proposed developing a hundred acres of campsites and paving three cross-island routes. Congress interrupted the plans by designating the island a wilderness area in 1978. A decade later, the US Fish and Wildlife Service used Horn to advance a captive-breeding program for red wolves, once an inhabitant of the broader South's bottomlands and coastal prairies. The Horn Island wolves flourished on the rabbit population that Anderson had known so well, but after ten years the service removed them to the eastern North Carolina wild. There had been too many encounters between *Canis lupus rufus* and *Homo sapiens*—the camper, sightseer, birder, Anderson aficionado, and weekend party boater.

After Anderson's death, every condo or hotel that went up on an island elsewhere in the Gulf reinforced the importance of seashore sanctuaries to wildlife. On Rancho Nuevo beach in Tamaulipas, Mexico, just south of the border, Kemp's ridleys had built some forty thousand nests in 1947. Thirty-one years later, when nests of this small, greenish-gray turtle totaled less than a thousand worldwide, American scientists collaborated with Mexican counterparts to use Padre's national seashore to reverse the trend.

Four of the five sea turtle species that lived in the Gulf—it was long after the soup-can days, yet each was an endangered or threatened species—laid eggs on Padre. The island was one of the few places in the world on the reproductive radar of the endangered Kemp's ridley. In 1987, Congress required state governments to adopt protective measures for sea turtles, and the Gulf states, sans one, established secure nesting areas and required shrimpers to use turtle exclusion devices (TEDs) in their nets. Defiant Baton Rouge legislators passed a law flouting the federal mandate and let shrimpers know that Louisiana wildlife officers would not check for TEDs (under pressure, the state reversed its truancy in 2015). Elsewhere, lights-out policies and yellow caution tape encircling nests patrolled by volunteers became common on developed beaches. The private, public, and government cooperation brought the Kemp's ridley back from the brink with an average population growth rate of fifteen percent a year.

Had Anderson lived to witness the turtle's changing fortune, it's easy to imagine a log entry congratulating the selflessness of the states participating in the national seashore, even as the increased traffic in island visitors would have irritated him. Toward the end (his own), Anderson had not only fewer turtles to draw; birdlife was on the wane too.

He first noticed a difference in the 1950s, most sadly in the brown pelican population, which was spiraling toward complete disappearance. Beginning in 1963, you couldn't find his favorite bird on the mainland of Louisiana, except stitched on the state flag, where it had been emblematically perched for five decades. In 1966, as if they were naming a highway for a fallen war hero, lawmakers selected the pelican as the state bird. By then, the chief ambassador of Gulf nature was missing in action from eastern Texas to the Florida Big Bend. No one knew where the confounding bird had gone. A favored theory early on, which let humans off the hook, was that storms or an anonymous avian pathogen had coursed through pelican colonies. Then, pelicans started disappearing from southern California too.

Scientists on the West Coast traced the cause to DDT streaming into the food chain after a manufacturing plant dumped thousands of gallons into Los Angeles County's sewer system. Infected birds were laying eggs with weakened shells that wouldn't hatch if the weight of the nesting parent didn't crush them first. In 1933, an ornithologist counted twenty-three hundred pelican nests on North Island in the Chandeleurs. Three decades along, the island sheltered only a hundred nestlings. The Chandeleurs' frequent visitor, Anderson, suspected chemical pollution. He was right. Since the war, farmers had been dowsing their fields in the Mississippi River basin with DDT, and down the river and into the food chain it went.

The US banned the general use of the chemical at the end of 1972. By spring, Gulf-coast newspapers were reporting fresh sightings of the "big-billed bird." The *Pensacola News Journal* called its return a "harbinger that nature will not desert mere humans if we but give it an opportunity to survive." The statement hits you over the head with its human self-interest, but the normally pro-business newspaper also had been a relentless supporter of the national seashore—as habitat for beachgoers as much as for birds.[7]

No group was more grateful for the DDT ban and the Gulf's protected habitat than binocular-wielding birders. Since midcentury, their passion had become one of the country's fastest-growing recreations. The Texas coast, at the confluence of the Central and Mississippi Flyways, was the favored destination among their flock. A lithe and sprightly—birdlike—woman was largely responsible for that.

Not much was known about the flyways before Connie Hagar and her husband, Jack, a former oilman, bought an eight-cottage tourist court in Rockport, amid Texas sabal palms and wind-twisted and -stunted coastal oaks. That was 1935, several years after Connie and her sister, Bert, traveling from their home near Dallas, had started seeking a coastal reprieve from the family plague, arthritis. They intentionally arrived with the feathered migrators, and Connie would fill pocket datebooks with precise notes of birds, habitats, and habits. By the time she and Jack moved to the coast, she knew more about resident and migratory avian life than most.

Professional ornithologists, all of them men, tended to laugh her off as nothing more than a twittering homemaker with a bird feeder outside her kitchen window. It is true that she went out in the field wearing a cotton dress and viewed the world of birds through trendy harlequin glasses (so did Rachel Carson). But her field was a nine-mile loop that she had astutely mapped out along the shore, through woods and prairies, around wetlands, and beside salt marshes to maximize her exposure to the widest variety of birds. The loop became her daily beat.

When the archbishop of American birding, Roger Tory Peterson, went to Rockport in 1948, he let Hagar be his guide and learned she was the real deal. The state named a bird sanctuary after her and subsequently used it as the nucleus of the Great Texas Coastal Birding Trail, created in the 1990s as a five-hundred-mile conjoined system of preserves, trails, and sanctuaries. By then, the more than six hundred species of birds in Texas, including the only Gulf nesting spot for white pelicans, on Padre, were generating major tourist dollars, as much as $90 million a year in the Rio Grande Valley alone, home to two national wildlife refuges.

WHEN HAGAR DIED at age eighty-seven in 1973, the Gulf had countless local and state bird sanctuaries and ten national wildlife refuges. Public pressure to control convulsive growth had created twenty-eight more federal refuges by the time the *Deepwater Horizon* platform exploded. But they, too, were in danger of going the way of the once-disappearing pelican. The amendment that Congressman Gene Taylor, who wanted to clean up the pollution in Mississippi Sound, proposed for the 2000 Water Resources Development Act included a major provision for shoreline restoration. This was not just beach building for tourists. Islands were sinking, shrinking, and ebbing away.

The National Park Service fretted most over historic Ship Island. The French had launched their search for the mouth of the Mississippi from there, and it remained the home of Civil War–era Fort Massachusetts—for now. Hurricane Camille opened a pass through the island in 1969, creating East and West Ship Islands, marooning the fort on the western remnant, and leaving it on the precipice of crumbling brick by brick into the sound.

Fortifying the old citadel turned into a constant battle. Between 1974 and 2002, the island required six nourishment projects. After Hurricane Katrina damaged the fort and demolished the visitor center, and after East Ship remained hidden underwater for a period in the aftermath of Hurricane Ike in 2008, the Army Corps of Engineers, loving the restoration business that it had, in part, created from previous shoreline-eroding projects, released a $1.5 billion revetment proposal for the Mississippi barriers. The proposal mentioned Ship Island 537 times.[8]

On the ecological front, a worse scenario than losing a historic structure would be losing the Chandeleurs. Barely elevated above sea level, they had always been among the higher-risk islands. A succession of lighthouses and Anderson's art form a historical record of land in danger. The US built the first lighthouse on the Chandeleurs in 1848, and a hurricane took it away four years later. Its replacement, delayed by the 1853 yellow-fever epidemic, was a handsome white-washed brick tower with a flame-sourced fourth-order Fresnel lens mounted at fifty feet. Storms diligently eroded the light's foundation, and by 1896 a new metal skeletal tower supported a slightly more powerful third-order lens at twice the height.

Anderson drew a picture of the light fifty years later. It stands above two keeper's dwellings and a long dock striking out over salt marsh. A boat and storage shed are attached to the dock. The sea is gentle, and a gull squats on a solitary piling in the foreground. By 1960, storms had carried away one of the dwellings, the boathouse, and most of the dock. Camille took the last dwelling nine years later. By then, the lighthouse had been automated. In 1998, Hurricane Georges consumed enough landmass to leave the light stranded in three feet of open water, looking more like a channel marker than a lighthouse. Finally, Katrina obliterated all evidence of the structure's existence. What had been dry land under the tower when Anderson drew it was seventeen feet of Gulf water in 2006. Some scientists say Katrina dealt a somber, lasting blow, and the Chandeleurs will be gone before the second half of the twenty-first century.

If that's true, the Chandeleurs' Breton National Wildlife Refuge, the country's second-oldest refuge, will also be gone. Anderson met the loggerhead, green, and Kemp's ridley turtles that visited the islands, and he was endlessly entertained by the two dozen species of sea- and shorebirds that fished the beachfront and salt marshes. More than half of them nested on the Chandeleurs, designated by the Audubon Society as a Global Important Bird Area. After their bout with DDT, brown pelicans used the Chandeleurs to regroup and build a major colony. Five oil spills associated with Hurricane Katrina endangered the pelicans and other Chandeleur birds, including North America's largest tern colony, and Katrina's storm surge caused permanent damage to the island's beaches and salt marshes, affecting all inhabitants and passers-through.

Like every barrier in this part of the Gulf, the Chandeleurs for migrating birds are a vital "hiatus." Since George Lowery used this word in the 1940s in conjunction with proving the cross-Gulf flyway, the number of birds traveling it had, by 2014, declined by half (and Mississippi's Cat Island, the former training ground of war dogs, had all but washed away). The fragmenting of habitat and breeding areas by seaside development, and to a lesser extent parasites in select species, lie behind the loss. Climate change is also redirecting birds and changing migration patterns. A principal factor, with perilous consequences, is the loss of landmass on the Gulf.[9]

Barrier islands are becoming less barriers than weakened sandspits, not to mention endangered species. That would be the case for those around Louisiana even without the worry of sea-level rise. Like the birds, sediment from the Mississippi River that replenished the islands and coast no longer lands on shores in the same volumes.

Nineteen

LOSING THE EDGE

By the twenty-first century, ten thousand miles of canals crisscrossed
Louisiana's great coastal wetlands, turning much of the region into
open pools of water, as shown here, contributing to the state's
land erosion crisis.

*The whole universe depends on everything fitting together just
right. If one piece busts, even the smallest piece . . . the entire
universe will get busted.*

HUSHPUPPY, *BEASTS OF THE SOUTHERN WILD* (2012)[1]

⁘ ─────────────────────────────

COASTAL MARSHES ARE EVERYWHERE ALONG THE GULF'S
edge. The long continental shelf, barrier islands, gentle breakwaters,

and sediment from the sea's many rivers inspire their proliferation. The Gulf husbands somewhere around half of the nation's coastal marshes, saltwater and fresh. They generously encircle bays, bayous, and islands, and trim estuarine terminuses of rivers.

At a place like Alabama's Bayou La Batre, where marshes bundle the shrimp docks in a snug shelter, they are so otherworldly that when one sees them, all thoughts of strife or hardship in the world seem thoroughly remote. The marshes draw your vision out to the infinity of grass and sky, and you are a speck on the big Earth, left adrift in the hugeness. Yet, if you allow, the marsh can be a sanctuary on a planet crowded by billions. The marsh is a living place. It is life that gives life.

Sidney Lanier called coastal marshes the "Vast of the Lord." He was moved by them as others are moved by mountains, and he composed long verse to honor them.

Ye marshes, how candid and simple and nothing-withholding and free
Ye publish yourselves to the sky and offer yourselves to the sea![2]

Alabama and, especially, Florida have sizable swaths of coastal marsh; Mississippi, a rake or two. They are most liberally present in Texas and Louisiana. Find Connecticut on a map of the US, and that's the size of Louisiana's coastal marshland. It is the heel and sole of the Louisiana boot. Nearly every foot of Gulf front is the same, reaching fifteen miles inland, a fifty-five-hundred-square-mile alluvial sweep matched by few places on the planet.

There is no single word to describe it. Wild, certainly. Graceful, that too. Breathtaking, yes. Cloud shadows slide silently across the expanse like so many migrating lakes, casting down on the flush Earth the sky's enormity in duplicate. There is room enough for sunlight to pour down in one corner and a dark thunderstorm to throb noiselessly in a farther corner. The marsh not only dominates your view; it catches you with its hushed sounds, and with its blended earthy and briny smells in the grass, mud, air, and water.

When referring to coastal marshes, it was once common to use the generally contemptuous term "waste," even among lovers of the wild. Texas naturalist Roy Bedichek found marshes "wanting." Yet there is nothing wanting or wasteful about them. Nor are they "empty"— another common characterization. Bedichek, in fact, would have been the first to concede that there is always a mullet's splash or a heron's croak to break the lonesome quiet, that marshes are aquatic Serengetis racing with life. Lanier saw them as an animated world unto themselves.[3]

Passeth a hurrying sound of wings that westward whirr.[4]

In Louisiana, a hundred or more bird species share the grassy bergs. They range from the smallest warblers on the Gulf Express to the year-round great blue heron. Weighing in between is the common gallinule, or marsh hen, a squat and ubiquitous resident vernacularly known as a swamp chicken or skitty coot. Two dozen kinds of migrating ducks bring out hunters in the fall. Family descendants of Edward McIlhenny continue to provide roosting platforms at Avery Island for hundreds of snowy egrets in the gene pool of those that first benefited from his protection.

Ospreys are regular visitors, flying many miles from home sometimes several times a day—an easy commute for these tremendous flying birds on their nearly six-foot wingspans. They live as solitary couples in great nests built to last a lifelong companionship. Rachel Carson saw an osprey nest that was six feet across at its base, a masterwork of beach-salvaged driftwood, oyster shells, conch egg casings, splintered boat oar, and a fisherman's boot, reinforced with twenty-four feet of fishing net and cork line. It was commodious enough for multifamily occupation in its lower parts—sparrows, starlings, wrens—so heavy that it strained the topmost branches of its forty-foot-tall loblolly host. When in the marsh, one or both of the fish hawks, as they are known—gray, white, and brown—shadow prey from high above, and the osprey itself is often stalked by a fish-stealing eagle.

An honest and most disciplined fisher is the great blue heron. It commonly takes its position standing still beside the grass, half hidden. Its S-shaped neck holds head, dagger bill, and yellow eyes furtively above the grass. It blends in as if it were an overtall sprout.

A league and a league of marsh-grass, waist-high, broad in blade,
Green, and all of a height, and unflicked with a light or a shade,
Stretch leisurely off, in a pleasant plain.[5]

The marsh is nothing if not for the grass. There is bulrush, needlerush, duck millet, and smartweed. Spartina species command the salt zones and create a prairie aesthetic of amber, green, and gray. Locals refer to spartina as cordgrass, or sometimes wire grass, marsh hay, or, in Cajun country, *paille chat tigré*—"hair of the tiger." In salt marshes, as with prairie grass on arid terra firma, flora diversity is low (it is higher in brackish water), but reproduction is great. The grass grows as densely as it does expansively—growing and dying, growing and dying. So much vegetation decomposes that the marsh is a naturally anaerobic place.

Between the little oxygen, salty water, and waterlogged base, the ancient grass has adapted to be exceptionally forgiving of extreme conditions. Its folded blades are resourcefully designed to store fresh rainwater. Unlike prairie grasses that multiply by throwing seeds into the wind—not an ideal strategy for the marsh—spartina regenerates and attains its upthrusting density through horizontal stems and lateral roots, known as rhizomes, that run under the mud.

But who will reveal to our waking ken
The forms that swim and the shapes that creep
Under the waters of sleep?[6]

Gulf marshes are home to otters, nutrias, minks, rabbits, and mice; snakes; and an array of turtles (Suwannee cooters, Mobile cooters, and diamondback terrapins). Butterflies live in salt marshes. Amphibians don't. The largest marsh denizens, alligators, prefer freshwater. The broad, wet gardens are nurseries of the sea—same as mangroves, estuaries, and coral reefs. They are quietly scored with natural looping channels, languid pathways of sea grass and oyster beds traveled by juvenile redfish, trout, drum, croaker, flounder, mullet, and sheepshead.

Blue crabs are central occupants. Scientists have a new understanding of the crabs' ecological vitality, manifested in their quotidian feeding habits. Gamboling sideways near the surface, using their swimmerets—paddle-like hind legs—they reach up with a claw to pinch a periwinkle snail from the grass. As with nutrias, an excess of these snails leads to overgrazing, which leaves a lot of leftover decaying matter, which makes for eutrophic waters and more dead grass. Crabs are also burrowers, and their digging, along with that of certain mussels and fungi, acts as an aerator by stimulating oxygen levels in the porous mud and plant detritus.

Much of the underwater animal life begins with "coffee grounds." That's what shrimpers call the brown and crumbly dead tissue of plants accumulated at the edges of marsh grass. The rotting matter that absorbs so much oxygen is also food for larvae and growing marine life, such as brown shrimp. Scientists once considered the shrimp as "detritivores," meaning they ate only the decaying vegetation. Researchers subsequently learned that grass detritus promoted the multiplication of nematodes, and that shrimp nibbled on the rotting grass to get to the minuscule worms.

Back in 1977, when all this was still speculation, Eugene Turner, the scientist who discovered the dead zone, conducted a study showing that the size of the shrimp population was directly related to the size and health of the marsh area—to wit, the nursery. It's no wonder that Louisiana has the highest-volume shrimp fishery in the country, that it's one of the most fruitful marine habitats in the world, that a biologist back in 1963 nicknamed the coast between Mobile and east Texas the "Fertile Fisheries Crescent."[7]

As the coffee grounds give refuge to underwater life, so the marsh provides refuge to humans. Nature knew what it was doing when it spread the quilt of marshes along the storm-ridden Texas and Louisiana coast. After the disaster of Hurricane Katrina, a lot of people were talking about the importance of preserving these natural storm buffers, as if this benefit to humankind were a new discovery. Mostly *forgotten* is more like it. Back in the 1840s, congressmen debating the Swamp Land acts were making that very point. Marshes also possess the capacity to filter foul water, much as oysters do. More recently, scientists have been studying the benefit of marshes, as well as mangrove forests and sea grasses, for sequestering carbon dioxide from the oceans and atmosphere, thus helping to slow climate change.

But nature can do only so much for humankind. The marshes' filtering and sequestering capacities have limits. Human behavior sometimes knows none.

And all of a sudden the sinister smell of a man,
Awaft on a wind-shift.[8]

IN THAT BLUSTERY YEAR OF 1988—the year of the first Toxics Release Inventory, *Time*'s "Filthy Seas" cover, the Texas ban on commercial net fishing, and the drought that devastated Apalachicola oyster beds but temporarily shrank the dead zone—Oliver Houck published a law-review article that abandoned the usual academic doctrinality. The opening sentence was a grabber: "We are involved in a war of extermination." The casualties of this war were "coastal resources," and stemming those casualties would be unlike "almost any other environmental struggle." Houck, former general counsel and vice president of the National Wildlife Federation, a veteran canoer of rivers across the land, happiest when outdoors with family or students, and recently professor at Tulane Law School in New Orleans, was advancing a reality check. "All over America, development is moving to the sea," he said, later to be echoed in public comment by the best hurricane tracker in his adopted hometown, Nash Roberts.[9]

Next door in Texas, nearly one-third of the population and nearly three-quarters of its industrial base had advanced on the coast. In all states, the permitting process for coastal development was so convoluted, underfunded, understaffed, bureaucratic, and political, Houck added—this time sounding like Eugene Turner describing a wicked problem—that "we have created a Dr. Seuss-like machine that produces occasionally good, but more often poor, compromises at the end of an elaborate pipeline." The overwhelmed EPA contemplated streamlining the process by distinguishing between important and unimportant wetlands—a step that the "construction-minded Corps," the military force behind the war of extermination, was encouraging.[10]

The consequences? The nation's estuaries were "rotten with conventional pollution." Houck's own home front was a petrochemical redoubt second only to Texas. Louisiana, too, had traded away its ecological soul for jobs and taxes and presumably a better quality of life. The Environmental Defense Fund rated Louisiana's beachfront water the fifth most contaminated in the country. Pollution affected more than one-third of its estuaries. Effective strategies for dealing with bad water were available, but it was unclear whether the resolve to deploy them existed. When Congress created the National Estuary Program in 1987, Houck noted, the Fertile Fisheries Crescent received no priority consideration like that afforded the Chesapeake Bay and Great Lakes.[11]

Even less resolve existed for tangling with a bigger gorilla: land erosion. The coast "is disappearing so rapidly that the measures needed to save it are almost at the limits of technology," Houck wrote, "to say nothing of economics and political will." He wasn't talking about tourist beaches either, which were not Louisiana's claim to fame. Coastal marshes were.[12]

Since the 1950s, the Gulf's two largest bays had been major losers of marshland. Channeling and fill dredging had triggered the disintegration of forty percent of Tampa Bay's marshes. Similar projects had left Galveston Bay with a deficit of thirty-five thousand acres, and continued to rob six inches of shoreline a year. But it was the marshiest place in the US—Louisiana—that was shrinking the fastest, accounting for eighty percent of the continental US wetland loss. Once secluded Cajun country, where only a few decades before a one-time boy movie star poling his pirogue with his pet raccoon encountered an oddity in the form of an oil-drilling rig, had become overrun with an "unimaginably large network of highways, causeways, pipelines, and canals." "Each one," said Houck, "destroys."[13]

Louisiana's is a naturally eroding coastline. It also is, or was, a naturally replenished coast, sustained, rebuilt, and reshaped by the Atchafalaya and Mississippi Rivers, both industrious land makers. Throughout its ten-thousand-year life, the Mississippi, one of those fidgety course-changing rivers, has been like a loose garden hose, swinging its end back and forth to the east and west—spraying not just water, but also a revitalizing sediment, across the upper Gulf. In satellite photos, you can see great dirty plumes swirling sediment in the Gulf as it approaches a resting place on the mud-brown coast. The Atchafalaya River, which diverts about thirty percent of the Mississippi's flow, faithfully tends to land-making to its west.

In its restless lifetime, the Mississippi has built the Louisiana coast up to fifty miles out, and made several deltas. Abandoned ones are now part of the state's famous coastal marshes. They would not exist, if not for the river's natural building materials. Nor would the barrier islands, such as Grand Isle and the Chandeleurs. Nor would the corridor of underground and undersea oil and gas reservoirs around Louisiana.

Thomas Hutchins, the British surveyor who charted parts of the upper Gulf in the eighteenth century, was one of the first to understand that the Mississippi River relocated landmass from the upper continent to the lower. Moving that load is a mean feat, though undeniably not surprising when you consider that the river pushes an average of 450,000 cubic feet of water into the Gulf every second. Imagine, then, two million dump trucks rumbling down the interstate toward the Gulf carrying midwestern dirt, 180 million tons a year. That's enough to build three hundred feet of Louisiana coast. This is what was happening before "improvements" were made.[14]

Improvements—or, more accurately, altering the river—began with the shovels and wheelbarrows of Bienville's French, who raised the first levee against the river. After New Orleans, city after river city demanded a levee. Farm irrigation and factories demanded dams. Navigation demanded jetties and passes. In 1862, Louisiana sisters Anne and Martha Cubitt dug (or, more likely, had slaves dig for them) a canal—a ditch really—across the riverbank to Ronde Bayou as a shortcut for their aging father, who poled his skiff into the bayou to oyster. When the river flooded that spring, their canal morphed to a wide-eyed hundred times its size as its banks eroded. Within eight years it was twenty-five hundred feet across. By 1950, the bayou was a wetland the size of New Orleans (now it's the Delta National Wildlife Refuge).

The Cubitt sisters were working with nothing more technologically advanced than human and mule power. Imagine, then, the unintended consequences resulting from engineers drawing on the muscle of steam and kinetics of mechanics. The Swamp Land acts opened the way for their smoke-puffing, clanking equipment to tame the river, under the sacred auspices of land reclamation, flood control, and navigation. They pursued their endeavors with an aggressiveness that compared with Union forces invading Confederate New Orleans.

In a venerable book titled *Rising Tide,* historian John Barry lays bare both the engineers' technological genius and their competitive spirit, among themselves and against the river's intemperate flow and flooding. Their genius depended on unproven science in controlling nature and a compulsion to "fix" the feral river. Levees were their first strategy. A rail and road bridge, connecting Missouri and Illinois and completed in 1874 by a self-taught civil engineer named James Buchanan Eads, was their second. Jetties were their third, and another Eads accomplishment.

A major flaw in the Big Muddy from the point of view of commerce was the constant buildup of sediment in the southern passes, disrupting shipping traffic between New Orleans and the Gulf. Eads, bald above an Abe Lincoln beard, touted by *Scientific American* as a "man of genius," tried to persuade the Corps that jetties were the solution. Built within the river's flow, they would increase the speed of the current, which in turn would scour the bottom and simultaneously deepen the river and mitigate flooding. Jetties would act as a constant hydraulic form of dredging, commanding the river to do the work usually assigned to less reliable and more expensive mechanical dredges.

Congress wanted thirty feet of water at the South Pass, deep enough for the most heavily laden cargo ships. Eads said if he failed to reach it, the government wouldn't have to compensate him. In 1879, jetties complete, inspectors sounded thirty feet, and Eads got paid. With smooth sailing through the pass assured, ship owners saved $5 million in maritime insurance, and New Orleans shot from the ninth to the second busiest cargo port in America (behind New York).[15]

Yet soon after South Pass opened, oyster fishers on Breton Sound, between the delta and Chandeleur Islands, noticed saltwater drowning freshwater marshes and ancient coastal forests. Martha Field wrote from Grand Isle in 1892, "The sparkling waters of bayou and bay slipping southward over the sands seem to have washed the unstable land away." What were they seeing?[16]

Five years later, Eads's chief assistant on the lower Mississippi, Elmer Corthell, gave some hint in a *National Geographic* article. He reported that marshland near the jetty was retreating, or more accurately subsiding, at a rate of slightly over half an inch a year—a consequence not of the Gulf rising, but of men engineering the river. His findings were no confession of a contrite professional, however. Corthell reasoned that the "great benefit"—and he believed "every human being on this continent" benefited—"accruing from" his and Eads's work "far outweighs the disadvantages to future generations from the subsidence of Gulf delta lands." Besides, the seer of America's future welfare argued, "when the time comes," engineers could "build a protective levee against the Gulf waters."[17]

In the meantime, Corthell's kindred built jetties in the Southwest Pass to accommodate increased ship traffic. And their professional organization eventually designated Eads's original jetties a National Historic Civil Engineering Landmark. Then, in 1914, the Department of Agriculture made an official pronouncement on erosion. It concluded that the Louisiana coast was secure, that natural sedimentation adequately offset erosion and subsidence, and that five thousand years of land-building was continuing uninterrupted. For the next five decades, engineers and geologists preached this gospel of equilibrium.

In the late 1960s, a Louisiana State University geographer named Sherwood "Woody" Gagliano came along to be the George Lowery of the sedimentation question. Having grown up in Louisiana and known many dry places that succumbed to water, Gagliano had retained a healthy skepticism that often serves good scientists. When the Corps concocted a proposal to reroute up to a third of the Mississippi's water to dry parts of Texas and New Mexico, he got funding to conduct a study of the implications for the Louisiana coast. What he and his research team discovered shocked the hell out of them: Louisiana was disappearing at a rate of 16.5 square miles a year. Radiocarbon dating of core samples revealed that the state first started losing its edge in the 1880s, the decade after Eads completed his jetties.

Not unlike the 1950s, the 1880s was a decade of portents, in the form of disappearances. Silas Stearns noted disappearing red snapper then, and William E. D. Scott, plume birds. Researchers subsequently calculated that since that time, the sediment load settling on the Louisiana coast had declined by nearly eighty percent. Most of the drop-off started in the 1950s, moving into what scientists call the beginning of the postdam period. Dams and their reservoirs along the Mississippi and its tributaries acted as traps holding back downstream deposits of sediment.

Research on the most famous Texas watercourse revealed the same problem. Designated an American Heritage River, the Rio Grande supports a dam every ninety miles—twenty-one altogether. If not for tributaries along its lower course, no water would spill from its mouth. Only a little does anyway. In the old days, tarpon fishers cast their lines while standing on the shore at a place called Tarpon Bend, and sediment from the river traveled out and up the shore to revitalize Padre Island. These days, nobody is casting for silver king. The fish can no longer enter the river's mouth, which is little more than a thin sheet of water, and swim up to Tarpon Bend. Sometimes the river doesn't even make it to the Gulf, denying Padre a major source of land nourishment.

Back up in Louisiana, Gagliano published his findings in 1970. Subsequent studies showed that the forfeiture of terra firma was greater than previously known—twenty-five to thirty-five square miles per annum. And Delaware was gone; that's how much Louisiana land dissolved from the 1930s to the end of the century: twenty-three hundred square miles. People accused the Gulf currents of stealing it. Dams were the culprit, though, and not the only one. Eads's national-landmark jetties, and other jetties, hastened the river's flow as intended, and levees did the same. The linear distances they covered on the Mississippi and its tributaries eventually exceeded the length of the river itself. They compelled the water to drive fast and hard, and as it did, it blasted through the shore drift and thrust much of the sediment far out across the Gulf's continental shelf and into the deep, rather than around to the coast.[18]

And there was more. When Eugene Turner was trying to solve the hypoxia mystery back in 1974, he got in a plane for a bird's-eye view of America's greatest marshland. What he saw left him thunderstruck. Canals crossed the marsh in every direction. Some looked like airport runways without ends; others, like neighborhood streets. Straight-edged and knifing the marsh into severed sections, they were clearly not nature's creations. Three-quarters of them were the webwork of the oil and gas industry, averaging eighty feet in width, used primarily for pipelines and supply and crew boats. By the time of Turner's illuminating plane ride, biologists were piecing together the ecological chain reaction from the canals—how they changed the flow of water in the marshes, sent saltwater where fresh should be, killed off grasses and oyster beds, and inhibited the incubatory capacity of wetlands. And each canal lost its original straight edges and doubled or more in width within a decade—the Cubitt-sisters effect.

Back in the 1920s, Percy Viosca, a Louisiana marine biologist, noticed that the "cutting of navigation and drainage canals" was "changing the conditions of existence" of Louisiana wetlands from their "very foundations." For a long time, his was a voice in the wilderness. Then, a handful of biologists discussed the issue at the 1948 symposium of the Louisiana Academy of Sciences, the year Robert J. Flaherty released his propaganda film. Several years later, a pipeline company owned by Esso (later renamed Exxon) quietly conceded that the canal had caused damage, and that repairing it would require more than a "few passes of a bulldozer, some shovel work, and a little seeding."[19]

A couple years later, in 1959, state biologists noted significant ballooning out of the twenty-plus miles of canals in Rockefeller Wildlife Refuge. When the canals were dug through the refuge, they were anticipated to serve as a model of symbiosis between oil and conservation. The year before Turner's flight, even the Corps of Engineers acknowledged "irretrievable marshland loss" in connection with pipeline construction. "The word had gotten that far," Houck wrote in a later law-review article, with an intended dig at the Corps.[20]

Houck had become aware of the "collapse" of coastal wetlands in the 1970s, when it was still a "big secret" that was "completely unattended" by the media and policy makers. As a lawyer, he had sued water polluters and spent seventeen years on a case to stop the Corps from drying up a big expanse of the Atchafalaya River basin. But the canals were a "much bigger issue." Houck first took the oil and gas industry to task in a 1983 law-review article, which cited a score of sources that connected canals to marshland loss. What Flaherty didn't propagate in his film about the friendly drilling crew and its benign presence is that another crew would soon come in to dig a pipeline access to Alexander Napoleon Ulysses LaTour's huggable wellhead, and others would be dug as the industry expanded in and offshore, until ten thousand miles of canals would lace Louisiana's marshy boot.[21]

Houck, Turner, and a number of others have said that the industry's greatest fallout has been inshore. At the same time, they have never disputed the horribleness of offshore oil spills. It was hard to forget the June 1979 blowout at the Ixtoc I exploratory well in Mexico's Campeche Bay, which had released an average of ten to thirty thousand barrels of oil a day for ten months.

Until BP and 2010, Ixtoc I was the largest marine oil spill in industry history. Oil lapped onto Mexican beaches up to a foot thick, much of it just as Kemp's ridleys were hatching at Rancho Nuevo, plundering the newly mobilized conservation efforts of biologists in Tamaulipas and Padre Island. Oil visited over 160 miles of US beaches, mainly in southern Texas. Fish landings in some areas fell by as much as seventy percent, and remained at a nadir for many years. The Kemp's ridley population teetered until the 1990s, before crawling toward recovery, only to be oiled again by the BP spill.

It would be foolish to minimize the initial impact and the decades-to-come aftershock of the *Deepwater Horizon* disaster. And maybe little comes from trying to make comparisons between offshore and onshore threats. Still, Turner and Houck have offered a valid point: Ocean spills are onetime events, most of them short-term and containable. They generate the words "crisis situation" across emergency communication networks. Minute-by-minute update reports race over the wires to be turned into breaking news, and the public won't tolerate the image of a suppurating well. Cleanup crews hit the beach with the sort of dispatch that FEMA deprived Hurricane Katrina victims. The truth is, the day-to-day, fairly routine assault from in- and onshore support infrastructure, as John Barry puts it, "doesn't have the drama of accidents."[22]

When the industry wants to open a new region to extraction, opponents tend to look outward too, where a platform might turn the water slick-black, or sully the view from a tourist beach. On occasions when Florida lawmakers start beating the oil drum to lift the only Gulf state's ban on offshore drilling, citizens and the hospitality lobby come out in force. On a cold but clear Saturday in February 2010, an assembly of ten thousand, organized by Seaside restaurant owner and surfer Dave Rauschkolb, joined hands on some ninety Florida Gulf beaches in a symbolic and prophetic defense of the shoreline. Two months later, the *Deepwater Horizon* drilling unit exploded. Oil touched panhandle beaches, tar balls washed up on peninsular shores, and diseased fish with dissolved BP oil in their livers were found off Sanibel.

The emphasis on outer-water dangers enabled the industry to concentrate on one issue. To defend its offshore activities, it developed a ready strategy, which harkens to 1953 and *Thunder Bay*'s all-American Steve Martin (James Stewart) holding up the golden shrimp. Of late, the industry holds up the red snapper, insisting that each of its nearly four thousand Gulf platforms is an artificial reef, and that the habitats they create have restored red snapper numbers. When *Thunder Bay* premiered in theaters, commercial fishers were having to go all the way to Campeche Bay for the Gulf's remaining snapper grounds. So few fish were biting by the 1960s that the long trip no longer made sense. Then, by the 1980s, recreational anglers were hooking red snapper and other fish left and right out on oil-drilling grounds.

Writing a popular book on the Gulf commissioned by Exxon Corporation, Bern Keating quoted a Louisiana State marine biologist, who said that whenever the industry sinks a platform, it creates a "flourishing colony" of sea life "where it used to be just empty sea." The world's highest concentration of offshore platforms had, in other words, become the world's largest complex of artificial reefs. Enlarging the eco-complex, the state of Alabama built artificial reefs off its shores by sinking old cars, buses, ships, army tanks, railcars, and construction rubble, developing twenty thousand of them and a new hot spot for catching red snapper.[23]

The red snapper population in some areas seems to have returned to nineteenth-century levels, with sixty percent of it concentrated in the petroleum-platform waters of the northwestern Gulf. Industry defenders argue that, thanks to the platforms, the snapper is new to Louisiana waters. That's not true, though. In the early twentieth century, commercial fishers were taking plenty of red snapper from the area. Still, many, including the Environmental Defense Fund and the five Gulf states, have opposed a Department of the Interior requirement that decommissioned platforms be dismantled, which usually means dynamiting them—to wit, blowing up fish, corals, artificial reef, and all.

The snapper story made the energy industry's presence more tolerable. But Rowan Jacobsen, author of *Shadows of the Gulf*, the perceptive postmortem of the BP spill, looks at the rigs qua reefs with a more discerning eye than many. He points out that the "breeding population of snappers in the Gulf has actually plunged by ninety-seven percent since World War II," much of it lost as bycatch in shrimp trawler nets and to recreational fishers seeking "easy pickings" around the rigs. And while there may be abundance swimming around them, there are also high levels of mercury from "produced water"—that which was injected into an oil or gas reservoir to force the mineral out, and from drilling mud, despite EPA efforts to regulate the dumping of mud at drill sites. Tests showed that mercury levels in rig fish and shrimp were as much as twenty-five times the levels in outliers and, consequently, dangerously high in people who frequently eat rig-caught seafood.[24]

Furthermore, what the industry incidentally contributed in terms of population growth by erecting platforms, each of which also perpetually put that environment at risk of spills and toxic dispersants in the event of one, could not make up for the losses inshore. Land deficits have not generated widespread public outrage anywhere equivalent to that engendered by a spill. No emergency crews have dispatched containment booms to encircle the agricultural runoff that keeps the dead zone alive. More than twelve million pounds of hazardous chemicals, most of it legally discharged, slipped down the Mississippi in the year of the BP tragedy, as in the year before and the year after—and all the years since then. Nearly three million pounds came from Exxon Mobil's Baton Rouge refinery, consistently among the country's top ten polluters.[25]

Raw-sewage discharges never seem to spare the Mississippi either.*

---

* Or elsewhere. During heavy rains in the summer of 2015, the city of St. Petersburg dumped fifteen million gallons of untreated waste into Boca Ciega Bay, threatening the public with *E. coli* contamination.

And until they disappear, Louisiana's nutrient-absorbing wetlands are the sole defense, in the absence of policy remedies, against the agricultural runoff feeding the dead zone.

Land erosion is also eating away at the cultural history of the coast. Mike Tidwell has written movingly about this in *Bayou Farewell*, an adieu to a people and place. It's more than the common story of the displacement of language, memories, and folk traditions. People are losing the physical place that has grounded their heritage for centuries—one drowned tree, telephone pole, road, and house at a time. By the time the culture is gone, there will be no land on which to place a historic marker or monument to commemorate the culture. As Tidwell writes, most of the hubbub after Katrina was about damage to New Orleans resulting from the degraded buffer in wetlands. Meanwhile, the folk down in the marshes were devastated, returning to vanished places, never to reemerge. Rita, barreling in just weeks later, was even worse than Katrina. All this loss was the truth that was trying to come out when Joseph Boudreaux sat down with film students in the aftermath of Rita and volunteered that, within a few decades of making *Louisiana Story*, "that's when the erosion's going."[26]

But life went on as usual. People still celebrated at the Louisiana Shrimp & Petroleum Festival at Morgan City. Gumbo and jambalaya could be had anytime, anywhere, in any quantity. Tidwell consumed his share with ambivalent relish. The dark cloud that hung over the fleeting physical landscape just didn't fully translate to the emotional landscape of the people who saw the changes up front and close and were most affected by them.

One reason was the fishers' general distrust of the government, which intensified its controversial presence with every levee it repaired, marsh it studied, new bridge it built, or old one it replaced, and when it told people to raise their houses and house trailers on stilts, to fish here but not there, and to put those damn TEDs on their nets. Combating the erosion would just mean more government in their lives.

Another reason was the immediacy of those lives. If you were a fisher, every day was a day not unlike the heron that fished the marsh—

a quest to make the quota for sustenance. Paying for groceries, making the truck and boat payments, hoping against needed repairs, and topping off the gas tanks and cell phone minutes didn't leave much room for thinking about the future.

But a main reason was that the shrimp were still running as thick as ever. The shrimp, oyster, and blue-crab takes in the years just prior to the oil spill kept peaking—and had been since the 1960s, as a matter of fact, all the time that scientists were squawking about erosion. In 2010, catches plummeted, but then immediately they started climbing back, returning to their prespill quantities by 2013. Louisiana was still the nation's best at netting shrimp.

Maybe the scientists were crying wolf. Maybe coastal erosion would mean nothing more than the inconvenience of moving to higher ground or driving over a bridge rather than on a road. Maybe pairing oil and shrimp like at the Morgan City festival wasn't so illogical or corrupt.

These catch peaks, however, have not surprised scientists. As Turner argued back in the seventies, marine production corresponds to the length of wetland shoreline: the longer, the more productive. The breakup of the Louisiana coast from canals and erosion, scientists have argued, has temporarily increased the length and thus the catch. As land continues to erode, the meeting between open water and wetland will eventually start shrinking, and so will productivity.[27]

In 1987, the EPA published *Saving Louisiana's Coastal Wetlands: The Need for a Long-Term Plan of Action*. A year later, a grassroots gathering of church groups, scientists, environmentalists, and fishers chartered the Coalition to Restore Coastal Louisiana (it had technically organized three years earlier) and published its own report with a sobering title framed as an implied challenge: *Coastal Louisiana: Here Today, Gone Tomorrow?* It called for the restoration of a half-million square miles of Cajun coast.

A spate of legislation trundled through the state legislature and Congress, as Tidwell writes. Local restoration projects to divert river water and sediment back toward Louisiana got under way, and there was success, including at Breton Sound, where a century before, oyster fishers had detected something amiss. This was potentially good news for the birds in the Chandeleurs. But the net loss of the entire coast was much greater than the modest gains of the smaller projects. It became clear that what was needed was a comprehensive and very expensive project—one that experts estimated would cost $14 billion.

The political initiative to produce those funds never materialized. Adding to these woes was the increasingly realistic problem of sea-level rise, which the 1987 EPA report prophesized: "If projections that the greenhouse effect will raise sea level one foot or more in the next fifty years are accurate, the need for immediate action is much greater than previously thought." At an alarming rate starting in 2011, NOAA began delisting places on the coast, now awash in the sea and history, some of them first put on maps drawn by the US Coast Survey.[28]

Two years later, John Barry—citizen, author, policy maker of late, the clean-shaven wavy-hair opposite of Eads—spearheaded a lawsuit against ninety-seven oil and gas companies, an industry that was simultaneously responsible for thirty-six percent of the state's GDP and thirty-six percent of the land loss. The suit demanded that the companies pay their share of the costs to restore coastal wetlands and Louisiana's future.

Epilogue

A SUCCESS STORY AMID SO MUCH ELSE

We who live today can only wonder; a rising sea could write a different history.

—Rachel Carson (1955)[1]

✦

There is a street in Venice, Louisiana, named Halliburton Road. You can enter "h-a-l-l-i-b-u-r-t-o-n" in a GPS navigation device and select a route to it. Venice, population 202 in 2010,

is down in the delta a short distance from the Mississippi's northernmost pass to the Gulf. Hurricane Katrina nearly wiped out the
little town in 2005, and five years later the *Deepwater Horizon* disaster
sent oil and chemical dispersants to its shores at Hospital Bay, sluicing
in through industry canals across a depleted marshland barrier. BP's
cement contractor for the *Deepwater* well was Halliburton Company.
Investigators determined that its work was deficient and responsible
for the fatal blowout.

From New Orleans, the drive to Halliburton Road starts out crossing the Huey P. Long Bridge over the Mississippi and onto State Road
23. After the first few miles, the highway begins ghosting the serpen-
tine river for the remaining seventy to Venice. As long as you stay on
blacktop, you cannot see one of the continent's most compelling natural features, mere feet away. Its waters are hidden behind an engineering structure, the Mississippi levee, mired in a long history of controversy. An imposing earthen embankment, grassy in spots and bare in
others, and precisely formed, the levee runs continuously off your left
shoulder. It is the only elevation on this slab of land and marsh, and
not fully integrated with either. The levee is both overlay and under-
score, an emphatic ethos that makes the river and the recipient sea
below it American.

Nine miles from Venice, within the hollow of a sharp bend, is Fort
Jackson, dwarfed by the levee crowding the fort's old but still-solid
brick walls. Park the car, climb the levee, and you find yourself at eye
level with the Mississippi, muddy green and unquestionably mighty.
Its powerful current and eddies, nevertheless, offer little resistance to
the persistent stream of container ships bound for New Orleans—just
as, 150 years before, the Confederate barricade lying across here failed
to turn back the Union attack-convoy ably guided by Coast Survey
assistant Joseph Smith Harris.

The eighteen-ship fleet would fit on board one of today's cargo vessels many times over. Stacked across each freighter's beam up to the
nose of its bridge are typically several thousand rectangular steel containers, each the size of a semitrailer truck—cornucopias that, upon

final delivery, spill the fruits of consumer culture. Coming from abroad, they carry the bulk of our daily lives: clothes, toys, furniture, kitchenware, garden tools, desktop and handheld electronics (including your GPS), even green-friendly stainless-steel water bottles— nearly the entire inventory of big-box retail stores.

In terms of tonnage moved, thirteen of the top twenty-five US water ports in 2013 were on the Gulf. They shipped out oil, chemicals, sulfur, salt, phosphate, seafood, cattle, grain, and forest products, and brought in mostly manufactured goods, exchanging the natural for the artificial. It can boggle the mind to think about where all the imported stuff originates and where it is heading as it passes through the hands of some 322 million Americans, and how much—beginning with packaging—will end up in landfills or floating ocean garbage patches, the latter ninety percent plastic—one the size of Texas—drifting the world. How do we clean up something like that? Highlighting these patches in her Mission Blue campaign, Sylvia Earle says we must eradicate them to save the oceans and ourselves.

Next to the levee, and beneath the container ships eerily passing overhead, the ramparts of Fort Jackson feel small and its past unimportant and forgotten, like an anonymous historical marker at a roadside rest stop. Once a defender of enslaved labor, the fort is the historical opposite of the many modern heliports that Highway 23 passes. Their sprawling parking lots are a motionless sea of vehicles—nearly all pickup trucks and most of them, inexplicably, white. They belong to the oil-and-gas platform crews airlifted to fourteen-day shifts offshore. Industry workers are well compensated, yet no less entrapped by their employers' economic dominance than by, and because of, the coveted material standard of living embodied in the shipping containers streaming the Mississippi.

Louisiana has been called a "petrocolonial" state, and it's hard to argue with that assertion. The legislature almost always votes the industry's calling, and the courts rarely decide against it. Big Oil, in turn, says it has done much good for the people and economy of Louisiana. It has also, according to the *New York Times*, "extracted about $470 billion in natural resources from the state in the last two decades."[2]

The goal of industry is not to provide jobs. It is to make a profit and pay dividends to stockholders, and bonuses to high-level executives. Oil and gas employment numbers have not climbed in proportion to the significant increase in domestic production. As in any industry, when cost-effective, automation gets the nod to replace workers. Furthermore, since *Deepwater Horizon* and the hydraulic fracking boom and cheaper onshore sources, the industry has cut back on more expensive offshore extraction. When oil prices collapsed in late 2015 and early 2016 (by sixty percent in a matter of months), at the very moment the US had returned as a global petroleum superpower, job growth in Texas and Louisiana dropped behind the rest of the nation. Oil-related tax revenues went into a spiral, and Standard & Poor's rating services reported that it expected to lower the credit rating of Louisiana, where roughneck employment had fallen off by more than twenty percent (some ten thousand jobs) in a twelve-month period.

Approached from the highway, Venice appears less in the character of a town than an industrial yard, a rock-still one after the oil price collapse. The GPS will direct you down a flat and treeless road, bordered on one side by a canal and on the other by utility lines strung low across power poles. They stake off a procession of giant steel storage tanks, construction and trash dumpsters, office trailers parked on mostly empty gravel lots, and sieges of idle work cranes pointing to Louisiana's big sky.

Off to the right, a dark mountain of mud rises beside your destination, Halliburton Road. The EPA regulates, though not terribly effectively, the dumping of sediment that the industry removes while drilling a well into the Gulf floor. Barges bring loads contaminated with mercury and other toxins back to land—via dredged canals—and pile them up just as municipalities do household garbage in landfills, sans the familiar gyre of cheering gulls. These are the Gulf-side's new mounds, rising in place of the shell-laden aboriginal mounds leveled for roadbeds—both, in their way, evidence of Gulf abundance, both serving the automobile culture. Driving around the far side of the brooding mud reveals a sportfishing resort, with a motel, restaurant, and marina of expensive recreational boats. From there to the horizon, wetland opens out like a landscape painting. It is an exquisite example of coastal Louisiana's expansive beauty, save for gas pipes occasionally periscoping out of the water. Louisianans have quietly reconciled themselves to living with this sort of discordant juxtaposition between nature and petrocolonialism. As has Venice, historically a fishing port.

Remarkably, through all the change, economic and environmental, Venice has managed to maintain its ranking in value of catch among the top ten commercial-fishing ports in the US. It is the only Gulf port to have done so in the twenty-first century. In 2000, half of the top fishing ports were on the Gulf. People talked about recovery after the BP accident, but these ports were losing ground before the spill. And since then, shrimp, oyster, and crab landings have failed to recover fully, and they may never, if the coastline continues to disappear. As Oliver Houck points out, while the oil may have reached a hundred yards inland, erosion goes on for miles. The bottom line is that the Gulf has become less and less a fishers' sea than industry's sea.

As this is being written, the same is true onshore, where energy riches have brought industrial squalor. Along State Road 23 and other coastal highways, the discards of Louisiana's biggest profit makers lie about everywhere: junkyards of rusting equipment, tumbles of rusting pipes, weedy plats of sidelined barges, also rusting. The most disquieting imprint is land loss. Houck conveyed a sad irony decades ago, repeated many times since: If Texas seized fifty square miles from Louisiana every year, the governor would call up the National Guard. Not so with Shell, Chevron, ExxonMobil, BP, and the rest.

Houses and house trailers all around the coast rise on stilts beside roadways washed or washing away, with telephone poles and leafless trees standing in water. You might be able to live with rusty pipes next door, but you can't live on vanishing land. State Road 1 out to Grand Isle leads over a nineteen-mile toll bridge opened in 2009 and elevated high above the drowned highway below. Google Earth shows a lacework of canals dissecting the land around and far out from the bridge. Most of the canals have ruptured into shapeless elongated forms, resembling a mass of distended arteries in a doomed body.

Viewing this scene makes clear the reason for the lawsuit that John Barry initiated. The plaintiff is the Southeast Louisiana Flood Protection Authority–East. After writing *Rising Tide*, and after seeing how the levees around New Orleans failed so miserably during Katrina, Barry sought an appointment to the authority's board of commissioners. Eventually, he and his colleagues concluded that restoration of coastal wetlands, as first-defense storm buffers, was as important to protecting New Orleans as levee reinforcement.

Federal law requires companies to repair environmental damage caused by their morphing creations and to fill them in once they no longer serve a purpose. But canal users typically shirked their responsibilities, and federal and state authorities rarely forced them to do otherwise. The state adopted a master plan for coastal restoration but lacked the estimated $30 billion (ballooned from an original $14 billion estimate, and, as of 2016, reaching estimates of $70 billion) that implementing it would cost. The energy industry endorsed the Coastal Master Plan and even conceded that its own activities contributed to land loss, yet, as with refilling old canals, made no offer to share the restoration expenses. It insisted that the levee system and accelerated river flow were the principal agents in wetland loss.

Barry, a former college football player and coach, became the broad shoulders and public face of the lawsuit, which had the unanimous support of the authority's commissioners. They reasoned that BP settlement money would go toward part of the restoration cost, and that ninety-plus oil, gas, and pipeline companies named in the suit should pay an $18 billion portion. Barry announced the suit in a press conference on July 24, 2013, and it drew endorsements from the state's newspapers and three former governors, but not the current one.

Governor Bobby Jindal said the authority had overstepped its boundaries and denounced the suit as "frivolous." The industry, calling it "ill-conceived, unwise, and divisive," dispatched seventy lobbyists to the capital to try to kill the case and, to no one's surprise, got its way. As land down on the coast continued to disappear, the legislature voted to rescind the suit. The flood protection authority responded by filing a request with the federal district court to rule on the legality of the state's actions. In February 2015, Judge Nannette Jolivette Brown dismissed the suit, maintaining that the authority had not demonstrated a "viable claim" against the defendants. Coastal residents and Barry predicted that the ruling would saddle taxpayers with the repair bill for the energy industry's reckless profit making, allowed by the state.[3]

When Barry's term on the authority expired, Jindal refused to reappoint him. So the book writer, who never considered himself an activist, founded a nonprofit group—Restore Louisiana Now—to help keep the lawsuit alive. The authority appealed the ruling to the Fifth US Circuit Court of Appeals and, as of this writing, awaits the court's actions. Attorneys told Barry that Judge Brown's decision was full of holes, and Houck said that the appeal stood on solid law, although both recognized that the Fifth Circuit has never ruled against oil and gas.[4]

IN LATE MARCH 2014, a container ship the length of two football fields steamed across Galveston Bay and sideswiped a tug-driven oil barge. Four thousand barrels of fuel oil poured into the water, and the US Coast Guard and hazmat crews went into damage control mode. Wind and waves pushed the offending substance into the Gulf—a lucky break for the bay, some said. All the same, shore currents transported oil and tar balls to beaches and marshlands along down the coast, beside the Great Texas Coastal Birding Trail. The kill report—three-hundred-plus birds, thirty-nine dolphins, and seventeen turtles—amounted to another lucky break. The commencement of spring migration was still a few weeks away. Wildlife just missed taking much heavier casualties. Texas newspapers said the event was another day in the life of the bay—just a little more so. Since 1985, it had suffered an average of 285 spills annually. No one knows the count dating back to 1918, when Sweet No. 16 delivered Galveston Bay and the Gulf their first dose of spilled oil.[5]

The event left people to wonder whether or not the Gulf was better protected against industry accidents since the *Deepwater Horizon* explosion. Production had started trending upward that year—in part because higher-yielding deepwater drilling was expanding sharply and at much greater depths than *Deepwater* had gone. Drilling in the farther bottom is more accident-prone than in shallow water. To offset the risk, the industry developed subsea robot technology that it claimed would seal a runaway well in forty-five seconds. Critics pointed out that the technology had not been tested at the new depths, and worried about the industry again becoming complacent in the pursuit of profit.

It did not grow complacent in trying to get its way. Oil executives and assorted members of Congress complained that the Obama administration had been slow to open new oil leases, and they challenged as too costly proposed new federal workplace safety and well control rules, which were to be finalized in 2016.

No new rules were proposed to regulate the stealthier onshore activities that have done far more damage to the great estuarine sea. Those activities persisted as unchanged destructive habits and unending old stories.

Alabama, Florida, and Georgia had yet to settle the dispute over the river water flowing into Apalachicola Bay, and many predicted that plucking the bay's famous oysters would soon come to pass as a way of life. Yet algal blooms didn't seem similarly doomed. In Florida, 2013 saw a record in manatee deaths associated with harmful algae. The next year, seventy-five percent of Florida voters supported a referendum initiative, known as Amendment 1, to restore its model property tax–supported trust fund for the state purchase of conservation land, which the legislature and Governor Rick Scott had gutted. The Sanibel-Captiva Conservation Foundation pushed for the purchase of privately held Everglades land for a reservoir that would significantly reduce nutrient flow down the Caloosahatchee, and thus curtail algal blooms.

The Florida legislature used none of the first round of trust fund money to buy conservation land (although it did dedicate part to covering damage awards for unrelated Civil Rights Act violations). A coalition of environmental groups sued the legislature, and as the case was awaiting its day in court, the Army Corps of Engineers in February 2016 sent a record discharge of agricultural wastewater down the Caloosahatchee River. Videos on YouTube of the coffee-dark release fanning across the estuary, killing oyster beds and fish and anything that could not escape it, horrified viewers—a mass devastation that evoked images of the Escambia Bay fish kills of the 1970s that everyone thought was a thing of the past. As the contamination pushed into the Gulf and along the coast, at the height of the tourist season— dubbed the "tourist season from hell"—hotel clerks warned guests about a "red tide." Many had come from as far away as Europe for fun and sun on a Gulf-side vacation only to be advised to stay out of the water and wear a face mask when walking the beach.

Three years earlier, a river up the coast had been in line for rescue, but not Gulf waters. After Koch Industries, privately held by brothers Charles and David Koch, bought Buckeye Technologies in 2013, Florida gave them a preliminary go-ahead to construct the long-before-proposed fifteen-mile pipeline to bypass all but the end of the Fenholloway River, where the pipe would be allowed to discharge up to fifty-eight million gallons per day of industrial waste (the pipe has not been completed as this book goes to press).

Buckeye was required to improve the treatment process first, but to hometown activist Joy Ezell, the new ownership and its pipe didn't add up to stewardship. She knew Koch Industries was one of the country's dirtiest concerns. According to *Rolling Stone* magazine, Ezell's bête noire dumped "more pollutants into the nation's waters than General Electric and International Paper combined." Linda Young, director of Florida Clean Water Network, said that the state's water-testing standards, to which Buckeye would be subjected, were substandard, and that no one had "mastered the art" of "privatizing profit and socializing pollution" better than the Koch brothers.[6]

Back in Pensacola, Young and the Bream Fishermen Association still could not get grass to grow in Escambia Bay in 2016. The lawsuit that fifty residents had brought eight years earlier against Monsanto and its successors—Pharmacia Corporation and Solutia Inc.—for the cleanup of residual PCBs was settled that year. The settlement included an undisclosed monetary award for the plaintiffs but no provision for mitigating the residual PCBs. "For me, it wasn't about the money," said Ernie Rivers, ninety years old and lamenting the payoff of a nearly fifty-year struggle. "I just wanted my bay cleaned up."[7]

In Perdido Bay, grass beds remained stable, but that was after a ninety percent decline since 1940. Jackie Lane continued to monitor the water quality, while wastewater and industrial discharges continued to deliver excessive nutrient loads and coliform bacteria, and again, old stories repeated.

Escambia County ranked twelfth on the latest Toxics Release Inventory, 2014, the EPA's annual measure of industrial discharges. Ascend Performance Materials (formerly Monsanto), situated on the Escambia River, was the heaviest polluter, mainly through atmospheric discharge. A lawsuit that Young brought in the early 2000s had forced the company to convert from discharging into the river to deep-well injection. International Paper, with its trail of waste into Perdido Bay, was the number two polluter.

Diane Wilson's Calhoun County now ranked thirty-five on the TRI rather than at the top as it had in 1988. Between then and 2014, total releases in the county had dropped by eighty-six percent, with no loss in industrial output. Alcoa was the environmental star, having reined in nearly the same percentage of poisonous discharges. Formosa, by contrast, which more than doubled its production capacity, increased its releases more than tenfold. All of that went into the air. Water discharges into Lavaca Bay declined slightly. In 2016, Formosa applied to increase the amount of copper and chloroform in its daily releases, at higher water temperatures, and clashed once again with Diane Wilson. This time she had the support of the Union of Commercial Oystermen, and Formosa retreated to existing content and temperature levels.

Harrison County, Mississippi, came in at number thirteen on the TRI. A DuPont plant manufacturing titanium dioxide was the primary culprit. But more than anything else, improperly treated municipal wastewater sickened Mississippi Sound. In 2015, the sound's beachside counties issued thirty-six "water contact" advisories and one beach closure, which lasted just over a week.

Five Gulf coast counties were among the top thirty on the TRI. You might add two Louisiana parishes that border the big river. Three of those five counties directly on the Gulf are in Texas, and two, Harris and Brazoria, made the top ten. Twenty petrochemical plants fouled the water and air in Brazoria, and nineteen of the heaviest polluters in Harris County were members of the energy industry. Accommodating nearly 350 daily ship and barge movements, the Houston Ship Channel had become the LA Freeway of Texas, with Galveston Bay as the cloverleaf. The Coast Guard temporarily shut down the channel in March 2015 after a bulk carrier and chemical tanker collided, spilling a flammable gasoline additive into the water.

And then there remained the matter of fertilizer runoff from faraway places. After the Midwest experienced an especially rainy and snowy winter and early spring, the 2016 Gulf dead zone expanded to a larger-than-average mass, nearly sixty-five hundred square miles—the same as the summer before and about what you'd get if you merged Rhode Island with Connecticut. Since the EPA set a goal in 2008 for shrinking the dead zone to nineteen hundred square miles, its annual size had averaged nearly three times that. Eugene Turner saw insignificant "movement forward" and even some "backsliding" from government agencies that were supposed to oversee a cleanup.[8]

Cast all this in with climate change and sea-level rise and, Turner says, "there is no bright future on the coast." Predictive models indicate as much as a seven-degree annual average temperature increase within the next century. One Texas scientist suggests imagining Corpus Christi moving climatically a hundred miles to the southwest.[9]

Warmer weather by 2016 was already encouraging wildlife to expand its territory in the other direction. Fishers were catching gray snapper up around Galveston, when previously they would have had to go down to the lower Laguna Madre to hook them. Binoculars on the upper Texas coast were spying some seventy bird species, including great kiskadees, Audubon orioles, and tropical kingbirds, that once had not ventured north of the Rio Grande Valley. The Guatemalan leafwing, blue-eyed sailor, and many other tropical butterflies crossed the Mexican border and started alighting on nectarous plants in Texas, and five species of tropical dragonfly had become transplants to Florida, where the invasive Cuban tree frog was making its way toward Georgia.

In Texas, scientists were seeing red and black mangroves follow northward-shifting plant hardiness zones. Twenty or thirty years before, black mangroves had occupied roughly sixty-five acres in the Aransas Bay area; in 2015, they inhabited some fifteen thousand acres. The cold-weather-sensitive red mangrove, the "walking tree" of native lore and once confined to south Florida and Mexico, had begun marching up the Texas coast as far north as Matagorda Bay.

Normally, one would welcome the propagation of an estuarine species like mangroves if the warming trend weren't also bringing higher water, and not just from melting Arctic ice. Water expands when it heats up. Warmer water also means hurricanes. Scientists expect the number of storms to drop but the intensity to increase. Sea-level rise complicates everything, from coastal restoration to beachfront condo living. A group of Tulane University geologists determined in 2015 that Gulf waters had risen five times faster in the last century than in the thousand years prior to modern industrialization.

NASA scientists reported that, a century in the future, the sea might be as much as seven feet higher, with much at stake for NASA: water would be lapping against the concrete walls of the Houston Space Center. It also would mean that the Houston Ship Channel would turn into a bay. Without duplicating the engineering feat that followed the 1900 hurricane in elevating the land, Galvestonians would likely lose their island city this time. Mobile and New Orleans would be in the tidal zone. All those industries located on the coast would lose out too—the industries that pumped tons of climate-warming CO_2 into the air and killed the sea grasses that could absorb the CO_2.

In bays across the Gulf, saltwater intrusion had already killed off freshwater marshes and coastal forests. What had been tidal flats in many places turned to open water. These changes were giving new life to seawall building, justified euphemistically as "coastal armoring" and "engineered protection." But remember, seawalls contribute to erosion. They destroy valuable marine and shoreside vegetation, and they don't stop the sea from going underneath and infiltrating the porous limestone that quarters the freshwater of the Floridan aquifer beneath Florida, Alabama, and part of Mississippi. Big, tall, earthen dikes, à la New Orleans and Holland, which many hold up as a model for combating the sea, are similarly useless above a limestone platform. The water goes under the dike and through the limestone.

For decades, saltwater in that manner had been contaminating municipal wells, forcing utilities to pipe in freshwater from sources farther inland. And seawalls don't facilitate the work of stormwater systems, which, when rain comes down hard, back up more frequently in coastal cities. Water falls from the sky, gurgles up through the ground, flows backward through stormwater drains, and washes in from the sea. An August 2015 study on storm surges in the US determined that five of the ten most vulnerable cities are on the Gulf. The Tampa/St. Petersburg metropolitan area was first on the list. New Orleans was second, Fort Myers fifth, Galveston-Houston sixth, and Sarasota seventh.[10]

The first principle in adapting to sea-level rise should be that ecosystems matter. It makes sense to let mangrove forests, marshlands, and sea grass beds thrive, not simply to provide habitat for fish and birds, but to stave off rising water and soak up carbon. In January 2016, a Chinese billionaire, Wenliang Wang, a stranger to the Gulf, pledged as much as $5 million to restore mangroves around Marco Island. On an individual level, home owners can make a difference by refraining from putting fertilizer and pesticides on their lawns, and by replacing grass with indigenous vegetation, while keeping in mind that the problem source is not just waterfront lawns. Many neighbor-hoods miles from the Gulf are serviced by stormwater systems that drain to the sea or into a river running to it. Individuals can also elect smart leaders.

That has not been the trend in the Gulf states. Before Jindal's second term ended in January 2016, all five governors were either climate-change deniers or doubters, and not one of them recognized human or industrial culpability. Nature alone took the rap. Typically, they saw climate change more as politics than as reality. In 2015, Jindal asked President Obama not to mention it during a Hurricane Katrina tenth-anniversary event in New Orleans.

According to Florida state personnel and contractors, Governor Rick Scott's administration instructed them to cease using the terms "global warming" and "climate change" in official communications, reports, and public presentations. His state's response to what it called "nuisance flooding" was to erect coastal armoring, while permitting more waterside condo construction, and to install shipping container–sized water abatement pumps, which burned fossil fuels. Relocating waterside residents was off the table.[11]

Texas US senator and 2016 Republican presidential candidate Ted Cruz called climate change the "pseudoscientific theory for a big-government politician who wants more power," and a ruse of scien-tists raking in millions from government-funded research grants. At the same time, he said the free-enterprise system should be trusted to develop effective responses to climate change. Cruz comes from Harris County, number ten on the 2014 TRI, and a principality of global warmers.[12]

THE GULF WAS ALSO FEELING the rippling effect of another kind of offshore oil business—fish oil—found in most homes in soap, margarine, lipstick, paints, pesticides, flooring, and health food supple-ments. The main source of the oil is menhaden, one of the most abun-dant finfish in coastal waters. Omega-3 fish oil supplements, which exploded in popularity in the 1990s to ward off heart disease, prostate cancer, and Alzheimer's, come mainly from menhaden, as do fish-variety foods fed to farm animals and the family cat and dog. You never find menhaden neatly arranged on ice at the seafood market; it is strictly a factory fish, pulverized and squeezed by the billions in a production-line process known as reduction. H. Bruce Franklin calls menhaden "the most important fish in the sea," which is the title of his gripping book about their contemporary plight.[13]

The importance of the fish is not its commercial worth but its ecological value. Marine birds feed heavily on them. The majority of the fish eaten by the pelicans that commercial fishers were shooting during the First World War were menhaden. They are a small fish that school in "closely packed, unwieldy masses," which in the nineteenth century reportedly reached up to forty miles long—commanding in size, yet as "helpless as flocks of sheep" in being the target of just about every larger carnivorous fish and mammal in the sea, from striped bass to whales.[14]

The description of these helpless masses comes from George Brown Goode, the distinguished ichthyologist who recruited Silas Stearns in the 1880s to write about the Gulf for the US Fish Commission's first comprehensive study. Referring to the menhaden's niche in the food chain, Goode said that if you ate fish from the sea, you were consuming "nothing but menhaden." If you were in the fish business, you were also probably dealing in menhaden. They were the country's largest fishery at the time—one that never lost its status. By 1948, the Gulf states were landing 103,000 metric tons of menhaden a year.[15]

Indians planted the fish with their crops as fertilizer, and they taught European settlers to do the same. As long as anyone can remember, menhaden were caught as baitfish for both recreational and commercial fishers. But the reduction industry has historically been the primary harvester, undertaken not by family fishers. One company, the Houston-based Omega Protein, with production facilities in Virginia, Louisiana, and Mississippi, strategically bought out smaller operations to forge a nearly complete monopoly in the fishery—one just shy of violating antitrust laws.

When Franklin was writing in 2007, Omega Protein—which was controlled by Malcolm Glazer, real-estate billionaire and owner of the Tampa Bay Buccaneers football team—operated sixty-one ships and half as many spotter planes, which meant, as one pilot told Franklin, the "menhaden had no place to hide." As early as the late nineteenth century, the Atlantic fishery was moving toward collapse, and by the 1960s, the Gulf fishery had surpassed it. Annual catch weights peaked two decades later, at more than two billion pounds of menhaden, and then began to drop steadily, down to half the level of the peak years by the time Franklin was writing. This decline was not surprising, given the efficiency of a fleet of spotter planes working with a fleet of boats that lassoed whole schools in gluttonous purse seines a third of a mile long, cinched tight between two boats when they were swollen with the commodity.[16]

In 2015, the industry reported that the menhaden fisheries in the Atlantic and Gulf were healthy, and that allowable harvest numbers should be increased. The Gulf States Marine Fisheries Commission (GSMFC), headquartered in Ocean Springs and founded by the five US Gulf states in 1949 to promote sustainable commercial fishing, agreed, saying the "stock is neither overfished nor is overfishing occurring," even though 2014 landings were twenty-five percent lower than the average of the previous five years.[17]

Franklin maintains that the dominant voice on the Department of Commerce's menhaden advisory committee is that of Omega Protein. Furthermore, since only three companies made up the menhaden industry—Omega and two small concerns that it had not absorbed—the DOC did not require them to publicize catch numbers. The rationale was that secrecy would keep the industry members competitive, though the fish they caught were a public, not private, resource.[18]

One thing was certain: the Gulf menhaden population had been significantly diminished. A decrease in its numbers affects other fish populations and the general health of the sea. The menhaden's primary food is phytoplankton. Menhaden are swimming filter feeders, counterparts to sedentary clams and oysters, with each adult sifting approximately four gallons of water per minute. Among the phytoplankton consumed are tons and tons of algae.

Franklin has argued tirelessly that the menhaden diet helps check algal blooms, an assessment that the GSMFC disputes. In an age when so many oyster and clam beds have disappeared and are disappearing, he writes, the menhaden schools are the "only remaining significant [natural] checks on the phytoplankton that cause algal blooms and dead zones." Scientists have recently pointed out that as human infractions, such as conducting extreme volumes of agricultural waste down the Caloosahatchee River, spur more and larger algal blooms, the menhaden's diet can turn the fish toxic and imperil the food chain—just like red snapper living around oil platforms.[19]

IN THE MIDST OF GLOOM, there are hopeful stories to be told about clean water and the protection of wildlife. There is even one about filter feeders, despite an event in 2015 that perplexed everyone. That spring, all the nesting birds vanished from Seahorse Key in Florida's Big Bend. When scientists investigated, the 165-acre island and roosting dynasty felt postapocalyptic. "Just the wind," said a wildlife ecologist. Originally a tall dune on the pre-ice-melt shore, Seahorse is among the Cedar Key chain of islands, and indeed, its shape resembles the marine species for which it is named. In the nineteenth century, the military used Seahorse as a transient center for Seminole it was removing to the West, some of whom had worked the Cuban fish ranchos. In 1929, President Hoover made it and twelve sibling islands a national wildlife refuge.[20]

Tens of thousands of pelicans, herons, egrets, ibises, spoonbills, and cormorants have continued ever since then to roost on Seahorse, but no one ever figured out why they abandoned ripe nests in 2015. Scientists identified potential culprits—raccoons, snakes, eagles, poison, disease, airboats, and food scarcity—but no guilty party. They pondered climate change and ruled that out—although researchers were seeing its effects in many ways: inundated marshlands and dying trees, including the one that gave Cedar Key its name.

Cedar Key had become something of an innocent bystander in the Anthropocene, what some have termed the epoch when human-induced environmental impact escalated to a planetary scale. Ever since the pencil factories shut down in the 1890s, and timbering early in the next century, the region had been lessening its environmental footprint, even as most of the Gulf had been pressing deeper ones. Cut woodlands had grown back in two national wildlife refuges and four state preserves, and, save for Buckeye's disastrous impact, the Big Bend largely eluded the trample of development and industry. Cedar Key remained a village of net and oyster fishers and crabbers, and preserved a charm as a last remnant of old Florida. The population in 2010 was 701, and the enveloping marshes were still the "vast sweet visage" that had inspired Sidney Lanier and John Muir.[21]

Cedar Key had evolved into an aquaculture success story too, which featured a clean environment and jobs, in clam farming. Two principal figures writing the success story—Suzanne Colson and Leslie Sturmer—styled Cedar Key's aquaculture "Clamelot," a spin on Camelot, an idyllic place of pure happiness.

Sturmer got her start in aquaculture at a Corpus Christi hatchery turning out redfish during the chef Paul Prudhomme era. After the 1988 drought, she took her experience to Apalachicola to head a job-retraining program in shellfish aquaculture. The fishers there didn't take well to government ideas and programs, and despite Sturmer's valiant effort, aquaculture struggled.

Meanwhile, Colson had her own dealings over on the Big Bend. A boatbuilder's daughter who had grown up on Long Island, Colson found her way to Florida, married an oysterman from Suwannee, and joined him on the water, where the salt air and marshes spoke to a sense of belonging. Then, in 1991, bacterial contamination traveling the Suwannee River forced the FDA to close oystering in Suwannee Sound, just north of Cedar Key. The sound is a natural artwork of looping islands—low-lying, grassy, and treeless. A long-ago biographer of the river called it America's most romantic.

Some say Maya paddled up from Yucatán and ascended to the river's rise at Okefenokee Swamp in Georgia. Spanish clerics proselytized at missions on its banks. Indians and Americans fought two wars across its water. The victors went on to foul it. Colson, whom Sturmer describes as a "come-to-Jesus person," meaning she's tenacious, was determined to get the river cleaned up and put oyster fishers back on the sound. "They didn't dirty the water," she says. "They didn't eff it up." She got herself appointed to the state's Suwannee River Water Management District and helped the town obtain federal grants to replace leaky septic tanks with a new wastewater treatment system. The water management district also implemented a best-management-practices program to encourage cattle and poultry operations upriver to reduce their runoff.[22]

While this was happening, Colson and others persuaded state officials to bring Sturmer and shellfish aquaculture to Suwannee. As in Apalachicola, Sturmer faced similar keep-the-government-out resistance. Still, with the help of Colson and others, she managed to get the program off the ground. Then, when Florida voters banned commercial gill-netting in 1994, some 150 Cedar Key commercial fishers had to turn in their nets, leaving men and women without a major part of their income.

"I will never get over" the net ban, says Mike Davis, whose family fished the Cedar Keys before the Civil War. "Neither will anybody else that was in the fishing business. We all feel like somebody died. It was wrong." Starting out, Sturmer signed up sixty-nine to train to work two-acre clam leases around the islands. It wasn't the same as getting out on the open water and chasing fish, but more like getting up in the morning for a nine-to-five and going to work in a cubicle. Yet it was still outdoors, and it provided a living.[23]

Colson didn't want the fishers to get "caught again by an environmental disaster." So she ran a successful campaign for a seat on the Cedar Key city commission. Her priority was clean water, and new

stormwater and sewage treatment systems. By 2000, clamming operations were farming 950 acres of Gulf floor. By the next year, every
last septic tank had been put out of service. The clean water prompted
the state to open thirty-seven hundred acres of previously closed harvesting grounds, including Suwannee Sound, ten years after the FDA
shut it down. In 2010, thirteen hundred submerged acres supported
206 clam farmers.

This was thirteen hundred acres of filter feeders that mitigated nitrogen and carbon levels while turning the water clearer, to the benefit
of sunlight-absorbing sea grass. Researchers calculated that the 136
million clams harvested from Florida leases in 2012 removed 25,000
pounds of nitrogen and 760,000 pounds of carbon from the environment, saving municipalities $100,000 in water treatment costs. Three-
quarters of the clams were sold outside the region. Locally, they generated income that exceeded the intake during net-fishing days, with
an annual economic impact of nearly $50 million. Beneficial to all, the
industry was ecologically sustainable.

Whether climate change will eventually swamp the successes in
Cedar Key remains to be seen. During tropical storms, ever-higher
floodwaters surge into the streets of the little downtown. Sea-level rise
has already disrupted the freshwater supply. But one clammer from
a longtime fishing family admitted to welcoming the return of the
sea. Maybe the storms and rising waters will chase away the snowbirds who plant invasive, fertilizer-loving turfgrass in the sand, and
the cursed sportfishing crowd that took away commercial nets, forced
market fishers out of family homes by driving up property taxes, and
pushed their weight around in the old fishing villages, turning some
of them into condo villages. Fisher folk, who know best how to live by
the sea, no matter the conditions, will then reclaim their waterfront.

Meanwhile, aquaculture has taken hold across the Gulf. Oyster
farming has been around Louisiana arguably for centuries. More
recently, the Nature Conservancy established a successful oyster reef
project, and Sherwood Gagliano, who in the 1960s delivered the bad
news about the state's shrinking coast, developed a central structure

used in that project. In Alabama, 2015 was a boom year for new oyster farms, and, despite earlier resistance, aquaculture had by then gained a foothold in Apalachicola.

Still, aquaculture, as in open-water fish farming, is subject to pitfalls common to raising stock on land: overdevelopment, overuse of antibiotics, and the spread of excrement nutrients, pollution, and diseases. The shrimp-farming business in Thailand and China, Louisiana shrimpers' biggest competitor, is notorious for ripping out mangroves and spiking the water with nutrients, running up ecological costs that exceed the economic benefits. All the while, on the other side of the globe, a historic little fishing village on the Gulf of Mexico has secured a healthy economy by restoring a healthy ecosystem.

ALTHOUGH HUMANS HAVE BEEN slow to learn it, preserving a vigorous and productive estuary nets a far better catch than does managed seafood production. Preservation is not control—just the opposite. It means managing our own behavior, not nature's. It means letting go, allowing nature to find its resonating beat. In this instance, we should abandon the impulse to lead and instead follow, holding ourselves to the precept that nature takes better care of itself than do humans.

Fortunately, every estuarine bay and river has at least one organized group defending its ecological integrity. Multiple concerns are doing the same for the larger Gulf. Think of them not as environmental but as public-interest groups. In working for the betterment of nonhuman life, they are working for our betterment too. They have made tremendous strides in bringing pulsating health back to rivers, bays, and the sea itself. Finishing the work they've begun bears all the logic in the world, and if we're lucky, their endeavors will one day write a new history.

"There will never be an end," wrote Wallace Stevens, "to this droning of the surf." The Gulf's is an ongoing story. In its longer version, humans are as the dinosaurs—only passing through, minor characters making a brief appearance, almost certainly briefer and in some ways no more important than our extinct predecessors. In our own eyes, we are neither insignificant nor ephemeral, and perhaps that's why we try to dominate nature, to convince ourselves that we are important and in command. Our decisions and behavior, indeed, do matter with regard to much existing life on Earth, including our own. We will live longer on this planet if we take command of our excesses, align ourselves with the natural balances that predate us and the biosphere that supports us, and understand that nature is most generous when we respect its sovereignty. We cannot destroy or control the sea, although we can diminish its gifts, and when we do, we turn away from our providence and diminish ourselves.[24]

Acknowledgments

The inspiring elements behind this book originated in childhood years in Mary Esther, when the Florida panhandle was a mostly quiet stretch of white sand on the Gulf of Mexico. Water and wildlife provided a surplus of attractions for my sometimes solitary circumstances and incessant fidgeting. The estuarine environment of Santa Rosa Sound, on which my family lived, became the cul-de-sac of my youth, where docks were the sidewalks, waterways the streets, a little motorboat my bicycle, and a rod and reel my bat and ball. From minuscule sea creatures to Goliath storms, the world of the Gulf furnished experiences—both wonderful and tragic—that shaped enduring sensibilities toward what we call nature.

Numerous people since have helped me make the shift from personal experiences and memory to objective research and writing. My gratitude begins with librarians, unsung partners involved in every nonfiction book. Those who graciously answered my call for assistance include the archival and librarian staffs at the universities of South Florida St. Petersburg, Florida, West Florida, Houston, and Texas; Texas A&M (at Corpus Christi), Tulane, and Mississippi State universities; and the public libraries in Apalachicola (FL), Houston (TX), Freeport (TX), Biloxi (MS), and Fort Myers (FL).

When it was time to do a final reading of the manuscript, the Sanibel-Captiva Conservation Foundation graciously lent me its cottage on the Gulf.

Many people helped get me to that point and deserve my appreciation. Among them are Barbara Albrecht, Sherry Arrant, Ray Arsenault, Shane Bernard, Kathy Bollerud, Ray Bollerud, Joe Browder, Jim Cusick, Dan D'Andrea, Tim

Delaney, Diana Dombrowski, Marsha Dowler, Joy Towles Ezell, Nick Foreman, Lynne Howard Frazer, Gary Garrett, Jorge Gonzalez, Robbie Gonzalez, Scott Graves, Caty Greene, Jennifer Guida, Karl Havens, Lee Irby, H. C. "Hank" Klein, Dean Lindsey, Bill Mahan, Jay Malone, Forrest Marcy, Marty Melosi, Gary Mormino, John Nemmers, Jack Payne, Betsy Perdichizzi, Leslie Poole, Lorraine Redd, Jack Rudloe, Jim Schnur, Ryan Schumacher, Courtney Smith, Bruce Stephenson, Leslie Sturmer, Geoff Sutton, Terry Tomlins-Walsh, Flo Turcotte, Kathy Turner, Frederic E. Vose, Christian Wagley, Chris Warren, and, not least of all, Ed White and Michelle Zacks (who shared her fabulous dissertation). Aaron Hoover, José Leal, Chris Morris, Paul Mueller, Nancy Rabalais, Margaret Ross-Tolbert, Gene Turner, Stefanie Wolf, and Linda Young graciously read parts of the manuscript. A true friend on many levels, Mary Santello hunkered down on demand with several sections in draft, written and visual, and offered advice on countless uncertainties. A champion of the project from the start, Cynthia Barnett read every word, some of them multiple times, from book proposal to epilogue. She was an inestimable and unfailingly supportive critic who, not to mention being a treasured friend, has been a true gift to my professional life.

A one-year sabbatical from the University of Florida gave welcome support, while month-long residential fellowships at Escape to Create (Seaside, FL) and the MacDowell Colony (Peterborough, NH), and the brilliant people who were part of the experience, were equally priceless gifts. I was fortunate to have Lisa Adams, my agent, believe in the value of this book from the start, and to connect me with the superlative editor Bob Weil and his talented assistant, Will Menaker; their advice and unflagging enthusiasm pushed me in key directions. The book benefited in immeasurable ways from the copyediting skills of Stephanie Hiebert, who rescued me from much more than typos and misspellings. Many thanks also to Anna Oler, Julia Druskin, and Steve Attardo for the fabulous design work, and Marie Pantojan and Rebecca Homiski for patiently navigating the book through production.

Finally, my family, Sonya Rudenstine and Willa Mae Davis Rudenstine, endured more than I had the right to ask of them. One of the most special moments came when Willa returned with me to my Gulf childhood and kayaked the very waters where this book found its beginning.

Notes

Prologue: HISTORY, NATURE, AND A FORGOTTEN SEA

1. H. F. Helmolt, *The World's History: A Survey of Man's Record*, vol. 1 (William Heinemann, 1901), xxv.
2. Edward O. Wilson, *Half Earth: Our Planet's Fight for Life* (Liveright, 2016), 211.
3. Charles Hallock, *Camp Life in Florida: A Handbook for Sportsmen and Settlers* (Forest and Stream Publishing, 1875), 336, 337; Helen Cooper, *Winslow Homer Watercolors* (Yale University Press, 1986), 234; Randall C. Griffin, *Winslow Homer: An American Vision* (Phaidon Press, 2006), 190.
4. Count Edward Wilczek, "The Historical Importance of the Pacific Ocean," in Helmolt, *World's History*, 566.
5. A couple of noteworthy exceptions include Robert S. Weddle, *Spanish Sea: The Gulf of Mexico in North American Discovery, 1500–1685* (Texas A&M University Press, 1985); and Kathleen DuVal, *Independence Lost: Lives on the Edge of the American Revolution* (Random House, 2015).
6. Fernand Braudel, *The Mediterranean and the Mediterranean World in the Age of Philip II*, vol. 1 (University of California Press, 1995), 20.
7. Walter Inglis Anderson, *The Horn Island Logs of Walter Inglis Anderson*, ed. Redding S. Sugg Jr. (Memphis State University Press, 1973), 28.
8. T. S. Eliot, "The Dry Salvages," in *Four Quartets* (Harcourt, 1973), 48.
9. Rowan Jacobsen, *Shadows on the Gulf: A Journey through Our Last Great Wetland* (Bloomsbury, 2011). Similarly, Terry Tempest Williams has dedicated a compelling chapter in her latest book to the events of the tragedy and its immediate aftermath. See *The Hour of Land: A Personal Topography of America's National Parks* (Sarah Crichton Books, 2016), 221–51.

Introduction: BIRTH

1. Quoted in Associated Press, "Scientists Say Flood Waters Threaten Gulf," *Christian Science Monitor*, August 17, 1993.
2. Stephen Crane, *Stephen Crane: Prose and Poetry* (Penguin, 1984), 707.

3. E. O. Wilson, *Naturalist* (Island Press, 1994), 7, 11; Edward O. Wilson, interview by the author, June 19, 2014.

4. Henry Major Tomlinson, *The Sea and the Jungle* (E. P. Dutton, 1920), 363.

5. Holly Stevens, ed., *Letters of Wallace Stevens* (University of California Press, 1996), 268.

6. Rachel Carson, *The Edge of the Sea* (Houghton Mifflin, 1983), 192.

7. Stevens, *Letters of Wallace Stevens*, 449, 655.

One: MOUNDS

1. Quoted in Marion Spjut Gilliland, *Key Marco's Buried Treasure: Archaeology and Adventure in the Nineteenth Century* (University of Florida Press, 1989), 94.

2. Charles Kenworthy, "Ancient Canals in Florida," *Forest and Stream* 5 (August 12, 1875): 8.

3. Frank Hamilton Cushing, "Relics of an Unknown Race Discovered," *Journal* (New York), June 21, 1896.

4. "Folk Lore of the Zuni," *Washington Post*, August 25, 1895; Alex F. Chamberlain, "In Memoriam: Frank Hamilton Cushing," *Journal of American Folklore* 13 (1900): 129; "In Memoriam: Frank Hamilton Cushing," *American Anthropologist* 2 (1900): 366.

5. Cushing, "Relics of an Unknown Race Discovered."

6. Ibid.

7. Ibid.

8. Ibid.

9. Ibid.; Frank Hamilton Cushing, *The Pepper-Hearst Expedition: Preliminary Report on the Exploration of Ancient Key-Dweller Remains on the Gulf Coast of Florida* (MacCalla, 1897), 20.

10. Cushing, "Relics of an Unknown Race Discovered"; Cushing, *Pepper-Hearst Expedition*, 3, 4.

11. Cushing, *Pepper-Hearst Expedition*, 7, 68.

12. Ibid., 8, 68; Frank H. Cushing, *Exploration of Ancient Key-Dweller Remains on the Gulf Coast of Florida* (University Press of Florida, 2000), 3, 4.

13. Cushing, *Exploration of Ancient Key-Dweller Remains*, 4; Phyllis E. Kolianos and Brent R. Wiesman, eds., *The Florida Journals of Frank Hamilton Cushing* (University Press of Florida, 2005), 22.

14. Kolianos and Wiesman, *Florida Journals*, 23.

15. Ibid., 23; Cushing, *Exploration of Ancient Key-Dweller Remains*, 28.

16. Wells M. Sawyer, "Memories," Wells M. Sawyer Collection, Special and Area Studies Collection, University of Florida; Wells M. Sawyer, "The Health" (undated verse), Sawyer Collection; Wells Sawyer to My Dear Weller, March 1896, Sawyer Collection; Kolianos and Wiesman, *Florida Journals*, 89–90.

17. Kolianos and Wiesman, *Florida Journals*, 59.

18. Randolph J. Widmer, "Introduction," in Cushing, *Exploration of Ancient Key-Dweller Remains*, xvi; Cushing, *Pepper-Hearst Expedition*, 112.

19. Cushing, *Pepper-Hearst Expedition*, 83.

20. Darcie A. MacMahon and William H. Marquadt, *The Calusa and Their Legacy* (University Press of Florida, 2004), 84.

21. Gilliland, *Key Marco's Buried Treasure*, 75; Sawyer, "Health."

Two: EL GOLFO DE MÉXICO

1. Joseph Conrad, *The Mirror of the Sea* (Harper & Brothers, 1906), 168.
2. Charles W. Arnade, "Who Was Juan Ponce de Leon?" *Tequesta* 27 (1967): 3.
3. Stan Ulanski, *The Gulf Stream: Tiny Plankton, Giant Bluefin, and the Amazing Story of the Powerful River in the Atlantic* (University of North Carolina Press, 2008), xii.
4. Carl Ortwin Sauer, *Sixteenth-Century North America: The Land and the Peoples as Seen by the Europeans* (University of California Press, 1975), 29.

Three: UNNECESSARY DEATH

1. Bernard Romans, *A Concise Natural History of East and West Florida*, ed. Kathryn E. Holland Braund (University of Alabama Press, 1999), 259.
2. William Carlos Williams, *In the American Grain* (New Directions, 1925), 44.
3. T. S. Eliot, "The Dry Salvages," in *T. S. Eliot: Poetry, Plays and Prose* (Atlantic, 2008), 141.
4. Marjory Stoneman Douglas, *Florida: The Long Frontier* (Harper & Row, 1967), 51.
5. Bernal Diaz del Castillo, *The Memoirs of the Conquistador Bernal Diaz del Castillo*, vol. 1, trans. John Ingram Lockhart (J. Hatchard Lockhart, 1844), 302–28.
6. Samuel Eliot Morison and Henry Steele Commager, *The Growth of the American Republic* (Oxford University Press, 1962), 33.
7. *The Account: Álvar Nuñez Cabeza de Vaca's Relación*, trans. Martin A. Favata and José B. Fernández (Arte Público Press, 1993), 46.
8. Robert F. Berkhofer, *The White Man's Indian: Images of the American Indians from Columbus to the Present* (Vintage, 1979), 5, 11.
9. Andre Reséndez, *A Land So Strange: The Epic Journey of Cabeza de Vaca* (Basic Books, 2009), 104, 121; *Account: Álvar Nuñez Cabeza de Vaca's Relación*, 23.
10. *Account: Álvar Nuñez Cabeza de Vaca's Relación*, 56.
11. Ibid.
12. Ibid.; Edward W. Kilman, *Cannibal Coast* (Naylor, 1959).
13. Robert A. Ricklis, *The Karankawa Indians of Texas: An Ecological Study of Cultural Tradition and Change* (University of Texas Press, 1996).
14. C. Herndon Williams, *Texas Gulf Coast Stories* (History Press, 2010), 13.
15. Albert S. Gatschet, *The Karankawa Indians, the Coast People of Texas* (Peabody Museum of American Archaeology and Ethnology, 1891), 56; Ricklis, *Karankawa Indians of Texas*, 10, 109–10.
16. William C. Foster, ed., *The La Salle Expedition to Texas: The Journal of Henri Joutel, 1684–1687* (Texas State Historical Association, 1998), 99.
17. Ricklis, *Karankawa Indians of Texas*, 61.
18. Douglas, *Florida: The Long Frontier*, 53.
19. David Ewing Duncan, *Hernando de Soto: A Savage Quest in the Americas* (University of Oklahoma Press, 1997), xx.
20. Michael Gannon, "First European Contacts," *The New Florida History*, ed. Michael Gannon (University Press of Florida, 1996), 23–30.
21. Lawrence A. Clayton, Vernon James Knight Jr., and Edward C. Moore, eds., *The De Soto Chronicles: The Expedition of Hernando de Soto to North America in 1539–1543*, vol. 1 (University of Alabama Press, 1993), 162.

22. Francis Parkman, *La Salle and the Discovery of the Great West* (Charles Scribner's Sons, 1915), 3.
23. Ann F. Ramenofsky and Patricia Galloway, "Disease and the Soto Entrada," *The Hernando de Soto Expedition: History, Historiography, and "Discovery" in the Southeast*, ed. Patricia Kay Galloway (University of Nebraska Press, 2006), 270–75.
24. Williams, *In the American Grain*, 44.

Four: A MOST IMPORTANT RIVER, AND A "MAGNIFICENT" BAY

1. Quoted in John D. Ware and Robert R. Rea, *George Gauld: Surveyor and Cartographer of the Gulf Coast* (University Presses of Florida, 1982), 37.
2. Joseph Conrad, *The Mirror of the Sea* (Harper & Brothers, 1906), 168.
3. Louis De Vorsey Jr., "The Impact of the La Salle Expedition of 1682 on European Cartography," in *La Salle and His Legacy: Frenchmen and Indians in the Lower Mississippi Valley*, ed. Patricia K. Galloway (University Press of Mississippi, 1982), 71.
4. Francis Parkman, *La Salle and the Discovery of the Great West* (Charles Scribner's Sons, 1915), 373; Christopher Morris, *The Big Muddy: An Environmental History of the Mississippi and Its People from Hernando de Soto to Hurricane Katrina* (Oxford University Press, 2012), 25.
5. Parkman, *La Salle*, 366.
6. Robert S. Weddle, *The French Thorn: Rival Explorers in the Spanish Sea, 1682–1762* (Texas A&M University Press, 1991), 82.
7. Richebourg McWilliams, *Iberville's Gulf Journals* (University of Alabama Press, 1991), 52.
8. Weddle, *French Thorn*, 136, 157.
9. Thomas Hutchins, *An Historical Narrative and Description of Louisiana, and West Florida* (University of Florida Press, 1968), facsimile reproduction of 1784 ed., xliv.
10. Newton D. Mereness, ed., *Travels in the American Colonies* (Macmillan, 1926), 489.
11. Thomas Hutchins, *A Topographical Description of Virginia, Pennsylvania, Maryland, and North America* (Burrows Brothers, 1904), 49.
12. Bernard Romans, *A Concise Natural History of East and West Florida*, ed. Kathryn E. Holland Braund (University of Alabama Press, 1999), 1, 3, 321, 348.
13. Ware and Rea, *George Gauld*, 61, 62.
14. Ibid., 24; Romans, *Concise Natural History*, 267.
15. Ware and Rea, *George Gauld*, 24; Romans, *Concise Natural History*, 262, 267.
16. Hutchins, *Historical Narrative*, 33.
17. Romans, *Concise Natural History*, 158.
18. Ibid., 126.
19. Ibid., 138.
20. Ibid., 142.
21. Ibid.
22. Ibid., 209–10.
23. Edward Charles Boynton, *History of West Point* (Applewood Books, 1864), 32.

Five: MANIFEST DESTINY

1. US Coast Survey, *Report of the Superintendent of the Coast Survey, Showing the Progress of the Survey during the Year 1862* (Government Printing Office, 1864), 92.
2. Anne P. Streeter, *Good Fences Make Good Neighbors: Joseph S. Harris and the U.S. Northwest Boundary Survey, 1857–61* (Trafford, 2012), 428.
3. US Coast Survey, *Report of the Superintendent*, 262.
4. Robert W. Tucker and David C. Hendrickson, *Empire of Liberty: The Statecraft of Thomas Jefferson* (Oxford University Press, 1990), 109.
5. Ibid.
6. T. D. Allman, *Finding Florida: The True History of the Sunshine State* (Atlantic Monthly Press, 2013), 65.
7. Roger G. Kennedy, *Mr. Jefferson's Lost Cause: Land, Farmers, Slavery, and the Louisiana Purchase* (Oxford University Press, 2003), 303.
8. Thomas Jefferson to James Monroe, October 24, 1823, in Thomas Jefferson, *The Wisdom of Thomas Jefferson*, ed. Kees De Mooy (Citadel Press, 2003), 106.
9. Thomas Jefferson to James Monroe, May 14, 1820, in Thomas Jefferson, *The Works of Thomas Jefferson*, vol. 12, ed. Paul L. Ford (G. P. Putnam's Sons, 1904), 160.
10. G. J. A. O'Toole, *The Spanish War: An American Epic—1898* (Norton, 1984), 38.
11. "The Ostend Manifesto" (Aix-la-Chapelle, October 15, 1854), historyofcuba.com, http://www.historyofcuba.com/history/havana/Ostend2.htm, accessed summer 2014.
12. Henry Nash Smith, *Virgin Land: The American West as Symbol and Myth* (Harvard University Press, 1978), 176.
13. US Coast Survey, *Report of the Superintendent*, 92.
14. Ibid., 90.
15. Ibid., 79.
16. Walt Whitman, "I Saw in Louisiana a Live-Oak Growing," in *Leaves of Grass* (Modern Library, 1892), 101.
17. US Coast Survey, *Report of the Superintendent*, 175; Bernard Romans, *A Concise Natural History of East and West Florida*, ed. Kathryn E. Holland Braund (University of Alabama Press, 1999), 262.
18. D. W. Meinig, *The Shaping of America: A Geographical Perspective on 500 Years of History*, vol. 1, *1492–1800* (Yale University Press, 1986), 410.
19. Michelle Honora Zacks, "From Table to Trash: The Rise and Fall of Mullet Fishing in Southwest Florida" (PhD diss., University of Hawaii, 2012), xix; Sidney Lanier, *Florida: Its Scenery, Climate, and History, with an Account of Charleston, Savannah, Augusta, and Aiken; a Chapter for Consumptives; Various Papers on Fruit-Culture; and Complete Hand-book and Guide* (J. B. Lippincott, 1876), 94.

Six: A FISHY SEA

1. Sidney Lanier, *Florida: Its Scenery, Climate, and History, with an Account of Charleston, Savannah, Augusta, and Aiken; a Chapter for Consumptives; Various Papers on Fruit-Culture; and Complete Hand-book and Guide* (J. B. Lippincott, 1876), 94.
2. H. C. "Hank" Klein, *Destin's Founding Father: The Untold Story of Leonard Destin* (Freeport, FL: Arturo Studios, 2017), 11–60.
3. Wallace Stevens, "Some Friends from Pascagoula," in *The Collected Poems of Wallace Stevens* (Vintage, 1990), 126–27; Lanier, *Florida*, 94; Edward King, *The Great South:*

A Record of Journeys in Louisiana, Texas, the Indian Country, Missouri, Arkansas, Mississippi, Alabama, Georgia, Florida, South Carolina, North Carolina, Kentucky, Tennessee, Virginia, West Virginia, and Maryland (American Publishing Company, 1875), 406; Bernard Romans, *A Concise Natural History of East and West Florida*, ed. Kathryn E. Holland Braund (University of Alabama Press, 1999), 185.

4. Philip Lee Phillips, *Notes on the Life and Works of Bernard Romans* (Florida State Historical Society, 1924), 124.

5. Ibid., 185.

6. Michelle Honora Zacks, "From Table to Trash: The Rise and Fall of Mullet Fishing in Southwest Florida" (PhD diss., University of Hawaii, 2012), 29; Clinton Newton Howard, *The British Development of West Florida, 1763–1769* (University of California Press, 1974), 40.

7. Phillips, *Notes on the Life and Works*, 185.

8. John Lee Williams, *The Territory of Florida: Or Sketches of the Topography, Civil and Natural History, of the Country, the Climate, and the Indian Tribes, from the First Discovery to the Present Time* (A. T. Goodrich, 1837), 25.

9. "Pensacola—A City of Manifest Destiny," *Stone & Webster Public Service Journal* (December 1908): 382–86.

10. Henry David Thoreau, *Walden, and On the Duty of Civil Disobedience* (Arc Manor, 2007), 178.

11. J. W. Collins, "Notes on the Red-Snapper Fishery," *Bulletin of the U.S. Fish Commission* 6 (1887): 299.

12. *Makers of America: An Historical and Biographical Work by an Able Corps of Writers*, vol. 2, Florida ed. (A. B. Caldwell, 1909), 360.

13. Ibid.

14. Collins, "Notes on the Red-Snapper Fishery," 299.

15. Jason T. Raup, "Fish On: Pensacola's Red Snapper Industry," *Florida Historical Quarterly* 85 (2007): 327.

16. Silas Stearns, "The Red-Snapper Fishery and the Havana Market Fishery of Key West, Florida," in *The Fisheries and Fishery Industries of the United States*, ed. George Brown Goode (Government Printing Office, 1887), 591.

17. "The Retail Markets," *New York Times*, January 7, 1883.

18. Silas Stearns to Professor S. F. Baird, April 17, 1878, Silas Stearns Papers, John C. Pace Library Special Collections, University of West Florida Archives.

19. Stearns, "Red-Snapper Fishery," 553–54.

20. William N. Lindall Jr. and Carl H. Saloman, "Alteration and Destruction of Estuaries Affecting Fishery Resources of the Gulf of Mexico," *Marine Fisheries Review* 39 (1977): 1.

21. Roy Bedichek, *Karánkaway Country* (Doubleday, 1950), 8; Clyde L. MacKenzie Jr., "History of Oystering in the United States and Canada, Featuring the Eight Greatest Oyster Estuaries," *Marine Fisheries Review* 58 (1996): 59.

22. Mark Kurlansky, *The Big Oyster: History on the Half Shell* (Random House, 2007), 165.

23. Ibid., 47; Stearns, "Red-Snapper Fishery," 563.

24. Stearns, "Red-Snapper Fisher," 579, 580.

25. John Steinbeck, *John Steinbeck Novels, 1942–1952* (Library of America, 2001), 101.

26. Jack Rudloe and Anne Rudloe, *Shrimp: The Endless Quest for Pink Gold* (FT Press, 2010), 31.

27. Martha Field, *Louisiana Voyages: The Travel Writings of Catharine Cole*, ed. Joan B. McLaughlin and Jack MacLaughlin (University Press of Mississippi, 2006), 5.

28. Bern Keating, *The Gulf of Mexico* (Viking Press, 1972), 55; Rudloe and Rudloe, *Shrimp*, 37, 39.

29. Kirk Munroe, "Sponge and Spongers of the Florida Reef," *Scribner's Magazine* 12 (1892): 640.

30. "Ten Fathoms Down in the Gulf," *Florida Highways* 10 (March 1942): 10–12, 14.

31. Field, *Louisiana Voyages*, 19; Zacks, "From Table to Trash," 129.

32. Mike Davis, interview by the author, October 28, 2011; Zacks, "From Table to Trash," 126; L. S. K., "Fishing in Florida," *New York Times*, December 25, 1876.

33. Zacks, "From Table to Trash," 87, 139.

34. Leo Lovel, *Spring Creek Chronicles: Stories of Commercial Fishin', Huntin', Workin' and People along the North Florida Gulf Coast*, ed. Ben Lovel (L. V. Lovel, 2000), 17, 18.

35. Jack Rudloe, *Time of the Turtle* (E. P. Dutton, 1979), 100.

36. Lovel, *Spring Creek Chronicles*, 11, 53; Leo Lovel, *Spring Creek Chronicles II: More Stories of Commercial Fishin', Huntin', Workin' and People along the Gulf Coast*, ed. Ben Lovel (Spring Creek Restaurant, 2004), 137.

37. Rudloe, *Time of the Turtle*, 3, 7–8.

38. John James Audubon, "The Turtles," in *Audubon in Florida*, ed. Kathryn Proby (University of Miami Press, 1974), 352.

39. Ibid.

40. Osha Gray Davidson, *Fire in the Turtle House: The Green Sea Turtle and the Fate of the Ocean* (Public Affairs, 2001), 70.

41. Corey Malcom, "Turtle Industry in Key West," *Sea Heritage Journal* 19 (2009): 5.

42. Audubon, "Turtles," 348.

43. Joint Resolution for the Protection and Preservation of the Food Fishes of the Coast of the United States, no. 22, 41st Cong., session 3, February 9, 1871, preamble.

Seven: THE WILD FISH THAT TAMED THE COAST

1. Richard L. Sutton, "The Initiation of Raymond: A Tarpon Story of Aransas Pass," *Forest and Stream* 44 (1924): 76.

2. I thank Randy Wayne White for sharing his life story with me at Doc Ford's Rum and Bar Grill in Sanibel on January 19, 2013.

3. Evan Williams, "The Relentless Randy Wayne White," *Fort Myers Florida Weekly*, March 3, 2010, http://fortmyers.floridaweekly.com.

4. Moise N. Kaplan, *Big Game Angler's Paradise* (Liveright, 1937), 97.

5. Frank Sargeant, *The Tarpon Book: A Complete Angler's Guide* (Larsen's Outdoor Publishing Group, 1991), 5.

6. John Dos Passos, "Under the Tropic," in *The Key West Reader: The Best of the West's Writers, 1830–1990*, ed. George Murphy (Tortugas, 1989), 86.

7. Accessible scientific studies of the tarpon are found in Jerald S. Ault, ed., *Biology and Management of the World Tarpon and Bonefish Fisheries* (CRC Press, 2010).

8. "Gulf Coast Byway," Texas Tropical Trail, http://thetropicaltraveler.com/blog/about/gulf-coast-byway, accessed summer 2013.

9. Otis Mygatt, "Some Tarpon Adventures," *Badminton Magazine of Sports and Pastimes* 1 (1895): 328.

10. John Waller Hills, *A History of Fly Fishing for Trout* (Philip Allan, 1921); C. B.

McCully, *The Language of Fly-Fishing* (Fitzroy Dearborn, 1992), 9–11; John McDonald, *The Origins of Angling* (Doubleday, 1963), 67–68; Dame Juliana Berners, *A Treatise of Fishing with an Angle* (Walking Lion Press, 2006), 86; Dame Juliana League, http://www.djlflyfishers.org, accessed summer 2013.

11. Izaak Walton, *The Compleat Angler or the Contemplative Man's Recreation* (S. Bagster, 1810), 39.

12. Walton, *Compleat Angler*, 243; *Philadelphia Inquirer*, March 12, 1878, clipping found in Hampton Dunn manuscript materials, Old Courthouse Heritage Museum, Inverness, FL.

13. Henry William Herbert, *Frank Forester's Fish and Fishing of the United States and British Provinces of North America* (W. A. Townsend, 1866), 12.

14. John James Audubon, *The 1826 Journal of John James Audubon* (University of Oklahoma Press, 1967), 5.

15. Charles Hallock, *An Angler's Reminiscences: A Record of Sport, Travel and Adventure* (Sportsmen's Review Publishing, 1913), 38.

16. "Qx," unidentified manuscript, in Hampton Dunn manuscript materials, Old Courthouse Heritage Museum, Inverness, FL; Charles Hallock, *Camp Life in Florida: A Handbook for Sportsmen and Settlers* (American News Co., 1876), 14, 30.

17. Kenworthy's dispatches in *Forest and Stream* appeared under the pseudonym Al Fresco on March 18 and 25; April 1, 8, 15, 22, and 29; May 13, 20, and 24; and June 10 and 17, 1875. Hallock reprinted them, along with other essays, in *Camp Life in Florida*. Quotes are from the book's following pages: 38, 40, 259.

18. Hallock, *Camp Life in Florida*, 341.

19. Ibid., 336, 341.

20. Ibid., 341; "Angling at Homosassa Florida," *American Angler* 3 (March 24, 1883): 185.

21. Helen Cooper, *Winslow Homer Watercolors* (Yale University Press, 1986), 234.

22. Peter Brazeau, *Parts of a World: Wallace Stevens Remembered: An Oral Biography* (Random House, 1983), 97; Sidney Lanier, *Florida: Its Scenery, Climate, and History, with an Account of Charleston, Savannah, Augusta, and Aiken; a Chapter for Consumptives; Various Papers on Fruit-Culture; and Complete Hand-book and Guide* (J. B. Lippincott, 1876), 94.

23. Robert Grant, "Tarpon Fishing in Florida," in *Angling*, Leroy M. Yale, A. Foster Higgins, J. G. A. Creighton, et al. (Charles Scribner's Sons, 1897), 182; James A. Henshall, *Camping and Cruising in Florida* (Robert Clarke, 1884), 192.

24. Randy Wayne White, *The Heat Islands* (St. Martin's Press, 1993), 119; White, *Sanibel Flats* (St. Martin's Press, 1990), 45, 108.

25. Randy Wayne White and Carlene Fredericka Brennen, *Randy Wayne White's Ultimate Tarpon Book: The Birth of Big Game Fishing* (University Press of Florida, 2010), 265.

26. Anthony Weston Dimock, *Wall Street and the Wilds* (Outing Publishing, 1915), 12.

27. Anthony Weston Dimock, *The Book of the Tarpon* (Outing Publishing, 1911), 15.

28. N. A. Bimon, "The Silver King," *Forest and Stream* 38 (1892): 394; Grant, "Tarpon Fishing in Florida," 183.

29. White and Brennen, *Randy Wayne White's Ultimate Tarpon Book*, 9, 50, 55, 227, 234.

30. Ibid., 122–23.

31. Ibid., 138.

32. Kevin Kokomoor, "'In the Land of the Tarpon': The Silver King, Sport, and the

Development of Southwest Florida, 1885–1915," *Journal of the Gilded Age and Progressive Era* 11 (2012): 191.

33. White and Brennen, *Randy Wayne White's Ultimate Tarpon Book*, 26–28; Kokomoor, "'In the Land of the Tarpon,'" 211–12.

34. White and Brennen, *Randy Wayne White's Ultimate Tarpon Book*, 55.

35. Theodore Roosevelt, *The Rough Riders: An Autobiography* (Library of America, 2004), 296.

36. Theodore Roosevelt, "Harpooning Devilfish," *Scribner's Magazine* 62 (1917): 293–305.

37. White and Brennen, *Randy Wayne White's Ultimate Tarpon Book*, 81.

38. Paul Hendrickson, *Hemingway's Boat: Everything He Loved in Life, and Lost, 1934–1961* (Alfred A. Knopf, 2011), 230; White and Brennen, *Randy Wayne White's Ultimate Tarpon Book*, 136.

39. R. M. S., "The Tarpon Record—How Long Do They Fight," *American Angler* 21 (1892): 327.

40. White and Brennen, *Randy Wayne White's Ultimate Tarpon Book*, 89.

41. Bimon, "Silver King," 394. Thanks to Gary Mormino for bringing this issue of the *Fort Myers Press* to my attention.

42. Kokomoor, "'In the Land of the Tarpon,'" 192, 212; White and Brennen, *Randy Wayne White's Ultimate Tarpon Book*, 167.

43. "In the Land of Tarpon," *New York Times*, March 5, 1893.

44. W. D. "The Land of the Tarpon," *Atlanta Constitution*, December 18, 1893; Martha Field, *Louisiana Voyages: The Travel Writings of Catharine Cole*, ed. Joan B. McLaughlin and Jack MacLaughlin (University Press of Mississippi, 2006), 10, 11.

45. Nellie D. S. Graham, "Tarpon Fishing at Port Aransas Pass," *Outing* 35 (February 1900): 473; Barney Farley, *Fishing Yesterday's Gulf Coast* (Texas A&M University Press, 2008), xi.

46. Zane Grey, *The Best of Zane Grey, Outdoorsman: Hunting and Fishing Tales* (Stackpole Books, 1992), 51.

47. Field, *Louisiana Voyages*, 5.

48. Farley, *Fishing Yesterday's Gulf Coast*, xiii.

49. "Harding Fights Fish 45 Minutes," *Washington Post*, November 10, 1920; "Harding Loses Fish," *New York Times*, November 9, 1920.

50. "Tarpon along Florida Coast," *New York Times*, April 2, 1912.

51. "Aransas Pass Tarpon Club," *Forest and Stream* 69 (1907):100.

52. "Fierce Fighting Tarpon," *New York Times*, July 21, 1895.

53. Randy Wayne White, "Fishing's Dirty Little Secret," *Tampa Tribune*, April 14, 2013.

Eight: BIRDS OF A FEATHER, SHOT TOGETHER

1. In Thomas Wright, ed., *Popular Treatises on Science Written During the Middle Ages, in Anglo-Saxon, Anglo-Norman, and English* (R. and J. E. Taylor, 1841).

2. "Notes from Field and Study," *Bird-Lore* 18 (March–April 1916), 103; "A Tropical Migration Tragedy," *Bird-Lore* 18 (1916): 103; W. T. Helmuth, "Extracts from Notes Made in the Naval Service," *Auk* 37 (1920): 255–61.

3. George H. Lowery Jr., "Evidence of Trans-Gulf Migration," *Auk* 63 (1946): 175–211.

4. Scott Weidensaul, *Living on the Wind: Across the Hemisphere with Migratory Birds* (North Point Press, 1999), 251.

5. John Muir, *A Thousand-Mile Walk to the Gulf* (Houghton Mifflin, 1998), 134.

6. Harriet Beecher Stowe, *Palmetto-Leaves* (James R. Osgood, 1873), 260, 261.

7. Quoted in "The Pinellas," *Medical Bulletin: A Monthly Journal of Medicine and Surgery* 29 (1907): 34.

8. W. E. D. Scott, "The Present Condition of Some of the Bird Rookeries of the Gulf Coast of Florida," *Auk* 4 (1887): 139–40.

9. Ibid., 276.

10. Ibid.

11. J. A. Allen, "The Present Wholesale Destruction of Bird-Life in the United States," *Science* 7 (1886): 192.

12. Minnie Moore-Willson, *Birds of the Everglades and Their Neighbors the Seminole Indians* (Tampa Tribune, 1920), 7.

13. Marjory Stoneman Douglas, *The Everglades: River of Grass* (Pineapple Press, 1997), 279.

14. *Life Histories of North American Marsh Birds, Orders Odontoglossae, Herodiones, and Paludicolae*, Smithsonian Institution United States National Museum Bulletin 135 (Government Printing Office, 1926), 149.

15. Edward A. McIlhenny, *How I Made a Bird City* (privately published by author, 1912), 2.

16. Shane K. Bernard, *Tabasco: An Illustrated History* (McIlhenny Co., 2007), 107; John Taliaferro, *In a Far Country: The True Story of a Mission, a Marriage, a Murder, and the Remarkable Reindeer Rescue of 1898* (Public Affairs, 2007), 228, 273.

17. McIlhenny, *How I Made a Bird City*, 7.

18. Terry L. Jones, "Alligator Tales: Stories from Louisiana's Alligator-Filled Past," *Louisiana Sportsman*, September 1, 2012, http://www.louisianasportsman.com, accessed fall 2013.

19. Mark Derr, *Some Kind of Paradise: A Chronicle of Man and the Land in Florida* (William Morrow, 1989), 136–37.

20. Oscar E. Baynard to A. J. Hanna, September 24, 1947, Plume Hunting folder, Alfred J. Hanna Papers, Special Collections, Rollins College, Winter Park, FL.

21. Oliver H. Orr Jr., *Saving American Birds: T. Gilbert Pearson and the Founding of the Audubon Movement* (University Press of Florida, 1992), 30–31.

22. George B. Sennett, "Destruction of the Eggs of Birds for Food," *Science* 7 (1886): 200.

23. Virginia Woolf, *The Diary of Virginia Woolf*, vol. 2, *1920–1924* (Harcourt Brace Jovanovich, 1978), 337.

24. Ella Lowery Moseley, "Fashion Has No Soul," *Washington Post*, November 10, 1901; Robin Doughty, *Feather Fashions and Bird Preservation: A Study in Nature Protection* (University of California Press, 1975), 54; McIlhenny, *How I Made a Bird City*, 1.

25. Woolf, *Diary of Virginia Woolf*, 2:337; "Poetry of Season's Hats: Grace in New Shapes," *Washington Post*, October 24, 1909.

26. "Activity of the Audubon Society Spells Death for Vagrant Cats Slinking about Saint Petersburg," *St. Petersburg Times*, January 10, 1915.

27. Martha R. Field, "Come South, Young Woman," in *The Congress of Women*, ed. Mary K. O. Eagle (Monarch, 1894), 776.

28. John Gould, *Handbook to the Birds of Australia* (published by the author, 1865), 410.

29. The US Biological Survey *Bulletin* 41 (1912) contains a list of game protection laws by state from 1776 to 1911, pages 20–46.

30. Frank Graham Jr., *The Audubon Auk: A History of the National Audubon Society* (University of Texas Press, 1992), 47.

31. "Third Audubon Warden Murdered," *Bird-Lore* 11 (January-February 1909): 52.

32. Robin W. Doughty, *Wildlife and Man in Texas* (Texas A&M University Press, 1989), 62.

33. Theodore Roosevelt, *A Book-Lover's Holidays in the Open* (Charles Scribner's Sons, 1916), 283, 288, 300.

34. John M. Parker, "Roosevelt as a Student of Birds," *Forest and Stream* 89 (1919): 627.

35. Graham, *Audubon Auk*, 123; Theodore Cross, *Waterbirds* (W. W. Norton, 2009), 13, 14.

36. Edward A. McIlhenny to May Mann Jennings, August 5, 1916, May Mann Jennings Papers, P. K. Yonge Library of Florida History, University of Florida, Gainesville. I thank Leslie Poole for bringing this letter to my attention.

37. Frank M. Chapman, *Camps and Cruises of an Ornithologist* (D. Appleton, 1908), 368.

38. John James Audubon, *The Audubon Reader* (Alfred A. Knopf, 2006), 526. Thanks to Gary Mormino for the following *Tampa Daily Times* articles from 1918: "Say, Folks, Whaddye Know about Old Man Pelican?" (February 17); "Fishermen Generally See, to Hold Pelican a Pirate" (February 28); "State Council of Defense Wants Pelican Protected" (March 2); "The Pelican: His Enemies Take a Swing at Him" (March 4); "The Pelican: Is Bird a Blessing or a Burglar?" (March 5).

39. Graham, *Audubon Auk*, 90.

40. Henry Hazlit Kopman, *Wild Acres: A Book of the Gulf Coast Country* (E. P. Dutton, 1946), 37.

41. Martha Field, *Louisiana Voyages: The Travel Writings of Catharine Cole*, ed. Joan B. McLaughlin and Jack MacLaughlin (University Press of Mississippi, 2006), 12.

42. Graham, *Audubon Auk*, 10.

43. "The Audubon Society of Louisiana," *St. Tammany Farmer*, December 27, 1902.

44. "Voice of the People: 'Ignoble and Cowardly,'" *Chicago Daily Tribune*, November 28, 1923.

Nine: FROM BAYSIDE TO BEACHSIDE

1. Rachel Carson, *The Edge of the Sea* (Houghton Mifflin, 1983), 1.

2. Anthony Weston Dimock, *The Book of the Tarpon* (Outing Publishing, 1911), 232, 256.

3. Carson, *Edge of the Sea*, 125.

4. Martha Field, *Louisiana Voyages: The Travel Writings of Catharine Cole*, ed. Joan B. McLaughlin and Jack MacLaughlin (University Press of Mississippi, 2006), 9.

5. Michael Welland, *Sand: The Never-Ending Story* (University of California Press, 2009), 19.

6. Carson, *Edge of the Sea*, 129.

7. Field, *Louisiana Voyages*, 10.

8. Martha R. Field, "Come South, Young Woman," in *The Congress of Women*, ed. Mary K. O. Eagle (Monarch, 1894), 776; Field, *Louisiana Voyages*, 123.

9. Lena Lenček and Gideon Bosker, *The Beach: The History of Paradise on Earth* (Viking Press, 1998), 40, 43.

10. Victor Hugo, *The Toilers of the Sea*, trans. Mary W. Artois (George H. Richmond, 1892), 25.

11. Bernard Romans, *A Concise Natural History of East and West Florida*, ed. Kathryn E. Holland Braund (University of Alabama Press, 1999), 8.

12. Charles Lawrence Dyer, *Along the Gulf* (Women of Trinity Episcopal Church, 1971), 1.

13. Jessica Brannon-Wranosky, "Corpus Christi History before La Retama," Corpus Christi Libraries, http://www.cclibraries.com/local_history/laretama/lrhistory.htm, accessed May 2012.

14. Louis H. Sullivan, *The Autobiography of an Idea* (Press of the American Institute of Architects, 1924), 295.

15. Robert H. Gore, *The Gulf of Mexico* (Pineapple Press, 1992), 152.

16. Alexander Agassiz, *Three Cruises of the United States Coast and Geodetic Survey Steamer "Blake"*, vol. 1, 2 (Houghton, Mifflin, 1888).

17. Wallace Stevens, *The Collected Poems of Wallace Stevens* (Vintage, 1990), 126.

18. Ibid., 128.

19. Sidney Lanier, *Florida: Its Scenery, Climate, and History, with an Account of Charleston, Savannah, Augusta, and Aiken, a Chapter for Consumptives; Various Papers on Fruit-Culture; and Complete Hand-book and Guide* (J. B. Lippincott, 1876), 115.

20. John Muir, *A Thousand-Mile Walk to the Gulf* (Houghton, Mifflin, 1916), 114, 134.

21. Ibid., 139, 140.

22. Ibid., 142.

23. Julian Ralph, "Coney Island," *Scribner's Magazine* 20 (1896): 12; H. Barbara Weinberg, Doreen Bolger, and David Park Curry, *American Impressionism and Realism: The Painting of Modern Life, 1885–1915* (Metropolitan Museum of Art, 1994), 119.

24. Mary Austin Holley, *Mary Austin Holley: The Texas Diary, 1835–1838* (University of Texas Press, 1965), 27, 29; "Surf Bathing," *Corpus Christi Daily Herald*, May 21, 1910.

25. Stephen Crane, *Stephen Crane: Prose and Poetry* (Penguin, 1984), 710.

26. "Corpus Christi, the Home of the Next Annual Convention," *Texas State Journal of Medicine* 3 (1908): 313; "The Life of Velasco," *Velasco Daily Times*, January 22, 1892.

27. Field, *Louisiana Voyages*, 9, 11, 12.

28. Ibid., 9.

29. Ibid., 3–11.

30. Ibid., 6, 123; Henry Lee, *The Octopus: Or, the "Devil-Fish" of Fiction and of Fact* (Chapman and Hall, 1875), 31.

31. Abby Sallenger, *Island in a Storm: A Rising Sea, a Vanishing Coast, and a Nineteenth-Century Disaster That Warns of a Warmer World* (Public Affairs, 2009), 5; James M. Sothern, *Last Island* (Cheri, 1980), 19.

32. Sothern, *Last Island*, 26.

33. Ibid., 36.

34. Field, *Louisiana Voyages*, 10; Charles Tenney Jackson, *The Fountain of Youth* (Outdoor Publishing, 1914), 293.

35. Albert Irving Clark, "The History of Galveston Island," *Texas Teachers' Bulletin* 14 (1927): 58.

36. Harvey H. Jackson III, *The Rise and Fall of the Redneck Riviera: An Insider's History of the Florida-Alabama Coast* (University of Georgia Press, 2012), 14.

Ten: OIL AND THE TEXAS TOE DIP

1. "Offshore Petroleum History," American Oil & Gas Historical Society, http://aoghs.org/offshore-history/offshore-oil-history, accessed fall 2014.

2. "Thunder Beast Breathes Again at World's Fair," *Wall Street Journal*, June 30, 1933.

3. Sinclair Oil Corporation, "Sinclair History," https://www.sinclairoil.com/history, accessed fall 2014.

4. Henrietta M. Larson and Kenneth Wiggins Porter, *History of Humble Oil and Refining Company: A Study in Industrial Growth* (Harper & Brothers, 1959), 6.

5. Judith Walker Linsley, Ellen Walker Rienstra, and Jo Ann Stiles, *Giant under the Hill: A History of the Spindletop Oil Discovery at Beaumont, Texas, in 1901* (Texas State Historical Society, 2002), 23.

6. Ibid., 34, 82.

7. Larson and Porter, *History of Humble Oil*, 1.

8. Walter Rundell Jr., *Early Texas Oil: A Photographic History, 1866–1936* (Texas A&M University Press, 1977), 38.

9. Linsley, *Giant under the Hill*, 226.

10. Patricia Meyers Benham, "Goose Creek Oilfield," *Handbook of Texas Online* http://www.tshaonline.org/handbook/online/articles/dog01, accessed fall 2014; Tommy Thompson, *Great Oil Fields of the Gulf Coast* (Houston Chronicle, 1967), 12–13; Rundell, *Early Texas Oil*, 119.

11. Craig Thompson, *Since Spindletop: A Human Story of Gulf's First Half-Century* (1951), 20, 21.

12. "Gusher Makes $33 a Minute," *Pittsburgh Gazette*, August 19, 1917.

13. *Houston Chronicle*, July 13, 1916, quoted in Olga Miller Haenel, "A Social History of Baytown, 1912–1956" (master's thesis, University of Texas, 1958), 7.

14. "Ohio Offshore Wells," American Oil & Gas Historical Society, http://aoghs.org/offshore-history/ohio-offshore-wells, accessed fall 2014. See Judith L. Sneed, "The First Over-water Drilling: The Lost History of Ohio's Grand Reservoir Oil Boom," *Oil-Industry History* 6 (2005): 49–53.

Eleven: OIL AND THE LOUISIANA PLUNGE

1. A. W., "'Thunder Bay' Shown at State on New Wide, Curved Screen," *New York Times*, May 21, 1953; Jeanine Basinger, *Anthony Mann* (Wesleyan University Press, 2007), 132.

2. Nola Mae Ross, "Heywood 1872 History," USGenWeb Project, Louisiana Archives, http://files.usgwarchives.net/la/jeffersondavis/history/heywood.txt, accessed fall 2014.

3. "Jennings Has Become Greatly Excited," *Dallas Morning News*, September 24, 1901; Ross, "Heywood 1872 History."

4. Ross, "Heywood 1872 History."

5. Diane Austin, Tyler Priest, Lauren Penney, et al., *History of the Offshore Oil and Gas Industry in Southern Louisiana*, vol. 1, *Papers on the Evolving Offshore Industry* (US Department of the Interior, 2006), 29.

6. Michael Gannon, *Operation Drumbeat: The Dramatic True Story of Germany's First U-Boat Attacks along the American Coast in World War II* (Harper & Row, 1990), 308, 310.

7. Ibid., xviii.

8. Alistair Cooke, *The American Home Front, 1941–1942* (Grove Press, 2007), 76.

9. John Samuel Ezell, *Innovations in Energy: The Story of Kerr-McGee* (University of Oklahoma Press, 1979), 154.

10. Ibid.

11. Ibid., 169.

12. Ibid., 165.

13. Ibid., 169.

14. Paul Rotha, *Robert J. Flaherty: A Biography* (University of Pennsylvania Press, 1983), 235.

15. Ibid., 235.

16. Robin L. Murray, *Film and Everyday Eco-disasters* (University of Nebraska Press, 2014), 165.

17. Alan Gevinson, ed., *Within Our Gates: Ethnicity in American Feature Films, 1911–1960* (University of California Press, 1997), 614.

18. "Fishermen in Gulf of Mexico in Contest with Oil Men," *New York Times*, June 8, 1947.

19. Diane Austin, *History of the Offshore Oil and Gas Industry in Southern Louisiana*, vol. 3, *Morgan City's History in the Era of Oil and Gas—Perspectives of Those Who Were There* (US Department of the Interior, 2008), 226.

20. Jason P. Theriot, *American Energy, Imperiled Coast: Oil and Gas Development in Louisiana's Wetlands* (Louisiana State University Press, 2014), 72.

21. Oliver Houck, "Who Will Pay to Fix Louisiana?" *Nation*, June 24, 2010, online edition, http://www.thenation.com/article/who-will-pay-fix-louisiana.

22. John McPhee, *The Control of Nature* (Noonday Press, 1993), 86.

23. Coastal Zone Information Center, *Outer Continental Shelf Impacts, Morgan City, Louisiana* (University of Southwestern Louisiana, 1977), 3.

24. *Revisiting Flaherty's Louisiana Story*, produced by Patricia A. Suchy, James V. Catano, and Adelaide Russo (Louisiana State University, 2006), DVD.

Twelve: ISLANDS, SHIFTING SANDS OF TIME

1. *The Gulf Islands: Mississippi's Wilderness Shore*, directed by Jay Woods and Robbie Fisher (Mississippi Public Broadcasting, 2009), DVD.

2. Unless otherwise noted, all Anderson quotes come from *The Horn Island Logs of Walter Inglis Anderson*, ed. Redding S. Sugg Jr. (Memphis State University Press, 1973).

3. Agnes Grinstead Anderson, *Approaching the Magic Hour: Memories of Walter Anderson* (University Press of Mississippi, 1989), 112, 148.

4. Sugg in Anderson, *Horn Island Logs*, 85.

5. Martha Field, *Louisiana Voyages: The Travel Writings of Catharine Cole*, ed. Joan B. McLaughlin and Jack MacLaughlin (University Press of Mississippi, 2006), 5.

6. *Letter of Hernando de Soto and Memoir of Hernando Escalante de Fontaneda*, trans. Buckingham Smith (1854), 14.

7. Rachel Carson, *The Edge of the Sea* (Houghton Mifflin, 1983), 246.

8. Susan Cerulean, *Coming to Pass: Florida's Coastal Islands in a Gulf of Change* (University of Georgia Press, 2015), 221.

9. Anderson, *Approaching the Magic Hour*, 174.

10. Roderick Nash, *Wilderness and the American Mind* (Yale University Press, 1982), 91.

11. Christopher Maurer, *Fortune's Favorite Child: The Uneasy Life of Walter Anderson* (University Press of Mississippi, 2003), 227.

12. Richebourg McWilliams, *Iberville's Gulf Journals* (University of Alabama Press, 1991), 42.

13. Maurer, *Fortune's Favorite Child*, 17; *Mississippi: The WPA Guide to the Magnolia State* (University Press of Mississippi, 1988), 292.

14. Nancy Sweezy, *Raised in Clay: The Southern Pottery Tradition* (University of North Carolina Press, 1994), 292.

15. Anderson, *Approaching the Magic Hour*, 128.

16. Maurer, *Fortune's Favorite Child*, 175.

17. Sugg in Anderson, *Horn Island Logs*, 31.

18. Anderson, *Approaching the Magic Hour*, 118.

19. Simon Winchester, *Atlantic: Great Sea Battles, Heroic Discoveries, Titanic Storms, and a Vast Ocean of a Million Stories* (Harper Collins, 2010), 197–99.

20. "Harding's Vacation Town Used by Gen. Taylor in 1848," *Washington Post*, November 10, 1920; Geoff Winningham, *Traveling the Shore of the Spanish Sea: The Gulf Coast of Texas and Mexico* (Texas A&M University Press, 2010), 118–19.

21. Rodman L. Underwood, *Waters of Discord: The Union Blockade of Texas during the Civil War* (McFarland, 2003); Frank Zoretich, *Cheap Thrills: Florida, the Bottom Half* (Pineapple Press, 1994).

22. C. H. Rockwell, "Death of John Gomez," *Forest and Stream* 55 (1900): 82; Charles Hallock, *An Angler's Reminiscences: A Record of Sport, Travel and Adventure* (Sportsmen's Review Publishing, 1913), 38.

23. Rockwell, "Death of John Gomez," 82.

24. James A. Henshall, *Camping and Cruising in Florida* (Robert Clarke, 1884), 189.

25. Gaspar Cusachs, "Lafitte, the Louisiana Pirate and Patriot," *Louisiana Historical Quarterly* 2 (1919): 434.

26. Anderson, *Approaching the Magic Hour*, 156–58; Maurer, *Fortune's Favorite Child*, 280–81.

27. Ed Regis, *The Biology of Doom: The History of America's Secret Germ Warfare Project* (Henry Holt, 1999), 64–76, 223–24.

28. Anderson, *Approaching the Magic Hour*, 96–98.

29. Ibid., 100.

30. Ibid., 174–75.

Thirteen: WIND AND WATER

1. *All Over but to Cry*, directed by Jennifer John Block (Fresh Media and National Hurricane Museum and Science Center, 2009), DVD.

2. Joseph Conrad, *Typhoon* (Doubleday, Page, 1908), 186.

3. Barry Keim and Robert A. Muller, *Hurricanes of the Gulf of Mexico* (Louisiana State University Press, 2009).

4. These frequency numbers come from Eric S. Blake and Ethan J. Gibney, "The Deadliest, Costliest, and Most Intense United States Tropical Cyclones from 1851 to 2010," National Oceanic and Atmospheric Administration Technical Memorandum, NWS NHC-6 (National Weather Service, August 2011), 21.

5. Cynthia Barnett, *Rain: A Natural and Cultural History* (Crown, 2015), 21.

6. Loretta Koonce Flowers, quoted by lawson at BeaumontEnterprise.com ("Mem-

ories of Hurricane Audrey"), June 27, 2007, http://beaumontenterprise.activeboard.com/index.spark?forumID=90886&p=3&topicID=12394316.

7. "WWL-TV Meteorologist Nash Roberts Dead at 92," *New Orleans Times-Picayune*, December 20, 2011.

8. Flowers, quoted by lawson at BeaumontEnterprise.com.

9. *All Over but to Cry.*

10. Ibid.

11. Mrs. John R. Smith, "My Battle with Audrey," *Personnel Panorama* 6 (July–August 1957), quoted at "NOAA History," National Oceanic and Atmospheric Administration, http://www.history.noaa.gov/stories_tales/hurricaneaudrey.html, accessed spring 2014.

12. *All Over but to Cry.*

13. Cathy C. Post, *Hurricane Audrey: The Deadly Storm of 1957* (Pelican, 2007), 120.

14. Stephen Crane, *Stephen Crane: Prose and Poetry* (Penguin, 1984), 709.

15. Gary Cartwright, *Galveston: A History of the Island* (Texas Christian University Press, 1998), 141.

16. Keim and Muller, *Hurricanes of the Gulf of Mexico*, 8.

17. "Galveston Still Healing 5 Years after Hurricane Ike," *Texas Tribune*, April 26, 2013.

18. Phil Scott, *Hemingway's Hurricane: The Great Florida Keys Storm of 1935* (International Marine, 2006).

19. Dominic Massa, "Legendary Meteorologist Nash Roberts Dies at 92," Houmatoday.com, December 19, 2010, http://www.houmatoday.com/article/20101219/ARTICLES/101219492.

20. Lew Fincher and Bill Read, "The 1943 'Surprise' Hurricane," National Weather Service Weather Forecast Office, Houston/Galveston, TX, National Oceanic and Atmospheric Administration, http://www.srh.noaa.gov/hgx/?n=projects_1943surprischurricane, accessed spring 2014.

21. New Orleans Weather Bureau, "Hurricane Warning and Advisory Number 7 Audrey, 10 PM CST June 26 1957," Weather Underground, http://www.wunderground.com/education/audrey.asp?, accessed spring 2014.

22. "Forecaster Is Right on Gulf Storms," *New York Times*, October 4, 1998.

23. Brian Altobello, *New Orleans Goes to War, 1941–1945: An Oral History of New Orleans during World War II* (1990), 67–68. On the Pacific fleet's frustration with typhoons, see *Command Summary of Fleet Admiral Chester W. Nimitz, USN, Nimitz "Graybook," 1 December 1941–31 August 1945*, vol. 6, especially pp. 2687, 2698, 2919.

24. These items were discovered by underwater archaeologists. See a special issue of the *Florida Anthropologist* devoted to the Luna shipwrecks: *Florida Anthropologist* 62 (September–December 2009).

25. Herbert Ingram Priestley, *The Luna Papers, 1559–1561*, vols. 1 and 2 (University of Alabama Press, 2010), xxvii.

26. Ibid., xxi.

27. Ibid., 7.

28. Thomas Jefferson, *Memoirs, Correspondence and Private Papers of Thomas Jefferson*, vol. 1, ed. T. J. Randolph (Henry Colburn and Richard Bentley, 1829), 61.

29. Hunter S. Thompson, "The Gonzo Salvage Company," in *The Key West Reader: The Best of the West's Writers, 1830–1990*, ed. George Murphy (Tortugas, 1989), 209, 211.

30. John Viele, *The Florida Keys: The Wreckers* (Pineapple Press, 2001), vi, 54–55; Kathryn Hall Proby, ed., *Audubon in Florida* (University of Miami Press, 1974), 338, 340.

31. Ernest Hemingway, "Who Murdered the Vets? A First-Hand Report on the Florida Hurricane," *New Masses* 16 (1935): 9–10; Jeffrey Myers, *Hemingway: A Biography* (Da Capp Press, 1985), 288.

32. Post, *Hurricane Audrey*, 68.

33. "Betsy Lashes New Orleans," *Chicago Tribune*, September 10, 1965.

34. "Lloyd's Last to Feel Impact of Hurricane Betsy's Winds," *Chicago Tribune*, December 24, 1965.

35. Transcript of audio of President Johnson in New Orleans following landfall of Hurricane Betsy, September 10, 1965, LBJ Presidential Library online, http://www.lbjlibrary.net/collections/quick-facts/lyndon-baines-johnson-hurricane-betsy/lbj-new-orleans-hurricane-betsy.html, accessed spring 2014.

36. Philip D. Hearn, *Hurricane Camille: Monster Storm of the Gulf Coast* (University Press of Mississippi, 2007), 28.

37. Dan Ellis, *All about Camille—The Great Storm* (CreateSpace, 2010), ii.

38. Flowers, quoted by lawson at BeaumontEnterprise.com.

39. *All Over but to Cry.*

40. Ibid.

41. Ibid.

42. Post, *Hurricane Audrey*, 91.

43. Ibid., 152.

44. *All Over but to Cry.*

45. Post, *Hurricane Audrey*, 298.

46. Ibid.

47. *Revisiting Flaherty's Louisiana Story*, produced by Patricia A. Suchy, James V. Catano, and Adelaide Russo (Louisiana State University, 2006), DVD.

48. Roger A. Pielke Jr., Chantal Simonpietri, and Jennifer Oxelson, *Thirty Years after Hurricane Camille: Lessons Learned, Lessons Lost*, Hurricane Camille Project Report (1999), 14.

49. Steven G. Wilson and Tomas R. Frischetti, *Coastline Population Trends in the United States: 1960 to 2008*, Current Population Reports (US Census Bureau, 2010); Blake and Gibney, "Deadliest, Costliest, and Most Intense."

Fourteen: THE GROWTH COAST

1. Archie Carr, *The Everglades* (Time-Life, 1973), 136.

2. Rachel Carson, *The Edge of the Sea* (Houghton Mifflin, 1955), 246.

3. Frank Hamilton Cushing, *The Pepper-Hearst Expedition: Preliminary Report on the Exploration of Ancient Key-Dweller Remains on the Gulf Coast of Florida* (MacCalla, 1897), 3.

4. John H. Davis Jr., "Mangroves," *Nature Magazine* 31 (1938): 551; Joseph Conrad, *Heart of Darkness* (Plain Label Books, 1983), 35.

5. Karl A. Bickel and Walker Evans, *The Mangrove Coast: The Story of the West Coast of Florida* (Coward-McCann, 1942), 3.

6. Carson, *Edge of the Sea*, 246.

7. Gary R. Mormino, *Land of Sunshine, State of Dreams: A Social History of Modern Florida* (University Press of Florida, 2005), 340.

8. David Dodrill, *Selling the Dream: The Gulf American Corporation and the Building*

of Cape Coral (University of Alabama Press, 2002), 231; Mormino, *Land of Sunshine*, 340–42.

9. Marian Coe, "Permit Sought from State for Huge Boca Ciega Fill," *St. Petersburg Independent*, May 14, 1958.

10. R. Bruce Stephenson, *Visions of Eden: Environmentalism, Urban Planning, and City Building in St. Petersburg, Florida, 1900–1995* (Ohio State University Press, 1997), 131–32.

11. Robert F. Hutton, *The Ecology of Boca Ciega Bay, with Special Reference to Dredging and Filling Operations . . .*, Technical Series no. 17 (Florida State Board of Conservation, 1956), 69, 78.

12. Martin A. Dykman, *Floridian of the Century: The Courage of Governor LeRoy Collins* (University Press of Florida, 2006), 163.

13. Ibid., 87.

14. Jon Wilson, *The Golden Era in St. Petersburg: Postwar Prosperity in the Sunshine State* (History Press, 2013), 73.

15. Nicholas Foreman, "The Owl and the Monitor: Nature versus Neighborhood in Cape Coral, Florida" (unpublished manuscript in the possession of the author, courtesy of Nicholas Foreman).

16. Ibid., 8.

17. "Human Hair Can Die of Thirst," *Life* 36 (1954): 93; Dodrill, *Selling the Dream*, 20.

18. Dodrill, *Selling the Dream*, 13.

19. Kenneth J. Schwartz, interview by David Dodrill, November 16, 1987, Samuel Proctor Oral History Program, University of Florida, Gainesville, Florida, 2; "People of Influence: The Rosen Brothers in Cape Coral," *Fort Myers News-Press*, August 28, 2014.

20. Cynthia Barnett, *Mirage: Florida and the Vanishing Water of the Eastern U.S.* (University of Michigan Press, 2007), 26.

21. Dodrill, *Selling the Dream*, 233; "People of Influence," *Fort Myers News-Press*.

22. Trevor Armbrister, "Land Frauds," *Saturday Evening Post* 236 (April 27, 1963): 17–23.

23. James M. Gavin, "Land Boom Echoes Way thru Florida," *Chicago Tribune*, July 4, 1965.

24. Dodrill, *Selling the Dream*, 232.

25. Dykman, *Floridian of the Century*, 162–63.

26. John D. MacDonald, *The Dreadful Lemon Sky* (Fawcett Books, 1964), 45.

27. "Motor Boating and Sailing Answers," John D. MacDonald Collection, box 148, folder 18, Special and Area Studies Collection, University of Florida, Gainesville, FL.

28. John D. MacDonald, "Why a Quarter-Century of Growth May Not Have Been Progress," *Florida Trend* 25 (1983): 34.

29. Stephenson, *Visions of Eden*, 56.

30. John D. MacDonald, "A Florida of Swamps and Silences," *New York Times*, August 15, 1982.

31. Ibid.; John D. MacDonald, *Dead Low Tide* (Fawcett, 1953), 19.

32. Hugh Merrill, *The Red Hot Typewriter: The Life and Times of John D. MacDonald* (Minotaur Books, 2000), 132.

33. MacDonald, "Florida of Swamps and Silences"; John D. MacDonald, *Barrier Island* (Knopf, 1986).

34. John D. MacDonald to Jerome Bernard, n.d., John D. MacDonald Collection, box 148, folder 2.

35. John D. MacDonald to Frank S. Freeman, December 20, 1967, John D. MacDonald Collection (JDMC), box 67, folder 8. And the following newspaper clippings in JDMC, box 71, folder 8: "Developer Gets Bay Fill Permit," November 26, 1956; "Filling in Bay Defense Heard," undated; "Further Filling of Bay Opposed," November 27, 1956.

36. John D. MacDonald to Paul Stannard, December 16, 1959, John D. MacDonald Collection (JDMC), box 69, folder 7; T. Carrington Burns (JDM pseudonym), "Off the Beat," *Newsmonth*, June 1960, JDMC, box 69, folder 7.

37. Jim Harrison, *Just before Dark* (Houghton Mifflin, 1999), 248; John D. MacDonald, *A Flash of Green* (Simon & Schuster, 1962; repr., Fawcett Gold Medal, 1984), dedication page.

38. MacDonald, *Flash of Green*, 24.

39. Ibid.

40. *Florida's Emerald Isle, Marco Island* (Hack Swain Productions, 1965), State Library and Archives of Florida, https://www.floridamemory.com/items/show/232443, accessed summer 2015.

41. John D. MacDonald, *Bright Orange for the Shroud* (Random House, 2013), 87.

42. Mormino, *Land of Sunshine*, 57.

43. "Sea Wall Project Began in 1925" and "Know Your Coast—Sea-Wall," undated newspaper clippings, M. J. Stevens Collection, Notebooks, box 10, McCain Library and Archives, University of Southern Mississippi, Hattiesburg.

44. US Fish and Wildlife Service, *Proceedings on Coastal Ecosystems of the Southeastern United States, February 18–22, 1981*, ed. Robert C. Carey and Paul S. Markovits (Office of Biological Services, USFWS, 1981), 48 https://archive.org/stream/proceedingsusfis 00care/proceedingsusfis00care_djvu.txt, accessed summer 2016.

45. John D. MacDonald, *Murder in the Wind* (Fawcett, 1956), 53.

46. John D. MacDonald, *Condominium* (J. B. Lippincott, 1977).

47. John D. MacDonald to Clark Kerr, February 11, 1965, John D. MacDonald Collection, box 70, folder 4.

48. James to John [MacDonald], n.d., John D. MacDonald Collection, box 67, folder 9; "Bay Bottom Purchase Off IIF Agenda," *Sarasota Herald Tribune*, December 17, 1964, and "Bayfill: Thrust and Riposte," *Sarasota Herald Tribune*, January 25, 1968; Pete Schmidt, "An Armada of Retirees Invades Sarasota Bay," *Sarasota Magazine* 16 (1994): 103.

49. Barnett, *Mirage*, 28; "Bay Bottom Purchase," *Sarasota Herald Tribune*, and "Bayfill: Thrust and Riposte," *Sarasota Herald Tribune*.

50. John Clark, *The Sanibel Report: Formulation of a Comprehensive Plan Based on Natural Resources* (Conservation Foundation, 1976).

Fifteen: FLORIDA WORRY, TEXAS SLURRY

1. Diane Wilson, *An Unreasonable Woman: A True Story of Shrimpers, Politicos, Polluters, and the Fight to Save Seadrift, Texas* (Chelsea Green, 2005), 355.

2. Anastasia Toufexis, "Our Filthy Seas: The Oceans Send Out an S.O.S.," *Time* 132 (1988): 44.

3. Paul Galtsoff, ed., *Gulf of Mexico: Its Origin, Waters, and Marine Life* (US Fish and Wildlife Service, 1954), 555.

4. Charles Lowery, interview by the author, August 27, 2013.

5. "Huge Fish Kill in Escambia Bay," *St. Petersburg Times*, September 3, 1970.

6. US Environmental Protection Agency, *Environmental and Recovery Studies of Escambia Bay and the Pensacola-Bay System, Florida* (EPA, 1975); Lowery, interview, August 27, 2013.

7. "Massive Kill Spotted in Florida Bay," *Chicago Tribune*, September 13, 1971.

8. Wilson, *Unreasonable Woman*, 382.

9. Ibid., 48.

10. Ibid., 322.

11. The information on pollution from these manufacturing plants was gathered in spring 2015 from the EPA's annual Toxics Release Inventory reports, accessible online at http://www2.epa.gov/toxics-release-inventory-tri-program. On the closing of the bay, see "EPA Superfund Program: Alcoa (Point Comfort)/Lavaca Bay, Point Comfort, TX," Environmental Protection Agency, https://cumulis.epa.gov/supercpad /cursites/csitinfo.cfm?id=0601752, accessed spring 2015.

12. Ibid., 36-37, 382.

13. Irene Hahn, "Plants, Pollution and Lavaca Bay," *Victoria Advocate*, August 23, 1989.

14. Bream Fishermen Association, "Our Mission," http://breamfishermen.org, accessed summer 2016; Lowery, interview, August 27, 2013.

15. J. D. Brown, interview by the author, May 2, 2013; Ernie Rivers, interview by the author, May 2, 2013.

16. Peter Behr, "Bay Recovers from Pollution," *Pensacola News*, February 21, 1975; "The Fish Are Biting Again in Escambia Bay Waters," *Escambia County Beacon* 2 (1976): 2.

17. Galtshoff, *Gulf of Mexico*, 555–73.

18. Deborah Cramer, *The Narrow Edge: A Tiny Bird, an Ancient Crab, and an Epic Journey* (Yale University Press, 2015), 145; Robert F. Hutton, *The Ecology of Boca Ciega Bay, with Special Reference to Dredging and Filling Operations . . .*, Technical Series no. 17 (Florida State Board of Conservation, 1956), 12.

19. Rivers, interview, May 2, 2013.

20. Jennifer Waters, "Harmful Fish," *Earth Issue*, no. 8 (April 10, 2008), http:// inweekly.net/article.asp?artID=7299.

21. R. F. Schneider, *Surveys of Perdido River and Bay, 1966–1967*, Report of Florida State Board of Health, Bureau of Sanitary Engineering for the Northwest Region (1967), 36.

22. *Jacqueline M. Lane v. International Paper Company and Department of Environmental Protection*, State of Florida Department of Environmental Protection, OGC case no. 01-0582, DOAH case no. 01-1490; Jackie Lane, interview by the author, August 27, 2013; *James H. Lane, Jacqueline M. Lane, and Robert C. Donnenwirth, on behalf of themselves and others similarly situated, Plaintiffs, v. Champion International Corp., et al., Defendants.* Civ. A. No. 93-0914-BH-M. US District Court, SD. Alabama, SD. 844 F. Supp. 724 (1994).

23. Joy Towles Ezell, interview by the author, November 11, 2011, and July 29, 2015; Will Lester, "State May Face Worse Pollution," *Gainesville Sun*, November 23, 1995; TaMaryn Waters, "Foley Cellulose Mill Plans River Restoration Project," *Tallahassee Democrat*, June 2, 2015; Julie Hauserman, "Dioxin at Mill Too High," *St. Petersburg Times*, February 9, 2001; Thomas B. Pfankuch, "Florida's Rotten River," *Florida Times-Union* (Jacksonville), June 5, 2002.

24. Ezell, interview, July 29, 2015; Pfankuch, "Florida's Rotten River."

25. Lester, "State May Face Worse Pollution."

26. *Jacqueline M. Lane v. International Paper Company*; Lane, interview, August 27, 2013; US Environmental Protection Agency, TRI Explorer, Release Reports, 2014 Dataset (March 2016), Inventory Facility Report, Escambia County, Florida, https://www.epa.gov/triexplorer, accessed summer 2016; Taylor Kirschenfeld, Robert K. Turpin, and Lawrence R. Handley, "Perdido Bay," US Geological Survey Publications Repository, 115-27, http://pubs.usgs.gov/sir/2006/5287/pdf/PerdidoBay.pdf, accessed summer 2016; William Rabb, "Suit Doesn't Rule Out Escambia Cleanup," *Pensacola Today*, October 21, 2014; Craig Pittman and Joni James, "DEP Chief Will Join Company He Helped," *St. Petersburg Times*, January 29, 2004; "Paper Plant to Eliminate Its Water Pollution," *GreenBiz*, June 6, 2001, https://www.greenbiz.com/news/2001/06/06/paper-plant-eliminate-its-water-pollution; *Tidings: The Newsletter of the Friends of Perdido Bay* 29, no. 1 (February 2016), http://www.friendsofperdidobay.com/Feb%2016.pdf.

27. Wilson, *Unreasonable Woman*, 150.

28. "Bayou Water . . . 'Just Sewer Water,'" *Houston Post*, January 8, 1967.

29. Oliver A. Houck, *Downstream toward Home: A Book of Rivers* (Louisiana State University Press, 2013), 112.

30. Wilson, *Unreasonable Woman*, 204.

31. J. Madeleine Nash, "The Fish Crisis," *Time* 150 (1997): 27.

32. William N. Lindall Jr. and Carl H. Saloman, "Alteration and Destruction of Estuaries Affecting Fishery Resources of the Gulf of Mexico," *Marine Fisheries Review* 39 (1977): 1–7.

33. James B. Blackburn, *The Book of Texas Bays* (Gulf Coast Books, 2005), 158.

34. Wilson, *Unreasonable Woman*, 158.

35. Louise Popplewell, "Alcoa to Study Ending Lavaca Bay Discharges," *Victoria Advocate*, August 8, 1995; Blackburn, *Book of Texas Bays*, 161–63.

36. "Company's Cleanup of Polluted Bay May Not Purge Acrimony," *Los Angeles Times*, February 13, 2005.

Sixteen: RIVERS OF STUFF

1. Curt D. Meine and Richard L. Knight, eds., *The Essential Aldo Leopold: Quotations and Commentary* (University of Wisconsin Press, 1999), 248.

2. Hermann Hesse, *Siddhartha* (Simon and Brown, 2013), 76.

3. Anastasia Toufexis, "Our Filthy Seas: The Oceans Send Out an S.O.S.," *Time* 132 (1988): 45.

4. Joby Warrick, "Death in the Gulf of Mexico," *National Wildlife* 37 (1999): 48.

5. R. Eugene Turner, interview by the author, April 7, 2015.

6. "Eugene Turner Named Boyd Professor," *LSU Research*, 2013, 18.

7. Turner, interview, April 7, 2015.

8. Vince Raffield, interview, provided on tape by Linda Raffield, December 12, 2011.

9. "Greeting from Bay County Florida" (1915 promotional brochure), facsimile on *Exploring Florida*, http://fcit.usf.edu/florida/docs/b/baycounty.htm, accessed summer 2015; US Environmental Protection Agency, *Water Quality Study, St. Andrew Bay, Florida* (EPA, 1975).

10. Paul Galtsoff, ed., *Gulf of Mexico: Its Origin, Waters, and Marine Life* (US Fish and Wildlife Service, 1954), 555, 569; Frederick Marryat, *A Diary in America: With*

Remarks on Its Institutions, vol. 2 (Longman, Orme, Brown, Green, Longmans, Paternoster Row, 1839), 143.

11. Nancy Rabalais, e-mail to the author, May 3, 2015.

12. R. Eugene Turner and Nancy N. Rabalais, "Changes in Mississippi River Water Quality This Century: Implications for Coastal Food Webs," *BioScience* 41 (1991): 144; Scott W. Nixon, "Enriching the Sea to Death," *Scientific American Presents* 279 (1998): 50.

13. Cynthia Barnett, *Mirage: Florida and the Vanishing Water of the Eastern U.S.* (University of Michigan Press, 2007), 114.

14. John Richards, interview by the author, December 13, 2011.

15. Committee on Environment and Natural Resources, *Scientific Assessment of Hypoxia in U.S. Coastal Waters* (Interagency Working Group on Harmful Algal Blooms, Hypoxia, and Human Health, 2010).

16. Karl Havens, Mark Brady, Erin Colborn, et al., "Lake Okeechobee Protection Program—State of the Lake and Watershed," in *2005 South Florida Environmental Report*, vol. 1, *The South Florida Environment—WY2004* (South Florida Water Management District, 2004), chap. 10, p. 2.

17. Sylvia A. Earle, *Sea Change: A Message of the Oceans* (G. P. Putnam's Sons, 1995), 179.

18. Scott Hamilton Dewey, *Don't Breathe the Air: Air Pollution and U.S. Environmental Politics, 1945–1970* (Texas A&M University Press, 2000), 176.

19. Edward O. Wilson and Alex Harris, *Why We Are Here: Mobile and the Spirit of a Southern City* (Liveright, 2012), 186.

20. Archie Carr, *A Naturalist in Florida: A Celebration of Eden* (Yale University Press, 1994), 24.

21. Ibid., 23.

22. Michael Fumento, "Hypoxia Hysteria," *Forbes* 164 (1999): 96, 97, 99.

23. Brian Clark Howard, "Mississippi Basin Water Quality Declining Despite Conservation," *National Geographic*, April 12, 2014, http://news.nationalgeographic.com/news/2014/04/140411-water-quality-nutrients-pesticides-dead-zones-science; Carolyn Lochhead, "Dead Zone in Gulf Linked to Ethanol Production," *SFGate*, July 6, 2010.

24. Lochhead, "Dead Zone in Gulf"; Cheryl Lyn Dybas, "Dead Zones Spreading in World Oceans," *BioScience* 55 (2005): 554.

25. Paul Greenberg, "A River Runs through It," *American Prospect*, May 22, 2013, http://prospect.org/article/river-runs-through-it.

26. Toufexis, "Our Filthy Seas," 44.

Seventeen: RUNOFF, AND RUNAWAY

1. Edward O. Wilson, interview by the author, June 19, 2014.

2. Ken Olsen, "Mississippi's Pearl: The Pascagoula," *National Wildlife* 48 (2010): 18.

3. Harvey H. Jackson III, *The Rise and Fall of the Redneck Riviera: An Insider's History of the Florida-Alabama Coast* (University of Georgia Press, 2012), 151; Wilson, interview, June 19, 2014.

4. Jackson, *Rise and Fall of the Redneck Riviera*, 89.

5. Ibid., 103.

6. Robert S. Davis, interview by the author, January 28, 2013.

7. Bruce Stephenson, e-mail to the author, August 10, 2015.
8. Davis, interview, January 28, 2013.
9. Ibid.

Eighteen: SAND IN THE HOURGLASS

1. Rick Bragg, "The Lost Gulf," *Garden & Gun*, August/September 2010, http://gardenandgun.com/article/lost-gulf.
2. Stefanie Wolf, beach tour narration, February 25, 2015, Sanibel Island, FL.
3. Ibid.; Sylvia Sunshine (Abbie M. Brooks), *Petals Plucked from Sunny Climes* (Southern Methodist Publishing House, 1880), 303.
4. Anne Morrow Lindbergh, *Gift from the Sea* (Random House, 2011), 28, 115.
5. Office of Geology, Mississippi Department of Environmental Quality, *Mississippi Coastal Geology and Regional Marine Study, 1990–1994: Final Report*, vol. 2 (US Geological Survey, n.d.), 198.
6. US National Park Service, *A Report on Our Vanishing Shoreline* (US Department of the Interior, 1955), 7.
7. "The Pelican Returns," *Pensacola News Journal*, May 6, 1973.
8. US Army Corps of Engineers, *Mississippi Coastal Improvements Program (MsCIP), Hancock, Harrison, and Jackson Counties* (2009).
9. George H. Lowery Jr., "Trans-Gulf Spring Migration of Birds and the Coastal Hiatus," *Wilson Bulletin* 57 (1945): 92–121.

Nineteen: LOSING THE EDGE

1. *Beasts of the Southern Wild*, directed by Benh Zeitlin (Cinereacah, Journeyman Pictures, 2012), DVD.
2. Sidney Lanier, *Poems of Sidney Lanier*, ed. Mary Day Lanier (Brown Thrasher Books, 1999), 16.
3. Roy Bedichek, *Karánkaway Country* (Doubleday, 1950), 23.
4. Lanier, *Poems of Sidney Lanier*, 18.
5. Ibid., 16.
6. Ibid., 18.
7. R. E. Turner, "Intertidal Vegetation and Commercial Yield of Penaeid Shrimp," *Transactions of the American Fisheries Society* 106 (1977): 411–16.
8. Lanier, *Poems of Sidney Lanier*, 33.
9. Oliver A. Houck, "Ending the War: A Strategy to Save America's Coastal Zone," *Maryland Law Review* 47 (1988): 358, 360.
10. Ibid., 362.
11. Ibid., 360.
12. Ibid., 358.
13. Ibid., 360.
14. These figures come from Michael J. Mac, Paul A. Opler, Catherine E. Puckett Haecker, et al., *Status and Trend of the Nation's Biological Resources*, vol. 1 (US Department of the Interior, US Geological Survey, 1998).
15. John M. Barry, *Rising Tide: The Great Mississippi Flood of 1927 and How It Changed America* (Simon and Schuster, 1997), 22.

16. Martha Field, *Louisiana Voyages: The Travel Writings of Catharine Cole*, ed. Joan B. McLaughlin and Jack MacLaughlin (University Press of Mississippi, 2006), 4.

17. E. L. Corthell, *A History of the Jetties at the Mouth of the Mississippi River* (John Wiley & Sons, 1881), vii; E. L. Corthell, "The Delta of the Mississippi River," *National Geographic* 8 (1897): 354.

18. Sherwood M. Gagliano, Hyuck J. Kwon, and Johannes L. van Beek, "Deterioration and Restoration of Coastal Wetlands," *Coastal Engineering Proceedings* 12 (1970): 1767–81.

19. Jason P. Theriot, *American Energy, Imperiled Coast: Oil and Gas Development in Louisiana's Wetlands* (Louisiana State University Press, 2014), 82;

20. Oliver A. Houck, "The Reckoning: Oil and Gas Development in the Louisiana Coastal Zone," *Tulane Environmental Law Review* 28 (2015): 198, 209.

21. Oliver Houck, interview by the author, December 1, 2015; Oliver A. Houck, "Land Loss in Coastal Louisiana: Causes, Consequences and Remedies," *Tulane Law Review* 58 (1983): 45–48, 169–70.

22. John Barry, interview by the author, December 8, 2015.

23. Bern Keating, *The Gulf of Mexico* (Viking Press, 1972), 62.

24. Rowan Jacobsen, *Shadows on the Gulf: A Journey through Our Last Great Wetland* (Bloomsbury, 2011), 137.

25. 18 discharges at ExxonMobil Baton Rouge, see the EPA's TRI Explorer, 2014 Dataset and earlier years, https://www.epa.gov/triexplorer; see also Jennifer Larino, "Louisiana Waterways among the Most Polluted in Nation, Report Says," *New Orleans Times-Picayune*, June 19, 2014.

26. Mike Tidwell, *Bayou Farewell: The Rich Life and Tragic Death of Louisiana's Cajun Coast* (Vintage, 2004); *Revisiting Flaherty's Louisiana Story*, produced by Patricia A. Suchy, James V. Catano, and Adelaide Russo (Louisiana State University, 2006), DVD.

27. J. A. Browder, L. N. May, A. Rosenthal, et al., "Modeling Future Trends in Wetland Loss and Brown Shrimp Production in Louisiana Using Thematic Mapper Imagery," *Remote Sensing of the Environment* 28 (1989): 45–59; Rex H. Caffey and Mark Schexnayder, "Floods, Fisheries, and River Diversions in Coastal Louisiana," in *Coastal Water Resources: Proceedings of the American Water Resources Association, May 13–15, 2002, New Orleans, LA*.

28. Louisiana Wetland Protection Panel, *Saving Louisiana's Coastal Wetlands: The Need for a Long-Term Plan of Action*, US Environmental Protection Agency report (1987), ii.

Epilogue: A SUCCESS STORY AMID SO MUCH ELSE

1. Rachel Carson, *The Edge of the Sea* (Houghton Mifflin, 1983), 246.

2. Nathaniel Rich, "Waterworld," *New York Times Magazine* (October 6, 2014): 32.

3. Mark Schleifstein, "Federal Judge Dismisses Levee Authority's Wetlands Damage Law Suit against Oil, Gas Companies," *New Orleans Times-Picayune*, February 13, 2015.

4. The case is Board of Commissioners of the Southeast Louisiana Flood Protection Authority-East et al. v. Tennessee Gas Pipeline Co. LLC et al.

5. Matthew Tresaugue, "Oil Spills in Galveston Bay a Routine Occurrence," *Houston Chronicle*, April 6, 2014; Matthew Tresaugue, "Latest Oil Incident Belies Painful Truth," *San Antonio Express-News*, April 6, 2014.

6. Tim Dinkinson, "Inside the Koch Brothers' Toxic Empire," *Rolling Stone*, Septem-

ber 24, 2014, http://www.rollingstone.com/politics/news/inside-the-koch-brothers-toxic-empire-20140924; Kate Bradshaw, "Environmentalists Tout New Study Highlighting the Influence of 'Corporate Polluters,'" *Creative Loafing*, February 24, 2015, http://cltampa.com/politicalanimal/archives/2015/02/24/environmentalists-tout-new-study-highlighting-the-influence-of-corporate-polluters#.VmncivkrJN0.

7. Ernie Rivers, interview by the author, August 24, 2016.

8. Eugene Turner, e-mail to the author, December 11, 2015.

9. Ibid.

10. *Most Vulnerable U.S. Cities to Storm Surge Flooding* (Karen Clark, 2015).

11. John Van Beekum, "In Florida, Officials Ban Term 'Climate Change,'" *Miami Herald*, March 8, 2015.

12. Thomas Kaplan, "Republicans on Campaign Trail Largely Ignore the Climate Deal," *New York Times*, December 13, 2015.

13. H. Bruce Franklin, *The Most Important Fish in the Sea: Menhaden and America* (Island Press, 2007), 7.

14. George Brown Goode, *A History of the Menhaden* (Orange Judd, 1880), 109.

15. Ibid., 110.

16. H. Bruce Franklin, "Net Losses: Declaring War on Menhaden," *Mother Jones*, March/April 2006, http://www.motherjones.com/environment/2006/03/net-losses-declaring-war-menhaden?page=3.

17. Gulf States Marine Fisheries Commission, "Current Status of This Species in the Gulf of Mexico Ecosystem" (2015 report on menhaden), http://www.gsmfc.org/profiles/Gulf_menhaden/Gulf%20Menhaden.php, accessed winter 2016.

18. Franklin, *Most Important Fish in the Sea*, 161–62.

19. Ibid., 9.

20. Tessa Stuart, "What Made All of Seahorse Key's Birds Jump Ship?" *Audubon*, July 15, 2015, https://www.audubon.org/news/what-made-all-seahorse-keys-birds-jump-ship.

21. Sidney Lanier, *Florida: Its Scenery, Climate, and History, with an Account of Charleston, Savannah, Augusta, and Aiken; a Chapter for Consumptives; Various Papers on Fruit-Culture; and Complete Hand-book and Guide* (J. B. Lippincott, 1876), 115.

22. Leslie Sturmer, interview by the author, October 7, 2011; Suzanne Colson, interview by the author, September 23, 2011.

23. Mike Davis, interview by the author, October 28, 2011; Colson, interview, September 23, 2011.

24. Wallace Stevens, "Fabliau of Florida," in *Wallace Stevens: Collected Poetry and Prose* (Library of America, 1997), 18.

Additional Selected Sources

Altobello, Brian. *New Orleans Goes to War, 1941–1945: An Oral History of New Orleans during World War II.* Brian Altobello, 1990.

Bailey, Conner, Svein Jentoft, and Peter Sinclair, eds. *Aquaculture Development: Social Dimensions of an Emerging Industry.* Westview Press, 1996.

Barnes, Jay. *Florida's Hurricane History.* University of North Carolina Press, 2007.

Bedichek, Roy. *Adventures with a Texas Naturalist.* University of Texas Press, 1994.

Boesch, Donald F., and R. Eugene Turner. "Dependence of Fishery Species on Salt Marshes: The Role of Food and Refuge." *Estuaries* 7 (1984): 460–68.

Brinson, Ayeisha A., Eric M. Thunberg, and Katherine Farrow. *The Economic Performance of U.S. Non-catch Share Programs.* NOAA Technical Memorandum NMFS-F/SPO 150. US Department of Commerce, National Oceanic and Atmospheric Administration, National Marine Fisheries Service, 2015.

Britton, Joseph. *Shore Ecology of the Gulf of Mexico.* University of Texas Press, 2014.

Cancelmo, Jesse, and John W. Tunnell. *Glorious Gulf of Mexico: Life below the Blue.* Texas A&M University Press, 2016.

Casas, Bartolomé de las. *The Devastation of the Indies: A Brief Account.* Translated by Herma Briffault. Johns Hopkins University Press, 1992.

Cerulean, Susan, Janisse Ray, and A. James Wohlpart, eds. *Unspoiled: Writers Speak for the Florida Coast.* Heart of the Earth, 2010.

Chipman, Donald E. "Alonso Avarez de Pineda and the Rio de las Palmas: Scholars and the Mislocation of a River." *Southwestern Historical Quarterly* 98 (1995): 369–85.

Crouse, Nellis Maynard. *Lemoyne d'Iberville: Soldier of New France.* Louisiana State University Press, 2001.

Cusachs, Gaspar. *Lafitte, the Louisiana Pirate and Patriot.* Louisiana Historical Society, 2013.

Cushing, Frank Hamilton. *Exploration of Ancient Key-Dweller Remains on the Gulf Coast of Florida.* University Press of Florida, 2000.

Day, John, and George Paul Kemp, eds. *Perspectives on the Restoration of the Mississippi Delta: The Once and Future Delta.* Springer, 2014.

Dean, Cornelia. *Against the Tide: The Battle for America's Beaches.* Columbia University Press, 1999.

Dickinson, William R. "The Gulf of Mexico and the Southern Margin of Laurentia." *Geology* 37 (2009): 479–80.

Dimock, A. W. *Florida Enchantments.* Outing Publications, 1908.

Doughty, Robert W. *Wildlife and Man in Texas: Environmental Change and Conservation.* Texas A&M University Press, 1983.

Durrenberger, E. Paul. *"It's All Politics": South Alabama's Seafood Industry.* University of Illinois Press, 1992.

Dyer, Charles Lawrence. *Along the Gulf.* Women of Trinity Episcopal Church, 1971.

Eidse, Faith. *Voices of the Apalachicola.* University Press of Florida, 2007.

Field, Martha R. "Come South, Young Woman." In *Congress of Women*, edited by Mary Kavanaugh Oldham, 776. Monarch, 1894.

Florida Department of Agriculture. *Third Biennial Report of the Florida Shell Fish Commission, Years 1917–18.* T. J. Appleyard, [1918].

Fontaneda, Hernando d'Escalente. *Memoir of Dr d'Escalente Fontaneda Respecting Florida. Written in Spain, about the Year 1575.* Glades House, 1944.

Frazer, Lynne Howard. *Silver King: The Birth of Big Game Fishing.* WGCU Film, 2012.

Galloway, William E. "Depositional Evolution of the Gulf of Mexico World." In *The Sedimentary Basins of the United States and Canada*, edited by Andrew Miall, 506–44. Elsevier, 2008.

"The Gentleman of Elvas: From *The Narrative of the Expedition of Hernando de Soto* (1557)." In *The Florida Reader: Visions of Paradise from 1530 to the Present*, edited by Maurice O'Sullivan and Jack C. Lane. Pineapple Press, 1991.

Green, Ben. *Finest Kind: A Celebration of a Florida Fishing Village*. Florida Historical Society, 2007.

Griffin, Randall C. *Winslow Homer: An American Vision*. Phaidon Press, 2006.

Hansen, Gunnar. *Islands at the Edge of Time: A Journey to America's Barrier Islands*. Island Press, 1993.

Hearn, Lafcadio. *Chita: A Memory of Last Island*. University Press of Mississippi, 2003.

Hoffman, Paul. *A New Andalucia and a Way to the Orient: The American Southeast during the Sixteenth Century*. Louisiana State University Press, 2004.

Holder, Charles Frederick. *The Big Game Fishes of the United States*. Macmillan, 1903.

Horowitz, Andy. "The BP Oil Spill and the End of Empire, Louisiana." *Southern Cultures* 20 (Fall 2014): 6–23.

Houde, Edward D., and Edward S. Rutherford. "Recent Trends in Estuarine Predictions of Fish Production and Yield." *Estuaries* 16 (1993): 161–76.

Howard, Clinton N. "Colonial Pensacola: The British Period." *Florida Historical Quarterly* 19 (1940): 114.

Hubbert, M. King. "Energy Resources." In *Resources and Man: A Study and Recommendations*, by the Committee on Resources and Man of the Division of Earth Sciences, National Academy of Sciences-National Research Council, 157–241. W. H. Freeman, 1969.

Huffard, R. Scott, Jr. "Infected Rails: Yellow Fever and Southern Railroads." *Journal of Southern History* 79 (2013): 80–95.

Humphreys, Margaret. *Yellow Fever in the South*. Johns Hopkins University Press, 1999.

Ingle, Robert M. *Sea Turtles and the Turtle Industry of the West Indies, Florida and the Gulf of Mexico*. University of Miami Press, 1974.

Jacobsen, Rowan. *Shadows on the Gulf: A Journey through Our Last Great Wetland*. Bloomsbury, 2011.

Jenkins, Peter. *Along the Edge of America*. Mariner Books, 1995.

Johnson, Sherry. "Climate, Community, and the Commerce of Florida, Cuba, and the Atlantic World, 1784–1800." *Florida Historical Quarterly* 80 (2002): 445–82.

Kahrl, Andrew W. "The Sunbelt's Sandy Foundation: Coastal Development and the Making of the Modern South." *Southern Cultures* 20 (2014): 24–42.

Kane, Harnett T. *The Golden Coast.* Doubleday, 1959.

Kasprzak, R. A. "Use of Oil and Gas Platforms as Habitat in Louisiana's Artificial Reef Program." *Gulf of Mexico Science* 16 (1998): 37–45.

Keating, Bern. *The Gulf of Mexico.* Viking Press, 1972.

Lowery, George H., Jr. *Louisiana Birds.* Louisiana State University Press, 1955.

Lugo, Ariel E., and Samuel C. Snedaker. "The Ecology of Mangroves." *Annual Review of Ecology and Systematics* 5 (1974): 39–64.

Maril, Robert Lee. *Texas Shrimpers: Community, Capitalism, and the Sea.* Texas A&M University Press, 1983.

McComb, David G., and J. U. Salvant. *The Historic Seacoast of Texas.* University of Texas Press, 1999.

McCracken, Karen Harden. *Connie Hagar: The Life History of a Texas Birdwatcher.* Texas A&M University Press, 1986.

Melosi, Martin, and Joseph Pratt, eds. *Energy Metropolis: An Environmental History of Houston and the Gulf Coast.* University of Pittsburgh Press, 2007.

Minor, H. E. "Goose Creek Oil Field, Harris County, Texas." *AAPG Bulletin* 9 (19265): 286–97.

Montrose, Jack. *Tales from a Florida Fish Camp and Other Tidbits of Swamp Rat Philosophy.* Pineapple Press, 2003.

Mullen, Patrick. *I Heard the Old Fishermen Say: Folklore of the Texas Gulf Coast.* University of Texas Press, 1978.

Norris, Thaddeus. *The American Angler's Book: The Natural History of Sporting Fish, and the Art of Taking Them.* E. H. Butler, 1864.

Nuñez Cabeza de Vaca, Álvar. *Chronicle of the Narváez Expedition: A New Translation: Contexts, Criticism.* Edited by Ilan Stevens. Translated by David Frye. W. W. Norton, 2013.

Ober, Frederick. *Juan Ponce de Leon.* Harper & Brothers, 1908.

Perdichizzi, Elizabeth McDonald, and Katherine Stephens Kirk. *Island Voices: They Came to Marco.* Edited by Marion Nicolay. Caxambas, 2006.

Pilkey, Orrin H., William J. Neal, Joseph T. Kelley, and J. Andrew G. Cooper. *The World's Beaches: A Global Guide to the Science of the Shoreline.* University of California Press, 2011.

Porch, Clay E., S. C. Turner, and M. J. Shirripa. "The Commercial Landings of Red Snapper in the Gulf of Mexico from 1872 to 1962." *Southeast Data, Assessment and Review* SEDA31-RD46 (2012): 2–12.

Powell, Lawrence N. *The Accidental City: Improvising New Orleans.* Harvard University Press, 2012.

Pratt, Joseph A. *Offshore Pioneers: Brown & Root and the History of Offshore Oil and Gas.* Gulf Professional, 1997.

Priest, Tyler. "Extraction Not Creation: The History of Offshore Petroleum in the Gulf of Mexico." *Enterprise and Society* 8 (2007): 227–67.

Rabalais, Nancy N., R. Eugene Turner, and William J. Wiseman Jr. "Gulf of Mexico Hypoxia, a.k.a. 'The Dead Zone.'" *Review of Ecology and Systematics* 33 (2002): 235–63.

Reiger, George. *Profiles in Saltwater Angling: A History of the Sport—Its People and Places, Tackle and Techniques.* Prentice Hall, 1973.

Roberts, William. *An Account of the First Discovery, and Natural History of Florida.* University Press of Florida, 1976.

Rudloe, Jack. *The Wilderness Coast.* Great Outdoors, 2008.

Salvador, Amos, ed. *The Gulf of Mexico Basin.* Geological Society of America, 1992.

Schmidy, David J. *Texas Natural History: A Century of Change.* Texas Tech University Press, 2002.

Schueler, Donald G. *Preserving the Pascagoula.* University Press of Mississippi, 1980.

Scott, William Earl Dodge. *The Story of a Bird Lover.* Outlook, 1903.

Seavey, J. R., W. E. Pine III, P. Frederick, L. Sturmer, and M. Berrigan. "Decadal Changes in Oyster Reefs in the Big Bend of Florida's Gulf Coast." *Ecosphere* 2 (2011): 1–14.

Sheffield, David A., and Darnell L. Nicovich. *When Biloxi Was the Seafood Capital of the World.* City of Biloxi, MS, 1979.

Streeter, Ann P. *Joseph Smith Harris and the U.S. Northwest Boundary Survey, 1857–1861.* Trafford, 2012.

Streever, Bill. *Saving Louisiana? The Battle for Coastal Wetlands.* University Press of Mississippi, 2001.

Sullivan, Charles, and Murella Hebert Powell. *The Mississippi Gulf Coast: Portrait of a People.* Windsor, 1985.

Swanton, John R. *Indian Tribes of the Lower Mississippi River Valley and the Adjacent Coast of the Gulf of Mexico.* Sagwan Press, 2015.

Tembanis, Arthur C., and Orrin H. Pilkey. "Summary of Beach Nourishment along the Gulf of Mexico Shoreline." *Journal of Coastal Research* 14 (1998): 407–17.

Turner, Frederick. *A Border of Blue: Along the Gulf of Mexico from the Keys to the Yucatán.* Henry Holt, 1993.

Tveten, John L. *Coastal Texas: Water, Land, and Wildlife.* Texas A&M University Press, 1982.

Ulanski, Stan. *The Gulf Stream: Tiny Plankton, Giant Bluefin, and the Amazing Story of the Powerful River in the Atlantic.* University of North Carolina Press, 2010.

Walsh, J. J., J. K. Jolliff, B. P. Darrow, J. M. Lenes, S. P. Milroy, A. Remsen, D. A. Dieterle, et al. "Red Tides in the Gulf of Mexico: Where, When, and Why?" *Journal of Geophysics Research* 111 (2007): 1–46.

Weber, David. *The Spanish Frontier in North America.* Yale University Press, 1994.

White, Nancy Marie, ed. *Gulf Coast Archaeology: The Southeastern United States and Mexico.* University Press of Florida, 2005.

Widmer, Randolph J. *The Evolution of the Calusa: A Nonagricultural Chiefdom of the Southwest Florida Coast.* University of Alabama Press, 1988.

Yergin, Daniel. *The Prize: The Quest for Oil, Money and Power.* Free Press, 1991.

Illustration Credits

Pages iv–v   Florida State Library & Archives

12   National Oceanic and Atmospheric Administration.

20–21   University of Florida Map & Imagery Collections

23   Florida State Library & Archives

41   Florida State Library & Archives

51   Annie Cole Cady, *The American Continent and Its Inhabitants before Its Discovery by Columbus* [Gebbie, 1894]

75   Florida State Library & Archives

94–95   David Rumsey Map Collection, http://www.davidrumsey.com.

97   Florida State Library & Archives

114   Mississippi Department of Archives and History

150   Useppa Island Historical Society

184   State Library of Louisiana

220–221   University of Florida Map & Imagery Collections

223   Florida State Library & Archives

261   Library of Congress

280   Universal Studios

304   Walter Anderson Museum of Art, Ocean Springs, MS

335   Portal to Texas History, https://texashistory.unt.edu; Corpus Christi Museum of Science and History

372–373   University of Florida Map & Imagery Collections

375   Florida State Library & Archives; photo by Robert M. Overton.

Index

African slaves and slavery, 101, 271
  Cuba and, 105, 119, 140
  on Gulf with Spanish, 55, 58, 67,
    68, 69, 70, 236, 352
  runaways to Gulf from colonies
    and U.S. states, 102, 103, 121–22
  in the U.S., 98, 105–6, 112, 141,
    196, 207, 247, 251, 353
  used on the U.S. Gulf, 90, 196,
    197, 271, 358, 497
Agassiz, Alexander, 240–41
Agassiz, Louis, 239, 240
Alabama
  fishing industry and, 128
  oysters and, 529
  shrimp and, 491
  U.S. annexation of, 110–11
Alaminos, Antón de, 48
  navigating the Gulf Stream,
    46–47
Alcoa Aluminum, 397, 418, 419,
    438, 518
alligators, 78, 229, 443, 493

hunting and, 135, 190, 198, 200–
    201, 293, 294
Allman, T. D., 101–2
Álvarez de Pineda, Alonso, 49, 72, 178
  first map of Gulf, 41–42, 48–50
American Ornithologists' Union,
    192, 193, 201, 205, 206, 208
Anclote River, FL, 32, 137, 139,
    190
Anderson, Agnes "Sissy," 305, 312,
    314, 316, 318, 327, 329–30, 331,
    334
Anderson, John, 304, 466
Anderson, Peter, 316
Anderson, Walter, 314, 316
  compared with other artists, 317,
    318–19
  Horn Island and, 304, 305, 306,
    307, 313, 317, 326, 327, 328,
    330, 331, 361, 465
  nature sensibilities of, 8, 306–8,
    312–13, 317–18, 326–27, 331–
    32, 334

Apalachee Bay, 60, 66, 78,

Apalachee Indians, 59, 69, 70, 73

Apalachicola Bay, FL
  ecological decline of, 447–48,
    452–55, 516
  oysters and, 130–31, 133, 147,
    446–48, 450, 453–55, 495, 516

Apalachicola, Chattahoochee, Flint
  Compact, 453–54

Aransas Pass, TX, 182, 189, 216

Arvida Corporation, 397–98, 399,
    402, 403–5

Atchafalaya River, 132, 282, 290,
    299, 449, 451, 497, 502

Atlanta, GA, 131, 238, 452–54,
    469

Atlantic Ocean, 5, 13, 17, 34, 70, 82,
    84, 157, 288, 356, 481
  comparisons with the Gulf, 10, 15,
    16, 17, 318–19, 482
  crossings of, 45, 46, 47, 49, 54, 77,
    89, 125, 345
  fishing and, 157, 163, 412, 524
  hurricanes and, 16, 252, 336–38,
    344, 348, 353, 361, 363
  See also Gulf Stream; Homer,
    Winslow

Audubon, John James, 189, 215, 217,
    218, 355
  Gulf birds and, 180, 206, 317, 342
  sea turtles and, 144–45

Audubon Society, 191, 194, 213,
    215, 432

bird wardens of, 201, 208–9
  local and state groups, 204–5, 207,
    210, 211, 217, 389, 392
  national organization of, 206–7,
    208, 209, 212, 219, 300, 407,
    489

Austin, Martha, 232–33, 237

Austin, Mary, 246–47

Austin, William, 232–33, 237–38

Avery, Daniel, 196, 197

Avery Island, LA, 198
  as bird sanctuary, 184, 199–200,
    213, 300, 492
  salt dome under, 197, 266, 267,
    293

Bache, Alexander, 47, 106–8

Bahama Islands, 34, 44, 52, 122,
    255, 361

Balli, Nicholas, 320–21

Barnett, Cynthia, 338, 452

Barry, John, 498, 503, 508, 514–15

Batty, Joseph H., 193–94

Bay of Campeche, Mexico, 48, 148,
    156, 186, 348, 503, 504

Bayou Chico, 424–25

Bayou La Batre, AL, 131, 132, 136,
    491

beaches
  erosion and restoration of, 475,
    479–82
  geological origins of, 224–27
  segregation and, 259

as tourist attraction on Gulf, 175,
247–60, 470–71

beachgoing

history of in western culture,
229–31, 245–47

trepidations about, 229–32, 238–
39, 250, 252

Beaumont, TX, 216, 265, 268,
269–70, 345, 424

Bedichek, Roy, 129, 492

Belvin, William T., 384–85, 386, 390

Bermuda High, 187, 337

Berners, Juliana, 157–58, 182

Bickel, Karl, 377, 410

Bienville, Jean-Baptiste Le Moyne
de, 80–81

establishes New Orleans and
builds first dike, 82, 235, 497

Big Cypress Swamp, FL, 31, 390

Biloxi, MS, 316, 330, 363, 364

boat- and shipbuilding industry of,
136–37, 289

French settlement of, 80, 81, 232

seafood industry of, 131–34, 234,
315

tourism and, 161, 233–34, 364,
379, 465, 467, 468

Biloxi Bay, 87, 315

French settlement and, 80, 81

birding, 2, 187, 188, 406, 484,
486–87

birds and ornithology

Audubon orioles, 520

black skimmers, 188

Blue Goose symbol, 406

common gallinules (marsh hen),
492

coots, 216, 317

cranes, 163, 177, 216

curlew, 333

ducks, 66, 109, 177, 188, 199, 212,
216–17, 274, 317, 333, 406, 492

eagles, 4, 19, 30, 142, 163, 242,
274, 492, 525

egg hunters and, 206, 208

egrets, 3, 30, 184, 188, 191–96,
199, 200–202, 211–13, 217, 331,
408, 480, 492, 525

feather trade and, 184, 190–94,
201–2, 203

Federal Duck Stamp Program,
406

flyways, 2, 186–87, 211, 218, 442,
486, 489

frigate birds (man-o'-war birds), 307

geese, 216, 217, 406

Gulf Express and, 188, 492

gulls, 123, 142, 187, 194, 207, 317,
331, 332, 488, 512

herons, 3, 30, 163, 188, 190–96,
306, 317, 331, 332, 492–93, 525

hummingbirds, 186

ibises, 30, 163, 188, 191, 192, 195,
525

ivory-billed woodpecker, 3, 196

migration across the Gulf, 185–89

birds and ornithology (*continued*)
ornithology, 185–86, 189, 192,
194, 196, 202, 211, 213, 217–18,
486–87
ospreys, 4, 30, 142, 163, 190, 274,
492
oystercatchers, 188
pelicans, 30, 142, 163, 176, 194,
202, 274, 304, 307, 317, 321,
332, 485–86, 489, 523, 525
pelicans as targets of Gulf fishers,
213–15
protection of, 184, 203–9, 210,
214, 215, 217, 219
purple gallinules, 317
redstarts, 187
red-winged blackbirds, 417
sanctuaries and preserves of,
207–13, 218–19, 300, 487
sandpipers, 185, 187, 189, 193,
199, 210, 216, 229
shearwaters, 316, 331
sparrows, 186, 188, 194, 492
spoonbills, 30, 188, 191, 194, 217,
274, 525
starlings, 492
terns, 188, 193, 194, 207
turkeys, 73, 80, 88, 109, 163,
417
warblers, 186, 187, 188, 377, 492
wood storks, 30, 188, 191, 194, 195
wrens, 492

bison, 37, 64, 67, 81, 88, 166, 172,
190, 191, 202, 218
Blackburn, Jim, 431–33, 436, 437
Boca Ciega Bay, FL, 56, 379, 398,
402, 409, 505
sea grass and, 379, 381, 382
Boca Grande Pass, 169, 175, 182,
183, 458
Bonaparte, Napoleon, 100, 101–2
Bosker, Gideon, 229, 230
Boudreaux, Joseph, 293, 369, 506
Bowles, William Augustus, 324
BP, 418
2010 oil spill and, 10, 272, 430,
463, 468, 502–5, 510, 513, 514
Bradley, Guy, 208
Braudel, Fernand, 6, 8, 10
Brazos River, 26, 246–47, 442, 460
pollution of, 182, 419
Bream Fishermen Association, 420,
421, 518
Brennen, Carlene Fredericka, 163
Breton Island, LA, and national
wildlife refuge, 210, 211, 488
Breton Sound, 132, 315, 499, 508
Brooks, Thomas E. 258
Brown, J. D., 421–22, 424
Brown, Marshall, 340
Brown, Nannette Jolivette, 515
Buckeye Industries (a.k.a. Buckeye
Technologies), 428–30, 517
Buffalo Bayou, TX, 432

Cabeza de Vaca, Alvar Núñez, 68, 232
envisions cattle ranching in Texas, 67, 416
Panifilo de Narváez expedition and, 57–58, 61–62
Texas years and escape to Mexico, 62–68, 377, 422
Calhoun County, TX, 416–17, 418, 419, 432, 433, 518
Caloosahatchee River, 168, 174, 384, 392, 404
pollution and, 456, 457, 516, 517, 525
Calusa, 64, 152, 155, 310, 389, 456
Cuban ranchos and, 120
European views of, 34–35
interactions with Spanish and, 34–40, 52, 73
population of, 33
trade with Cuba and, 119
way of life with estuaries, 34–39, 385
Cameron Parish, LA, 303
hurricanes and, 339–40, 359, 360–361, 365–69, 370
Cape Coral, FL, 382, 387, 388–93, 396, 404, 405, 409
Captiva Island, FL, 169, 172, 405, 406, 408, 477, 479, 482
Carr, Archie, 142, 460
Carson, Rachel, 18, 223, 224, 385, 398, 486, 492

Gulf of Mexico and, 227, 310, 376, 377–78, 380, 410
sea-level rise and, 509
Cat Island, MS, 308, 315, 328, 483, 489
cedar trees, 90, 243–44
Cedar Key(s), FL, 31, 140, 162, 377, 525
aquaculture and, 526–29
commercial fishing and, 145, 148, 527
pencil industry and, 243–44
sea-level rise and, 528
Chandeleur Islands, LA, 210, 211, 329–32, 485, 499
sea-level rise and, 488–89, 497, 508
Chapman, Frank, 194, 202–7, 209, 213, 215, 217
Charlotte Harbor, FL, 34, 167
estuary and, 27–28
feather industry and, 192, 208, 210
Juan Ponce de León at, 45
pollution of, 459
population growth around, 399
preservation of, 409
Chattahoochee River, 131, 452–54
Chevelier, Jean (a.k.a. Alfred Leche-velier), 192, 194, 458, 459
Chickasaw Indians, 88, 91
Choctawhatchee Bay, FL, 79, 116, 258

Choctaw Indians, 88, 91

Civil War, 31, 122, 133, 142, 237, 353

   Gulf blockade during, 197, 240, 271, 274, 322, 325

   nature and war during, 98–99

   See also Mississippi River

Clement, Jules, 284–85

climate change, 9, 489, 495, 519, 520, 522, 526, 528

Cline, Isaac, 343–44, 345

Coalition to Restore Coastal Louisiana, 507

coastal marshes, 3, 90, 110, 286, 482, 515, 521, 526

   ecology of, 490–95

   erosion of, 496 (*see also* Louisiana coastal marshes)

Cobb, Sewall C., 123, 124

Coden, AL, 353

Collier, Barron, 31, 169, 181, 248, 399

Collier County, FL, 31, 390

Collier, Maggie Eliza (McIllvaine), 31, 33, 400

Collier, William D., 24, 25, 30–32, 37, 147, 400

Collins, Joseph, 129

Collins, LeRoy, 381, 382, 393, 404

Colson, Sue, 526–28

Columbus, Christopher, 44, 45, 46, 60

   encounter with Gulf of Mexico and Gulf Stream, 42–43

Conrad, Joseph, 76, 151, 335–36, 376

Cooke, Alistair, 289

Cooper, James Fenimore, 25, 241

Corpus Christi, TX, 62, 235, 248, 289, 335, 418, 422, 526

Corpus Christi Bay, 65, 177, 248, 422

Cortés, Hernán, 48, 49, 53–54, 352

Cortez, FL, 140, 148

Corthell, Elmer, 499

Covacevich, Jacob D., 136–37

crabs, 3, 29, 36, 56, 59, 60, 61, 142, 144, 146, 156, 248, 296, 332, 460, 494

   blue, 29, 61, 65, 66, 116, 117, 125, 126, 417, 421, 494, 507

   fiddler, 29, 449

   grapsid, 125

   hermit, 29, 311, 477, 479

   industry in, 117, 128, 131, 248, 417, 437, 455, 507, 513, 526

   pollution and, 426, 437, 445

   stone, 61, 317, 479

Crane, Hart, 242

Crane, Stephen, 14–16, 242, 247, 345

Creek Indians, 88, 91, 120, 324, 421

creosote industry, 236, 238, 287, 424–25

Cross, Ted, 212, 408

Cuba, 4, 28, 34, 65, 103, 236, 255, 289, 344, 363
  agriculture and, 53, 82, 85, 355, 462
  American manifest destiny and, 101, 103–5
  fishing industry and, 114, 119, 138, 141, 144
  Gardens of the Queen coral reef, 462
  Gulf geography and, 17, 18
  Spanish period in, 38, 42–44, 48, 52, 53, 54–55, 68, 70, 73, 82, 122, 324, 326
  See also Spanish-American War
Cubitt sisters, 497–98, 501
Cushing, Frank Hamilton, 74, 151, 154, 377, 400, 479
  aboriginal relationship with nature and, 28, 30, 35, 36, 37, 39–40
  archaeology research in Florida of, 25, 26, 27–33, 34–35, 38–39
  mangroves and, 376, 410
  Zuni Indians and, 25–26
cypress trees, 3, 31, 34, 59, 60, 90, 110, 136, 195, 196, 265, 276, 277, 298, 299, 428

Darling, Jay "Ding," 406–7, 408
Dauphin Island, AL, 308, 353, 483
Davis, Jefferson, 284, 364
Davis, Mervyn Bathurst, 205

Davis, Mike, 140, 527
Davis, Robert, 471–74
DDT (dichlorodiphenyltrichloroethane), 416, 485–86, 489
Deepwater Horizon oil platform, 10, 272, 430, 455, 487, 503–4, 510, 512, 516
deer, 36, 64, 67, 73, 88, 90, 109, 201, 310, 325, 417
De la Cosa, Juan, 42–43
Delmonico's, 140, 202, 249
De Pourtalès, Louis François, 239–40
Destin, FL, 161, 258
  late-20th-century boom, 469–70, 471
Destin, Leonard, 114–17, 121, 149, 161, 354, 422
devilfish, 172, 210, 250
Dimock, Anthony Weston, 165–66, 175, 181, 223–24
Disston, Hamilton, 456
dolphinfish, 161
dolphins, bottlenose and others, 56, 113, 143, 297, 394, 421, 431, 433, 515
Douglas, Marjory Stoneman, 69, 195
dredge and fill, 31, 378–82, 383, 388–90, 392, 395–98, 400, 404, 407, 409, 410, 431, 469
Dry Tortugas, 45, 112, 144, 148, 206, 310

Duany, Andrés, 473
Duckworth, Joseph, 349
dune lakes, 259, 471, 475
Dunn, Patrick, 321–22
DuPont Chemical, 418, 438, 519
Dupuis, Laura, 335, 340, 348, 367
Durnford, Charles D., 24–27
Dutcher, William, 207, 208, 209, 218

Eads, James Buchanan, 498–500
Earle, Sylvia, 457, 464, 511
East Florida, colony of, 7, 83, 118
Edison, Mina, 168, 173, 385
Edison, Thomas, 165, 168, 385
Elevenmile Creek, 426–27
Eliot, T. S., 9, 52, 347
Emerson, Ralph Waldo, 242, 243
Endangered Species Act, 436, 483
Energy Policy Act, 461
Escambia Bay, FL
   fish kills and, 413–16, 425, 517
   pollution of, 413–16, 420
   sea grass and, 421, 425, 426, 431
Escambia River, 87, 414, 415, 421, 425, 518
estuaries, 10, 133, 299, 380
   aboriginal life and, 26, 30, 35, 39, 41, 57, 61, 67, 68, 69, 74 (*see also* Calusa, way of life with estuaries; Karankawa, way of life)
   commercial fishing and, 129, 131–32, 463–64

defined, 26–27, 28, 64–65
destruction of, 9, 182, 274, 279, 346, 402, 409, 413, 416, 420, 435, 447, 455–56, 460, 482, 496, 517
mangroves and, 377, 520
marine life and, 29, 30, 37–38, 60, 142, 152, 156, 170
natural wealth of, 8, 23, 26, 29, 64, 66, 444, 492, 493–94
protection and restoration of, 454, 459, 463, 464, 529
Spanish and, 55–56, 62, 66
U.S. Gulf distinctiveness and, 26, 162, 444, 516
   See also specific bays, bayous, and sounds; Trinity-San Jacinto Estuary
ethanol, 461–62
ExxonMobil (and earlier incarnations), 270, 286, 502, 504, 505, 513
Ezell, Joy Towles, 428–30, 517

Farley, Barney, 180
Farragut, David, 98, 99, 107, 197, 322
Faulkner, William, 242, 319, 467
FEMA (Federal Emergency Management Agency), 369, 424, 475, 503
Fenholloway River, 428–30, 517
Field, Martha (a.k.a. Catherine Cole), 135, 140, 178, 205, 216,

224, 227–228, 248, 252, 260,
308, 499

fish

bass, 117, 153, 155, 160, 163, 322,
452, 523

density of, 4, 113, 117, 412

drum, 66 (*see also* fish: redfish)

fish oil industry, 522–25

flounder, 117, 412, 417, 460, 493

grouper, 117, 121, 129, 136, 141,
163, 377, 412

mackerel, 117, 161, 177, 412

menhaden, 126, 412, 522–525

mullet, 61, 65, 113, 114, 116, 117,
119, 129, 139–43, 146, 147, 153,
156, 178, 394, 417, 421, 423,
424, 493

pompano, 119, 125, 126, 138, 155,
322

redfish (red drum), 61, 65, 66, 125,
178, 322, 331, 434, 493, 526

red snapper, 114, 125–27, 129,
136, 148, 153, 434, 457, 504–5,
525

sea trout, 65

sharks, 15, 30, 36, 56, 113, 187,
239, 250

sheepshead, 61, 125, 163, 493

sturgeon, 117, 443, 453, 454

tarpon, 24, 27, 139–40, 150–57,
163–83, 189, 190, 216, 223, 248,
254, 272, 287, 322, 342, 377,
385, 418, 423, 456, 458, 479,
500

tuna (also skipjack), 18, 65, 155,
412

See also fishing, commercial; fishing, sport

fishing, commercial, 115, 127, 213–
15, 379, 417–19, 523

British rejection of, 118

Cuban ranchos and, 118–22, 135,
140, 525

declining yields in, 147–49, 382,
412, 433–35, 500, 507

diversity of fishers and, 128,
132–33, 135, 137

early, 1, 31, 113, 118–19

Gulf comparison with other fisheries regions, 128–29, 148, 412,
513

ice and refrigeration and, 123–24,
135

New England influence, 7, 8, 114,
117, 121–125, 129, 141, 414

Northeastern U.S. and, 128, 129

Spanish rejection of, 67

See also specific states

fishing, sport, 1, 3, 31, 60, 140, 233,
342, 379, 382, 396, 412, 469,
504–5, 513, 523

connection to Gulf tourism, 149,
150, 152–55, 156–57, 161,
163–64, 167–71, 174–80

conservation and, 181, 182,
420–21

economics of, 161, 412

history of, 157–61

fishing, sport (*continued*)
manhood and, 171–73
overfishing and, 9, 181–83
popularity with northerners, 1, 4, 31, 141, 149, 163, 164, 176–78, 181–82
women and, 173–74
fishing, subsistence, 37, 66, 140, 421
Flagler, Henry, 167, 355–57
Flaherty, Robert J., 292–98, 302, 502
Flint River, 103, 134, 452
Florida
clams and (*see* Cedar Key(s), FL)
fishing industry and, 108, 115, 116, 128 (*see also specific cities*)
oysters and, 116, 421, 431, 447, 517, 526, 527 (*see also* Apalachicola Bay, FL)
sea turtles and, 29, 30, 36, 38, 117, 145
shrimp and, 60, 116, 117, 128, 421, 448, 455
Spanish naming of, 44–45
U.S. acquisition of, 103–94, 120
Florida Big Bend, 60, 111, 428, 485, 525, 526
Florida Everglades, 168, 175, 192, 208, 212–13, 361, 390, 456, 468, 516
Florida Keys, 4, 18, 85, 111, 112, 144, 165, 208, 217, 462
origins of, 309–10

Overseas Highway, 357–59
Overseas Railroad, 355–57, 358
See also Key West, FL
Floridan aquifer, 89, 232, 428, 442, 521
Florida Reef, 85, 112, 240, 410, 462
Florida Straits, 17, 18, 111–12, 119, 240, 252, 289, 338, 354, 462
Flowers, Loretta, 339, 340, 350, 365, 367
Forbes, Edward, 239
Foreman, Nick, 385
Forest and Stream, 4, 24, 325
on bird protection, 207, 217
on Gulf fishing, 164, 168, 175, 181
Formosa Plastics, 418, 420, 431, 432, 436–38, 518
Fort Jackson, 99, 510
Fort Myers, FL, 152, 382, 404, 410, 521
tarpon fishing and, 153, 167–68, 175–76
Fort Walton Beach, FL, 324, 363, 364, 470
Franklin, Benjamin, 25, 91
Franklin, H. Bruce, 523, 524, 525
Fumento, Michael, 461
Furen, Albert, 379, 380, 381
Furs, Jerry, 340, 366, 367

Gagliano, Sherwood "Woody," 500, 501, 528

Gaillard, John, 271–73, 274, 279

Galveston Bay, 65, 66, 79, 202, 271, 419

    degradation of, 419, 431–32, 436, 460, 496, 519

    fishing and, 131, 132

    oil spills and, 279, 432, 515–16

Galveston Bay Foundation, 431

Galveston, TX, 14, 62, 66, 153, 189, 205, 322, 326, 424

    as beach resort, 247, 252–53, 343

    fishing and, 148, 161, 520

    hurricanes and, 205, 247, 252–53, 268, 337, 311, 341–47, 350, 356

    port of, 342, 419

    sea-level rise and, 520, 521

Gasparilla Island, FL, 175, 192, 193, 324

Gauld, George, 91

    Gulf survey work of, 84–87, 106

    view of Pensacola and, 75, 84

Gerdes, Ferdinand, 97, 107–8, 355

Gomez, John, 324–25

Goode, George Brown, 127–28, 523

Good Roads Movement, 256

Goose Creek Oil Field (and Tabbs Bay), 261, 271–75, 277–78, 279, 284

Goose Creek, TX, 271, 274, 275, 279

Goss, Porter, 407, 408

Granday, Armand, 145, 146

Grand Isle, LA, 182, 248–50, 252, 300, 361, 497, 499

Great Texas Coastal Birding Trail, 487, 515

Green brothers (Hyman, Irving), 380, 382, 394

Grey, Zane, 157, 165, 170, 176, 179

Griffith, D. W., 360, 366–67, 368, 369

Griffith, Geneva, 360, 366–67, 368, 369

Griffith, Leslie, 360, 366–67, 368, 369

Grinnell, George Bird, 206–7

Gulf American Corporation, 388, 391–92

Gulf Islands National Seashore, 482–84, 485, 486

Gulf of Mexico

    dead zone and, 2, 444–46, 448– 52, 455, 458, 461–64, 494, 495, 506, 519

    dumping biological weapons in, 328–29

    early deep-sea exploration of, 240–41

    early tourism and, 232–35, 238–39 (*see also* beaches; *individual cities and states*)

    European discovery and early mapping of, 41, 43, 45, 48–49, 83–87

    geological origins of, 12–14, 89

    historical research and, 4, 5, 6–7, 8–11

Gulf of Mexico (*continued*)
  manifest destiny and, 100–6,
    112–13
  physical geography of, 16, 17, 50,
    85, 240–41
  Pleistocene epoch and, 13, 19, 195,
    226
  post–World War II, development
    and growth and, 375, 378–40,
    391, 402–5, 407–10, 469–71, 495
  sea-level rise and, 438, 480,
    520–21
  U.S. expansion in (*see* Manifest
    Destiny)
  World War II and, 288–89,
    327–30
Gulf Oil Corporation, 270, 273, 277,
  295, 298
Gulf Shores, AL, 465, 470–71,
  483
Gulf Stream, 12, 42, 55, 104, 338,
  436
  anatomy of, 17–18
  discovered and used by the Span-
    ish, 45–47
  mapping and, 47, 107

Hagar, Connie, 486–87
Haiti, 43, 101–2
Halliburton Corporation, 509–10,
  512
Hallock, Charles, 161–62, 207
Harding, Florence, 179–80, 434
Harding, Warren. G., 179–80, 322

Harris County, TX, 424, 432, 519,
  522
Harris, Joseph Smith, 98, 99, 100,
  107–8, 109, 112, 312, 510
Harrison County, MS, 369, 519
Harrison, John, 106
Harvey, John Hale, 249
Havana, Cuba, 17, 23, 19, 168,
  401
  feather market and, 206
  fish market and, 116, 117, 119,
    121, 124
  Spanish colonial period and, 43,
    54, 55, 68, 73, 82
Hawley, Christine B. M., 150,
  173–74, 181, 182, 434
Hearst, Phoebe A., 32
Hemenway, Harriet, 207
Hemingway, Ernest, 18, 156, 165,
  170, 173, 242, 353, 358–59
Herbert, Henry William, 159–60
Hershey, Terry, 432
Hesse, Hermann, 441, 443
Heywood, Scott, 183–86
Higgins, Patillo, 265–67, 270, 271
Hispaniola, 43, 44, 46, 52
Homer, Winslow, 6, 7, 8, 9
  as angler, 3–4, 163–64
  Atlantic Ocean and, 3, 5, 15, 163,
    318–19
  Gulf of Mexico and, 3–5, 15, 60,
    163–64, 242, 245
Homosassa River, 3, 4, 5, 15, 60,
  166, 245

Homosassa Springs, FL, 162–63, 377

Hornaday, William T., 218

Horn Island, MS, 79, 317, 327

military occupation of, 306, 328–29, 330, 416

national seashore and, 483–84

See also Anderson, Walter

horseshoe crabs, 142

Houck, Oliver, 299fn21, 433, 495–96, 502, 503, 513, 515

Houston Ship Channel, 419, 519, 520

Houston, TX, 57, 153, 252, 342, 343, 345

pollution and, 424, 432

as port city, 414

sea-level rise and, 521

Hughes, Howard, Sr., 274, 277

Humble Oil, 269, 279, 294, 300

Humboldt, Alexander, 43

Humm, Harold J., 402

hunting

American liberty and, 158–59

commercial, 31, 81, 91, 135, 200–201, 202, 299 (*see also* birds and ornithology: feather trade and)

conservation and, 158, 217–18, 219

sport, 31, 154, 158, 166, 177, 189–90, 203, 216–19, 229, 248, 279, 286, 420, 492

subsistence, 36, 37, 49–50, 57, 62, 67, 81, 88, 158–59, 199

hurricanes, 2, 36, 76, 82, 108, 231, 260, 292, 311, 330, 356, 361, 480

1559 storm, 352

1906 storm, 353

1861 storm, 353

1926 storm, 405–6

anatomy of, 335–39, 348, 349

Audrey, 339, 341, 347, 348–50, 351, 359–60, 365–68, 369, 370

Betsy, 307–8, 333, 360–62, 363, 484

Camille, 311, 360, 363–64, 368, 369, 467, 480, 487, 488

Carla, 346

Elena, 339

first tracked by plane, 349

Florence, 348

frequency in Gulf, 337

Galveston storm 1900, 205, 247, 252–53, 268, 311, 341–47, 356

Georges, 347, 488

Ike, 346–47

Ivan, 424

Katrina, 337, 338, 341, 363, 369, 370, 438–39, 465, 468, 487, 488, 494, 506, 510, 514, 522

Labor Day storm 1935, 358–59

property damage and, 338, 346–47, 370–71

Rita, 369, 506

sea-level rise and, 489, 520

See also Atlantic Ocean; Cameron Parish, LA; New Orleans, LA; Pacific Ocean; Pensacola, FL

Hutchins, Thomas, 84, 85, 87,
    91–92, 100, 106, 311, 497
Hutton, Robert, 380–82

Iberville, Pierre Le Moyne d', 200,
    213, 330
  discovery of Mississippi River,
    79–80, 314, 315
  settlements on Gulf and, 80–81
Indians, 6, 24, 25, 37, 66–67, 83,
    114, 115, 178, 233, 322, 523
  American interactions with, 527
  British interactions with, 88–89,
    90–91, 103
  Cuban ranchos and, 120, 121
  enslavement of, 43, 44, 48, 53, 54,
    58, 69, 70, 71, 73, 74, 119, 352
  European diseases and, 49, 53, 73,
    91, 232
  European views and, 57, 61, 62,
    63, 88, 89–90, 232
  fishing and, 144 (*see also* Calusa,
    way of life with estuaries;
    Karankawa, way of life; shell
    mounds)
  French interactions with, 77, 78,
    79
  Gulf population of, 41, 57
  hunting and, 36, 49–50, 57, 62, 67,
    80, 81, 88, 91
  Spanish interactions with, 44, 49,
    51, 52, 59, 61, 63–64, 68–70, 71,
    73, 102
  See also specific Indian groups

International Paper Company, 426–
    27, 430–31, 466–67, 518
islands, 61, 62
  as bird habitat and migration
    stops, 188, 193
  development of, 308–10, 311
  erosion of, 487–89
  estuaries and, 131, 415
  popular imagination and, 312, 319,
    323–24
  as protective barriers, 239, 308–9,
    489
  sea-level rise and, 439, 489
  See also Mississippi
Ixtoc I oil spill, 502–3
Izaak Walton League, 181

Jackson, Harvey, 258, 259, 470
Jacobsen, Rowan, 10, 505
Jefferson, Thomas, 6–7, 100–102,
    104, 112, 113, 354
Jindal, Bobby, 514–15, 522

Karankawa, 73, 341
  cannibalism myth and, 63
  Spanish interactions with, 63, 320,
    417
  way of life, 63–64, 66–67, 231,
    271
  white views of, 63–64
Keim, Barry, 337
Kenworthy, Charles, 24, 162
Kerr-McGee Oil Industries, 290–92,
    294, 299, 360

Key West, FL, 16, 17, 18, 65, 112, 121, 156, 356, 358
  Labor Day Hurricane and, 358–59
  poem by Wallace Stevens and, 242–43
  seafood market of, 115, 124, 145, 206
  shipwrecking (salvage) industry and, 116, 353–55
  sponges and, 138, 355
Kircher, Athanasius, 47
Kirk, Claude, 392, 404
Koch Industries, 517
Kurlansky, Mark, 130

Lacey Act, 207
Lafitte, Jean, 325–26
Laguna Madre, TX, 65, 66, 178, 320, 322
  sea grass and, 65
Lane, Jackie, 427, 430–31, 518
Lanier, Sidney, 117, 162, 164, 242, 377, 452, 491, 492, 493, 495, 526
Larson, Erik, 343
La Salle, Robert
  descent of Mississippi River and, 77, 80
  Gulf expedition of, 66, 77–79, 87, 232
Last Island, LA, 248, 250–52
Lavaca Bay, sea grass and, 431
Lee, Charles, 389, 392
Lenček, Lena, 229, 230

Lindbergh, Anne Morrow, 477–78
Louisiana
  Cajun culture and, 128, 135, 141, 293, 295, 296–97, 299, 302, 303, 359, 493, 496, 507
  nutria and, 201
  oil and gas industry, 285–86, 297–303, 497, 501, 502–3, 507–8, 510, 511–15 (*see also* Kerr-McGhee Oil Industries; oil: Caddo Lake and, first off-shore wells and)
  oysters and, 81, 132, 133, 147, 198, 297, 298, 299, 436, 498, 499, 501, 507, 513, 528
  sea-level rise and, 489, 519
  shrimp and, 128, 297, 300–301, 302, 494, 504, 505–6, 507, 513
Louisiana coastal marshes, 18, 19, 102, 110, 111, 229, 248
  canals and, 298–99, 490, 496–98, 501–2, 513–15
  erosion and, 303, 496, 498–502, 506–8, 513–15
  restoration of, 514–15
  sea grass and, 493, 495
Louisiana Purchase, 6, 100, 102
Louisiana Shrimp & Petroleum Festival, 301–2, 506
Louisiana Story, 303, 369
  See also Flaherty, Robert J.
Lovel, Leo, 142, 143
Lowery, Charles, 414–16, 420–21, 431

Lowery, George H. Jr., 186, 217–18, 489, 500
Lucas, Anthony, 267, 270, 271, 284, 292
Ludwig, John, 248–49
Luna y Arellano, Tristan de, 351–52

MacDonald, Dorothy, 393, 394
MacDonald, John D., 393–99, 400, 402–3, 404, 483
McGee, Dean, 290–91, 297
McGhee, Gilbert, 421
McIlhenny, Edmund, 197 98
McIlhenny, Edward Avery
    bird protection and, 195–96, 201, 204, 209, 211–13, 250, 300, 492
    conservationists and, 218–19
    hunting and, 217, 218–19
    Louisiana Story and, 293, 294
    nutria farming and, 201, 203
    Tabasco business and, 198
    trips to Artic north of, 198–200
McIlhenny, John, 198
Mackle brothers (Elliot, Frank, Robert), 399–400, 401, 409
MacLeod, Columbus, 208–9
malaria, 33, 70–71, 108, 236, 244
manchineel tree, 52, 354
mangroves, 30, 31, 50, 108, 313, 358
    carbon sequestration of, 410, 521
    climate change and, 520
    destruction of, 375, 377–79, 382, 383, 389, 392, 396, 398, 402, 409, 529
    habitat of, 29, 32, 56, 65, 111, 152, 156, 179, 191, 195, 211, 310–11, 331, 376–78, 379, 385, 394, 402, 478
    negative views of, 111, 377, 378, 380, 386, 395–96, 402
    protection and restoration of, 393, 405, 407, 409, 521
    shoreline protectors and, 310, 377, 400
    species on Gulf and, 28–29
manifest destiny, 112
    See also Cuba; Gulf of Mexico; West Florida
Mann, Anthony, 282–83, 290, 294, 296, 299, 302
Marco Island, FL, 30–31, 147, 154, 164, 311, 409, 520
    archaeological research on, 24, 25, 31, 32–33
    growth and, 375, 399–401
Marryat, Frederick, 448
Matagorda Bay, 66, 78, 79, 481
Matlacha Pass, 37, 384, 385, 388, 409
Matthiessen, Erard, 407
Mediterranean Sea, 6, 137, 139, 229, 230
    Gulf of Mexico comparisons and, 16–17, 18, 84
Meinig, Donald W., 112–13
Mellon, Andrew W., 267, 270
Mellon, Robert B., 267, 270
Menard, Michael, 342

Migratory Bird Act, 215
Miles, Franklin, 384, 387
Mississippi, 89, 115, 210, 309
 barrier islands of, 310, 322, 483,
  488 (*see also specific islands*)
 coast of, 109, 110, 233, 256, 305,
  319, 368, 369, 401, 480, 481,
  483, 491
 fishing industry and, 114, 117,
  128, 133, 137, 147, 467, 523 (*see
  also* Biloxi, MS)
 oysters and, 80, 85, 133–34, 233,
  234, 238, 315, 327
 pollution and, 424, 448, 450, 468,
  519
 seawall and, 480
 shrimp and, 315
 sport fishing and 161, 177, 467
 tourism and, 161, 232–34, 259,
  369–70, 401, 467, 468, 480 (*see
  also* Biloxi, MS; Ocean Springs,
  MS)
 U.S. annexation of, 110
Mississippian culture, 72–73, 88
Mississippi River, 18, 24, 70, 84,
  102, 186, 241, 242, 289, 327
 basin and watershed of, 13–14,
  75–76, 440, 441, 446, 450, 451,
  463, 489
 Civil War and, 98–99, 107, 322,
  510
 delta of, 75–76, 78, 87, 363, 481
 European discovery and, 48–49,
  70–71, 72, 77–82, 100, 200, 314

international rivalries and, 79, 83,
  87, 88, 92, 101
 jetties and, 498–501
 levees and, 235, 501, 510
 pollution and, 432, 445, 446,
  448–49, 450, 489, 505
 sediment flow and, 76, 78, 109,
  224, 225, 319, 481, 489, 497–99,
  500
 See also Gulf of Mexico: dead zone
  and
Mississippi Sound, 79, 232, 306,
  311, 353, 368
 pollution of, 424, 466–68, 519
 tourism and, 467
Mobile, AL, 19, 168, 234, 309, 322,
  494
 British and, 87
 fish market and, 234, 124, 234
 French and, 81, 88, 90
 pollution and, 424
 rainiest city and, 339
 sea-level rise and, 520
Mobile Bay, 79, 87, 111, 131, 247,
  309
 Jubilee and, 459–60
 pollution and, 459–60
 sea grass and, 436
mollusks, 3, 37, 38, 129, 144, 185,
  225, 241, 427, 445, 477–80
Monroe, James, 103, 104
Monsanto Company, 425–26, 518
Morgan City, LA, 133, 282–83, 299,
  301, 506, 507

mosquitoes, 29, 315
diseases and, 33, 235–38, 244 (*see also* malaria; yellow fever)
as irritant, 33, 36, 64, 108, 111, 210–11, 264, 323, 380, 383, 384
species of, 236, 237
Muir, John, 188
Gulf trip and, 243–44, 526
Muller, Robert A., 337
Mullet Key, FL, 322–23, 328, 380, 382
Mustang Island, TX, 178, 321
Myakka River, 28, 394

Naples, FL, 147, 176, 180, 181
Narváez, Panfilo de, 109
Gulf expedition of, 53–62, 65, 67, 68, 69, 70, 71, 72, 352
National Estuary Program, 496
National Hurricane Center, 341, 363, 364, 370, 471
National Oceanic and Atmospheric Administration, 341, 369, 445, 460, 508
Native Americans. *See* Indians
nature
human relationship with, 9–10, 11, 38, 64, 135, 202–3, 244, 383, 385–86, 445, 530
views of European explorers and, 57, 81, 314, 315–16
New Orleans, LA
Civil War and, 98–99, 107, 197, 322, 498
founding of, 82

hurricanes and, 350, 351, 358, 361–62, 363, 522 (*see also* hurricanes: Audrey, Betsy, Katrina, Rita)
international rivalry and, 82–83, 87, 91, 101, 103, 326
levee and, 99, 235, 277, 361, 363, 497, 514, 521
port city of, 117, 124, 125, 126, 234, 236–37, 289, 342, 354, 414, 498–99, 510
sea-level rise and, 520
society in, 98
yellow fever and, 108, 234–37
New York, 314, 319, 321, 382, 386, 395, 448, 499
feather trade and, 193, 194, 202–3, 206, 207, 210, 211, 244
Gulf seafood and, 126, 145, 447
Gulf tourism and, 164, 170, 173, 176, 179, 181–82
migrants to Gulf and, 388, 390, 393, 405, 407
oysters and, 129–30
Nicholson, Eliza Jane Poitevent Holbrook, 227–28
Nolen, John, 394–95, 396

oak trees, 109, 110, 122, 138, 162, 196, 208, 233, 248, 306, 365, 368, 385, 389, 398, 486
Ocampo, Sebastian de, 43–44, 48
Ocean Springs (a.k.a. Biloxi and East Biloxi), MS, 305, 306, 314, 316, 468, 480, 524

as early beachside resort, 232–33,
234, 237–38, 315

Spanish settlement as Biloxi,
80–81

O'Hare, Ralph, 349

oil

artificial reefs and, 302, 303,
504–5

Caddo Lake and, 276–77

early commercial uses of, 268–69

early prospectors and, 264–65,
271, 286

first Gulf spill and, 279

first offshore wells and, 280, 282,
287–88, 290–92

geological origin of, 263–64

origin myth of, 261–63, 272, 297,
302

overwater drilling and, 275–79

salt domes and, 261, 266–67, 271,
285, 286

seismograph exploration and, 286,
290, 295–98

spills (*see* BP; Galveston Bay; Ixtoc
I oil spill)

Spindletop strike and, 264–68,
269, 270, 271, 274, 278, 283,
284, 294, 345, 418

See also Goose Creek Oil Field;
Louisiana; Pacific Ocean; *specific
oil companies*; Texas

Omega Protein Company, 523–24

Ovando, Nicholas de, 43–44

Overseas Highway, 357–59

Overseas Railroad, 355–57, 358

oysters, 29, 81, 114, 117

beds of as navigational hazard, 61,
80, 85, 325

habitat of, 36, 38, 56, 60–61, 80,
132–33, 311, 448, 493, 526

industry and market of, 117, 131–
32, 315, 411–12, 455, 518

loss of, 147, 296, 297, 298, 431,
436, 447–48, 453–54, 501, 507,
513, 516, 517, 525

native peoples and, 5, 36, 61, 64,
80, 129, 271

road bedding and, 233 (*see also*
shell mounds)

species of, 29, 130–31

tools and weapons of natives and,
35, 231, 479

See also shell mounds; *specific bays;
specific states*

Pacific Ocean, 5, 6, 42, 53, 348, 412

Gulf of Mexico comparisons and,
10, 17

hurricanes and, 336, 351

oil and, 276

Padre Island, TX, 65, 328, 422, 481,
487, 503

erosion of, 500–501

geological origin of, 319–20

history of, 320–23

national seashore and, 323, 482–
83, 484

Panama City, FL, 259, 426, 447, 471

Parkman, Francis, 72, 77, 78, 79
Pascagoula, MS, 19, 107, 133,
    233–34
Pascagoula River, 80, 85, 309, 466
Pass Christian, MS, 233–34, 238,
    363–64
Peace River, FL
    estuary and, 28
    phosphate industry and, 175, 458
Pearl River, 132, 309, 441
Pearson, T. Gilbert, 215, 218–19
PCBs (polychlorinated biphenyl),
    416, 419, 425–26, 518
Pensacola Bay, 131
    British period and, 75, 84
    pollution of, 414, 415, 421, 422,
        423–24
    sea grass and, 436, 518
    Spanish period and, 86, 352
Pensacola, FL, 106, 417, 421
    British period and, 24, 86–87,
        90–91
    fishing industry and, 122–25, 127,
        129, 145, 148, 153, 414
    growth and, 483
    hurricanes and, 81, 352, 353, 424
    pollution and, 413–16, 422, 423–
        27, 430, 518
    Spanish period and, 80, 91, 103,
        352–53
    tourism and, 257–58, 259, 260, 414
Pensacola Beach, FL, 259–60, 483
Pepper, William, 25, 32
Peralta, Gerald, 363–64

Perdido Bay, FL, 426, 430
    sea grass and, 427, 518
Perdido River, 81, 102, 426, 441
pesticides, 383, 390, 416, 451–52,
    485–86, 489, 521, 522
Petit Bois Island, 308, 311, 329, 330,
    483
petrochemical pollution, 431, 432,
    433, 436–37, 496, 505
Peterson, Roger Tory, 487
Philadelphia, PA, 25, 27, 32, 139,
    159, 246, 456
Pine Island, FL, 155, 168, 324, 384,
    405
Pine Island Sound, FL, 37, 248, 388
    Calusa and, 152
    Cuban ranchos and, 120
    as an estuary, 28, 131, 152
    sport fishing and, 169
Pinellas County, FL, 192, 379, 380,
    393, 410, 481
pine trees, 110, 136, 316–17, 243, 389
    as construction material, 36, 80,
        122, 175, 287, 424
    Gulf region and, 59, 60, 89, 90,
        110, 111, 175, 228, 243, 260,
        306, 333, 385, 400, 421, 471
    naval stores and pulp industries
        and, 60, 90, 123, 426, 447
pirates, 47, 214, 323–26, 477
Plant, Henry, 175, 176, 458
Plater-Zyberk, Elizabeth, 473
Pleistocene epoch, 13, 19, 195, 226
Polk, James K., 104–5

Ponce de León, Juan, 53, 174, 377
death of, 52, 352
Dry Tortugas and, 112, 144
first Gulf entrada of, 34, 35, 38,
44, 45, 48
Florida encounters of, 35, 45, 52,
152, 231, 354
Gulf Stream discovery of, 45–46
Port Aransas, TX (formerly Tarpon,
TX), 148, 156, 161, 178, 182,
248, 287
Port Arthur, TX, 360, 411, 418
Port Lavaca, TX, 416, 417
Powell, John Wesley, 25–26, 33
Poynter, Nelson, 379–80, 381, 382,
397
Price, William Armstrong, Jr., 226
Procter & Gamble, 428–29
Prudhomme, Paul, 434, 526
pulp industry pollution, 426–427,
428–30
Punta Gorda, FL, 28, 193, 154, 167,
172, 458
Punta Rassa, FL, 161, 384
Putnam, Frank W., 33

Rabalais, Nancy, 449–50, 451, 457,
459–63
Raffield, Vince, 446–47, 448, 450, 455
Randell, Ted, 404
Ratner, Leonard, 381–82
Rauschkolb, Dave, 503
red tides, 422–23, 517 (*see also*
sponges)

Reed, Nathaniel P., 404
rice, cultivation on Gulf, 90, 215,
250, 271, 279, 284, 285, 286,
298
Richards, John, 454
Ricklis, Robert, 63–64, 67
Ringling, John, 254, 394, 397
Rio de las Palmas, 55, 59
Rio Grande, 55, 65, 76, 178, 441,
442, 520
diminished flow of, 182, 500
sediment flow of, 225, 226, 319,
481
Rio Grande Valley, 431, 487, 520
Rio Pánuco, 72, 178
rivers, ecology of, 440–44 (*see also
specific rivers*)
Rivers, Ernie, 421–22, 423, 518
Roberts, Nash, 339–41, 348, 350–51,
361–64, 370
Rockport, TX, 178, 486, 487
Rogel, Juan, 38–39
Romans, Bernard, 51, 91, 111
on commercial fishing in Gulf,
118–19
Indian observations of, 88, 89–90
Mobile observations of, 87–88, 90,
459
Pensacola observations of, 86, 87
as surveyor in the Gulf, 84–90,
106, 117, 232
Romantics, 241–45, 246
Roosevelt, Franklin, 156, 180, 269,
287, 394, 406

Roosevelt, Theodore, 160, 171, 172, 198, 205, 250
  bird conservation and, 209–12, 217, 330, 332
Rosen, Jack, 382–83, 384
Rosen, Leonard, 382–83, 384
Rowe, Thomas, 153–54, 255–56, 379
Rowland, Thomas, 275
Rudloe, Anne, 136
Rudloe, Jack, 136, 143, 144
Ruge, John G., 132, 133
Ruth, Babe, 254–55
Rutherford, Walter, 365–66, 367

St. George Island, FL, 188, 328, 448
St. Johns River, FL, 27, 242
St. Petersburg, FL, 204, 214
  bird sanctuaries and, 212
  post–World War II boom and, 378–82, 391, 393, 397
  real-estate boom of the 1920s and, 254–55, 395
  sea-level rise and, 521
Sanibel-Captiva Conservation Foundation, 407, 457, 516
Sanibel, FL, 151, 152, 377, 477, 482, 504
  growth management of, 405–9, 457, 479
San Jacinto River, 66, 271
Santa Rosa Island, FL, 86, 116, 227, 257, 258, 324, 352, 470, 483
Sarasota Bay, 394, 397, 409

Sarasota, FL, 148, 161, 182, 192, 257, 377, 457
  post–World War II growth, 393–99, 403–5, 410
  real-estate boom of 1920s and, 254
  sea-level rise and, 521
Saunders, E. E., 125, 127
Save Our Bays, 403–4
Sawyer, Wells Moses, 23, 32, 33, 39–40
Sayles, Edwin Booth, 63
Scott, Rick, 522
Scott, William Earl Dodge, 189–90, 191, 192–93, 194, 206
Seadrift, TX, 416, 417, 433, 438
sea grass, 134, 379, 402, 527
  habitat of, 29, 37, 56, 60, 140, 145, 421
  loss of, 296, 381, 392, 415, 421
  See also specific bays and rivers
Seale, Tom, 290, 291, 292
sea-level rise, 9, 347, 439, 519–22, 528
  See also Carson, Rachel; Gulf of Mexico; islands; *specific cities*; US Environmental Protection Agency
Seaside, FL, 472–75, 503
sea turtles, 18, 45, 112, 114, 117, 138, 142, 327, 443, 488
  consumption of turtles and eggs, 145–46, 232
  industry in, 137, 143–45
  protection of, 211, 433, 484–85, 503
  species of, 144, 484

See also Audubon, John James; *specific states*

seawalls, 28, 253, 346, 389, 396, 401–3, 409, 410, 480, 481, 521

Seixas, Cecile, 205

Seminole, 91, 116, 166
    conflicts between U.S. and, 102–3, 121, 154, 322, 384, 405, 526
    Cuban ranchos and, 121–22

sewage pollution, 2, 130, 238, 247, 381, 422–25, 430–32, 453, 456, 458, 462, 467, 506, 518, 519, 527, 528

shell mounds, 30, 36, 37, 49, 69, 401, 512
    Gulf region density of, 4–5, 23, 24, 28, 129
    as road bedding, 133, 395, 479

Ship Island, MS, 80, 314, 315, 322, 364
    sea-level rise and, 487

shrimp, 29, 36, 56, 60, 114, 131, 138, 156, 198, 234, 332, 412
    industry and, 134–36, 140, 143, 144, 147–48, 248, 287, 296–97, 433, 484–85, 505, 529
    species of, 65, 135–36, 494
    See also specific states

Sigsbee, Charles, 240–41

Sinclair Oil Corporation, 261–63, 272, 273, 279

Singer, John V., 320–21, 323

Smith, John, 27, 28, 30, 69
    first hooked tarpon and, 154, 155, 168–69, 385

Smithsonian Institution, 25, 127

Soto, Hernando de, 109
    encounter with Texas oil, 71, 265
    Gulf expedition of, 68–72, 76, 352
    legacy of, 72–73

Southeast Louisiana Flood Protection Authority–East, 514, 515

Spain and the Spanish
    Christianity and, 38–36, 55, 59, 62–63, 199, 352
    colonizing the Caribbean basin and, 42–47, 48, 52
    desire for gold and silver of, 18, 24, 44, 46, 47, 48, 53, 54, 55, 58, 59, 68, 70, 74, 76, 82, 458
    navigation and the New World and, 46–47, 54–55
    pigs of in New World, 43, 53, 69, 70, 73, 88, 235
    See also specific Spanish conquistadors

Spanish-American War, 172, 198, 210, 322

sponges, 29, 241
    habitat of, 117, 138, 266
    industry in, 117, 129, 355 (*see also* Tarpon Springs, FL)
    red tide and, 423

Stagg, Mrs. George T., 174, 179

Standard Oil, 168, 283, 287, 293–95, 355, 356

Stearns, Silas, 125, 126–49, 500, 523

Stevens, Wallace, poetry and observations of, 16, 18, 117, 164, 242, 287, 529
Stewart, James, 264, 275, 280, 281–83, 290, 291, 296–97, 302, 504
Stowe, Harriet Beecher, 190, 242
Straits of Yucatán, 13, 17, 18, 48, 77, 86, 338, 363
Sturmer, Leslie, 526–28
Sugg, Redding S., 313
Sullivan, Louis, 238, 314
Swamp Land acts, 495

Tabasco sauce, 197–98, 300
Tampa Bay, 85, 111, 175, 254, 394
    Cuban ranchos on, 120, 121
    description of, 56, 66, 87
    estuary and, 56, 64–65, 409, 459, 464
    feather trade and, 191–92
    marshes and, 496
    phosphate industry and, 458–59
    pollution of, 457–59
    restoration of, 459, 464
    sea grass and, 379, 436, 459
    Spanish and, 55, 56, 57–58, 68
Tampa Bay Estuary Program, 459
Tampa, FL, 19, 124, 148, 153, 167, 257, 289, 325
    growth of, 254
    port of, 192
    sea-level rise and, 521
    Spanish-American War and, 172, 210, 322

Tampico, Mexico, 150, 178, 179, 181
Tariff Act, 207
Tarpon Bay, 152, 168, 407
Tarpon Springs, FL, 60, 162, 190, 410
    sponges and, 32, 137–39, 423
    sport fishing and, 161, 168
    tourism and, 138
Taylor, Gene, 467–68, 487
Ten Thousand Islands, 192, 201, 310–11, 409
terrapins, 248–49, 332, 493
Texaco, 270, 281, 294, 297
Texas
    coastal environment of, 110, 225–26
    independence and U.S. annexation, 104–5, 108, 122, 342
    oysters and, 64, 65, 66, 78, 129, 147, 271, 275, 342, 438, 518
    petrochemical industry and, 295, 297, 303, 411, 416–20, 431–33, 435–39
    sea turtles and, 145, 515
    shrimp and, 65, 66, 275, 297, 417, 437
Thoreau, Henry David, 123, 243, 313
Thunder Bay, 264, 274–75, 280–83, 290–92, 296–97, 299, 300, 302, 504
Tidwell, Mike, 506, 507
Tierra Verde, FL, 380, 394, 399
Tin Can Tourists, 256–57, 377

Time, "Filthy Seas" article, 412–13, 418, 444, 463–64, 495

Tippetts, Katherine, 204, 205, 212, 217

Tocobaga Indians, 58–59, 73

Tombigbee River, 87

Toxics Release Inventory (TRI), 418, 426, 518

Trahan, Jimmy, 340, 348, 366, 367

Trinity River, 66, 342

Trinity–San Jacinto Estuary, 66, 274

tupelo trees, 196, 453

Turner, R. Eugene, 502–3
  coastal canals and, 501, 507
  Gulf dead zone and, 445–46, 448, 449–50, 451, 457, 459, 461–63, 494, 495, 519

Union Carbide, 418, 433, 438

US Army Corps of Engineers, 9, 277, 328, 399, 409, 453, 454, 480, 488, 517
  navigation projects of, 323, 381, 431, 448, 456, 458, 481

US Coast Survey, 47, 99, 106, 250, 312, 340, 510
  biological study of Gulf and, 239–41
  mapping the Gulf and, 97, 100, 107–112, 325, 354, 355, 376–78

US Environmental Protection Agency, 380, 418, 429, 438, 505, 507

fish-kill study of, 415, 416

lax oversight of 420, 426, 436, 496, 512, 519

offshore chemical incinerator and, 416

pollution reduction and, 422, 425

sea-level rise and, 508

Toxics Release Inventory and, 418, 426, 518

US Fish Commission, 127–28, 141, 147, 149, 523

US Fish and Wildlife Service, 378, 380, 406

US Geological Survey, 309, 428

US Weather Bureau, 341, 343–44, 349, 350, 358, 359, 360

Usseppa Island, FL, 150, 169–70, 171, 173, 181, 248

Velázquez de Cuéllar, Diego, 44, 46, 53

Veracruz, Mexico, 53, 182

Viosca, Percy, 501–2

vom Hofe, Edward, 170–71, 174

Walton, Izaak, 157–59, 162, 166, 178

Wang, Wenliang, 521

Ward, Charles Willis, 211–12

War of 1812, 102, 103, 326

Warren, Andrew Fuller, 123, 124, 125, 127, 129

WaterColor, 474–75

Weddle, Robert, 68, 79

Welch, Benny, 367–68

West Florida, 7
  British colony of, 75, 83, 86
  manifest destiny and, 101
  Republic of, 102
  Spanish colony of, 101, 102, 103,
    110–11, 120, 352

White, Randy Wayne, 151–55,
    165–66, 168, 182–83, 408

Whitman, Walt, 109, 241

Wilczek, Edward, 5–6

Williams, James, 108, 110

Williams, Ted, and tarpon fishing,
    165

Williams, William Carlos, 52, 73–74

Wilson, Alexander, 189

Wilson, Diane, 411
  as activist, 416–20, 429, 431–33,
    436–438, 464, 518

Wilson, Edward O., 3, 15, 459, 460,
    465, 466

Wood, William Halsey, 164–67,
    172, 189, 377, 456
  hooking first tarpon and, 153–54,
    155, 168–69

Woolf, Virginia, 203, 204

Yarborough, "Smilin' Ralph,"
    482–83

yellow fever, 71, 108, 192, 235–38

Young, Linda, 425–26, 428, 429,
    431, 517, 518

Yucatán, Mexico, 13, 14, 17, 34, 43,
    48, 43, 83, 241, 422, 527
  bird migration and, 185–86, 187
  continental shelf and, 19

Zacks, Michelle, 119, 140